LEGAL TERMINOLOGY

WEST LEGAL STUDIES

Options.

Over 300 products in every area of the law: textbooks, CD-ROMs, reference books, test banks, online companions, and more – helping you succeed in the classroom and on the job.

Support.

We offer unparalleled, practical support: robust instructor and student supplements to ensure the best learning experience, custom publishing to meet your unique needs, and other benefits such as West's Student Achievement Award. And our sales representatives are always ready to provide you with dependable service.

Feedback.

As always, we want to hear from you! Your feedback is our best resource for improving the quality of our products. Contact your sales representative or write us at the address below if you have any comments about our materials or if you have a product proposal.

Accounting and Financials for the Law Office • Administrative Law • Alternative Dispute Resolution Bankruptcy • Business Organizations/Corporations • Careers and Employment • Civil Litigation and Procedure • CLA Exam Preparation • Computer Applications in the Law Office • Contract Law Court Reporting • Criminal Law and Procedure • Document Preparation • Elder Law • Employment Law • Environmental Law • Ethics • Evidence Law • Family Law • Intellectual Property • Interviewing and Investigation • Introduction to Law • Introduction to Paralegalism • Law Office Management Law Office Procedures • Legal Nurse Consulting • Legal Research, Writing, and Analysis • Legal Terminology • Paralegal Internship • Product Liability • Real Estate Law • Reference Materials Social Security • Sports Law • Torts and Personal Injury Law • Wills, Trusts, and Estate Administration

---

West Legal Studies
5 Maxwell Drive
Clifton Park, New York 12065-2919

For additional information, find us online at:
www.westlegalstudies.com

LEGAL
TERMINOLOGY

S. WHITTINGTON BROWN

THOMSON

DELMAR LEARNING

Australia Brazil Canada Mexico Singapore Spain United Kingdom United States

WEST LEGAL STUDIES

Legal Terminology
by S. Whittington Brown

Vice President, Career Education Strategic Business Unit:
Dawn Gerrain

Director of Editorial:
Sherry Gomoll

Editor:
Shelley Esposito

Senior Developmental Editor:
Melissa Riveglia

Editorial Assistant:
Brian E. Banks

Director of Production:
Wendy A. Troeger

Production Editor:
Matthew J. Williams

Director of Marketing:
Wendy E. Mapstone

Marketing Specialist:
Gerard McAvey

Marketing Coordinator:
Erica Conley

Cover Design:
Joe Villanova

COPYRIGHT © 2006 Thomson Delmar Learning, a part of The Thomson Corporation. Thomson, the Star Logo, and Delmar Learning are trademarks used herein under license.

Printed in the United States
1 2 3 4 5 XXX 09 08 07 06 05

For more information contact Delmar Learning, 5 Maxwell Drive, Clifton Park, NY 12065-2919.

Or find us on the World Wide Web at www.delmarlearning.com or www.westlegalstudies.com

Library of Congress Cataloging-in-Publication Data

Brown, S. Whittington.
    Legal terminology / S. Whittington Brown.—
    1st ed.
      p. cm.—(West Legal Studies Series)
    Includes index.
    ISBN 1-4018-2012-3
    1. Legal research—United States. 2. Legal assistants—United States—Handbooks, manuals, etc. I. Title. II. Series.
    KF240.B767 2006
    349.73—dc22   2005011965

NOTICE TO THE READER

Publisher does not warrant or guarantee any of the products described herein or perform any independent analysis in connection with any of the product information contained herein. Publisher does not assume, and expressly disclaims, any obligation to obtain and include information other than that provided to it by the manufacturer.

The reader is notified that this text is an educational tool, not a practice book. Since the law is in constant change, no rule or statement of law in this book should be relied upon for any service to any client. The reader should always refer to standard legal sources for the current rule or law. If legal advice or other expert assistance is required, the services of the appropriate professional should be sought.

The Publisher makes no representation or warranties of any kind, including but not limited to, the warranties of fitness for particular purpose or merchantability, nor are any such representations implied with respect to the material set forth herein, and the publisher takes no responsibility with respect to such material. The publisher shall not be liable for any special, consequential, or exemplary damages resulting, in whole or part, from the readers' use of, or reliance upon, this material.

DEDICATION

To my wife, Karyn, who said, "Why don't you?"

CONTENTS IN BRIEF

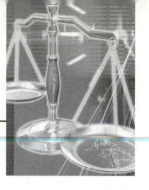

CONTENTS

CHAPTER 3   CRIMINAL PROCEDURE   37

CHAPTER 12   REAL ESTATE TRANSACTIONS   213

CHAPTER 13   AGENCY   225

CHAPTER 15   SECURITIES   257

CHAPTER 16   SECURITIES REGULATION   275

CHAPTER 17   ANTITRUST   291

CHAPTER 25   DISCRIMINATION IN EMPLOYMENT AND BY STATE ACTION   455

PREFACE

"The secret to understanding any profession is to understand its language." This observation was made by Dr. Will Sweetzer years ago in a public personnel management course the author was taking at Rhodes College. Part of learning any profession is familiarizing oneself with the terminology used in that profession.

Legal Terminology is a textbook for two- and four-year college students. It is also valuable for law students, working paralegals, legal assistants and legal secretaries. The text is a direct result of the author's experiences in teaching legal terminology without a comprehensive text. In speaking with students, the author learned their frustrations with existing books on legal terminology. Their options were very limited: Either use existing texts, where terminology is presented in dictionary format, or use a legal dictionary. There was no context for students to see how legal terminology is used in the profession, and contextual application is essential to true understanding.

ORGANIZATION

Each chapter in this text follows the same format. The introduction gives the student an idea of the subject matter that will be discussed. Basic terminology is presented first, followed by more detailed terminology arranged by topic or classification. The first time a key word or phrase is used, it is in boldface type for emphasis. When necessary, a pronunciation key follows the term. Throughout each chapter, terms are applied in legal scenarios. Cases that either defined or created the terminology or that are examples of the terminology in use are cited and discussed in many chapters.

The chapters themselves are arranged in a natural progression: Students are exposed to broad topics before moving on to more detailed areas. The text opens with the American legal system: our courts and the personnel that make up these courts. The appendix consists of the Constitution and a listing of the court system for each state.

Chapter 2, Criminal Law, deals with basic principles of criminal law and the general definitions of specific crimes against persons and property. Criminal liability and culpability are also discussed in this chapter. Chapter 3, Criminal Procedure, is similar to Chapter 8, Constitutional Law, but it deals with the law that protects the rights of the accused and the criminal trial process. Specific cases and examples are used throughout this chapter to explain concepts.

Chapters 4 and 5, Civil Procedure I and II, show the student how a civil case progresses through the court system, from the initial filing of the lawsuit all the way through an appeal. Chapter 6, Administrative Law, discusses the basic principles of administrative law and covers specific federal agencies.

Chapter 7, Evidence, is more specific and shows students how cases are proven in court. It covers admissible and inadmissible evidence, real and demonstrative evidence, character evidence, the rules of hearsay, and privilege. Chapter 8, Constitutional Law, deals with the legal basis for our entire system of government, our court systems, and how basic rights within those court systems are protected. Many cases are referred to in this chapter because of the nature and importance of Constitutional law.

Chapter 9, Torts, Chapter 10, Contracts, and Chapter 11, Property, introduce the student to these legal concepts, which serve as the basis for all other areas of law. Chapter 12, Real Estate Transactions, is part of property law and deals with the specific topic of buying and selling real estate. Chapter 13, Agency, and Chapter 14, Business Organizations, deal with the law of agency and sole proprietorships, partnerships, corporations, limited liability companies, and franchises. How each is formed, the liability each faces, and how each may be dissolved are discussed.

Chapter 15, Securities, deals with types of securities and the rights and responsibilities that exist with each type. Chapter 16, Securities Regulation, deals with the law that relates to the buying and selling of securities. Chapter 17, Antitrust, discusses the methods used by companies to control markets, what methods are legal and illegal, and the methods used by the government to enforce antitrust laws.

Chapter 18, Labor and Employment Law, deals with employer-employee relations: the formation of labor unions, union representation, the dissolution of unions, the Family and Medical Leave Act, OSHA, COBRA, and Workers' Compensation. Chapter 19, Debtor-Creditor Relations, discusses the types of credit available, how it is determined who gets credit, how credit agreements are enforced, secured and unsecured transactions, and bankruptcy. Chapter 20, Commercial Paper, discusses the different substitutes for cash that are used by individuals and businesses. Chapter 21, Intellectual Property, deals with a third type of property and covers patents, copyright, trademarks, and trade secrets.

Chapter 22, Domestic Relations, covers the topics of relations before marriage, marriage, divorce, adoption, surrogate parenthood, paternity, property division, child custody and support, and remarriage. Chapter 23, Decedent Estates, discusses wills, trusts, estates, and the effects of dying without a will. Chapter 24, Products Liability and Consumer Protection, is about the areas of law that provide for consumer protection from harmful products and sales practices.

Chapter 25, Discrimination in Employment and by State Action, discusses discrimination in the workplace based on race, religion, sex, and age. Chapter 26, Environmental Protection, and Chapter 27, Cyberspace Law, present two new areas of law that deal with the protection of the environment and attempts to regulate the use of computers and the Internet.

FEATURES

Legal terminology is not an easy subject to make interesting. In addition, learning new vocabulary can present hurdles for even serious students. Therefore, this text includes features not available in other texts.

- An introduction to each chapter tells the student what will be covered in that chapter.
- The first time a key word or phrase is used, it is in boldface type for emphasis. The definition for each term closely follows its first use.
- As often as possible, legal terms are used in context.
- A pronunciation key is provided for some of the more complicated terms.
- Abundant examples further clarify the terminology and demonstrate how legal vocabulary is applied in real-life situations.
- Terminology is provided in narrative rather than dictionary form.
- Cases using the terminology or principles under discussion are cited and discussed in the text.
- Exhibits are used extensively to summarize definitions, to compare and contrast terms, to show tests used by the courts, and to provide additional information.
- A chapter summary condenses and distills the essential information presented.
- A chapter review lists the key words and phrases for each area of law covered.
- The end-of-chapter exercises include short answer questions, fill-in-the-blank questions, and fact situations that require students to apply what they have learned.
- Terminology in each chapter is presented in order from basic to more complex.

- The text is comprehensive. The instructor can select those subjects he or she wishes to emphasize during the semester.
- The text is designed for continued use as a resource for students as they progress to a more advanced study of law.
- The text is flexible enough that the instructor can incorporate local laws into his or her instruction.

Everyone in the legal profession—attorney, paralegal, legal secretary, law clerk, court reporter, investigator—must know legal terminology. The only way legal professionals can effectively communicate with others in the profession is to speak the same language. That is the purpose of this book: to introduce and explain the language used by legal professionals.

SUPPLEMENTAL TEACHING MATERIALS

- The **Instructor's Manual with Test Bank** is available in printed version and online at *www.westlegalstudies.com* in the Instructor's Lounge, under Resource. The manual contains a proposed syllabus, related Web sites, teaching suggestions, answers to the review questions after each chapter, and a test bank featuring multiple choice and true-false questions. Suggestions as to areas where an instructor can supplement the text with local examples are also identified.
- **Online Companion**™ – The Online Companion™ Web site can be found at *www.west legalstudies.com* in the Resource section of the Web site. The Online Companion™ contains additional chapters on oil and gas law, insurance, tax law, disability law, and military law can be found on the Web site. These supplemental chapters follow the same format as the chapters in the text.
- **Web page** – Come visit our Web site at *www.westlegalstudies.com,* where you will find valuable information specific to this book such as hot links and sample materials to download, as well as other West Legal Studies products.
- **Westlaw**® – West's on-line computerized legal research system offers students "hands-on" experience with a system commonly used in law offices. Qualified adopters can receive ten free hours of Westlaw®. Westlaw® can be accessed with Macintosh and IBM PC and compatibles. A modem is required.
- **Survival Guide for Paralegal Students,** a pamphlet by Kathleen Mercer Reed and Bradene Moore, covers practical and basic information to help students make the most of their paralegal courses. Topics covered include choosing courses of study and note-taking skills.
- **West's Paralegal Video Library** – West Legal Studies is pleased to offer the following videos at no charge to qualified adopters:
  - *The Drama of the Law II: Paralegal Issues Video*
    ISBN 0-314-07088-5
  - *The Making of a Case Video*
    ISBN 0-314-07300-0
  - *ABA Mock Trial Video—Product Liability*
    ISBN 0-314-07342-6
  - *Arguments to the United States Supreme Court Video*
    ISBN 0-314-07070-2

> Please note the Internet resources are of a time-sensitive nature and
> URL addresses may often change or be deleted.
> **Contact us at westlegalstudies@delmar.com**

ACKNOWLEDGEMENTS

A person cannot attempt a project of this size without the support and encouragement of many people. The most important person to my efforts is my wife, Karyn. I came home one night, frustrated by the limitations placed on me by existing texts for legal terminology and said that I was tempted to write a textbook myself. Karyn looked at me and said, "Why don't you?" Thank you for saying that to me. I could not have done this without your love, your support, and your belief in me. Thanks also to Jim Roomsburg, who first hired me to teach at Pulaski Technical College. I think it has worked out, don't you? Many thanks as well to Bob Glidewell, who reviewed the first chapter and let me know I was on the right track, and who provided encouragement and advice during this entire process.

A big thank you to the staff at Thomson Delmar Learning, West Legal Studies for believing in me and this project and for deciding to publish the work. A special thanks to editorial assistants Lisa Flatley and Sarah Duncan, who promptly answered even the simplest of questions quickly.

Many thanks to my family: my parents, Frank and Madge, for their support throughout the years; to Bill and Maxine, who have passed on but who I know are still proud; to my sister Candy, to my brother Paul, and to my brother-in-law and sister-in-law Mike and Susan. Thanks also to my friends who provided support and were so proud of this: Harold, Holly, Samantha, Amy, Shirley, Bob, Calvin, Charlie, Joe, Margo, Randy, Brenda, and to R.S. #2—you know who you are.

Thanks to my students, past, present, and future. Those who have gone on to law school, those who are in the profession, and those still working on entering the profession—it is for you that I wrote this book.

I would also like to thank the reviewers for their many valuable suggestions.

Donna Ayala
UniveralClass.com, Inc.
New York, NY

Debbie Bailey
Amarillo College
Amarillo, TX

Eli Bortman
Babson College
Wellesley, MA

Linda Delorme
Olympic College
Bremerton, WA

Susan DeMatteo
Boston University
Boston, MA

Dora Dye
City College of San
    Francisco
San Francisco, CA

Kathleen Fisher
National Center for
    Paralegal Training
Atlanta, GA

Luci Hoover
Private Law Practice
Rockford, IL

Kent Kauffman
Ivy Tech State College
Ft. Wayne, IN

Linda Murphy
Cuyahoga Community
    College
Cleveland, OH

Linda Potter
Saginaw Chippewa Indian
    Tribe
Mount Pleasant, MI

Susann Shanahan
Central Technology Center
Sapulpa, OK

Ruby Weems
Kaplan College
Detroit, MI

Linda Wilke
Central Community
    College
Grand Island, NE

Marilyn Wudarki
North Idaho College
Coeur D'Alene, ID

TABLE OF CASES

CHAPTER 1

The Legal System and the Legislative Process

INTRODUCTION

In order to understand legal terminology and the manner in which it is used, it is important to understand the legal system that it is used in and how new laws are created. It is important to know the types of laws, the different court systems, and how they interact with each other. Laws are classified according to how they are created—the source of the law. Courts are classified according to the type of cases that can be heard, what type of court it is, the authority a court has, and where the court is located in the judicial hierarchy.

A legislature is one source of law in the United States, so it is important to know how bills are introduced, where bills are introduced, and how they are considered and passed. In order to understand the law and the legal terms related to the law, it is helpful to understand the terms that describe the process by which law is written and the process of passing the law. The Congress of the United States is the focus of this chapter; most states' legislatures are fashioned after it. The terms and the examples used in this chapter apply to U.S. Congress, and also to most state legislatures. There are terms to describe the members of a legislature, the houses in the legislature, and the process of passing laws. There are also terms to describe proposed laws and what the laws are designed to create.

THE U.S. LEGAL SYSTEM

The legal system in the United States is an **adversary** (*ad*-ver-sa-ree) **system:** a system of laws, rules, and procedures wherein parties oppose each other. Each party is seeking the result that is most favorable to him or her and may have representation to argue his or her position to the person or body that ultimately makes the decision regarding the controversy between the parties.

COMMON LAW

The foundation of the legal system in the United States is rooted in the common law system that originated in England around 1066. William the Conqueror, the first true king of England, determined that in order to have stability in England, there had to be a uniform system of laws and courts. The system that was put in place is the system of common law. **Common law** is the body of law that comes from judicial decisions; it is judge-made law, what the judge determines the outcome of the case is to be. The written decisions of the judges contain the relevant facts of the dispute, the legal rationale and reasoning applied by the court, and the outcome of the case. These cases are published and serve as precedent for all future cases. **Precedent** (*pres*-e-dent) is a past decision (case) that may be binding upon future cases. When a judge is presented with a case where the facts are identical or similar enough to a previous case that has been decided, the judge will apply that past case to the present dispute. This practice is known as using the doctrine of stare decisis. **Stare decisis** (star-*e*-de-*si*-sis) requires that when a court has set a principle of law as being applicable to a certain set of facts, that court and all other courts will follow that principle and apply it to all future cases. When a court is presented with the same or similar facts as an earlier case that has been decided, the court will follow the principles of law established in the earlier case. For example, two people are in a dispute as to where a property line is. The court looks at previous decisions regarding property disputes to see if this issue has been addressed by another court. If so, the court may base its decision upon what the earlier decisions said. Exhibit 1-1 demonstrates the difference between precedent and stare decisis.

EXHIBIT 1-1 DIFFERENCE BETWEEN PRECEDENT AND STARE DECISIS

Precedent – The actual written decision of a court issued to resolve a dispute between the people who are suing each other

Stare Decisis – The doctrine that states courts will use precedents of courts as a guide to determine how to rule on a current case that is pending before the court.

STATUTORY LAW, CONSTITUTIONAL LAW, AND REGULATORY LAW

The court system in the United States is not limited to just using common law; it also consists of statutory law, constitutional law, and regulatory law. **Statutory** (sta-*choo*-tore-ee) **law** is the body of law that is created by state legislatures and the U.S. Congress. Whenever Congress or a state legislature passes a new law, it becomes statutory law. **Constitutional law** is law that is based on interpretations of the United States Constitution and the constitutions of the different states. In other words, when a court interprets part of a state constitution or the United States Constitution, this interpretation is constitutional law. Regulatory (*reg*-yoo-le-tore-ee) law originates from the rules and regulations of administrative agencies and the court decisions interpreting them. For example, any regulations issued by the Internal Revenue Service and any court decision interpreting those regulations are regulatory law. See Exhibit 1-2, Classifications of Law.

EXHIBIT 1-2 CLASSIFICATIONS OF LAW

Common Law – Law made by judges; judge-made law; comes from written decisions of judges

Statutory Law – Law that is created by state legislatures and by the U.S. Congress

Constitutional Law – Law that comes from interpretations by a court of the U.S. Constitution and of state constitutions

Regulatory Law – Law that comes from the rules and regulations of administrative agencies and the court cases interpreting those rules and regulations

---

CIVIL AND CRIMINAL COURTS

The court system in the United States is divided into state courts, which are operated by the states, and federal courts, which are operated by the federal government. **Courts** are defined as organs of the government, belonging to the judicial department, whose function is the application of the law to controversies brought before them. Courts are also responsible for the public administration of justice. The person who presides or governs over the court proceedings is the **judge,** the officer of the court who administers and answers questions concerning the law. Judges are either elected or appointed. The court system is the network of courts in a particular jurisdiction—a system of courts in a state or in the federal government.

There are many ways to characterize courts, the first being by the type of case that can be presented to each. A court can be a civil court, which is charged with resolving controversies between private parties or with determining private rights. For example, a couple seeking divorce would take their case to civil court. Civil courts also deal with cases involving contract disputes, property disputes, and personal injuries. A **criminal court** is responsible for the administration of criminal laws and the punishment for wrongs against society. If someone is charged with violating either state or federal criminal laws, the trial to determine either innocence or guilt takes place in these courts. In civil court cases, private citizens bring the case to court; in criminal court cases, the state or the federal government is always the party that brings the case to court. Private individuals cannot charge someone with a crime in state or federal courts; only the government has the authority to charge people with crimes. Refer to Exhibit 1-3 for a summary of the differences between civil and criminal courts.

EXHIBIT 1-3	CIVIL COURT OR CRIMINAL COURT
CIVIL COURT	*CRIMINAL COURT*
Cases are brought by one person or company against another person or company	Cases are brought by the government against a person or a company
Determines the controversy between the private parties	Determines innocence or guilt of a person charged with a crime
Determines private rights	Determines punishment for a crime

JURISDICTION OF COURTS

A second way to distinguish courts is by their jurisdiction, that is, their power or authority to hear different types of cases. A court can be one of general jurisdiction (joo-ris-*dik*-shen), one that has unlimited power to hear civil and criminal cases. State circuit courts and federal district courts are examples of courts of general jurisdiction because they have the authority to hear a wide array of civil and criminal cases. A court of limited jurisdiction is one with authority to only hear certain types of cases. These courts do not have the power or authority to hear a broad range of cases. The type of cases these courts can hear is limited to a few types or even just one type. For example, bankruptcy court is a court that hears only bankruptcy cases; juvenile courts hear cases regarding minors; probate court hears cases dealing with wills, estates, and guardianships.

Courts can further be classified by where they fit into the judicial hierarchy, whether the court is a lower court or a higher court. The term *lower court,* or the court below, refers to a trial court whose decision has been appealed. The *higher court,* or the court above, is a term that refers to an appellate court. The **trial court** is a generic term used to describe courts where civil and criminal actions are started at either the state or federal level. The **appellate court** (a-*pel*-et) is a generic term used to identify the courts that have authority to review the decisions of the trial court. Cases do not start in appellate courts; these are the courts where an appeal of a decision of the trial court is brought. The term kangaroo court does not describe a type of court, but rather what can happen in court. It refers to a sham legal proceeding in which a person's rights are totally ignored and the results are a foregone conclusion because of the bias of the court. In other words, the disposition of the case is determined by how the court feels about the parties rather than by the information presented.

In order for a court to hear a particular case, it must be the court of competent jurisdiction, the court that has the power under the law to rule on a certain type of case. You cannot bring an appeal in municipal court; you cannot have a trial in an appellate court; and you cannot bring a criminal case in a civil court or a court of limited jurisdiction, such as a bankruptcy court. The trial court does not have the authority to hear an appeal of a case from another trial court. A bankruptcy court does not have the authority to hear a divorce case or to resolve a contract dispute. See Exhibit 1-4.

EXHIBIT 1-4	GENERAL CLASSIFICATIONS OF COURTS

I. JURISDICTION

General Jurisdiction – The court has the authority to hear several types of cases.

Limited Jurisdiction – The court has the authority to hear only a few types of cases or even just one type of case (e.g., bankruptcy).

Competent Jurisdiction – The court has the authority to hear the type of case that has been presented to it.

II. JUDICIAL HIERARCHY

Trial Court/Court Below – The court where all cases are first brought; the first court to hear the case.

Appellate Court/Court Above – The court where the losing party at trial can ask for a review of the trial.

FEDERAL JURISDICTION

If someone wishes to file a lawsuit in federal court, that person cannot just file the case with the federal court clerk. In order to file a case in federal court, the plaintiff must demonstrate **federal jurisdiction,** the power of the federal court to hear the case presented to it. Federal jurisdiction is based on Article III of the U.S. Constitution, federal law, diversity of citizenship, or the presentation of a federal question. See Exhibit 1-5 for a summary of federal jurisdiction based on the U.S. Constitution and Exhibit 1-6 for an example of federal jurisdiction based on a federal statute.

EXHIBIT 1-5	FEDERAL JURISDICTION BASED ON THE U.S. CONSTITUTION

Article III, Section 2.

(1) The judicial power shall extend to all cases, in law and equity, arising under this Constitution, the laws of the United States, and treaties made, or which shall be made, under their authority;—to all cases affecting ambassadors, other public ministers and consuls;—to all cases of admiralty and maritime jurisdiction;—to controversies to which the United States shall be a party;—to controversies between two or more states;—between a state and citizens of another state;—between citizens of different states;—between citizens of the same state claiming lands under grants of different states, and between a state, or the citizens thereof, and foreign states, citizens or subjects.

(2) In all cases affecting ambassadors, other public ministers and consuls, and those in which a state shall be party, the Supreme Court shall have original jurisdiction. In all the other cases before mentioned, the Supreme Court shall have appellate jurisdiction, both as to law and fact, with such exceptions, and under such regulations as the Congress shall make.

Diversity of citizenship refers to the creation of federal jurisdiction because the parties are from two different states or one of the parties is a citizen of the United States and the other party is an alien. A federal question is a case involving the interpretation and application of the U.S. Constitution, federal statutory law, or treaties.

EXHIBIT 1-6	FEDERAL JURISDICTION BASED UPON FEDERAL STATUTES

42 U.S.C. § 2004-e, The Civil Rights Act of 1964.

In any proceeding instituted by the United States in any district court of the United States under this section in which the Attorney General requests a finding of a pattern or practice of discrimination pursuant to subsection (e) of this section the Attorney General, at the time he files the complaint, or any defendant in the proceeding, within twenty days after service upon him of the complaint, may file with the clerk of such court a request that a court of three judges be convened to hear and determine the entire case. A copy of the request for a three-judge court shall be immediately furnished by such clerk to the chief judge of the circuit (or in his absence, the presiding circuit judge of the circuit) in which the case is pending. Upon receipt of the copy of such request it shall be the duty of the chief justice of the circuit or the presiding circuit judge, as the case may be, to designate immediately three judges in such circuit, of whom at least one shall be a circuit judge and another of whom shall be a district judge of the court in which the proceeding was instituted, to hear and determine such case, and it shall be the duty of the judges so designated to assign the case for hearing at the earliest practicable date, to participate in the hearing and determination thereof, and to cause the case to be in every way expedited.

STATE AND FEDERAL COURT SYSTEMS

Each state and the federal government has its own court system. The types of courts each state might have are similar to each other, and the state courts are similar to the federal courts. There are trial courts and appellate courts in each system; the difference is the authority each of these courts has to rule on various areas of the law.

STATE COURT SYSTEM

State court systems vary from state to state. However, there are characteristics that the different court systems have in common. In general, a state court system may consist of a municipal court, a circuit court, a chancery court, a probate court, an appellate court, and a supreme court. A **municipal court** is a court that has a territorial limitation to the city or county where it is created; it usually hears minor criminal cases and may hear small civil cases. For example, the municipal court may only hear civil cases that started in a specific city or county, and in which the amount in controversy is $1,500 or less. The amount of money, or the value of the lawsuit, cannot be over $1500. For example, a landlord is suing a former tenant for unpaid rent. If the amount of unpaid rent is $1500 or less, the landlord may sue in municipal court. A municipal court may or may not be a **court of record,** which is a court that is required to keep a record of its proceedings.

A **circuit court** can hear cases that originate from several counties within its circuit. The court may meet in different parts of its circuit; it usually can hear criminal and civil cases, and it is a court of record. There is no limitation on the amount in controversy for civil actions. For example, if a landlord is suing a former tenant for $2000 in back rent, the case will be brought to circuit court. **Juvenile court** has the authority to hear cases involving **juvenile delinquency,** the illegal behavior of a minor, and cases of abused and neglected dependent children. Juvenile court may or may not be a court of record.

Chancery court or **equity court** is a court of **equity** (*ek*-wi-tee)—justice administered on the basis of fairness rather than by statute. Equity court is not restricted by laws and regulations; it can fashion its rulings to ensure that equity is reached, that it is fair to the parties involved. For example, if a person is suing another because the terms of a contract have not been fulfilled, the person suing may want the terms of the contract met rather than monetary damages. The **chancellor** is the judge who presides over the chancery court. Chancery court does not hear criminal actions; it only hears certain types of civil cases. **Probate court** is responsible for the administration of wills and estates. It may appoint guardians, and it may approve the adoption of minors. For example, if parents wish to become the guardian of their adult child, they would bring the guardianship case to probate court. Probate court and chancery court are courts of record. Some states combine chancery and probate court into one court, and other states have combined circuit court with chancery court and probate court.

Each state also has at least one appellate court, which may be an intermediate court of appeals or a supreme court. These courts hear appeals either from the lower courts, or further appeals from the state's intermediate court of appeals. For example, a state may have a court of appeals that hears most civil and criminal appeals. Its supreme court may hear appeals from certain administrative agencies, criminal cases where the penalty is death or life imprisonment, and civil cases concerning constitutional issues. See Exhibit 1-7 for a summary of state courts.

EXHIBIT 1-7	DIFFERENT TYPES OF STATE COURTS

1. **Municipal court** – Court of a city or a county that hears minor criminal offenses and small civil cases; small claims court
2. **Circuit court** – Trial court at the state level; can hear civil and criminal cases and may hear appeals from municipal court
3. **Equity court** – Hears cases that involve an issue of equity rather than law; there is no traditional legal remedy available, so the court will fashion a remedy based on what is fair
4. **Probate court** – Hears cases involving wills and trusts, guardianships, and adoptions
5. **Juvenile court** – Hears civil cases involving minors (e.g., child abuse or neglect cases) and criminal cases involving minors and/or juvenile delinquents
6. **Court of appeals** – An intermediate appellate court; hears certain types of appeals
7. **Supreme court** – Highest court in the state; an appellate court that has the power to interpret state law

See Appendix B for a listing of the type of court in each state.

FEDERAL COURT SYSTEM IN GENERAL

The primary federal court system consists of United States district courts, the United States courts of appeals, and the United States Supreme Court. **District courts,** which are courts of record, are the trial courts of the federal court system that hear civil and criminal cases. Each state is divided into one or more judicial districts, and each district has at least one district court. Generally, district courts hear cases involving questions of federal law and cases involving citizens of two states or disputes between two states.

Court of appeals constitute the first level of appellate court in the federal court system. The United States is divided into thirteen circuits, and there is a court of appeals for each circuit. See Exhibit 1-8. There are usually nine appellate judges for each court, with panels of three judges hearing different appeals. However, when the court is presented with an issue of great importance or impact, the court may meet **en banc** (ən *bænk*), which means all of the judges of the court will hear the case and render a decision.

EXHIBIT 1-8 | FEDERAL COURT CIRCUITS

FIRST CIRCUIT
Maine
New Hampshire
Rhode Island
Puerto Rico

FOURTH CIRCUIT
Maryland
North Carolina
South Carolina
Virginia

SEVENTH CIRCUIT
Illinois
Indiana
Wisconsin

TENTH CIRCUIT
Colorado
Kansas
New Mexico
Oklahoma
Utah
Wyoming

SECOND CIRCUIT
Connecticut
New York
Vermont

FIFTH CIRCUIT
Louisiana
Mississippi
Texas

EIGHTH CIRCUIT
Arkansas
Iowa
Minnesota
Missouri
Nebraska
North Dakota
South Dakota

ELEVENTH CIRCUIT
Alabama
Florida
Georgia

THIRD CIRCUIT
Delaware
New Jersey
Pennsylvania
Virgin Islands

SIXTH CIRCUIT
Kentucky
Michigan
Ohio
Tennessee

NINTH CIRCUIT
Alaska
Arizona
California
Hawaii
Idaho
Montana
Nevada
Oregon
Washington
Guam
Mariana Islands

U.S. Court of Appeals for the Federal Court
D.C. Circuit—Washington D.C.

The **U.S. Supreme Court** is the highest court in the United States. Nine justices—a title given to judges at the appellate level—serve on the Supreme Court. All justices are nominated by the President of the United States, approved by the U.S. Senate, and serve for life. Article III of the U.S. Constitution created the Court, which means that the Supreme Court is a constitutional court. The U.S. Supreme Court consists of the Chief Justice and eight associate justices.

SPECIAL FEDERAL COURTS

There are also additional special courts in the federal court system; each has its own limited jurisdiction and powers. The **United States Bankruptcy Court** is a federal trial court of record that has limited jurisdiction because it only hears bankruptcy cases. It is presided over by a bankruptcy judge. This federal court is the only court that has the authority to hear bankruptcy cases; no other federal or state court can hear this type of case.

The **United States Tax Court,** which is authorized by § 7441 of the Internal Revenue Code, is a court of record and has limited jurisdiction. If the Commissioner of the Internal Revenue Service determines that there are deficiencies in the amount of income, estate, or gift taxes paid and the taxpayer challenges that determination, then the U.S. Tax Court hears the case and determines if there was a deficiency or an overpayment of taxes. Its decisions may be appealed to a U.S. court of appeals and to the U.S. Supreme Court.

The **United States Claims Court** is authorized by 28 U.S.C. § 1491 and is also a court of limited jurisdiction. Anyone who has a claim against the United States because of the Constitution, a federal statute or regulation, a contract dispute, or a claim for other damages may file his or her claim with this court. Appeals are to the **U.S. Court of Appeals for the Federal Circuit.** The U.S. Court of Appeals for the Federal Circuit was established in 1982 and is authorized by 28 U.S.C. § 1295. This court is an appellate court that has the authority to hear appeals of decisions from the United States Claims Court, decisions from the Patent and Trademark Office, copyright decisions, decisions from the U.S. Court of International Trade, the Merit Systems Protection Board, and the Court of Veterans Appeals, and decisions from the United States International Trade Commission regarding unfair import practices.

Other special federal appellate courts are the U.S. Court of Veterans Appeals, the U.S. Court of Military Review, and the U.S. Court of Military Appeals. The **U.S. Court of Appeals for Veterans Claims,** which was created by 38 U.S.C. § 4051 in 1988, hears appeals of decisions made by the Board of Veterans Appeals. The **U.S. Courts of Military Review,** for the U.S. Army, Navy, Air Force, Marine Corps, and Coast Guard, were created in 1968 by the Military Justice Act of 1968, 10 U.S.C. § 866. These are intermediate criminal appellate courts that hear and review court martial convictions related to the different services. Each is made up of one or more panels of military justices; each panel consists of at least three members. The court may choose to sit as a panel or may meet en banc. The **U.S. Court of Military Appeals** was established in 1950 by 10 U.S.C. § 867. It is a civilian (not a military) appellate court that is responsible for reviewing criminal court martial convictions from every branch of military service. If a soldier is found guilty of a criminal offense, this is the court that hears the appeal of the conviction. The court consists of three civilian judges who are appointed by the President of the United States. It is responsible for reviewing cases where the sentence is death, a prison sentence of a year or longer in a military prison, or punitive discharge from the military. The decisions of this court may be appealed to the U.S. Supreme Court.

The **U.S. Court of International Trade** is made up of a chief judge and eight additional judges. This court has jurisdiction over civil cases against the United States arising out of federal laws governing import transactions. It also makes determinations as to whether workers, firms, and communities are eligible for adjustment assistance under the Trade Act of 1974. The court also has jurisdiction over cases initiated by the United States to recover customs duties, to recover on custom bonds, or to seek civil penalties for fraud or negligence. See Exhibit 1-9 for the federal court structure.

OFFICERS OF THE COURT

The **officers of the court** is a collective term that refers to the different personnel who make up the court system, each with a different role in the legal process. The official designation for each of these persons helps describe his or her role in the legal process.

GENERAL PERSONNEL

The **clerk of the court** is responsible for filing pleadings, motions, judgements, and other documents related to the trial. The clerk will also issue service of process and keep the records of the court proceedings. The **bailiff** (*bail*-if) is the officer of the court in charge of

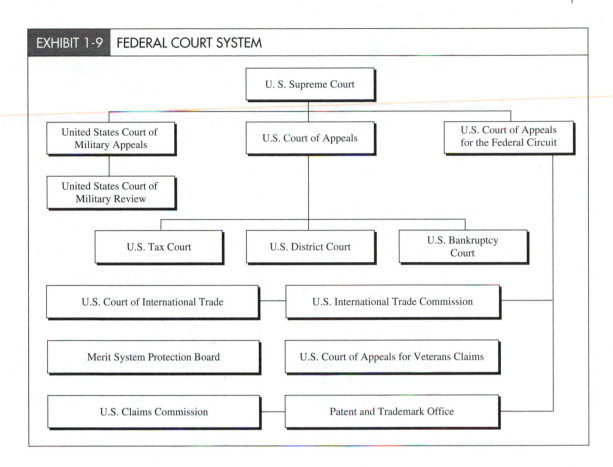

EXHIBIT 1-9 FEDERAL COURT SYSTEM

keeping order during the court session. This person keeps custody of the jury and of any prisoners while they are in court.

JUDGES

There are several different tiers of judges and judicial officers, depending on the amount of authority they have to conduct hearings and the type of hearings they can conduct. A **magistrate** is an inferior judicial officer. A **justice of the peace** is a judicial magistrate who has limited jurisdiction over civil and criminal matters. The civil matters are usually limited to performing marriages, and the criminal matters are usually limited to minor criminal offenses. A committing magistrate is an inferior judicial officer who has the authority to conduct a preliminary hearing of a person who is charged with a crime to determine if there is sufficient evidence to hold the person for trial or not. In some jurisdictions, this magistrate also has the power to determine whether or not bail should be granted. A United States magistrate is a judicial officer, appointed by federal district court judges, who has many of the powers of the district court judge. The magistrate may hear motions and other pre-trial matters in both civil and criminal cases, and may even conduct civil or misdemeanor criminal trials if the parties involved agree. These magistrates are prohibited by law from presiding over criminal cases where the person is charged with a felony and may not even preside over the selection of a jury for a felony case.

A judge is an officer of the court who presides over the entire court, is responsible for controlling the proceedings of the court, and issues decisions regarding questions of law. This term is usually assigned to trial level courts. A **justice** is a judge of the U.S. Supreme Court and the supreme courts of the states; the term also applies to judges of appellate courts. The **chief justice** is the presiding, most senior, or principal judge of a court. A **presiding judge** is the judge that directs, controls, or regulates the court proceedings; he or she is the chief officer of the court. For example, the presiding justice of the U.S. Supreme Court is the Chief Justice. The Chief Justice is appointed by the President, and is not necessarily the justice with the longest length of service on the court. Each of the other justices of the court is referred to as an **associate justice.** For example, there are nine justices on the U.S. Supreme Court. The Chief Justice is the presiding justice, and the remaining eight justices are associate justices of the Supreme Court. Refer to Exhibit 1-10 for a summary of court personnel.

EXHIBIT 1-10	COURT PERSONNEL

1. **Clerk of the Court** – Person responsible for filing all pleadings and other documents in the case files
2. **Bailiff** – Person responsible for maintaining order in the courtroom during court proceedings
3. **Justice of the Peace** – Judicial magistrate possessing very limited authority over certain civil and criminal matters
4. **Committing Magistrate** – Inferior judicial official possessing the authority to conduct a criminal preliminary hearing
5. **U.S. Magistrate** – Judicial officer appointed by a federal judge to hear motions and pre-trial matters in federal civil and criminal cases
6. **Judge** – Officer of the court who presides over the entire court; is responsible for controlling the proceedings of the court and issuing decisions regarding the law
7. **Justice** – Judge of the U.S. Supreme Court and the appellate courts of the different states
8. **Chief Justice** – Presiding, most senior, or principal judge of a court

THE LEGISLATIVE PROCESS

Some laws in the United States are derived from common law. Others are created by the state and federal legislatures. Such laws are created when bills are introduced and passed in response to the needs or requests of the legislature's constituency.

BASIC STRUCTURE OF THE LEGISLATURE

A **legislature** is a department, assembly, or body of people who make statutory laws for a state or for the United States. The legislature of the United States is the **United States Congress.** (The term *congress* refers to a formal meeting of delegates or representatives.) The United States Congress was created by Article I, Section I of the U.S. Constitution. It is a **bicameral** (bi-*cam*-er-all) legislature, meaning that it is divided into two separate chambers: the Senate and the House of Representatives. Most states also utilize a bicameral legislature. The **U.S. House of Representatives** has 435 elected representatives from all fifty states. The number of representatives from each state is determined by the state's population; each state is entitled to at least one representative. Members of the House of Representatives serve a two-year term of office. They are called Congressmen or Congresswomen, but technically that term refers to a person who is a member of Congress, so it could apply to senators as well. The number of representatives each state is entitled to is determined by **apportionment,** which is the process used to distribute legislative seats among the "units" entitled to representation. Districting is the establishment of the geographical boundaries of each such unit. **Reapportionment** is the realignment or redrawing of legislative districts based on changes in population as indicated by the U.S. Census, which occurs every ten years. The **U.S. Senate** is considered the "upper" chamber of Congress and has 102 members, two from each state and two from the District of Columbia. **Senators,** the elected members of the Senate, serve a six-year term. Senators and representatives are also known as legislative officers, the members of the legislative body whose duties are the enactment of laws. Exhibit 1-11 summarizes the make-up of the United States Congress and Exhibit 1-12 lists how many representatives each state currently has in Congress.

EXHIBIT 1-11	UNITED STATES CONGRESS

Created by Article I, Section 1 of the United States Constitution

Bicameral Legislature – Two separate chambers

House of Representatives – The number of representatives is determined by each state's population; currently 435.

Senate – Two senators are elected from each state (regardless of that state's population) and two are elected from the District of Columbia, for a total of 102.

Representatives serve for two years.

Senators serve for six years.

EXHIBIT 1-12	NUMBER OF REPRESENTATIVES FROM EACH STATE

Alabama – 7	Alaska – 1	Arizona – 6	Arkansas – 4
California – 52	Colorado – 6	Connecticut – 6	Delaware – 1
D.C. – 1	Florida – 23	Georgia – 11	Hawaii – 2
Idaho – 2	Illinois – 20	Indiana – 10	Iowa – 5
Kansas – 4	Kentucky – 6	Louisiana – 7	Maine – 2
Maryland – 8	Massachusetts – 10	Michigan – 18	Minnesota – 8
Mississippi – 5	Missouri – 9	Montana – 1	Nebraska – 3
Nevada – 2	New Hampshire – 2	New Jersey – 13	New Mexico – 3
New York – 31	North Carolina – 12	North Dakota – 1	Ohio – 19
Oklahoma – 6	Oregon – 5	Pennsylvania – 21	Rhode Island – 2
South Carolina – 6	South Dakota – 1	Tennessee – 9	Texas – 31
Utah – 3	Vermont – 1	Virginia – 11	Washington – 9
West Virginia – 3	Wisconsin – 9	Wyoming – 1	

LEGISLATIVE SESSIONS

A Congressional session refers to the period of time the legislature is meeting for the transaction of business. *Session* can refer to a particular day, or it can refer to the entire period of time the legislature meets, from the first day to adjournment *sine die.* **Adjournment** is the postponing or setting aside of business of a session until another time and place. For example, the House of Representatives could adjourn until April 4 at 9:00 A.M.—a definite date and time are set for when the House will meet again. **Sine die** (*sán*iy *dáy*) means "without day." When a legislature adjourns sine die, it adjourns without setting another date and time when it will reassemble. This adjournment occurs at the end of the legislative session.

The primary business the legislature is conducting is legislative business, which is the function of making laws and the process of the enactment of laws. **Enactment** is the method or process by which a bill becomes law. When something is enacted, it is established by law, and **legislation** is the actual making of the law. It is also a term used when referring to the laws enacted by Congress. In order to create a new law, a bill, which is a draft of a proposed law, is introduced for consideration. Each bill introduced will have an **enactment clause** included at its beginning, which states the authority by which it is being made. This identifies the bill as legislation arising from the proper legislative authority. For example, a federal statute may read, "Be it enacted by the Senate and House of Representatives of the United States of America in Congress Assembled."

THE STATUS OF BILLS

As the bill proceeds through the legislative process, different terms indicating its status are assigned to it. When a bill goes into committee for consideration, it may be amended; this process is called **marking up.** The committee goes through the bill section by section, revising and amending its language. If the revisions are extensive enough, a new bill with a new number may be introduced. The bill that has gone through this process is the **marked-up bill. Engrossment** is the process of writing the bill in its final form, including all amendments, prior to the final vote on the bill. An **engrossed bill** is a bill that is in its final format—one that is ready to be voted on by the entire legislature. When a bill has been passed by both houses of the legislature, has been signed by the appropriate officers from the legislature, and is being forwarded to the President or governor for signature, it is known as an **enrolled bill.** See Exhibit 1-13. Once both houses have approved the bill, it becomes an **act** or a **legislative act,** a piece of legislation that has been approved by both houses of Congress.

EXHIBIT 1-13 | **TYPES OF BILLS**

1. **Marked-Up Bill** – Bill that has been amended or revised
2. **Engrossed Bill** – Bill that is in its final format and is ready to be voted on by the entire legislature
3. **Enrolled Bill** – Bill that has been passed by both houses of a legislature and that is ready to be signed by the president or governor

---

VETO OF A BILL

An act becomes law when the president or the governor of the state signs the act. If the president or governor disagrees with the act, he or she may veto it. A **veto** is the refusal of the president or governor to sign into law a bill that has been passed by the legislature. At the federal level, a message is usually sent to Congress explaining why the act has been vetoed. At the federal level, Congress can **override the veto.** A veto override occurs when Congress, by a two-thirds vote of both houses, passes the legislation again. Because the veto has been overridden, the act becomes law because it passed by a two-thirds vote. A **pocket veto** is also a veto of the legislation, but it is not a written veto. The president or governor takes no action on the act; it is not rejected, but it is also not approved before the legislature adjourns. If the bill is not acted upon before the legislature adjourns, the act is vetoed: it is said the president or governor has put it "in his or her pocket." A line item veto is a power given to some state governors, but it does not exist at the federal level. **Line item veto** is the power a governor has to veto items in appropriation bills without vetoing the entire bill. The governor can pick and choose which parts of the appropriation act he or she will approve and disapprove. Refer to Exhibit 1-14 for the process by which a bill becomes law.

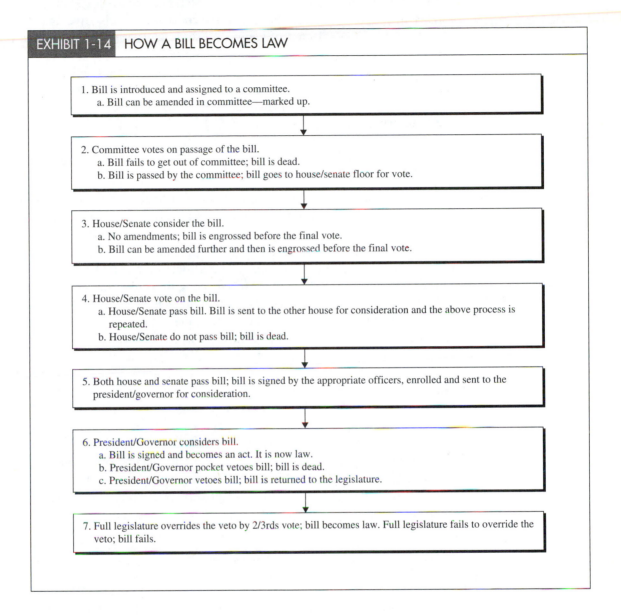

EXHIBIT 1-14   HOW A BILL BECOMES LAW

1. Bill is introduced and assigned to a committee.
   a. Bill can be amended in committee—marked up.

2. Committee votes on passage of the bill.
   a. Bill fails to get out of committee; bill is dead.
   b. Bill is passed by the committee; bill goes to house/senate floor for vote.

3. House/Senate consider the bill.
   a. No amendments; bill is engrossed before the final vote.
   b. Bill can be amended further and then is engrossed before the final vote.

4. House/Senate vote on the bill.
   a. House/Senate pass bill. Bill is sent to the other house for consideration and the above process is repeated.
   b. House/Senate do not pass bill; bill is dead.

5. Both house and senate pass bill; bill is signed by the appropriate officers, enrolled and sent to the president/governor for consideration.

6. President/Governor considers bill.
   a. Bill is signed and becomes an act. It is now law.
   b. President/Governor pocket vetoes bill; bill is dead.
   c. President/Governor vetoes bill; bill is returned to the legislature.

7. Full legislature overrides the veto by 2/3rds vote; bill becomes law. Full legislature fails to override the veto; bill fails.

GRANDFATHER CLAUSES AND SPECIAL SESSIONS

Sometimes legislation that has been passed initiates the regulation of a business or profession that has not previously been regulated, or it may apply a new requirement to existing regulations or legislation. This type of legislation may contain a **grandfather clause,** a provision in the legislation that exempts those already in the system or position that is being regulated. For example, people who have no degree in social work are being licensed as social workers. A legislature passes a law that states that only people with a degree in social work can become licensed social workers. But it also contains a grandfather clause that states that those who do not have a degree but who are licensed on the effective date of the act may continue to be licensed. Any new applicant must meet the new standard, but those who are already licensed may continue to be licensed.

At the state level, if an issue arises when the legislature is not in session, the governor may call an **extraordinary session** of the legislature. These sessions meet in the intervals between regular sessions and are usually limited to considering the matters specified by the governor in calling the session. In some states, when the legislature is not in session, the legislative council meets. The **legislative council** is a legislative agency composed of legislators and other selected officials who study legislative problems and plan strategy between the regularly scheduled legislative sessions.

At the local level, a city council has the authority to pass legislation affecting local matters such as zoning, building regulations, and safety measures (for example, speed limits within the city). The enactments of the legislative body of a municipality are referred to as **ordinances.**

TYPES OF BILLS

There are four special types of bills: the appropriations bill, the authorization bill, the public bill, and the private bill. An **appropriations bill** is a bill that deals with the raising and spending of public money. It specifies how much money may be spent for a particular purpose. The bill that actually authorizes the spending of the public funds that have been appropriated for a specific purpose is an **authorization bill.** A **private bill** is legislation that deals with an issue that is a private, personal, or local issue only. This bill is for a particular purpose and no other. Legislation that is for the benefit of the whole "community" (in the case of the U.S. Congress, the entire United States) is known as a **public bill.**

One special type of bill, an **omnibus bill,** contains legislation dealing with several different issues at the same time. Its purpose is to compel the president or the governor of a state to sign the bill because it contains measures he or she approves of. It also contains measures he or she might not approve of, but in order to enact laws he or she favors, the president or governor also has to approve laws he or she may not favor. Congress may also pass a **resolution,** which is a formal expression of an opinion of the legislature adopted by vote. The resolution is to express an opinion about some issue or matter, and it has only a temporary effect. The resolution can be a **concurrent resolution,** one that is passed or adopted in one house of the legislature with the other house concurring or agreeing. A joint resolution is one that is passed or adopted by both houses of the legislature. The types of bills are summarized in Exhibit 1-15.

EXHIBIT 1-15 TYPES OF BILLS
1. **Appropriations Bill** – Deals with the raising and spending of money; states what money will be spent for
2. **Authorization Bill** – Authorizes the money that has been appropriated to actually be spent
3. **Private Bill** – Deals with a private or personal matter only; bill is for a particular purpose
4. **Public Bill** – Benefits the entire community
5. **Omnibus Bill** – Deals with several different issues at the same time

CONCLUSION

In the legal system used in the United States, certain terms are used to describe the court itself (trial court or appellate court) and certain terms describe types of courts. For example, a circuit court may hear civil and criminal cases; a court of general jurisdiction can hear a broad category of cases; a court of limited jurisdiction can hear only certain types of cases. Courts are further described in terms of where they fit into the judicial hierarchy: a municipal court, a circuit court, a court of appeals, or the Supreme Court. Courts at the federal level include U.S. district courts, which are trial courts; U.S. courts of appeals, which are intermediate appellate courts, and the U.S. Supreme Court, the highest court in the country. The term *judge* refers to the deciding official at the trial level; *justice* refers to appellate court judges.

Terms that indicate where the law comes from include *common law* (law that is made by judicial decision) and *statutory law* (law that is written and passed by legislatures). Before legislation becomes law, it is first a bill that may be marked up, then engrossed, and finally enrolled. Once a bill passes the legislature, it can still be vetoed by either the governor of a state or the president, but the veto can be overridden. The terms in this chapter all refer to where laws come from, how they are created, and the institutions and persons responsible for applying and interpreting them.

CHAPTER 1 REVIEW

KEY WORDS AND PHRASES

act
adjournment
adversary system
appellate court
apportionment
appropriations bill
associate justice
authorization bill
bailiff
bicameral
chancellor
chancery court
chief justice
circuit court
common law
concurrent resolution
congress
constitutional law
court
court of record
criminal court

district court
en banc
enactment
enactment clause
engrossed bill
equity
equity court
extraordinary session
grandfather clause
judge
justice
juvenile court
juvenile delinquency
legislation
legislature
line item veto
magistrate
marked-up bill
municipal court
omnibus bill
ordinance

overriding a veto
pocket veto
precedent
private bill
probate court
public bill
reapportionment
resolution
sine die
stare decisis
statutory law
trial court
veto
U.S. House of
  Representatives
U.S. Senate
United States Bankruptcy
  Court
United States Congress

REVIEW QUESTIONS

SHORT ANSWER

1. What is a court of record?

2. What is the difference between a court of limited jurisdiction and one of general jurisdiction?

3. Which courts are the trial courts of the federal system?

4. Probate court hears what type of cases?

5. Which court is the highest court in the United States?

6. Who presides over hearings in chancery court?

7. How is *juvenile delinquency* defined?

8. What type of system is in place in the United States?

9. What does it mean when the court meets en banc?

10. What term is used to refer to a legislature's adjourning without setting a date for its next meeting?

11. What is the difference between an act and a bill?

12. What type of bill gives permission to spend money?
13. What type of bill sets the amount of money that can be spent?
14. What is the difference between a legislature's regular session and a special session?
15. How long do U.S. senators serve?
16. How long do U.S. representatives serve?
17. What is an omnibus bill?
18. What is the difference between a public bill and a private bill?
19. What is a resolution?

FILL IN THE BLANK

1. A bill that makes amendments to an existing law is _____.
2. A legislature made up of two separate houses is referred to as _____.
3. The authority an executive officer has to veto specific spending items in a bill is a _____.
4. The clause that makes a law effective is known as the _____ clause.
5. What is the difference between a veto and a pocket veto?
6. The types of opinions an appellate court can issue are _____

   _____

   _____
7. Judge-made law is also termed _____.
8. The _____ hears appeals from the United States Tax Court.
9. Claims against the federal government are presented in the _____ court.
10. Federal Bankruptcy Court is a court of _____ jurisdiction.

FACT SITUATIONS

1. Henry has lost his appeal in the highest state court. Where else can he file his appeal?
2. Suzanne has filed an appeal with the U.S. Court of Appeals regarding a decision the court made in her case against her former employer. One of the issues on appeal is the same one raised by several other appeals filed subsequently to hers. What phrase is used to describe the entire Court of Appeals' decision to hear the appeal?
3. The United States is suing an importer of goods for failing to pay custom duties. Which court has authority to hear this case?
4. A soldier is tried and convicted of murder in a military court. Where may he file an appeal of his conviction? If he is not satisfied with that decision, where else may he appeal his case?
5. The IRS audits Drew's tax returns and determines that he owes $1,000 in back taxes. If Drew wishes to contest this determination, where does he bring his case?
6. Congress has voted to allow the Department of Justice to spend $800,000 to fill three new federal judgeships. Which types of legislation must Congress have passed to allow the Department of Justice to receive and spend this money?
7. Enrique has asked his senator to introduce a bill that gives his business a tax break for five years. What type of bill will the senator introduce?
8. The United States basketball team wins the Olympic gold medal. What sort of legislation would Congress pass to congratulate the team on this victory?

9. Congress passes a bill that the president opposes, but for political reasons, the president does not want to veto it outright. He leaves the bill sitting on his desk for several days. What has the president done and what, if anything, can Congress do?

10. Congress passes a bill that deals with the rights of the disabled, minimum wage laws, and food and drug labeling laws. What type of bill did Congress pass?

CHAPTER 2
Criminal Law

INTRODUCTION

Any study of criminal law includes a study of the crimes themselves and the procedures used prior to trial and during trial in order to ensure that the rights of the accused are protected. In this chapter, what constitutes a crime and how crimes are classified will be discussed. Mens rea and actus rea will be covered, and the mental states required to commit crimes will be explained. The chapter also explores crimes against persons (assault, battery, kidnapping, manslaughter, and murder), as well as crimes against property (forgery, counterfeiting, embezzlement, blackmail, and robbery). Sexual offenses are covered, as well as how a person can be held criminally liable for simply participating in the planning, carrying out, or cover-up of a crime.

GENERAL PRINCIPLES

Generally, a **crime** is a positive or negative act in violation of penal law; it is an offense against a state or the United States. If a person breaks a law, then that person has committed a crime. How serious a crime has been committed depends on how the crime is classified and what actions constitute the crime.

CAPITAL AND CONTINUOUS CRIMES AND CRIMES OF PASSION

The most serious crime is a **capital crime,** which is punishable by death. An example of such a crime is capital murder. A **continuous crime** consists of a series of acts that extend beyond the period the crime was initially committed. For example, carrying a concealed weapon is a continuous crime: the crime began when the person concealed the weapon, and it continues as long as the weapon remains concealed on the person. A **crime of passion** is a crime committed in the heat of extreme emotional distress suddenly aroused by an immediate and reasonable provocation. The provocation for the crime can be an act or it can be verbal. For example, a husband and wife get into an argument that becomes heated; one spouse picks up an object and strikes the other spouse with it. There is no plan to do this; it happened in the "heat of the moment."

ACTUS REA AND MENS REA

In order for a person to commit a crime, he must perform the **actus rea** (*ahk*-tus *ray*), the criminal act—the physical aspect of the crime, the act itself—and he must have the necessary **mens rea** (*menz ray*), the criminal intent to do the act (a guilty mind). Each definition of a crime includes the actus rea and the mens rea, which together make up the criminal activity. In order for a person to be convicted of committing a crime, both the actus rea and the mens rea have to be proven. If both are not shown, then legally a person cannot be convicted of having committed a crime. In other words, not only must a crime have been committed, but the person responsible for the crime must have had the necessary mental intent. If both of these are not present, then the person cannot be convicted of committing the crime. Refer to Exhibit 2-1 for the necessary elements of a crime.

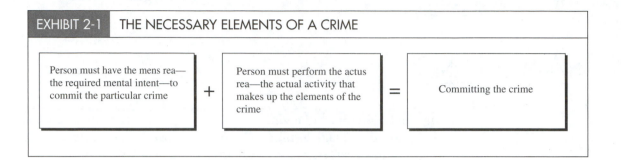

EXHIBIT 2-1 THE NECESSARY ELEMENTS OF A CRIME

| Person must have the mens rea—the required mental intent—to commit the particular crime | + | Person must perform the actus rea—the actual activity that makes up the elements of the crime | = | Committing the crime |

THE FOUR MENTAL STATES

According to the Modal Penal Code, there are four **culpable** (*kul-pa*-bull), or guilty, mental states: purposely, knowingly, recklessly, and negligently. One of these mental states is identified for each crime; this identifies the mental state that must be proven in order to convict someone of a crime. A person acts **purposely,** or intentionally, when it is his conscious objective to engage in conduct of that nature or to cause such a result. For example, if a person goes into a bank with a gun, approaches a teller, and informs the teller that "This is a hold-up," the conscious objective of the person—what the person intended to do—was rob the bank. A person acts **knowingly** when she is aware that it is almost certain that her conduct will cause a particular result. For example, if a person fires a weapon at another person, she may not intend to kill that person, but she knows that it is almost certain that if the bullets she is firing hit the victim in the right place, the victim will be killed. A person acts **recklessly** when he *consciously disregards* a substantial and unjustifiable risk that certain results will occur. The risk must be of a nature and a degree that constitutes a gross deviation from the standard of care a reasonable person would use in the same situation. For example, a driver of a vehicle starts down a very steep hill that is covered with ice. Children are playing at the bottom of this hill. There is a risk that if the person goes down the hill, he will not be able to control his vehicle and may injure one or more of the children. Most drivers would choose not to go down the hill until the children are gone or would use an alternate route. However, this driver chooses to go down the icy hill, and accelerates as he is going down the hill. His act is considered reckless. A person acts **negligently** when she *should be* aware of a substantial and unjustifiable risk that certain circumstances exist or that certain results will occur. The four mental states are summarized in Exhibit 2-2. Exhibit 2-3 features examples of actus rea and mens rea in a criminal statute.

EXHIBIT 2-2 THE FOUR CULPABLE MENTAL STATES

1. **Purposely** – Intent to engage in the criminal conduct
2. **Knowingly** – Almost certain that the conduct will result in a crime
3. **Recklessly** – Intend to disregard the risk that criminal conduct will occur
4. **Negligently** – Should be aware of the risk that criminal conduct will occur

---

EXHIBIT 2-3 | **ACTUS REA AND MENS REA IN CRIMINAL STATUTES**

5-41-202. Unlawful acts regarding computers.

(a) A person commits an unlawful act regarding a computer if the person **knowingly** (**mens rea**) and without authorization

  (1) Modifies, damages, destroys, discloses, uses, transfers, conceals, takes, retains possession of, copies, obtains or attempts to obtain access to, permits access to or causes to be accessed, or enters data or a program which exists inside or outside a computer, system, or network (**actus rea**).

(b) An unlawful act regarding a computer is a Class A misdemeanor.

5-41-206. Computer password disclosure.

(a) A person commits computer password disclosure if the person **purposely** (**mens rea**) and without authorization discloses a number, code, password, or other means of access to a computer or computer network (**actus rea**).

(b) Computer password disclosure is a Class A misdemeanor.

FELONY OR MISDEMEANOR

There are several ways to classify crimes. One such classification is as a felony or misdemeanor. A **felony** (*fel*-a-nee) is a crime of graver or more serious nature than one designated as a misdemeanor. Felonies are usually punishable by at least a year in prison. Examples of crimes that are felonies include murder, rape, arson, kidnapping, and manslaughter. A **misdemeanor** (mis-de-*mee*-ner) is an offense that is lesser than a felony and is usually punishable by fine, penalty, forfeiture, or imprisonment somewhere other than in a penitentiary. Examples include assault, some cases of battery, and theft below a certain dollar amount. Crimes can also be classified as crimes against the person or crimes against property.

CRIMES AGAINST THE PERSON

Crimes against the person are crimes that affect the physical or mental well-being of another. This classification includes such crimes as assault, battery, kidnapping, murder, manslaughter, and rape. Refer to Exhibit 2-11 for a listing of the crimes against the person.

ASSAULT AND BATTERY

Assault (ə-*salt*) is the willful attempt or threat to inflict injury upon the body of another. The person committing the assault must have an apparent present ability to do so, and the display of force must give the victim reason to fear or expect immediate bodily harm. These conditions are important to the definition of *assault*. For example, a person who is five feet tall and weighs 100 pounds does not commit the crime of assault by threatening to beat up the heavyweight boxing champion of the world. However, if the same person threatens the champion with a .357 magnum pistol, then an assault has taken place because he now has the present ability to carry out the threat.

    Aggravated assault is carried out with the intention of committing an additional crime; in other words, something more than assault takes place. Aggravated assault can be the threat that, if something is not done, further harm will result. For example, a person can be threatened with a gun and told that if he does not give up all his money, he will be shot. The assault is the threat to shoot the victim; the additional crime is the robbery. A simple assault is unaccompanied by any circumstances of aggravation; the assault is the only crime that was committed. The threatening of bodily harm to another is enough for simple assault to be charged. See Exhibit 2-4 for a summary of the types of assault.

EXHIBIT 2-4	ASSAULT

Assault – Attempt or threat to carry out bodily harm on another person; perpetrator must have the present ability to carry out the threat

Simple Assault – The assault is the only crime committed

Aggravated Assault – Assault with the intention of carrying out another crime

Battery (*bat*-er-ee) is intentional and wrongful physical contact with a person without his consent that involves an injury or offensive touching. Physical harm does not have to take place; a touching that is offensive is enough. Simple battery does not result in serious bodily injury; it can include grabbing or fondling. **Aggravated battery** causes violent injury to a person and may involve the use of a deadly weapon. For example, if a person is shot with a pistol, there has been violent injury involving the use of a deadly weapon; thus, aggravated battery has taken place. Aggravated battery can also be committed by a person who hits a victim with a hammer, causing a concussion and broken bones; there was a violent injury, but it was carried out with something other than a deadly weapon. See Exhibit 2-5 for a summary of the types of battery.

EXHIBIT 2-5	BATTERY

Battery – Intentional physical contact with another person without that person's consent; physical harm is not required

Simple Battery – Physical contact only; there is no injury to the person who is touched or fondled

Aggravated Battery – Battery that results in serious injury to a person; a deadly weapon may be involved

An assault can take place without a battery, a battery can take place without an assault, and an assault and battery can take place concurrently. **Assault and battery** is the unlawful touching of another that is without any justification; the threat of immediate bodily harm is followed by actual bodily harm. See Exhibit 2-6.

EXHIBIT 2-6	ASSAULT AND BATTERY

Assault and Battery – A threat of bodily harm is made followed by the actual infliction of bodily harm; there must be the threat of contact, followed by the actual contact.

Important Note: There can be an assault *without* a battery, and there can be a battery *without* an assault.

If assault is threatening a person with a hammer, then battery is actually hitting that person with the hammer. Assault is an example of an **inchoate crime** (in-kow-ət), one that tends to lead to the commission of another crime or that is part of another crime. Assault is an inchoate crime because it can lead to or be part of a battery.

KIDNAPPING

Kidnapping, which is classified as a felony, is the unlawful taking and carrying away of a person against his will by force, fraud, threats, or intimidation. **Kidnapping for ransom** occurs when an individual is detained for the purpose of getting money from the person kidnapped or from another as the price for the person's release. **Ransom** is the price demanded or paid to have a kidnapped person released from captivity. The ransom demanded does not have to be actually paid in order for it to be considered ransom; the demand is enough. Also, ransom does not have to be money; it can be whatever is demanded or used to release the person being held. For example, ransom could be payment of $100,000 or it could be the demand that a contract worth $100,000 be signed.

MURDER AND MANSLAUGHTER

Manslaughter is the unjustifiable, inexcusable, and intentional killing of another human being without premeditation and malice. **Malice** is the intentional doing of a wrongful act without just cause or excuse, with an intent to inflict an injury. **Premeditation** is the decision or plan to commit a crime, but it does not have to exist for a set period of time prior to the crime being committed. If an intentional act causes the death of a person but there is no malice or premeditation involved, the person who commits the act has no intention of performing a wrongful deed; then, the act is manslaughter, not murder.

Voluntary manslaughter is committed with design or intention; it was the person's intent to kill another human being, but there is no premeditation—no planning involved prior to committing the act. **Involuntary manslaughter** is the unlawful killing of a person while another crime that is a misdemeanor, not a felony, is being committed. For example, a person is driving too fast and hits a pedestrian. The misdemeanor is the violation of the speed limit, which was occurring when the victim was hit by the car. Involuntary manslaughter also occurs when a person is committing a lawful act that might produce death in an unlawful manner.

Murder is the unlawful killing of another person with malice aforethought, either expressed or implied by the killer's conduct. To be charged with murder, a person must have deliberately thought about committing the murder, and then acted on his or her intent. Refer to Exhibit 2-7 for the distinctions among manslaughter, involuntary manslaughter, and murder.

EXHIBIT 2-7	DISTINCTIONS AMONG MURDER, MANSLAUGHTER AND INVOLUNTARY MANSLAUGHTER

Murder – **Intentional** killing of another person **with** premeditation and malice; there *must* be intent, premeditation, and malice.

Manslaughter – **Intentional** killing of another person **without** premeditation and without malice; there *must* be intent with no premeditation and no malice.

Involuntary manslaughter – **Unintentional** killing of another person while **committing a misdemeanor;** *no* intent, *no* premeditation, *no* malice while committing a misdemeanor.

If a person causes the unintentional death of another while committing a felony, then the person has also committed murder; this is the **felony murder doctrine.** For example, if someone kidnaps a victim and causes the victim's death in the course of the kidnapping, he or she can be charged with felony murder. The felony that was committed was the kidnapping of the person; the murder of the person took place as a result of the kidnapping.

RAPE AND SEXUAL OFFENSES

Rape is unlawful sexual intercourse with a woman or a man without his or her consent. Rape can be committed when a person's resistance is overcome by force or fear or by the use of drugs or intoxicants of which the victim has no knowledge. If a person is incapable of giving consent to sexual activity because she or he is drugged or intoxicated, having sex with her or him can be considered rape. **Statutory rape** is sexual intercourse with a person who is under the statutory age of consent. This does not necessarily mean the sexual intercourse involved a minor. The statutory age of consent for sexual activity may be lower than the age of majority, or it could be higher than the age of majority. The offense of statutory rape may be either with or without the victim's consent, and ignorance about her or his age is not a defense. If the person is a minor he or she cannot give "consent," and ignorance about the person's age is not allowed to be a defense. See Exhibit 2-8.

EXHIBIT 2-8	RAPE

A common law, only men could commit the crime of rape, and only women could be the victims of the crime of rape.

Rape – Unlawful sexual intercourse with a man or woman without his or her consent; if consent is obtained through force or fear, or the victim is too drunk or drugged to resist, then there is no consensual sex, and the act is an act of rape.

Statutory Rape – Sexual intercourse with a person who is under the age of consent; even if the victim "consents" to the activity, it is still statutory rape because consent is not a defense.

What constitutes sodomy and carnal abuse varies from state to state, so definitions of these crimes tend to be quite general. **Sodomy** (*sod*-ə-mee) is oral or anal sex between humans or between humans and animals. Carnal (*kar*-nal) abuse is generally defined as the indulgence of sensual/sexual pleasures with the sexual organs of another person without actual penetration and without consent. This can include fondling. **Sexual abuse** is an illegal sexual act performed against a minor by a parent, guardian, relative, or acquaintance; the sexual act can be vaginal, anal, or oral in nature. Indecent exposure is the exposure to the sight of others of the private parts of the body in a lewd or indecent manner in a public place. Some federal statutes define sex crimes; one such statute is the **Mann Act,** or the White Slave Traffic Act, which is found at 18 U.S.C. § 2421. The Mann Act makes the transportation of a woman or a child in interstate or foreign commerce for the purpose of prostitution or other immoral act a federal crime. Refer to Exhibit 2-9 for an example of a state sexual offenses statute.

EXHIBIT 2-9 STATE SEX OFFENSE STATUTES

Section 13A-6-61
Rape in the first degree.

(a) A person commits the crime of rape in the first degree if:
  (1) He or she engages in sexual intercourse with a member of the opposite sex by forcible compulsion; or
  (2) He or she engages in sexual intercourse with a member of the opposite sex who is incapable of consent by reason of being physically helpless or mentally incapacitated; or
  (3) He or she, being 16 years or older, engages in sexual intercourse with a member of the opposite sex who is less than 12 years old.

Section 13A-6-63
Sodomy in the first degree.

(a) A person commits the crime of sodomy in the first degree if:
  (1) He engages in deviate sexual intercourse with another person by forcible compulsion; or
  (2) He engages in deviate sexual intercourse with a person who is incapable of consent by reason of being physically helpless or mentally incapacitated; or
  (3) He, being 16 years old or older, engages in deviate sexual intercourse with a person who is less than 12 years old.

Source: Code of Alabama

There are crimes against a person that do not necessarily involve physical harm or contact with the person. **Bribery** (*bry*-buh-ree) is the offering, giving, receiving, or soliciting of something of value for the purpose of influencing the action of an official in the discharge of his or her public or legal duties. Put more simply, bribery is a gift given to a public official to influence his or her behavior while in office. For bribery to occur, the person bribed must be a public official, and the payment must be intended to influence his or her behavior. **Extortion** (eks-*tor*-shun) is the obtaining of the property of another person by threatening that person with one of the following.

1. Bodily injury or the commission of another crime against the person
2. An accusation of a criminal offense
3. Exposure of a secret that would tend to subject the person to hatred, contempt, or ridicule
4. The taking or withholding of an action as a public official or causing a public official to take or withhold a certain action
5. Testifying or providing information or withholding information with respect to a legal claim or defense
6. Any other act that would not benefit the person

In order for extortion to occur, there must be a demand for money that is coupled with a threat to perform one of the above-listed acts. **Blackmail,** which is a form of extortion, is the unlawful demand of money or property under the threat to do bodily harm, injure property, accuse of a crime, or expose a disgraceful act or deed. A person who blackmails someone is also committing extortion. However, extortion has a broader definition than blackmail, so certain conduct that is extortion might not be considered blackmail. Refer to Exhibit 2-10 for a summary of the differences among bribery, extortion, and blackmail.

EXHIBIT 2-10   THE DIFFERENCES AMONG BRIBERY, EXTORTION, AND BLACKMAIL

Bribery is **giving** something to a **public official** to influence her or his behavior while in office. The person *must* be a public official and the payment *must* be to influence behavior.

Extortion is the **taking** of the property of another person by **threatening** that person with either bodily injury or the commission of another crime against him or her; an accusation of a criminal offense; exposure of a secret that would tend to subject the person to hatred, contempt, or ridicule; the taking or withholding of an action as a public official or causing a public official to take or withhold a certain action; testifying or providing information or withholding information with respect to a legal claim or defense; or any other harm which would not benefit the person.

Blackmail, a form of extortion, is the unlawful **demand** of money or property **under the threat** to do bodily harm, to injure property, to accuse of a crime, or to expose a disgraceful act or deed.

    Loansharking is the lending of money at excessive and illegal interest rates, with the threat or use of extortion to enforce repayment of the loan. For example, the victim borrows money at an interest rate of 75% and is told that if repayment is not made, serious physical injury will occur.

    See Exhibit 2-11 for a listing of crimes against a person.

EXHIBIT 2-11   CRIMES AGAINST THE PERSON

PHYSICAL HARM OR CONTACT	SEXUAL OFFENSES	NO PHYSICAL HARM OR CONTACT
Assault	Rape	Bribery
Battery	Statutory rape	Extortion
Assault and battery	Sodomy	Blackmail
Kidnapping	Sexual abuse	Loansharking
Manslaughter	Carnal abuse	
Murder	Indecent exposure	

CRIMES AGAINST THE PROPERTY

A second broad classification of crimes is **crimes against the property**—those in which the object of the crime is property as opposed to a person. This classification includes such crimes as arson, embezzlement, larceny, theft, robbery, and burglary.

ARSON

One of the most serious crimes against property is **arson,** which occurs when a person starts a fire or causes an explosion with the intent to destroy a building or occupied structure belonging to someone else, or destroys or damages his own or someone else's property with the intent to collect insurance for the loss. Refer to Exhibit 2-12 for an example of a state statute defining arson.

EXHIBIT 2-12	STATE STATUTES, ARSON

806.01 Arson.

(1) Any person who willfully and unlawfully, or while in the commission of any felony, by fire or explosion, damages or causes to be damaged:

    (a) Any dwelling, whether occupied or not, or its contents;

    (b) Any structure, or contents thereof, where persons are normally present, such as: jails, prisons, or detention centers; hospitals, nursing homes, or other health care facilities; department stores, office buildings, business establishments, churches, or educational institutions during normal hours of occupancy; or other similar structures; or

    (c) Any other structure that he or she knew or had reasonable grounds to believe was occupied by a human being, is guilty of arson in the first degree.

Source: Florida Statutes

EMBEZZLEMENT

Embezzlement (em-*bezl*-ment) is the willful taking of another's money or property, usually by fraudulent means, when the embezzler has lawful possession of the money or property. The embezzler has lawful possession usually because of an office or position he or she holds. The person committing embezzlement is converting another's property to his or her own use and possession. For example, a sports agent uses his client's money to buy boats and cars for his family. The agent has lawful possession of his client's money because the client gave him that authority, and he has that authority because he is the person's agent. When the agent takes the client's money and converts it to his own use, he embezzles.

LARCENY, THEFT, ROBBERY, AND BURGLARY

Larceny (*lar*-sen-ee) is the taking of goods or property of another person without that person's consent and against the will of the owner or possessor with the intent to convert the use of the property to someone other than the owner. **Petty larceny** is the larceny of goods or property whose value is below a statutory limit (for example, items valued at less than $1,000). **Grand larceny** is the larceny of goods or property whose value is above the statutory limit (for example, items whose value is at least $1,000). **Theft** is the popular or more commonly used term for *larceny*. Someone who breaks into a car and takes the portable CD player that the victim left on the front seat has just committed theft or larceny. The player was taken without the owner's consent and the person taking it intends either to sell it or use it herself. Larceny or theft becomes robbery when, in the course of the theft, the person inflicts serious bodily injury on another, threatens or puts another in fear of immediate serious bodily injury, or commits or threatens to immediately commit any felony. Someone who approaches a jogger, threatens him with a knife, and takes his portable CD player has just committed the crime of robbery. The person converted the property to his own use and did so by threatening the victim with bodily injury.

    Burglary is the entering of a building or occupied structure with the purpose of committing a crime. An additional crime does not have to take place: breaking into the building is the crime. For example, breaking into someone's home is burglary; actually taking items from the home is larceny. It is not burglary if a person enters a building that at the time is open to the public to commit a crime. For example, it is not burglary if a criminal walks into a bank during regular working hours and commits larceny. It is burglary if the criminal breaks into the bank after hours with the intent to commit larceny. The crime that is committed once the person breaks into the building does not have to be robbery. If a person breaks into a building to commit arson, he or she has also committed burglary. See Exhibit 2-13 for the differences among larceny, robbery, and burglary.

EXHIBIT 2-13	THE DIFFERENCES AMONG LARCENY, ROBBERY, AND BURGLARY

Larceny/Theft – Taking away of the property of another person without his consent and against his will with the intent to never return the property and to put it to some other use

Robbery – Larceny becomes robbery when a person inflicts or threatens immediate serious bodily injury, or commits or threatens to commit a felony while the larceny is taking place

Burglary – The entering of a building or occupied structure with the purpose of committing a crime. No robbery or larceny has to take place to have burglary; entering the building or structure is the actual burglary

FORGERY AND COUNTERFEITING

Forgery is the creation of a false document or the material alteration of a document with the intent to defraud someone. Forgery includes signing a person's name without his authorization or consent. A person who steals another person's checks and signs that person's name to a check has committed forgery. The intent is to defraud a merchant by paying for goods or services with a stolen check, and this intent is carried out by signing someone else's check. **Counterfeiting** is the copying or imitating of something without authority and with the intent to deceive or defraud someone by passing off the copied item as being genuine or original. This term is most commonly applied to the unauthorized copying of money, but it can apply to other items as well. A person can counterfeit travelers' checks, contracts, tickets to events, paintings, videotapes, CDs, and audiotapes. What is required is that the original is copied without permission and that the copy is represented to be an original with the intent to defraud someone. See Exhibit 2-14 for a list of crimes against property.

EXHIBIT 2-14	CRIMES AGAINST THE PROPERTY

ARSON	EMBEZZLEMENT	LARCENY	PETTY LARCENY
Grand larceny	Burglary	Forgery	Counterfeiting
	Theft	Robbery	

DRUG OFFENSES

Because each state and the federal government have statutes that deal with the manufacture, sale, and use of illegal drugs, there are different statutes dealing with the same type of crimes with differing penalties for essentially the same offense. However, common phrases are coming into use to describe drugs, drug use, and drug paraphernalia.

DRUGS IN GENERAL

A **drug** is any substance that is recognized as such by the official United States Pharmacopoeia, the Official Homeopathic Pharmacopoeia of the United States, or the Official National Formulary. Drugs include substances intended to be used in diagnosing, curing, mitigating, treating, or preventing diseases in people or animals; substances intended to affect the function or structure of the body of people or animals; and substances that are a component of any of the above-listed substances.

A **controlled substance** is a drug, a substance, or an immediate precursor as defined by Schedules I through IV. An immediate precursor is a substance that has been designated as the compound commonly used or produced in the manufacture of a controlled substance. In other words, an immediate precursor is another drug that is commonly used to manufacture the controlled substance. Manufacture refers to the production, the preparation, the compounding, the conversion of, or the processing of a controlled substance. In other words, when someone is charged with manufacturing a controlled substance, the person is charged with the process used to make the controlled substance. When someone is charged with possession with intent to deliver, he or she is involved in the actual, constructive, or attempted transfer of a controlled substance from one person to another in exchange for money or anything of value.

A **narcotic drug** is any drug identified as such by order of the Director of the U.S. Department of Health. Narcotic drugs are addictive and pose a danger to public health and safety. Narcotic drugs also include substances that are manufactured by either extraction from vegetation, by chemical synthesis, or by a combination of extraction and chemical synthesis. For example, opium comes from the gum of poppy plants, and the gum is processed further to create heroin. One of the steps in processing cocoa leaves into cocaine is to soak the cocoa leaves in kerosene.

The following substances are considered narcotic drugs: opium, opiates, and derivatives of opium or opiates; poppy straw and concentrates of poppy straw; coca leaves, unless the cocaine, ecgonine, and derivatives have already been removed from the leaves; cocaine and its salts; ecgonine and its derivatives; and any combination of these substances.

SCHEDULES OF CONTROLLED SUBSTANCES

Different schedules, or listings, of substances are used to designate types of controlled substances. Each schedule has different criteria. **Schedule I** substances have a high potential for abuse, have no accepted medical use in the United States, and are not safe for use in medical treatments. **Schedule II** substances have a high potential for abuse and are accepted for medical use in the United States, but only with severe restrictions because their abuse may lead to severe psychological or physical dependence. In other words, drugs under Schedule II are very addicting, can be abused very easily, and their use in the medical field is very controlled.

A **Schedule III** substance has less potential for abuse, and has accepted medical uses in the United States. Its abuse may lead to moderate or low physical dependence, but strong psychological dependence. A **Schedule IV** substance has a low potential for abuse, has currently accepted medical uses in the United States, and creates only limited physical or psychological dependence. A **Schedule V** substance has the lowest potential for abuse, is currently accepted for medical use in the United States, and has the lowest potential to create either physical or psychological addiction. **Schedule VI** substances are the most dangerous of all the controlled substances. These substances are not accepted for medical use in the United States, and are not safe for use even under direct medical supervision. These substances carry a high psychological and physiological dependence, and their use creates a definite risk to public health. See Exhibit 2-15.

EXHIBIT 2-15 | SCHEDULE OF CONTROLLED SUBSTANCES

1. **Schedule I** – Very addictive; high potential for abuse; no accepted medical uses
2. **Schedule II** – Very addictive; high potential for abuse; accepted medical uses
3. **Schedule III** – Moderately addictive; lesser potential for abuse; accepted medical uses
4. **Schedule IV** – Limited potential for addiction; low potential for abuse; accepted medical uses
5. **Schedule V** – Lowest potential for addiction; low potential for abuse; accepted medical uses
6. **Schedule VI** – Highest potential for addiction; highest potential for abuse; no medical uses at all, accepted or otherwise

---

DRUG PARAPHERNALIA

The possession of drug paraphernalia can also be a crime. **Drug paraphernalia** are items, equipment, or materials that are used or intended to be used to plant, cultivate, grow, harvest, process, prepare, test, analyze, package, store, or conceal controlled substances. Items used to manufacture, compound, convert, or produce controlled substances are also considered drug paraphernalia, as are items used to inject, ingest, or inhale a controlled substance.

The term also refers to items that are used, intended to be used, or are designed to ingest, inhale, or somehow get into the human body marijuana, cocaine, hashish, or hashish oil. These items include pipes, water pipes, carburetion tubes or devices, smoking and carburetion masks, roach clips (objects used to hold burning material that has become too small or too short to hold in the hand), miniature spoons and vials used for cocaine chamber pipes, electric pipes, air-driven pipes, chillums, bongs, and ice pipes or chillers.

OTHER CRIMES

Some crimes involve only the person committing the crime, while others are deemed victimless crimes.

DWI/DUI

Driving while intoxicated (DWI) or driving under the influence (DUI) is the operation of a motor vehicle while under the influence of intoxicating liquor or drugs. A showing of complete intoxication is not required; all that has to be shown is that the person's ability to operate the vehicle is impaired. If a person is stopped because she has been drinking, all that is required to show impairment is that she is over the legal limit for blood/alcohol levels established by the state in which the violation occurred.

PROSTITUTION

A person commits the crime of **prostitution** if he or she is a member of a house of prostitution or otherwise engages in sexual activity as a business. The crime of prostitution can also be charged if a person is within view in any public place for the purpose of being hired to engage in sexual activity. Prostitution can be classified as a **victimless crime**—a crime that generally only involves the criminal and that has no direct victim.

CRIMINAL ACTIVITY

There are other terms that relate to criminal activity and criminal liability. These terms relate to whether the person helped in the commission of the crime, helped with the planning of the crime, or helped after the crime was committed. There are terms that relate to racketeering and whether or not a person is asking or encouraging another to commit a crime.

ACCESSORIES, ACCOMPLICES, AND CONSPIRACY

An **accessory** is a person who was not present when a crime was committed, but who aided in the commission of the crime. He or she may have commanded the crime be committed, given advice, or instigated or helped conceal the crime. An **accessory before the fact** is a person who ordered, provided counsel, encouraged, or aided another person to commit the crime, but who was not actually present when the crime was committed. An **accessory after the fact** is a person who knows that a crime has been committed and provides aid to the criminal in helping him or her escape punishment. An **accomplice** is a person who knowingly, voluntarily, and with the same intent joins the principal offender in the commission of a crime and who is actually present when the crime is committed. **Accomplice liability** is the criminal responsibility of one who acts with another before, during, or after the commission of a crime. Both an accomplice and an accessory engage in **aiding and abetting** (*ay*-ding and a-*bet*-ing), assisting, encouraging, planning or facilitating the commission of a crime.

Conspiracy refers to a combination of or agreement between two or more people for the purpose of committing, by their joint effort, a criminal act. Conspiracy to commit an act can be a separate criminal offense from the actual commission of the criminal act.

RACKETEERING AND RICO

Racketeering is an organized conspiracy to commit the crime of extortion. Racketeering also includes the attempt to extort money. The classic example of racketeering is the "protection" offered by organized crime: Pay a certain amount of money each week for "protection," or physical harm will befall you or your business. In order to more successfully prosecute organized crime, Congress passed the **Racketeer-Influenced and Corrupt Organizations Act (RICO)**. According to RICO, United States Code (U.S.C.) § 1961, certain activities are considered illegal. These racketeering activities are "any act or threat that involves murder, kidnapping, gambling, arson, robbery, bribery, extortion, dealing in obscene materials, or dealing in controlled substances."

SOLICITATION

Solicitation is the asking, encouraging, or requesting of a person to commit a criminal act. For example, the crime of solicitation of prostitution involves asking a person to commit an act of prostitution. The crime solicited does not have to be committed; all that is required is that the perpetrator sought to have the crime committed.

CONCLUSION

The terms and phrases in this chapter are all related to general criminal law principles. Some crimes are committed against a person. These include assault, battery, manslaughter (voluntary and involuntary), murder, and sex offenses such as rape. What crime a person is charged with when he or she kills someone depends on the mental state of the perpetrator at the time of the killing and whether there was premeditation and malice.

Rape generally consists of non-consensual sexual activity, or sexual activity that occurs when resistance is overcome by threat, force, drugs, or alcohol. Other sex offenses, such as statutory rape or carnal abuse, can vary from state to state. Crimes like extortion, blackmail, bribery, and loansharking are considered to be crimes against a person, even though there may not be any physical harm suffered by the victim. The threat of physical harm is enough to have these offenses classified as crimes against the person.

Crimes can also be committed against property. Such crimes include arson (the burning of property), embezzlement (the taking of property by someone who is lawfully in possession of the property), larceny (the stealing of a person's property), or robbery, when another crime is being committed while the larceny is taking place.

A person does not actually have to carry out a crime in order to be criminally liable. Planning a crime, helping before or after a crime, or asking that a crime be committed are all criminal offenses. Crimes involving drugs are another category, and include such activities as the possession of drugs or the use or possession of material or equipment used to ingest, enhance, manufacture, or transport drugs.

Individual states will have more specific designations of the offenses described, the different levels of the offense, and the punishment for violation of the criminal law. But these classifications are all based on the same basic principles of criminal law.

KEY WORDS AND PHRASES

accessory	drug paraphernalia	murder
accomplice	embezzlement	narcotic drug
actus rea	extortion	petty larceny
aggravated assault	felony	premeditation
aiding and abetting	felony murder doctrine	prostitution
arson	forgery	Racketeer-Influenced and
assault	grand larceny	Corrupt Organizations Act
assault and battery	inchoate crime	(RICO)
battery	involuntary manslaughter	racketeering
blackmail	kidnapping	rape
bribery	knowingly	sexual abuse
burglary	larceny	sodomy
capital crime	loansharking	solicitation
conspiracy	malice	statutory rape
controlled substance	Mann Act	theft
counterfeiting	manslaughter	victimless crime
crime of passion	mens rea	voluntary manslaughter
culpable	misdemeanor	
driving while intoxicated		
(DWI)		

REVIEW QUESTIONS

SHORT ANSWER

1. What makes an act a crime of passion?
2. What is the difference between robbery and theft?
3. What is premeditation?
4. What are the four culpable mental states?
5. What is the difference between manslaughter and murder?
6. Prostitution is what type of crime?
7. What is the difference between conspiracy and solicitation of a crime?
8. What is meant by premeditation?
9. What is RICO?
10. What is the difference between assault and aggravated assault?
11. What is a crime of passion?
12. Give five examples of drug paraphernalia.
13. What is the difference between embezzlement and extortion?
14. Who could commit a rape under common law?
15. How does one become an accomplice to a crime?
16. What schedule of drugs has no medical use whatsoever?

17. What is considered to be aiding and abetting?

18. How does a person commit burglary?

19. What is a victimless crime?

20. What is considered to be sodomy?

FILL IN THE BLANK

1. Someone murders another person while committing a felony. This is known as _____.

2. A crime that tends to lead to the commission of another crime is a _____.

3. When someone asks someone else to commit crime, this is _____.

4. Lending money at high interest rates is _____.

5. What makes the crime of manslaughter involuntary _____?

6. When someone breaks into a building intending to commit a crime, the crime of _____ has been committed.

7. The intent to carry out a crime is _____.

8. The actual elements of a crime are _____.

9. A crime that is punishable by death is a _____.

10. A person who helps plan a crime but does not participate in the actual commission of the crime is an _____.

11. A crime that consists of a series of events is known as a _____.

12. When someone copies another person's signature, this is the crime of _____.

FACT SITUATIONS

1. Sam threatens to hit Ralph with a baseball bat and then does. What crimes have been committed?

2. Randy helps Terry and Jerry plan to break into a factory and set a fire. Terry and Jerry carry out this act. What crimes can each of the three be charged with and why?

3. Henry is a sports agent who steals money he was responsible for investing from his client. What crime did Henry commit?

4. Martha discovers some embarrassing information about David. She tells him that if he pays her $10,000, she will not make the information public. What crime has Martha committed?

5. Marco approaches a woman standing on a street corner and says he will pay her $100 if she will have sex with him. She is an undercover police officer. When Marco discovers this, he offers her the $100 to forget the whole thing and let him walk away. With what crimes may Marco be charged?

6. Henry, who is twenty, takes a fifteen-year-girl whom he thinks is sixteen across state lines to a motel so they can have sex. The age of consent in the state he took her to is sixteen. What statutes did Henry violate?

7. Margaret steals a dress worth $150. With what crime may she be charged?

8. While taking a necklace from Susan, William hits her. With what crimes can William be charged?

9. Peter has just robbed a bank. He flags down Richard, a friend of his, jumps in Richard's car, and tells Richard what happened. Richard agrees to help Peter get away from scene of the crime. What crime is Richard committing? What is he?

10. Alex breaks into a bank with the intent to rob it. But before he can rob the bank, he sets off a silent alarm. Alex leaves the bank without stealing anything. What crime has Alex committed, if any?

CHAPTER 3

Criminal Procedure

INTRODUCTION

In the previous chapter, terms related to criminal law were discussed; in this chapter, terms related to criminal procedure are presented. Many of the same terms associated with civil procedure also apply to criminal procedure. However, criminal procedure begins before the case is even filed; it extends into the investigation of the crime and the gathering of evidence, when a search warrant is needed and when police can search without a warrant. How someone is charged with a crime can vary; conviction and appeals are also part of criminal procedure. Several criminal procedure concepts originated from Supreme Court cases, such as the right to be free from unreasonable searches and seizures, the right to remain silent, and the right to a jury trial, so some terms discussed in Chapter 8, Constitutional Law, are also presented in this chapter.

GENERAL CONSTITUTIONAL PRINCIPLES

The U.S. Constitution protects the rights of people accused of crimes. The protection of rights helps prevent abuse of the government's power to investigate and prosecute people accused of crimes and those who violate the criminal laws. The protections are in the Constitution and in the amendments to the Constitution.

WRIT OF HABEAS CORPUS, BILL OF ATTAINDER, AND EX POST FACTO LAWS

The first of the rights guaranteed by the Constitution is the **writ of habeas corpus** (*rit* of *habe*-ee-us *kor*-pus). The writ literally means "You have the body." The writ of habeas corpus is a court order directing a governmental official having a person in custody to present the prisoner in court and explain to the court why the prisoner is in jail. If it is found a prisoner is being held illegally, then the court can order the prisoner's release. This right is invoked often after an initial appeal of a criminal conviction has been denied. The prisoner alleges that he or she is being held illegally, and requests that the writ be granted to force the state to prove that it is not holding the person illegally.

The Constitution prohibits **ex post facto laws,** laws that make a particular act a crime that was not a crime at the time it was committed. An ex post facto law can also be a law that increases the punishment for a crime after it was committed, or lessens the burden of proof necessary to prove a crime. For example, a person is serving a ten-year sentence for a violation of the federal Mann Act. Congress passes a new law stating that all people currently serving time for a violation of the Mann Act and all people convicted in the future of violation of the Mann Act will serve a fifteen-year sentence. This would be an ex post facto law because it increases the punishment of a person who has already been convicted—a measure that is illegal under the U.S. Constitution. Article I, Section 9, Clause 3—the part of the Constitution that prohibits ex post facto laws—applies to the federal government and to the states. An ex post facto law can also remove one of the elements of a crime, making it easier for the State to prove the crime. For example, to prove a person guilty of manslaughter, the State must prove that the defendant knowingly, with malice aforethought, caused the death of another person. If there is a new statute passed eliminating the need to prove the criminal intent of knowingly committing the crime, or any criminal intent, this is an ex post facto law. Because the State no longer has to prove the mental intent of the defendant, proving the crime just became easier; all the State would have to show is that the defendant caused the death of another.

The Constitution prohibits the passage of a **bill of attainder,** a legislative act that imposes punishment without the benefit of trial on individuals or on a specific group. For example, if the current penalty for being a convicted spy is imprisonment twenty years, Congress cannot pass a law stating that all people convicted of spying on the United States between June and August of 2001 will serve life sentences without the possibility of parole. The law would be illegal because it applies to a group of people who have already been convicted, and it only applies to that group of people. See Exhibit 3-1 for a summary of these rights.

EXHIBIT 3-1	CONSTITUTIONAL PROTECTIONS

1. **Writ of Habeas Corpus** – "You have the body." A prisoner requests the writ when he is alleging he is being held illegally. If issued, the prisoner must be presented in court and reasons shown why he is being held.
2. **Ex Post Facto Law** – "After the fact." Three categories constitute an ex post facto law.
   a. Conduct that was not criminal when it was done is made criminal and a person is charged after the fact.
   b. Punishment for a crime is increased and a person who is serving time for that crime has his sentence increased.
   c. One element of a crime is removed so it is easier for the prosecution to prove its case.
3. **Bill of Attainder** – Imposes punishment on a particular group of people without the benefit of a trial.

FOURTH, FIFTH, SIXTH, EIGHTH, AND FOURTEENTH AMENDMENTS

The **Fourth Amendment** protects people from unreasonable searches and seizures without a warrant. The general rule is that the police cannot conduct a search until they have demonstrated to a court that they have probable cause to search and a warrant is issued. However, as will be discussed later, there are many exceptions to this general rule. The **Fifth Amendment** gives an accused the right to a grand jury indictment, safeguards against double jeopardy, ensures that a person cannot be compelled to testify against himself or herself, and guarantees that a person cannot be deprived of life, liberty, or property without due process. The **Sixth Amendment** protects the right to a speedy and public trial, the right to trial by a jury of one's peers, the right to know the charges against one, the right to confront the witnesses against one, and the right to counsel. The Sixth Amendment applies to the federal government only. In the case of *Gideon v. Wainwright,* the Supreme Court made the guarantee that every criminal defendant is entitled to legal counsel applicable to the states through the due process clause of the Fourteenth Amendment. The **Eighth Amendment** protects the right to bail and prohibits cruel and unusual punishment. The **Fourteenth Amendment** makes the right to due process applicable to the states. See Exhibit 3-2 for a summary of the rights protected by these amendments. Now, what does all this mean?

EXHIBIT 3-2	RIGHTS PROTECTED BY THE CONSTITUTION
Fourth Amendment	No unreasonable searches and seizures; the police must have a warrant
Fifth Amendment	No self-incrimination
	Grand jury indictment required
	No double jeopardy
	Federal Due Process of Law Clause
Sixth Amendment	Speedy and public trial
	Trial by jury of peers
	Right to know the charges against one
	Right to confront witnesses
	Right to counsel
Eighth Amendment	Right to bail
	No cruel and unusual punishment
Fourteenth Amendment	Right to due process on the state level

SEARCH AND SEIZURE

The **Fourth Amendment** protects people from unreasonable searches and seizures by the government. The **search** is the looking for or seeking out that which is concealed from view; the **seizure** is the act of taking property because of some violation of the law. The general rule under the Fourth Amendment is that the government cannot conduct a search without a search warrant. However, there are many exceptions to the requirement for a search warrant that have been created by the Court over the years. This area of criminal procedure is constantly changing.

SEARCH WARRANTS

A **search warrant** is an order in writing issued by a justice or other magistrate in the name of the state that authorizes law enforcement officials to search for and seize any property that constitutes evidence of the commission of a crime. One thing the police search for is **contraband**—any property that is illegal to produce or possess. For example, it is illegal to produce, grow, and possess marijuana, so marijuana is considered contraband. Contraband also includes items that are exported or imported into a country against its laws—in other words, smuggled goods. If a person brought into the United States cigars from Cuba, the cigars would be considered contraband because it is against the law to bring Cuban cigars into the United States. There are two types of contraband. The first is **contraband per se:** property that is illegal to possess. Because it is illegal to possess cocaine, cocaine is contraband per se. **Derivative contraband** is property that is legal to possess, but is used to perpetrate or commit a crime. For example, it is legal to possess some of the ingredients to make crystal methamphetamine, but it is illegal to use those ingredients to make the drug.

AUTOMOBILE EXCEPTION

There are several exceptions to the general rule that there must be a search warrant before a legal search can take place. One is **automobile exception.** If there is probable cause to believe that a car has been used to commit a crime (even a traffic offense) that the people in the car have committed a crime, or that there is evidence of crimes in the vehicle, the police may stop the car, detain the driver and passengers, and search them and any containers or packages found in the car. **Probable cause** is defined as reasonable grounds for belief in certain alleged facts that is more than mere suspicion, but less than the evidence required for conviction. In other words, there is enough information to lead someone to believe that there may be evidence of crime. Probable cause is more than suspicion, but it does not have to be at the level needed to convict someone of the crime in a court of law.

TERRY EXCEPTION

The **Terry Exception,** which was first announced in *Terry v. Ohio,* allows police officers to search without a warrant people the police think are armed and dangerous. See Sidebar 3-1. This exception has been expanded to cover stops when the police have reasonable cause to believe that a person has committed or is about to commit a criminal offense. The Terry Exception allows only a limited, quick, pat-down search of a person. If contraband is found that might justify an arrest, a full search can be made.

SIDEBAR 3-1 *TERRY V. OHIO*

Facts: A police officer watched as two men, Chilton and Terry, walked up and down a street, pausing to look into the same store window a total of twenty-four times. Each time they would meet with another man, Katz, and talk. Suspecting the three were planning to rob the store, the officer approached all three men and asked their names. When all three mumbled something, the officer spun Terry around and did a pat-down search. He found a pistol in Terry's overcoat pocket. He also found a pistol when he searched Chilton. All three were arrested, and Terry and Chilton were charged with carrying concealed weapons. The defense made a motion that the weapons not be allowed to be admitted, but the Court denied the motion to suppress.

Issue: The issue before the court was whether or not this was a valid search because it occurred without a warrant.

Decision: The Supreme Court ruled that a reasonably prudent officer, when confronted with circumstances that lead him to believe that his safety or the safety of others is in danger, may make a reasonable search for weapons in the possession of the person he believes to be armed and dangerous.

Although the police must secure a search warrant whenever practical, the procedure cannot be followed when swift action based on the spot observations of a "beat" policeman is required.

The reasonableness of any particular search and seizure must be assessed in light of the particular circumstances.

Source: United States Reports

VALID ARREST, SEARCH FOR EVIDENCE, AND BORDER SEARCH EXCEPTIONS

If a search is subsequent to a **valid arrest,** the police may make a warrantless search of persons involved in the arrest, the area under those persons' immediate control, and any possessions they take with them to detention. The police can also make a protective sweep of the surrounding area to make sure it is clear and safe from any illegal items. When there is probable cause to make an arrest, even if the arrest is not made, limited searches are permitted if necessary to preserve easily destroyed evidence. This is the **searches for evidence exception.** The purpose of this exception is to allow searches for items that the accused can destroy easily. Searches based on voluntary consent—permission—are allowed even if the person is not told he has the right to say no.

The **border search exception** allows searches of a person and the goods she or he brings with her or him when crossing the border. Border officials can also open mail that is crossing the border if they have reasonable cause to suspect it contains merchandise sent contrary to the law.

PLAIN VIEW AND STOP AND FRISK

The **plain view exception** allows an officer to seize evidence without a warrant if the officer is lawfully in a position from which the evidence can be viewed. In other words, the evidence is in plain sight. The material can be seized if it is immediately apparent to the officer that the items seen are evidence of a crime or contraband, or if the officer has probable cause to believe that the evidence uncovered is contraband or evidence of a crime. For example, a police officer stops someone for speeding. When the officer approaches the car, she sees a bag of marijuana sitting on the car seat next to the driver. The officer can seize the evidence of the crime—the bag of marijuana—without a warrant because she is lawfully in a position where the evidence can be seen. The marijuana is in plain sight, and it is contraband.

If **exigent** (*ex*-ə-jent) **circumstances** exist, searches can be conducted without a warrant. If the officer does not have time to obtain a warrant before evidence is destroyed or a criminal escapes capture, when there is a need to preserve life or avoid serious injury, a search may be performed without a warrant. The police may perform a **stop and frisk** by running their hands lightly over a suspect's outer garments to determine if the person is carrying a concealed weapon. The search must stop short of any activity that could be considered a violation of the Fourth Amendment. For example, the police receive a report that a bank has just been robbed. The suspect is armed and on foot, and they have a description of the suspect. If they see someone matching that description running down the street a short distance from the bank that was robbed, they may stop and frisk that person. But the search they are allowed to perform without a warrant is limited to looking for a concealed weapon. See Exhibit 3-3 for a summary of the exceptions to the requirement for a search warrant.

EXHIBIT 3-3 | EXCEPTIONS TO THE REQUIREMENT FOR SEARCH WARRANTS

Terry Exception – Police can search people that may be armed and dangerous.

Search Subsequent to Valid Arrest – Police can search areas under a suspect's immediate control and any possessions the suspect takes into detention.

Searches for Evidence – Police can conduct limited search to preserve easily destroyed evidence.

Consent – The person agrees to the search.

Border Search – Police can search people and items crossing the border.

Plain View Exception – Officer is lawfully in a place where he can see the evidence.

Stop and Frisk – Police officer suspects a person has committed a crime; he stops the person and runs his hands lightly over the suspect's outer garments.

Outside of these exceptions, a **warrantless search,** a search performed without a search warrant, is illegal. The police have to obtain a search warrant from a magistrate after they indicate that they have probable cause to justify issuing the warrant. A **general search warrant,** one that authorizes the police to search a person or place without limit, has been declared unconstitutional. In order to be valid, a **specific warrant** must be issued—one that describes what is to be searched and what is to be seized.

If evidence is obtained by illegal search and seizure, it is considered illegally obtained evidence. Illegally obtained evidence is evidence that is obtained in violation of the defendant's rights because there was no warrant and no probable cause to arrest the person or because the warrant was defective and no valid grounds existed for the seizure. Illegally obtained evidence is subject to the exclusionary rule, which was announced in *Mapp v. Ohio*. See Sidebar 3-2.

SIDEBAR 3-2 *MAPP V. OHIO*

Facts: The police, responding to a tip about the location of a suspect, went to Mapp's home, knocked on the door, and demanded that they be let in. Mapp refused to allow the police to enter unless they produced a warrant. Three hours later, four additional police officers arrived and the police attempted to enter the home again. When Mapp did not immediately come to the door, the police forced their way in. Mapp demanded to see a search warrant, and one of the officers held up a piece of paper, saying it was the warrant. Mapp grabbed it, but the officers took it away from her. The police did an extensive search of the home and found some pornographic material in Mapp's possession. She was charged with and convicted of the possession of obscene material.

Issue: The issue before the Court was whether this was a valid, warrantless search and whether the exclusionary rule applied to the states.

Ruling: The Supreme Court made the exclusionary rule applicable to the states by writing:
   "All evidence obtained by searches and seizures in violation of the Constitution is, by that same authority, inadmissible in a state court." The exclusionary rule is an essential part of both the Fourth and Fourteenth Amendments.

Source: United States Reports

The **exclusionary rule** (eks-*kloo*-zhen-air-ree rule) states that any illegally obtained evidence is inadmissible in any court of law, that is, it is excluded from admission into evidence. The evidence may also be excluded because of the **Fruit of the Poisonous Tree Doctrine,** which was first announced by the Supreme Court in *Wong Sun v. United States*. The doctrine states that not only is the illegally obtained evidence excluded, but all evidence that has been found that is related to the illegally obtained evidence is also excluded. If there is illegally obtained evidence, and this evidence is used to get a search warrant or it creates probable cause to seize additional evidence, all of the evidence obtained because of the use of the illegally obtained evidence is also excluded from trial. The rationale for the rule is that the additional evidence would not have been discovered if it was not for the illegally obtained evidence.

ARREST

The requirement for a warrant also applies when someone is arrested. **Arrest** is the deprivation of a person of his or her liberty by legal authority. An arrest is the taking of a person into custody for the purpose of holding him or her to answer to a criminal charge.

TYPES OF WARRANTS

An **arrest warrant** is a written order of the court that is made on behalf of the government, based upon a criminal complaint, that directs law enforcement to arrest a person and bring him or her before the court. A **bench warrant** is an arrest warrant that is issued by the court based upon a finding of contempt of court, where an indictment exists, or where a witness failed to appear when subpoenaed to Court. An arrest can also take place without a warrant.

WARRANTLESS ARREST AND THE KNOCK AND ANNOUNCE RULE

A **warrantless arrest** is the arrest of a person without a warrant. A warrantless arrest is permissible if the arresting officer has reasonable grounds to believe that the person has committed a felony or a misdemeanor amounting to a breach of the peace in the presence of the officer. If there is a warrantless arrest, the **McNabb-Mallory Rule** applies. This rule states that the suspect who is arrested without a warrant must be promptly brought before a magistrate or else any incriminating statement made by him will be suppressed (will not be allowed to be used in any trial). This rule comes from *McNabb v. United States* and from *Mallory v. United States.* See Exhibit 3-4.

EXHIBIT 3-4	THE MCNABB-MALLORY RULE

The McNabb-Mallory Rule applies when a person is arrested without a warrant. The person must be brought before a magistrate promptly, or any incriminating statement made by the person will not be admissible at any trial.

When serving the arrest or search warrant, the **knock and announce rule** applies. A police officer must knock and announce his or her authority and purpose before entering into the home. The door of the home can be broken down by the police only after he or she first states his or her authority and purpose for demanding admission.

PROCEDURES SUBSEQUENT TO ARREST

When a person is arrested, there are procedures that the police are required to follow and certain procedures they choose to follow. Constitutional protections apply to these procedures to help protect the rights of a person accused of a crime.

INTERROGATIONS

When a suspect is arrested, the police will conduct an interrogation by questioning the suspect in an effort to gain information to solve the crime. There are two classifications of interrogation. An **investigatory interrogation** is the questioning of a person by police officers in a routine manner when the investigation has not yet reached the stage where an accusation can be made. The person being questioned is not in legal custody, and his or her freedom of movement has not been limited in any significant way. A **custodial interrogation** is the questioning of a person who has been taken into custody by police officers or has otherwise been deprived of his or her freedom of movement. See Exhibit 3-5 for a summary of the differences between these types of interrogations. It is important to note that custody can take place without the person actually having been placed under arrest. Custody can take place anywhere, provided there has been a limitation of the person's freedom of movement. However, in order for the interrogation to be used in any subsequent proceeding, the person being questioned must be advised that he or she has the right to have counsel present and the right to not answer questions. The person in custody must also be advised of the possible consequences if he or she does answer questions.

EXHIBIT 3-5	THE DIFFERENCE BETWEEN CUSTODIAL AND INVESTIGATORY INVESTIGATIONS

1. **Investigatory**
   a. Investigation is **not** concentrating on **one person.**
   b. Person is **not** in **custody.**
   c. **Freedom of movement** is **not** limited.
2. **Custodial**
   a. Investigation **is** concentrating on **one person.**
   b. Person **is** in **custody.**
   c. **Freedom of movement** is limited.

CONFESSIONS AND ADMISSIONS

One of the purposes of an interrogation is to gain a confession or admission. A **confession** is a voluntary statement made by one person charged with a crime, communicated to another person, in which the person admits or acknowledges that he or she is guilty of the crime he or she is charged with or that is being investigated. As part of the confession, he or she may also disclose the circumstances of the crime and whether there were other participants in the crime. In this situation, the **Escobedo Rule,** established in *Escobedo v. State of Illinois* might apply. The Escobedo Rule applies when a police investigation begins to focus on a particular person, the person the investigation is concentrating on is in custody, the person requests and is denied counsel, and/or the person has not been warned of his or her right to remain silent. Any statement given by the person is inadmissible in any criminal trial. See Exhibit 3-6.

EXHIBIT 3-6	FACTORS OF THE ESCOBEDO RULE

1. Police investigation concentrates on one person; the person is now a suspect.
2. The person is in custody.
3. The person requests and is denied counsel OR
4. The suspect has not been warned of his or her right to remain silent.

Result – Any statement given is inadmissible in any criminal proceeding.

Classifications of confessions are based on the circumstances under which the confession is given. A **voluntary confession** is one made spontaneously by a person and is free from any influencing situations. The person confessing has freely chosen to do so. An **involuntary confession** is one that is given because of hope, a promise made, fear of violence or actual violence, torture, or threats. An **implied confession** is one in which the defendant does not admit to the crime verbally. However, guilt is deemed admitted because the defendant places himself or herself at the mercy of the court and asks for a light sentence for the crime. The guilt is implied because of statements made to the court. An **indirect confession** is one that is inferred from the conduct of the defendant, not by what he or she says, but by his or her actions. A **judicial confession** is a guilty plea or some other similar action or conduct in court during a judicial proceeding. This type of confession indicates to the court that the person is admitting guilt for the crime.

Interlocking confessions occur when two or more people who are charged with the same crime confess, the confessions are substantially the same, and both are consistent with each other regarding the major elements of the crime. If there is a joint trial, such confessions are admissible. See Exhibit 3-7 for the types of confessions and admissions.

EXHIBIT 3-7 CONFESSIONS AND ADMISSIONS

1. **Voluntary confession** – Confession made spontaneously by a person, free from any influencing situations. The person confessing does so freely.

2. **Involuntary confession** – Confession given because of hope, a promise made, fear of violence or actual violence, torture, or threats.

3. **Implied confession** – Confession in which the defendant does not admit to the crime verbally. However, guilt is deemed admitted because the defendant places himself at the mercy of the court and asks for a light sentence for the crime. The guilt is implied because of the statements made to the court.

4. **Indirect confession** – A confession that is inferred from the conduct of the defendant, not by what he says, but by his actions.

5. **Judicial confession** – A guilty plea or some other similar action or conduct in court during a judicial proceeding.

6. **Interlocking confessions** – Two or more people are charged with the same crime. All the parties confess, the confessions are substantially the same, and each is consistent with the others regarding the major elements of the crime.

However, prosecutors need to make sure they are not committing the **Bruton error,** a legal principle that was established in the case of *Bruton v. United States.* The Bruton error arises when there is a joint trial and the confession of one defendant that implicates another defendant is admitted into evidence. The first defendant did not testify and the second defendant has maintained his innocence. The error is that the second defendant did not have the opportunity to confront his accuser and subject him or her to cross-examination. The first defendant implicated the second by his or her admission, but did not take the stand to do so. See Exhibit 3-8.

EXHIBIT 3-8 BRUTON ERROR

1. A joint trial is held.
2. The confession of one defendant is entered into evidence.
3. That defendant does not take the stand.
4. The confession implicates another defendant in the trial.
5. The other defendant has maintained his innocence.

It is important to note that a confession is different from an admission. An **admission** is an acknowledgment of the facts *tending* to prove guilt, but the person *does not* admit to all the necessary elements of the crime. He or she stops short of a full confession. The defendant may admit he was in the area when the crime took place, that he had the opportunity to commit the crime, and that he had the means to do so, but he does not admit that he did, in fact, commit the crime.

DUE PROCESS OF LAW

The Fifth Amendment protects **due process of law** (due process), which is the established rules and regulations that restrain those in government who exercise power. Due process protects our civil rights by limiting government's ability to interfere with them.

PROCEDURAL DUE PROCESS AND SUBSTANTIVE DUE PROCESS

There are two types of due process: procedural due process and substantive due process. **Procedural due process** deals with the methods used to enforce the law, not the law itself. It sets a limit on how government exercises its power to limit rights. It used to apply only to criminal proceedings, but has been expanded to cover almost any type of governmental proceeding. **Substantive due process** is primarily a limit on what the legislature can do, a limit on the laws that Congress can pass. All laws that Congress passes must be fair and reasonable in content—what the law says—as well as how the law is applied.

FIFTH AMENDMENT

The **Fifth Amendment** states that a person cannot be compelled to testify against himself or herself. When an individual says, "I refuse to answer on the grounds that it may tend to incriminate me," he or she is **pleading the Fifth.** According to the Fifth Amendment, a person has the right to remain silent about a crime he or she is accused of not only at trial, but also during any interrogation by the police or any other officer of the court. A person will plead the Fifth because he or she does not want to incriminate himself or herself—that is, expose himself or herself to a criminal charge. The right to remain silent is waived if a person is granted immunity, or exemption from being prosecuted. There are two types of immunity. **Use immunity** prevents the prosecution from using the testimony to prosecute. **Transactional immunity** prevents a person from being prosecuted for any crime related in the compelled testimony. Once this immunity is granted, the witness no longer has a constitutional right to remain silent.

MIRANDA RIGHTS

The Miranda warnings are an offshoot of the right to remain silent. Prior to the case of *Miranda v. Arizona,* the police could conduct custodial interrogations—the questioning of someone after he or she was in custody without advising the person of any rights he or she had or the possible consequences of answering questions. The Supreme Court ruled that no federal or state conviction would stand if the evidence used against the person were obtained because of a custodial interrogation unless prior to questioning the person was informed of his or her **Miranda rights.** If the Miranda warnings are not given, this error can lead to a conviction being reversed. See Sidebar 3-3. The actual Miranda warnings are listed in Exhibit 3-9.

SIDEBAR 3-3 *MIRANDA V. ARIZONA*

Facts: In *Miranda,* four cases were combined into one: *Miranda v. Arizona; Vignera v. New York; Westover v. United States;* and *California v. Stewart.* In all four cases, the defendant was in police custody and was questioned by police officers, detectives, or a prosecuting attorney in a room where he was cut off from the outside world. None of the defendants was given a full warning about his rights at the beginning of the interrogation. In all four cases, the defendants gave oral confessions, and in three of the cases, signed confessions. All four defendants were convicted.

Issue: The issue before the court was whether these confessions violated the Fifth Amendment right against self-incrimination.

Ruling: The Court stated that the privilege against self incrimination is the "essential mainstay of our adversary system" and guarantees to the person the "right to remain silent unless he chooses to speak in the unfettered exercise of his own will." In the absence of any other effective measures, the following procedures to safeguard the Fifth Amendment privilege must be observed: The person in custody must, prior to interrogation, be clearly informed that he has the right to remain silent, and that anything he says will be used against him in court; he must be clearly informed that he has the right to consult with a lawyer and to have the lawyer with him during interrogation; and that if he is indigent, a lawyer will be appointed to represent him.

All four convictions were reversed by the Supreme Court.

Source: United States Reports

EXHIBIT 3-9	MIRANDA RIGHTS

Established by the Supreme Court in the case of *Miranda v. Arizona*

1. You have the right to remain silent.
2. If you choose not to remain silent, everything that you say can and will be used against you in a court of law.
3. You have the right to have an attorney present during questioning.
4. If you cannot afford an attorney, one will be appointed to represent you.
5. You have the right to terminate this interrogation at any stage of the interrogation.

EIGHTH AMENDMENT

The Eighth Amendment bans **cruel and unusual punishment,** which is punishment that amounts to torture or barbarity or any punishment so disproportionate to the offense as to shock the moral sense of the community. An example of cruel and unusual punishment is a twenty-year sentence in a maximum security prison imposed for shoplifting.

Cases alleging cruel and unusual punishment have been brought before the U.S. Supreme Court many times in its history. For example, in 1947, the case of *Louisiana v. Reswerber,* in which Willie Francis, a sixteen-year-old man who had been convicted of murder in Louisiana, was argued before the Supreme Court. Mr. Francis was convicted and sentenced to die in the electric chair. On the date of his execution, Mr. Francis was strapped into the electric chair and electricity was passed through his body. However, because of a malfunction in the chair, the current was not powerful enough to kill him. While the chair was being repaired, he sought to have the execution stopped. The argument brought before the Court was that the second execution attempt violated the double jeopardy clause and the due process clause of the U.S. Constitution. The Supreme Court disagreed, stating that the equipment failure did not bring due process into play, and holding that this was not cruel and unusual punishment because that principle applies to the methods used, not how much pain is caused by the selected method.

The Eighth Amendment also states that excessive **bail,** the monetary amount for or condition of pretrial release from custody normally set by the judge at the initial appearance, is not allowed. Bail is designed to ensure that the person will appear in court in the future and that he or she will remain within the court's jurisdiction. If someone **jumps bail,** he or she has left the jurisdiction of the court, has gone into hiding, or has failed to appear at subsequent hearings. If the defendant jumps bail, the money that was posted for bail is forfeited. Excessive bail is defined as bail set in an amount that is more than reasonably sufficient to prevent the evasion of the law by the accused person by fleeing or concealment. Excessive bail is an amount of money that is clearly disproportionate to the offense the person is charged with. For example, bail set in the amount of $100,000 for a person who is charged with shoplifting a $50 item could be considered excessive. Instead of being granted bail, a defendant may be released on his or her **own recognizance.** The defendant is released before trial on the condition of his or her promise that he or she will show up for trial. No bond is required when a person is released on his or her own recognizance.

CRIMINAL PRE-TRIAL PROCEDURES

When a person is charged with a crime, certain processes and procedures must be followed according to case law and rules. These procedures take place before the criminal trial actually begins and are designed to help protect the rights of anyone who is accused of committing a crime.

INDICTMENT OR INFORMATION

If a person is charged with a federal crime, the Fifth Amendment guarantees him or her the right to a **grand jury**—a jury of inquiry. The duty of a grand jury is to determine whether probable cause exists that a crime has been committed and whether an indictment should be issued. Probable cause is reasonable cause or reasonable grounds for belief in certain alleged facts. An **indictment** (in-*dite*-ment) is a formal written accusation of the commission of a crime that is issued when it is determined there is sufficient evidence to charge someone with a crime. A **grand jury indictment** is a formal written accusation of a commission of crime that is issued by the grand jury that conducted an inquiry into the circumstances of the crime and that determined there was sufficient information to charge someone with a crime. A **joint indictment** is issued when several defendants are named in the same indictment and there is enough information to charge more than one person with the crime. The people charged can be conspirators or accessories before or after the fact (see Chapter 2, Criminal Law). Some states use a grand jury to issue an indictment for every criminal charge brought against a person. See Exhibit 3-10.

EXHIBIT 3-10	CHARGING SOMEONE WITH A CRIME

I. FEDERAL COURT

Grand Jury Indictment – Right guaranteed by the Fifth Amendment. Prosecutor presents evidence to the grand jury that there is probable cause that a crime has been committed. If the grand jury decides that sufficient information has been presented to show that a crime was committed, it will issue the indictment.

II. STATE COURT

Prosecuting Attorney – Decides to file an information, so there is no grand jury indictment. A preliminary hearing can be held during which information is presented to the court. The court decides if there is sufficient information for a criminal case to proceed.

An **information** is an accusation made by a public prosecutor without the intervention of a grand jury. The grand jury has not met, and has not handed down an indictment; it is the public prosecutor who has decided to file criminal charges. If there is no grand jury, then there may be a **preliminary hearing** by a judge to determine whether a person who is charged with a crime should be held for trial. The question before the court is this: Is there sufficient evidence produced by the state to establish that there is probable cause to believe a crime has been committed and that the defendant committed it?

The indictment, information, or preliminary hearing is the start of the **criminal prosecution,** an action or proceeding begun in the appropriate criminal court on behalf of the public for the purpose of securing the conviction and punishment of one accused of a crime. The defendant may be charged with a misdemeanor, a felony, or a capital crime. A **capital crime** is one for which the penalty may be **capital punishment**—the death penalty. The **prosecuting attorney,** the public official who is appointed or elected to conduct criminal prosecutions on behalf of the state or federal government, will be the person who conducts the trial for the "people," the state. The prosecuting attorney is also known as the prosecutor, or the person who carries out the trial in the name of the government, seeking to prove that the person charged with a crime is guilty of that crime.

EXTRADITION

If an indictment or information is obtained against the defendant, but the defendant is in another state or even another country, extradition must take place. **Extradition** is the surrender by a state or country to another state or country of a person accused of an offense who is within the state or country. For example, a person is charged with rape in Tennessee, and it is discovered that he is in jail in Arkansas. Tennessee would apply for extradition, the request that Arkansas send the defendant to Tennessee to stand trial for rape. Extradition also applies to a person who has been convicted of a crime in another state.

ARRAIGNMENT

Once the indictment or information has been obtained, or it has been found that there is sufficient evidence to hold the defendant for trial, **arraignment** occurs. Arraignment is the procedure by which the accused is brought before the court to enter a plea to the criminal charge. The defendant can enter a **guilty plea,** an admission in open court that the defendant is responsible for and did commit the criminal act he or she is charged with; a **not guilty plea,** a denial that he or she is responsible for the criminal act; or a plea of **nolo contendere.** See Exhibit 3-11. *Nolo contendere* literally means "I will not contest it," and it has the same legal effect as pleading guilty although it is not technically a guilty plea. The defendant is not contesting the fact that he or she is charged with the crime, and acknowledges that he or she will be treated in the same manner as he or she would have been had he or she pleaded guilty. After a plea of nolo contendere, the court may sentence the defendant because the defendant did not contest the allegations made by the state.

EXHIBIT 3-11	PLEAS AT ARRAIGNMENT

During arraignment, the defendant will enter one of the following pleas to the criminal charges.

1. **Not Guilty** – The person is *not* responsible for the crime with which he or she is charged.
2. **Guilty** – The person *is* responsible for the crime with which he or she is charged.
3. **Nolo Contendere** – "I will not contest it." The person is pleading neither guilty nor not guilty, but declares he or she will not contest the charges against him or her. This has the same effect as a guilty plea.

NOT GUILTY BY REASON OF INSANITY; NOT COMPETENT TO STAND TRIAL

The defendant may also enter a plea of **not guilty by reason of insanity,** which means that, at the time the defendant committed the crime, he or she was insane and thus could not conform his or her conduct to the requirements of law, or was unable to form the necessary criminal intent because he or she was not aware of the criminal nature the act committed. If this defense is raised, both the defense and the prosecution can have the defendant examined to determine if he or she was legally insane at the time of the crime or if he or she was insane at the time of the crime *and* is still insane. Another plea is that the defendant is **not competent to stand trial,** which is different from a plea of not guilty by reason of insanity. Not competent to stand trial means that the defendant lacks the capacity to understand the nature of the proceedings, is unable to consult with counsel, or is unable to assist with the preparation of his or her defense. Incompetency to stand trial can be caused by a mental illness, by mental retardation, or by any temporary incapacity. If this plea is entered, it must be determined if the person will ever be competent to stand trial. If it is determined that the defendant will never be competent to stand trial, then the defendant can be found not guilty by reason of insanity or by reason of mental defect. If competency can be restored, then the trial does not take place until such time as the defendant is competent to stand trial. See Exhibit 3-12.

EXHIBIT 3-12 THE MENTAL ILLNESS PLEAS

Instead of pleading guilty, not guilty, or nolo contendere, the defendant pleads not guilty by reason of insanity or not competent to stand trial.

1. **Not Guilty by Reason of Insanity** – At the time the defendant committed the crime, he or she was insane and could not conform his or her conduct to the requirements of law. At the time of the crime, the defendant could not form the necessary mental intent to commit the crime. The defendant is not guilty because, in order to be found guilty of committing a crime, the state must prove the elements of the crime and that the defendant had the necessary intent.

2. **Not Competent to Stand Trial** – The defendant lacks the capacity to understand the nature of the proceedings, is unable to consult with counsel, or is unable to assist with the preparation of his or her defense.

If a defendant is not mentally ill or mentally retarded, he or she can involve the **diminished capacity doctrine.** This doctrine states that if a person's mental capacity was so diminished by intoxication, trauma, or mental disease that he or she did not possess the required mental intent to commit the offense he or she is charged with, he or she cannot be found guilty of the crime. In other words, the person was so intoxicated or so traumatized that he or she was incapable of conforming his or her conduct to that expected of society, and that he or she did not fully understand the import of the act. The burden of proof of diminished capacity is on the defendant, who raises this defense.

PLEA BARGAINING AND DISMISSING THE CASE

The defendant may also enter into a negotiated plea at this time. In a negotiated plea, the defendant agrees to plead guilty to the pending charge or a reduced charge if the prosecutor agrees to recommend a sentence less severe than the maximum allowed by the particular statute. A **plea bargain** is an arrangement made in which the defendant agrees to plead guilty to a lesser offense. At any time prior to the jury's reaching its verdict, the prosecutor and defendant may enter into a plea bargain.

If the prosecutor decides not to proceed with the case, he may nolle prosequi (*no-liy pro-se-kwi*) or **nol. pros.** the case. This is a voluntary formal entry on the record by the prosecuting attorney in a criminal case by which he declares he will no longer prosecute the case.

Prior to the case going to trial, the prosecution is required to disclose to the defendant all the evidence it has gathered about the case. This can include evidence that proves the defendant's guilt as well as **exculpatory evidence,** evidence or information that justifies the defendant's actions, excuses the conduct, or clears the defendant of any guilt. Exculpatory evidence tends to show the innocence of the defendant. If the prosecution does not provide this information, then it is considered Brady material. The name comes from the case of *Brady v. United States.* **Brady material** is information or evidence the government has or knows about that is relevant to the defendant's innocence or guilt that is not disclosed to the defendant in time for the trial. The effect is that the defendant is denied due process of law because the government suppressed evidence. For example, a defendant is charged with kidnapping by the government. There is evidence to indicate the defendant was involved, but the government also has a videotape of another person confessing to the crime and stating the defendant was not involved. This information is to be provided to the defendant. If it is not, it is Brady material because it goes to the innocence or guilt of the defendant.

SUPPRESSION HEARINGS

Before the criminal trial, a **suppression hearing** will be held. This is a hearing during which the defendant, through his or her attorney, attempts to prevent the introduction of evidence that the defense alleges was obtained illegally. The defense seeks the suppression—the exclusion from evidence—of information that can be used against the defendant. **Suppression of evidence** is the actual ruling by the trial judge that the evidence the prosecution wishes to use against the defendant will not be admitted into evidence at trial because it was illegally obtained. Usually the evidence the defendant does not want admitted is **incriminating evidence,** evidence that tends to prove the guilt of the defendant or, combined with other evidence, tends to prove the guilt of the defendant. The defense will also seek to suppress any incriminating statements, statements that tend to prove the guilt of the defendant or, when combined with other facts, may tend to prove the guilt of the defendant.

See Exhibit 3-13 for a summary of criminal pre-trial procedure.

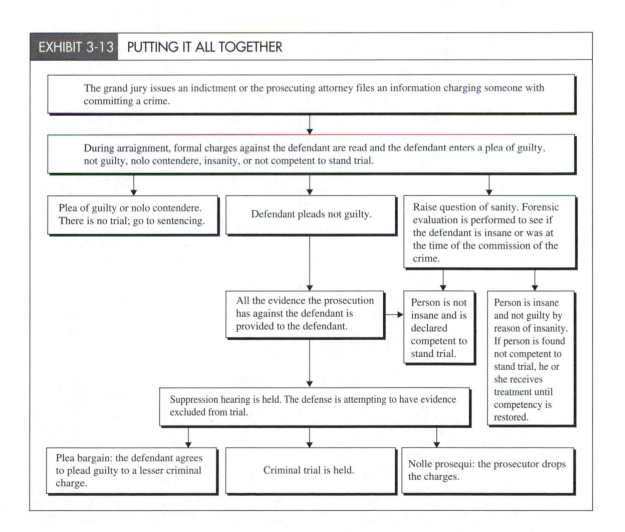

EXHIBIT 3-13 PUTTING IT ALL TOGETHER

The grand jury issues an indictment or the prosecuting attorney files an information charging someone with committing a crime.

During arraignment, formal charges against the defendant are read and the defendant enters a plea of guilty, not guilty, nolo contendere, insanity, or not competent to stand trial.

Plea of guilty or nolo contendere. There is no trial; go to sentencing.

Defendant pleads not guilty.

Raise question of sanity. Forensic evaluation is performed to see if the defendant is insane or was at the time of the commission of the crime.

All the evidence the prosecution has against the defendant is provided to the defendant.

Person is not insane and is declared competent to stand trial.

Person is insane and not guilty by reason of insanity. If person is found not competent to stand trial, he or she receives treatment until competency is restored.

Suppression hearing is held. The defense is attempting to have evidence excluded from trial.

Plea bargain: the defendant agrees to plead guilty to a lesser criminal charge.

Criminal trial is held.

Nolle prosequi: the prosecutor drops the charges.

CRIMINAL TRIAL

There are several similarities between a criminal trial and a civil trial. There are opening arguments, the plaintiff or prosecutor presents the state's case first, and the defense has the right to cross-examine all witnesses. The defense then presents its case, the prosecution can cross-examine all witnesses, and can call rebuttal witnesses. Closing arguments are then presented to the jury or to the court, whichever is the finder of fact. But there are certain elements that are unique to a criminal trial.

FAIR AND IMPARTIAL JURY AND TRIAL

When facing criminal charges, a defendant is entitled to a fair and impartial jury and trial. A **fair and impartial jury** is one chosen to hear evidence and render a verdict without any predetermined opinions concerning the innocence or guilt of the defendant. Every member of the jury must be **fair and impartial;** each must not already have an idea as to whether the defendant is innocent or guilty. A **fair and impartial trial** is a hearing before a disinterested and impartial judge or tribunal; the court does not have any interest in how the case is decided. What makes a trial fair is that the defendant's legal rights are safeguarded, witnesses are compelled to appear and testify, there is adequate time to investigate and prepare a defense, witnesses are allowed to testify, and the defendant has the right to face his or her accusers. See Exhibit 3-14.

EXHIBIT 3-14	ELEMENTS OF A FAIR TRIAL

1. The jury has no preconceived ideas about the guilt or innocence of the defendant.
2. The court does not have an interest in the outcome of the trial.
3. Witnesses were required to appear and testify and did so.
4. Adequate time to investigate and prepare the case was allowed.
5. Defendant was allowed to confront his or her accusers and subject them to cross-examination.

The right a defendant has to confront his or her accusers, as well as all witnesses against him or her, is guaranteed a person by the **confrontation clause** contained in the Sixth Amendment. The defendant has the right to confront all witnesses against him or her, face to face, so that the defendant may make any objection he or she has to the witness testifying, subject the witness to cross-examination, and allow the witness to identify him or her. These rights are collectively known as the right of confrontation.

RIGHT TO A SPEEDY TRIAL

The Sixth Amendment also requires the defendant to receive a **speedy trial,** one that is held as soon after the indictment as the prosecution, using reasonable diligence, can prepare for it. The U.S. Supreme Court in the case of *Barker v. Wingo* established a four-factor test to be used to determine if the defendant did indeed receive a speedy trial:

1. The length of the delay
2. The prosecution's justification for the delay
3. Whether and how the defendant asserted the right to a speedy trial
4. What prejudice to the defendant was caused by the delay (see Exhibit 3-15)

EXHIBIT 3-15	FACTORS USED TO DETERMINE IF THE DEFENDANT RECEIVED A SPEEDY TRIAL

BARKER V. WINGO

1. How long was the delay between indictment and the start of the trial?
2. What was the prosecution's reason for the delay?
3. When and how did the defendant assert the right to a speedy trial?
4. What prejudice—harm—was caused to the defendant by the delay?

Prejudice, when applied to the speedy trial requirement, refers to impairment of the defendant's ability to present an effective defense. The term also refers to any threat to the psychological, physical, or financial situation of the defendant caused by a delay in the proceedings.

BURDEN OF PROOF

Once the trial begins, many of the same procedures used in civil court are followed. The burden of proof is on the prosecution and the burden is beyond a reasonable doubt. **Reasonable doubt** is doubt based on reason and arising from the evidence or lack of evidence; it is doubt that a reasonable man or woman might have. The term **beyond a reasonable doubt** means that the facts proven and evidence presented tend to prove guilt beyond any doubt that a reasonable man or woman might have. This does not mean that all doubt of guilt or innocence is removed; it means that a *reasonable* person has no *reasonable* doubts about guilt or innocence. The defendant has a **presumption of innocence:** the government has the burden of proving every element of a crime beyond a reasonable doubt and the defendant has no burden to prove his or her innocence. Thus, according to law, the defendant is innocent until proven guilty.

Several principles relate to proving guilt beyond a reasonable doubt. One such principle is the **equal access rule.** This rule states that finding contraband on the premises occupied by the defendant is not enough evidence to sustain a conviction if it is shown that another person also had an equal opportunity to commit the crime and had the same access to the contraband. For example, a person is charged with possession of marijuana with intent to deliver. If the marijuana is found in the defendant's apartment, this is not sufficient evidence to support a conviction if it is shown the defendant's roommate also had access to the marijuana.

DEFENSES

After the prosecution has presented evidence of the defendant's guilt, the defendant may come forward with evidence of his or her innocence. There are several defenses a person may declare in a criminal proceeding. The first is an alibi. An **alibi** places the defendant at a location removed from the scene of the crime at the time the crime was committed. Another defense available is **self-defense,** the protection of one's person or property from injury attempted by another. The person must believe that he or she is in immediate danger of unlawful bodily harm and that the use of force was necessary to avoid the danger. The **fighting words doctrine,** first announced by the Supreme Court in *NAACP v. Clairborne Hardware Co., Mississippi,* is a defense to a criminal charge. The doctrine states that the use of fighting words, words whose very utterance inflicts injury or tends to incite an immediate breach of the peace, is a legitimate defense. (See Chapter 6, Constitutional Law.) Another defense is **entrapment,** which is defined as actions by officers or agents of the government that induce a person to commit a crime that was not contemplated by the person. The actions of the police were intended to start a criminal prosecution against the person. An official or agent of the government cannot originate the idea of the crime and then induce or encourage another person to engage in the crime when the person is not inclined to do so. The entrapment defense declares that the person had no predisposition—no inclination—to engage in the criminal activity before the government agents or the police suggested the crime be committed. See Exhibit 3-16 for a summary of these defenses.

EXHIBIT 3-16 SUMMARY OF CRIMINAL DEFENSES

1. **Alibi** – The defendant was somewhere else doing something else when the crime was committed.
2. **Self defense** – The defendant was protecting his or her person or property from harm attempted by another person.
3. **Fighting Words Doctrine** – The defendant was goaded into a fight because of what was said to him or her.
4. **Entrapment** – The police originated the idea of committing the crime and encouraged the criminal activity.

JURY VERDICTS

According to the Sixth Amendment, every defendant is entitled to a trial by jury in which the issues of fact are to be determined by the verdict of a jury that is duly selected, impaneled and sworn. A **verdict** is the formal decision or finding by a jury that is reported to the court. The U.S. Constitution requires that a jury have six members; federal statutes require a jury to have twelve members. The vote of the jury to either convict or acquit the defendant must be unanimous. A **conviction** is a judgment or sentence from the finder of fact, either the judge or jury, that the accused is guilty as charged. An **acquittal** is the legal and formal certification of the innocence of a person who has been charged with a crime; it is a finding of not guilty. If the jury is unable to reach a verdict because it is hopelessly deadlocked, it is a **hung jury.** For example, a defendant is charged with kidnapping. The jury has deliberated, voted several times, and each time the vote is nine to three for conviction. This is a hung jury; it cannot reach a unanimous verdict. If there is a hung jury, the court can declare a mistrial. Technically, a **mistrial** is an erroneous or invalid trial. The court can declare a mistrial because of an extraordinary event, a prejudicial error that cannot be corrected at trial, or because of a deadlocked jury. A mistrial might be declared because of the death of one of the attorneys, or because there is evidence that a sequestered jury has seen news reports about the case.

SENTENCING

Upon conclusion of the trial, if the defendant is found guilty, the next phase involves sentencing. **Sentencing** is the post-conviction stage of the criminal process during which the defendant is brought before the court for the imposition of the sentence. The **sentence** is the judgment that is formally pronounced upon the defendant by the court after the defendant has been convicted. Criminal sentences are usually fines, terms of imprisonment, or probation.

PROBATION

Probation allows the convicted defendant to be released into the community under the supervision of a probation officer instead of being incarcerated. The defendant has to be found eligible for probation; it is not a right, but an alternative. If the defendant fails to comply with the terms of the probation, it may be revoked and the defendant may serve the remainder of his or her sentence in prison.

CONCURRENT AND CONSECUTIVE SENTENCES

When the court sentences a defendant, the sentences may run concurrently or consecutively. **Concurrent sentences** are served at the same time. If a person is sentenced to five years for one crime and ten years for a second crime and the sentences are to run concurrently, the five- and ten-year sentences run at the same time, so the sentence is served in ten years. **Consecutive sentences** are sentences of confinement that follow each other. For example, a person is convicted of two counts of burglary. The court orders that the ten-year sentences are to run concurrently. Both sentences are served at the same time, so the maximum amount of time the person will spend in prison is ten years. Another defendant is convicted of first degree murder and robbery. The sentences are ten years for the robbery and forty years to life for the murder. At the conclusion of the robbery sentence, the sentence for the murder conviction begins. The defendant will be in prison for ten years, serving time for the robbery conviction, and then will serve the forty years to life for the murder conviction. In an effort to mitigate the sentence—make it less severe—the attorney for the defendant may bring to light **mitigating circumstances.** These do not provide a justification or an excuse for the crime committed, but may be considered when sentencing the defendant. Some examples of mitigating circumstances are whether or not this was a first offense, the circumstances surrounding the offense, or the remorse shown by the defendant.

DEFERRED, INDETERMINATE, INTERLOCUTORY, AND MANDATORY SENTENCES

Other terms are used to further describe the types of sentences imposed. A **deferred sentence** is one that is postponed until a future time. For example, a defendant is tried and convicted, and is sentenced to serve two years in prison. A deferred sentence may not start until three months later. Because sentence is deferred, the defendant is told when to report and where to report to when he or she begins serving the sentence. An **indeterminate sentence** is a form of a sentence of imprisonment that states that the term of imprisonment shall be for not less than or more than so many years. The sentence cannot be less than the minimum amount allowed, but can be no more than the maximum amount allowed. The minimum amount the sentence can be is one day; the maximum amount the sentence can be is life. An **interlocutory sentence** is a temporary sentence imposed upon the defendant pending final sentencing. A **life sentence** is the maximum sentence as far as time that can be imposed by the law. Life sentences are imposed for the most serious of criminal offenses, and extend for the remaining natural life of the defendant. A **mandatory sentence** is imposed when the judge is required to sentence the defendant to a specific period of time for a specific crime; there is little if any discretion given to the court regarding the length of the sentence. For example, in order to combat the increase in drug trafficking, a state legislature passes a law stating that the absolute minimum amount of time a person convicted of selling drugs may be sentenced to is seven years. No sentence less than seven years is authorized; probation is not an option. The court is mandated to sentence every defendant convicted of drug dealing to at least seven years in prison. Mandatory sentences are often used with habitual criminals, persons who keep committing crimes. Mandated sentences are derived from **habitual offender statutes** that are passed by different states authorizing more severe penalties for repeat offenders up to and including life imprisonment.

MINIMUM, MAXIMUM, SPLIT, AND SUSPENDED SENTENCES

A **maximum sentence** sets the limit beyond which the defendant cannot be held in prison any longer. For example, the maximum sentence for arson is forty years. If the defendant is convicted of arson, he or she cannot serve more than forty years for the crime. The **minimum sentence** is the least amount of time the defendant can spend in prison before becoming eligible for parole or release. In sentencing, the court may declare that the defendant is sentenced for a period of seven to fifteen years, and is eligible for parole after serving five years. The minimum sentence would be five years because the defendant has to serve at least five years before he or she becomes eligible for parole. A **split sentence** is one in which part of the time is served in prison and the rest is served by the defendant on probation or on some other conditions established by the court. A **suspended sentence** is the postponing or altogether withholding of sentencing after conviction, or the postponing of the imposition of the sentence after it has been announced by the court. For example, a defendant is convicted of embezzlement. The court sentences the defendant to ten years in prison, but suspends seven of those years contingent upon the defendant repaying the victims the amount of money that was embezzled. As long as payments are made, the defendant does not have to serve seven years of the sentence. But if the defendant fails to meet the conditions of the suspended sentence, the remaining sentence can be imposed upon him or her. See Exhibit 3-17 for a summary of criminal sentences.

EXHIBIT 3-17	TYPES OF CRIMINAL SENTENCES

1. **Probation** – Defendant is supervised in the community.
2. **Deferred Sentence** – Sentencing is delayed until some time in the future.
3. **Concurrent Sentences** – Sentences are served at the same time.
4. **Consecutive Sentences** – Sentences are served one after the other.
5. **Indeterminate Sentence** – A definite length of sentence is not set. Minimum and maximum lengths of sentence are stipulated.
6. **Interlocutory Sentence** – A sentence that is imposed prior to the final sentencing.
7. **Mandatory Sentence** – The court is required to sentence the defendant to a certain length of time.
8. **Maximum Sentence** – The longest period of time someone can be imprisoned for a particular offense.
9. **Minimum Sentence** – The shortest period of time someone can be imprisoned for a particular offense.
10. **Split Sentence** – Part of the sentence is served in prison; the rest of the sentence is served on probation.

DOUBLE JEOPARDY

The Fifth Amendment prohibits **double jeopardy** in stating that, after a conviction or an acquittal, a person cannot be prosecuted for the same offense. The state has one chance to get a conviction. If the state fails to convict and the defendant is acquitted, the defendant can never be tried for that same offense. The state also cannot appeal an acquittal. The Fifth Amendment also states that a person cannot be punished twice for the same offense. The Fifth Amendment is made applicable to the states through the Fourteenth Amendment. If the defendant is convicted, the state is prohibited from imposing an excessive fine or excessive punishment by the Eighth Amendment to the Constitution.

APPEALS

If a defendant is convicted (found guilty), he or she may file an appeal of the conviction, seeking either a new trial or a dismissal of the case. Generally the basis for the appeal is that there was some error at trial that prevented the defendant from receiving a fair and impartial trial.

PLAIN ERROR RULE

The general rule is that the appellate court will not consider an argument about an error at trial unless the error or issue was raised at trial. The defendant/appellant must have done something to indicate that this was an issue during the trial in order to preserve it for purposes of appeal. An exception to that rule is the **plain error rule,** which states that if an error affected a substantial right of the defendant, the error may be considered as part of a motion for a new trial or an appeal even if the issue was not raised at trial. However, there must be a clear showing of injustice or that a miscarriage of justice will result if the conviction is not reversed.

REVERSIBLE ERRORS, ERRORS IN LAW, AND FUNDAMENTAL ERRORS

On appeal, the defendant is trying to show that a reversible error happened in the trial. A **reversible error** is an error that would cause the appellate court to reverse the decision that is being appealed. It is a substantial error that might have prejudiced the rights of the defendant who is appealing the decision. A defendant may also claim there was an **error in law,** which is a mistake by the court in how the law was applied to the case at trial. An error in law occurs if the court rules that evidence is admissible when it should have been ruled inadmissible, or if the court gives improper instructions to the jury. The most serious error is a **fundamental error,** a mistake so serious that if it is not corrected it will result in the denial of fundamental due process to the defendant. Fundamental error is a mistake so egregious that it renders a judgment totally void. For example, if a defendant is denied the right to counsel or is denied the right to cross-examine witnesses against him or her, fundamental errors have occurred. A denial of these rights is denial of due process of law. Thus, the conviction is void.

HARMFUL ERROR AND HARMLESS ERROR

A **harmful error** is a mistake that more likely than not affected the verdict or the decision of the court. Examples of harmful error include admission of information into evidence that should have been excluded, allowing a witness to testify when testimony should not have been allowed, or not granting certain defense motions. If this type of error occurs, it does not mean the conviction is void; however, harmful error can be the basis for reversal of the conviction. The **harmless error doctrine** states that minor or harmless mistakes that happened during a trial do not require the reversal of the decision by the appellate court, provided these mistakes did not deny the defendant due process and did not affect the final outcome of the case. In other words, the error was not prejudicial to the rights of the defendant. Whenever an error is alleged as part of an appeal, the defendant is seeking either a reversal of the conviction and a dismissal of the case or reversal of the conviction and a new trial. A **new trial** is a re-examination of the facts, or some part of the facts, by the same court after a verdict by the jury or a decision of the court.

NEWLY DISCOVERED EVIDENCE AND EFFECTIVE ASSISTANCE OF COUNSEL

Another basis for appeal is **newly discovered evidence**—evidence that is new and that applies to a material fact or evidence that relates to a fact in issue, discovered by one of the parties after the verdict has been reached. This newly discovered evidence can be used as a basis for new trial, but it is not mandatory that the defendant receive a new trial. Another basis for appeal may be that the defendant was denied effective assistance of counsel. **Effective assistance of counsel,** when applied to criminal proceedings by the Sixth Amendment to the Constitution, means counsel reasonably likely to render reasonably effective assistance. Whether or not a person received effective assistance of counsel is determined by looking at the totality of the circumstances indicated in the record of the criminal proceeding. Did counsel conduct discovery? Did counsel object and file motions as needed? Did counsel conduct reasonable cross-examination and give valid arguments? Failure to have performed these duties can result in a reversal of the conviction. See Exhibit 3-18 for a summary of the basis of appeals of a criminal conviction.

EXHIBIT 3-18 | **BASIS OF APPEALS OF A CRIMINAL CONVICTION**

1. **Error in Law** – A mistake in how the law was applied during the trial was made.
2. **Fundamental Error** – A violation of the defendant's fundamental rights occurred during trial.
3. **Harmful Error** – A mistake that more likely than not affected the verdict or decision of the court was made at trial.
4. **Newly Discovered Evidence** – Evidence that is new and important that neither the prosecution nor defendant had at the first trial has come to light.
5. **Ineffective Assistance of Counsel** – The defendant's attorney did not conduct discovery, did not investigate, made no objections at trial, filed few if any motions, and made poor arguments.

OTHER POST-CONVICTION REMEDIES

Even if a defendant's appeal fails, there are other ways that a criminal conviction can be eliminated or removed from the records of a court. Other post-conviction remedies are issued either by the executive or judiciary branch of government.

COMMUTATION OF SENTENCE

The first post-conviction remedy is a commutation of a criminal penalty. **Commutation** (kom-yoo-*tay*-shun) is the lessening of a criminal penalty that makes the penalty less severe than the sentence that was originally imposed. For example, a prisoner on death row may have his sentence commuted or reduced to life imprisonment by the governor.

PARDONS

A **pardon** is an action by the executive branch of government (by the President of the United States or the governor of a state) that mitigates or sets aside the punishment imposed for a crime. The pardon not only sets aside the punishment, but also restores any civil rights that were taken away from the defendant because of the criminal conviction. Different types of pardons may be granted. The first is an absolute or full pardon. An **absolute** or **full pardon** frees the defendant and sets aside the conviction without any conditions being attached. The conviction and the time served by the defendant are totally eliminated.

A **conditional pardon** is granted when certain conditions have been met; the pardon is not effective until the conditions are met. The defendant must perform some act or some event must take place before the pardon becomes effective. For example, a defendant may have to admit to the crime committed and apologize to the victim before the pardon becomes effective. A **general pardon** is given to every defendant who either participated in certain criminal activity or who violated a certain statute. For example, the President of the United States might grant a pardon to everyone who participated in a riot that began during a political rally. If some activity is decriminalized (declared no longer illegal) by the passing of a statute, all defendants convicted of violating the old law can receive a general pardon.

EXPUNGEMENT OF RECORD

Another post-conviction remedy is the **expungement of record,** the process whereby the record of a criminal conviction is either destroyed or sealed after a certain period of time. Juvenile records are often expunged after defendants reach the age of majority. One way records can be expunged is if a court of appeals reverses a conviction and then orders the expungement of the defendant's criminal record. Another way records can be expunged is if the conditions set by a court after conviction or set by statute have been complied with.

CONCLUSION

The entire purpose of criminal procedure is to make sure that every person's constitutional rights are protected. These rights include the right to be free from unreasonable searches and seizures, the rights a person has if he or she is accused or arrested, the right to a fair and speedy trial, and the right to appeal.

The police can search without a warrant in several circumstances, e.g., when searching for concealed weapons, to preserve evidence of a crime, if the evidence is in plain view, or if it is subject to a lawful arrest. However, if a search is illegal, then any information gathered is subject to the exclusionary rule and the fruit of the poisonous tree doctrine.

When someone is arrested, he or she must be informed of his or her Miranda rights: the right to remain silent, to have an attorney present during questioning, to have an attorney appointed to represent him or her, and the right to halt all questioning. Also, if arrested without a warrant, the person has the right to be brought before a magistrate. See Exhibit 3-19 for a summary of cases establishing criminal procedure principles.

EXHIBIT 3-19	CRIMINAL PROCEDURE CASES AND THE PRINCIPLES CREATED

1. *Terry v. Ohio* – Police can search people they suspect are armed and dangerous or who have committed or are about to commit a crime.
2. *Mapp v. Ohio* – Any illegally obtained evidence is inadmissible in court.
3. *Wong Sun v. United States* – All evidence that is related to illegally obtained evidence is inadmissible (fruit of the poisonous tree doctrine).
4. *McNabb v. United States, Mallory v. United States* – Person who is arrested without a warrant must be brought before a magistrate promptly or any statements will be excluded from evidence.
5. *Miranda v. Arizona* – Establishes the Miranda warnings. (See Exhibit 3–9.)

During the pre-trial phase, the defendant has the right to see all the evidence the state has accumulated against him. The defense can request that certain information be excluded from trial. The defense can raise the issue of the sanity of the defendant at the time the crime was committed or the defendant's present mental state.

During trial itself, the defendant has the right to a fair and speedy trial and the right to confront all witnesses against him or her. A defendant can only be tried once for a particular crime. If the state loses, the defendant cannot be tried again for the same crime, and the state does not have the right to appeal an acquittal. The defendant can appeal a conviction by raising the arguments of fundamental error, harmful error, newly discovered evidence, or ineffective assistance of counsel.

If the appeal is not successful, the defendant can seek a pardon, commutation of a sentence, or expungement of the record.

CHAPTER 3 REVIEW

KEY WORDS AND PHRASES

acquittal
alibi
arraignment
arrest
automobile exception
bail
bench warrant
beyond a reasonable doubt
bill of attainder
capital punishment
concurrent sentences
confession
consecutive sentences
contraband
conviction
cruel and unusual
  punishment
custodial interrogation
diminished capacity
  doctrine
double jeopardy
due process of law

entrapment
ex post facto law
exclusionary rule
expungement of record
extradition
Fifth Amendment
Fruit of the Poisonous Tree
  Doctrine
full pardon
fundamental error
general pardon
grand jury
habitual offender statutes
harmless error doctrine
hung jury
indictment
information
jump bail
knock and announce rule
McNabb-Mallory Rule
Miranda rights

mistrial
nolo contendere
plain view exception
plea bargain
pleading the Fifth
presumption of innocence
probable cause
procedural due process
reasonable doubt
reversible error
search
search warrant
seizure
stop and frisk
substantive due process
suppression of evidence
suspended sentence
Terry Exception
verdict
warrantless search
writ of habeas corpus

REVIEW QUESTIONS

SHORT ANSWER
1. What is entrapment and how does it happen?
2. What are the Miranda warnings?
3. What happens to evidence that is subject to the fruit of the poisonous tree doctrine?
4. What is the Terry exception?
5. What are the elements of the plain view exception?
6. What is the stop and talk exception?
7. What is the difference between consecutive and concurrent sentences?
8. What is an admission?
9. What is the border search exception?
10. What is bail?
11. What is meant by *cruel and unusual punishment?*
12. What is the Escobedo Rule and to what does it apply?
13. What is the Equal Access Rule?

14. What are exigent circumstances?

15. What is the Knock and Announce Rule?

16. What was the holding of the court in *Mapp v. Ohio?*

17. When is a grand jury indictment required?

18. What is the McNabb-Mallory Rule?

19. What is meant by "pleading the Fifth"?

20. What is reasonable doubt?

21. What is reversible error?

22. What is the difference between a general search warrant and a specific warrant?

23. What is considered self-defense?

24. What does the Sixth Amendment protect?

25. What is transactional immunity?

FILL IN THE BLANK

1. The case of *Gideon v. Wainwright* gives people charged with a crime the right _____.

2. *Wong Sun v. the United States* established the _____ doctrine.

3. The hearing during which the defense attempts to have evidence excluded is called the _____.

4. The doctrine of _____ means a defendant cannot be tried for the same crime twice.

5. A search for weapons is allowed under the _____ to the requirement for a search warrant.

6. When a jury cannot reach a verdict, this is known as a _____.

7. Cars are stopped and searched between the United States and Canada. This can happen because of the _____.

8. A law that increases the punishment of a person after he or she has been sentenced is an _____.

9. _____ means "You have the body," and is a court order to show why a person is being held in jail.

10. The Fifth Amendment says the _____ must issue a _____ in order to charge someone with a crime.

FACT SITUATIONS

1. Officer Richards stops a car that he suspects may have been the getaway vehicle used in a bank robbery. Under what exception, if any, can he search the car?

2. If Officer Richards sees what he thinks is an illegal substance on the car seat, under what principle can he seize the illegal substance?

3. If Officer Richards arrests the people in the car, what rights must he advise them of and what are these rights called?

4. A person is found not guilty at trial. What else is this called?

5. Herman was charged with embezzling $500,000 from the bank where he worked. He was found not guilty at trial. After the not guilty verdict, he wrote a best-selling book about how he stole the money. Can he be charged again? Why or why not?

6. The police seize evidence without a search warrant. Because of this evidence, they discover even more evidence. At a hearing, it is ruled that the initial evidence was obtained illegally. The defense moves to exclude the rest of the evidence. What results and why?

7. Ted is convicted for the third time of the same drug offense. Under what statutes may he be sentenced?

8. Sidney is out on bail but fails to appear at the next two scheduled hearings. What has Sidney done?

9. Larry is charged with assault and battery. The court releases him prior to trial without requiring him to post bail. What has the court done?

10. After the jury has convicted a defendant, his attorney finds out the jury had access to newspapers even though they were sequestered. What can the attorney ask the court to do?

11. Sarah is convicted of prostitution. Instead of sending her to jail, the court allows her to stay free if she meets certain conditions. What is this called?

12. Gordon fights the police when they try to arrest him for suspected DWI. With what else might he be charged?

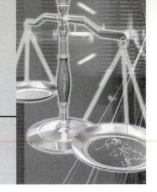

CHAPTER 4

Civil Procedure—Part I: Pleadings, Discovery, Remedies, and Pretrial Procedures

INTRODUCTION

In the previous chapter, courts and our legal system in general were discussed. In this chapter, what happens in those courts and in that system will be discussed. This chapter deals with the start of the lawsuit: who has the right to sue, how it is determined where to bring suit, and what is filed to start the lawsuit. Persons being sued must be put on notice that they are being sued, what they are being sued for, and how to respond. Once the person has been put on notice, the discovery phase of the lawsuit—the process where each side learns about the other side's case—begins. This chapter also deals with the remedies that are available to those who bring action against a defendant.

CIVIL PROCEDURE: PRETRIAL

Civil courts operate using the **Rules of Civil Procedure,** which are rules that govern the civil proceedings in state and federal courts. These rules set out how a civil lawsuit is started and how it proceeds through the courts to its conclusion. Each state has its own version of the rules; the Federal Rules of Civil Procedure govern federal courts. Many states have based their rules of civil procedure on the federal version. The Rules of Civil Procedure are classified as **procedural** (pro-*seed*-jer-el) **law. Substantive** (*sub*-sten-tiv) **law** is the law that fixes duties and establishes rights and responsibilities among and for people. Procedural law sets out when and how a person can sue someone; substantive law sets out what a person can sue someone for. See Exhibit 4-1.

INITIATION OF THE LAWSUIT

Henry is driving his car down the road when Jonathan runs a red light and hits the side of Henry's car. Henry is not hurt, but the car sustains over $4,000 in damage. Jonathan refuses to pay, saying he did not run a red light and that he is not responsible for the accident. Jonathan's insurance company, Fly-By-Night Insurance, believes him and refuses to pay. Henry decides to retain an attorney and file suit, a generic term meaning any proceeding by one person against another in a court of law. Henry is about to enter into litigation involving Jonathan and Fly-By-Night. **Litigation** (lit-i-*gay*-shen) is legal action that includes all

EXHIBIT 4-1	SUBSTANTIVE LAW OR PROCEDURAL LAW

1. **Substantive Law** – Law that determines rights and responsibilities among different people. This is the law that establishes what one person can sue another for.
2. **Procedural Law** – Law that determines how one person can sue another person. This law sets out the process that is to be followed when one person is suing another person.

the proceedings associated with a lawsuit. Henry can file the suit because he has **standing to sue**—a stake in the controversy that can be presented to the court. Henry has a tangible interest that is legally protected and that will be directly affected by the lawsuit. Henry's interest in the lawsuit is forcing Jonathan and his insurance company to pay for repairs to his vehicle. Once the decision to file the suit is made, the case proceeds to the next stage, the pleadings stage.

JURISDICTION

The first decision that is made is where the lawsuit will be filed: Which court will the case be filed in and where is that court located? The lawsuit must be filed in a court that has **jurisdiction** (joo-ris-*dik*-shen), authority granted to the court by law to hear certain types of cases and to render decisions. Jurisdiction is the authority to inquire into the facts, apply the law, make decisions, and declare judgment, the final decision of the court resolving the dispute and determining the rights of the parties involved. A lawsuit must be filed in a court that has been given the authority by statute or other means to hear this type of case. Because this is a civil case, it cannot be filed in criminal court; it must filed in a civil court.

Jurisdiction is further broken down into several categories. The first category is **subject matter jurisdiction,** or the power of the court to hear the particular type of case before it. For example, bankruptcy court is a civil court, but it cannot hear a divorce case even though a divorce is a civil matter. Bankruptcy court has subject matter jurisdiction over bankruptcy only and therefore can only hear bankruptcy cases. Probate court cannot hear a criminal case because probate court only has subject matter jurisdiction over probate matters—wills, trusts, estates, and guardianships.

The second type of jurisdiction is **in personam** (in-per-*soh*-nam) **jurisdiction** which is the power a court has over a defendant's person. The court must have in personam jurisdiction (authority) over the defendant in order to be able to issue a judgment for which the defendant will be personally responsible. There is no in personam jurisdiction issue with a plaintiff because the plaintiff chooses the court where the lawsuit will be filed, and therefore subjects himself to the court's jurisdiction.

In rem jurisdiction is the power the court has over a thing—not a person—so that the court can enter a judgment that determines every person's right with regard to this thing. For example, three people argue over who owns a piece of real estate. In rem jurisdiction gives the court the authority to determine who owns the property. The court has the authority, because of in rem jurisdiction, to decide everyone's right to this piece of property. **Quasi in rem** (*kway*-sye-in-rem) **jurisdiction** is the court's jurisdiction over a piece of property, real or personal, that is not the subject matter of the lawsuit. For example, a bank has loaned a person money. The person has moved to another state, has not repaid the loan, and has no intention of ever repaying the loan. But the person still has property in the state. The bank sues to obtain judgment against the person and asks the court to exercise quasi in rem jurisdiction over the property. The property is not the subject matter of the suit; the loan is the subject matter, and the bank sued because the person defaulted on paying the loan back. The bank gets its judgment and the court declares that the bank can sell the property to get its money back. The court can do this because, by virtue of quasi in rem jurisdiction, it has the authority to declare what rights the defendant still has to the property. In order to use quasi in rem jurisdiction, the property must be within the geographical limits of the court, that is, within the court's authority. For example, a court in Arkansas cannot exercise quasi in rem jurisdiction to determine the interests a person has in land that is in Texas. Quasi in rem jurisdiction is an example of a legal fiction. A **legal fiction** is defined as a situation created by the law to permit the court to dispose of a matter before it. The court really does not have jurisdiction over the property, but in order to dispose of the matter before it, the law allows the court to exercise jurisdiction over the property.

Concurrent (kon-*ker*-ent) **jurisdiction** is the jurisdiction of different courts over the same subject matter within the same area. In other words, there can be more than one court in the location where a lawsuit can be filed that have the authority to hear a particular case. The plaintiff selects which court to originally file the suit in, but the defendant has the right to request that the case be transferred to another court. For example, a plaintiff might file a case in state court, but it could also be filed in federal court. Because the state court and the federal court have concurrent jurisdiction, the defendant could request that the case be transferred to the federal court. See Exhibit 4-2 for a summary of the different types of jurisdictions.

EXHIBIT 4-2	TYPES OF JURISDICTION

1. **Subject Matter Jurisdiction** – The court has the authority to hear the type of case before it.
2. **In Personam Jurisdiction** – The court has authority over the people who are involved in the case before it.
3. **In Rem Jurisdiction** – The court has authority over property, so it can rule on issues regarding the property.
4. **Quasi in Rem Jurisdiction** – The court takes authority over property even though the property is not what the lawsuit is about. The court uses this to obtain jurisdiction over a person.
5. **Concurrent Jurisdiction** – More than one court has the authority to hear a particular case.

VENUE AND FORUM

A case must also be filed in the proper **venue** (*ven*-yoo). *Venue* is defined as the place where the suit is brought; it is the place where either party may request the case be tried. *Venue* does not refer to jurisdiction (the authority a court has to hear a case), but rather to the physical site where a case can be heard. For example, there may be several divorce courts in a state, all of which have the authority to hear a divorce case. However, the case must be brought in a court that is in the proper location within the state—the court that has the proper venue. In federal court, venue is based on where the cause of action arose or where the parties reside or conduct their business. The plaintiff chooses where the case is filed, but the defendant can request a **change of venue,** or removal of the case that has begun in one court or district from that court or district to another court or district. In civil cases, this change may be permitted in the interests of justice or for the convenience of the parties. For example, a person who is suing files the case in the county where he lives. The person who is being sued can request that the case be moved to the county where the actionable incident took place because that is where the physical evidence and most of the witnesses are located. See Exhibit 4-3.

The **forum** (*for*-em) is the particular court where the case may be brought. The plaintiff also makes the initial choice as to the forum where the case is filed. For example, there may be several divorce courts in a county. The plaintiff chooses where he will file the case. The forum selected should be the **forum conveniens** (*for*-em kon-*viy*-yenz), or the court or judicial district in which it is most appropriate to bring the case taking into account the best interests of the parties. If the defendant is not satisfied with the court selected, then he or she would file a forum non conveniens motion. **Forum non conveniens** (*for*-em non kon-*viy*-yenz) is the discretionary power a court has to decline jurisdiction of a particular case if it believes the best interest of the parties would be better served by having another court hear the case. When this motion is filed, the defendant is asking the court to determine that another court is better suited to hear the case than the court selected by the plaintiff. See Exhibit 4-3 to see how the proper court is determined. One thing this is designed to prevent is **forum shopping,** an attempt by the plaintiff to have his case tried in a particular court or jurisdiction because he feels he will receive a more favorable judgment.

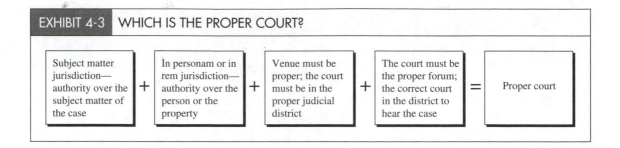

EXHIBIT 4-3 WHICH IS THE PROPER COURT?

Subject matter jurisdiction—authority over the subject matter of the case	+	In personam or in rem jurisdiction—authority over the person or the property	+	Venue must be proper; the court must be in the proper judicial district	+	The court must be the proper forum; the correct court in the district to hear the case	=	Proper court

PLEADINGS AND THE PARTIES

A lawsuit or case in civil court starts when a **petition** (pə-*tish*-en), a formal written application to a court that contains the cause of action, is filed with the clerk of the court. A petition is sometimes referred to as a *complaint;* these terms can be used interchangeably. The term **cause of action** refers to the facts that give a person the right to judicial relief from the actions of another and the right to request judicial action on this matter. In other words, a cause of action is what one person is suing another for—the events that give a person the right to file a lawsuit against someone else. **Filing,** in the legal sense, is the delivery of an instrument or other paper to the proper official for the purpose of its being kept as a matter of record. The proper official is usually the clerk of the court where the plaintiff is filing the lawsuit. The **plaintiff** (*plain*-tif) is the person who is bringing the cause of action. The **defendant** (de-*fen*-dent) is the person the cause of action is being brought against. In the example used earlier in this chapter, Henry would be the plaintiff, and Jonathan and Fly-By-Night Insurance would be the defendants. All of the parties to a lawsuit—that is, all of the people involved in the suit—are known as **litigants** (*lit*-i-gents).

A plaintiff is required to bring all claims against a particular defendant in the same cause of action; failure to do so will subject the plaintiff to the **entire controversy doctrine.** This rule states that the plaintiff must raise all claims against the defendant that arose from the same transaction or occurrence or he or she is barred from bringing them up in any subsequent actions. The plaintiff must state all claims that he or she has against the defendant because of this particular activity or he is prevented from bringing them up in any subsequent proceeding.

By filing a petition, the plaintiff is saying, "I have a claim, a cause of action, and a right to demand something against the defendant." Another term for *petition* is **complaint;** the original, initial pleading that begins an action under the rules of civil procedure. Because of the claim being made, the plaintiff is also known as the claimant, the one who is claiming or asserting a right.

Every petition will have a **caption,** or heading, that contains the name of the parties, the name of the court, the docket or file number, and the title of the action. For example, a caption might read: "In the Chancery Court of Pulaski County" (the name of the court), "Heath v. Heath" (the name of the parties), "P-98-01" (the file number), "Petition for Divorce" (the title of the action). The petition will also contain **allegations** (al-ə-*gay*-shəns), which are statements the plaintiff hopes to prove. The allegations, if proven, should establish the facts necessary for the plaintiff to have a case and to be successful if the allegations are true. The petition will conclude with the **prayer for relief,** the part of the petition where the plaintiff states the relief he wants or the amount of damages he is alleging he is entitled to. For example, the prayer for relief could state: "The plaintiff prays that this court issue an injunction prohibiting the defendant from _____, and requests $10,000 in compensatory damages, and $200,000 in punitive damages." This is a required element of the petition. See Exhibit 4-4 for an example of the different parts of a petition.

EXHIBIT 4-4	PARTS OF A PETITION/COMPLAINT

1. CAPTION

IN THE CIRCUIT COURT OF PULASKI COUNTY, ARKANSAS

NINTH DIVISION

HEATH		PLAINTIFF
v.	Case No. E98-974	
HEATH		DEFENDANT

PETITION FOR DIVORCE

2. ALLEGATIONS

1. The plaintiff and defendant were married on June 22, 1998, in Little Rock, Arkansas.
2. The defendant has committed adultery, has beaten the plaintiff, and has failed to support the plaintiff since they have been married.
3. The plaintiff is entitled to a majority of the marital property because of the defendant's actions.
4. The couple has two minor children and the defendant has a continuing obligation to support his children and should be ordered to pay child support.

3. PRAYER

Wherefore, the plaintiff prays that this court grant her a final divorce, that she receive a majority of the property accumulated during the marriage, that the Court apply the child support chart and set a reasonable amount of child support based upon the number of children and the defendant's salary, and for all other appropriate relief that she is entitled to.

If Henry and his attorney found out there were many Fly-By-Night clients who were involved in automobile accidents and that Fly-By-Night was refusing to pay in every case, they might consider filing a class action suit. A **class action lawsuit** is one brought by a group of people who have a common legal position and a common claim against the opposing party. The plaintiffs all have the same legal rights, and the court can efficiently and fairly adjudicate all of their rights in a single hearing. See Exhibit 4-5. Whatever decision the court reaches is binding upon every member of this class.

EXHIBIT 4-5	REQUIREMENTS FOR A CLASS ACTION LAWSUIT

1. **Numerosity** – Proposed class is so numerous that it is not practical to have all of the potential plaintiffs join in the suit.
2. **Commonality** – One or more common questions of law or fact affect the rights of all or a substantial number of the members of the proposed class.
3. **Typicality** – The claims of the representatives of the class are typical or the same of the claims of all of the members of the class.
4. **Adequacy of Representation** – The named plaintiffs must adequately represent the interests of the class. This is determined by whether or not the plaintiff's attorney will adequately protect the interests of the class and if there is any conflict of interest between the plaintiffs that are representing the class and the rest of the class members.

Source: *Federal Rules of Civil Procedure, Rule 23*

SUMMONS

Once the petition is filed, the plaintiff must notify the defendant that a lawsuit has been filed against him or her. The defendant must receive a summons, which is issued by the clerk and delivered to the sheriff or other authorized person. The sheriff or other person is required to notify the person named (the defendant) that a suit has been filed against him or her and that he or she is required to file an answer to the complaint. The summons is in effect a **writ** (*rit*), a written court order directing that a sheriff or other judicial officer do what is commanded by the order—in this case, serve notice of the lawsuit on the defendant.

There are several ways to serve a summons on a defendant, to get **service of process** or the actual delivery of the summons and complaint by an authorized person to the defendant. The first way is actual service, whereby the summons and complaint are physically delivered to the defendant personally or, in most states, left with a responsible person at the defendant's place of residence. **Constructive** or **substituted service** is the mailing of the summons to the last known address of the defendant or causing notice of the suit to be published in a newspaper. Substituted service may also be to an attorney who is authorized to accept service on behalf of the defendant. **Service by publication** is the publishing of the notice directed to an absent or nonresident defendant in a newspaper as an advertisement provided the newspapers used meet the conditions set by the statute or the Rules of Civil Procedure. Once the defendant has been served, the person who actually served the defendant will submit **proof of service**—evidence that service was made on the defendant. This is also known as return of service. Henry's attorney knows where Jonathan lives, so he is able to have the sheriff serve him the summons. Exhibit 4-6 summarizes the types of service of process.

EXHIBIT 4-6	TYPES OF SERVICE OF PROCESS

1. **Actual Service** – The summons and complaint are delivered to the defendant in person.
2. **Constructive/Substituted Service** – Mailing the summons to the defendant's last known address. It may also be sent to the attorney who represents the defendant.
3. **Service by Publication** – Warning notice is published in a newspaper advising the defendant that a lawsuit has been filed against him or her and stating how he or she should respond.

Serving Fly-By-Night proves to be more difficult. Upon investigation, it is determined that the company has no offices or agents in the state. Jonathan got the insurance by calling an 800 number, which he found in advertising brochures Fly-By-Night had sent into the state, hoping to generate business.

Because there is no one to serve in the state, Henry's attorney will attempt service by the use of a long arm statute. A **long arm statute** is a state statute that provides for jurisdiction over persons or corporations who are not residents of the state, but who have voluntarily gone into the state either directly, by agent, or by communication with people in the state, and transacted business. The cause of action arises out of the transaction. This statute allows the state to extend its "long arm" across state lines and exercise authority (jurisdiction) over someone who is not a resident of the state where the court is located. According to *International Shoe Company v. State of Washington,* the non-resident defendant must have sufficient **minimum contacts** (sufficient contact with the state, such as conducting business in the state) so as not to violate the defendant's rights to due process. See Sidebar 4-1 for a summary of this case.

SIDEBAR 4-1 *INTERNATIONAL SHOE COMPANY V. STATE OF WASHINGTON*

Facts: International Shoe Company, a Delaware Corporation headquartered in St. Louis, Missouri, manufactured and distributed shoes and footwear in several states. Between 1937 and 1940, the only contact the company had with the state of Washington was the salesmen who displayed samples of ISC's products, solicited orders from prospective buyers, and sent the orders to headquarters for acceptance. Managers in St. Louis supervised the salesmen and paid them commissions (totalling over $31,000 annually) based on sales. ISC filled orders by shipping its products to the buyers' residences in the state of Washington. Payments were collected at the place of shipment prior to delivery. Washington state had an unemployment compensation fund financed by mandatory annual employer contributions based on percentages of employee salaries. The Commissioner served an order and notice of assessment for delinquent contributions upon an ISC salesman in Washington and sent a copy of the order and notice by registered mail to ISC in St. Louis, Missouri. ISC appeared before the Washington office of unemployment, asking that the order and assessment be set aside because: (1) the service on the salesman was not service on the company; (2) ISC was not a Washington corporation and did not conduct business there; (3) ISC did not authorize its Washington agents to receive service of process; and (4) ISC was not an employer under the statute.

Issue: Was having salesmen and conducting business in a state sufficient minimum contacts to allow the state of Washington to exercise personal jurisdiction over ISC and therefore compel ISC to make payments to the state's unemployment compensation fund?

Ruling of the Court: A corporation does not have a physical location in the same sense as a natural person since the corporate personality is a legal fiction. The location of a corporation is determined by its activities and dealings in a state. Due process permits a state court to assert personal jurisdiction over an out-of-state corporate defendant provided that the defendant has minimum contacts with the state so that the suit does not offend traditional notions of fair play and substantial justice. The term *minimum contacts* refers to the nature and quality of the defendant's activities in the state and the relationship between those activities and the legal action.

ISC had continuous and systematic contacts with the state of Washington through its employment of salesmen, marketing efforts, product sales, and profit derived in the state. The continuous and systematic contacts were related and gave rise to the legal action against it because ISC employed workers in the state and incurred a tax obligation under Washington law.

Source: Federal Reports

See Sidebar 4-2 for the case of *World-Wide Volkswagen v. Woodson,* which is an example of a determination being made about whether there were sufficient minimum contacts.

SIDEBAR 4-2 *WORLD-WIDE VOLKSWAGEN V. WOODSON*

Facts: The Robinsons purchased an Audi from World-Wide Volkswagen, an Audi dealer in New York. On a trip to Arizona, the Robinsons were injured in an automobile accident that took place in Oklahoma. The Robinsons sued the Audi Corporation, the importer of the Audi they bought, and World-Wide Volkswagen in Oklahoma state court. World-Wide Volkswagen objected to the trial court in Oklahoma exercising jurisdiction over it. World-Wide argued it did no business in Oklahoma, so there were not sufficient minimum contacts. Judge Woodson, the trial judge in Oklahoma, disagreed. World-Wide appealed the decision to the United States Supreme Court.

Ruling of the Court: The Supreme Court ruled that not only did World-Wide Volkswagen not have minimum contacts with Oklahoma, it had *no* contact with Oklahoma at all. Their business was limited to selling cars on the East Coast. Just the fact that a car they sold wound up in Oklahoma was not a sufficient minimum contact for a court to exercise jurisdiction over World-Wide. For there to have been minimum contact, there must have been an intent to do business in the state. A firm must have made an effort to do business in a state to become subject to the jurisdiction of its courts.

Source: United States Reports

In our scenario, because Fly-By-Night has made an effort to do business in the state, and actually has done business in the state, the summons can be sent to Fly-By-Night and the court will exercise jurisdiction over the company using the long arm statute.

DEFENDANT'S ANSWER TO BEING SUED

Once he or she is served, the defendant is required to file an **answer,** which is the response of the defendant to the plaintiff's complaint, denying it in part or in whole. By filing an answer, the defendant has entered his or her **appearance**—the coming into court as a party to a suit. The defendant is submitting himself or herself to the jurisdiction of the court. The defendant's appearance can be made by the actual party or by his or her attorney. The petition and the answer are collectively known as the **pleadings,** the documents that contain the formal allegations by the parties to the suit of their claims and defenses that have the intended purpose of showing what it is hoped will be proven at trial.

At this point of the proceedings, the defendant is required to raise any affirmative defense he or she might have. An **affirmative defense** (a-*fer*-ma-tiv de-*fense*) attacks the plaintiff's legal right to bring the cause of action. It does not attack the truth of the claim; rather, it says that the plaintiff has no legal right to bring the suit at all. See Exhibit 4-7. An example of an affirmative defense is **statute of limitations** (*stat*-shoot of lim-i-*tay*-shənz)—a statute that sets out the maximum amount of time someone has to bring a certain cause of action. Under a statute of limitations, Henry has a certain amount of time to actually sue Jonathan and Fly-By-Night. If the period of time to file suit is two years and Henry does not sue until two and a half years later, then Jonathan and Fly-By-Night have the affirmative defense of statute of limitations. Jonathan was not sued within the time established by statute, so now he cannot be sued for hitting Henry's car. Because Jonathan cannot be held liable, Fly-By-Night Insurance Company cannot be made to pay. However, if there is a revival statute, the cause of action may still be brought against the defendant. A **revival statute** is a state or federal statute that authorizes a revival of action. If certain conditions are met, a cause of action that is barred by a statute of limitations can still be brought against a defendant.

EXHIBIT 4-7	AFFIRMATIVE DEFENSES

These affirmative defenses are listed in Federal Rules of Civil Procedure, Rule 8(C).

1. Accord and Satisfaction – (see Chapter 19, Debtor Creditor Relations)
2. Arbitration and Award – (see this chapter)
3. Assumption of the Risk – (see Chapter 9, Torts)
4. Contributory Negligence – (see Chapter 9, Torts)
5. Discharge in Bankruptcy – (see Chapter 19, Debtor Creditor Relations)
6. Duress
7. Estoppel – (see Chapter 10, Contracts)
8. Failure of Consideration – (see Chapter 10, Contracts)
9. Fraud – (see Chapter 9, Torts)
10. Illegality
11. Laches
12. License – (permission to do a certain act)
13. Payment
14. Res Judicata – (the matter has already been decided by a court and cannot be litigated again)
15. Statute of Frauds – (see Chapter 10, Contracts)
16. Statute of Limitations – (see above)

A defendant can file a **cross-claim,** which is a claim against a co-party (a party having a like status to the defendant) stating that the co-party is liable for some or all of the harm suffered. For example, Jonathan might make a cross-claim against his insurance company, stating that the company is responsible for payment of the damages to Henry's car. Jonathan could also file a **counterclaim,** which is a claim against the plaintiff that, if established, will defeat or diminish the plaintiff's claim: "I am not liable to Henry for the damage to his car because he is the one who ran the red light. He is responsible to me for the damage to my car." See Exhibit 4-8.

EXHIBIT 4-8	DEFENDANT'S RESPONSES TO A COMPLAINT

1. **Answer** – Response to the plaintiff's complaint filed by the defendant that usually denies all the allegations made in the complaint
2. **Affirmative Defense** – Attacks the plaintiff's legal right to bring the claim at all
3. **Cross-claim** – A claim that another defendant is liable for some or all of the harm caused
4. **Counterclaim** – Claim that is made against the plaintiff that defeats or lessens the plaintiff's claims
5. **Raise a Defense Under Rule 12(b)**
   1. Lack of jurisdiction over the subject matter
   2. Lack of jurisdiction over the person
   3. Improper venue
   4. Insufficiency of process
   5. Insufficiency of service of process
   6. Failure to state a claim for which relief can be granted
   7. Failure to join a necessary party

Source: Federal Rules of Civil Procedure

If the defendant fails to file an answer, a default judgment may be entered against him or her. A **default judgment** is a judgment entered against a party who has failed to defend against a claim that has been brought by another party. If there is a cross-claim or a counterclaim and the party fails to answer, then default judgment can be entered against them also. If Henry failed to respond to Jonathan's counterclaim, Henry could have a default judgment entered against him. If Fly-By-Night failed to respond to Jonathan's cross-claim, it could have a default judgment entered against it.

Once the petition has been answered, Henry and his attorney discover some errors in the petition as well as some additional facts that will make their case stronger. Because of this, they may want to amend the petition to correct the errors and allege the additional information. The legal definition of amend (ə-*mend*) is "to improve; to change for the better by removing defects or faults." **Amendment of the complaint** involves changing or modifying the complaint for the better. In order to amend the complaint, Henry's attorney must file a **motion,** an application to the court for the purpose of obtaining a rule or order directing some act be done in favor of the moving party (the party that made the motion). In this situation, Henry and his attorney are asking the court to grant an order allowing them to amend their original petition.

DISCOVERY

Once all of the initial pleadings have been filed, the case moves to the next phase, which is the discovery phase. **Discovery,** which is governed by the Rules of Civil Procedure, is the obtaining of facts and information about the case from the other party in order to assist the party's preparation for trial. Discovery can include depositions, interrogatories, production of documents, requests for admissions, and physical and mental examinations. However, physical or mental examinations can only be performed if the physical or mental status of one of the parties is an actual issue at trial.

INTERROGATORIES

Interrogatories (in-te-*raw*-ge-toh-reez) are written questions that are propounded (pro-*pound*-ed)—offered or proposed—and submitted by one party to another that are to be answered in writing, usually under oath. Interrogatories can ask about the facts of the case: What time did the accident take place? What happened? Who witnessed the event? Were there injuries? What is the nature of the injuries? Who treated the injuries? Who will you call as witnesses? Will any of the witnesses be expert witnesses? If so, what is their area of expertise? The other party may object to some of the questions as being too broad or too vague to be answered, or on the grounds that an item is not related to the lawsuit. The purpose of interrogatories, and all types of discovery, is to discover information about the other party's case.

PRODUCTION OF DOCUMENTS AND REQUESTS FOR ADMISSIONS

Production of documents is a request from one party to another that documents in the other party's possession or control be provided to the first party. The answering party can make copies of the requested documents or, if the records are too large to copy, may give the other party access to view the documents and copy those they want. Requests may be for police reports, reports to insurance companies, repair bills, and medical bills. A **request for admission** is a written statement of fact concerning the case that is submitted to an adverse party who is required to either admit or deny the statement in writing. Facts that are admitted are established and do not need to be proven at trial. Failure to respond to these requests can result in all admissions not specifically denied being considered admitted. For example, in our scenario, Henry's attorney would want admissions regarding who was driving the car, what time the accident took place, that it was Jonathan's fault that the accident took place, and that his insurance is liable for all harm caused.

DEPOSITIONS

A **deposition** (dep-ə-*zish*-en) is the asking of oral questions of the other party or witnesses for the other party. The deposition is taken under oath and outside the courtroom, usually at one of the attorney's offices. A **transcript** (*tran*-skript), a word for word account, is made of the deposition. The person whose deposition is taken is called the **deponent** (di-*po*-nənt). The attorneys in our case would want to take depositions of Henry, Jonathan, any police officer who investigated the accident, any witness to the accident, and all other potential witnesses. The purpose of deposing is to discover what each person knows about the accident and to try to establish what happened prior to trial. A deposition can be used in court during the questioning of the person who gave that particular statement. Exhibit 4-9 is a summary of the different types of discovery.

EXHIBIT 4-9	TYPES OF DISCOVERY

1. **Interrogatories** – Written questions submitted to the other side that must be answered in writing
2. **Request for Production of Documents** – Request for documents that are sent to the opposing side; copies of documents must be provided or access to the original documents given
3. **Request for Admission** – Request for the other side to admit to certain facts about the case
4. **Depositions** – Questioning of witnesses for the other side about the case, on the record

REMEDIES

A **remedy** is the method used to enforce a right or to prevent the violation of a right; it is the method whereby a wrong that has been done is redressed or compensated. Which remedy is available to the plaintiff depends upon the type of injury that was suffered. Henry would seek a civil remedy against Jonathan and Fly-By-Night Insurance. A **civil remedy** is a remedy granted by the law to a private person in a civil court for an injury to his private, individual rights. Henry is entitled to a civil remedy because he has the right to operate his vehicle without being hit by another vehicle. A **criminal remedy** is one granted by the law to the public in general for an injury to the public's rights caused by the criminal activity.

LEGAL AND EQUITABLE REMEDIES

If a remedy is a civil remedy, it can either be a legal remedy or an equitable remedy. A **legal remedy** is available in a court of law under the particular circumstances of the case. It is based on the law—what the statutory law or common law says is available for the harm. For example, money to pay for the damage to Henry's car would be a legal remedy. An **equitable** (*ek*-wi-tebl) **remedy** is one that is not based on the law, but on what is fair, or right, in a particular situation. Remedies available at law are more rigid than those available in equity. This principle allows the court to create whatever remedy is necessary to see that justice is carried out, that the injured party is returned to the position he or she would have been in had it not been for the wrongful act.

DAMAGES

More specific types of remedies are also available. The first of these is damages. **Damages** are defined as the compensation or indemnity that may be recovered in court by any person who has suffered a loss or injury because of the unlawful act, omission, or negligence of another person. Damages are usually a monetary amount awarded to compensate the person for the harm caused. There are several different classifications of damages. The first is **actual damages,** the amount awarded to the injured party for the actual loss or injury suffered. Actual damages are to pay the injured party for the exact amount of the loss suffered. For example, the actual damages suffered by Henry are the cost of repairing his vehicle, any medical bills he incurred as a result of the accident, and lost wages. **Compensatory damages** are intended to compensate the injured party for the harm caused, to restore him or her to the position he or she was in before the harm or injury. They are the equivalent of actual damages. **Punitive** (*pew*-nə-tive) **damages** are awarded because the wrong done to the plaintiff was made worse because of violence, malice, or fraud. Punitive damages are designed to punish the defendant and to serve as a warning against this type of conduct in the future.

Other classifications of damages include future damages and nominal damages. **Future damages** are awarded for future losses the plaintiff will suffer because of the injury caused by the defendant. Examples of future damages are future pain and suffering, or a diminished or lessened ability to earn money in the future because of the injury. **Nominal damages** are awarded when a right of the plaintiff was violated, but the plaintiff suffered little if any harm. Nominal damages are often awarded when there is technical invasion of a right; a small amount of money, usually $1, is awarded. See Exhibit 4-10.

EXHIBIT 4-10	TYPES OF MONETARY DAMAGES

1. **Actual/Compensatory Damages** – The amount of the actual harm or loss suffered by the injured party. These damages compensate the person for what was actually lost.
2. **Punitive Damages** – Damages that are awarded because of the wrong that was done to the plaintiff. The person responsible is punished because of the wrongdoing done to the injured party. These serve as a warning to others not to do this type of conduct.
3. **Future Damages** – Damages for the future losses the plaintiff will suffer because of the conduct of the defendant.
4. **Nominal Damages** – Damages awarded because rights of the plaintiff were violated, but no actual harm was caused by the plaintiff.

Nominal damages were awarded in the antitrust lawsuit the U.S. Football League filed against the National Football League. Sidebar 4-3 gives the facts and outcome of the case.

SIDEBAR 4-3 *UNITED STATES FOOTBALL LEAGUE V. NATIONAL FOOTBALL LEAGUE*

In 1984, the United States Football League (USFL) sued the National Football League (NFL) under the antitrust provisions of the Sherman Antitrust Act. The USFL, which was a professional football league that played in the summer, announced plans to move to the fall and compete directly with the NFL. Part of the competition was to sue the NFL. The league sought actual damages of $567 million, which, under antitrust law, when trebled, would amount to more than $1.7 billion.

The USFL argued that the NFL, which had contracts with ABC, NBC, and CBS, had pressured the networks to not televise the USFL in the fall. The league also claimed that the NFL had followed the practices outlined in the Porter Presentation, a package compiled by a Harvard professor to show the NFL how to conquer its new competitor.

The jury that heard the case ruled that the NFL was guilty of monopolizing professional football and of using predatory tactics, but it ruled against the rest of the USFL's claims. It did not find that the NFL controlled or attempted to control the television market. The jury felt that the USFL had abandoned its original plan to patiently build fan support while containing costs and had instead pursued a merger with the NFL. The move to the fall also caused the abandonment of major markets and led to further fan skepticism. The jury ruled that although the USFL was harmed by the NFL's monopolization of pro football, most of the upstart league's problems were the result of its own mismanagement.

Because of this, the jury awarded the USFL $1 in damages which was tripled under antitrust law to $3. The rights of the USFL were violated because of the actions of the NFL, but no real harm was caused by the NFL.

Source: United States District Court

EQUITABLE REMEDIES

Rather than seek monetary damages, the injured party may seek an equitable remedy. One type of equitable remedy is **restitution** (res-ti-*tew*-shen), the actual restoration of the injured party to the condition or position he or she was in prior to the loss or injury. It can also be used to place the injured into the position or condition he or she would have been in had it not been for the harm caused. Another type of equitable remedy is a **constructive trust,** which is created when a defendant, because of fraud, duress, or any other unconscionable or questionable conduct, has obtained property that he should not be allowed to own and enjoy. The defendant is required to return or transfer the property to the person who should be the rightful owner. A party that is seeking an equitable remedy should first make sure that he or she has not done anything wrong with regard to the events that lead up to the injury because the clean hands doctrine applies when an equitable remedy is sought. The **clean hands doctrine** states that a person who is seeking an equitable remedy in court cannot take advantage of any wrong he or she has committed. The person seeking the equitable remedy must come before the court with "clean hands"; that is, he or she performed no act that violated a principle of equity. If the person does not have "clean hands," he or she may not receive the remedy.

Sometimes more than one type of remedy may be available to the plaintiff. However, if one is awarded, the plaintiff cannot also receive the other. The plaintiff will have to make an **election of remedy:** he or she must determine and state the remedy he or she seeks. Once the remedy is chosen, the plaintiff is barred from receiving the other remedy.

SETTLEMENT

At any time prior to going to trial, and even up to the point before the case has gone to the jury, the parties can reach a **settlement,** a resolution of the conflict to which both parties agree. There is a meeting of the minds of the parties involved in a controversy as to a way to end it. For example, Fly-By Night might agree to admit to liability and to pay Henry less than he is asking for but an amount that is agreeable to Jonathan. It is less than Jonathan was seeking at trial, but it helps Jonathan avoid the expense and time of a trial where the results are uncertain. Sometimes a settlement is a **structured settlement,** in which the defendant agrees to make periodic payments to the plaintiff for the harm caused for the rest of the plaintiff's life. This type of settlement is usually in the form of an initial lump sum payment with the remaining payments coming from an annuity that is funded by the defendant. The agreed amount is usually a large amount of money and is designed to compensate the plaintiff over a period of time because of continuing medical bills and other expenses related to the injury. Structured settlements are commonly used in personal injury cases where the plaintiff is no longer able to work and will have ongoing medical expenses.

PRETRIAL PROCEDURES

Before the case is ever presented to a judge or a jury for decision, there are certain things that can happen to preserve the status quo. Motions can be made either to limit the issues at trial or even decide the case without going to trial.

PRELIMINARY INJUNCTIONS AND TEMPORARY RESTRAINING ORDERS

Any time before trial, the parties may attempt to maintain the status quo pending trial. For example, Henry, Jonathan, or Fly-By-Night may request a preliminary injunction. An **injunction** (in-*junk*-shen) is a court order prohibiting someone from doing some specific act or commanding someone to undo some wrong or injury. A **preliminary injunction** is one entered before trial, but should only be granted if the party requesting it can show that he or she will probably be successful on the merits at trial, that there is a likelihood of irreparable harm to him or her unless the injunction is granted, or that the harm to him or her outweighs the harm caused to others if the request is denied. An injunction is issued only after there has been a hearing by the court. A **permanent injunction** remains in effect until the final action in a lawsuit. In other words, the injunction remains in effect as long as the cause of action is pending in a court. The injunction ends when the case is finally dismissed and closed.

A **temporary restraining order (TRO)** is an order to maintain the status quo pending a hearing on an injunction. It is to be granted only in exceptional circumstances. The TRO is granted only if it appears clear from specific facts shown by **affidavit** (a-fi-*day*-vit) (a written or printed statement of facts, made voluntarily under oath) or by a verified complaint that immediate and irreparable injury, loss, or damage will result, and that either the party has attempted to give notice to the other side but has been unsuccessful, or there are reasons that such notice is not required. See Exhibit 4-11. A TRO may be granted without giving notice to the other party that the TRO has been requested. If this happens, there is to be a hearing as soon as possible to determine if the TRO needs to remain in effect.

EXHIBIT 4-11	THE DIFFERENCE BETWEEN A PRELIMINARY INJUNCTION AND A TEMPORARY RESTRAINING ORDER

Preliminary injunctions are issued after there has been a hearing on the request, the party requesting the injunction proves probable success at trial, and there will be irreparable harm if the injunction is not granted.

Temporary restraining orders are issued only if there is a showing that immediate and irreparable harm will result if the TRO is not granted. The TRO can be issued without a hearing or notice to the other side. If it is granted, a hearing must be held as soon as possible.

PRETRIAL MOTIONS

Upon completion of discovery, the parties may file several **pretrial motions**—motions filed before trial—seeking favorable rulings from the court. A **motion in limine** (lim-e-*nee*), which is a pretrial motion, may be filed. This motion requests the court to prohibit the other side from referring to or offering evidence on matters so highly prejudicial to the moving party that harm to the moving party cannot be prevented. The defendants may file a **motion to dismiss,** requesting that the case be dismissed because it does not state a claim for which the law provides a remedy, or it is in some way legally insufficient. Either party may file a **motion to strike,** which is a request to remove from any pleading any insufficient defense, or redundant, immaterial, or scandalous matter.

Either party may also file a motion for summary judgment. **Summary judgment** is a procedural device whereby one or both of the parties asks the court to issue a ruling based on the pleadings. There is no dispute as to the material facts; there are no inferences drawn from the undisputed facts; there is no question as to the applicability of the law to the situation. In short, there is no need to go to trial; the court can decide the case based on the information before it.

PRETRIAL CONFERENCES AND SUBPOENAS

In this scenario, there is no settlement, the motion to dismiss is denied, and there is no summary judgment. The parties are going to **trial,** which is the judicial examination and determination of issues of fact, law, or both between the parties to the action. Before the trial actually begins, the parties may engage in a **pretrial conference,** which is a meeting with the judge. The purpose of this meeting is to narrow the issues to be tried, secure stipulations as to matters and evidence to be heard, and to take whatever other steps are necessary to aid in the disposition of the case.

Prior to the trial, the plaintiff and his or her attorney will want to ensure that their witnesses and the documents they need will be present. To ensure that witnesses will be present, the attorney arranges to have a **subpoena** (sub-*peen*-uh), which is a court order directing a person to appear at a certain time and certain place to give testimony upon a certain matter, issued. In order to assure that necessary documents will be available at trial, a **subpoena duces tecum** (sub-*peen*-uh *doo*-ses *tee*-kum), an order directing that specific documents and other materials be brought at a certain time and certain place, is also issued. The subpoena duces tecum is addressed to the person who has custody and control of the documents: It directs that person to appear and verify that these are the records requested and that they are either the originals or accurate copies of the originals.

Before trial, or even during trial, either party to the lawsuit might ask for the recusal of the judge. **Recusal** (re-*kew*-zal) is the process through which a judge is disqualified from hearing a lawsuit because of self-interest, bias, or prejudice. The judge can recuse himself or herself if he or she believes the case presents a conflict of interest for him or her. If a judge fails to recuse himself or herself and it is established on appeal that he or she should have, this can be the basis for reversing the court's decision.

Exhibit 4-12 shows the stages of a lawsuit from the injury that leads to the lawsuit through the pretrial stage.

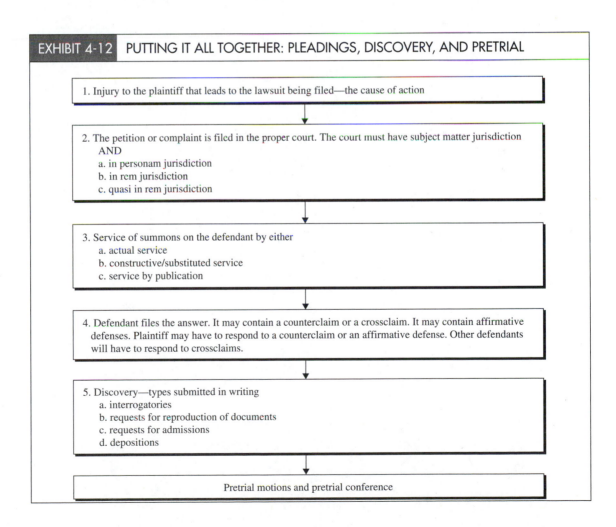

EXHIBIT 4-12 | PUTTING IT ALL TOGETHER: PLEADINGS, DISCOVERY, AND PRETRIAL

1. Injury to the plaintiff that leads to the lawsuit being filed—the cause of action

2. The petition or complaint is filed in the proper court. The court must have subject matter jurisdiction
   AND
   a. in personam jurisdiction
   b. in rem jurisdiction
   c. quasi in rem jurisdiction

3. Service of summons on the defendant by either
   a. actual service
   b. constructive/substituted service
   c. service by publication

4. Defendant files the answer. It may contain a counterclaim or a crossclaim. It may contain affirmative defenses. Plaintiff may have to respond to a counterclaim or an affirmative defense. Other defendants will have to respond to crossclaims.

5. Discovery—types submitted in writing
   a. interrogatories
   b. requests for reproduction of documents
   c. requests for admissions
   d. depositions

Pretrial motions and pretrial conference

CONCLUSION

In this chapter, words and phrases that describe the start of the lawsuit and the proceedings that take place before the trial were discussed. The lawsuit starts with the filing of the complaint in the proper court based on jurisdiction, venue, and the proper forum. Once the complaint has been filed, the defendant must be served with the complaint so he or she can be put on notice that he or she is being sued. Service can be done in person, by publication in a newspaper, or by sending the summons to the last known address of the defendant. The defendant must file an answer, and if he or she fails to do so, then default judgment can be entered against him or her. The next phase is discovery: using interrogatories, requests for production of documents, requests for admissions, and depositions to discover information about the other side's case.

The plaintiff is seeking either a legal or equitable remedy. A legal remedy can be damages, compensatory or actual, punitive, and future. If the plaintiff's case is weak, he or she may recover only nominal damages. Prior to trial, the parties may seek a temporary restraining order or an injunction to maintain the status quo before trial. Parties may also file pretrial motions to either limit issues at trial or win the case before it ever gets to trial. In order to ensure that witnesses and documents will be present at trial, subpoenas and subpoena duces tecums are issued by the court.

KEY WORDS AND PHRASES

actual damages
affidavit
affirmative defense
allegation
amendment of the
  complaint
answer
appearance
cause of action
change of venue
class action lawsuit
clean hands doctrine
compensatory damages
complaint
concurrent jurisdiction
constructive service
constructive trust
counterclaim
cross-claim
damages
default judgment
defendant
deponent
deposition

discovery
election of remedy
entire controversy doctrine
equitable remedy
forum conveniens
forum non conveniens
forum shopping
future damages
in personam jurisdiction
in rem jurisdiction
injunction
interrogatories
jurisdiction
legal fiction
long arm statute
minimum contacts
motion in limine
nominal damages
permanent injunction
petition
plaintiff
prayer for relief
preliminary injunction
pretrial conference

pretrial motion
procedural law
production of documents
proof of service
quasi in rem jurisdiction
recusal
request for admission
restitution
revival statute
service by publication
service of process
standing to sue
statute of limitations
structured settlement
subject matter jurisdiction
subpoena
subpoena duces tecum
substantive law
summary judgment
temporary restraining order
  (TRO)
venue
writ

REVIEW QUESTIONS

SHORT ANSWER

1. What is the difference between in personam jurisdiction and in rem jurisdiction?
2. What term refers to the person who brings the lawsuit?
3. How can service be obtained on someone out of state?
4. What type of statute allows a court to take jurisdiction over a defendant who is out of state?
5. What are minimum contacts?
6. What is the difference between a cross-claim and a counterclaim?
7. What is a statute of limitations?
8. A statute of limitations is an example of what? When must it be raised?
9. How does one enter one's appearance?
10. What is venue?
11. What motion will the parties file if the issue is how the law applies to the facts?

12. What is election of remedy and what is its effect?

13. What is the difference between a temporary restraining order and a preliminary injunction?

14. If a person fails to respond to a complaint, what can happen?

15. What is a motion in limine?

16. What is the difference between a subpoena and a subpoena duces tecum?

17. What does a party have to show to get a temporary restraining order?

18. What is the difference between interrogatories and depositions?

19. What is a legal fiction?

20. What is restitution?

FILL IN THE BLANK

1. The authority a court has to hear a case is _____.

2. The burden of proof in a civil case is _____.

3. The ways a person can be served are: _____

_____

_____

4. A request for written documents is known as a _____.

5. A _____ can be given to maintain the status quo, and it is issued without having a hearing.

6. A request can be made to the judge to _____ himself or herself from hearing the case because of a conflict of interest.

7. The law that determines how the case is to proceed is known as _____.

8. The right a person has to bring a lawsuit is known as _____.

9. The actual location of the court is known as _____.

10. The requirement that all issues be brought before the court in the same lawsuit is known as _____.

FACT SITUATIONS

1. What can a state court use to get jurisdiction over a person who is located in another state but is doing business in the state where the court is located?

2. Theresa has made diligent effort to locate a person she needs to sue, but has not been successful. To what sort of service can Theresa now resort?

3. Jackson is injured in a car wreck that is not his fault. He has accumulated doctor's bills, a hospital bill, and the ambulance bill. He missed work because of the injuries he sustained, and had to undergo physical therapy. He suffered a great deal of pain because of the accident. What type of damages can he claim for each of the above?

4. One attorney sends requests for admissions to another attorney. Two months later, the requests still have not been responded to. What consequences might ensue?

5. Bill is afraid that Dillon will destroy the property that Bill is claiming is his that is in Dillon's possession. What can Bill petition the court for to maintain the status quo?

6. Henrietta sues an antique dealer for fraud, but it is shown in trial that Henrietta knew the item she was buying was not a genuine antique. What sort of damages, if any, might Henrietta receive?

7. Roberto is suing Calvin, but Calvin has fled to another state. Calvin has real property in the state where Roberto lives. The real property is not the subject matter of

the lawsuit. Roberto goes to court and asks the court to exercise what over Calvin's property?

8. If the property was the subject matter of the lawsuit, what sort of jurisdiction could the court exercise over the property?

9. Juana was injured in a car accident. She has doctor's bills totaling $10,000, $4,000 in car repair bills, plus pain and suffering and lost wages. For what types of damages can Juana sue?

10. Margaret has filed suit against Amanda in one county. However, Amanda and all of the witnesses reside in a different county. What can Amanda request?

CHAPTER 5

Civil Procedure—Part II: Trial, Appellate Procedures, and Alternate Dispute Resolution

INTRODUCTION

In Chapter 4, the civil trial process was discussed up to the point of the start of the trial. In this chapter, the civil trial process will be discussed: the terms used to describe trial courts, the types of hearings that can be held, how the jury is selected, broad types of evidence, witnesses and how they may be questioned, who is the finder of fact, and what can happen once a decision is made. The appellate process—what the party that lost at the trial level can do—is also discussed. Briefs, the authority the appellate court has, and the types of opinions the appellate court can issue are also explained. Alternatives to civil trials are explored: mediation, arbitration, mini-trials, and neutral case evaluation. The chapter details the different types of alternate dispute resolution and the parties involved in the process.

TRIAL PROCEEDINGS

Before the trial actually starts, several variables must be determined. Who is the finder of fact? Who will actually decide the case? What type of hearing will be held before the finder of fact? If there is a jury, how will the jury be selected? All of these questions must be answered before the actual trial ever starts.

COURTS, HEARINGS, AND JURIES

When the trial begins, it will be conducted by the **trial court,** the court with the jurisdiction to rule on the issues between the plaintiff and defendant. It is the court of original jurisdiction, where all evidence is first received and recorded, the first court to consider the litigation. The trial can be a **bench trial,** which is a trial held before the judge, without a jury. In this type of trial, the judge will be the finder of fact. It can be a **jury trial,** which is a trial held before a **jury,** a body of men and women selected according to law and sworn to inquire into the matter and declare the truth based on the evidence presented to them. In a jury trial, the jury is the finder of fact. See Exhibit 5-1. The hearings may be *in camera* (in-*kam*-er-a), meaning "in chambers" or in private. An *in camera* **hearing** is held in a place that is not open to the public. For example, an *in camera* hearing may be held in the judge's chambers or a courtroom where all spectators are excluded. In an ex parte (ex-par-*tay*) hearing, only one side is present and the court hears only one side of the case.

EXHIBIT 5-1	DIFFERENT HEARINGS AND FINDERS OF FACT

Jury Trial – A trial where a jury is the finder of fact
Bench Trial – A trial where the court is the finder of fact
In Camera **Hearing** – A hearing that is held in private
Ex Parte Hearing – A hearing where only one of the parties is present before the court

The **jurors,** or members of the jury, are drawn from the **jury panel,** a group of prospective jurors who are summoned to appear on a certain day. In order to determine a person's qualification and suitability to serve on the jury, attorneys for both sides subject potential jury members to *voir dire* (*vwär* dir), the examination of prospective jurors. If an attorney does not want a person to be on the jury, he or she can request that the person not serve and give a specific reason as to why the person is not suitable. This is a **challenge for cause,** and each side has an *unlimited* number of challenges for cause. The court, however, must accept the reason before the person will be dismissed. If the court rejects the reason given, or the attorney does not want the person on the jury but cannot think of an objection that will be acceptable to the court, he or she may use a peremptory (per-*emp*-ter-ee) challenge—the challenge of a juror without giving a reason. If a **peremptory challenge** is used, the potential juror is excused from serving and the attorney does not have to give a reason. Each side has a *specified, limited,* number of peremptory challenges. The stated goal is to arrive at an **impartial** (im-*par*-shəl) **jury,** one that does not favor one side more than the other. Once enough jurors have been selected from the jury pool, the jury is **impaneled** (im-*pan*-eld), which is the making up of the list of the jurors by the clerk of the court. See Exhibit 5-2 for a summary of the jury selection process.

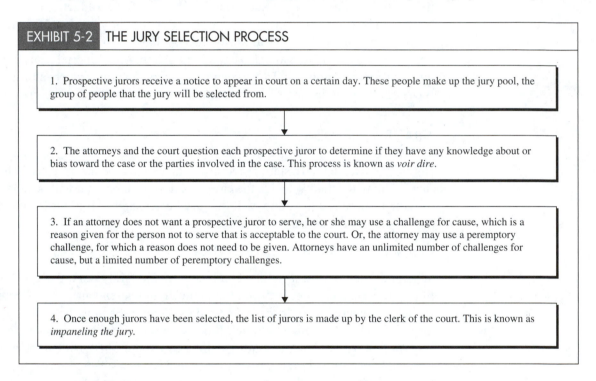

EXHIBIT 5-2 THE JURY SELECTION PROCESS

1. Prospective jurors receive a notice to appear in court on a certain day. These people make up the jury pool, the group of people that the jury will be selected from.

2. The attorneys and the court question each prospective juror to determine if they have any knowledge about or bias toward the case or the parties involved in the case. This process is known as *voir dire.*

3. If an attorney does not want a prospective juror to serve, he or she may use a challenge for cause, which is a reason given for the person not to serve that is acceptable to the court. Or, the attorney may use a peremptory challenge, for which a reason does not need to be given. Attorneys have an unlimited number of challenges for cause, but a limited number of peremptory challenges.

4. Once enough jurors have been selected, the list of jurors is made up by the clerk of the court. This is known as *impaneling the jury.*

WITNESSES AND EVIDENCE

Once the jury is selected, the actual trial begins. In most cases, the plaintiff has the **burden of proof,** the responsibility to prove the fact or facts in dispute between the parties on an issue raised between the parties in the cause of action. In civil trials, the burden of proof is a **preponderance** (pre-*pon*-der-ense) **of the evidence**—evidence that is of greater weight or more convincing than the evidence offered in opposition to it. In the scenario from the previous chapter, Henry has the responsibility to prove by a preponderance of the evidence that Jonathan ran the red light, that he has insurance, and that either Jonathan or his insurance should pay damages.

Henry's attorney will do this by presenting **evidence:** testimony, written documents, exhibits, material items, photographs, or other items that tend to prove the existence or nonexistence of a fact. (See Chapter 7.) **Witnesses**—people who were present or who have knowledge of certain facts—will be called to testify. A witness may be qualified as an **expert witness:** one who, because of education or experience, possesses knowledge regarding a subject that the general public does not. If a witness is declared by the court to be an expert witness, then the witness is allowed to give an opinion based on his or her expertise.

Every witness that is called will undergo **direct examination,** which is the first questioning of a witness by the party on whose behalf he or she is called. The other side may object to some of the questions asked during direct examination. Say, for example, the following question is asked: "On April 19th, 2000, while you were standing on the corner of Capital and Broadway, did you see the defendant run a red light and hit my client's car?" The defense could object because this is a **leading question,** one that instructs the witness how to answer. A leading question suggests the answer to the witness or puts words in his or her mouth to be echoed. Generally, leading questions require only a yes or no answer, or give the answer wanted in the question. See Exhibit 5-3.

EXHIBIT 5-3	HOW A WITNESS MAY BE QUESTIONED

1. **Direct Examination** – Questions asked by the attorney who called the person as a witness; the first questioning of a witness. Leading questions may not be used.
2. **Cross Examination** – Questions asked by the attorney for the other side after direct examination. Leading questions may be used.
3. **Leading Questions** – Questions that suggest or give the answer to a witness; can be used on cross-examination or if the witness is declared hostile.

If the witness is a **hostile witness**—one who shows extreme hostility or enmity toward the party that called him or her as a witness—the party or his or her attorney is allowed to treat the witness as if he or she were a witness for the other side. Essentially the attorney is allowed to cross-examine his or her own witness. In this situation, the attorney may ask leading questions because "cross-examination" is occurring. However, the court must declare the witness hostile *before* this type of questioning can take place. See Exhibit 5-4 for the types of witnesses.

EXHIBIT 5-4	TYPES OF WITNESSES

1. **Witness** – A person who has knowledge about certain facts related to the case.
2. **Expert Witness** – A person who, because of education or experience, has knowledge regarding a subject that the general public does not. An expert witness can give his or her opinion if he or she is classified as an expert by the court.
3. **Hostile Witness** – The witness is so hostile to the side that called him or her that the attorney is allowed to treat her as a witness for the other side.

If a witness starts testifying about what someone else told him, the objection of hearsay may be made. **Hearsay** (*here*-say) is an out-of-court statement made by someone other than the person testifying offered in evidence to prove the truth of the matter asserted. Hearsay is **inadmissible** (in-ad-*miss*-a-bel) **evidence;** it cannot be admitted or received into the record. (For further discussion of hearsay, refer to Chapter 7.) The **record** is the written account of the court proceeding, including exhibits, that is prepared by a proper court official, and is permanent evidence of the matter. However, there are twenty-four exceptions to the hearsay rule, the last being that the court can deem a statement **admissible evidence,** meaning that it is relevant, pertinent, and proper to be considered by the court/jury in reaching a decision. (See Chapter 7.)

Each witness may also undergo **cross-examination,** which is the questioning of the witness by the party opposed to the one who called him or her. Cross-examination is usually limited to the subjects raised on direct examination, and leading questions may be used. The purpose of cross-examination is to **impeach** the witness, that is, to dispute, deny, or contradict what the witness has testified to. The other side wants to call the credibility of the witness into question.

Attorneys for both sides may introduce **exhibits**—papers, documents, charts, photographs, and so on—to the court during a trial. If an exhibit is accepted into evidence, it becomes part of the case.

If evidence is ruled to be inadmissible, then a **proffer** (*praw*-fer)—the offer of testimony or a document into evidence—may be made. This evidence is made part of the record, but it is presented outside the sight and hearing of either the jury or the judge, if the judge is the decision-maker. When rendering a decision, the judge or jury cannot consider this evidence. It is introduced as a basis for an appeal, the argument on appeal being, "This is evidence the court should have considered, but did not."

A plaintiff and his or her attorney want to establish a **prima facie** (*pry*-muh *fay*-shee) **case,** one that is sufficient to prove what was alleged until contradicted or overcome by other evidence. A prima facie case exists when enough evidence has been presented to force the defendant to proceed with the case. Failure to establish a prima facie case can lead to the case being dismissed. The prima facie case is created by presenting **direct evidence,** that which directly proves a fact without the reliance on inference or presumption. A prima facie case can also be made with **circumstantial evidence,** evidence of facts and circumstances from which the existence or non-existence of a fact in dispute may be inferred.

VERDICT, DIRECTED VERDICT, JUDGMENT NOV, MISTRIALS, AND JUDGMENTS

At the conclusion of a case, the defendant is allowed to make a motion for directed verdict. A **directed verdict** is granted when the plaintiff has failed to establish a prima facie case. In a prima facie case, the trial judge orders the entry of a **verdict** (*ver*-dikt): the formal decision of a jury upon the matters or questions submitted to them during trial. However, with a directed verdict, the jury is not allowed to consider the case because, as a matter of law, there can be only one verdict. In effect, the court is telling the jury, "This is the decision you will reach because no other decision can be reached."

If the court denies the motion for a directed verdict, the defendant must present his or her case. After this segment of the trial, the plaintiff may also ask for a directed verdict, arguing that the defendant has not presented any defense to excuse himself or herself from responsibility. As a matter of law, the plaintiff contends, the defendant is responsible and judgment should be entered on behalf of the plaintiff. Upon the conclusion of the defendant's case, the plaintiff is allowed to call a **rebuttal witness,** whose testimony will refute or disprove facts presented by the opposing party. More than one rebuttal witness may be presented. If no rebuttal witnesses are called, the case is ready to be presented to the jury. See Exhibit 5-5.

EXHIBIT 5-5	WHAT CAN HAPPEN AT THE END OF THE PLAINTIFF'S AND THE DEFENDANT'S CASES

Plaintiff

1. The defendant can move for a directed verdict. The plaintiff has failed to meet the burden of proof. There is only one way the jury can vote, so the judge tells the jury how to decide the case.

Defendant

1. The plaintiff can move for a directed verdict. The defendant has failed to raise a sufficient defense. There is only one way the jury can vote, so the judge tells the jury how to decide the case.

2. Call rebuttal witnesses, who refute some of the allegations made by witnesses called by the defendant.

In order for the jury to consider the case—to determine who wins—the jury has to be instructed about the law. **Jury instructions** are directions given by the judge to the jury concerning what the law is and how it is to be applied to the case. Jury instructions may be drafted by each side and submitted to the court for its consideration. Once the court reviews these drafts, it will issue the set of instructions it deems appropriate. Many states and the federal courts have model jury instructions—standard instructions to be given to a jury based on the type of case heard. For example, there may be model instructions if the case is about personal injury involving a car wreck.

The case is then given to the jury, who begin their deliberations. The jury members weigh, consider, and discuss the evidence and the case in order to arrive at their decision. If the jury are irreconcilably divided in their opinions and cannot agree upon any verdict unanimously, they are referred to as a **hung jury.** A hung jury can be the basis for a **mistrial** (*mis*-try-el), an invalid trial that has been terminated prior to its normal conclusion. A mistrial can also be declared for some extraordinary event or for prejudicial error that cannot be corrected. Let's return to the scenario begun in Chapter 4, involving Henry, Jonathan, and Fly-By-Night. The jury emerges from deliberations with a verdict for Henry, saying Jonathan was responsible for the accident and Fly-By-Night has to pay for the damage to Henry's car. Not satisfied with this decision, Fly-By-Night makes a motion for a **judgment NOV** or **judgment non obstande veredicto** (non ob-*stan*-day ver-*dik*-toe). Judgment NOV literally means "a judgment notwithstanding the verdict." It is a verdict entered by the court for the plaintiff or the defendant, even though the jury has ruled for one or the other. In essence, the judge substitutes his or her judgment for the judgment of the jury. See Exhibit 5-6 for a summary of the difference between a directed verdict and a judgment NOV. When this motion is denied, Fly-By-Night requests that the court **poll the jury.** During this procedure, the court asks each individual juror what his or her verdict was, and if each still agrees with that verdict. This is a tactic used to see if one juror will change his or her vote, causing the decision not to be unanimous. Once again, Fly-By Night loses. See Exhibit 5-6.

EXHIBIT 5-6	DIFFERENCE BETWEEN A DIRECTED VERDICT AND A JUDGMENT NOV

Directed Verdict – The court tells the jury how to rule on a case. The jury never gets to consider the case.

Judgment NOV – The jury did reach a decision, but the court sets it aside and enters a different decision.

Once these matters have been disposed of, the court will enter its **judgment** (*juj*-ment), its official decision regarding the rights and claims of the parties to the action. This is the final decision of the court resolving the dispute.

Judgment and *order* are often used interchangeably. The court enters judgment for Henry and directs Fly-By Night to pay the amount determined by the jury to fix the car and for other damages.

CONTEMPT OF COURT

If Fly-By-Night refuses to pay, Henry could request the court to issue an **order to show cause.** A show cause order directs someone to appear as directed and show to the court reasons why its judgment has not been complied with, or should not be complied with. Failure to show the court adequate reasons as to why its order or judgment has not been complied with or why it should not be complied with can lead to a finding of contempt of court.

Contempt of court is any act that is designed to embarrass, hinder, or obstruct the court in the administration of justice. Contempt of court is found when a person is a party to a proceeding that is under the court's authority and the party willfully disobeys or fails to comply with that court's lawful orders. There are two classifications of contempt of court: civil and criminal. **Civil contempt** is a willful failure to comply with the orders of the court. For example, if an absent parent ignores a court order directing that he pay child support, the court can hold him in civil contempt of court. As a result of a finding of civil contempt of court, the court can order the person confined in jail until he is in compliance with the court order, for example, until he paid a certain amount of the past due child support. **Criminal contempt** is conduct in the presence of the court that shows a lack of respect for the court and its proceedings. Criminal contempt is punishable by fine or by incarceration for a specific period of time. See Exhibit 5-7.

| EXHIBIT 5-7 | TYPES OF CONTEMPT OF COURT |

Civil Contempt

    a. Committed away from the court.
    b. Failure to comply with a court order.
    c. Incarceration is for an indefinite period of time.

Criminal Contempt

    a. Committed in the presence of the court.
    b. Shows lack of respect for the court.
    c. Incarceration is for a definite period of time.
    d. A fine may be levied.

Exhibit 5-8 shows the entire trial process.

| EXHIBIT 5-8 | THE TRIAL PROCESS |

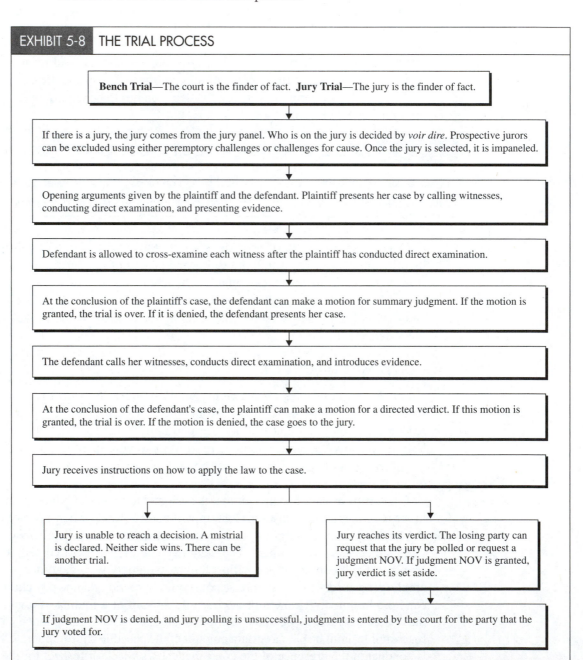

Bench Trial—The court is the finder of fact. **Jury Trial**—The jury is the finder of fact.

If there is a jury, the jury comes from the jury panel. Who is on the jury is decided by *voir dire*. Prospective jurors can be excluded using either peremptory challenges or challenges for cause. Once the jury is selected, it is impaneled.

Opening arguments given by the plaintiff and the defendant. Plaintiff presents her case by calling witnesses, conducting direct examination, and presenting evidence.

Defendant is allowed to cross-examine each witness after the plaintiff has conducted direct examination.

At the conclusion of the plaintiff's case, the defendant can make a motion for summary judgment. If the motion is granted, the trial is over. If it is denied, the defendant presents her case.

The defendant calls her witnesses, conducts direct examination, and introduces evidence.

At the conclusion of the defendant's case, the plaintiff can make a motion for a directed verdict. If this motion is granted, the trial is over. If the motion is denied, the case goes to the jury.

Jury receives instructions on how to apply the law to the case.

Jury is unable to reach a decision. A mistrial is declared. Neither side wins. There can be another trial.

Jury reaches its verdict. The losing party can request that the jury be polled or request a judgment NOV. If judgment NOV is granted, jury verdict is set aside.

If judgment NOV is denied, and jury polling is unsuccessful, judgment is entered by the court for the party that the jury voted for.

APPELLATE PROCESS

IN GENERAL

The party that has lost the trial still has options available to him or her. An appeal of the court's decision can be filed with the appropriate court of appeals. When such an appeal is filed, the losing party will present argument that the trial court made various errors that require that its decision be reversed or that a new trial be ordered.

FILING THE APPEAL

Rather than run the risk of contempt of court, Fly-By-Night decides to **appeal** (ə-*peel*). It will request that a superior court review the decision of the trial court. The superior court is the **appellate** (ə-*pel*-et) **court,** the court having jurisdiction to review the lower court's decision. The superior court that the case is appealed to will have to be a court that has appellate jurisdiction, the power and authority to review the case from the lower court. Fly-By-Night is the **appellant** (ə-*pel*-ent), the party that is appealing the decision; Henry is the **appellee** (ə-pel-*ee*), the party against whom the appeal is made. The appellee is the person who received the judgment he or she wanted, and is also known as the respondent.

Fly-By-Night will file a **notice of appeal,** the document that gives notice of an intention to appeal. If the appellee is also dissatisfied with the judgment of the court, a **cross-appeal**—an appeal by the appellee—could also be filed. When this notice of appeal is filed, the **record on appeal**—the official documentation of all the proceedings in the court about the case, including the pleadings, exhibits, and the transcript of all the hearings in the court—is sent to the appellate court along with a **certification of record on appeal,** the formal acknowledgement of the questions for appellate review signed by the trial judge. If corrections need to be made in the record to accurately reflect what happened at trial, those corrections may be made **nunc pro tunc** (nunk *pro* tunk). This term is literally translated "now for then," and it refers to the inherent power of the court to correct errors in the record at a later time to accurately reflect what happened at trial.

BRIEFS, ORAL ARGUMENTS, AND PERFECTING THE APPEAL

All parties to an appeal will prepare and file **briefs,** written arguments containing a summary of the facts of the case, the applicable laws, and an argument as to how the law applies to the facts supporting the party's position. The appellant will give reasons why the trial court was wrong and why its decision should be reversed; the appellee will give reasons why the trial court was correct and why its decision should be upheld. People who were not involved in the litigation, but who may have an interest in the outcome of the case may file an amicus curiae brief. **Amicus curiae** (a-*mee*-kəs *koo*-ree-eye) literally means "a friend of the court." This kind of brief is filed by a person who was not a party to the litigation, but who nonetheless has a strong interest in the issues before the court or in the outcome of the appeal.

After the briefs are submitted, one or both of the parties or the appellate court itself may request that oral arguments be heard. **Oral arguments** are presented before the appellate court, and focus on why the judgment of the court below should be reversed, modified, or affirmed. The time to present these arguments is limited, and the justices of the court may question the attorney about his or her position.

PERFECTING THE APPEAL AND THE FINAL DECISION RULE

Before it is submitted to the appellate court for consideration, the appeal must move through a process referred to as **perfecting the appeal.** The submission of documents and all procedures must be in compliance with the Rules of Appellate Procedure, which govern the appellate proceedings in state and federal courts. (See Sidebar 5-1 for an example of what can happen if these rules are not complied with.) Each state has its own version of the rules, and the Federal Rules of Appellate Procedure govern federal appellate courts. Many of the state's versions are based on the federal version. If all the necessary information has not been submitted to the court, it can dismiss the appeal.

SIDEBAR 5-1 *LAFOLLETTE V. SAVAGE*

Facts: LaFollette had sued Savage over a business deal that had fallen through. The jury ruled for Savage and the trial court denied LaFollette's motion for judgment NOV. LaFollette appealed this decision.

Ruling: The appellate court stated that LaFollette had alleged in his appeal that the record included no credible evidence to support the jury's verdict in favor of Savage. "Our consideration of plaintiff's arguments is met at the outset by a rather formidable obstacle. Plaintiffs included in the record on appeal only portions of the trial transcript and none of the numerous documentary exhibits admitted into evidence at trial." Because a complete transcript is to be filed with the federal court, the appeal was dismissed.

Source: Federal Reporter

Another type of appeal that may be filed is an interlocutory appeal. An **interlocutory** (in-ter-*lok*-yə-tore-ee) **appeal** is an interim appeal. The trial court has made a decision on a matter pending before it, and one of the parties has filed an appeal of that decision. The decision that is appealed is not the final decision of the court, but rather a decision on some matter relating to the trial. For example, a decision regarding the admissibility of evidence, the dismissal of one party from the case, or the dismissal of part of the lawsuit could be appealed. A reversal of the trial court decision is sought.

In federal courts, the final decision rule applies. This rule states that appeals to federal courts of appeals must be based on the final decision of the district court. The **final decision** is the ruling of the court that leaves nothing open to further litigation; it settles the rights of the parties with regard to the issues raised in the lawsuit. In other words, the lawsuit is over unless the decision is reversed or set aside on appeal. The purpose of this rule is to prevent piecemeal litigation. U.S. courts of appeals, in order to limit the number of appeals from a particular case, will not hear an appeal on the case until the final order has been entered by the U.S. district court. Exhibit 5-9 shows the appeal process.

TYPES OF OPINIONS ISSUED BY THE APPELLATE COURT

When the appellate court has decided the case, it will issue its written order. It may contain a majority opinion, concurring opinions, and dissenting opinions. The **majority opinion** is the opinion of the appellate court with which a majority of the justices agree. The **concurring opinion** is the opinion of those justices who agree with the outcome of the case, but for reasons other than the ones stated in the majority opinion. The **dissenting opinion** is the opinion of the justices of the appellate court who do *not* agree with the majority at all; and who would have reached a different decision. Reasons for

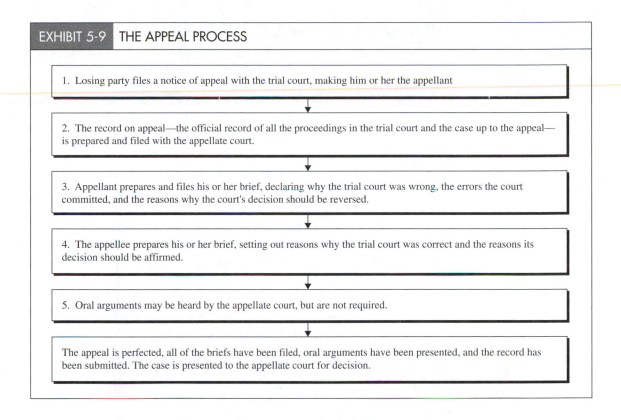

EXHIBIT 5-9   THE APPEAL PROCESS

1. Losing party files a notice of appeal with the trial court, making him or her the appellant

2. The record on appeal—the official record of all the proceedings in the trial court and the case up to the appeal—is prepared and filed with the appellate court.

3. Appellant prepares and files his or her brief, declaring why the trial court was wrong, the errors the court committed, and the reasons why the court's decision should be reversed.

4. The appellee prepares his or her brief, setting out reasons why the trial court was correct and the reasons its decision should be affirmed.

5. Oral arguments may be heard by the appellate court, but are not required.

The appeal is perfected, all of the briefs have been filed, oral arguments have been presented, and the record has been submitted. The case is presented to the appellate court for decision.

their dissent may or may not be put in writing. See Exhibit 5-10. All three opinions may contain **dicta** (*dik*-tah), or written statements of one or more of the justices that go beyond the facts of the case before them and are therefore not binding in future cases as legal precedent.

EXHIBIT 5-10   TYPES OF APPELLATE COURT OPINIONS

Majority Opinion – A majority of the justices agree with the decision. It sets out who won the appeal and the reasons why.

Concurring Opinion – Written by justices who agree with who won the appeal, but do not agree with the reasons why.

Dissenting Opinion – Written by justices who disagree with who won the appeal and disagree with the reasons why.

In its decision, the appellate court may uphold, modify, or reverse the decision of the trial court. If the decision is reversed, the case can be dismissed or it can be remanded to trial court. **Remand** occurs when the appellate court sends a case back to trial court and orders that court to conduct limited new hearings and enter a judgment "not inconsistent with this ruling." The trial court is ordered to hold a new hearing about part of the case, taking into account what the appellate court said in its decision, or is ordered to have an entirely new trial. If a new trial is ordered by the appellate court, this trial is referred to as a **trial de novo** (deh-*noh*-voh).

Returning to the scenario begun in Chapter 4, the decision of the trial court is upheld, and Fly-By-Night has to pay for the damages caused by Jonathan, the person they insured. Unfortunately for Jonathan, his policy is cancelled by Fly-By-Night, and he must seek new insurance.

ALTERNATIVE DISPUTE RESOLUTION

Because of the rising costs of litigation, more and more cases are being resolved through alternative dispute resolution. Alternative dispute resolution (ADR) refers to procedures used to resolve disputes by means other than trials. Instead of going to court, the people involved use an alternate means of resolving their dispute. ADR includes arbitration, mediation, and mini-trials, and is being used in commercial cases, labor disputes, divorce actions, and tort claims.

ARBITRATION

Arbitration (ar-bi-*tray*-shen) is the process whereby a neutral third party—someone who is not involved in the dispute and who does not know either of the parties—hears both sides of the dispute from the people involved and then gives a decision that resolves the dispute. The neutral person is chosen by the parties or appointed by the court, and is referred to as the **arbitrator** (ar-bi-*tray*-tor). Sometimes one of the parties does not want to participate in arbitration. If one of the parties is forced to come to arbitration because of an earlier agreement or a statute mandating arbitration, it is referred to as **compulsory arbitration**: The dispute has to go to arbitration because the agreement or the law requires the dispute to go to arbitration. The parties to the dispute do not have any choice about whether or not the issue will go to arbitration. **Voluntary arbitration** is agreed to by mutual consent of the parties without any coercion: Both of the parties involved in the dispute freely agree that the dispute will be resolved by arbitration.

In **final offer arbitration**, the arbitrator must choose the final offer of one party or the other to resolve the dispute; there is no compromise. This is the arbitration process currently used in major league baseball. The team owner argues his or her case for the salary he or she wants to pay, the player makes his case for the salary he wants to receive, and the arbitrator chooses between the two. The arbitrator cannot change either offer, and he or she cannot form his or her own offer.

In contract law, there are two types of arbitration: interest arbitration and grievance arbitration. **Interest arbitration** involves the settlement of a dispute about the terms of a contract between different parties. The people who entered into the contract cannot agree who is supposed to do what under the contract or what terms should or should not be in the contract. **Grievance arbitration** involves a hearing about the violation of a contract or an interpretation of one of the contract's terms. Grievance arbitration is used when one of the parties to a contract does not do what he or she is required to do under the contract or when there is a dispute as to what part of the contract means. Exhibit 5-11 summarizes the different types of arbitration.

EXHIBIT 5-11   TYPES OF ARBITRATION

1. **Compulsory Arbitration** – One of the parties is forced to come to arbitration because of an agreement or because of law.
2. **Voluntary Arbitration** – Arbitration that is agreed to by the mutual consent of the parties.
3. **Final Offer Arbitration** – The arbitrator must accept the final offer of one of the parties to the dispute because there is no compromise.
4. **Interest Arbitration** – The settlement of a dispute about the terms of a contract between the different parties.
5. **Grievance Arbitration** – Arbitration about the violation of a contract or an interpretation of one of the contract's terms.

An **award** in arbitration is the arbitrator's decision. It may or may not involve money. The award of the arbitrator is not absolutely final; it can be set aside if corruption or fraud is proven. The award can also be set aside if the conduct of the arbitrator indicates there was bias or corruption against a party. Types of conduct that shows bias or corruption on the part of the arbitrator include the following.

    a. Refusal to postpone a hearing when good cause is shown

    b. Refusal to hear evidence that is material and pertinent to the issue

    c. Failure to use authority properly

Sometimes the parties wish to enter into arbitration, but there is no provision in their earlier agreement to allow arbitration to take place. A **submission agreement** is a special contract entered into when there is no arbitration clause in a contract; the parties agree to settle the matter by arbitration. The submission agreement specifies the following.

    1. How the arbitrator will be selected

    2. The nature of the dispute

    3. Any restrictions on the arbitrator's authority to resolve the dispute

    4. The place where the arbitration will take place

    5. The date by which the arbitration must be scheduled

MEDIATION

Mediation (mee-dee-*ay*-shun) is an informal process whereby a neutral third party helps the parties in a dispute try to reach a mutually agreeable solution. The **mediator** (mee-dee-*ay*-tor) is the neutral third party who guides the parties through the process and helps them reach settlement. Mediation is different from arbitration because the mediator has no authority to actually resolve the dispute. Exhibit 5-12 lists the steps of mediation. The mediator cannot make a decision that is binding on the parties involved. The parties themselves must come to an agreement about how they will resolve their dispute; the mediator simply takes them through the process.

EXHIBIT 5-12	MEDIATION PROCESS

Step 1 – The mediator makes an opening statement, explaining the mediation process to the participants.

Step 2 – The parties to the mediation express their positions.

Step 3 – The mediator invites the parties to talk to each other about the situation and encourages them to reach agreement.

Step 4 – The mediator meets privately with each side. These discussions are not revealed to the other side.

Step 5 – The parties are brought back together. Possible solutions are proposed.

Step 6 – If solution is agreed upon, mediation is successful. If solution is not agreed upon, mediation has failed.

The mediator is supposed to be a neutral party who takes people through the mediation process. However, sometimes, the mediator injects himself or herself too much into the process. Sidebar 5-2, the case of *Vitakis-Valchine v. Valchine*, recounts an example of what can happen when the mediator becomes too involved in the process.

SIDEBAR 5-2 *VITAKIS-VALCHINE V. VALCHINE*

Kalliope Vitakis-Valchine and Dennis Valchine were involved in a divorce proceeding when they entered court-ordered mediation. Both of them had attorneys present during the mediation. A twenty-three-page agreement was prepared during the mediation that resolved all the matters regarding the divorce. A month after the mediation, Kalliope moved to have the agreement set aside because she alleged she was coerced by her husband, her husband's attorney, and by the mediator to enter into the agreement. She testified that the mediator threatened to report her to the judge for failing to agree to a reasonable marriage settlement, and that even if she disagreed with the agreement, she could request the court to set it aside. The trial court denied her motion and she appealed.

The appellate court reversed and remanded the trial court, stating that the mediator was acting as an agent of the court in court-ordered mediation. If the allegations are true, then the mediator abused his position. If there is merit to the complaints of Ms. Kitakis-Valchine, then the mediator violated the Rules for Mediators and the settlement should be set aside.

Source: Arkansas Reports

MINI-TRIAL

A **mini-trial** is a voluntary, informal form of dispute resolution. Unlike mediation or arbitration, where attorneys are not used, attorneys play a role in a mini-trial. Also involved are representatives or officials from each side of the dispute who have the authority to settle the dispute. During the mini-trial, the attorneys for each side make a brief presentation of their case to the officials from each side. There may also be a neutral third party advisor present to give a non-binding advisory opinion about the possible outcome of the case if it went to full trial. At the end of the case presentations, representatives from each side attempt to reach a settlement of the dispute.

EARLY NEUTRAL CASE EVALUATION

Early neutral case evaluation occurs when the parties select a neutral third person and explain their positions to him or her. This person evaluates the strengths and weaknesses of the respective cases and then provides this information to the parties. The parties involved then use this information to help reach settlement of their dispute.

See Exhibit 5-13 for a summary of the types of alternate dispute resolution.

EXHIBIT 5-13	TYPES OF ALTERNATE DISPUTE RESOLUTIONS

Arbitration – A neutral third party resolves the dispute between the parties.

Mediation – A third party takes the parties through a process in an effort to reach a settlement of the dispute. A settlement may or may not be reached.

Mini-Trial – Attorneys for each side present arguments to a representative of the other side. A neutral third party may give an opinion as to which side would win at trial. The representatives then meet and try to reach a settlement.

Early Neutral Case Evaluation – A neutral third party hears both sides of the dispute and then gives an evaluation of the cases. The parties use this information to try to reach a settlement.

CONCLUSION

In a bench trial, the court is the finder of fact. In a jury trial, the jury is the finder of fact. If a jury is used, it must be selected from the jury pool using *voir dire*. The plaintiff and the defendant will attempt to prove their case by the use of witnesses, expert witnesses, and evidence. Some evidence is admissible; other evidence is inadmissible for various reasons and cannot be considered by the jury. Witnesses are subject to direct examination and cross-examination, but can only be asked leading questions on cross-examination. The plaintiff has the right to call rebuttal witnesses. If the case goes to the jury, the jury receives instructions on how the law is to apply to the case before them.

The party the jury rules against has several alternatives available. He or she can request a judgment NOV, he or she can poll the jury, or he or she can file an appeal of the court's decision. If an appeal is filed, briefs will be prepared by both of the parties involved in the lawsuit, and people who have an interest in the outcome of the case may file amicus curie briefs. The court will consider the appeal and then issue a ruling that may affirm, reverse, or reverse and remand the case. The decision will be contained in the majority opinion. There may be concurring and dissenting opinions.

If the parties wish to avoid a trial, they may use arbitration, in which a third person resolves their dispute, or mediation, in which a third person takes them through a process whereby they attempt to reach an agreement. A mini-trial or early neutral case evaluation may take place to help one party determine whether or not to proceed with a lawsuit.

CHAPTER 5 REVIEW

KEY WORDS AND PHRASES

admissible evidence
amicus curiae
appeal
appellant
appellate court
appellee
arbitration
arbitrator
briefs
burden of proof
certification of record on
 appeal
challenge for cause
circumstantial evidence
concurring opinion
contempt of court
cross-appeal
cross-examination
direct evidence
direct examination
directed verdict

dissenting opinion
early neutral case
 evaluation
evidence
expert witness
hearsay
hostile witness
hung jury
impanel
impartial jury
impeach
in camera hearing
inadmissible evidence
interlocutory appeal
judgment non obstande
 veredicto (NOV)
jury
jury instructions
leading question
majority opinion
mediation

mediator
mini-trial
mistrial
notice of appeal
nunc pro tunc
oral arguments
order to show cause
perfecting the appeal
poll the jury
preponderance of the
 evidence
prima facie case
proffer
rebuttal witness
record
record on appeal
remand
trial de novo
verdict

REVIEW QUESTIONS

SHORT ANSWER

1. What is the difference between a directed verdict and a judgment NOV?
2. What is a summary judgment? When is it requested? Who can ask for it?
3. What makes a person an expert witness?
4. What is polling the jury and when does it take place?
5. If someone who was not involved in the trial wants to file a brief in the appellate case, what type of brief will he or she file?
6. When a jury cannot reach a decision, what term applies?
7. What is an order to show cause?
8. What is the difference between a peremptory challenge and a challenge for cause?
9. The group of people the jury is selected from is known as what?
10. What is a mistrial and when can it be declared?
11. What does *nunc pro tunc* mean?
12. What is ADR?
13. What is the difference between mediation and arbitration?

14. What is a mini-trial?

15. What is meant by a final order?

FILL IN THE BLANK

1. When everything has been presented to the appellate court, this is known as _____.

2. What are the three different opinions that an appellate court can enter?

_____

_____

_____

3. When a person disobeys a court order, the court can enforce its order using _____.

4. When a person shows disrespect to the court in the presence of the court, the person may be held in _____.

5. At the conclusion of the defendant's case, the plaintiff may call a _____ to disprove or refute the testimony of witnesses called by the defendant.

6. A method of alternate dispute resolution used to settle a dispute about what contract terms mean is _____.

7. The questioning of prospective jury members is known as _____.

8. The party that called a witness can use leading questions with a witness when the witness is classified as a _____.

9. The burden of proof in most civil cases is _____.

10. When the court is contemplating holding a person in contempt, it will issue a _____.

FACT SITUATIONS

1. All the justices of an appeals court decide to hear an appeal rather than a panel of judges. What is this known as?

2. The attorney for the plaintiff calls a witness and asks, "On September 22, you were standing on the corner of 7th and Main, correct? While you were standing there, you saw the defendant run the red light, correct?" The defense attorney objects. What is the basis for his objection?

3. The Court enters an order directing Bradley to pay $100 a week in child support. Bradley does not pay any child support. What can the court do to enforce its order?

4. Max attempts to introduce into evidence some documents relating to a contract. The other side objects to their admission and the court upholds the objection. What can Max do to make these documents part of the record?

5. Candy and Mike are adopting a child. The court orders everyone not connected with the case to leave the courtroom. What type of hearing is this?

6. After the jury has reached its decision, the attorney for the losing side wants to make sure all of the jurors voted the same way. What will the attorney do to determine how the jurors voted?

7. Inga calls Dimitri to the stand and questions him about his education, his work experience, if he has written any articles or books, and concentrates on his knowledge about accounting practices. What is Inga trying to do with Dimitri?

8. Ahmed is questioning prospective jurors about their knowledge of the case and the parties involved. Ahmed wants to strike a prospective juror from the jury pool, but does not have a specific reason to have the person removed. However, he does not want that person on the jury. What can Ahmed do to keep the person off the jury?

9. The jury in a personal injury case has been unable to reach a verdict. Half want to rule for the plaintiff; the other half want to rule for the defendant. They have taken several votes and have been unable to reach a decision. What type of jury is this?

10. Margaret has called Ricardo as a witness, but Ricardo is openly aggressive toward her. Ricardo is argumentative with her, is not answering her questions, and gives information that was not requested. What can Margaret do with regard to Ricardo?

CHAPTER 6

Administrative Law

INTRODUCTION

The more complex our society has become, the more complex laws passed by state legislatures and the U.S. Congress have become. But these laws give broad directions only; details are not included. Congress cannot write laws designed to deal with every possible situation and issue that may arise across the country because of the passage of a new law. To bridge this gap, administrative agencies are given the legal responsibility to write rules and regulations designed to deal with more specific situations. These agencies are given the responsibility to further define and refine the broad laws passed by Congress and state legislatures.

Administrative law deals with the creation of administrative agencies, where they get their power, what powers they have, how they can exercise those powers, and how the courts interpret the agency's exercise of that power. This chapter describes the major administrative agencies of the United States government and some of the more important agencies and commissions that have been created by Congress.

PART I. ADMINISTRATIVE LAW IN GENERAL

GENERAL PRINCIPLES

What constitutes administrative law and how is it created? **Administrative law** is a body of law created by administrative agencies in the form of rules, regulations, orders, and decisions that carry out the regulatory powers and duties given to the agencies. **Administrative agencies** are governmental bodies responsible for administering and implementing legislation passed by Congress or by a state legislature. Because of the complexity of issues before them, Congress and the states pass general statutes and then give power to certain administrative agencies to further interpret and carry out the laws. It is the responsibility of the agency to issue rules and regulations that further interpret the statute that has been passed, to issue regulations as required by the statute, or to enforce those laws. Examples of these types of agencies include the Equal Employment Opportunity Commission (EEOC), which is responsible for issuing and enforcing regulations regarding employment discrimination; the Securities and Exchange Commission (SEC), which is responsible for issuing and enforcing regulations regarding the stock market; and the Department of Labor, which is responsible for issuing and enforcing rules regarding the minimum wage, overtime, and the Family and Medical Leave Act.

TYPES OF FEDERAL AGENCIES

An administrative agency may be a **state agency**, an administrative agency that has been created by a state legislature, or a federal agency. A **federal agency** is an agency that may be classified in one of three ways.

99

1. One of the executive **departments,** the major administrative divisions of the executive branch of the government. Some examples of a department at the federal level are the Treasury Department, the State Department, or the Department of Labor.

2. A **government corporation,** a corporation that is government created and controlled. The Legal Services Corporation is an example of a government corporation. (See below.)

3. Another agency that has been established in the executive branch of the government, such as a board or commission. Two examples of such an agency are the Equal Employment Opportunity Commission or the National Labor Relations Board. These boards or commissions may stand alone, or they may be part of one of the departments of the executive branch of government.

REGULATORY AND INDEPENDENT ADMINISTRATIVE AGENCIES

Administrative agencies are further classified as either regulatory or independent administrative in nature. It is possible for an agency to be both, taking into account its authority and how long its members may serve the agency. If the agency is a **regulatory agency,** it has the power to issue and enforce regulations. Examples of federal agencies that have regulatory authority include the following.

1. The Internal Revenue Service has the authority to issue regulations concerning income tax and other tax codes.

2. The Department of Labor has the authority to issue regulations concerning wage and hour laws and the Family and Medical Leave Act.

3. The Occupational Safety and Health Administration (OSHA) has authority to issue regulations regarding workplace safety.

A federal agency may also be an **independent administrative agency**, one whose appointed head and members serve for a fixed period of time and cannot be removed from office by the President except for reasons that are defined by Congress. See Exhibit 6-1 for a listing of some of this nation's independent administrative agencies.

EXHIBIT 6-1	INDEPENDENT AGENCIES OF THE FEDERAL GOVERNMENT

Commodity Futures Trading Commission (CFTC)
Federal Communications Commission (FCC)
Federal Election Commission (FEC)
Federal Deposit Insurance Commission (FDIC)
Federal Trade Commission (FTC)
Consumer Product Safety Commission (CPSC)
Legal Services Corporation (LSC)
Equal Employment Opportunity Commission (EEOC)
National Labor Relations Board (NLRB)

AUTHORITY OF AN ADMINISTRATIVE AGENCY

In order to carry out its mission of writing and enforcing rules and regulations, an agency must have the authority to do so. The authority to write rules and regulations, to enforce those rules or parts of the statute to issue licenses, or to carry out any administrative duty comes from an **enabling statute**—a statute that gives the authority to perform certain activity to the agency. Administrative agencies may have the authority to issue rules and regulations regarding a certain area of government, society, or the law for which the agency is responsible. If the agency has **rulemaking authority,** then it has the power to issue a rule regarding an area for which the agency has responsibility. For example, the Centers for Medicare and Medicaid Services is responsible for issuing regulations regarding various Medicare and Medicaid programs. A regulation is a rule or order issued by an administrative agency; these rules and orders have the force and effect of law. See Exhibit 6-2.

EXHIBIT 6-2	C.F.R. 825.200 FMLA REGULATIONS

How much leave may an employee take?

(a) An eligible employee's FMLA leave entitlement is limited to a total of 12 workweeks of leave during any 12-month period for any one, or more, of the following reasons:
  (1) The birth of the employee's son or daughter, and to care for the newborn child;
  (2) The placement with the employee of a son or daughter for adoption or foster care, and to care for the newly placed child;
  (3) To care for the employee's spouse, son, daughter, or parent with a serious health condition; and,
  (4) Because of a serious health condition that makes the employee unable to perform one or more of the essential functions of his or her job.

(b) An employer is permitted to choose any one of the following methods for determining the "12-month period" in which the 12 weeks of leave entitlement occurs:
  (1) The calendar year;
  (2) Any fixed 12-month "leave year," such as a fiscal year, a year required by State law, or a year starting on an employee's "anniversary" date;
  (3) The 12-month period measured forward from the date any employee's first FMLA leave begins; or,
  (4) A "rolling" 12-month period measured backward from the date an employee uses any FMLA leave (except that such measure may not extend back before August 5, 1993).

Source: Code of Federal Regulations

The agency or its head will also have **administrative authority**, the power to carry out the terms of the law that created it as well as to make regulations for the conduct of business that comes before it. See Exhibit 6-3. For example, the Equal Employment Opportunity Commission has the administrative authority to issue regulations regarding employment discrimination and regulations regarding how complaints will be investigated and handled by the Commission.

EXHIBIT 6-3	REGULATIONS REGARDING THE ENFORCEMENT OF THE FAIR LABOR STANDARDS ACT

(a) **Investigations and inspections**

The Administrator or his designated representatives may investigate and gather data regarding the wages, hours, and other conditions and practices of employment in any industry subject to this chapter, and may enter and inspect such places and such records (and make such transcriptions thereof), question such employees, and investigate such facts, conditions, practices, or matters as he may deem necessary or appropriate to determine whether any person has violated any provision of this chapter, or which may aid in the enforcement of the provisions of this chapter. Except as provided in section 212

Continued

Continued

of this title and in subsection (b) of this section, the Administrator shall utilize the bureaus and divisions of the Department of Labor for all the investigations and inspections necessary under this section. Except as provided in section 212 of this title, the Administrator shall bring all actions under section 217 of this title to restrain violations of this chapter.

(b) **State and local agencies and employees**

With the consent and cooperation of State agencies charged with the administration of State labor laws, the Administrator and the Secretary of Labor may, for the purpose of carrying out their respective functions and duties under this chapter, utilize the services of State and local agencies and their employees and, notwithstanding any other provision of law, may reimburse such State and local agencies and their employees for services rendered for such purposes.

(d) **Homework regulations**

The Administrator is authorized to make such regulations and orders regulating, restricting, or prohibiting industrial homework as are necessary or appropriate to prevent the circumvention or evasion of and to safeguard the minimum wage rate prescribed in this chapter, and all existing regulations or orders of the Administrator relating to industrial homework are continued in full force and effect.

Source: Code of Federal Regulations

Agencies also derive their authority from inspection laws. **Inspection laws** authorize the inspection and examination of various kinds of merchandise that are intended for sale, especially food, with the intent to determine whether the merchandise is fit for its intended use. For example, the Food and Drug Administration will conduct an inspection of a food processing plant to ensure that standards for safe food production are being met. Inspection laws also may allow for inspections to determine employee safety, building and construction safety, health conditions of food processors or restaurants, or motor vehicle safety. For example, the Occupational Safety and Health Administration is authorized to inspect worksites for safety violations. See Exhibit 6-4.

EXHIBIT 6-4	OSHA INSPECTION LAWS 29 U.S.C. § 15-657

Section 657. Inspections, investigations, and recordkeeping

(a) Authority of Secretary to enter, inspect, and investigate places of employment; time and manner. In order to carry out the purposes of this chapter, the Secretary, upon presenting appropriate credentials to the owner, operator, or agent in charge, is authorized –

(1) to enter without delay and at reasonable times any factory, plant, establishment, construction site, or other area, workplace or environment where work is performed by an employee of an employer; and

(2) to inspect and investigate during regular working hours and at other reasonable times, and within reasonable limits and in a reasonable manner, any such place of employment and all pertinent conditions, structures, machines, apparatus, devices, equipment, and materials therein, and to question privately any such employer, owner, operator, agent, or employee.

Source: United States Code

Agencies also receive authority to act because of their ability to issue **licenses,** a permit to pursue some occupation or to engage in some business that is subject to regulation. With all of these powers—the power to implement rules and regulations, the power to inspect, and the power to issue licenses—an agency can determine if there is a violation of a regulation, or even if an administrative crime has been committed. An **administrative crime** is an offense that consists of a violation of an administrative rule or regulation that carries with it a criminal sanction. For example, if a taxpayer deliberately fails to pay income tax, or utilizes a deduction that the IRS says is improper, he or she may face criminal sanctions for income tax evasion. See Exhibit 6-5 for a summary of how an administrative agency may derive its power.

EXHIBIT 6-5	HOW AN ADMINISTRATIVE AGENCY GETS ITS POWER

1. **Rulemaking Authority –** The power to issue rules and regulations about an area that the agency is authorized to regulate by the enabling statute.
2. **Administrative Authority –** The power to carry out the terms of the law; the agency actually enforces as well as interprets the law.
3. **Inspection Laws –** The authority to inspect and examine merchandise, buildings, construction, worksites, and health conditions in order to determine if there are safety violations.
4. **Licensing Authority –** The authority to issue a license that allows someone to enter some occupation or to allow a business to conduct a certain activity.

SUNSET LAWS AND THE FREEDOM OF INFORMATION ACT

Two types of statutes affect how an agency does business: sunset laws and freedom of information acts. These laws affect how long a particular agency is in existence and can mandate the release of information regarding the business of the agency to qualified people who ask for it.

Some administrative agencies are established with no time limit on how long they may be in existence; other agencies may be governed by a **sunset law**, which is a statute that requires a periodic review of the agency and its purpose to determine if the agency's continued existence is needed or justified. A sunset law may also state that the legislature that created the agency must take positive steps to allow the agency to continue in existence by a stated certain date, or the agency will cease to exist. In other words, the legislature has to pass another enabling statute by a certain time or the agency will be disbanded. If the legislature does not act, the enabling statute—the statute that created the agency—is no longer effective, so the agency ceases to exist.

Because government is service to the public, and funded by the public, the public has a right to have knowledge and information about the business of government. This right has been codified into freedom of information acts, not only at the federal level but also at the state level of government. A **freedom of information act (FOIA)** is a statute that makes documents generated by federal agencies and state governments available to the public upon request. A freedom of information act request is the actual request for documents that may contain the information the person is seeking. Generally the request has to be for an existing document; a government body is not required to create a new document to meet the request. Also, only a citizen of the United States or a citizen of the state may make a request for the documents. Upon request, the government must release the documents for viewing to the private citizen or provide the requester with copies of the specified documents. Certain documents are not subject to release under FOIA; these are usually listed in the statute. For example, at the federal level, documents that contain trade secrets, documents that concern national security, or documents that would be an invasion of personal privacy are not releasable under the FOIA. See Exhibit 6-6 for parts of the federal Freedom of Information Act.

| EXHIBIT 6-6 | EXCERPTS FROM THE FEDERAL FREEDOM OF INFORMATION ACT 5 U.S.C. § 552 |

§ 552. Public information; agency rules, opinions, orders, records, and proceedings

(a) Each agency shall make available to the public information as follows:

(2) Each agency, in accordance with published rules, shall make available for public inspection and copying—

(A) final opinions, including concurring and dissenting opinions, as well as orders, made in the adjudication of cases;

(B) those statements of policy and interpretations which have been adopted by the agency and are not published in the Federal Register;

(C) administrative staff manuals and instructions to staff that affect a member of the public;

(D) copies of all records, regardless of form or format, which have been released to any person under paragraph (3) and which, because of the nature of their subject matter, the agency determines have become or are likely to become the subject of subsequent requests for substantially the same records; and

(E) a general index of the records referred to under subparagraph (D); unless the materials are promptly published and copies offered for sale.

(3) (E) An agency, or part of an agency, that is an element of the intelligence community (as that term is defined in section 3(4) of the National Security Act of 1947 (50 U.S.C. 401a(4))) shall not make any record available under this paragraph to—

(i) any government entity, other than a State, territory, commonwealth, or district of the United States, or any subdivision thereof; or

(ii) a representative of a government entity described in clause (i).

Source: United States Code

THE PROMULGATION PROCESS

In order to issue its rules and regulations, an agency is required to follow the promulgation process provided for in an administrative procedures act. An **administrative procedures act** is the law that governs the practice and proceedings before the administrative agency and may govern how an agency will perform its day-to-day business. **Promulgation** is the process that the agency follows to formally issue its rules and regulations. See Exhibit 6-7 for an example of an administrative procedures act.

| EXHIBIT 6-7 | EXAMPLE OF AN ADMINISTRATIVE PROCEDURES ACT |

25-15.203. Rules – Required Rules – Public inspection.

(a) In addition to other rule making requirements imposed by law, each agency shall:

(1) Adopt as a rule a description of its organization, stating the general course and method of its operations, including the methods whereby the public may obtain information or make submissions or requests;

(2) Adopt rules of practice setting forth the nature and requirements of all formal and informal procedures available, including a description of all forms and instructions used by the agency;

(3) Make available for public inspection all rules and all other written statements of policy or interpretations formulated, adopted, or used by the agency in the discharge of its functions;

(4) Make available for public inspection all orders, decisions, and opinions.

(b) No agency rule, order, or decision shall be valid or effective against any person or party, nor may it be invoked by the agency for any purpose, until it has been filed and made available for public inspection as required in this subchapter. This provision shall not apply in favor of any person or party with actual knowledge of an agency rule, order, or decision.

21-25-204 Rules – Procedure for adoption.

a) Prior to the adoption, amendment, or repeal of any rule, the agency shall:

(1)(A) Give at least thirty (30) days' notice of its intended action. The third-party period shall begin on the first day of the publication of notice.

(B) The notice shall include a statement of the terms or substance of the intended action or a description of the subjects and issues involved and the time, the place where, and the manner in which interested persons may present their views thereon.

(C) The notice shall be mailed to any person specified by law and to all persons who have requested advance notice of rule-making proceedings.

(2)(A) Afford all interested persons reasonable opportunity to submit written data, views, or arguments, orally or in writing.

(B) Opportunity for oral hearing must be granted if requested by twenty-five (25) persons, by a governmental subdivision or agency, or by an association having no fewer than twenty-five (25) members.

(C) The agency shall fully consider all written and oral submissions respecting the proposed rule before finalizing the language of the proposed rule and filing the proposed rule as required by subsection (d) of this section.

Source: Arkansas Code Annotated

At the federal level, during the first step of the promulgation process, the rules or the agency are written internally (within the agency) and then are reviewed internally. After the internal review, a notice of rule making is published in the *Federal Register.* The *Federal Register* is published daily, and will contain the proposed rules and give an address where interested people may send comments. It is also used to make the public aware of the final federal regulations. The *Federal Register* is the first place the new, final regulations appear.

If the promulgation process is an informal one, the comments are mailed to the agency. If the process is a formal, rule-making process, there are public meetings where people can appear and provide their comments to the agency on the record. These meetings or hearings are known as an **investigatory hearings.** An investigatory hearing is authorized by the enabling statute. This information gathered at the hearing is used by the agency to determine the desirability of proposed rules.

The agency may or may not take public comments into consideration in issuing their final rules. Final rules are first published in the *Federal Register,* but will eventually be published in the **Code of Federal Regulations,** the annual accumulation of executive agency regulations published along with the regulations that are still in force. See Exhibit 6-8.

EXHIBIT 6-8 FEDERAL PROMULGATION PROCESS

Federal agency writes the proposed rule or regulation and it undergoes an internal review.

↓

Notice of the proposed rule is published in the *Federal Register*. The public is told where to submit comments to the rule and when those comments are due.

↓

Comments are received and reviewed by the agency. They may or may not be considered by the agency. Changes may or may not be made to the regulations.

↓

Final agency rule is first published in the *Federal Register* and then is published and incorporated into the *Code of Federal Regulations.*

ENFORCEMENT PROCESS

ADMINISTRATIVE HEARINGS

If an agency is responsible for enforcing rules and regulations, then because of due process of law requirements, there must be a procedure in place to determine if a rule or regulation was actually violated and what the penalty will be for the violation. If a violation of a rule or regulation is found, the agency may request an **administrative hearing**—a proceeding before the administrative agency consisting of arguments, a trial, or both to determine if a violation of the rules or regulations occurred and what sanctions should be imposed. Procedural rules in an administrative hearing are more relaxed than in a court hearing.

The hearing may take place before an **administrative board,** a body that has the authority to conduct a quasi-judicial hearing, a hearing officer, or an **administrative law judge (ALJ).** The hearing officer or the ALJ is the person who presides over an administrative hearing with the power to administer oaths, take testimony, rule on questions of evidence, regulate the proceedings, and make agency determinations of fact.

Another type of hearing before the agency is an adjudicatory hearing. An **adjudicatory hearing** is a formal hearing that involves the agency and a private party, that are engaged in a complaint or controversy. The agency may be alleging a violation of its rules or regulations or be seeking revocation of license or other sanction, and the other party is disputing the allegations. An adjudicatory hearing is a little less formal than a court of law, and is designed to protect the right the "defendant" has to due process of law. The party has a right to know what rules or regulations he or she has allegedly violated, the right to confront the people who are accusing him or her of the violation, the right to be represented by an attorney, the right to call witnesses, the right to cross-examine any witnesses against him or her, and the right to present arguments to the finder of fact.

TYPES OF OPINIONS ISSUED BY AN ALJ

If an administrative law judge is the finder of fact, there are two types of decisions he or she can issue, and one type of opinion he or she can request. If the ALJ is trying to decide a difficult or controversial matter, he or she may request an advisory opinion from a court prior to rendering a decision. An **advisory opinion** is given by a court at the request of the government or an interested party indicating how the court would rule on a matter if litigation develops. In other words, either the agency or another interested person can ask a court how it would rule if the same issue were presented to it. The advisory opinion is not a binding decision of the court; it is the court's *opinion* on how it would rule, given this particular set of facts. That opinion may change once the full case is presented to the court.

The ALJ may be authorized to give one of two types of decisions. An **initial decision** is one given by an administrative law judge that will become final and binding unless one of the parties appeals the decision to the full commission, who will then review the decision. A **recommended decision** does not become a final, binding decision until either the full commission or the head of the agency accepts it. See Exhibit 6-9.

EXHIBIT 6-9 | OPINIONS INVOLVED IN ADMINISTRATIVE HEARINGS

Advisory Opinions – An opinion given by a court at the request of the government or an interested party indicating how the court would rule on a matter if litigation develops. This is not a binding decision; it is advisory only.

Initial Decision – A decision given by an administrative law judge that will become final and binding unless one of the parties appeals the decision to the full commission.

Recommended Decision – A decision by an administrative law judge that does not become a final, binding decision until either the full commission or the head of the agency accepts it.

CITIZEN SUIT PROVISIONS

Sometimes the agency is not the only one that can enforce rules and regulations. An alternative to the agency enforcing the regulations exists if the enabling statute includes a **citizen suit provision.** A citizen suit provision is a provision in the statute that gives private citizens a right to bring a suit before a federal court to force compliance with the law passed by Congress. In other words, instead of the federal agency bringing a suit to enforce the law or regulations, a private citizen can bring a case requesting that the law be enforced. This is usually done if the citizen believes the administrative agency is failing to act or has not acted appropriately. The cost of bringing the suit is borne either by the government or the defendant if the private citizen wins the lawsuit.

APPEALS

BASIS FOR AN APPEAL

If the defendant in the administrative proceeding is not satisfied with a decision, he or she has the right to appeal the decision to a court of law for judicial review. **Judicial review** is the power of the court to review decisions of another department or level of government. In order for the court to hear the appeal, the person bringing the appeal must state a reason for the appeal—explain why the decision of the administrative agency is in error and should be reversed. The appellant might argue that the decision of the agency is **arbitrary and capricious,** and that willful and unreasonable actions have been taken by the agency without consideration for or in disregard of the facts or law. The defendant may also allege there was an **abuse of discretion:** a failure to exercise sound, reasonable, and legal judgment.

However, before a person can appeal to a court of law, he or she must satisfy the **exhaustion of administrative remedies** doctrine. This doctrine states that relief must be sought through all of the appropriate agency channels before a person can request a court to hear the case and grant relief. In other words, a person must exhaust all the appeals available through the agency itself before the appeal can be filed with a court. The exhaustion of administrative remedies requirement is usually established by statute. For example, before a person can sue someone in federal court for discrimination, he or she must present the claim to the EEOC first. The EEOC has the right to investigate a complaint for up to ninety days before a person can request a right to sue letter. The right to sue letter must be issued by the EEOC before a person can file a case of employment discrimination in federal court.

STANDARD ON APPEAL

When the case is appealed to a court, the court will apply a standard of review that will be used to determine whether or not to uphold the agency decision or reverse it. The standard that will be used by the court is the **substantial evidence rule**—evidence that a reasonable mind might accept as adequate to support a conclusion. Put another way, this is evidence that a reasonable person would accept as being enough to support a decision made by the agency. The reviewing court is to defer to the agency determination so long as, upon review of the whole record, there is substantial evidence upon which the agency could reasonably base its decision. The standard is *not* if the *court* would reach a different conclusion. The standard is whether sufficient evidence was presented to support the conclusion reached by the agency.

Taking the evidence into account, the court may affirm or reverse the agency's decision or issue a **declaratory judgment,** which determines what the rights and responsibilities of the parties are.

PART II. SPECIFIC AGENCIES OF THE UNITED STATES GOVERNMENT

INTRODUCTION

Administrative agencies at the federal level are divided into the departments that make up the presidential Cabinet, departments that are not part of the Cabinet, bureaus, agencies, and commissions that are part of the different departments, and agencies and commissions that stand on their own. These agencies oversee numerous government programs, enforce a myriad of federal laws, and perform investigations, including investigations related to law enforcement. The directors of some of the agencies serve as advisors to the President of the United States.

DEPARTMENTS OF THE UNITED STATES

IN GENERAL

In the executive branch of the government of the United States, there are fourteen departments that are considered cabinet-level departments. This means that the heads of these departments, the respective secretaries, are members of the President's **Cabinet,** an advisory board that counsels the President. The Cabinet-level departments are the Department of Agriculture, the Department of Commerce, the Department of Defense, the Department of Education, the Department of Energy, the Department of Health and Human Services, the Department of Housing and Urban Development, the Department of the Interior, the Department of Justice, the Department of Labor, the State Department, the Department of Transportation, the Department of the Treasury, the Department of Veterans Affairs, and the Department of Homeland Security. See Exhibit 6-10 for when each these Cabinet-level departments was created.

EXHIBIT 6-10	FORMATION OF THE PRESIDENT'S PRESENT CABINET

1789
Department of State
Department of the Treasury
Department of Justice

1849
Department of the Interior

1862
Department of Agriculture

1903
Department of Commerce

1913
Department of Labor

1949
Department of Defense

1965
Department of Housing and Urban Development

1966
Department of Transportation

1977
Department of Energy

1980
Department of Education
Department of Health and Human Services

1988
Department of Veterans Affairs

2002
Department of Homeland Security

DEPARTMENTS OF JUSTICE AND TREASURY

The main purpose of the **Department of Justice** is to enforce federal law, to furnish legal counsel in federal lawsuits that the United States is involved in, and to interpret laws affecting other departments. The Department of Justice gives legal opinions to other departments regarding how laws affect them. The Justice Department is responsible for all the suits in the Supreme Court that the United States is party to or has an interest in, for the federal penal system, and for investigating and detecting violations of federal law. It represents the government in legal matters, rendering legal advice and opinions to the heads of the executive departments and to the President. The Attorney General of the United States is the head of the Department of Justice and is a member of the President's Cabinet.

The **Department of the Treasury,** one of the oldest departments of the executive branch of the federal government, has four basic functions.

1. It formulates and recommends financial, tax, and fiscal policies.
2. It serves as a financial agent for the U.S. government.
3. It provides certain types of law enforcement.
4. It manufactures coins and currency.

The law enforcement agencies are set out later in this chapter.

DEPARTMENTS OF STATE, DEFENSE, AND HOMELAND SECURITY

The **State Department** is one of the oldest and smallest departments in the executive branch. The purpose of the department is to support other agencies of the United States in the coordination of international activities, such as foreign policy and relations with other countries.

A fundamental belief of the founding fathers was that there should be civilian control of the military. The **Department of Defense** is an example of the application of that principle. The president of the United States is the commander in chief of the armed forces. The president and the secretary of defense, who is a civilian, are part of the **National Command Authority**. All directions for military operations come from the National Command Authority. The Department of Defense is responsible for all military installations, troops, and civilians of the Army, the Navy, the Air Force, and the Marine Corps, as well as for the training and equipping of the armed forces and all its debts.

The newest department of the President's Cabinet is the **Department of Homeland Security**. Established by the Homeland Security Act of 2002, its purpose is to prevent terrorist attacks within the United States, reduce the vulnerability of the United States to terrorism, and minimize the damage and assist in the recovery from terrorist attacks that may occur within the United States. There are four major sections of the department: Border and Transportation Security; Emergency Preparedness and Response; Science and Technology; and Information Analysis and Infrastructure Protection.

DEPARTMENTS OF VETERANS AFFAIRS, COMMERCE, EDUCATION, TRANSPORTATION, AND HOUSING AND URBAN DEVELOPMENT

The **Department of Veterans Affairs** administers a system of benefit programs for veterans and their dependents. These benefits include compensation for disabilities or death related to military service, pensions, education and rehabilitation, home loan guaranty programs, and a comprehensive medical program.

The **Department of Commerce** promotes domestic and international business and commerce. Anything affecting interstate commerce (see Chapter 8, Constitutional Law) can be regulated by the Department of Commerce.

The **Department of Education** is responsible for the development, administration, and coordination of the President's educational programs. It is responsible for the administration of laws related to education passed by Congress, and administers most of the federal assistance that is given to the states for education.

The **Department of Transportation** is responsible for ensuring that the nation's transportation systems are fast, safe, efficient, accessible, and convenient. The DOT develops and coordinates policies that will provide an efficient and economical transportation system. It is responsible for shaping and administering the policies and programs that are designed to protect and enhance the safety and efficiency of the nation's transportation system and services.

The mission of the **Department of Housing and Urban Development** is to provide a decent, safe, and sanitary home and suitable living environment for every American. It tries to accomplish this mission by doing the following.

1. Creating opportunities for homeownership
2. Providing housing assistance for low-income persons
3. Working to create and rehabilitate affordable housing
4. Enforcing fair housing laws
5. Establishing programs to assist the homeless
6. Spurring economic growth in distressed neighborhoods
7. Helping communities develop housing

DEPARTMENTS OF AGRICULTURE, INTERIOR, AND HEALTH AND HUMAN SERVICES

The **Department of Agriculture** is responsible for enhancing and supporting the agricultural industry in the United States. It is responsible for ensuring a safe, affordable, nutritious food supply; for caring for agricultural, forest, and range lands; for supporting the development of rural communities; for providing economic opportunities for farm and rural residents; and for expanding the global markets for American agricultural and forest products and services.

The **Department of Energy** is responsible for the research and development of energy technology, energy conservation, the nuclear weapons programs, regulation of energy production and use, and the pricing and allocation of energy resources. The Department of the Interior oversees agencies that are responsible for Indian affairs, mining, fish, and wildlife, geological research, land use, national parks and monuments, territories, conservation, and flood control.

The **Department of Health and Human Services** is responsible for protecting the health of Americans and for providing human services. Health and Human Services fulfills this mission through several different agencies: the National Institute of Health; the Food and Drug Administration; the Centers for Disease Control and Prevention; the Indian Health Service; the Health Resources and Services Administration; the Substance Abuse and Mental Health Services Administration; the Centers for Medicaid and Medicare Services; the Administration for Children and Families; the Administration on Aging; and the U.S. Public Health Services Commissioned Corps.

SPECIFIC AGENCIES

Many different federal agencies are classified based on whether they are an independent agency or an agency of an existing department and by what their duties and responsibilities are. Some are engaged in law enforcement, while others are primarily regulatory agencies. See Exhibit 6-11 for an example of the agencies within an executive department.

EXHIBIT 6-11	BUREAUS, COMMISSIONS, AND SERVICES UNDER THE DEPARTMENT OF JUSTICE

1. Bureau of Alcohol, Tobacco, and Firearms
2. Community-Oriented Policing Services
3. Drug Enforcement Agency
4. Federal Bureau of Investigation
5. Federal Bureau of Prisons
6. Office of Legal Policy
7. U.S. Marshall Service
8. U.S. Parole Commission

LAW ENFORCEMENT AGENCIES

The **Bureau of Alcohol, Tobacco, and Firearms (ATF)** is a law enforcement bureau within the Department of the Treasury. ATF is responsible for the enforcement of federal laws regarding alcohol, tobacco, firearms, explosives, and arson. It is also responsible for the collection of any taxes related to tobacco, firearms, or alcohol. The **Secret Service** is also part of the Department of the Treasury. One of the missions of the Secret Service is to protect the President of the United States. Former presidents and certain presidential candidates also receive Secret Service protection. Another function of the Secret Service is to investigate and suppress the use of counterfeit money in the United States. The Secret Service has exclusive jurisdiction over anything regarding the counterfeiting of U.S. obligations and securities. U.S. obligations and securities include U.S. currency and coins, U.S. Treasury checks and bonds, food stamps, WIC vouchers, and U.S. postage stamps.

The **Drug Enforcement Agency (DEA)** is an agency of the Department of Justice, and is responsible for the enforcement of the controlled substance laws and regulations of the United States. The DEA concentrates on organizations and the principal members of the organizations that are responsible for the growth, manufacture, or distribution of controlled substances in the United States or that are meant for the United States.

The **Bureau of U.S. Citizenship and Immigration Services**, which was formally known as Immigration and Naturalization Service (INS), and which was an agency of the Department of Justice, is now part of the new Department of Homeland Security. USCIS is responsible for enforcing the laws regarding the regulation of admission of aliens into the United States, the naturalization process, and other alien benefits. Working with the State Department, the Department of Health and Human Services, and the United Nations, USCIS also works with the admission and resettlement of refugees. See Exhibit 6-12.

EXHIBIT 6-12	LAW ENFORCEMENT AGENCIES

Bureau of Alcohol, Tobacco, and Firearms – Part of the Treasury Department
Secret Service – Part of the Treasury Department
Drug Enforcement Agency – Part of the Justice Department
Citizenship and Immigration Services – Part of the Department of Homeland Security

MONEY AND PEOPLE

The **Bureau of Engraving and Printing** is exclusively responsible for designing, engraving, and printing U.S. paper currency. It is also responsible for printing postage stamps, treasury securities, and security documents for other federal agencies. The **Census Bureau** is part of the Department of Commerce, and is responsible for the collection and provision of information about the people and economy of the United States. The Census Bureau is responsible for conducting the census that is mandated by the U.S. Constitution every ten years.

PEOPLE'S HEALTH AND WELL-BEING

The **National Institutes of Health** (a collective of a number of medical research organizations) supported over 35,000 research projects nationwide in 2004. The **Food and Drug Administration (FDA)** assures the safety of food and cosmetics and the safety and effectiveness of prescription drugs, biological products, and medical devices. The Centers for Disease Control and Prevention provides a system of health surveillance to monitor and prevent disease outbreaks, implements disease prevention strategies, and maintains national health statistics. The **Centers for Disease Control and Prevention** also provides immunization and workplace safety services and environmental disease prevention. The **Substance Abuse and Mental Health Services Administration** works to improve the quality and availability of substance abuse prevention programs, addiction treatment, and mental health services. This Administration provides funding to the states to support drug treatment and mental health services through federal block grants. All of these agencies are part of the Department of Health and Human Services.

The Department of Health and Human Services also includes agencies that are responsible for providing human services as well as medical services. The **Centers for Medicare and Medicaid Services**, formally the Health Care Financing Administration, administers the **Medicare** program, which provides health care coverage to elderly and disabled persons. It also administers the **Medicaid** program, which provides health care coverage to low-income people, nursing home coverage to low-income elderly people, and the Children's Health Insurance Program, which provides medical coverage to children. The **Administration for Children and Families** administers the state-federal welfare program, the Temporary Assistance to Needy Families, the national child support enforcement system, funding for childcare, and Head Start. It also provides support to the states' foster care and adoption assistance programs. The **Administration on Aging** is responsible for implementing several federal programs for the elderly that are mandated by the Older Americans Act. See Exhibit 6-13 for a summary of these agencies.

EXHIBIT 6-13	THE DIFFERENT AGENCIES OF HEALTH AND HUMAN SERVICES

National Institutes of Health – Medical research agency

Food and Drug Administration – Product safety agency

Centers for Disease Control and Prevention – Prevent disease outbreaks and the spreading of disease

Substance Abuse and Mental Health Services Administration – Improve the quality and availability of different programs

Centers for Medicare and Medicaid Services – Responsible for administering the Medicaid and Medicare programs

Administration for Children and Families – Administers different welfare programs.

Administration on Aging – Administers different federal programs that assist the elderly.

INDUSTRY-REGULATING AGENCIES

The **Commodity Futures Trading Commission (CFTC)** is an independent federal agency that is charged with the protection of participants in the commodities market. It is responsible for issuing and enforcing regulations against manipulative or abusive trading practices and fraud. It is also responsible for the regulation of the commodities markets and the people who work for those markets.

The **Nuclear Regulatory Agency (NRA)** is responsible for the regulation of commercial nuclear power and nuclear power plants in the United States. The Nuclear Regulatory Agency is an agency of the Department of Energy and is responsible for preparing regulations regarding the use of nuclear power, inspecting plants, and enforcing those regulations. It is also responsible for responding to emergency situations involving nuclear power.

The **Federal Communications Commission (FCC)** is responsible for the regulation of interstate and international communications by radio, television, wire, satellite, and cable. The FCC issues licenses that allows business to operate, and investigates and handles any complaints about communication and its regulation.

ELECTIONS

The **Federal Election Commission (FEC)** is an independent agency that is responsible for the enforcement of the Federal Election Campaign Act. The Federal Election Commission is responsible for the disclosure of campaign finance information, for enforcing limits on legal contributions and prohibiting illegal contributions, and for overseeing the public financing of presidential elections.

BANKS AND BANKING

The **Federal Deposit Insurance Corporation (FDIC)** is the federal agency that regulates the banking industry. The FDIC promulgates rules and regulations regarding how banks are to conduct business and is responsible for monitoring the banking industry for compliance with these rules and regulations. The FDIC also provides insurance for depositors of funds with FDIC-insured banks. If a depositor is threatened with the loss of his or her money because the bank or savings association in which he or she has an account is going out of business, the FDIC will guarantee his or her deposits up to $100,000.

Banks that are members of FDIC pay annual premiums to the agency. These monies are split between two funds: the Bank Insurance Fund (BIF) and the Savings Association Insurance Fund (SAIF). The BIF covers losses suffered by depositors of banks, and the SAIF covers losses suffered by depositors of savings associations.

CONSUMER PROTECTION AND ADVOCACY

The **Federal Trade Commission (FTC)** is the government agency responsible for enforcing federal antitrust laws and federal consumer protection laws. Its main purpose with regard to consumer protection is to eliminate unfair and deceptive trade practices. The **Consumer Product Safety Commission (CPSC)** is an independent agency that was created in 1972. It is responsible for overseeing the safety of over 15,000 kinds of consumer products. It establishes voluntary standards for safety, issues bans on consumer products if there is no standard that will protect the public, obtains recalls of products, conducts research on potential product hazards, and receives and responds to consumer complaints and questions. It does not have authority over automobiles or other onroad vehicles, tires, boats, alcohol, tobacco, firearms, foods, drugs, cosmetics, pesticides, and medical devices. Other federal agencies also have responsibility in these areas.

The **Legal Services Corporation** is an independent agency that is responsible for helping provide civil legal assistance to those who cannot afford it. The Agency itself does not provide legal services, but gives grants to local agencies that deliver the services. These local agencies are prohibited from taking on criminal cases and cases on a contingent fee basis. They are also prohibited from litigating class action suits, challenges to welfare reform, attempts to collect attorney's fees, lobbying, litigation on behalf of prisoners, and drug related evictions from public housing. The **Small Business Administration (SBA)** is the government agency that provides financial, technical, and managerial assistance to small businesses. It provides business loans, serves to guarantee loans, provides disaster loans, and provides venture capital to small businesses.

The **National Transportation Safety Board (NTSB)** is a federal agency that is part of the Department of Transportation. It is responsible for the investigation of the following kinds of transportation accidents.

  a. All U.S. civil aviation accidents and some public-use aircraft accidents
  b. Selected highway accidents
  c. Railroad accidents involving passenger trains or any train accident that involves at least one fatality or major property damage
  d. Major marine accidents and any marine accident involving a public and nonpublic vessel
  e. Pipeline accidents that involve a fatality or substantial property damage
  f. Releases of hazardous materials from all forms of transportation
  g. Selected transportation accidents that involve problems of a recurring nature

Some other federal agencies are discussed in other chapters of this text: the Securities and Exchange Commission (SEC)—Chapter 17; the Equal Employment Opportunity Commission (EEOC)—Chapter 25; the National Labor Relations Board (NLRB)—Chapter 19; the Occupational Safety and Health Administration (OSHA)—Chapter 19; and the Food and Drug Administration (FDA)—Chapter 24.

CONCLUSION

As our society has become more and more complex, it has become more and more difficult for legislatures to write laws that sufficiently deal with all situations that can arise. Administrative law helps fill in gaps in the legislation.

KEY WORDS AND PHRASES

abuse of discretion
adjudicatory hearing
administrative agency
administrative board
administrative crime
administrative hearing
administrative law
administrative law judge (ALJ)
administrative procedures act
advisory opinion
arbitrary and capricious
Bureau of U.S. Citizenship and Immigration Services
cabinet
citizen suit provision
Code of Federal Regulations
declaratory judgment
department
Department of Agriculture
Department of Commerce
Department of Defense
Department of Education
Department of Energy
Department of Health and Human Services
Department of Homeland Security
Department of Housing and Urban Development
Department of Justice
Department of the Treasury
Department of Transportation
Department of Veterans Affairs
Drug Enforcement Agency (DEA)
exhaustion of administrative remedies
federal agency
Federal Communications Commission (FCC)
Federal Deposit Insurance Commission (FDIC)
Federal Register
Food and Drug Administration (FDA)
freedom of information act (FOIA)
government corporation
inspection laws
investigatory hearing
judicial review
Legal Services Corporation
license
Medicaid
Medicare
National Transportation Safety Board (NTSB)
promulgation
regulatory agency
rulemaking authority
Secret Service
Small Business Administration (SBA)
State Department
substantial evidence rule

REVIEW QUESTIONS

SHORT ANSWER

1. What is administrative law?
2. What is promulgation?
3. What is the *Federal Register,* and what is its purpose?
4. What is the standard of proof in a judicial review?
5. What is an arbitrary and capricious act?
6. What is a declaratory judgment?
7. What are inspection laws?
8. What is an administrative crime?
9. What is a license?
10. What is the difference between Medicare and Medicaid?
11. What is rule-making authority?
12. What is the promulgation process?
13. What are the Cabinet-level departments?

14. What is an independent agency?

15. What is the role of the Department of the Interior?

16. What are inspection laws?

17. What is the purpose of the Department of Education?

18. What is a citizen suit provision?

19. What is the purpose of the Legal Services Corporation?

FILL IN THE BLANK

1. The first notice of rule making is published in the _____.

2. The process an agency follows °to formally issue rules and regulations is _____.

3. The Department of _____ promotes domestic and international business and commerce.

4. The Department of _____ oversees agencies responsible for Indian affairs.

5. The _____ suppresses the use of counterfeit money in the United States.

6. The major administrative division of the executive branch of government is the _____.

7. An agency whose appointed head and appointed members serve for a fixed period of time and cannot be removed from office by the President except for reasons that are set by Congress is known as _____.

8. A _____ is a rule or order that is issued by an administrative agency.

9. A _____ is a statute that requires the review of an agency to determine if its continued existence is warranted.

10. An _____ is a law that governs how an agency performs its day-to-day business.

FACT SITUATIONS

1. Cheri wishes to obtain information about the bidding process on a recently awarded government contract. Which statute may she use to try to get this information?

2. Inspectors discover several violations of food health rules in a restaurant owned by Felicia Rumbaurer. The agency wants to revoke Ms. Rumbaurer's license to run the restaurant. What will the agency hold to be able to take this kind of action taken against Ms. Rumbaurer?

3. The administrative law judge is unsure about how to rule on a case pending before the agency. What can the ALJ request for guidance? From whom can he or she request it?

4. Emmaline is fed up with a junk yard that is not in compliance with federal regulations regarding fencing around the yard. The appropriate federal agency is not enforcing the rules. Emmaline files a suit in federal court to have the regulations enforced. What sort of provision must have been in the law to allow her to·do this?

5. An agency has an internal appeal process in addition to its regular hearings. Eugene has lost the regular hearing and is planning on appealing the matter directly to federal court. What doctrine or rule might prevent Eugene from doing so?

6. Jamal and Carletta wish to adopt a child from overseas. Which agency will they work with to get the necessary papers to bring the child into the United States?

7. Willem is suspected of operating a counterfeiting ring that duplicates U.S. currency and documents. Which agency will conduct the investigation into Willem's activities?

8. A horrible accident happened when a large commuter plane crashed onto an interstate. Which agency will be responsible for investigating the accident to determine what happened?

9. Several banks are going out of business because of a series of bad loans that businesses defaulted on. Depositors are losing their money. Which federal agency can they file a claim with to get their money back?

10. Several people are offended by a radio show hosted by a "shock jock." They object to the language that is used by the host and the subject matter of the show. To which federal agency can the people make a complaint?

INTRODUCTION

An attorney proves his or her case through the presentation of evidence; failure to provide sufficient evidence to the finder of fact can result in the case being lost. This chapter sets out the number of ways that evidence is classified, from very broad categories down to more specific categories. Evidence can be classified by what type of evidence it is, how important the evidence is, or even how relevant the evidence is to the case. The chapter sets out how and when evidence can be admitted by setting out in detail the method used to introduce something into evidence. The different burdens of proof are discussed along with which burden of proof applies to the different types of cases and how this burden can shift from one side to the other. Hearsay evidence that is inadmissible is presented as well as the many exceptions to the hearsay rule. Privileged communications, to whom they apply, and how privilege can be raised to exclude proposed evidence are discussed in detail. Other ways that information can be excluded are also highlighted.

GENERAL CLASSIFICATIONS OF EVIDENCE

A plaintiff can allege anything he or she wants: The hard part is proving the allegation. Failure to prove the facts that are the basis for the cause of action means the person loses the case. Proving the facts that are essential to winning the case is accomplished through the introduction of evidence.

ADMISSIBLE AND INADMISSIBLE EVIDENCE AND LAYING THE FOUNDATION

Evidence is anything that is used to prove the existence or nonexistence of a fact. Evidence can be testimony given orally and under oath; it can also be written records, tape recordings, videotapes, photographs—anything that tends to prove the existence or nonexistence of a fact. There are many ways that evidence is classified. For example, evidence can be classified as admissible or inadmissible, as direct or circumstantial, or as real, relevant, or irrelevant. **Admissible evidence** is relevant to an issue in the case and can be admitted under rules of evidence. **Inadmissible evidence** is evidence that cannot be admitted or considered under state or federal rules of evidence or case law. For example, evidence obtained as a result of an illegal search and seizure is inadmissible. The information obtained cannot be entered into evidence during the criminal trial. See Exhibit 7-1. Courts at the federal and state level have rules that establish what kind of evidence is admissible and what kind is inadmissible.

EXHIBIT 7-1 ADMISSIBLE OR INADMISSIBLE EVIDENCE

Evidence is admissible if it is relevant to an issue that is before the court and if it can be admitted under the applicable rules of evidence of case law. In order for evidence to be admissible, it must be either direct or circumstantial, relevant, competent, and material.

Evidence is inadmissible if it is irrelevant to the issue that is before the court or if it cannot be admitted under the applicable rules of evidence of case law. If evidence is irrelevant, incompetent, or immaterial, then it is inadmissible and will not be considered by the finder of fact.

In order for something to be admitted into evidence, the foundation must be laid. The phrase **laying the foundation** refers to establishing the relevancy and validity of the item or testimony the attorney wishes to have put into evidence. For example, an attorney wants to ask an expert witness her opinion about certain facts. Before the expert will be allowed to give her opinion, the attorney must establish the witness's qualifications to be an expert and to give her opinion. In a criminal case, if the prosecution wishes to introduce an item into evidence, the prosecution must show the **chain of custody.** The custody or possession of the item must be shown from the time it was seized up to the time it is offered into evidence. See Exhibit 7-2. For example, a bag of cocaine has been seized and now the prosecution wants to introduce it into evidence. In order for it to be admitted, the prosecution must have the officer who seized it testify as to how he took control of it and identified it. The prosecution will also have to show where the cocaine was secured, how it was taken to the crime lab for testing, and how it was taken from the crime lab to where it was locked up until it was offered as evidence at trial.

EXHIBIT 7-2 LAYING THE FOUNDATION: ESTABLISHING THE CHAIN OF CUSTODY

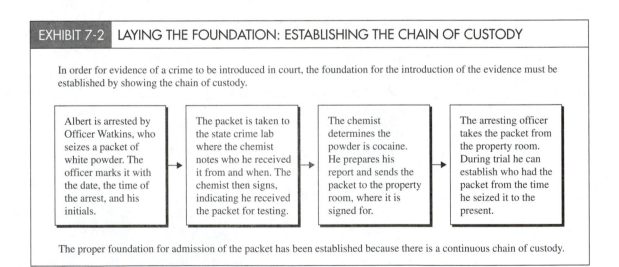

In order for evidence of a crime to be introduced in court, the foundation for the introduction of the evidence must be established by showing the chain of custody.

| Albert is arrested by Officer Watkins, who seizes a packet of white powder. The officer marks it with the date, the time of the arrest, and his initials. | The packet is taken to the state crime lab where the chemist notes who he received it from and when. The chemist then signs, indicating he received the packet for testing. | The chemist determines the powder is cocaine. He prepares his report and sends the packet to the property room, where it is signed for. | The arresting officer takes the packet from the property room. During trial he can establish who had the packet from the time he seized it to the present. |

The proper foundation for admission of the packet has been established because there is a continuous chain of custody.

DIRECT EVIDENCE, CIRCUMSTANTIAL EVIDENCE, AND PRESUMPTIONS

Evidence can be direct or circumstantial. **Direct evidence** shows or tends to show the existence of a fact that is in question. The fact is shown without any inference or presumption. In other words, this evidence, by its existence, proves a fact in question. For example, if David and Bob are involved in a lawsuit over a contract, the contract itself is direct evidence of its terms. **Circumstantial** or **indirect evidence** is evidence that requires a logical chain of events to prove the existence of a fact. It is not based on actual personal knowledge, but rather on presumption and inference. **Inference** is the process by which logical conclusions are reached by using facts already proven or admitted to. **Presumption** is a rule of law stating that because a basic fact exists, another fact also exists. See Exhibit 7-3 for the distinctions between direct and circumstantial evidence.

EXHIBIT 7-3	DIRECT OR CIRCUMSTANTIAL EVIDENCE

Direct Evidence – Evidence that shows or tends to show the existence of a fact directly; no inference or presumption has to be made. Because the evidence shows this, the fact is established.

Circumstantial Evidence – Evidence that shows the existence of a fact indirectly. An inference or a presumption has to be made in order for the fact to be established using circumstantial evidence.

Certain inferences are allowed to be drawn from certain facts. For example, Mario is charged with the murder of his wife, Isabella. There is no body, so there is no direct evidence that she has been murdered. Mario states that Isabella left him and he has no idea where she is. Circumstantial evidence has to be used to prove that she is, in fact, dead. Several people testify that Mario repeatedly threatened his wife and said many times that he wished she were dead. No one has heard from her since she disappeared; no money has been withdrawn from bank accounts in her name, and none of her credit cards have been used. Investigation reveals Mario had the carpets in the home cleaned the day after Isabella's disappearance; a small amount of blood matching her blood type was found in the carpet. A small amount of blood matching her type was also found on one of the kitchen knives. Shortly before Isabella disappeared, Mario increased substantially the amount of life insurance he carried on her. None of these facts are direct evidence that Isabella is dead, but when weighed as a whole, a logical conclusion that she was, in fact, dead could be reached.

A **rebuttable presumption** is one that, once it is shown, shifts the burden of proof to the defendant. What is shown by the presumption is deemed proven unless the defendant can produce evidence to show that the presumption cannot be made. In other words, certain facts are deemed proven unless the defendant can produce sufficient evidence to prove that the presumed fact is not true. The defendant has to **rebut**—defeat or take away—the effect of the presumption by showing that the presumption is not true. See Exhibit 7-4.

EXHIBIT 7-4	REBUTTABLE PRESUMPTIONS

Presumption – Because one fact exists, it can be assumed that another fact exists.

Rebuttable Presumption – The burden of proof shifts to the other side because of the showing of a presumption. If it cannot be rebutted, then the presumption is deemed to be true.

COMPETENT, INCOMPETENT, RELEVANT, AND IRRELEVANT EVIDENCE

Competent evidence is evidence that the court will admit into the record. A **competent witness** is a witness who is legally qualified to testify—one who can understand the meaning of the oath. The term also refers to an individual who has personal knowledge about an issue before the court. **Incompetent evidence** is not admissible into a court of law because of an established rule of evidence. Rules of evidence do not allow for incompetent evidence to be introduced.

Relevant evidence is evidence that has the tendency to make the existence of a fact at issue more probable or less probable. This evidence has a logical relationship to the issues of the case. **Irrelevant evidence** has little or no tendency to prove or disprove an issue of fact that is being contested. It is immaterial or irrelevant to the issues of the case, and has no logical relationship to the case. For example, in Mario's criminal trial, the fact that he increased the amount of life insurance on his wife's policy and by how much is relevant. What Mario was wearing when he increased the amount of the policy is irrelevant.

MATERIAL AND IMMATERIAL EVIDENCE

Material evidence is evidence that tends to influence the final decision of the finder of fact—the judge or jury—because of its logical connection to the issue that is in dispute. The testimony of an eyewitness to a crime is material evidence because it tends to establish what happened and who did the act. This eyewitness may also be a material witness, one who can give testimony that relates to a particular matter that no one else can or that very few other people can. **Immaterial evidence** is evidence that is unlikely to have any influence over the finder of fact with regard to the issue brought before the court. It does not tend to prove an alleged fact, and it is usually inadmissible into the record. See Exhibit 7-5 for a summary of the distinctions between material and immaterial evidence.

EXHIBIT 7-5	MATERIAL AND IMMATERIAL EVIDENCE

Material Evidence and Witnesses – Evidence the tends to influence the finder of fact; it tends to establish what happened or who did what. A material witness is a witness who can give testimony only a few other people can. A material witness may be the only one who can testify about a particular matter.

Immaterial Evidence – Evidence that will have no influence over the finder of fact regarding any issue brought to court. It does not tend to prove any issue in the case.

NARRATIVE, REAL, AND DEMONSTRATIVE EVIDENCE

Evidence is usually presented in response to questions asked by attorneys or by the court. **Narrative evidence** is testimony given in a narrative form, with no questions being asked of the witness. For example, Mario is asked to explain his whereabouts the day his wife disappeared. He explains in detail where he was that day with no interruptions.

Sometimes evidence is not testimony, but actual objects. **Real evidence** is evidence that is provided by the thing itself. There is no description involved: Rather, the evidence is presented to be viewed or inspected. Real evidence might be photographs of a crime scene that are enlarged so the finder of fact can view them; narrative evidence might be testimony about the crime scene given by the investigating officer. Real evidence can also be classified as autoptic evidence or demonstrative evidence. **Autoptic evidence** consists of the thing itself. For example, the kitchen knife taken from Mario's home that had traces of Isabella's blood on it is autoptic evidence; the knife is the thing itself. Testimony might be given about the weapon, but the weapon itself is autoptic evidence. The knife may also be classified as **tangible evidence,** that which can be seen or touched. Tangible evidence is also referred to as real evidence. **Demonstrative evidence** is evidence that is perceived by the senses. It can be seen, heard, felt, tasted, or smelled without the intervention of testimony. Demonstrative evidence might be maps and diagrams of an accident scene, photographs of a crime scene, models, charts, medical illustrations, or X-rays. See Exhibit 7-6.

EXHIBIT 7-6	REAL EVIDENCE

Real Evidence – Evidence that is the thing itself. Real evidence is the actual physical object, photographs of the object, or a demonstration that appeals to the senses.

Autoptic Evidence – The actual physical object. There is no description; the thing itself is shown.

Demonstrative Evidence – Evidence that is seen, heard, felt, tasted, or smelled without the intervention of testimony.

CHARACTER EVIDENCE

Character evidence relates to a person's standing in the community. Essentially, it is evidence about a person's reputation. A general rule is that evidence about a person's bad reputation cannot be introduced into evidence unless the person makes his or her character an issue at trial. See Exhibit 7-7 for when character evidence can be used.

EXHIBIT 7-7	USE OF CHARACTER EVIDENCE

Character evidence relates to a person's reputation or standing in the community.

The prosecution cannot put into evidence the defendant's past bad acts, such as criminal charges or convictions, or bad reputation **unless the defense presents evidence of the defendant's good character first.**

For example, the prosecution cannot present as evidence the fact that Mario has a past criminal record for spousal abuse in order to get a conviction unless Mario (through his attorney) presents evidence of his good character first. If the defense puts into evidence testimony from others about Mario's good character—how much he loved Isabella and would never hurt her—then the prosecution could introduce into evidence Mario's past conviction for spousal abuse. The evidence presented by the prosecution would be **rebuttal evidence** because it explains, disproves, or disputes evidence introduced by the other side. Rebuttal evidence tends to explain or contradict evidence the other side has presented. The defense presents evidence of the defendant's good character in order to rebut—defeat, refute, or take away—the effect of evidence showing Mario may have killed his wife. The plaintiff presents evidence of the defendant's past criminal record to rebut the character evidence presented by the defense. See Sidebar 7-1, *Burley v. State of Arkansas,* for an application of these principles.

SIDEBAR 7-1 *BURLEY V. STATE OF ARKANSAS*

Facts: Burley was convicted of murder in the second degree. It was alleged she caused the death of a three-year-old child by forcing a rectal thermometer into the child with enough force to tear the rectal wall, ultimately causing the death of the child. Information about her being charged in the past with child abuse was introduced into evidence. The trial court allowed testimony that there had been an investigation into a battery committed against a three-year-old child. The battery consisted of several bruises on the child's buttocks and "a mark that looked like it had been made with something other than a hand." The investigator testified that, after interviewing the child and the child's grandmother, he concluded that the appellant had committed the battery. One basis for her appeal was that the introduction of this information violated Rule 404 of the Rules of Evidence regarding the introduction of character evidence.

Ruling of the Court: Evidence of other crimes, wrongs, or acts is not admissible to prove the character of a person in order to show that he acted in conformity therewith. It may, however, be admissible for other purposes, such as proof of motive, opportunity, intent, preparation, plan, knowledge, identity, or absence of mistake or accident.

The test for admission of prior bad acts under Rule 404(b) is whether the evidence offered has independent relevance to a fact of consequence in the case. *Id.* Also, there must be a degree of similarity between the prior bad act and the present crime. To be probative, the prior criminal act must require an intent similar to that required by the charged crime. Finally, if the evidence of a prior bad act is independently relevant to the main issue, rather than merely to prove that the defendant is a criminal, then the evidence of that conduct may be admissible with a cautionary instruction by the court.

In this case, the only testimony, or tangible evidence, of a prior bad act was an opinion offered by Detective Juhl. There is nothing here but an unsubstantiated allegation. Rule 404(b) cannot apply without proof of an actual act being committed.

Reverse and remanded for a new trial.

Source: Arkansas Reports

FABRICATED, PRIMA FACIE, PROBATIVE, AND SCINTILLA EVIDENCE

Fabricated evidence is evidence that is made up or altered after the fact with the intent to deceive the finder of fact. An example is a fabricated fact, one that is made up and that has no foundation in truth. For example, Mario testifies that he was out of town the day that Isabella was murdered; he was 500 miles away and did not return until two days later. However, the prosecution produces credit card receipts from a gas station in the town where Mario and Isabella lived bearing the date that Mario said he was out of town. Mario gave fabricated evidence: his testimony about where he had been that day. If a fabricated fact is given in court, the witness who testified as to the fact may be guilty of the crime of **perjury.** The elements of perjury are the willful statement of a fact in a judicial proceeding, given under oath, either in open court or by an affidavit, known by the witness to be a false statement. See Exhibit 7-8.

EXHIBIT 7-8	ELEMENTS OF PERJURY

1. Willful statement of fact
2. In a judicial proceeding
3. Given under oath
4. In open court or by affidavit
5. Known by the witness to be a false statement

All these elements have to be proven to convict someone of perjury.

Prima facie evidence is evidence that is sufficient to establish the existence of a fact or a group of facts, but that may be contradicted by other evidence that shows the opposite may have been true. Parties will produce prima facie evidence during the presentation of their case, and if no evidence is introduced to refute the evidence already admitted, then that fact is deemed proven. A **scintilla of evidence** refers not to a type of evidence, but rather to the amount of evidence presented. A scintilla of evidence is the smallest amount of evidence that can be introduced.

Probative evidence has the effect of proof: It is evidence that tends to prove or does, in fact, prove an issue. A probative fact is one that tends to prove or does prove the fact. **Proof**

is the establishment of a fact by evidence. In other words, probative evidence is evidence that either establishes or tends to establish a fact that is an issue at trial. *Proof* is not the same as *evidence:* proof is anything that will establish a fact, whereas evidence relates to proof that is admissible in a trial.

BURDEN AND STANDARDS OF PROOF

In any case pending before a court, evidence is used to help the parties meet their burden of proof with regard to the allegations they have made against each other. The **burden of proof** is the requirement that a fact or facts that are in dispute between parties be established by evidence.

BURDEN OF PERSUASION AND OF GOING FORWARD

There are two distinct principles of burden of proof: burden of persuasion and burden of going forward. The **burden of persuasion** is the requirement that the party that bears the burden of proof convince the finder of fact that all the required elements of the case are, in fact, present. For example, in a criminal case the prosecuting attorney has the burden of proving that the defendant did all the elements that make up the crime and that he or she possessed the necessary mental intent when he or she committed the act. If the defendant is charged with battery, then the prosecutor must prove that the defendant hit the victim, that the blow caused harm, and that the defendant acted with the necessary mental intent.

Burden of going forward is a shift of the burden of proof. One party to the case has introduced evidence in support of a claim. The burden now shifts to the other party to present evidence to dispute the claim. In our example, the prosecuting attorney has introduced evidence that Mario increased the amount of life insurance on his wife, that blood was found in the home and on a knife, that the carpets were cleaned the day after Isabella disappeared, and that Mario lied about his whereabouts the day of his wife's murder. The burden of proof has now shifted to Mario, who must present evidence to overcome the inference (see above definition) that he murdered his wife, Isabella. Mario has to produce evidence to show why he was in town when he said he was not, that he had a legitimate reason for increasing the life insurance, why blood was in his home and on a knife in his home, and that there was a legitimate reason why the carpet was cleaned the day after Isabella disappeared.

STANDARDS OF PROOF

The term **standard of proof** refers to how convincing the evidence presented must be in order for the party to be in compliance with his or her burden of proof. There are three general standards of proof: proof beyond a reasonable doubt, proof by clear and convincing evidence, and proof by a preponderance of the evidence. Proof **beyond a reasonable doubt,** the highest burden of proof, is the burden of proof in a criminal case. Proof beyond a reasonable doubt is evidence that fully satisfies the trier of fact; it is entirely convincing. A reasonable person would not have any reasonable doubt as to the guilt of the person charged with the crime. **Clear and convincing** proof establishes a reasonable certainty in the truth of a fact in controversy; the truth of the facts asserted is established with reasonable certainty. **Preponderance of the evidence,** the lowest burden of proof, is used in civil cases. When all the evidence that has been introduced is considered, a preponderance of that evidence shows that it is more likely than not that the alleged fact is true. The fact that is being sought to be proven is more likely to be true than not. Exhibit 7-9 lists the types of burdens of proof.

EXHIBIT 7-9 | BURDEN OF PROOF

Highest: Beyond a Reasonable Doubt – This burden is used in criminal trials only. A reasonable person has no doubt about the guilt or innocence of the defendant.

Middle: Clear and Convincing – There is reasonable certainty that the facts stated are true. This burden is used in civil trials.

Lowest: Preponderance of the Evidence – It is more likely than not that the facts stated are true.

HEARSAY

One of the general rules of evidence is that hearsay is inadmissible into evidence. **Hearsay** is an out-of-court statement offered to prove the truth of the matter asserted. Hearsay includes testimony by a witness as to what other people know or what they told him or her. The person who made the original statement that the witness is attempting to testify about is the **declarant. Double hearsay** is a hearsay statement that contains even more hearsay. For example, Phillip attempts to testify as to what Isabella told him that Mario told her. Phillip's statement is hearsay within hearsay and is inadmissible in court.

However, there are often exceptions to general rules of law with regard to hearsay; over twenty-four such exceptions exist. Some of these exceptions are the business record exception, past recollection recorded, present sense impression, state of mind, dying declaration, excited utterance, and statements of a physical condition.

VERBAL STATEMENTS WHEN THE DECLARANT IS AVAILABLE AS A WITNESS

The first set of exceptions to the hearsay rule states that hearsay is admissible into evidence even though the person who made the statement is available as a witness. Another person is allowed to testify about what the person said, even though the person who made the statement is available to testify. This is the **present sense impression:** Any statement that describes or explains an event or condition made while the person perceived the event or condition is admissible. For example, if a person saw a car speeding by and commented on how fast the car was moving, a person who heard this statement could testify about what he or she heard. An **excited utterance** is a statement made about a startling event or condition made while the declarant was under the stress of the excitement caused by the incident. An excited utterance is a statement made almost simultaneously with the event. It is one that the utterer did not have time to think about. See Exhibit 7-10.

EXHIBIT 7-10 | PRESENT SENSE IMPRESSION OR EXCITED UTTERANCE

Present Sense Impression – A statement that explains an event or condition made while the person perceived the event.

Excited Utterance – A statement made about a startling event or condition made while the utterer is still excited about the incident and does not have time to think about what she or he saw.

The **state of mind exception** applies when the declarant is describing his or her then-existing mental, emotional, or physical condition, when he or she makes a statement about his or her present intent to do something. For example, if Mario said to Phillip, "My life would be better off without Isabella. I really hate her!", Phillip could testify about what

Mario said because Mario's statement indicated how he felt about Isabella at that time. If Isabella said that she was hurting because Mario had hit her, her statement could be admitted because it indicated how Isabella felt at that particular time. **Statements for medical diagnosis or treatment**—those made to a doctor regarding a person's current physical condition, pain, past or present symptoms, and medical history—are admissible. See Exhibit 7-11. For example, Dr. Hedges would be allowed to testify that Isabella told him that she was suffering from severe pain in her abdomen because Mario hit her there. Dr. Hedges could also testify about Isabella's medical history.

EXHIBIT 7-11	STATE OF MIND AND STATEMENTS FOR MEDICAL DIAGNOSIS

State of Mind Exception – The declarant is describing his or her then existing mental, emotional, or physical condition.

Statements for Medical Diagnosis or Treatment – Statements made to a doctor regarding a person's current physical condition, pain, past or present symptoms, and medical history. Such statements are admissible because a person generally will not lie about how he or she is currently feeling or about his or her condition when seeking medical treatment.

WRITTEN STATEMENTS WHEN THE DECLARANT IS AVAILABLE AS A WITNESS

A hearsay statement can be in a document, making the document itself inadmissible into evidence unless one of the following exceptions is found to apply. A **recorded recollection** is a memorandum or other written record about a matter produced by a witness when that witness was able to recall the matter in question. See Exhibit 7-12. In order for a recorded recollection to be admitted into evidence, the following four elements must be met.

1. The witness does not remember or does not remember accurately the information contained in the record;
2. The witness made the record close to the time of the event;
3. The witness had firsthand knowledge of what was written down; and
4. The witness can verify the accuracy of the record.

For example, Susan is testifying about items that were stolen from her home. She is unable to remember all the items taken, but she made an inventory the day after the robbery happened for her insurance claim. This inventory could be admitted into evidence.

EXHIBIT 7-12	CRITERIA FOR RECORDED RECOLLECTION

1. The witness does not remember or does not remember accurately the information contained in the record;
2. The witness made the record at or near the time of the event;
3. The witness had firsthand knowledge of what was written down; and
4. The witness can verify the accuracy of the record.

These criteria must be met in order to show the likelihood of the validity of the information contained in the records.

The **business record exception** to the hearsay rule states that all original, routine records that are maintained may be introduced into evidence. The documents must be shown to be kept in the routine order of business, and it must be shown that the entry was made at or near the time of the actual transaction. A witness also can testify about an **absence of entry in business records.** If records are kept in the normal course of business, the lack of such a record can be introduced to show that the transaction did not occur. See Exhibit 7-13 for a summary of these exceptions. For example, Michael is charged with allowing a friend to take merchandise from the store where he works without paying for it. At this store, all sales are to be rung up at the registers. Video surveillance tapes show someone bringing a DVD player and a pack of gum to the counter where Michael works. Receipts reveal that the only sale entered is the sale of the gum. The lack of a record of sale of a DVD player is evidence that Michael allowed someone to take an item from the store without paying for it.

EXHIBIT 7-13 | BUSINESS RECORDS

Business Records – In order to be admissible as evidence, business records must be shown to be:

1. Original and routine
2. Kept in the routine order of business
3. Made at or near the time of the transaction

Absence of Entry in Business Records – The lack of records can be used to show that a transaction did not take place if it is shown that

1. The records are kept in the routine order of business
2. An entry would have been made at or near the time of the transaction
3. There are no entries that have been made

Business records are admissible because, as a rule, businesses strive to keep accurate and complete records.

Public records are also exceptions to the hearsay rule. These are records that describe the actions of a government agency, that describe subjects the agency is responsible for examining and reporting on, or that contain facts that were uncovered in an official investigation. For example, an airline is being sued for injuries caused by a plane crash. The allegation is pilot error during the landing. Even though the pilot and the air traffic controller are available to testify, a tape recording or transcript of their communication is admissible. The hearsay rule does not exclude records of vital statistics (birth, marriage, and death certificates) if the reports regarding such statistics are made to a public agency under statutory law. The absence of public record exception is very similar to the exception for an absent entry in business records: Testimony or certified public records are admissible if they show the nonexistence of a matter that would ordinarily be in the public records.

The **records of religious organizations exception** applies to statements of births, marriages, divorces, deaths, legitimacy, ancestry, relationships by blood or marriage, or other similar facts. Such records are admissible if they are contained in a regularly kept record of a religious organization. The marriage, baptismal and similar certificates exception allows statements contained in those documents to be introduced into evidence if each of the following conditions exists:

1. An authorized public or religious official conducted the ceremony.
2. The certificate was issued shortly after the ceremony was performed.
3. The certificate was issued by the official who conducted the ceremony.

The **family record exception** provides that statements of fact concerning personal or family history recorded in family Bibles, genealogies, charts, engravings on rings, inscriptions on family portraits, and tombstones are admissible into evidence.

Records of property documents—those that establish or affect an interest in property—are admissible if the following criteria are met.

1. The document contains a property right.
2. The record of the document was made in a public office according to statutory law.
3. The record is used to prove the content, the execution, or the delivery of the original document.

If these criteria are not met, then the record is not admissible as an exception to the hearsay rule. The statements in property documents exception applies to statements in documents that establish or affect a property right if the statement is relevant to the purpose of the document. However, these statements are not admissible if later transactions regarding the property contradict the statements in the document. The **statements in ancient documents** exception applies to statements contained in a document that has been authenticated and that is twenty years old or older.

Statements made in market reports and commercial publications, which contain market quotations, tabulations, lists, directories or other published compilations used and relied on by the public or people in particular occupations, are also exceptions to the hearsay rule. For example, if someone is suing because of stock fraud, he or she could use statements in the *Wall Street Journal* about the stability of the stock and the stock price on a certain date in question. If a person is testifying as an expert witness and uses statements from a text, then the learned treatise exception applies. According to this exception, statements from a learned treatise can be used if the publication is established as reliable by the witness, by other expert testimony, or by the court, and if the statements are used in either direct examination or cross-examination.

STATEMENTS WHEN THE DECLARANT IS UNAVAILABLE

When a person is unavailable as a witness, hearsay statements may be admissible into evidence.

If one of a number of conditions is met (see Exhibit 7-14), hearsay statements may be admitted into evidence. If a person is claiming privilege, the court must first rule that the privilege is valid. Statements made outside of court may then be introduced into evidence. For example, a wife claims the husband and wife privilege and refuses to testify against her spouse. Statements she made outside the hearing regarding the spouse's criminal activity could then be introduced into evidence. Similarly, if a person refuses to testify in court, statements made by him or her outside the court about the same subject matter may be introduced into evidence.

EXHIBIT 7-14	CRITERIA FOR ADMISSION OF HEARSAY WHEN THE DECLARANT IS UNAVAILABLE AS A WITNESS

1. Privilege
2. Refusal to testify, even when ordered to do so by the court
3. Inability to be present to testify because of death or physical illness
4. Testimony declaring a lack of memory
5. Absence from the hearing; noncompliance with the party requesting attendance

Two other exceptions to the hearsay rule, based on the unavailability of the declarant, are the dying declaration and the statement against interest. A **dying declaration** is a statement made by a person who believes he or she is dying about how he or she received injury, and about who inflicted the injury. See Exhibit 7-15. The injured person does not actually have to die; all that is required is that the person thinks he or she is dying. A **statement against interest** is a statement made that is not in the declarant's financial or property best interest, that may expose the declarant to civil or criminal judgment, or that may eliminate a cause of action against another person.

EXHIBIT 7-15 | ELEMENTS OF A DYING DECLARATION

1. The statement is made by a person who **believes he or she is dying.**
2. The statement is about **how** he or she received the injuries causing death, and about **who** inflicted the injuries.
3. The person **does not** actually have to die.
4. The person **must have thought** he or she was dying when the statement was made.

This statement is admissible because it is assumed that a person does not want to face God having just lied about something.

STATEMENTS THAT ARE NOT HEARSAY

Certain types of statements may appear to be hearsay but are not under the rules of evidence. The first is a **prior inconsistent statement:** a statement given at an earlier hearing, deposition, or other proceeding where the declarant was under oath and subject to cross-examination that is inconsistent with testimony given at a later trial or hearing. The prior inconsistent statement can be used to impeach the credibility of the person testifying. A **prior consistent statement** is one given at an earlier hearing, deposition, or other proceeding where the declarant was under oath and subject to cross-examination that is consistent with testimony given at a later trial or hearing and that is used to counter a claim that the declarant lied or was pressured to testify. This is used to increase the credibility of the witness by showing that he or she has maintained the same statement over a period of time. A statement of **prior identification** identifies a person if the declarant saw the person he or she is identifying. In order for the statement to be entered into evidence, the declarant must be testifying at a later trial or hearing and is subject to cross-examination. For example, if a witness cannot identify a defendant in a criminal trial because the defendant has changed his or her appearance, statements made by the witness at a police line up are admissible. An **admission by a party/opponent** is when a person who is one of the parties involved in a court case either makes a statement that is not in that person's best interest or gives some indication that such a statement has been made. The statement does not have to be made by the person involved in the case; it can be made by someone authorized to speak on behalf of the person, such as an agent. However, the statement the agent gives on behalf of the person must be a statement about something that is within the scope of the agency relationship, and it must have been made during the agency relationship. An admission can also be a statement that was made by a co-conspirator in furtherance of a conspiracy. Exhibit 7-16 is a summary of exceptions to the hearsay rule.

EXHIBIT 7-16	SUMMARY OF THE EXCEPTIONS TO THE HEARSAY RULE

Declarant Available as a Witness

I. Verbal Statements

1. Present sense impression
2. State of mind
3. Excited utterance
4. Statements for medical diagnosis

II. Written Statements

1. Recorded recollection
2. Absence of entry in business records
3. Records of vital statistics
4. Records of religious organizations
5. Family record
6. Ancient documents
7. Learned treatise
8. Business records
9. Public records
10. Absence of public record
11. Birth/Marriage certificates
12. Property records
13. Market reports

Declarant Unavailable as a Witness

I. Verbal Statements

1. Dying declaration
2. Statement against interest

PRIVILEGE

Certain communications are protected from disclosure. The Federal Rules of Evidence no longer recognize these communications per se, but do rely on common law to determine if they exist. Several states recognize these communications in their state rules of evidence. A **privileged communication** is a statement made by certain people within a protected relationship that the law protects from forced disclosure on the witness stand. A person who claims one of the privileges cannot be forced to testify about what was said in a conversation with the other person in the relationship. **Privileged evidence** is evidence whose introduction cannot be compelled. Some examples include governmental secrets, the identity of an informant, grand jury proceedings, and an attorney's work product. See Exhibit 7-17 for a listing of privileges.

EXHIBIT 7-17	PRIVILEGED COMMUNICATIONS

Communications between the following people are privileged and cannot be disclosed unless the parties agree to the disclosure.

1. Husband and wife
2. Priest and penitent
3. Work product rule
4. Doctor and patient
5. Attorney and client

HUSBAND/WIFE, DOCTOR/PATIENT, AND PRIEST/PENITENT

Spousal communication is protected by the **husband/wife privilege.** Any confidential statements between a husband and wife during the existence of a legal marriage are protected from forced disclosure. This privilege can even extend to anyone who heard the communication between the husband and wife. The **doctor/patient privilege** protects communication between a doctor and a patient when the patient has consulted the doctor for medical treatment and diagnosis. In order for the privilege to apply, there must be a doctor/patient relationship, the information communicated must be intended to remain confidential, and the communication must be for the purpose of diagnosis and treatment. Because of the **priest/penitent privilege,** the seal of the confessional bars testimony as to the communication between the person making a confession and a priest who is hearing the confession.

ATTORNEY/CLIENT AND WORK PRODUCT

The **attorney/client privilege** applies to all client communications with an attorney when the client believes he or she is consulting an attorney to obtain legal advice. The communication must be made in confidence and it must be made to an attorney for the privilege to apply. The **work product privilege** applies to trial materials prepared by an attorney if the documents reveal the attorney's mental process, if using the documents would turn the attorney into a witness instead of an advocate, and if the information is available from other sources. This is not an absolute privilege; it is a conditional privilege, and the three listed conditions must be met.

OTHER EVIDENTIARY TERMS

Other terms that deal with types of evidence and the admissibility of evidence are often used. **Parol evidence** is oral or verbal testimony given by witnesses in court. The **parol evidence rule** states that if a contract is put in writing, the terms of the contract cannot be amended or altered by verbal testimony in court unless mistake or fraud in the writing of the contract is alleged. The **golden rule** is more of a rule of arguments before the court. It states that the jury cannot be asked to put itself in the place of the person who has been injured, or to render a verdict as if they or a member of their family were the injured party. In other words, an attorney cannot ask the jury to treat others as they would like to be treated. A **rape shield statute** is one that prevents a victim's past sexual conduct from being introduced into evidence. It prevents the victim's past sexual conduct from being used against her or him when he or she is testifying against a defendant.

CONCLUSION

Terms related to evidence come from federal or state rules of evidence as well as from common law regarding evidence. In order to be admitted into the record as evidence, information must be relevant to the issues before the court, and it must be material. The proper foundation for admission must be established. Evidence can be direct or circumstantial; that is, it can directly prove what is alleged, or it can prove what is alleged by inference. Evidence can create presumptions—facts that are presumed to exist—unless the other side overcomes those presumptions.

Evidence is used to help parties meet their burden of proof. The highest burden of proof is beyond a reasonable doubt; this is the burden in criminal cases. The lowest burden of proof is preponderance of the evidence.

Hearsay is an out-of-court statement offered to prove the truth of the matter asserted. The general rule is that hearsay is inadmissible into evidence because it is inherently unreliable. However, hearsay can be admitted into evidence if particular circumstances make the statements inherently more reliable. Exceptions to the hearsay rule include excited utterances, statements for medical diagnosis, business records, and dying declarations. Hearsay can also be used to show contradiction or consistency in a person's testimony.

The laws of evidence provide for protection of certain communications between classifications of people. Put another way, conversations between certain people are privileged, protected from disclosure. Such conversations occur between a husband and wife, a priest and penitent, or an attorney and his or her client.

KEY TERMS AND PHRASES

admissible evidence
admission by a
  party/opponent
attorney-client privilege
beyond a reasonable doubt
burden of going forward
burden of proof
business record exception
chain of custody
character evidence
circumstantial evidence
clear and convincing
competent evidence
competent witness
declarant
demonstrative evidence
direct evidence
doctor/patient privilege

dying declaration
evidence
excited utterance
golden rule
hearsay
husband/wife privilege
immaterial evidence
inadmissible evidence
inference
irrelevant evidence
material evidence
material witness
parol evidence
parol evidence rule
preponderance of the
  evidence
present sense impression
presumption

priest/penitent privilege
prima facie evidence
prior inconsistent statement
privileged communication
privileged evidence
probative evidence
proof
rape shield statute
rebuttal evidence
recorded recollection
relevant evidence
scintilla of evidence
standard of proof
state of mind exception
statements for medical
  diagnosis or treatment
tangible evidence
work product privilege

REVIEW QUESTIONS

SHORT ANSWER

1. What is meant by *burden of proof?*
2. What is the difference between direct evidence and circumstantial evidence?
3. What is hearsay?
4. What is the golden rule?
5. What is a rape shield statute?
6. For each of the following, state the elements of the hearsay exception.
   - Business records
   - Past recollection recorded
   - Excited utterance
   - Present sense impression
   - Prior inconsistent statement
   - Recorded recollection
   - Spontaneous exclamation
   - State of mind
   - Statement against interest
   - Statement for medical diagnosis
7. What is a privilege?

8. What is a scintilla of evidence?

9. What is the parol evidence rule?

10. What is the priest/penitent privilege? Who can claim the privilege?

11. What makes a witness a material witness?

FILL IN THE BLANK

1. Evidence given orally and under oath is _____ evidence.

2. A statement given by a person who believes death is imminent about how he or she was injured and identifying who is responsible for the injuries is the _____ exception to the hearsay rule.

3. Hearsay is _____ offered to prove _____.

4. A statement by a person about an event he or she witnessed made before he or she had the opportunity to think about what he or she saw is the _____ exception to the hearsay rule.

5. A reasonable certainty that the facts given are true is the _____ burden of proof.

6. _____ shifts the burden of proof.

7. An attorney cannot introduce _____ unless the defense puts the defendant's character into evidence.

8. A statement made by a person when he or she is shocked or surprised by an event is the _____ exception to the hearsay rule.

9. When the chain of custody of a piece of evidence in a criminal case is established in court, this is known as _____.

10. Evidence that requires a logical chain of events before a conclusion can be reached is _____.

FACT SITUATIONS

1. During a trial for rape, the defendant's attorney asks the victim about her past sexual conduct. Can the prosecution object? What, if anything, is the basis for the objection?

2. A wife is asked about her husband's criminal conduct. Can she refuse to answer? What can be the basis for her refusal?

3. Ivan thought he was dying and confessed to robbing several people. Can these statements be admitted into evidence? Why or why not?

4. While witnessing an accident, a person screams out several things. Another person is attempting to testify about what was said. What exception to the hearsay rule applies?

5. A man is talking to his doctor about his physical condition. Can the doctor testify about what he or she was told? If he or she can, is this an exception to the hearsay rule? If so, which one? Could someone else testify about what he or she heard the person say to the doctor? What exception, if any, would apply?

6. The prosecution calls someone to testify about the criminal background of the defendant. Can this be done? Why or why not? Under what circumstances, if any?

7. Wolfgang is called to testify about contract negotiations. He is only asked a couple of questions before he starts giving very long, detailed answers to general questions. What sort of testimony is Wolfgang giving?

8. During closing arguments, one of the attorneys asks the jury to put themselves in the place of the plaintiff when determining how much money in damages she should receive for her injuries. Is this allowed? Why or why not?

9. Richards is called to testify about business records in a trial. He establishes that these records are required to be kept every day, and that they are records of transactions. However, there is no record of the transaction that the plaintiff claims was made. What hearsay exception applies?

10. A detective is called to the stand to testify about an arrest she made a year ago. She took extensive notes when she made the arrest, and inserted those notes into a case file. She cannot remember all the details of the arrest and wants to look at her notes. Can she do this? Why or why not?

11. The prosecution attempts to get copies of the notes that Mario's attorney has made about his case for Mario's defense. What can Mario's attorney argue to keep the prosecution from seeing this information?

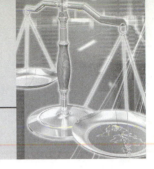

CHAPTER 8

Constitutional Law

INTRODUCTION

Any study of constitutional law is a study of the U.S. Constitution, its articles, its clauses, its amendments, and the cases interpreting those provisions. It is the law that is based on the interpretation of the U.S. Constitution, which is the supreme law of the land. It is also the law that is based on the interpretation of each state's constitution, which is that state's supreme law. This chapter provides an overview of constitutions and how the Supreme Court developed its power to determine if a law or a case complies with the U.S. Constitution. Constitutional officers and how they are selected are discussed. The chapter also deals with the enumerated and implied powers of the Constitution. Specific clauses of the Constitution—for example, the commerce clause, the full faith and credit clause, and the privileges and immunities clause—and their impact on the law are explored. Civil rights guaranteed by the Constitution are discussed, rights such as freedom of the press, religion, expression, and speech; due process, equal protection under the law, and the right to privacy are also addressed. Key amendments to the Constitution are the focus of the latter portion of the chapter.

OVERVIEW OF CONSTITUTIONAL LAW

A **constitution** (kon-sti-*too*-shun) is the fundamental law of a nation or a state. It may be written or unwritten. Constitutional law establishes the character and conception of a nation's or state's government; it establishes the basic principles to which its internal life is to conform. Constitutional law organizes government, regulating, distributing, and limiting the functions of its different departments and establishing the extent and manner of the exercise of power. A constitution is a charter of government that derives its entire authority from the people being governed.

AMENDING THE CONSTITUTION

The Constitution of the United States is over 200 years old and has been amended only twenty-six times. An **amendment** (a-*mend*-ment) is the changing or alteration of something for the better. Alteration may be made by means of modification, deletion, or addition. Amendments to a constitution are designed to modify the constitution, delete something from it, or make an addition to it. See Exhibit 8-1 for a summary of the amendments.

EXHIBIT 8-1	SUMMARY OF CONSTITUTIONAL AMENDMENTS
Amendments 1–10 – The Bill of Rights
Amendments 12, 17, 20, 22, 23, and 25 – Public office amendments
Amendments 15, 19, 24, and 26 – Voting rights amendments
Amendment 13 – Ended slavery
Amendment 18 – Established Prohibition
Amendment 20 – Repealed Prohibition
Amendment 16 – Gave Congress authority to create income tax

The first ten amendments to the U.S. Constitution are known collectively as the **Bill of Rights.** They provide for individual rights, freedoms, and protections. Six of the amendments deal with matters concerning public office: These are the Twelfth, Seventeenth, Twentieth, Twenty-Second, Twenty-Third, and Twenty-Fifth Amendments. Four of the amendments deal with the right to vote: the fifteenth gave former slaves the right to vote; the nineteenth gave women the right to vote; the twenty-fourth made poll taxes illegal; and the twenty-sixth lowered the voting age to 18. Four amendments—the thirteenth, the eighteenth, the sixteenth, and the twentieth—made changes that affected American society. The thirteenth ended slavery; the eighteenth established Prohibition (the declaring as illegal the making and selling of alcoholic beverages in the United States), and the twentieth repealed Prohibition. The Sixteenth Amendment is the least popular amendment: it gives Congress the authority to tax income.

Constitutional law is the area of law that deals with the organization, powers, and frame of government, the distribution of political and governmental authority and functions, and the fundamental principles that regulate the relationship between the government and citizens of a nation or state. Constitutional law deals with the interpretation of the U.S. Constitution and its amendments and whether other laws are in agreement.

CONSTITUTIONAL QUESTIONS

The U.S. Supreme Court becomes involved in constitutional law when a **constitutional question**—a legal issue that requires an interpretation of the Constitution for its resolution—is presented to it. A constitutional question asks: "Is the issue, deed, or act in question constitutional or unconstitutional?" If something is **constitutional** (kon-sti-*too*-shen-el), it is consistent with the Constitution, authorized by the Constitution, and does not conflict with any provision of the Constitution. If something is declared **unconstitutional** (un-kon-sti-*too*-shen-el), it is not consistent with the Constitution. It conflicts with one of the provisions and is therefore illegal.

JUDICIAL REVIEW

The principle of laws or actions being unconstitutional and the power of **judicial review**—the power of courts to review decisions of another department or level of government—are not articulated in the Constitution. These powers and principles were established by the Supreme Court in the case of *Marbury v. Madison.* See Sidebar 8-1.

SIDEBAR 8-1 *MARBURY V. MADISON*

Facts: William Marbury had been appointed Justice of the Peace by John Adams, the outgoing president. Thomas Jefferson, the newly elected president, told his Secretary of State, James Madison, not to deliver the commission to William Marbury. Marbury sued, using a federal law that stated that the U.S. Supreme Court could issue a writ of mandamus, a court order directing a government official to perform his official duties, in this case, a court order directing James Madison to deliver the judicial commission to William Marbury.

Ruling: The Court ruled that Mr. Marbury was entitled to receive the commission, and that a writ of mandamus was the proper remedy. However, the Supreme Court was not the Court to seek the mandamus from because the federal law that gave the Supreme Court the authority to issue the mandamus conflicted with the powers specifically granted to Congress and the Supreme Court by the U.S. Constitution. The Court wrote, "An act of the legislature repugnant to the constitution is void." The statute was unconstitutional because it violated provisions of the Constitution and was, therefore, illegal.

Source: United States Reports

CONSTITUTIONAL OFFICES AND OFFICERS

The U.S. Constitution establishes our system of national government by designating its offices and officers. A **constitutional office** is a public position or office that is created by the Constitution. For example, the Office of the President of the United States and seats in the Senate and the House of Representatives are constitutional offices. These offices are distinguished from a statutory office, which is an office created by the legislature. For example, the Equal Employment Opportunity Commission was created by legislation, so the Office of the Commissioner of the EEOC is a statutory office. A **constitutional officer** is a government official whose office was created by the U.S. Constitution or a state constitution, and whose tenure and term of office are fixed and defined by that constitution. For example, the President of the United States is a constitutional officer because the office was created by the U.S. Constitution and the term of office is fixed by the Constitution. See Exhibit 8-2.

EXHIBIT 8-2	CONSTITUTIONAL OFFICERS, SELECTION PROCESS, AND TERMS OF OFFICE

President of the United States – Elected by the Electoral College; each term is four years; limited to two terms in office or a maximum of ten years.

Representatives – Popularly elected; serve in the House of Representatives; each term is two years.

Senators – Popularly elected; serve in the Senate; each term is six years.

Supreme Court Justices – Nominated by the president and confirmed by the Senate; serve for life.

SELECTION OF CONSTITUTIONAL OFFICERS

The U.S. Constitution also sets out how certain constitutional officers are selected for office. Members of the House and Senate are elected by the voters in their home state. Members of the U.S. Supreme Court are appointed by the president, approved by the Senate, and serve for life. The president is selected using the electoral process and the Electoral College. The **electoral process** (ee-*lek*-tor-all) is a generic term for the method by which a person is elected to public office; for example, a person is elected by winning the popular vote. The **Electoral College** is a body of **electors** (ee-*lek*-tors), selected from each state, who cast their state's electoral votes to elect the president and vice president. The term *electoral college* also refers to the whole body of such electors, the people who actually vote for president. Exhibit 8-3 shows the number of electors from each state.

EXHIBIT 8-3	THE ELECTORAL COLLEGE

STATE

State		State		State	
Alabama	9	Georgia	13	Maryland	10
Alaska	3	Hawaii	4	Massachusetts	12
Arizona	8	Idaho	4	Michigan	18
Arkansas	6	Illinois	22	Minnesota	10
California	54	Indiana	12	Mississippi	7
Colorado	8	Iowa	7	Missouri	11
Connecticut	8	Kansas	6	Montana	3
Delaware	3	Kentucky	8	Nebraska	5
D.C.	3	Louisiana	9	Nevada	4
Florida	25	Maine	4	New Hampshire	4

Continued

Continued

New Jersey	15	Oregon	7	Utah	5
New Mexico	5	Pennsylvania	23	Vermont	3
New York	33	Rhode Island	4	Virginia	13
North Carolina	14	South Carolina	8	Washington	11
North Dakota	3	South Dakota	3	West Virginia	5
Ohio	21	Tennessee	11	Wisconsin	11
Oklahoma	8	Texas	32	Wyoming	3

Total electoral votes: 538

Electoral votes required to win the presidency: 270

Each state has one electoral vote for every member of the House of Representatives and the Senate from that state.

CONSTITUTIONAL POWERS

The Constitution grants power to the different branches of government and also limits that power. The distribution of power among the three branches of the federal government and state governments is based on the doctrine of **separation of powers** (sep-ə-*ray*-shun ov *pow*-erz). One branch is not allowed to assume the powers of any of the other branches. The legislative branch is given the power to make laws, the executive branch is given the power to carry out laws, and the judicial branch is given the power to interpret laws.

Congress, the president, and the Supreme Court are granted specific powers by the Constitution. These are known as **enumerated powers** (e-*nyoo*-mə-ray-ted) powers. See Exhibit 8-4 for a summary of these powers.

EXHIBIT 8-4	SUMMARY OF THE ENUMERATED POWERS

CONGRESS	PRESIDENT	SUPREME COURT
Set taxes	Commander in Chief	Highest court in the land
Borrow money	Make treaties	
Regulate interstate commerce	Appoint ambassadors	
Establish rules for naturalization	Appoint federal officers	
Establish rules for bankruptcy	Appoint federal judges	
Coin money	Appoint Supreme Court justices	
Set punishment for counterfeiting	Fill vacancies in the Senate	
Establish post offices	Deliver State of the Union address	
Establish post roads	Recommend laws to Congress	
Create patents	Approve laws passed by Congress	
Create inferior federal courts		
Punish piracy		
Declare war		
Raise and support armies		
Provide and maintain a navy		
Establish rules and regulations for the military		
Call the militia into action		
Govern Washington, D.C.		

ENUMERATED POWERS OF CONGRESS

The enumerated powers of Congress are listed in Article I, Section 8 of the Constitution. They are:

1. To set and collect taxes, duties, imposts and excises, to pay the debts of, and to provide for the common defense of the United States.
2. To borrow money.
3. To regulate commerce with foreign nations, states, and Indian tribes.
4. To establish rules of naturalization and bankruptcy.
5. To coin money, set its value, and fix standard weights and measures.
6. To provide for the punishment of counterfeiting.
7. To establish post offices and post roads.
8. To create patents.
9. To create courts inferior to the Supreme Court.
10. To punish piracy and felonies committed at sea.
11. To declare war and grant letters of marquee and reprisal.
12. To raise and support armies.
13. To provide and maintain a navy.
14. To make rules for the regulation of the armed forces.
15. To call the militia (the National Guard) to enforce the laws of the United States, to put down rebellions, and to repel invasions.
16. To provide for the organizing, arming, and disciplining of the militia (the National Guard).
17. To govern the area now known as Washington, D.C.

Article I, Section 8, Clause 18 is the **necessary and proper clause** of the Constitution; the term necessary and proper means "appropriate and adapted to carrying into effect a given objective." This clause authorizes Congress to make all laws necessary and proper to carry out the enumerated powers of Congress and all other powers vested in the government of the United States. According to *Julliard v. Greenman,* the powers that are necessary and proper are not limited to just the powers that are absolutely and indispensably necessary without which the enumerated powers cannot be carried out. They also include all appropriate means that are necessary to accomplish the purpose and that, in the judgment of Congress, will most advantageously effect it. According to *Kinsella v. United States,* the clause is not a grant of power but a declaration that Congress possesses all of the means necessary to carry out its specifically granted powers.

ENUMERATED POWERS OF THE PRESIDENT AND THE SUPREME COURT

The enumerated powers of the Presidency are the following.

1. To serve as the Commander in Chief of the armed forces and the state militias if they are called into federal service.
2. To make treaties, appoint ambassadors, appoint people to federal offices, and nominate justices to the Supreme Court, all with the advice and consent of the Senate.
3. To fill vacancies in the Senate.
4. To deliver a State of the Union address to Congress.
5. To recommend laws to Congress.
6. To approve laws passed by Congress.

The U.S. Supreme Court does not have any enumerated powers other than the declaration that it is the highest court in the country; all of its other powers have come from its decisions.

IMPLIED POWERS

The different branches of the federal government also have **implied powers**—that are not granted in express terms, but exist because they are necessary and proper to carry into effect some expressly granted power. This doctrine was articulated by the Supreme Court in the case of *McCulloch v. Maryland.* See Sidebar 8-2.

SIDEBAR 8-2 *MCCULLOCH V. MARYLAND*

Facts: Congress had created a national bank, the Bank of the United States, and the state of Maryland imposed a tax on the national bank. McCulloch was a clerk in the bank who refused to pay the tax. McCulloch was charged with failing to pay the tax and the case wound up in the Supreme Court.

Issues: There were two questions presented to the Court: Did Congress have the authority to establish the bank? and Did Maryland have the authority to interfere with congressional powers?

Ruling: The Court ruled that Congress's power was not limited to the enumerated powers. Instead, Congress possessed unenumerated powers not explicitly outlined in the Constitution. Put more simply, there are implied powers.

The Court also said, according to the Supremacy Clause, that the State of Maryland could not legally tax an entity of the United States government, in this case the Bank of the United States.

Source: United States Reports

Implied powers also come from another source besides the enumerated powers. The Supreme Court stated in the case of *Kohl v. United States* that the implied powers of the federal government, based on the Necessary and Proper Clause, permit one implied power to be combined with another implied power to create a third implied power. The ability to combine implied powers to create another implied power is known as the **penumbra** (pe-*num*-bra) **doctrine.**

EXAMPLES OF IMPLIED POWERS

One example of an implied power is the **police power** of the federal government. This is the power of a state or the federal government to take all necessary steps to protect the health, safety, and welfare of its citizens. This principle was first announced in the case of *New York v. Miln.* A state law required all vessels docking in New York City to provide a list of passengers and to post security against the passengers from becoming a public burden. Miln, who was the master of a ship, refused to comply with the law. The law was challenged on the basis that it violated the commerce clause (see below), but that issue was ignored. The Court applied what became known as "police power": the right of a sovereign to take whatever steps are necessary to protect the health, safety, and welfare of its citizens.

POWER OF FEDERAL LAW OVER STATE LAW

Sometimes a state government and the federal government pass conflicting laws dealing with the same subject matter. Certain constitutional provisions and principles apply if such a conflict exists.

SUPREMACY CLAUSE

If a state law conflicts with a federal law, then the **supremacy clause** (soo-*prem*-ə-see klawz), Article VI, Clause 2, applies. This clause states that all laws that are created because of the Constitution and the powers it grants, and all treaties entered into under the authority of the United States, shall be the supreme law of the land. In other words, laws passed by the federal government are legally superior over any part of state law that conflicts with the federal law. The case of *McCulloch v. Maryland* also reinforced the principle that the Constitution is the supreme law of the land. According to the supremacy clause, the state of Maryland could not legally tax an entity of the United States government, in this case the Bank of the United States.

PREEMPTION DOCTRINE

Because of the supremacy clause language, the **preemption** (pree-*emp*-shən) **doctrine** was adopted by the Supreme Court. This doctrine states that certain matters are of such national importance compared to state or local laws that federal laws will take precedent over any other. In other words, a state may not pass or enforce a law that conflicts with federal law. Even if the state passed a law in an area first, if there is subsequent federal law, the state law that conflicts with the federal law is preempted, or done away with. When the Constitution and acts of Congress give to the federal government exclusive power over certain matters, then the states may not pass or have any law governing that area; this is referred to as **federal preemption.** For example, the regulation of interstate commerce is a power given to Congress by the Constitution. Because of the commerce clause, no state can pass a law that attempts to regulate or that places an undue burden on interstate commerce. The states are prohibited from regulating interstate commerce because of the preemption doctrine.

COOLEY DOCTRINE

The **Cooley** (*kool*-ee) **doctrine,** which was established by the case of *Cooley v. Board of Wardens,* is another limitation on the power of states because of the supremacy clause. Pennsylvania state law required that ships entering or leaving the port of Philadelphia hire a local pilot; if not, the ship's owner would be fined. Cooley was a ship owner who refused to hire a local pilot and refused to pay the fine. He challenged the constitutionality of the law, saying that this was an area to be regulated by Congress—not the states. The Cooley doctrine states that a state is deprived of all regulatory power in certain areas if there is a national interest or there is a need for one uniform system or plan of regulation. The court ruled that pilotage of the ships in and out of the port demanded local rules to cope with varying local conditions. In other words, there was no national interest at stake, so there was no need for uniform regulation. See Exhibit 8-5 for a summary of these different principles.

EXHIBIT 8-5	WHY FEDERAL LAW IS SUPREME OVER STATE LAW

1. **Supremacy Clause** – Article IV, Clause 2: All laws that are created because of the Constitution and the power it grants, e.g., laws passed by Congress, are legally superior to any state law that is in conflict.

2. **Preemption Doctrine** – Certain issues and matters are so important on a national scale that federal law is superior to any state law. If a state passes a law that conflicts with a federal law, the state law is done away with. Also, if the federal government passes laws in a particular area, the states are prohibited from passing any laws in said area.

3. **Cooley Doctrine** – A state is deprived of all regulatory power in certain areas if there is a national interest at issue or if there is a need for one uniform system or plan of regulation.

LIMITATIONS ON POWERS

The Constitution not only grants power, but provides limitations on power given to government. **Constitutional limitations** are the provisions of the Constitution, specifically Article I, Section 9, that limit or restrict the legislature in the types of laws that it may enact. According to Article I, Section 9, Congress cannot:

1. Suspend the right to a writ of habeas corpus
2. Pass bills of attainder or ex post facto laws
3. Place taxes or duties on articles exported from a state
4. Withdraw money from the treasury without an appropriation
5. Grant titles of nobility in the name of the United States

COMMERCE CLAUSE

Perhaps the clause that gives Congress the most power is the **commerce clause** (*kom*-erss klawz), which states "Congress shall have the power to regulate commerce with foreign nations, and among the several states, and with the Indian Tribes." This clause grants Congress the power to regulate anything that affects interstate commerce.

COMMERCE

Commerce is the exchange of goods, productions, or property of any kind; the buying, selling, and exchanging of articles. The term **affecting commerce** applies to any activity that touches or concerns business or industry either favorably or by being burdensome, or obstructing commerce or the free flow of commerce. Commerce with foreign nations is commerce between citizens of the United States and citizens or governments of another nation. Congress's power to regulate this type of commerce applies to every type of commercial transaction between the United States and citizens and governments of other nations. Commerce with Indian tribes is commerce with a tribe as an entity or with individuals belonging to an Indian tribe. See Exhibit 8-6.

EXHIBIT 8-6	THE COMMERCE CLAUSE DEFINED

Congress has the authority to regulate

1. **Commerce** – The exchange of goods, productions, or property of any kind; the buying, selling, and exchanging of articles.
2. **With Foreign Nations** – Commerce between citizens of the United States and citizens or governments of other nations.
3. **Indian Tribes** – Commerce with the tribe itself or with individuals belonging to an Indian tribe.
4. **Between the states** – Interstate commerce; commerce between or among the states of the union or between points in one state and points in another state.

INTRASTATE OR INTERSTATE COMMERCE

Intrastate commerce (*in*-tra-state *kom*-erz) is commerce that is carried on between the different states of the union within the limits of a single state; that is, the commercial transaction is carried out entirely in one state. Congress has no power to regulate commerce that is entirely intrastate. **Interstate commerce** (*in*-ter-state *kom*-erz) is the commercial trading or the transportation of persons or property between or among the several states of the union, or from or between points in one state and points in another state. Interstate commerce was first defined in the case of *Gibbons v. Ogden.* New York state law gave two people the exclusive right to operate steamboats on waters within the state. If someone from out of state wanted to operate a steamboat on New York state waters, he would have to obtain an operating permit from the state of New York. The validity of this law was challenged, the allegation being that it violated the interstate commerce clause. The court ruled that the law did violate the interstate commerce clause, and that Congress had the authority to regulate the navigation of waters between the states.

BALANCING OF INTERESTS

Sometimes the states and Congress will have common interests with regard to commerce and are called upon to interact with each other. If a dispute arises, the doctrine of the balancing of interests is used. **Balancing of interests** is used by the Court when it examines the interplay between state actions involving intrastate commerce and federal laws regarding interstate commerce. If there is a legitimate state interest and no clear congressional intent to preempt the field, the state action will be upheld. The case of *Southern Pacific Company v. Arizona ex rel. Sullivan* illustrates this position. Arizona had passed a law that limited the operation of trains that had more than 14 passenger cars or more than 70 freight cars. If the train exceeded those numbers, it would have to stop at the Arizona border and another train would have to be brought in to pull the extra cars. The state argued that this was a safety measure. The Court rejected this argument, saying the use of more trains would produce more accidents and would result in additional costs of several million dollars a year. Arizona's argument failed the balancing test; the negative impact the Arizona law had on interstate commerce outweighed any safety concerns of the state.

FULL FAITH AND CREDIT/PRIVILEGES AND IMMUNITIES

The framers of the Constitution wanted to ensure that the national government and each state recognized the laws of other states. The framers also wanted to ensure that a visitor to another state would be given the same rights and privileges as the citizens of that state. Thus, a person who was a citizen of New York state who visited Pennsylvania would be treated the same as a citizen of Pennsylvania.

FULL FAITH AND CREDIT CLAUSE

The **full faith and credit clause,** Article IV, Section 1 states: "Full faith and credit shall be given in each state to the public acts, records and judicial proceedings of every other state." This means that the states are required to recognize the legislation, public records, and judicial decisions of other states in the United States as being valid.

FAUNTLEROY DOCTRINE

There are situations where one of the parties will attempt to challenge the validity of a court decision from one state in another state's court: "Do not give this judgment full faith and credit because of these reasons . . ." That was the situation in *Fauntleroy v. Lum,* the decision that created the **Fauntleroy doctrine.** See Exhibit 8-7. Fauntleroy was attempting to enforce a judgment from a Missouri court in Mississippi. Lum challenged a court order from Missouri, saying it violated Mississippi law and that Mississippi would not enter a judgment like the one entered by Missouri. The Court rejected this argument, saying that

Mississippi had to give full faith and credit to the judgment from Missouri. According to the Fauntleroy doctrine, a state must give full faith and credit to a judgment of a sister state if the state had jurisdiction to render it even though the judgment is based on a cause of action that is illegal in the state in which enforcement is brought.

EXHIBIT 8-7	FAUNTLEROY DOCTRINE

Established in *Fauntleroy v. Lum*

A state must give full faith and credit, recognize as valid, a judgment from another state even if the judgment comes from a cause of action that does not exist or is illegal in the state where enforcement of the judgment is sought.

PRIVILEGES AND IMMUNITIES CLAUSE

The **privileges and immunities clause** (*priv*-i-lej and im-*yoon*-i-teez klawz), Article IV, Section 2 states: " The citizens of each state shall be entitled to all privileges and immunities of citizens in several states." The purpose of this clause is to place the citizens of each state on the same footing as citizens of other states. The privileges and immunities clause provides that the advantages that result from being a citizen of a state extend to everyone who enters the state.

INDIVIDUAL RIGHTS

GENERAL PRINCIPLES

The Constitution also provides for the protection of certain civil and political rights described as **inalienable** (in-*ail*-en-able). These rights cannot be surrendered or transferred without the consent of the person possessing the rights. In other words, certain rights are so fundamental that the only way a person can be deprived of them is if that person agrees to their being taken away. **Civil rights** are those that belong to every citizen of a state or country. These include the rights of property, marriage, equal protection, freedom of contract, and trial by jury. **Political rights** grant power to participate directly or indirectly in the establishment or administration of government: the right to vote, the right to hold political office, and the right of petition. See Exhibit 8-8 for a summary of these rights.

EXHIBIT 8-8	CLASSIFICATIONS OF INDIVIDUAL RIGHTS

I. Inalienable Rights – Right of paramount importance: the only way they can be taken away from a person is if the person agrees to have them taken away.
   1. Freedom of speech
   2. Freedom of religion
   3. Freedom of association
   4. Due process of law

II. Civil Rights – Rights belonging to every citizen of the state and the United States.
   1. Property
   2. Marriage
   3. Equal protection
   4. Freedom of contract
   5. Trial by jury

III. Political Rights – The right to participate either directly or indirectly in the establishment or administration of government.

1. Right to vote
2. Right to hold office
3. Right of petition

These rights receive constitutional protection. **Constitutional protection** guarantees rights such as due process, equal protection under the law, and the fundamental provisions of the First Amendment—freedom of speech, press, and religion. A **constitutional liberty** or **freedom** is a freedom enjoyed by the citizens of a country or state that is protected by the Constitution.

FREEDOM OF CONTRACT

Freedom of contract is a basic right reserved to the people by Article I, Section 10 of the Constitution that a state cannot violate, even under sanction of a direct legislative act. The specific limitation is on the impairing of the obligation of contracts. The Constitution prohibits any law that is designed to weaken a contract, lessen its value, or impair it in any respect or to any degree. Any law that changes the intention and legal effect of the parties, giving to one a greater and to the other a lesser interest or benefit, or that imposes conditions not included in the contract, dispenses with the performance of a condition, or impairs the obligation of the contract is considered illegal and void. Something that nullifies or materially changes existing contract obligations is allowed to remain valid.

FIRST AMENDMENT RIGHTS

The Bill of Rights provides constitutional protection for many of the civil and political rights that are enjoyed in the United States. The **First Amendment** guarantees the basic freedoms of speech, religion, press, and assembly, as well as the right to petition the government for the redress of grievances. See Exhibit 8-9.

EXHIBIT 8-9	FIRST AMENDMENT RIGHTS

1. **Freedom of association –** the freedom to peacably assemble
2. **Freedom of expression –** freedom of speech, religion, and press
3. **Freedom of press –** the right to publish and distribute one's thoughts and views without governmental restriction
4. **Freedom of religion –** the freedom to individually believe and to practice or exercise one's belief. Civil authorities may not intervene in the affairs of a church. A church may not exercise its authority through the state.
5. **Freedom of speech –** the right to express one's thoughts and views without governmental restriction

These rights are protected, but that does not mean that government cannot or does not have the ability to limit them. In determining if the limitation is permissible, the balancing test is used. The **balancing test** is the doctrine by which the Court weighs the constitutionally protected rights of the individual against the rights of the state to protect all of its citizens from the invasion of their rights. This doctrine is used primarily in cases involving freedom of speech and equal protection.

FREEDOM OF SPEECH

Some of the limitations that are placed on speech derive from the fighting words doctrine, the clear and present danger doctrine, and from laws regarding obscene materials. The **fighting words doctrine** is a First Amendment doctrine that declares that certain utterances—statements—are not constitutionally protected as free speech if they are inherently likely to provoke a violent response from the audience. This doctrine was established in the case of *NAACP v. Clairborne Hardware Co., Mississippi.* In 1966, the local chapter of the NAACP organized a boycott of white-operated businesses until certain demands to end discrimination were met. Local businesses sued for earnings that were lost from 1966 to 1972. One of their bases for liability was that Charles Evers, the secretary of the NAACP, had given speeches that threatened violence if blacks did not comply with the boycott. The Court stated that fighting words, words that promote immediate violence, are not protected by the First Amendment. However, Mr. Evers's words were not fighting words, so his speech was protected by the First Amendment: he could not be held liable for the harm suffered by the businesses because he was exercising his First Amendment rights.

The **clear and present danger doctrine** was created by *Schenk v. United States.* It states that governmental restrictions on First Amendment freedoms of speech and press will be upheld if necessary to prevent grave and immediate danger to interests that government may lawfully protect. During World War I, Schenk was mailing circulars to men who had been drafted suggesting that the draft was a "monstrous wrong motivated by the capitalist system." Schenk advised only peaceful action, such as petitioning to repeal the Conscription Act. In this situation, the Court declared that Schenk's speech was not protected. Whether or not speech violates the clear and present danger doctrine is determined on a case-by-case basis. "The question in every case is whether the words used are used in such circumstances and are of such a nature as to create a clear and present danger that will bring about the substantive evils that Congress has the right to prevent" (*Schenk v. United States*). During times of war, speech that would be tolerable in peacetime can be punished because of the circumstances.

CENSORSHIP

One area of free speech that is looked at narrowly by the Court is the area of censorship. **Censorship** (*sen*-sor-ship), is the actual review of publications, movies, and plays for the purpose of prohibiting the publication, distribution, or production of material that is objectionable because it is considered obscene, indecent, or immoral. The **censor** (*sen*-sor) is a person who examines publications—books, magazines, films, and the like—for objectionable material or content. Historically the Court has been very protective of free speech and has not favored censorship.

One form of censorship is prior restraint. **Prior restraint** (*pry*-er re-*straynt*) is a method used by public officials to deny or restrain the use of a particular forum to state something before it can be stated. In the case of *Near v. Minnesota,* Jay Near published a "scandal sheet" in which he attacked local officials, saying they were associated with gangsters. The state of Minnesota used a state law to enjoin, or stop, the publication of the newspaper. The Supreme Court ruled that the First Amendment prohibits the imposition of a restraint on a publication before it is published. Any system of prior restraints of expression bears a heavy presumption against its constitutional validity, and the government carries a heavy burden of showing justification for impositions of such a restraint. There are three exceptions: publications creating a clear and present danger to the country, obscene publications, and publications that invade the zone of personal privacy. None of these exceptions applied in this case.

Another example of an attempted use of prior restraint is *New York Times v. United States,* also known as the Pentagon Papers case. The administration of President Richard Nixon attempted to prevent the *New York Times* and the *Washington Post* from publishing materials belonging to a classified Defense Department study regarding U.S. involvement in Vietnam. Nixon argued that prior restraint was necessary to protect the national security. The Court ruled that the government did not overcome the heavy presumption against prior restraint because it was not shown how the release of this information would jeopardize national security.

OBSCENE MATERIALS

If published material is considered to be obscene, it is not protected speech under the First Amendment. However, what is considered obscene material is another area that is highly debated. Are pictures and movies of people engaged in sexual activity obscene materials? Are publications like *Playboy, Playgirl,* or *Penthouse* obscene? What about paintings of people in the nude, or photographs of violent activity? Something is considered **obscene** (ob-*seen*) if it is objectionable or offensive to accepted standards of decency, and it tends to corrupt the public morals by its indecency or lewdness. As a result of the ambiguity inherent in the definition of *obscene,* what is considered obscene in one area of the country may not be considered obscene in another.

MILLER V. CALIFORNIA TEST FOR OBSCENITY

The current test used to determine if a work is obscene, particularly a work that describes or depicts sexual conduct, was created by the Court in *Miller v. California.* Miller conducted a mass mailing advertising the sale of "adult material." Some of the people who received this mailing complained to the police and Miller was convicted of distributing obscene material. He challenged his conviction, arguing that what he sent out was protected by the First Amendment. However, the Supreme Court ruled that material that is considered to be obscene is not entitled to First Amendment protection. The Court indicated that to determine if something is obscene, the trier of fact must determine:

1. If, after applying contemporary community standards, a reasonable person would find that the work, taken as a whole, appeals to prurient interest, or
2. Whether the work depicts or describes in a patently offensive way sexual conduct specifically defined by the applicable state statute, or
3. Whether the work taken as a whole lacks serious literary, artistic, political, or scientific value.

Contemporary community standards are defined as those held by reasonable people: Would reasonable people find any literary, political, or scientific value in the material under discussion when it is considered as a whole? Note that the test is not whether a *part* of the material may be obscene; the proper standard is that the material as a *whole* is obscene. **Prurient** (pru-ee-ent) **interest**, another one of the criteria of obscenity listed in *Miller v. California,* is defined in *Brockett v. Spokane Arcades, Inc.* as a shameful or morbid interest in nudity, sex, or excretion. In order for material to be considered obscene, the **dominant theme**—the prevailing, governing, influencing or controlling idea of the material, *when taken as a whole*—appeals to a prurient interest in sex. See Exhibit 8-10 for a summary of the test for obscenity.

EXHIBIT 8-10	WHEN IS SOMETHING OBSCENE?

1. The work **violates contemporary community standards** by appealing to a person's prurient interest.
2. The work depicts sexual conduct in a **patently offensive way.**
3. The entire works **lacks serious literary, political, or scientific value.**
4. The **dominant theme** of the work appeals to prurient interest.

Two cases that applied this standard were *Jenkins v. Georgia* and *Barnes v. Glen Theatre, Inc.* In *Jenkins v. Georgia,* Jenkins, a theatre manager, was convicted under the Georgia obscenity law when he showed *Carnal Knowledge,* a critically acclaimed film starring Jack Nicholson and Ann-Margret. The Court stated that the Georgia statute prohibited only "hard core sexual conduct." Because the movie did not contain any such scenes, it was not obscene and was entitled to First Amendment protection. The conviction was overturned.

In *Barnes v. Glen Theatre, Inc.,* Glen Theatre and the Kitty Kat Lounge in Indiana operated clubs featuring totally nude dancers. Indiana law required dancers to wear pasties and a G-string when performing. The owners of the club sued to stop the enforcement of the law. The Supreme Court ruled that, even though nude dancing is a form of expressive activity, the public indecency statute was justified because of the substantial government interest in protecting order and morality.

PANDERING

Pandering is another type of speech that is considered obscene and is not entitled to First Amendment protection. To **pander** (*pan*-der) is to cater to the gratification of the lust of another. The **pandering of obscenity,** as defined in *Ginzburg v. United States,* is the business of purveying textual, pictorial, or graphic matter openly advertised to appeal to the prurient interest of customers or potential customers by either blatant and explicit advertising or subtle and sophisticated advertising. Such conduct is not protected by the First Amendment. Ginzburg was convicted of violating a federal obscenity statute when he sent advertisements through the mail about how and where three different obscene publications could be obtained. He challenged his conviction, stating that the advertisements themselves were not obscene and, therefore, protected. The Court upheld the conviction because the sole emphasis of the advertising was for material that had prurient appeal. This was a "pornographic" communication that lay beyond the protection of the First Amendment.

FREEDOM OF THE PRESS

As indicated earlier, **freedom of the press**—the right to publish and distribute one's thoughts and views without governmental restriction—is protected by the First Amendment and by the Supreme Court. An example of how freedom of the press has been protected is found in the area of libel, in *New York Times v. Sullivan.* The *New York Times* had run a full-page ad alleging that the arrest of Martin Luther King, Jr., in Alabama was part of a campaign to destroy King's efforts to integrate public schools and encouraging blacks to register to vote. L. B. Sullivan, the city commissioner of Montgomery, Alabama, filed suit against the *Times,* alleging libel and defamation. The court ruled that because Sullivan was a public figure, the publication of all facts—even false ones—are protected by the Constitution unless there is actual malice involved.

FREEDOM OF RELIGION

The First Amendment also provides for freedom of religion: "Congress shall make no law respecting an establishment of religion, or prohibiting the free exercise thereof." According to *Everson v. Board of Education,* this language, known as the **establishment clause,** prohibits a state or the federal government from any of the following.

1. Setting up a church.
2. Passing laws that aid one or all religions.
3. Giving preference to one religion.
4. Forcing belief or disbelief in any religion.

The following two cases are examples of how the establishment clause has been applied to different situations.

In *Lynch v. Donnelly,* the city of Pawtucket, Rhode Island, annually erected a Christmas display located in the city's shopping district. It included a Santa Claus, a Christmas tree, and a nativity scene. Donnelly sued Lynch, the mayor of Pawtucket. The Court ruled that the display did not violate the establishment clause because it was not designed to advocate a particular religious message. The display merely depicted the historical origin of the holiday. In *Engel v. Vitale,* the Board of Regents for the State of New York authorized a short, voluntary prayer to be said at the beginning of each school day. The Court ruled that neither the nondenominational character nor the voluntariness of the prayer saved the practice from being unconstitutional. In other words, by providing the prayer, the state of New York was officially approving religion.

In the case of *Lemon v. Kurtzman,* the Court announced the **Lemon test,** which is used to determine if state action violates the establishment clause of the First Amendment. The three parts to this test follow.

1. Do the principal effects of the action neither inhibit nor advance religion?
2. Does the action have a neutral impact on religion?
3. Does the act not foster "excessive government entanglement with religion"? (See Exhibit 8-11.)

EXHIBIT 8-11	THE LEMON TEST

If *any* of these provisions is violated, the action *violates* separation of church and state.

1. The activity neither inhibits nor advances a religion.
2. The activity has a neutral impact on religion.
3. The activity does not create excessive government entanglement with religion.

If the action at issue violates any one of the elements of the Lemon test, there is a violation of the establishment clause.

For example, the case of *Edwards v. Aguilard* dealt with a Louisiana law that prohibited the teaching of the theory of evolution in public schools unless creation science was also taught. (Creation science is the belief that advanced forms of life appeared suddenly on Earth.) The Court ruled that this statute failed all three parts of the Lemon test: its purpose was not clearly secular; its primary effect was to advance the viewpoint that a supernatural being created mankind, which is the doctrine of certain religions; and the law entangled the interests of church and state.

DUE PROCESS OF LAW AND EQUAL PROTECTION

Perhaps the two most important clauses for the protection of individual rights and liberties are the principles of due process of law and equal protection of the law. **Due process of law** is the regular course of the administration of law through courts of justice. It is a course of legal proceedings according to the rules and principles that have been established in our legal system for the enforcement and protection of private rights.

DUE PROCESS CLAUSES

Two **due process clauses** are delineated in the Constitution. The first clause is contained in the Fifth Amendment and states: "No person shall . . . be deprived of life, liberty, or property without due process of law." The Fifth Amendment only applies to actions of the federal government. The **Fourteenth Amendment,** which states ". . . nor shall any State deprive any person of life, liberty, or property without due process of law," protects a person against state actions. There are two aspects to due process: procedural (a person is guaranteed fair proceedings) and substantive (a person is protected against unfair government interference or the taking of his or her life, liberty, or property). **Due process rights** are those so fundamentally important that they require compliance with due process standards of fairness and justice. They include procedural and substantive rights of citizens against government actions that may cause the denial of life, liberty, or property. **Procedural due process** (pro-*see*-jur-al dew *pro*-sess) is the guarantee of procedural fairness derived from the Fifth and Fourteenth Amendment due process clauses. The right to procedural due process applies when it is shown that there has been a deprivation of a significant life, liberty, or property interest as established in the case of *Cooley v. Board of Wardens.* The procedure that is used to deprive someone of a significant life, liberty, or property interest must be fair—a person's rights may not be violated. For example, in a case where a person has received the death penalty, the criminal process that led to that result must have protected the rights of the accused.

Substantive due process (*sub*-stan-tiv dew *pro*-sess) is a second doctrine that originates from the due process clauses of the Fifth and Fourteenth Amendments. Substantive due process requires legislation—the law itself—to be fair and reasonable in its content as well as how it is applied. Law must not be discriminatory in its content and it cannot be applied in a discriminatory manner.

EQUAL PROTECTION CLAUSE

The only **equal protection clause** in the Constitution is contained in the Fourteenth Amendment. This clause states that no state shall deny to any person within its jurisdiction the equal protection of the law. The term **equal protection of the law** means that no person or class of person can be denied the same protection of the law enjoyed by other persons or other classes in like circumstances in their lives, liberty, and property. The equal protection doctrine means that similarly situated people must receive similar treatment under the law. Exhibit 8-12 summarizes these two principles of law.

EXHIBIT 8-12	DUE PROCESS AND EQUAL PROTECTION

Due Process Clauses – The Fifth Amendment applies to the federal government; the Fourteenth Amendment applies to state government. A person cannot be denied life, liberty, or property without due process of law.

Substantive Due Process – The law itself must be fair and must apply to all people the same way.

Procedural Due Process – The process used to determine if someone is to be denied life, liberty, or property must be fair.

Equal Protection Clause – Laws and actions by government must be applied to people in the same way.

RIGHT TO PRIVACY

A right that is not found in any specific guarantee of the Constitution is the right to privacy. The Supreme Court, however, has recognized that some zones of privacy may be created by more specific constitutional guarantees, thereby imposing limits on governmental power.

CREATION OF THE RIGHT TO PRIVACY

The **right to privacy** is interpreted as the right to be left alone, to be free from unwarranted publicity, and to live without unwarranted interference by the public in matters with which the public is not necessarily concerned. This doctrine was first articulated in the case of *Griswold v. Connecticut.* Griswold was the Executive Director of the Planned Parenthood League of Connecticut. She gave information, instruction, and other medical advice to married couples about birth control. She was convicted under a Connecticut statute that prohibited the provision of counseling and other medical treatment to married persons for purposes of preventing pregnancies. The Court stated that even though the Constitution does not explicitly protect a general right to privacy, the various guarantees within the Bill of Rights create zones of privacy. The First, Third, Fourth, and Ninth Amendments create the constitutional right to privacy in marital relations. The Connecticut statute conflicted with the exercise of this right and was therefore null and void.

ROE V. WADE

The right to privacy serves as the basis for other rights not expressly granted by the Constitution. For example, this right has been extended to include a woman's right to an abortion. In the case of *Roe v. Wade,* Roe, a Texas resident, wanted to terminate her pregnancy by abortion. Texas only allowed abortions if the mother's life was in danger. The Court ruled that a woman's right to an abortion falls within the right to privacy recognized by *Griswold v. Connecticut* and is protected by the Fourteenth Amendment. It further declared that the state cannot interfere with this right during the first trimester of the pregnancy, and can only become involved in the second and third trimester. *Roe v. Wade* remains one of the most controversial Supreme Court decisions.

OTHER PROVISIONS OF THE CONSTITUTION

Other provisions of the Constitution cover treason, selection of public officials, the length of service for public officials, and other protections of citizens of the United States.

TREASON

The Constitution contains provisions regarding the rights of people who are accused of crimes, but does not specify what actions are crimes. **Treason** (*tree*-son) is the only crime defined by the Constitution. According to Article III, Section 3, treason is the levying of war against the United States or the giving of aid and comfort to enemies of the United States. **Aid and comfort** is a term used to refer to any assistance, counsel, or encouragement to an enemy of the United States. The aid does not have to be successful; simply attempting to provide aid and comfort may be enough to establish this standard under the definition of treason.

SECOND AND THIRD AMENDMENTS

The **Second Amendment** to the Constitution is the amendment that people use to argue that they have a right to bear arms. What the amendment actually says is: "A well-regulated **militia** [a body of citizens in a state enrolled as a military force that is not engaged in actual service except in emergencies] being necessary to the security of a free State, the right of the people to keep and bear arms shall not be infringed." There is a great deal of debate over the meaning of this amendment. Does it mean that only a person in the militia has the right to bear arms? Or, does a citizen have a right to bear arms even if he or she is not in the militia? The **Third Amendment** prohibits the government from forcing private citizens to allow soldiers to live with them in times of peace. In the times of war, soldiers can be quartered in private homes only if it is allowed by law and under the conditions set out in the law.

FOURTH, FIFTH, SIXTH, AND EIGHTH AMENDMENTS

The **Fourth Amendment** states that people shall be free from unreasonable searches and seizures, and that search warrants can only be issued if there is probable cause supported by oath or affirmation. The warrant must also describe the place to be searched and the items to be seized. The **Fifth Amendment** states that, in federal criminal cases, there has to be a grand jury indictment unless the case involves the military or militia. This amendment also prevents double jeopardy, states that a person cannot be compelled to testify against himself or herself in a criminal matter, states that a person cannot be deprived of life, liberty, or property without due process of law, and provides that, if private property is taken for public activity, just compensation must be paid. The **Sixth Amendment** guarantees that in a criminal action the defendant has the right to a speedy trial. This right is also guaranteed by Rule 50 of the Federal Rules of Criminal Procedure. A speedy trial is one that is as soon as the prosecution, using reasonable diligence, can prepare for it. The case of *Barker v. Wingo* established four factors to be used to determine if a defendant did indeed receive a speedy trial.

1. The length of any delay
2. The government's justification for the delay
3. If and when the defendant asserted the right to a fair and speedy trial
4. The prejudice caused by the delay

The Sixth Amendment also gives a person the right to an impartial jury, the right to be informed of the charges against him or her, the right to confront the witnesses against him or her, the right to compulsory process (subpoena) for witnesses in his or her favor, and to have assistance of counsel to prepare a defense. This amendment only applies to federal cases, but parts of it have been extended to the states. For example, the case of *Gideon v. Wainwright* extended the right to counsel to state criminal proceedings. The Eighth Amendment prohibits excessive bail and fines and prohibits cruel and unusual punishment.

PUBLIC OFFICIAL AMENDMENTS

The **Twelfth Amendment** changed how the president and vice president of the United States are elected. Prior to the Twelfth Amendment, the person who received the most electoral votes became president, and the person who received the second most votes was declared vice president. The Twelfth Amendment provided that people vote for president and vice president in terms of their designated offices. **The Seventeenth Amendment** changed how senators are selected from the states. Prior to this amendment, senators were selected by the different state's legislative bodies. Since the ratification of this amendment, senators have been elected in a popular election, the same way representatives are elected.

The **Twentieth Amendment** changed the date the president and vice president leave office and clarified the order of succession if the president-elect dies before he or she can take office. The **Twenty-Second Amendment** placed a limit on the number of times a person can be elected president and imposed term limits. A person can only serve two full terms as president; if he or she is completing someone else's term, he or she must serve less than two years of the remaining term or he or she can only run one more time. Thus, the longest period of time someone can serve as president is ten years.

The **Twenty-Third Amendment** gave three electoral votes to Washington, D.C. The **Twenty-Fifth Amendment** clarifies the order of succession if the president dies, resigns, or is removed from office. The vice president is first in the order of succession to the presidency. It also contains provisions regarding what to do if the president becomes unable to carry out the duties of the office. See Exhibit 8-13 for a summary of these amendments.

EXHIBIT 8-13	CONSTITUTIONAL OFFICER AMENDMENTS

Amendment 12 – Candidates for offices of president and vice president must be stated

Amendment 17 – Senators are selected by popular vote

Amendment 20 – Changed the date the president and vice president take office and clarified the order of succession to the presidency if the president-elect dies

Amendment 22 – Declared term limits for the presidency

Amendment 23 – Gave Washington, D.C. three electoral votes

Amendment 25 – Clarified the succession to the presidency if the president dies

---

VOTING AMENDMENTS

The **Fifteenth Amendment** gave the right to vote to males who were former slaves. At the time of this amendment, women could not vote. The **Nineteenth Amendment** prohibited the denial of the right to vote because of sex. The **Twenty-Fourth Amendment** prohibited the use of poll taxes or any other tax to prevent people from exercising their right to vote. The **Twenty-Sixth Amendment** gave citizens who are eighteen years or older the right to vote. This amendment lowered the voting age from twenty-one to eighteen.

SIXTEENTH, EIGHTEENTH, TWENTY-FIRST, AND TWENTY-SEVENTH AMENDMENTS

The Sixteenth Amendment authorized the imposition of income tax. The Eighteenth Amendment made the manufacture, sale, or transportation of intoxicating beverages illegal in the United States; this amendment was reversed by the Twenty-First Amendment. The Twenty-Seventh Amendment prohibits Congress from voting itself a raise and having it become effective in the same session. Such a raise is effective only after the next election of representatives.

CONCLUSION

Constitutional law serves as a basis for all other laws in our country. Any time Congress passes a law, it must be in compliance with the Constitution and it must be under one of the powers granted to Congress. Any law any state passes must also be in agreement with the provisions of the Constitution.

The Constitution established our system of government, creating the legislative, executive, and judicial branch, establishing their respective powers, and imposing checks on those powers. Congress has the most enumerated powers—powers specifically listed in the Constitution—while the judiciary has the fewest. The power of the judiciary has come from the decisions of the Supreme Court that have interpreted the role of the courts in government. The powers of the branches of government are not limited to the listed, enumerated powers; government has additional powers because of the implied powers and the penumbra doctrines.

The Constitution also places specific limits on the power of government—limitations that protect the civil rights of the citizens of the United States. Freedom of speech, the press, religion, and assembly are protected by the Constitution and by cases interpreting its provisions. Life, liberty, and property are protected by the due process clauses, and the equal protection clause of the Fourteenth Amendment helps ensure that laws are applied to every person in the same way.

The United States Constitution is an amazing document, especially considering how seldom its basic provisions have been amended. Most amendments either added something to the Constitution or made some minor adjustment to the way government operates. There has been no major change to the Constitution or to our system of government for over two hundred years.

Exhibit 8-14 contains a brief summary of the key cases mentioned in this chapter.

EXHIBIT 8-14	SUMMARY OF KEY CASES

Marbury v. Madison – Established the doctrine of judicial review

McCulloch v. Maryland – Established the implied powers doctrine and the supremacy of federal law over state law

Kohl v. United States – Established the penumbra doctrine: combine one implied power with another implied power to create a third implied power

Gibbons v. Ogden – Defined interstate commerce for the first time

Schenk v. United States – Created the clear and present danger doctrine

Miller v. United States – Established the current test of obscenity. Referred to contemporary community standards and prurient interest

Lemon v. Kurtzman – Established the Lemon test to determine if right to freedom of religion has been violated

Griswold v. Connecticut – Established the right to privacy

Gideon v. Wainwright – Extended the right to an attorney to include cases in state courts

KEY WORDS AND PHRASES

affecting commerce
aid and comfort
balancing test
Bill of Rights
censorship
civil rights
clear and present danger
  doctrine
commerce clause
constitution
constitutional law
constitutional question
contemporary community
  standards
Cooley doctrine
dominant theme
due process clause
due process of law

due process rights
Electoral College
enumerated powers
equal protection clause
equal protection of the law
establishment clause
federal preemption
Fifth Amendment
fighting words doctrine
First Amendment
Fourteenth Amendment
freedom of the press
full faith and credit clause
implied powers
interstate commerce
judicial review
Lemon test
necessary and proper clause

obscene
pandering of obscenity
penumbra doctrine
police power
preemption doctrine
prior restraint
privileges and immunities
  clause
procedural due process
prurient interest
right to privacy
separation of powers
substantive due process
supremacy clause
treason
unconstitutional

REVIEW QUESTIONS

SHORT ANSWER

1. What is the Bill of Rights and when was it passed?
2. Where is the due process clause found?
3. What are the constitutional offices of the federal government?
4. What is the clear and present danger doctrine?
5. What is the Lemon test?
6. What liberties and freedoms does the First Amendment protect?
7. What is the difference between enumerated and implied powers?
8. What is the police power?
9. What is the difference between interstate and intrastate commerce?
10. What is meant by the term *equal protection of the law?*
11. What is pandering of obscenity?
12. What is the preemption clause?
13. What is the Cooley doctrine?
14. What is a constitutional freedom?
15. What is the difference between interstate and intrastate commerce?
16. What is the balancing test?
17. What must be presented for the Court to decide to hear a case?

18. What is the process used to elect the president of the United States?
19. What is the only crime defined by the Constitution and what is its definition?
20. What is the right to privacy?
21. What is meant by separation of powers?
22. What is the free exercise clause?
23. Who actually votes for the president of the United States?
24. What is meant by the term *freedom of contract?*

FILL IN THE BLANK

1. Congress has the power to regulate commerce with _____, _____, and among _____.
2. The three elements of the Lemon test are _____

   _____

   _____
3. Providing aid and comfort to the enemy is _____.
4. The _____ doctrine states one implied power can be combined with another implied power to create a third implied power.
5. Two permissible limitations on freedom of speech are _____

   _____
6. The _____ clause prohibits the government from creating or showing favoritism to a particular church or religion.
7. If material appeals to _____, then it can be considered obscene.
8. When a matter is of such national importance that states are prohibited from enacting any laws governing that area, this is known as the _____.
9. The case of *Marbury v. Madison* established the power of _____.
10. The number of electors each state has is based on the number of _____ and _____ each state has.

FACT SITUATIONS

1. A law that states single people are not allowed to drink is passed. Married people are allowed to drink. What provision of the Constitution might this law violate?
2. A state passes a law barring married couples from purchasing condoms. What right might this law violate?
3. Ernest wishes to appeal his case to the U.S. Supreme Court. What sort of question must be raised on appeal?
4. What will the Court issue if it decides to hear the case?
5. The governor wants to stop a statewide paper from printing photos of him with his mistress. What is the governor trying to do? Is it permissible?
6. Fred wants to have a judgment enforced in another state. That state does not recognize Fred's cause of action as being valid. Will the state have to enforce the judgment? Why or why not?
7. Mike prints a pamphlet urging defense industry workers to go out on strike. The country is at war at the time. The government stops the publication of the pamphlet. Can the government do this? Why or why not?

8. A person goes into a crowded movie theater and yells, "Fire!" Is this protected speech?

9. The legislature passes a law that requires state employees to begin each workday in public prayer. Is this allowed? Why or why not?

10. A state tries to set minimum standards on what exotic dancers must wear. What principle can the state use to control this freedom of speech and expression?

11. A state starts charging out-of-state companies for doing business in the state. Can the state do this? If not, why not?

12. The governor allows a nativity scene to be displayed in the Capitol. The governor also allows a person to read a gospel story about the birth of Christ during the Christmas season. What test might the Supreme Court apply to this situation?

13. A state attempts to make criminal certain sexual activity between married couples. What rights are being potentially violated by the state?

CHAPTER 9

Torts

INTRODUCTION

Just as criminal law provides for "remedies" that are available to the state to punish people who violate other people's rights by breaking the law, tort law provides for civil remedies for people who have had their rights violated by the actions of others. In fact, some torts can also be crimes. Tort law provides a method of compensation for a private person who has been injured by the intentional or negligent acts of another person or persons.

This chapter defines what a tort is and describes intentional torts and torts based upon negligence. Who can commit a tort as well as who can be held liable and why are discussed. The types of damages that can be received for the harm caused and the defenses that can be raised to tort claims are also presented.

GENERAL PRINCIPLES

A **tort** is a private or civil wrong or injury, other than an action for a breach of contract, for which the court will provide a remedy in the form of a cause of action for the damages suffered. A tort is a violation of a duty imposed by law for which a person may sue another person, in court, for damages. In order to sue someone using tort law, there must be harm caused or about to be caused, and there must be the possibility of being compensated by a lawsuit seeking payment of damages.

LIABILITY AND TORTFEASORS

If someone commits a tort, he or she can be held liable for his or her conduct. Being held *liable* means being bound or obliged in law or equity to provide compensation to another for harm caused by one's actions or by one's failure to act. **Liability** (lye-ə-*bil*-i-tee) is a legal obligation to do, pay, or make good something, and this obligation may be enforced by a court of law.

Conduct, either by commission or omission, that may subject a person or business to liability under the principles of the law of torts is described as *tortious*. Tortious conduct can lead to a person's being forced to pay someone else for the harm caused by his or her action or inaction. The **tortfeasor** (*tort*-fee-zer) is the person or business that commits the tort. For example, if a person commits the act of trespass, he or she is a tortfeasor. The person's conduct is tortious because it may subject him or her to liability for any harm caused by the conduct. If the conduct damages property, the trespasser can be liable for the cost of repairing the damage. **Joint tortfeasors** are two or more people who are liable for the same injury to a person or property; if two or more people commit the tort, then each can be held liable for the act. For example, if three people commit a battery on a person (see below for a definition of *battery*), then all three are potentially liable. All three are joint tortfeasors. See Exhibit 9-1.

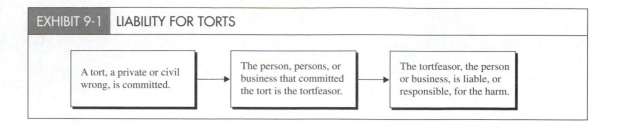

EXHIBIT 9-1   LIABILITY FOR TORTS

A tort, a private or civil wrong, is committed. → The person, persons, or business that committed the tort is the tortfeasor. → The tortfeasor, the person or business, is liable, or responsible, for the harm.

INTENTIONAL TORTS

Torts are broken down into two categories: intentional torts and negligence. Assault, battery, assault and battery, false imprisonment, fraud, intentional infliction of emotional distress, invasion of privacy, libel, malicious prosecution, misrepresentation, slander, trespass to land, and trespass to chattels are all intentional torts.

ASSAULT AND BATTERY

Assault is the willful attempt or threat to inflict injury upon the person of another. The threat can be verbal or physical. Verbally threatening to hit someone with a bat while waving a bat in front of that person is a form of assault. In order for there to be assault, there must be an apparent ability to carry out the threat, and the victim must have reason to fear or expect immediate bodily harm. For example, a professional football player in full gear cannot be assaulted by a six-year-old child: The child has no apparent ability to carry out a threat, and the football player, in all likelihood, would not be afraid of a six-year-old. However, a heavyweight boxing champion's threat to knock someone out could be construed as assault because the champion could successfully carry out the threat. Someone's pointing a gun at another person is also a threat because of the action of pointing the gun. No words need to be spoken; the act in itself is enough to constitute assault.

Battery is intentional and wrongful physical contact with a person without his or her consent that involves some injury or offense. Battery is also understood as unauthorized, unwanted, or unconsented to touching. A battery victim does not need to be aware that contact is about to happen; the physical contact is sufficient. If someone sneaks up behind someone else and hits that person on the head with a baseball bat, battery has taken place even though the victim did not know who or what hit him or her. The fact that the person was hit with the baseball bat is enough to establish the tort of battery.

Assault and battery occurs when the threat of physical contact is followed up with actual physical contact. For example, if someone threatens someone else with a baseball bat and then actually hits that person with the bat, assault and battery have taken place. Assault, battery, and assault and battery are torts. They can also be crimes. (See Chapter 2, Criminal Law.)

CONVERSION

Conversion (kən-*ver*-zhen) is the unauthorized assumption and exercise of ownership over goods or personal property of another person that deprives the owner of his or her property permanently or for an indefinite time. For example, if Ingrid takes a CD belonging to Fritz, treats it like it is her own, and has no intention of ever returning the property to Fritz, then Ingrid has committed the tort of conversion. She has deprived the rightful owner of the possession and enjoyment of his property and she has done so with the intent to make the property hers permanently or for an indefinite period of time. Conversion can also be a crime and is generally considered to be theft. (See Chapter 6, Criminal Law.) The person who is entitled to ownership of the goods has the right to **replevin** (rĭ-plĕ-vĭn), or recovery, of the goods or personal property. Refer to Exhibit 9-2 for a summary of a conversion and replevin.

EXHIBIT 9-2	CONVERSION AND REPLEVIN

Conversion takes place when a person takes the property of another with the intent of keeping it permanently or for an indefinite period of time. The rightful owner is deprived of the use of his or her property.

Replevin is the right of the property owner to take back, or recover, what was wrongfully taken.

FALSE IMPRISONMENT

False imprisonment is the intentional confinement of a person without lawful cause, without the person's consent, and for an appreciable length of time. This length of time can be very short or quite long; the person can be physically detained, but detainment is not a requirement. False imprisonment can occur by way of a verbal command: If a reasonable person believes that he or she cannot leave an area, he or she can allege false imprisonment. For example, a storekeeper suspects Lee of shoplifting and tells her not to leave the store until the police arrive. If the storekeeper does this with no evidence that Lee actually shoplifted something, and if Lee does not leave the store because she reasonably believes she cannot leave the premises, then this can be false imprisonment. If a police officer tells a person not to move, but has no probable cause to believe a crime has been committed, and the person does not move, then this also can be the tort of false imprisonment. False imprisonment can also be considered a crime. See Exhibit 9-3 for a summary of the elements of false imprisonment.

EXHIBIT 9-3	ELEMENTS OF FALSE IMPRISONMENT

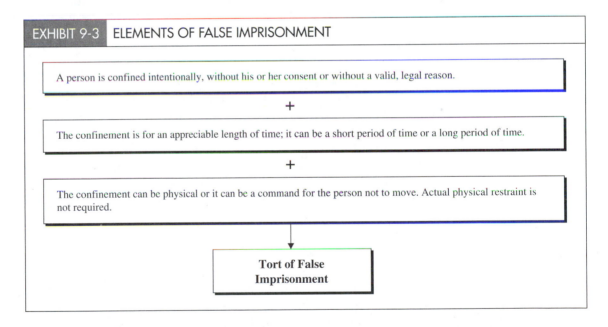

A person is confined intentionally, without his or her consent or without a valid, legal reason.

+

The confinement is for an appreciable length of time; it can be a short period of time or a long period of time.

+

The confinement can be physical or it can be a command for the person not to move. Actual physical restraint is not required.

Tort of False Imprisonment

In one documented case of false imprisonment, a woman was arrested because of crimes her sister had committed. Her sister had stolen her identification and was using her ID to write hot checks. The woman was able to prove that her sister had stolen her ID and that she had not written all the checks drawn on her account. The court ordered her released immediately; however, the county kept her in general lockup for another day and a half. The woman was not released until her attorney went to court a second time on her behalf. Only after the court ordered her immediate release for the second time was she released. The period of time she spent in jail after the first order from the court was false imprisonment.

FRAUD AND MISREPRESENTATION

In tort law, **fraud** is the false representation of a present or past material (important) fact made by one person to another who relies on this representation, takes some action, and then suffers some harm or loss because of the information. The false information that is given can be given verbally or in writing. For example, Kate wants to sell her car to Ahmed. She tells him that the car is in perfect working order and that it has never been in an accident. In reality, the car has transmission problems, the brakes are almost inoperative, and the car was hit by an SUV, which caused the frame to be bent. Kate intentionally withholds all this information from Ahmed, and Ahmed, relying on what Kate says, buys the car. Kate has committed the tort of fraud against Ahmed because fraud, in tort law, is always a positive, intentional act.

Misrepresentation in tort law is very similar to fraud. Misrepresentation is manifestation by words or conduct from one person to another that amounts to an assertion that does not agree with the facts. In other words, misrepresentation is an untrue statement of fact or conduct that does not agree with fact. The difference between fraud and misrepresentation is that fraud occurs via a verbal or written statement, whereas misrepresentation can take place as a result of the conduct of a person. A statement is not necessary for the tort of misrepresentation, but is a requirement for the tort of fraud. A statement that a car has never been in an accident when it actually had been hit in the rear by another car is fraud. Misrepresentation by conduct occurs when an individual turns back the odometer of a car he or she is attempting to sell, when someone shows a falsified document, or when a person writes a check knowing that there are not sufficient funds to cover it. In these latter examples, there is no verbal statement that is false; the misrepresentation is the actual conduct of the person.

INVASION OF PRIVACY AND DEFAMATION

Every person has a right to privacy (see Chapter 8, Constitutional Law, for more on the right to privacy). If someone takes the image or likeness of a person without that person's consent and uses it, publicizes private matters about that person that the public has no legitimate concern about, or wrongfully intrudes into the person's private life and activities, then the tort of **invasion of privacy** occurs. The action taken must have caused mental suffering (often interpreted as shame or humiliation) to the victim in order for invasion of privacy to have occurred. For example, if a company uses Mirelis's picture without her consent in an advertising campaign for revealing lingerie, then the company has committed the tort of invasion of privacy. A public figure, such as a politician or Hollywood celebrity, has a lesser expectation of privacy because he or she has chosen to be in the public eye, reducing their right to privacy by their own action.

Invasion of privacy is a tort concerning the truth about someone; the tortfeasor has told the truth, but that truth is something the person did not want the public to know. **Defamation,** on the other hand, is the communication of false information about someone. This false information, which is published or communicated to a third person, injures the victim's reputation or good name, holding him or her up to ridicule, scorn, or contempt. Defamation must involve a false statement, the statement must be published to a third person, and it must cause injury. The person hearing the information does not have to believe the statement is true. The fact that it was published is enough. Defamation is another tort that can also be a crime.

Defamation can take place in the business world, where it is termed *disparagement.* **Disparagement** is the intentional defamation of a business, a product, or a service. This defamation intentionally communicates false information about a business, a product, or a service to a third person, and it causes injury to the business.

Defamation is further broken down into two types: libel and slander. **Libel** (*lie*-bəl) is defamation that is in writing, has been printed, or is a picture or a sign. As with invasion of privacy, public figures have less protection from libel than private citizens because they have chosen to subject themselves to public scrutiny. According to the case of *New York Times v. Sullivan* 376 U.S. 254, 84 S.Ct. 710, 11 L.Ed. 2d 686, in order for a public figure to be able to sue for libel, the public figure must show malice was intended before he or she can successfully sue. *Malice,* in regard to libel, is the reckless disregard for the truth or untruth of a published statement. See Sidebar 9-1 for the decision in *New York Times v. Sullivan.*

SIDEBAR 9-1 *NEW YORK TIMES V. SULLIVAN*

Facts: L. B. Sullivan, who was a commissioner of the city of Montgomery, Alabama, sued the *New York Times* for libel because of an advertisement run in the *Times* titled "Heed Their Rising Voices." The advertisement was about the Civil Rights Movement in the South. It described some of the events that had been happening, and it asked for donations to help aid the movement. The article derogated actions of the police, but did not mention L. B. Sullivan by name. Mr. Sullivan claimed libel because he was the commissioner of police at the time, and officers' actions could be imputed to him. Not all of the statements made in the advertisement were totally accurate.

Decision of the Court: Expression does not lose the constitutional protection to which it would otherwise be entitled because it appears in the form of a paid advertisement.

Factual error, content defamatory of official reputation, or both, are insufficient to warrant an award of damages for false statements unless "actual malice"—knowledge that statements are false or in reckless disregard of the truth—is alleged and proved.

The judgment of the trial court in favor of Sullivan was reversed by the U.S. Supreme Court.

Source: United States Reports

Malice (*mal*-iss) is the intentional doing of a wrongful act without just cause or excuse, with the intent to inflict an injury; it is a conscious violation of the law. There is no presumption of malice when a public figure is involved because of the First Amendment freedoms of speech and press. In order to prove malice, it must be shown that:

1. The defendant published the material either knowing it to be false or
2. Recklessly published it without regard as to whether it was true or false. See Exhibit 9-4.

EXHIBIT 9-4	ELEMENTS OF MALICE

1. Person acted intentionally.
2. The act is illegal.
3. There is no justification for the illegal act.
4. There is intent to cause injury.

Slander is spoken defamation—a statement of false information communicated to a third person that causes injury. The statement does not have to be heard by the person it was directed against; it can be heard by someone else. Slander differs from libel in that it is *spoken* rather than written.

MALICIOUS PROSECUTION

If a civil or criminal action is brought against someone with malice and without probable cause to believe that the charges in the complaint can be sustained, upon conclusion of the case the defendant can sue for **malicious prosecution** (mə-*lish*-us pross-e-*kyoo*-shun). Suit brought after the first case is dismissed; the plaintiff in the first case becomes the defendant in the second case. In order to prove malicious prosecution, each of the following must be shown.

1. A legal action was commenced against the person who is now the plaintiff.
2. The action was brought by the person who is now the defendant.
3. The case was dismissed in favor of the person who is now the plaintiff.
4. There was no probable cause to bring the case.
5. Malice was present.
6. The current plaintiff suffered harm because of the first action.

Malicious prosecution applies to both criminal and civil cases. An example of criminal malicious prosecution is a prosecuting attorney's filing criminal charges against an individual when all the evidence indicates someone else is guilty. An example of a civil case of malicious prosecution is a person's suit against a grocery store for injuries suffered in a fall when the person was actually injured while working on his lawn. See Exhibit 9-5 for a summary of the elements of malicious prosecution.

EXHIBIT 9-5	ELEMENTS OF MALICIOUS PROSECUTION

1. A case (civil or criminal) was brought against someone.
2. It was brought by someone **who is now the defendant.**
3. The case was **dismissed in favor of the person the case was brought against.**
4. There was **no probable cause** to bring the case.
5. The original case was brought **because of malice.**

NUISANCE

The term **nuisance** (*noo*-sense) has a very broad meaning in legal vocabulary and an exact definition cannot be given. Generally speaking, a nuisance is something that endangers life or health, is offensive to the senses, violates the laws of decency, or obstructs the reasonable and comfortable use of property. Nuisance is broken down into three categories: public, private, and mixed. A **public nuisance** is one that affects an indefinite number of people, all the residents of a neighborhood, or all people coming within the range of it. The nuisance is public even though the extent of the harm or damage impacting each individual may be unequal. Thus, the nuisance is considered "public" because of the *number* of people it affects—not because of *how* it affects them. A Christmas display that consists of over 5 million red lights could be a public nuisance. It could cause traffic jams because people slow down and stop to look at it. People might park on residents' yards to view it, dropping trash or causing other damage. The display might prevent people from being able to get home in a timely manner because of traffic problems. The display does not impact everyone in the same way: It has a different impact on immediate neighbors than it does on people who live in other neighborhoods or on people who drive past it. However, it has sufficient enough impact on an indefinite number of people that it can be classified as a public nuisance. Another example of a public nuisance is a meat rendering plant near a residential neighborhood. The actual nuisance is the obnoxious smell from the plant that travels to the neighborhood when the wind blows a certain direction. The smell may affect different people in different ways and to varying degrees. The key is the number of people affected by the smell.

A **private nuisance** is any wrongful act that destroys or deteriorates the property of an individual or a few people. The interference with another person's right to the lawful use and enjoyment of his or her property is also regarded as a private nuisance. If someone sets up an automobile painting shop in his or her garage that causes surrounding property values to decrease, or if the smell and fumes produced by the shop prevent neighbors from being able to be outside for any length of time, then the shop is a private nuisance.

A **mixed nuisance** combines the elements of a private and a public nuisance; both the general public and private individuals are affected. A mixed nuisance is public in that it affects many people or all of the community, and it is private because, in addition to the effect it has on the general public, it causes special injury to a private right. The Christmas lights referred to earlier are an example of a mixed nuisance. They cause harm to the general public (traffic jams) as well as harm to private citizens (damage to private property). See Exhibit 9-6 for a summary of the differences among public, private, and mixed nuisances.

EXHIBIT 9-6 | PUBLIC, PRIVATE, AND MIXED NUISANCES

Public Nuisance – A nuisance that affects an indefinite number of people, or all the residents of a neighborhood, or all people coming within the range of the nuisance. The nuisance is a public nuisance because of the number of people it affects, not necessarily how it affects them.

Private Nuisance – Any wrongful act that destroys or causes deterioration of the property of an individual or a few people. A private nuisance is also the interference with another person's right to the lawful use and enjoyment of property.

Mixed Nuisance – Any nuisance that affects the general public as well as private individuals. The nuisance is public because it affects many people or all of the community, and it is private because, in addition to the effect it has on the general public, it also has causes special injury to a private right.

TRESPASS

Trespass is the unauthorized intrusion or invasion of private premises or land of another person. A trespass action can be brought by any person who is actually and exclusively in possession of the property; it does not have to be brought by the owner of the property. For example, Brett is renting an apartment. His is the only name on the lease; he is in actual and exclusive possession of the leased premises. If someone entered the apartment without his permission, Brett could sue for trespass. If someone enters a person's property without that person's permission, the person who entered has committed a trespass; however, in order for that person to be held liable, there must be intentional intrusion or negligence. The person who actually commits the trespass is the **trespasser.**

A **trespass to land** is any physical entry upon land, whether one walks on it, throws something onto it, or throws something over it. This is because a property owner's right to land includes the air above it, the ground itself, and what is below it. If an oil company drills at an angle through a property owner's land to get to a pool of oil, it has committed a trespass to land. If a deer hunter shoots across someone else's property, he has committed a trespass to land because the bullet travels over that person's property.

A **trespass to chattels** is the unlawful and serious interference with the possessory rights of another to personal property. Trespass to chattels is considered to be the "little brother" to conversion. Trespass to chattels can be a temporary interference, whereas conversion requires either permanent deprivation or deprivation for an indefinite period of time.

An **attractive nuisance** is a tort that contains elements of trespass and of nuisance. An attractive nuisance is something that is so tempting to children that they cannot resist it; they have to trespass to get to the nuisance. The landowner must take reasonable steps to protect children from the nuisance or face possible liability. See Exhibit 9-7 for an example of an attractive nuisance.

| EXHIBIT 9-7 | EXAMPLE OF AN ATTRACTIVE NUISANCE |

1. The pool is something children cannot ignore.
2. The pool is tempting to children, but it can also be dangerous to children because of the possibility of drowning.
3. The owner is required to take reasonable steps to protect the children from the hazard. The owner might:
   a. Put up a privacy fence with a gate.
   b. Lock the gate of the fence.

The fact that children trespassed onto the land is not a defense to an attractive nuisance lawsuit for damages.

WRONGFUL DEATH

A **wrongful death** is one that was caused by either the willful (intentional) or negligent act of another. A person can face a criminal action of murder or manslaughter and then face civil liability for wrongful death. The accused does not have to be criminally convicted in order for the plaintiff to be successful in a wrongful death case. A **wrongful death action** is the lawsuit brought on behalf of the deceased person's beneficiaries. It is a separate claim—not the continuation of any claim that the deceased person had. For example, a person files a lawsuit against the operator and the company that owned an 18-wheeler that struck his vehicle, causing extensive personal injuries. The person who filed the personal injury lawsuit later dies as a result of the injuries sustained. The beneficiaries could not continue the personal injury lawsuit because they were not the ones injured. However, they could file a wrongful death action against the operator and the owner of the vehicle because the death was by the driver's intentional or negligent act. The difference between wrongful death, which is a tort, and negligent homicide, which is the *crime* of causing the death of a person by negligent or reckless conduct is the conduct. The conduct for negligent homicide does not have to be willful, it can be negligent; the conduct for wrongful death can be willful.

NEGLIGENCE

Negligence is the second area of tort law where a person can be held liable for his or her actions. **Negligence** is the omission (neglecting to perform) of what the law requires, or the failure to do something that a reasonably careful person *would* do under the same or similar circumstances.

BREACH OF DUTY

Negligence is a breach of a duty of care owed to another person who will suffer an injury because of that breach. **Breach of duty** is any violation or omission of a legal or moral duty. For example, there is a foot of snow on the ground. A reasonably careful person would not drive down a steep hill at eighty miles an hour. A person who would go down that hill at eighty miles an hour is acting negligently, and would be held liable for any harm caused by his or her negligent act.

DEGREES OF NEGLIGENCE

There are several types or degrees of negligence. The first is **ordinary negligence:** the omission of care that a reasonably careful person usually would take. **Gross negligence** is the intentional failure to perform a duty, or the reckless disregard of the consequences of one's actions that affect the life and property of another. Gross negligence amounts to an indifference to a present legal duty respecting the rights of others. Gross negligence implies a degree of inattention greater than the degree of inattention implied by ordinary negligence. A driver who speeds down an ice-covered hill into a group of people who are clearly visible is guilty of gross negligence. **Slight negligence** is the failure to exercise a great deal of care; it is the absence of the degree of care that a person of *extraordinary* care and foresight would use. Medical specialists and trustees (see the chapter on wills, trusts, and estates) are two examples of persons who have the duty of extraordinary care and foresight. Because of their education or because of the position they are in, they have a greater duty of care than other people.

Negligence per se, or negligence in law, is the nonobservance of a duty prescribed by law. Negligence per se is conduct—either an action or an omission—that may be declared and treated as negligent because it is in violation of a statute or municipal ordinance. For example, a person goes through a stop sign without stopping. This is a violation of a statute or ordinance, and because there is a failure to exercise reasonable care, there is negligence per se. See Exhibit 9-8 for a summary of these types of negligence.

EXHIBIT 9-8	DEGREES OF NEGLIGENCE

1. **Slight Negligence** – Ignoring a high duty of care imposed because of education of position.
2. **Ordinary Negligence** – Ignoring the care a reasonably careful person would take.
3. **Gross Negligence** – Intentional failure to exercise regular care; the failure affects another person's life or property.

Willful negligence is the intentional performance of an act in disregard of the risk known, a risk so great that it is highly probable that harm will result. Willful negligence is very close to gross negligence. A **willful and wanton act** is an aggravated form of negligence that is committed with an intentional or reckless disregard for the safety of others or with an intentional disregard of a duty necessary to the safety of another's property. This intentional or reckless disregard is the actual act of willful negligence. Willful and wanton acts differ from **willful neglect,** which is the intentional disregard of a plain or manifest duty rather than the intentional disregard of the safety of another. For example, a parent who refuses to take care of his or her child is committing willful neglect, while a parent who leaves a child unattended in a car when the temperature is 100 degrees is committing a willful and wanton act.

There are circumstances when someone else is responsible for the negligent acts of another. **Imputed negligence** is the doctrine that places upon one person the responsibility for the negligence and the harm caused by another person. This responsibility exists as a result of the special relationship between the parties. A husband can be responsible for the conduct of his wife, a parent can be responsible for the conduct of his or her child, an employer can be responsible for the conduct of his or her employees, a driver can be responsible for the conduct of his or her passengers, a principal can be responsible for his or her agent. Another way that people can be held responsible for the negligence of another is through the doctrine of vicarious liability. **Vicarious liability** (vy-*kehr*-ee-us ly-e-*bil*-i-tee) is the imposition of the liability of one person upon another person simply because of the relationship between the two. Some of the same examples apply: parent and child, employer and employee, a principal and his or her agent. See Exhibit 9-9 for a summary of the differences between imputed negligence and vicarious liability.

EXHIBIT 9-9 THE DIFFERENCE BETWEEN IMPUTED NEGLIGENCE AND VICARIOUS LIABILITY

Imputed Negligence – One person is responsible for the negligent act *and* the harm caused by the negligent act of another person. Responsibility for the negligent act is placed on the person because of a special relationship. A parent is responsible for the acts of his or her child; an employer is responsible for the acts of its employees.

Vicarious Liability – Liability of one person is imposed on another person simply because of the relationship between the two people. Paying for the harm caused is the responsibility of someone other than the person who committed the tort.

CAUSATION

In order for a person to be held liable for a negligent act, it must be shown that there was **causation** (kaw-*zay*-shən)—a logical link between the negligent conduct and the harm caused. For example, because the driver ignored the stop light, his car hit another car. If the driver had paid attention to the stop sign, the accident would not have taken place. Sometimes negligent acts do not cause immediate injury. Instead, the negligent act starts a chain of events that causes the injury. This sequence of events is termed **proximate causation,** a natural and continuous sequence of events, unbroken by any intervening cause, that produce an injury and without which the result would not have occurred. However, this does not mean a person is responsible for all harm caused by his or her actions. See Exhibit 9-10 for a flow chart showing the connection between causation, negligence, and liability for negligence.

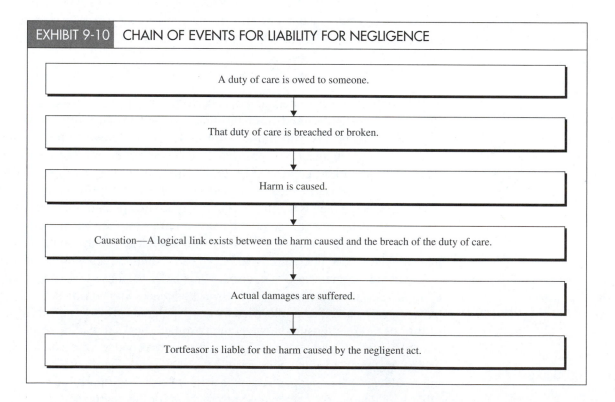

EXHIBIT 9-10 CHAIN OF EVENTS FOR LIABILITY FOR NEGLIGENCE

A duty of care is owed to someone.

That duty of care is breached or broken.

Harm is caused.

Causation—A logical link exists between the harm caused and the breach of the duty of care.

Actual damages are suffered.

Tortfeasor is liable for the harm caused by the negligent act.

The most famous example of the application of proximate causation to negligence is the case of *Palsgraf v. Long Island Railroad* 248 N.Y. 339, 162 N.E. 99. This case was decided in 1928 by the Court of Appeals for New York. See Sidebar 9-2 for the facts and decision in *Palsgraf v. Long Island Railroad.*

> **SIDEBAR 9-2** *PALSGRAF V. LONG ISLAND RAILROAD*
>
> **Facts:** Helen Palsgraf, the plaintiff, was standing on the platform of the Long Island Railroad, waiting for her train. A railroad employee, a guard, was on the same platform, along with a railway scale. As another train was leaving the station, a man came running onto the platform, carrying a package. He jumped onto the train, but it looked like he would fall off. The guard standing on the platform and another guard on the train grabbed the passenger and helped him into the train. As they were helping him, the package he was carrying fell onto the tracks. The package contained fireworks that exploded when they hit the rails. The force from the explosion caused the railway scale to tip over and hit Ms. Palsgraf, injuring her badly. The identity of the person carrying the package was never discovered. Ms. Palsgraf sued, and the case wound up before the New York Court of Appeals.
>
> **Issue:** Was this chain of events foreseeable enough for the Long Island Railroad to be liable for the injuries to Helen Palsgraf?
>
> **Decision of the Court:** The appeals court ruled that proximate cause did not exist. This chain of events was not foreseeable—it was too farfetched for there to be negligence. There was no way the railroad employee could have known that the package the man was carrying contained explosives, and thus he was not negligent in helping him board the train. No reasonable person could have reasonably predicted the chain of events. The railroad did not fail to exercise reasonable care, the degree of care that an ordinarily careful person would exercise in the same or similar circumstances.
>
> *Source: New York Reports*

The **Palsgraf rule,** which is derived from this case, states that a person who is negligent is liable only for harm or injury that is **foreseeable** (for-*see*-a-bəl) (reasonably anticipated harm or injury likely to result from a certain act or omission), and not for every injury that follows from his or her negligence. The test to see if something is foreseeable is the question: "Could a reasonably prudent man have known that his conduct or actions would lead to this result?"

RES IPSA LOQUITOR

Sometimes negligence can be shown by the legal doctrine of **res ipsa loquitor** (res *ip*-sa low-kwater), which means "the thing speaks for itself." For example, because the accident happened, the defendant was negligent; the accident is one that does not ordinarily occur unless there is negligence. Res ipsa loquitor is used sometimes in cases of **dangerous instrumentality,** the inherent capability of an object or act to place people in peril. For example, res ipsa loquitor comes into play when a boat or car is carelessly used because a boat or a car does not ordinarily injure someone if it is used appropriately. A person might allege: "I was injured because the car was being used in a negligent manner." Negligence is inferred because there was an accident; because there was an injury, there was negligence.

DEFENSES TO TORT CLAIMS

The first defense to tort action is **consent** or agreement—approval of what is going to happen. For example, the defendant argues that the person consented to the contact, so there is no battery; the defendant alleges that the person consented to remaining in one place, so there is no false imprisonment. **Assumption of the risk** is another defense in tort law. According to this defense, a plaintiff cannot recover for an injury received when he or she voluntarily exposes himself or herself to a known and appreciated danger. The requirements of this defense are:

1. The plaintiff has knowledge of the facts creating a dangerous condition.
2. The plaintiff knows the condition is dangerous.

3. The plaintiff appreciates the nature of the danger.

4. The plaintiff voluntarily exposes himself or herself to the danger. See Exhibit 9-11.

EXHIBIT 9-11 | THE DEFENSE OF ASSUMPTION OF THE RISK

1. The person **knows** the facts that create the dangerous condition.
2. The person **knows** the condition is dangerous.
3. The person appreciates—**understands**—the nature of the danger.
4. The person **voluntarily** exposes himself or herself to the danger.

The person must have knowledge of the danger.

For example, a person who plays football in the NFL cannot sue another player for a violent block. The player has knowledge of the facts about the NFL; he knows playing in the NFL can be dangerous; he appreciates the nature of the danger or violence; and he plays anyway.

In a negligence case, **comparative negligence** and **contributory negligence** may be a defense or a way to lessen a tortfeasor's liability. Contributory negligence is conduct that the plaintiff is responsible for that amounts to a breach of duty the law imposes on people to protect themselves from injury. When it takes place at the same time as the defendant's conduct, it also contributes to the proximate cause of the plaintiff's injury. The defense alleges that the plaintiff was also negligent and that was the reason why the plaintiff was injured. Even if the defendant was negligent, the plaintiff was also negligent and contributed to the harm he himself suffered. In many states, contributory negligence has been replaced by the doctrine of comparative negligence. Negligence is measured in terms of percentage, and any damages awarded are reduced by the percentage of negligence that is attributable to the plaintiff. For example, a plaintiff is awarded $100,000, but it is determined that he is 40% responsible for the harm he suffered. His award is reduced by 40%, $40,000, so the defendant is only liable for $60,000. In some jurisdictions, if the plaintiff is more than 50% responsible, he or she recovers nothing. In other jurisdictions, the plaintiff's award is still reduced by the percentage of fault, even if the plaintiff's fault is more than 50%. The case of *Wassell v. Adams* is an example of comparative negligence being applied to a tort case. Refer to Sidebar 9-3.

SIDEBAR 9-3 *WASSELL V. ADAMS*

Facts: The plaintiff, Susan Wassell, was visiting her fiancé. The motel where she was staying was close to a high-crime area. At 1:00 a.m., she was awakened by someone knocking on her door. When she looked out the peephole, she did not see anyone. Thinking it was her fiancé, she opened the door. A stranger came into the room. Wassell ran outside, but the person caught her, dragged her back inside, and raped her. Wassell sued the hotel owner for negligence because of the failure to warn her of the danger. The jury awarded her $850,000, but found that she was 97% responsible for the harm. The defendants were only 3% responsible for the harm, so Wassell only was awarded $25,500 in damages.

Issue: Was application of the doctrine of comparative negligence correct in this situation?

Ruling of the Court: In this case, either the plaintiff or defendant could have avoided the injury. The defendants had a duty to warn, to exercise a high degree of care to protect their guests from assaults on motel premises. The cost to the defendants of warning all their female guests about the dangers of the neighborhood would be nominal.

However, it is unlikely the warning would have stopped the attack. Because the plaintiff thought the man who knocked was her fiancé, she would have opened the door anyway. Everyone—or at least the average person—knows better than to open the door to a stranger in the middle of the night.

The decision of the jury was affirmed.

Source: Arkansas Reports

Another defense to a tort claim is **intervening cause.** This defense posits that there is an independent cause, not related to the original act or omission, that intervenes and destroys the causal connection between the negligent act of the defendant and the wrongful injury. In other words, something happens to break the causal connection; the defendant's action is no longer the proximate cause of the plaintiff's injury. A second event intervened and actually caused the injury to the plaintiff. Refer to Exhibit 9-12 for a summary of the application of intervening cause.

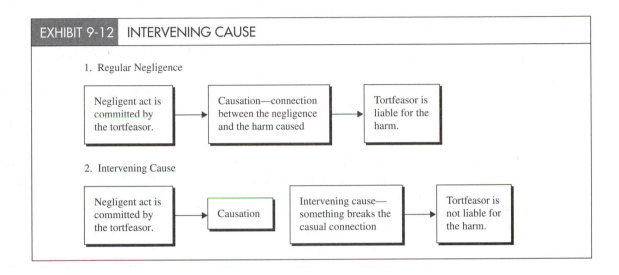

EXHIBIT 9-12   INTERVENING CAUSE

1. Regular Negligence

Negligent act is committed by the tortfeasor. → Causation—connection between the negligence and the harm caused → Tortfeasor is liable for the harm.

2. Intervening Cause

Negligent act is committed by the tortfeasor. → Causation → Intervening cause—something breaks the casual connection → Tortfeasor is not liable for the harm.

The **last clear chance doctrine** is a defense that can be used by the plaintiff in a tort case. The defendant alleges that the plaintiff's negligence is what caused the injury—not the negligence of the defendant. The plaintiff can counter this by showing that even though the plaintiff was negligent, the defendant had the last clear chance to prevent the injury. The defendant commits a negligent act and the plaintiff also acts negligently; the defendant had the last clear chance to prevent the injury, so the plaintiff can still recover damages from the defendant.

LIABILITY

If more than one tortfeasor is found to be liable, the tortfeasors can be held jointly and severally liable. **Joint and several liability** applies when each tortfeasor can be held entirely responsible for the harm caused by all of the tortfeasors. It does not matter that the tortfeasor was only responsible for 10% of the harm; he or she can be held liable for the entire amount of damages (see Chapter 21, Products Liability and Consumer Protection, about joint and several liability and market share liability). Another concept in tort law is **strict liability,** which is liability without fault. If a person committed the act, he or she is liable regardless of whether he or she was negligent or acted in a willful, deliberate way. Strict liability—liability without fault—is used frequently in products liability cases (see Chapter 24, Products Liability and Consumer Protection, for more on strict liability).

The **rescue doctrine** can also impose liability on a tortfeasor. The rescue doctrine states that a tortfeasor, who by his negligence has endangered the safety of another person, may be held liable for the injuries suffered by a third person who attempts to rescue the person and save him from being injured. The tortfeasor can be held liable for the harm caused to the person whose safety he endangered.

DAMAGES IN TORT LAW

Damages in tort law are the sum of money awarded to a person injured by the tort of another. Injury must be shown in order to collect any damages. **Injury** is defined as any wrong or damage to another, to his or her rights, to his or her reputation, or to his or her property. There are four types of damages in tort law: compensatory damages, punitive damages, special damages, and nominal damages. (See Chapter 4, Civil Procedure—Part 1.) The first type, **actual or compensatory damages,** are designed to compensate the injured party for the injury sustained and nothing more. The purpose of compensatory damages is to restore the injured party to the position he or she was in before the injury happened. For example, Calvin hits Yvonne's vehicle while she is driving it. The repair bill is $4,500, and Yvonne's medical bills total $5,000. Actual damages total $9,500. If Yvonne had to rent a car, then the cost of the rental car would also be a part of the actual damages.

Punitive damages may be awarded to the plaintiff in addition to any compensatory damages received. These damages are to help ease the harm caused by wrong that was done to him or her. Damages for mental anguish are an example of punitive damages. Punitive damages are also designed to punish the wrongdoer for conduct that was fraudulent or malicious; the purpose is to punish the defendant for his or her behavior or to make an example of him or her. **Pain and suffering** is another type of punitive damages that can be awarded. The term is used to describe the physical and mental discomfort the plaintiff suffered. For example, in addition to the actual loss caused by Calvin's hitting her car, Yvonne wants punitive damages for the pain she suffered as a result of having been injured and having to undergo testing and treatment.

Special damages are the third type of damages available in a tort claim. These are actual damages that are not necessarily the result of the actual injury, but are a natural and direct consequence of the action. Special damages must be specifically asked for in the pleading. Failure to request special damages precludes their being awarded.

Nominal damages, a fourth type of damages, are a small amount of money awarded to a plaintiff in a case where there is no substantial loss or injury, but where there has been an invasion of rights or a breach of duty. For example, someone trespasses onto another person's land, but causes no damage. Technically a tort has been committed: A person who had no right to be on the land entered onto it. However, no real harm has been done. Suit could be brought against the trespasser, but if it is successful, the property owner would receive only nominal damages. Such damages are usually in the amount of one dollar to show that a tort was committed, but no real harm occurred.

An injured party is required to try to lessen the harm caused by the tortious conduct of a defendant. That is, the injured party has a duty to mitigate the damages caused by the tortfeasor's conduct. The term **mitigation of damages** refers to the duty of the injured party to take whatever steps are necessary and reasonable to lessen the harm caused by the defendant's conduct. The plaintiff may not recover damages for the effect of the injury if the effect could have been avoided or lessened; this is known as the **avoidable consequences doctrine**. A person who is injured has a duty to minimize the injury and therefore the damages. An injured party cannot sit back, do nothing, and attempt to maximize the amount of money he or she can collect.

CONCLUSION

Tort law provides for a remedy whenever a person is harmed by either the deliberate act or the negligent act of another person. The harm can be caused by intentional torts such as assault, battery, false imprisonment, fraud, misrepresentation, trespass, libel, or slander. Harm can also be caused by negligent acts—one person's breaking the duty or care that he or she owes to other people. Negligence can be gross, ordinary, or even slight, depending upon the severity of the breach of duty. There is some crossover between torts and crime, as a person can commit a tort that is also a crime.

In order for a person to be liable—responsible for the harm caused by a tort—it must be shown that the person committed the tort, that there was harm caused by the tort, and that either the tort was the direct cause of the harm or that the tort set off a chain of events that led to the harm. However, the harm caused must have been foreseeable when the tort occurred; it cannot be the result of an unlikely chain of events. Intervening events can break the chain of causation so that the tortfeasor is not responsible for the harm.

Sometimes people other than the tortfeasor can be responsible for the harm caused by the tortfeasor. Tort law sets out damages that are available: These can be compensatory, punitive, special, and nominal damages. Tort law also states what defenses are available. These include intervening cause, voluntary assumption of the risk, contributory negligence, and comparative negligence. Tort law serves as the basis for other, more specific, types of laws that also provide a remedy for harm caused.

CHAPTER 9 REVIEW

KEY WORDS AND PHRASES

assault
assault and battery
assumption of the risk
attractive nuisance
battery
breach of duty
causation
comparative negligence
compensatory damages
contributory negligence
conversion
damages
dangerous instrumentality
defamation
false imprisonment
fraud
gross negligence

invasion of privacy
joint and several liability
joint tortfeasors
liability
libel
malice
malicious prosecution
misrepresentation
mitigation of damages
mixed nuisance
negligence
nominal damages
nuisance
pain and suffering
Palsgraf rule
private nuisance
proximate causation

public nuisance
punitive damages
replevin
res ipsa loquitur
slander
strict liability
tort
tortfeasor
trespass
trespass to land
trespasser
vicarious liability
willful and wanton act
willful negligence
wrongful death
wrongful death action

REVIEW QUESTIONS

SHORT ANSWER

1. What actions can be torts and crimes?

2. What is the difference between libel and slander?

3. What are the elements of assault?

4. What are the elements of a battery?

5. Can you have an assault without a battery?

6. What is required for a person to commit the tort of false imprisonment?

7. What is wrongful death?

8. What is the attractive nuisance doctrine?

9. What is proximate cause?

10. What is the difference between comparative negligence and contributory negligence.

11. Describe the types of damages available in tort law.

12. What are some of the defenses available in tort law?

13. Explain the concept of res ipsa loquitor.

14. Explain what the Palsgraf Rule is.

15. Describe the different types of negligence.

16. What are the necessary elements for assumption of the risk?

17. What is the last clear chance doctrine?

18. What happens to a tortfeasor's liability if there is intervening cause? Why does this happen?

19. What are the elements of a wrongful death case?

20. Define *invasion of privacy*.

FILL IN THE BLANK

1. Defamation that is spoken is _____ and defamation that is written is _____.

2. When someone intentionally commits a wrongful act, without justification or excuse, the person is acting with _____.

3. The obligation a person has to reduce the harm caused by another's actions is known as _____.

4. Something that affects a small group's enjoyment of property is _____, and something that affects a large group's enjoyment of property is _____.

5. When someone is responsible for the actions of another person because of the relationship between the two, this is known as _____.

6. When someone receives a small amount of money to indicate that a right was interfered with but there was no real harm, they have received _____.

7. An award that is designed to serve as a warning to others and to punish the wrongdoer is known as _____.

8. If a tortfeasor is held liable for the harm caused to one person and to another person who tried to help, this is known as the _____.

9. Liability without fault is also known as _____.

10. The doctrine that allows someone to assume one fact exists because of the existence of another fact is known as _____.

FACT SITUATIONS

1. Michael is threatened and then hit with a baseball bat. What tort(s) were committed?

2. Harold and Maude have an old swing set in their backyard that their children used to play on. Their children are now grown, but the swing set is still there. If children are injured playing on the swing set, what tort principle might apply?

3. John Henry is suing the manufacturer of Regrow, a hair restorer product for damages. Regrow caused the loss of his remaining hair as well as second-degree burns to his scalp. What damages might be available to John Henry and why?

4. A storekeeper stops Bonnie because he thinks she is a shoplifter. He tells Bonnie not to move while he goes to call the police. He then leaves. Nothing is preventing Bonnie from leaving, but she feels she cannot leave. Bonnie is not a shoplifter. What tort may the storekeeper have committed?

5. Roberto's minor son hit someone in the mouth with a brick, causing the person to need three root canals and crowns. Under what doctrine is Roberto responsible for his minor son's tort?

6. Tom and Charles were involved in an automobile accident. Tom sues Charles for damages. Charles claims that Tom's negligence was part of the reason for the accident. What defense has Charles raised?

7. Roxanne, who is out deer hunting, fires her rifle across Betsy's property. What tort has just been committed?

8. Martha is driving down the road and sees a picture of herself on a billboard advertisement. She did not know her likeness was going to be used. What tort has been committed?

9. David and Jerry were both involved in the plan to use Martha's likeness. What are David and Jerry considered to be?

10. James's massive Christmas display causes traffic jams and accidents. People are also walking across his neighbors' lawns, dumping trash on them. What is this classified as?

CHAPTER 10

Contracts and Sales

INTRODUCTION

When the term *contract* is mentioned, most people immediately think of long, complicated documents filled with the proverbial fine print they have been cautioned to read carefully. To be sure, some contracts are quite complicated. However, many of the contracts people enter into every day are not complex documents.

The law of contracts consists of two distinct areas: common law and the Uniform Commercial Code. The **Uniform Commercial Code** is a model statute adopted in some form by each of the states. The UCC regulates commercial transactions such as sales (contracts), commercial paper and transactions, bank deposits and collections, and secured transactions. The remaining law of contracts is governed by common, or judge-made, law.

The first part of this chapter deals with the types of contracts that exist under common law and how these contracts are formed. Contractual law regarding offers, acceptance, consideration, capacity, and compliance is explored. The second part of the chapter deals with the Uniform Commercial Code as it applies to contracts for the sale of goods. Major differences between common law and the Uniform Commercial Code in terms of their requirements and their vocabulary are discussed.

The chapter concludes with an explanation of the remedies available to a party who believes a breach of contract has occurred.

THE COMMON LAW OF CONTRACTS

A contract does not have to be a complicated document filled with fine print and hidden dangers for the unsuspecting. Contracts can be very simple documents; they do not even have to be in writing. A **contract** (*kon*-tract) is an agreement between two or more people that creates an obligation to do or not to do something. There are many classifications of contracts; these classifications are based on how an act is to be performed, when it is to be performed, what is given in consideration of the act performed, and who the parties to the contract are.

FORMATION OF A CONTRACT UNDER COMMON LAW

According to common law, a definite series of events and elements must be present in order for there to be a valid, enforceable contract. Exhibit 10-1 shows the various elements and what must be present to have a valid contract under common law. The definitions of the various elements follow.

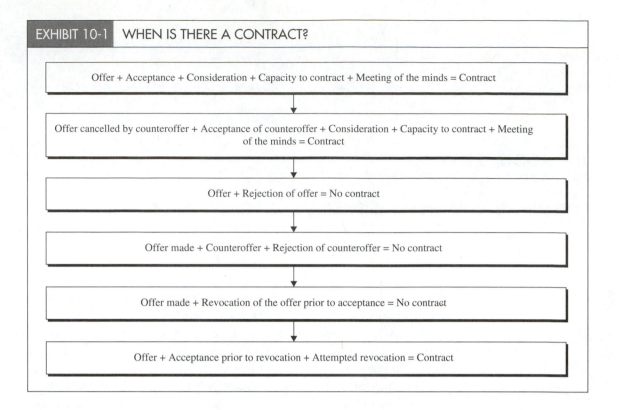

EXHIBIT 10-1 WHEN IS THERE A CONTRACT?

Offer + Acceptance + Consideration + Capacity to contract + Meeting of the minds = Contract

Offer cancelled by counteroffer + Acceptance of counteroffer + Consideration + Capacity to contract + Meeting of the minds = Contract

Offer + Rejection of offer = No contract

Offer made + Counteroffer + Rejection of counteroffer = No contract

Offer made + Revocation of the offer prior to acceptance = No contract

Offer + Acceptance prior to revocation + Attempted revocation = Contract

CAPACITY TO CONTRACT

In order to enter into a valid contract (that is, in order for a contract to be formed), there must be legal capacity to contract, an offer to enter into a contract, acceptance of the offer, and consideration. **Capacity to contract** refers to a person's ability to enter into a legally binding agreement. In order to have capacity to contract, the person must be mentally competent. **Mental capacity**—competency—is the ability to understand the nature and effect of the act one is engaging in; one must understand that he or she is entering into a contract and must be able to comprehend the duties and obligations that are the terms of the contract.

Minors, intoxicated persons, and persons who are insane either lack the ability to enter into a contract or have only partial ability to enter into a contract. A minor may enter into a contract, but has the right to cancel the contract with no liability. In other words, a contract with a minor is voidable at the option of the minor. A person who claims a contract is void because he or she was intoxicated at the time the contract was made will have to prove that the degree of intoxication was such that he or she did not have sufficient mental capacity to understand what he or she was entering into. Similarly, a person with mental illness who claims a contract he or she has entered into is void bears the burden of proof of that claim: he or she will have to show that he or she did not have the mental capacity needed to enter into a contract. See Exhibit 10-2.

EXHIBIT 10-2 CAPACITY TO CONTRACT

STATUS	EFFECT
Minor	Voidable contract at the option of the minor.
Intoxicated	Voidable contract at the option of the person if he or she can prove intoxication.
Mental Illness	Declared insane by a court, the contract is void.
	Mentally ill but not declared insane by a court, the contract is voidable.

OFFER, ACCEPTANCE, AND MEETING OF THE MINDS

A contract is formed when there is an offer and an acceptance—when the offer that is made is accepted by the person to whom the offer is made. An **offer** (*off*-er) is a proposal to perform a certain act or pay an amount of money in return for a certain act. The person who made the offer is expecting either acceptance of the offer, rejection of the offer, or a counteroffer. The person who made the offer is the **offeror** (*off*-er-or); the person who the offer is made to is the **offeree** (off-er-*ee*). If the offer is accepted by the offeree, a contract is formed; there is a **meeting of the minds,** which is an essential element of a contract and is understood to mean that there is a mutual agreement and assent that a contract has been entered into and that the parties understand the terms and conditions contained therein. If the offer is rejected by the offeree, there is no contract.

COUNTEROFFER, REVOCABLE OFFER, AND THE MAILBOX RULE

A **counteroffer** is an offer by the offeree to the offeror that proposes a bargain different than the one proposed by the offeror. For example, Jose offers to sell a Leroy Neiman print to Enrique for $2,000. Enrique makes a counteroffer for the print of $1,700. When there is a counteroffer, the original offer is cancelled and the counteroffer becomes the new offer. In the example, Enrique's counteroffer cancels the original offer, and his counter offer becomes the new offer. A **revocable** (*rev-ə-kəy*-bəl) **offer** is one that may be withdrawn by the person who made the offer before the offer is accepted. For example, an offer might read, "You have 24 hours to accept this offer." In other words, the offer will be considered withdrawn after 24 hours. An **irrevocable** (ir-*rev-ə-kə*-bəl) **offer** is one that cannot be withdrawn after it is made without the consent of the offeree.

If an offer can be withdrawn without the consent of the offeree, and it is withdrawn prior to the terms of the contract being accepted, then there is no contract. There has been no meeting of the minds because the offer has been withdrawn and the offeree cannot accept what is no longer an offer. The withdrawal of the offer is generally effective when it has been communicated to the offeree; however, the mailbox rule may apply to the situation. The **mailbox rule** states that an acceptance of an offer is effective when it is deposited in the mail and a withdrawal of the offer is not effective until it is received by the offeree. If the offeror sends a revocation of the offer to the offeree, but the offeree mails an acceptance before he receives the revocation, there is a valid contract. In other words, an acceptance is effective when it is mailed, and a revocation is effective when it is received by the offeree. Refer to Exhibit 10-3 for a summary of the mailbox rule.

Sometimes there may be a question as to whether an offer has been made, and if it has, whether it has been accepted. That was the situation in the famous "Case of the Carbolic Smoke Ball." Refer to Sidebar 10-1.

SIDEBAR 10-1 *CARLILL V. CARBOLIC SMOKE BALL COMPANY*

Facts: The Carbolic Smoke Ball Company ran an ad for the smoke ball, saying the company would pay £100 to any person who got sick with the flu after using the ball three times daily for two weeks following the instructions provided with the product. The plaintiff purchased the ball and used it as directed. When she got sick with the flu, she sued for the £100 reward. The trial court awarded her the £100. The Carbolic Smoke Ball Company appealed.

Issue: Was there an offer and acceptance so that a valid contract was formed?

Ruling: The offer to pay the £100 was an offer made to anyone who would perform the conditions, and the performance of the conditions was acceptance of the offer. Notification of the acceptance did not have to take place before the performance. The offer was a continuing offer; it was never revoked. By the nature of the offer, the company did not expect to be notified of any acceptance prior to the performance—the use of the smoke ball. This was a valid contract.

Source: Queen's Bench Reporter

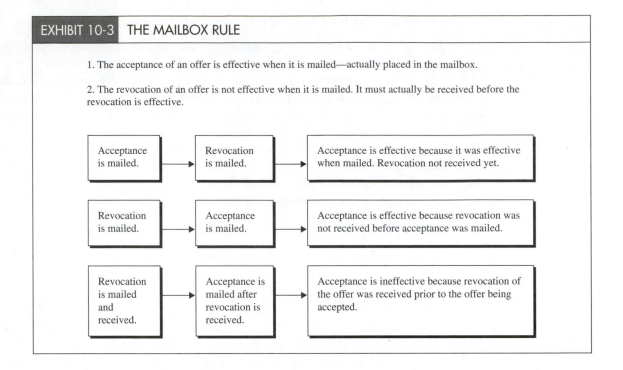

EXHIBIT 10-3 THE MAILBOX RULE

1. The acceptance of an offer is effective when it is mailed—actually placed in the mailbox.

2. The revocation of an offer is not effective when it is mailed. It must actually be received before the revocation is effective.

| Acceptance is mailed. | → | Revocation is mailed. | → | Acceptance is effective because it was effective when mailed. Revocation not received yet. |

| Revocation is mailed. | → | Acceptance is mailed. | → | Acceptance is effective because revocation was not received before acceptance was mailed. |

| Revocation is mailed and received. | → | Acceptance is mailed after revocation is received. | → | Acceptance is ineffective because revocation of the offer was received prior to the offer being accepted. |

TYPES OF ACCEPTANCE

An **acceptance** is an agreement to be bound by the terms of the contract. Acceptance can be **conditional,** which means that the offer is accepted if a certain condition is met. A conditional acceptance is a counteroffer because it is different from the original offer; it adds a provision that must be met in order for the offer to be accepted. The original offeror must accept the condition, and the condition must occur before there is a valid acceptance. An **express acceptance** is the stated acceptance of the terms of the contract; this is also referred to as an *absolute acceptance.* For example, "Will you paint my house for $1,000?" is the offer; the express (or absolute) acceptance is "Yes, I will paint your house for $1,000." An **implied acceptance** is the acceptance of the terms of the contract by words or acts indicating the offeree's intent to accept the contract. For example, an offeree does not verbally accept the contract, but starts to perform what has been asked of him or her. See Exhibit 10-4.

EXHIBIT 10-4 TYPES OF ACCEPTANCE

Acceptance – The agreement to be bound by the terms of the contract.

Conditional Acceptance – The offer is accepted if a certain condition is met. A conditional acceptance is a counteroffer because it is different from the original offer; it adds a provision that must be met in order for the offer to be accepted.

Express Acceptance – The stated (spoken) acceptance of the terms of the contract; also called an *absolute acceptance.*

Implied Acceptance – The acceptance of the terms of the contract by words or acts indicating the offeree's intent to accept the contract.

CONSIDERATION

Consideration is the inducement, the reason, or the cause of someone's entering into a contract. Consideration is a right, an interest, or a benefit going to one party. It is also some detriment, loss, or responsibility that is given to or undertaken by the other party. Consideration is a basic and necessary element of a binding contract; it is the reason why the contract is formed. There are several types of consideration, depending on when it is agreed upon, when it is paid, how it is stated, and its amount. **Concurrent consideration** arises at the same time or when the promises made in the contract are simultaneous. For example, if Enrique and Jose reach agreement about what buildings will be painted at the same time and what price will be paid for the act the promises are considered simultaneous.

Continuing consideration is consideration that extends over a period of time. For example, in return for a painting, Pamela will make a series of payments: Rather than being tendered all at once, her consideration will be spread out over a period of time. **Express consideration** is explicitly stated in the contract or other instrument. In the written contract for the sale of the painting to Pamela, it is stated how much she will pay for the painting each month, and how much the total purchase price is.

Implied consideration is consideration that is inferred from the acts or the situation of the parties. There is no definite amount of price set; rather, the consideration is implied. **Nominal consideration** has no relationship to the actual value of the contract or the article that the contract is about. For example, Vladimir and Irina want to transfer their property to their children. For the sum of $1, they transfer title of their property to their children. The $1 that is paid is nominal consideration because it has no relationship to the actual value of the property that is sold. **Sufficient consideration** is consideration that is deemed by law to be of enough value to support the contract between the two parties. If Vladimir and Irina's home appraised for $240,000 and they sold it to their children for $220,000, then this would be deemed sufficient consideration because what was paid was close to the actual value of the property.

Executory consideration is given for something that is to happen in the future. For example, Yukiko and Emiko might agree that Yukiko will pay Emiko now for painting that Emiko will start in three months. Emiko's painting will start at a definite time in the future, but Yukiko has already provided her consideration for the contract. **Executed consideration** is given before or at the time of entering into the contract. It has already been received, so it is considered executed.

STATUTE OF FRAUDS

The **statute of frauds** states that some contracts must be in writing to be enforceable; such contracts are valid, but in order to be enforced, they must be in writing. The contract can be a valid contract, but if it is not in writing, then the provisions of the contract cannot be enforced in a court of law. According to the statute of frauds, in order to be enforceable, the following contracts must be in writing:

1. A contract for the sale of land or real estate
2. A contract that will take longer than a year to perform
3. A promise to pay the debt of another
4. A promise by the administrator or executor of an estate to pay the debts of the estate rather than using the assets of the estate to pay the debts
5. A contract where the consideration for the contract is marriage
6. A contract for the sale of goods under the U.C.C. where the amount is more than $500. See Exhibit 10-5 for a summary of the statute of frauds.

| EXHIBIT 10-5 | STATUTE OF FRAUDS |

In order to be enforceable, the following types of contracts *must* be in writing.
1. A contract for the sale of land or real estate.
2. A contract that will take longer than a year to perform.
3. A contract to pay the debt of another person.
4. A contract of the executor of an estate to be personally responsible for the debts of the estate.
5. A contract where the consideration for the contract is marriage.
6. Under the U.C.C., a contract for the sale of goods where the amount is over $500.

Remember: *Legality* and *enforceability* **are two different things. A contract can be legal but unenforceable.**

For example, Donna agrees to pay Ann's monthly credit card bill because Ann does not have enough money. They do not put this agreement into writing. Donna makes a few payments, and then decides Ann can pay her own bills and quits making payments. Ann cannot sue Donna to force Donna to resume the payments she agreed to make. The contract was legal for them to enter into, but it is unenforceable because it was not in writing; the Statute of Frauds had been violated. If the contract was in writing, then Ann could sue Donna to force her to continue to make the payments agreed to because the statute of limitations was complied with.

TYPES OF CONTRACTS

EXPRESS OR IMPLIED CONTRACTS

An **express contract** is an actual agreement of the parties. The terms of the contract are openly declared in distinct and explicit language at the time the contract is entered into, either orally or in writing. For example, Jose approaches Enrique, a painter, and enters into an agreement for Enrique to paint Jose's house for $1,000. This is an express contract because the terms of the agreement are clearly stated and were openly declared when the agreement was reached.

An **implied contract** is one that has not been created and for which there is no written evidence of the agreement of the parties. The contract is implied by law based on the acts and conduct of the parties. An implied contract can be created when one of the parties, without being asked to, renders a service expecting to be paid, and the other party knows the services are being performed and accepts the benefits of those services. See Exhibit 10-6.

| EXHIBIT 10-6 | EXPRESS OR IMPLIED CONTRACT? |

Express Contract – The parties to the contract specifically state, either in writing or verbally, what the terms of the contract are.

Implied Contract – There is no specific agreement between the parties (nothing is said or put in writing), but the contract is implied by the parties' conduct.

For example, Yukiko asks Emiko how much Emiko will charge to paint her house. Emiko quotes a price of $1,000. Yukiko thanks Emiko and says she wants to shop around before she decides. Emiko, thinking that Yukiko will not find anyone willing to work more cheaply, starts to make arrangements to paint Yukiko's house. A couple of days later, Emiko shows up at Yukiko's house and starts to paint. When Yukiko sees Emiko doing this, she takes no action because she has not found another painter. Emiko is performing a service, expecting to be paid. Yukiko knows the service is being performed, says nothing, and accepts the painting of her house. According to these facts, an implied contract would be found to exist.

INDIVISIBLE AND DIVISIBLE CONTRACTS

An **indivisible contract** is a contact as a whole; every provision of it must be performed to have a complete contract. If a person fails to perform any part of the contract, then the person has failed to perform the entire contract. If Enrique only paints half of Jose's house, then he fails to perform the entire contract; the contract cannot be considered complete until the whole house is painted. The parts of the house that have been painted cannot be separated from the rest of the house, so the contract to paint the house is an indivisible contract.

A **divisible contract** is one in which the different provisions or parts are considered to be independent of each other. Performance of one of the provisions of the contract is considered to be completion of that part of the contract. The entire contract is not deemed complete until the entire contract is complete, but it can be said that part of the contract is complete. For example, if the contract between Enrique and Jose is for Enrique to paint more than one building, when one building is painted, that part of the contract will be considered complete. If there is a **breach of contract**—the failure without legal excuse to perform any promise that is part of the contract or the entire contract—the damages caused by the breach are limited to the portions of the contract that have not been completed. See Exhibit 10-7.

EXHIBIT 10-7	DIVISIBLE OR INDIVISIBLE CONTRACT?

Divisible Contract – Different parts of the contract can be performed and be completed. The contract can be partially performed.

Indivisible Contract – The contract must be performed entirely. The contract cannot be partially performed.

FURTHER CLASSIFICATIONS OF CONTRACTS

A **conditional contract** is a type of contract that exists only upon the happening of a condition that is expressly stated in the contract. If the condition is not met, there is no contract formed. If there is a clause in Emiko's and Yukiko's contract that reads that Emiko will paint Yukiko's house if and only if she can obtain the necessary paint at or below a certain cost, the contract does not exist until Emiko is able to obtain the paint at the agreed upon price. If she cannot obtain the paint at that price, then the condition has not been met, and the contract will never be formed.

An **entire contract** is a contract in which the completion of the promise on one side of the contract is a **condition precedent** (pree-*see*-dent), something that must happen first before the other side of the contract is to be performed. With an entire contract, one person does not have to perform his or her part of the contract if the condition for his or her performance has not been met. For example, Pamela wants to buy a painting from Dennis, and they agree that Pamela will pay $1,000 for the painting. But Dennis also states in the contract that Pamela must make a donation to the Humane Society before he will sell her the painting for $1,000. Pamela must make the donation to the Humane Society before the rest of the contract has to be performed, so this contract has a condition precedent and is considered to be a whole contract. See Exhibit 10-8.

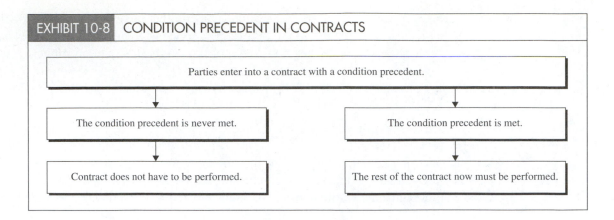

EXHIBIT 10-8 CONDITION PRECEDENT IN CONTRACTS

Parties enter into a contract with a condition precedent.

The condition precedent is never met.

The condition precedent is met.

Contract does not have to be performed.

The rest of the contract now must be performed.

A **severable** contract is one in which each part of the contract may be considered a distinct contract. One contract at a time is performed, but they are all contained in the same instrument or document. The parts of the contract can be broken up, severed, and each part can be treated like a separate contract. For example, Harold and Maude agree that Harold will pay Maude $50 a bushel for Maude's corn as it ripens. There is no maximum or minimum amount stated because it is not known how much corn will ripen. Each purchase of the ripened corn for the stated price can be considered a separate contract.

A **joint and several contract** is a contract made by two or more **promisors** (prom-i-*sors*)—the people who make a promise or agree to do something in the contract who are jointly bound to fulfill the promises in the contract. If one promisor does not complete the contract, then the other promisor must perform the entire contract. A joint and several contract can also be a contract with two or more **promisees** (prom-i-*sees*)—the people with whom the promise or agreement was made and who are jointly entitled to receive the benefits of the contract. If one promisee is unable to receive all of the benefits of the contract, then the other promisee will receive all of the benefits. See Exhibit 10-9 for a summary of the two parties to a contract.

EXHIBIT 10-9 TWO PARTIES TO A CONTRACT

Promisor – The person who made a promise or agreed to do something in the contract; is bound to fulfill the promises in the contract.

Promisee – The person who the promise or agreement was made with; is entitled to receive the benefits of the contract.

A **gratuitous contract** is one that is for the benefit of a person with no profit or advantage promised or received as consideration. Nothing of value is given for the performance of the contract. In an **onerous** (*own*-er-ous) **contract,** something is given or promised for the performance of the contract, but is unequal in value to what is bargained for. For example, Martha states she will pay Stewart's Lawn Service $500 if they will mow her lawn. This would be an onerous contract because the amount that will be paid is far more than the going rate for lawn mowing.

In a **unilateral** (yoon-ə-*lat*-er-el) **contract,** only one of the parties has to perform or make an express agreement. For example, a concert promoter wants a band to perform at a site the promoter owns, and under the contract the band will be responsible for all publicity, advance ticket sales, and appearing to play. For all of this work, including performing, the band will receive a percentage of revenue from the ticket sales. This contract can be considered unilateral because the promoter does not have to do anything prior to the concert; all work promoting the concert is being provided by the band. In a **bilateral** (by-*lat*-er-əl) **contract,** both parties are required to perform or to make an express agreement. If the band is responsible for performing and the promoter is responsible for all ticket sales and publicity, then the contract is a bilateral contract. An **unconscionable** (un-*kon*-shən-ə-bl) **contract** is one in which the terms of agreement are so excessive, unreasonable, or one-sided that the contract will not be enforced. For example, Calvin agrees to sell the painting he inherited from his grandfather for $10 to Hobbs when he receives it from the estate. What Calvin actually receives is an original Picasso, and he refuses to comply with the contract. Because the painting is worth millions instead of $10, Calvin can argue that the contract should not be enforced because it is unconscionable. An **unenforceable contract** is one that has been breached, but for which there is no legal remedy available because of certain defenses, such as the statute of frauds or the statute of limitations. For example, a company signs a contract with a supplier for the delivery of goods, but the supplier breaches the contract and the company gets the goods from someone else at a cheaper cost. Three years after the contract was breached, the company decides to sue the original supplier. The statute of limitations for a breach of contract suit is two years. The time to bring the lawsuit has passed, and therefore the contract is unenforceable. See Exhibit 10-10.

EXHIBIT 10-10	FURTHER CLASSIFICATIONS OF CONTRACTS

Conditional Contract – One or more conditions must be met before there is a contract.

Severable Contract – Each part of the contract can be considered a separate contract.

Joint and Several Contract – Multiple parties to the contract; one promisee can receive all the benefits, or one promisor can be forced to perform the entire contract.

Gratuitous Contract – No profit or benefit promised or received as consideration for the contract.

Onerous Contract – The consideration is not equal to the value of the contract.

Unilateral Contract – Performance from one of the parties to the contract only.

Bilateral Contract – Performance from both parties to the contract.

Unconscionable Contract – Terms of the agreement are so unreasonable and one-sided that the contract will not be enforced.

Unenforceable Contract – Contract is broken, but there is no legal remedy available.

EXECUTED, EXECUTORY, VOID, AND VOIDABLE CONTRACTS

An **executory** (ek-se-kyoot-*tor*-ee) **contract** is a contract in which some future act or acts must still be performed. The contract has not yet been completed. An **executed** (ek-se-kyoot-ed) **contract** is one that has been fully performed; there is nothing else to be done by either party. For example, when Emiko has finished painting Yukiko's house, the contract has been executed.

A **voidable** (*voyd*-ə-bəl) **contract** may be canceled by one of the parties because of a defect or illegality without the party's facing liability for breaching the contract. The contract is valid, but it may be canceled by one of the parties without fear of penalty. For example, recall that someone under the age of 18 cannot enter into a binding contract. Tamara, who is a minor, buys a four-wheel ATV from the local dealer. Tamara makes a few payments, gets tired of the ATV, and cancels the contract. The dealer can get the ATV back, but it cannot enforce the sales contract against Tamara because Tamara is a minor: She can cancel the contract and not face liability. A **void** (*voyd*) **contract** is not a contract at all; it is an arrangement to perform an illegal act or activity. One cannot enter into a valid contract to perform an illegal act. For example, Ricardo enters into an agreement to purchase 50 pounds of cocaine from a drug dealer. If he does not receive the cocaine, he cannot sue the dealer under contract law. The agreement was to perform an illegal act, and thus is invalid under contract law. See Exhibit 10-11.

EXHIBIT 10-11	VOID, VOIDABLE, EXECUTORY, AND EXECUTED CONTRACTS

Executory Contract – The contract has not been fully performed.

Executed Contract – The contract has been fully performed; there is nothing left to do.

Voidable Contract – One of the parties can cancel the contract and not be held liable for contract breech.

Void Contract – Not a contract at all; an agreement to perform an illegal act.

SUBCONTRACTS AND QUASI-CONTRACTS

A **subcontract** is the delegation of the responsibility for performance of part of a contract to another party. When a subcontract is entered into, someone other than one of the original parties to the contract is given the responsibility for performing part of the contract. For example, Shirley enters into a contract with a contractor for the contractor to build her dream home. The contractor is not licensed to wire the home for electricity, so the contractor enters into a contract with an electrician to perform the wiring of the home. The contractor has delegated part of his responsibility to build the home to a subcontractor; a subcontract has been entered into.

A **quasi** (*kway*-zye) **-contract** is not a contract at all. Rather, it is legal remedy under contract law. Quasi-contracts were created at common law to be used in situations where there was no contract but justice required that the situation be treated as if a contract had been entered into. When the court determines that a situation should be treated as if the parties did, in fact, enter into a contract even though no contract exists at all, it is imposing the legal remedy of quasi-contract.

CONTRACT CLAUSES, BREACH OF CONTRACT, AND DEFENSES

Contracts have different clauses with different terms that apply to those clauses. If a contract is not performed according to its terms, that nonperformance can be considered a breach of contract. Which type of breach of contract has occurred depends on the circumstances of the non-performance. Even if a contract is breached, there are certain defenses that can be raised.

CONTRACT CLAUSES

Contracts are made up of different **clauses.** A clause can be a single paragraph or subdivision of a legal document. Clauses can be very lengthy or as short as a single sentence. Different terms apply to specific clauses that may be found in contracts. The term **boilerplate** refers to a clause or language that has definite, invariable meaning regardless of the contract in which it is found. In other words, boilerplate is standard language in a contract.

A contract may have a **hold harmless** clause, which provides that one party to the contract has agreed not to hold the other party to the contract responsible for any damage or liability caused by the agreement or transaction. A contract may also have an **escape clause** that allows one of the parties to the contract to cancel or back out of the agreement without performance without facing liability for breach of contract. For example, a door-to-door sales contract that contains an escape clause of three days provides that the purchaser has three days from the date the contract is signed to cancel the contract and not face any liability. This escape clause may also be considered a boilerplate clause—language used in every door-to-door sales contract. See Exhibit 10-12 for a summary of standard contract clauses.

EXHIBIT 10-12 STANDARD CONTRACT CLAUSES

Boilerplate – A clause or language that is commonly used in contracts that has definite meaning without variation regardless of which contract it is in.

Hold Harmless – A clause indicating that one party to the contract has agreed not to hold the other party to the contract responsible for any damage or liability caused by the agreement or transaction.

Escape Clause – A clause that allows one of the parties to the contract to cancel or back out of the agreement without performance without facing liability for breach of contract.

BREACH OF CONTRACT

As stated earlier, breach of contract is the failure to perform the terms of the contract. There are several ways that a contract can be breached. A **material breach** is a violation of the contract that is substantial and significant and that usually excuses the non-breaching party from any further performance. For example, Hobbs and Calvin enter into a contract for the sale of a painting. When it comes time to complete the deal, Hobbs refuses to sell the painting. This is a material breach, and Calvin is excused from paying for the painting. A material breach not only excuses the non-breaching party from performing, but also gives him or her the right to sue. A **partial breach** is a violation of one part of the contract only. A partial breach is less significant than a material breach. It gives the non-breaching party the right to sue, but does not excuse that party from completing his or her part of the contract. For example, Yukiko has paid Emiko to paint her house and barn. Emiko has completed the painting of the house, but has not painted the barn. Emiko informs Yukiko that she has done all she is going to do under the contract. Part of the contract has been performed, but part has not, so Emiko has partially breached the contract. Yukiko can sue Emiko for the part of the contract that has not been performed, but cannot recover the full value of the contract because part of it was performed.

Constructive breach occurs when the party who is obligated to perform commits an act that prevents the performance of the rest of the contract or declares, before performance is due, that he or she will not perform his or her part of the contract. Emiko is to start painting Yukiko's house on May 1, but on April 15th, she informs Yukiko that she has changed her mind and does not intend to paint the house at all. This is constructive breach because Emiko stated she would not perform her part of the contract before she was obligated to start performing the contract.

Continuing breach occurs when the act constituting the breach happens over a long period of time or is a series of events happening at short intervals. Some types of breach of contract allow the non-breaching party to perform a rescission of contract. See Exhibit 10-13 for a summary of the types of breach of contract.

EXHIBIT 10-13 BREACH OF CONTRACT

Material Breach – A violation of the contract that is substantial and significant and that usually excuses the non-breaching party from any further performance of the contract.

Partial Breach – A less significant breach of contract because it is a violation of the contract as to one part of the contract only. It gives the non-breaching party the right to sue, but *does not* excuse the party from completing his or her part of the contract.

Constructive Breach – The party who is obligated to perform does some act that prevents the performance of the rest of the contract, or declares, before performance is due, that the contract will not be performed.

Continuing Breach – The act constituting the breach happens over a long period of time or is a series of events happening at short intervals.

Sometimes the question before a court in a case of contract breach is "What was promised, and can that promise be enforced?" That was the situation in the case of *Hawkins v. McGee*. See Sidebar 10-2 for a summary of this case.

SIDEBAR 10-2 *HAWKINS V. MCGEE*

Facts: McGee sustained a severely burned hand from contact with an electrical wire. Hawkins, the doctor, stated, "I will guarantee a 100% restoration of the hand." The doctor removed scar tissue from the palm of the burned hand and grafted skin from McGee's chest onto his palm. The hand was not 100% restored, and was covered with dense, matted hair. McGee sued for breach of contract. The jury awarded damages to McGee, but the judge set aside the jury verdict.

Issue: Was this a valid contract? If so, what was the proper measurement of damages?

Ruling: The court was correct in submitting the issue of whether this was a contract to the jury. The actions of the defendant (asking several times to operate on the hand because of his desire to experiment with skin grafting) and the promise he made could be construed as an offer under contract law. The offer was accepted, so a proper question was the amount of damages to be awarded.

The purpose of damages in contract law is to put the plaintiff in as good a position as he would have been had the defendant kept his contract. Pain and suffering is not a proper damages award in contract law. The proper measure of damages was the value of a good hand, which is what the doctor promised, and the value of the hand in its current condition.

New trial ordered.

Source: New Hampshire Reports

Rescission (ree-*sizh*-ən) **of contract** is the right of a party to cancel—rescind—a contract because of default (the breach of the contract by the other party). Rescission of contract is an undoing of the contract from the time the contract began. But not every type of contract breach or default allows for rescission.

DEFENSES

There are certain defenses to breaches of contract under the common law of contracts. One such defense is **commercial impracticability,** which is used when a situation makes the performance of a contract unreasonably expensive, injurious, or costly to one of the parties. **Impossibility of performance** is another potential defense, and is applied in a situation where a party to a contract cannot legally or physically perform the contract. Another defense that one of the parties may present is that the contract is an **adhesion** (add-*he*-zhen) **contract**—a take-it-or-leave-it contract that favors the seller and is unfair to the buyer to the point that it is unconscionable or a violation of public policy to enforce its terms.

CONTRACTS UNDER THE U.C.C.

Article 2 of the Uniform Commercial Code, a uniform law that has been adopted in all fifty states dealing with commercial transactions, governs the sale of goods. A **sale** is a contract between two parties for the transfer of property from one person to another for consideration. The parties are the **seller** or **vendor,** the person selling the goods or contracting to sell goods, and the **buyer** or **purchaser,** the person paying for and obtaining the goods or contracting to buy the goods. See Exhibit 10-14.

EXHIBIT 10-14	WHAT IS A SALE?

Under the UCC, a sale is a contract between the seller and buyer for the transfer of goods for consideration.

A good is something that can be packed in boxes, loaded and stacked onto a pallet, wrapped up, and shipped.

GOODS

Under the UCC, **goods** are items of merchandise, supplies, raw materials, or finished goods. They are moveable at the time they are identified for the purpose of the contract. Goods are tangible objects that can be packed in boxes, loaded and stacked onto a pallet, wrapped up, and shipped. A future good is a good that is not in existence and is not identified at the time of the sale; it is something that will be produced in the future.

Other terms are used to further describe goods that are part of a contract. A **lot** is a parcel or a single article that is the subject matter of a separate sale or delivery that may or may not be enough to fully perform a contract. A lot may be enough to satisfy a contract, or it may take several lots before the terms of the contract are satisfied. A **commercial unit** is a unit of goods identified by the commercial use in that area as a single whole for the purposes of the sale. A commercial unit can be one item (a machine or a car), a set of articles (a group of furnishings), or a quantity (a bale of hay, a gross, or even a carload).

TYPES OF SALES

A **sales contract** is a contract for the transfer of ownership of goods from a seller to a buyer for a fixed price in money, paid or agreed to be paid by the buyer. The contract may be for a present sale or a sale in the future. For example, Rodney enters into an agreement with Randy to purchase from Randy's factory 10,000 sweaters, deliverable immediately. This is a sales contract because there is an offer, an acceptance, and consideration, and the subject matter of the contract is goods.

There are several types of sales under the UCC. The first is an **absolute sale:** the passing of property to a buyer upon completion of the bargain. For example, Rodney orders sweaters from Randy's Clothing and pays for them at the time they are ordered. The bargain is completed when the sweaters are delivered to Rodney, so this is an absolute sale. A **present sale** is one accomplished by the making of the contract. In a **conditional sale,** the transfer of title is dependent on the performance of a condition, usually the payment of the purchase price. For example, a store purchases 20 cases of toothpaste that are delivered to the store, but title does not pass until the toothpaste is paid for by the store. A **bulk sale** is the sale of all or a substantial part of a seller's material, supplies, merchandise, or other inventory in the regular course of business. For example, Rodney contacts Randy's Clothing and says he will buy every sweater Randy has in stock, making this a bulk sale.

An **executory sale** is one for which terms and conditions have been agreed upon, but which has not been carried out in full. For example, Wally World Supermarket has entered into an agreement with Meats R Us for certain cuts of meat, and the amounts, price, and delivery times have been agreed to. Part of the meat has been received, but because part of the meat has yet to be delivered, the sale has not been carried out in full; it is an executory sale. An **executed sale** is final and complete; nothing remains to be done by either party before title to the subject matter of the sale can transfer. Using the example above, once all the meat has been delivered, the sale has been completed.

A **private sale** is negotiated between the buyer and seller privately; there has been no notice of the sale by advertisement or public notice. A **public sale** is a sale made after there has been public notice issued. See Exhibit 10-15 for a summary of the types of sales.

EXHIBIT 10-15	TYPES OF SALES

Absolute Sale – A sale whereby the goods pass to the buyer upon completion of the bargain; nothing is left to be done under the agreement.

Present Sale – A sale that is accomplished by the making of the contract. When the contract is formed, there is a present sale.

Continued

Continued

Conditional Sale – A sale in which the transfer of title is dependent upon the performance of a condition, usually the payment of the purchase price.

Bulk Sale – The sale of all or a substantial part of the seller's material, supplies, merchandise, or other inventory that takes place in the regular course of business.

Executory Sale – A sale in which the terms and conditions have been agreed upon, but which have not been carried out in full.

Executed Sale – A sale that is final and complete. Nothing remains to be done by either party before title to the goods can transfer.

SALES CONTRACTS

Certain types of contracts apply to sales. A **blanket contract** covers a number or group of products, goods, or services for a fixed period of time. For example, Wally World enters into an agreement with Supply Co. that, for one year, Wally World will purchase cleaning supplies from Supply Co. An **open-end contract** is one in which certain terms—usually the price—are deliberately left open. The terms that are not established in an open-end contact will be established at a later time. In an **output contract,** one party agrees to purchase another party's entire output of a particular product. For example, Wally World might enter into an output contract to purchase all the action figures that Lucasco can produce over a two-year period of time.

Another type of agreement a buyer and seller can enter into is a **pyramid sales scheme,** which is illegal in many states. A pyramid sales scheme is an arrangement in which a buyer of goods is promised a payment from the seller of the goods for each additional buyer he locates. The more buyers the seller obtains, the more money the seller will make.

BREACH OF A SALES CONTRACT

A sales contract, like any other type of contract, can be breached by the parties. However, different terms apply to sales contracts for a breach of contract, depending on the circumstances surrounding the breach. **Anticipatory breach** occurs when one party to the contract notifies the other party that he or she has no intention of performing his or her obligations under the contract. For example, Wally World is informed by Meats R Us that it has found another buyer for the meat who will pay a higher price. Meats R Us declares that it will do business with the new purchaser and not with Wally World. This breach can be reversed prior to the date for performance if the other party has not acted upon the breach. For example, if the second deal falls through, Meats R Us can inform Wally World that it will now perform the terms of the original contract. However, the party who did not breach the contract can sue for breach of contract before the performance date when he or she receives notice of the anticipatory breach.

A sales contract can also be terminated or cancelled. A sales contract is **terminated** when one of the parties, according to the terms of the agreement or the law, puts an end to the contract for something other than breach of the contract. When the contract is terminated, any duties that have not yet been performed are discharged, but the rights for past performance still exist. For example, a sales contract is cancelled. Not all the goods have been delivered, but the buyer still has to pay for goods already received. A sales contract is **can-**

celled when one party ends the contract because the other party has breached the contract. Any duties that have not been performed are discharged, but the party who cancelled the contract can still sue for breach of contract.

REMEDIES FOR BREACH OF CONTRACT

If any type of contract is breached, the non-breaching party may sue for monetary damages or for specific performance. **Specific performance** is the remedy wherein the breaching party is required to perform the contract exactly as originally agreed upon. If there was a mutual mistake or a mistake on one side made in the contract, then one or both parties may seek reformation of the contract. **Reformation** is the court-ordered correction of a written contract to accurately reflect what the parties intended when they entered into the agreement. It is considered an equitable remedy.

CONCLUSION

Common law and statutory law control contract laws. Which law applies is determined by the type of contract being entered into. If it is a sales contract, then the Uniform Commercial Code applies; if it is not a sales contract, then the common law of contracts will apply. The contract is a sales contract if the item that is being sold is a *good* as defined by the UCC.

Under the common law of contracts, there has to be an offer and an acceptance and one must be the mirror image of the other. Under the UCC, the acceptance can contain different terms and conditions and still be an acceptance. Under common law, all the terms of an agreement have to be disclosed. Under the UCC, key terms such as *price* and *delivery time* can be left open and the contract will remain valid.

The same terms can have different meanings depending on what type of contract is being entered into. The remedies available for a breach of contract may also be different, so the first, most important question is which contract law applies to a given situation.

Both the UCC and common law require adequate consideration—the reason for entering into a contract—in order to have a valid contract. Performance is required under both areas of the law, and the remedies available under common law and the UCC are similar.

A version of the statute of frauds exists for both common law and the UCC. In both versions, certain types of contracts must be put in writing in order for the contract to be enforceable. The contract can be valid, but it may be unenforceable in a court of law.

Contracts can be bilateral (performance due from both sides) or unilateral (performance due from one side only). Contracts can be express (clearly stated) or implied (created because of the conduct of the parties). Acceptance and consideration can also be express or implied.

Breach of contract can be material (affecting the whole contract) or immaterial (unimportant to the contract). Breach can happen once or it can be continuing; it can be actual or constructive. The innocent party can request specific performance, reformation, or other remedies that attempt to put him or her in the position he or she would have been in had it not been for the contract breach.

CHAPTER 10 REVIEW

KEY WORDS AND PHRASES

acceptance
anticipatory breach
bilateral contract
boilerplate
breach of contract
bulk sale
capacity to contract
commercial unit
condition precedent
conditional acceptance
conditional contract
conditional sale
consideration
constructive breach
contract
counteroffer
divisible contract
escape clause
executed contract

executed sale
executory contract
executory sale
express acceptance
express consideration
express contract
goods
gratuitous contract
implied acceptance
implied consideration
implied contract
irrevocable offer
mailbox rule
material breach
meeting of the minds
offer
open-end contract
output contract
partial breach

public sale
purchaser
pyramid sales scheme
quasi-contract
reformation
rescission of contract
revocable offer
sales
sales contract
severable contract
specific performance
statute of frauds
unconscionable contract
unenforceable contract
Uniform Commercial Code
unilateral contract
void contract
voidable contract

REVIEW QUESTIONS

1. What is an express contract?

2. What is the difference between an indivisible contract and divisible contract?

3. What is breach of contract?

4. What is a condition precedent?

5. What is an onerous contract?

6. What is a voidable contract?

7. What is a void contract?

8. What is an executory contract?

9. What is a quasi-contract?

10. What contracts must be in writing to be enforceable?

11. What is the effect of a counteroffer?

12. What is consideration?

13. What is a material breach?

14. What is the difference between a unilateral and bilateral contract?

15. Who does not have the ability to enter into a contract?

16. In the case of a voidable contract, what is the legal effect of a person's canceling the contract?

17. What is a pyramid sales scheme?

18. What is a conditional contract? What is the result if the condition is never met?

19. What is the difference between an executed sale and an executory sale?

20. What is a tender offer?

FILL IN THE BLANK

1. Items of merchandise, raw materials, or finished products are _____.

2. When goods transfer from the seller to the buyer upon completion of the bargain, this is a _____.

3. A party buys every good that is produced by a factory. This is a _____.

4. Certain terms of the contract are not established in the contract. This is known as a _____.

5. If someone refuses to perform his or her obligations under a contract, it is known as _____.

6. A seller refuses to ship items purchased. This is _____.

7. If the seller ships the items after he said he would not and before the buyer has bought them from someone else, this is _____.

8. A contract is basically rewritten. This is _____.

9. A court orders someone to do what he or she is supposed to do under a contract. This is _____.

10. When there are still goods to be delivered, this is an _____. When the goods have been shipped and paid for, this is an _____.

11. Consideration that has no relationship to the actual value of the contract is known as _____.

FACT SITUATIONS

1. Kyle and his friends plan a weekend at Las Vegas. They enter into an agreement with one of the hotels for the room rate and the services that will be available. Before they can go to Las Vegas, gambling is outlawed there. What type of contract is the agreement with the hotel?

2. Sam's Suzuki Motorcycles enters into a sales contract with Josh for the purchase of a new Suzuki ATV. Josh is seventeen when he signs the sales contract. What sort of contract is this?

3. What liability does Josh face if he cancels the contract?

4. Victor enters into a contract for the sale of some land to Rita. They do not put their agreement in writing. Rita later backs out of the deal because she found other land that she liked more that was cheaper. Victor sues her for breach of contract. What is a possible outcome and why?

5. Kahlil and Jawan enter into a contract for Jawan to purchase rugs from Kahlil, who manufactures rugs. They sign an agreement, but leave how much the rugs will cost open. The price will be set at the time the rugs are delivered. Is this a valid contract? Why or why not?

6. Paul and Frank enter into a contract that will take longer than a year to perform. They do not put the contract in writing. Is this a valid contract? Why or why not?

7. Ricki and Vicki enter into a contract, but they both make a mistake as to the amount of goods to be shipped and the price to be paid. What if anything can be done to fix the terms of the contract?

8. William enters into a contract with a national discount store to provide them with 100,000 units of his product. Prior to the shipping date, another discount store offers him a better price for his product. He notifies the first store that he is canceling their contract. What has William just done? What remedies are available?

9. Issac talks to Abraham about Abraham building a swimming pool for Issac. They discuss a price and a start date, but do not actually agree to anything. Abraham shows up on the date discussed and starts to put in a swimming pool. Issac sees this and says nothing. When Abraham finishes, Issac refuses to pay. Abraham sues for breach of contract. What would be the result of the lawsuit?

10. Jesus enters into an agreement with Estefan for the delivery of 2,000 pounds of meat. One thousand pounds is delivered, and then Estefan calls Jesus and says he will deliver no more meat. What type of breach is this?

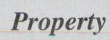

CHAPTER 11
Property

INTRODUCTION

Property is a very broad term that can refer to real estate, personal possessions, and even the product of someone's thoughts. This chapter deals with property law: with how people own property, with how ownership of property is passed from person to person, and with the different ownership interests in property a person can have. One area of property law discussed deals with what happens when a person leaves his or her property with another for safekeeping. The chapter also explains limitations that are placed on the use of property by covenants, zoning, and easements, and concludes with a discussion of laws governing leasing and tenancy.

GENERAL PRINCIPLES

TYPES OF PROPERTY

The legal definition of **property** (*prop*-er-tee) is "anything that is the subject of ownership." Property includes not only the right to ownership and possession, but also the right of use and enjoyment of property for a legal purpose. **Personal property** is all property that is the subject of ownership that is not real property. **Real property** is land, items that are fixed to the land, and whatever is erected or growing on the land. Real property includes houses, things attached to houses, trees and plants, and storage buildings.

ESTATES

The interest a person has in real or personal property is called an **estate.** An **absolute estate** is full and complete ownership or interest in the property. A **conditional estate** is an interest in the property that will not exist unless some event happens first.

TRANSFER OF PROPERTY

In the transfer of ownership of real property, certain terms apply to the buyer and seller, to how ownership is transferred, and to what is used to transfer ownership. There are also terms that apply to what is actually being transferred from one person to the other as a result of the sale or transfer of ownership.

PARTIES INVOLVED AND TITLE

Wells and Audrey are looking for property on which to build their dream home. They find a lot they want and decide to buy it. Upon their purchase of the property, it will be transferred by a **grant,** a conveyance of property. The person who is transferring the property is the **grantor** (gran-*tor*); the person receiving it is the **grantee** (gran-*tee*). Vito, the person owning the property, is the grantor; Wells and Audrey will be the grantees. When Wells and

Audrey purchase the property, they will receive title to the land. **Title** is the formal right of ownership of the property. Title is the means by which the owner of the real property has the possession of the property. Wells and Audrey will have an estate in the real property that was transferred to them by a grant. The way they have possession is by the title.

DEEDS

When the grantor sells the property, the grantees will also receive a **deed,** a written document that transfers title to real property from the grantor to the grantee. See Exhibit 11-1 for the differences among an estate, a title, and deeds.

EXHIBIT 11-1	THE DIFFERENCES AMONG AN ESTATE, A DEED, AND A TITLE

Estate – *What* an individual owns; the property itself.
Deed – The document that *transfers* ownership of property from one person to another.
Title – Evidence of ownership; the person owns property when he or she has title to the property.

Wells and Audrey want a **warranty deed** from Vito, a deed in which the grantor warrants good, clear title to the property. If there are no problems with the title, the property can pass to Wells and Audrey free and clear by warranty deed. If there are problems with the title, the couple may accept a **quitclaim deed,** which conveys whatever title, interest, or claim a person has in property. The deed does not claim or warrant that the title is valid; it only transfers whatever rights the grantor has, if any. If Vito gives Wells and Audrey a quitclaim deed, he will be passing them whatever title he has. In effect, he is saying, "I am passing whatever title I have to you. It may be no title at all, but that is what I am giving to you." See Exhibit 11-2.

EXHIBIT 11-2	WARRANTY AND QUITCLAIM DEEDS

Warranty Deed – The grantor warrants—promises—the grantee that he or she will receive good, clear title to the property that is being sold. The grantor is promising that he or she is the owner of the property and that he or she is passing title with no problems.

Quitclaim Deed – The grantor is giving a deed conveying whatever title, interest, or claim he or she has in the property. The deed does not claim or warrant that the title is valid. It only transfers whatever rights the grantor has, *if any.*

TITLE

Wells and Audrey do not want to take a chance with a quitclaim deed. When they decide to buy the property, they will have a title search performed. A **title search** is an examination of the records of the registry of deeds to determine if the title to the property is good. The person doing the title search is looking for a **cloud on title**—an outstanding claim or encumbrance on the property that affects or impairs the title of the owner. Such claims and encumbrances include mortgages, judgments, tax levies, and liens. Any claim against the property will have to be cleared before good title can pass. For example, if there is a mortgage on the property, then Vito will have to pay off the mortgage before he can pass clear title to Wells and Audrey. The person who requested the title may receive an **abstract of title,** which is a complete history of the title: who has owned the property, what encumbrances were on the property, when or if they have been cleared, and the current status of the title.

If it appears that Vito has clear title, but for some reason he is unable to pass clear title, then he has color of title. **Color of title** is the appearance that a person has clear title, but is unable to pass good title to a purchaser. If Vito has color of title, after the transfer of title from Vito, Wells and Audrey, the purchasers, could file a **quiet title action.** This is a proceeding where the plaintiff—the person who purchased the property—brings into court all claimants to the property and forces them to either prove their claim or be prevented from ever asserting it against the purchasers. A quiet title action serves to clear the title for the purchasers. See Chapter 12, Real Estate Transactions, for more terms related to the transfer and sale of real property.

ESTATES IN PROPERTY

Different terms indicate what type of estate a person holds in property. These terms indicate how long a person may own or use the property, what interest he or she has in the property, and what can happen to that interest.

FEE SIMPLE AND FEE TAIL

The most common estate is **fee simple absolute,** which is an estate without limitation or condition. The owner of the property and his or her heirs are entitled to ownership of the property forever, with no limitations or conditions. Fee simple absolute is the maximum interest a person can have in land; it is total ownership. A **fee simple conditional** estate refers to property conveyed on the condition that something must be done or not done. When this condition is met, the owners have fee simple absolute; if this condition is not met, title is not passed. Before title is passed, Vito could set as a condition that Wells and Audrey must pay him $10,000 for the property. Upon the receipt of the $10,000, which is the purchase price, Wells and Audrey will have a fee simple absolute estate in the property.

A **fee simple defeasible** (de-*fee*-si-bəl) is a fee grant of an estate that may be defeated or done away with by the happening of some future event. The estate may last forever, or it may end if a specified event occurs. If Vito is a baseball fan, he might put a condition in the sale of the property that if the Chicago Cubs win the World Series within 10 years of the sale of the property, title to the property will return to him. Wells and Audrey have to agree to this condition if they want ownership of the land. If the Cubs do not win the World Series in 10 years, then Wells and Audrey would have fee simple absolute. But if the Cubs win the Series in that ten-year period, the property would revert to Vito.

A **fee simple determinable** is a transfer of property that creates a fee simple and that also has a provision that provides for the ending of the estate upon the occurrence of a specified event. Fee simple defeasible can defeat—do away with an estate—if a specific event happens or does not happen. A **fee tail** is how an estate passes by inheritance; fee tail limits the inheritance of the estate to the children of the grantee. If Wells and Audrey own property by a fee tail, then only their children can inherit the property; title cannot pass to anyone else by inheritance.

Another estate in property is the **timeshare interest.** This is defined as the interest in property that a person has purchased which gives him or her the right to use and occupy the accommodations, facilities, or recreational sites for less than a full year during a set period of time. A timeshare interest does not have to be a right to use the property every year, but the right to use the property must be for at least three years. See Exhibit 11-3 for a summary of the different estates in property.

EXHIBIT 11-3 ESTATES IN PROPERTY

Fee Simple Absolute – Ownership of property with no limitations, restrictions, or conditions. The maximum ownership interest a person can have in property.

Fee Simple Conditional – Ownership of the property passes when a condition has been met.

Fee Simple Defeasible – Ownership of the property can be done away with if some future event happens or does not happen.

Fee Simple Determinable – Ownership is fee simple absolute, but can end if a specific event happens in the future.

Fee Tail – Ownership of the property is transferred by inheritance; property can only be inherited by the children of the owners.

Timeshare Interest – An interest in property that a person has purchased that gives him or her the right to use and occupy the accommodations, facilities, or recreational sites for less than a full year during a set period of time.

JOINT OWNERSHIP OF PROPERTY

If property is owned by two or more people at the same time, they can hold title to the property in one of three ways, or by three different estates. A **joint tenancy with right of survivorship** is an estate where each tenant has an individual interest in all the property and an equal right to enjoyment of the property. Upon the death of a tenant, his or her interest passes to the remaining tenants. The entire tenancy belongs to the last surviving tenant. For example, Mike and Candy leave their home and property to their three sons, Adam, Stuart, and Drew as joint tenants with right of survivorship. All three have an equal right to the possession of the entire estate. The one who would eventually inherit the entire estate is the one who lives the longest.

A **tenancy in common** refers to joint ownership in which each tenant holds an undivided interest in the estate. The tenants do not have a right to possession of the entire estate, only a portion of the estate. The interest in the tenancy does not end upon the death of a tenant; it is a right that can pass by inheritance. If Candy and Mike left their property to their sons as tenants in common, each son would own an undivided one-third of the property. The number of shares in the estate is determined by the number of people who have a right to the property though the tenancy in common. Adam, Drew, or Stuart could file a **partition of the property action.** This is a civil action where one or more of the tenants asks the court to divide the property equally among the tenants.

A **tenancy by the entirety** (*ten*-en-see by the en-*ty*-re-tee) is created between a husband and wife. Wells and Audrey, as husband and wife, would hold title to the property, the entire estate, with the right of survivorship. Upon the death of one spouse, the other spouse inherits the entire property. If Wells died first, Audrey would have fee simple absolute in the property. If Audrey died first, Wells would have fee simple absolute. See Exhibit 11-4 for a summary of the ways property can be owned by more than one person.

EXHIBIT 11-4 JOINT OWNERSHIP OF PROPERTY

Joint Tenancy with Right of Survivorship – An estate where each tenant has an individual interest in all the property and an equal right to enjoyment of the property. Upon the death of a tenant, his or her interest passes to the remaining tenants. The entire tenancy belongs to the last surviving tenant.

Tenancy in Common – Each tenant holds an undivided interest in the estate. The tenants do not have a right to possession of the entire estate, but rather only a portion of the estate. The interest in the tenancy does not end upon the death of a tenant. It is a right that can pass by inheritance.

Tenancy by the Entirety – A tenancy that is created between a *husband and wife*. Husband and wife hold title to the property—the entire estate—with the right of survivorship. Upon the death of one spouse, the other spouse inherits the entire property.

LIFE ESTATES

Another way someone can have an estate in property is by a **life estate,** an estate whose duration is for the life of the person holding it. Upon the person's death, the life estate ends. For example, Wells and Audrey give Audrey's mother Maxine a life estate to a piece of property that has a home on it. As long as Maxine is alive, she has the right to occupy the home and the property. When Maxine passes away, the right to occupy the property returns to Audrey. A **life estate pur autre vie** is a life estate for the life of another. For example, Wells and Audrey give Kyle a life estate pur autre vie, for the life of Audrey. Kyle has the right to occupy the property as long as Audrey is alive. Upon Audrey's death, Kyle's estate—his right to occupy the property—ends, and the right to occupy the property reverts back to Wells.

REMAINDER INTERESTS

The right to possess property after a life estate has ended is known as the **remainder** (re-*mane*-der), the remaining part of the estate after another estate has ended. The **remainder interest** is the property that actually passes to the next person after the expiration of the estate. The person who receives the remainder interest is known as the **remainderman** (re-*mane*-der-mən).

The right to receive the remainder may not be absolute. A remainder can be given to one person with a provision stating that it goes to someone else if a contingency that is stated is met. This is known as a **remainder vested subject to being divested.** The remainderman has the remainder interest in the property, but if a certain condition is met or is not met, then the remainder interest will transfer to someone else. For example, Audrey is entitled to the remainder interest in an acre of land if she is married at the time the remainder becomes effective. If she is not married, the remainder interest will pass to her brother Henry.

ADVERSE POSSESSION

Adverse possession is a method of obtaining title to real property. Adverse possession must be

1. Actual—the adverse user must in fact use or possess the property
2. Open—the use of the property must be visible, so the owner is on notice
3. Hostile—the use must be without the permission of the owner
4. Exclusive—the use must not be shared by others
5. Continuous—there can be no interruption in the possession of the property for the period of time set by statute.

If Luca puts up a fence on his property that occupies a foot-wide strip of Eli's land, and if Eli is aware of it, and if the fence was put up without his permission, and if Luca is not sharing the use of the land with anyone else, then, after the statutory period of time, Luca would own the foot-wide strip. If at any time during the statutory period Eli tells Luca to move his fence, then the period of time for adverse possession would start all over again. Adverse possession is not designed as a legal means for someone to take someone else's property. Rather, it is used to settle minor property disputes. See Exhibit 11-5 for a summary of the elements of adverse possession.

EXHIBIT 11-5	ELEMENTS OF ADVERSE POSSESSION

Actual – The adverse user in fact uses or possesses the property.

Open – The use of the property is visible, so the owner is on notice.

Hostile – The property is used without the permission of the owner.

Exclusive – The use of the property is not shared with others.

Continuous – There can be no interruption in the possession of the property for the period of time set by statute.

BAILMENTS

When the term *bailment* is mentioned, people tend to think of posting money so someone can be released from jail. In property law, *bailment* has an entirely different meaning. A **bailment** (*bayl*-ment) is the delivery of personal property by one person to another person for a specific purpose. The bailment may be beneficial to one or both of the parties involved. At the conclusion of the bailment, the personal property is returned to the owner.

PARTIES INVOLVED IN A BAILMENT

The person who delivers the property is the **bailor** (bayl-*or*); the person who receives the property is the **bailee** (bayl-*ee*). When you deliver your car to a paid parking lot, you become involved in a bailment. You "give" your car to the attendant when you hand over your keys; in essence, you are giving the attendant control over your personal property. The purpose of the delivery of the property—your car—is for your car to be parked on this lot. At the conclusion of the bailment (when you come to get your car), your car is returned to you.

TYPES OF BAILMENTS

Other terms further define bailments. An **actual bailment** is a bailment where there has been actual or constructive delivery of the personal property. A **constructive delivery** is an action that does not give physical possession, but rather a possessory right to the property. A **bailment for hire** is a contract in which the bailor agrees to compensate the bailee for the bailment. A **bailment for mutual benefit** is a bailment where the parties contemplate some compensation in return for the benefits of the bailment that the bailor will receive. For example, you deliver your car to the auto dealership to be repaired. You have turned over possession of your personal property to another person, creating a bailment. The mutual benefit is that your car will be fixed and the mechanic will be paid for fixing it.

A **gratuitous bailment** is one only for the benefit of the bailor; the bailee is not expecting any compensation or benefit from the bailment. For example, your neighbor is going on vacation and he leaves his car at your house, in your possession. All you do is start it every morning to make sure the battery does not go dead. Your neighbor, the bailor, is receiving the benefit of seeing that his battery does not go dead; you, the bailee, are not receiving any benefit from the bailment. In a **bailment lease,** a person obtains possession of personal property before it is paid for by agreeing to make rental payments on the property. The bailee enjoys the property as long as the rental price is paid, the rental payments apply to the purchase price, and he or she becomes the owner after completing the payments. For example, Maria goes to a local rent-to-own business and rents a color TV. She is allowed to leave the store with the TV, and she retains possession as long as she makes the rental payments. The rent Maria pays also applies to the purchase price of the TV. When the amount of rent paid equals the purchase price, Maria owns the TV. See Exhibit 11-6 for a summary of the types of bailments.

EXHIBIT 11-6   TYPES OF BAILMENTS

Actual Bailment – A bailment where there has been actual delivery of personal property or a constructive delivery, which is an action that does not give physical possession but rather possessory right to personal property.

Bailment for Hire – A contract in which the bailor agrees to pay the bailee for the bailment.

Bailment for Mutual Benefit – A bailment where the parties think there will be some type of compensation in return for the benefits of the bailment that the bailor will receive.

Gratuitous Bailment – A bailment only for the benefit of the bailor; the bailee is not expecting any compensation or any benefit from the bailment.

Bailment Lease – A person obtains possession of personal property before it is paid for by agreeing to make rental payments on the property.

LIMITATIONS ON THE USE OF PROPERTY

Limitations can be imposed on the use of property; some of these are established by covenants, easements, and zoning laws. These limitations can be passed from one owner of the property to the next, they can be permanent or temporary, they can limit what can be done with the property or what type of building can be built on the property, or grant someone else limited use of the property.

COVENANTS

A **covenant** (*kov*-ə-nənt) is an agreement in the deed stipulating that something shall or shall not be done with the property. A covenant may also be a promise made about the property. A **covenant for quiet enjoyment** is an assurance that there are no defects in the title, and that the grantee—the person purchasing the property—will not be disturbed by people with claims or liens against the property. A **covenant running with the land** is one that cannot be separated from the land; in other words, title to the property cannot be transferred without this covenant. Statements like "No storage shed will be put on the land," or "Only certain types of fences can be erected upon the land," or "All vehicles must be stored in a garage" are examples of covenants. See Exhibit 11-7.

EXHIBIT 11-7 COVENANTS

Covenant – An agreement stated explicitly in the deed to do or not do something with the real estate.

Covenant for Quiet Enjoyment – An assurance that there are no defects in the title, and that the grantee—the person purchasing the property—will not be disturbed by people with claims or liens against the property.

Covenant Running with the Land – A covenant that cannot be separated from the land; title to the property cannot be transferred without this covenant.

EASEMENTS

An **easement** (*eez*-ment) is the right to use the property of another, an interest one person has in the land of another. An **access easement** is the right a person has to enter and leave his own property by passing over the adjoining property of another. For example, Amy and Kim own adjoining lots of property. In order to get to her property, Kim has to drive over to Amy's property. Kim may obtain an easement to get to her property by crossing over Amy's property. A **private easement** is one that is restricted to one or a few individuals. A person may have an easement to walk over someone else's property to reach his or her own property, but he or she is the only person with this right.

The person who has the easement has a right of ingress and egress. **Ingress** (*en*-gress) is the right to enter property or the actual act of entering property. **Egress** (*ee*-gress) is the right to exit property or the actual act of exiting property. A **public easement** can be used by the public generally or an entire community. Examples include sidewalks through property, power lines, phone lines, and cable TV lines that run over or under property. See Exhibit 11-8.

ZONING

Zoning is the division of a city or town into districts and the setting of regulations about what the land can be used for and the physical dimensions of the buildings that can be built in those areas. An area can be zoned residential, multiple family dwelling (apartments), commercial, business, or manufacturing. A **zoning map** is created by a zoning ordinance and sets out the various zoning districts.

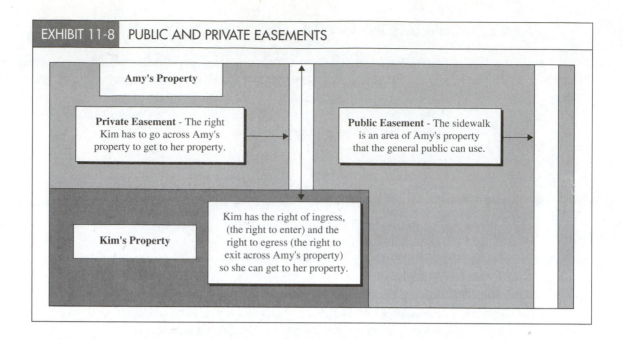

EXHIBIT 11-8 PUBLIC AND PRIVATE EASEMENTS

Amy's Property

Private Easement - The right Kim has to go across Amy's property to get to her property.

Public Easement - The sidewalk is an area of Amy's property that the general public can use.

Kim's Property

Kim has the right of ingress, (the right to enter) and the right to egress (the right to exit across Amy's property) so she can get to her property.

Several different terms are used to describe types of zoning and what they attempt to accomplish. **Cluster zoning** is the setting aside of land by the land developer for parks, schools, or other public needs in housing developments. **Density zoning** is a type of cluster zoning that regulates open spaces, density of population, and use of land. **Conditional zoning** is the imposing of specific restrictions on the landowner as a condition of a zoning change. These restrictions generally do not apply to other property that is zoned the same way; the conditions apply because of where the property is located. For example, a parcel of land is zoned residential, but a church congregation purchases the land and builds a new church. The city places a limitation on the height of the church building that would not ordinarily be placed on a church because of where the building is located.

Spot zoning is the changing of the zoning of a particular piece of land not taking into consideration the zoning plan for the area. An example of spot zoning is allowing a business to erect a new office building in the middle of a residential area. **Exclusionary zoning** is any form of zoning ordinance that tends to exclude specific classes of persons or businesses from a particular district or zone. Exclusionary zoning can be for a valid community purpose: For example, a residential area can exclude an adult entertainment oriented business. Exclusionary zoning can also be illegal: For example, zoning established to keep minority families and businesses out of certain areas is against the law.

A **special use permit** is a permitted exception to zoning ordinances. It is granted when a property owner wants to use his or her property in a way that the zoning regulations expressly permit *if* the conditions specified in the regulations are met. A **variance** is the permission to depart or deviate from the literal—actual—requirements of a zoning ordinance because of the special circumstances regarding a person's property. In effect, it is a waiver of the strict interpretation of the zoning law that remains in substantial compliance with the ordinance and that maintains the ordinance's spirit and purpose. See Exhibit 11-9.

EXHIBIT 11-9	ZONING

Zoning – The division of a city or town into districts; the setting of regulations about what the land can be used for and the physical dimensions of the buildings that can be built in those areas.

Cluster zoning – The setting aside of land by the land developer for parks, schools, or other public needs in housing developments.

Density Zoning – A type of cluster zoning that regulates the open spaces, density of population, and use of land.

Conditional Zoning – The imposing of specific restrictions upon the landowner as a condition of a zoning change.

Spot Zoning – The changing of the zoning of a particular piece of land, not taking into consideration the zoning plan for the area.

Exclusionary Zoning – Any form of a zoning ordinance that tends to exclude specific classes of persons or businesses from a particular district or zone.

LEASES

Sometimes a person does not own property but will rent it from the owner for a definite period of time and for a definite purpose. Certain terms describe this relationship, the type of lease that exists, and what the person can do with the leased property.

LANDLORDS, LEASES, AND TENANTS

The **landlord** is the owner of the estate in land—the owner of the rental property—who has leased the property to another person. The **lease** is the contract for the exclusive possession of the land—the agreement between the landlord and tenant. By way of the lease, the owner is giving up possession and use of the property for consideration and for a definite period of time. The landlord also has imposed upon him or her a **warranty of habitability,** which is an implied warranty that the leased premises are properly maintained and fit for habitation at the time the lease is entered into. The warranty of habitability also provides that the property will remain fit for habitation during the term of the tenancy. When the lease expires, the landlord has the absolute right to retake control of and use the property.

The landlord is the **lessor** of the property; the person who rents the property is the **tenant** or **lessee.** The **landlord tenant relationship** is the contractual, legal relationship between the lessor and the lessee regarding the occupation of the property. Because the lease is a contract, there must be consideration; in this case, **rent** is the consideration paid for the use or occupation of the property. In some cities, **rent controls** place restrictions or limitations on the maximum amount of rent that may be charged on rental property.

LEASEHOLDS

The **leasehold** is the estate in real property that is held by the lessee/tenant under a lease. There are four principal types of leaseholds: an estate for years, a periodic tenancy, a tenancy at will, and a tenancy at sufferance. An **estate for years** is the right to possess the estate for a determined and fixed period of time that is agreed upon by the lessor and the lessee. For example, a lease may be for six months, for $3,600 in rent, payable monthly in the amount of $600. A **periodic tenancy** is one that runs from week to week, month to month, or year to year, and that is subject to termination at the end of the rental period. A

tenancy at will is a tenancy by permission of the owner or landlord, but without a fixed period of time. A tenancy at will can be created by an express contract or it can be implied at law based on the parties' conduct. A tenancy at will has an uncertain duration and either party may terminate it with proper notice. A **tenancy at sufferance** is a tenancy created when a person who had a tenancy holds over, or remains in possession of the property after the tenancy expires. In other words, the tenant is allowed to stay by the landlord, but he has no interest in or right to possession of the property. A landlord can end a tenancy at sufferance at any time. See Exhibit 11-10 for a summary of the types of tenancies.

EXHIBIT 11-10	TYPES OF TENANCIES

Estate for Years – The right to possess property for a set period of time that is stated in the lease.

Periodic Tenancy – A tenancy that runs week to week, month to month, or year to year and that can be terminated at the end of each tenancy.

Tenancy at Will – A tenancy by the permission of the owner of the property or the landlord; there is no set period of time.

Tenancy at Sufferance – A tenancy created when a person who had a tenancy remains in possession of the property after the tenancy expires. He or she is allowed to stay by the landlord, but has no interest in or right to possession of the property.

When a landlord no longer wishes to lease premises to a tenant or a tenant wishes to vacate leased premises, a notice to quit may be given. A **notice to quit** is a written notification given by a landlord to a tenant stating that he or she wishes to repossess the leased property and that the tenant is required to remove himself or herself from the property when the lease expires. If the tenant has possession of the property by a tenancy at will or a tenancy by sufferance, the notice to quit means to vacate the premises immediately. This term can also apply to a written notice a tenant gives a landlord stating the tenant's intention to vacate the leasehold and when that will take place.

There are further classifications of leases under the four principal leaseholds. The lease can be a **concurrent lease**—one that begins before the earlier lease expires. The lessee is entitled to the rent from the previous lease starting on the date his or her lease begins. A **gross lease** requires the lessee to pay a flat sum for rent. The landlord is required to pay all expenses—taxes, water, utilities, insurance, and any other expenses associated with the property—out of this sum. In a **net lease** arrangement, the tenant not only pays rent, but also pays the expenses associated with the leased property: taxes, utilities, and insurance. A **graduated lease** takes into consideration future increases in operating expenses; rent can increase as operating expenses increase. An **index lease** provides for increases in rent according to increases in the consumer price index. See Exhibit 11-11.

EXHIBIT 11-11	FURTHER CLASSIFICATIONS OF LEASES

Concurrent Lease – A lease that begins before the current lease expires.

Gross Lease – The tenant pays a flat fee for rent to the landlord and the landlord uses this money to pay all the expenses of the property.

Net Lease – The tenant pays rent and those expenses associated with the property (e.g., taxes, utilities, and insurance).

Graduated Lease – The rent increases as the operating expenses of the lease increase.

Index Lease – Rent increases are based on the consumer price index.

LEASING A RIGHT TO USE THE LAND

A person who owns property owns certain rights in the property that can be leased out while the person retains ownership of the property itself. A person who owns **mineral lands**—lands that contain deposits of minerals that are useful or valuable in sufficient quantity to make their extraction worthwhile—can lease or sell the right to mine minerals that are on the property. A **mineral lease** grants a lessee the right to mine property for oil, gas, or minerals. The rent is usually based on the amount or the value of the mineral taken from the land. The landlord retains all other rights in the property. The person who has the lease has **mineral rights**—the right to take minerals from the land. The person who owns the property has mineral rights unless they are leased or sold. The owner also has mineral rights if he or she has **mineral royalties**—the income received from the lessee for the right to mine the land. This amount is usually based on the amount of the mineral that is removed from the land. A **mineral deed** indicates transfer of ownership of the minerals in the land. The owner of the property sells the minerals in the land to someone else and gives that party a mineral deed. Even if the property owner has leased or sold the mineral rights, he or she can still lease part of the land. A **top lease** is a lease granted on property that already has a mineral lease. A top lease is for the top of the property; the mineral lease is for what is below the property. See Exhibit 11-12.

EXHIBIT 11-12	MINERAL LEASES

Mineral Lease – A lease in which the lessee has the right to mine the property for oil, gas, or minerals. The rent is usually based on the amount or the value of the mineral taken from the land.

Mineral Rights – The interest the person who has the mineral lease has in the minerals in the land; the right to take minerals from the land.

Mineral Royalties – The income received from the lessee for the right to mine the land. The amount of royalties is usually based on the amount of the mineral that is removed from the land.

Mineral Deed – Indicates transfer of ownership of the minerals in the land. The owner of the property sells the minerals in the land to someone else and gives that party a mineral deed.

If a business leases property, it may be by a **percentage lease;** the amount of rent is based on a percentage of the gross or net profits of the business with a minimum amount set as the rent. This kind of lease is used when the location of the property is an important part of its value. A **sublease** is a lease executed by the lessee to another person giving that person the same estate for a shorter period of time. The sub-lessee has a leasehold that is for a shorter period of time than the leasehold of the original lessee. For example, Sam has a lease for a year. He has to go out of town on business for several months, so he subleases his property to Diana for six months.

EVICTIONS

If the lessee fails to pay rent, then the landlord has a **landlord warranty.** This warrant allows a landlord to place a lien on the personal property of the tenant and sell that property at public sale. This is used to compel payment of the rent or the observance of some other provision in the lease. If a group of tenants have disagreements with the landlord, they may conduct a **rent strike,** an organized undertaking in which rent is withheld until the problems between the tenants and the landlord are resolved.

If the tenant fails to pay rent per the lease agreement, the landlord has the legal remedy of eviction. **Eviction** is defined as the deprivation of a person of the possession of land or rental property either by re-entry or a legal proceeding. The legal proceeding to force eviction may be a **forcible entry and detainer.** This proceeding restores the possession of the land to the person who transferred possession by contract. It is designed to establish not who owns the property, but who has the right to possess the property. Additional terms further define and classify evictions. An **actual eviction** is the physical expelling of the tenant out of all or part of the leased premises. In a **constructive eviction,** the landlord does not physically remove the tenant from the premises, but takes some action that causes the premises to be unfit or unsuitable to be occupied. For example, a landlord might cut off one or more of the utilities that make the premises habitable. If the tenant chooses to leave the premises, he or she has been constructively evicted.

In a **total eviction,** a tenant is totally deprived of his or her rights to property. A **partial eviction,** in contrast, occurs when the tenant is deprived of only a portion of his or her rights to property. Depending on what the tenant is deprived of, a partial eviction could turn into a constructive eviction. In a **retaliatory eviction,** a landlord begins eviction proceedings against the tenant because he or she does not like some action or behavior of the tenant. For example, a tenant might complain about the premises not being repaired, participate in a tenants' union, or organize a rent strike. His or her landlord might arrange a retaliatory eviction. See Exhibit 11-13 for the types of evictions.

EXHIBIT 11-13	BEING EVICTED

Actual Eviction – The physical removal of the tenant from the leased property.

Constructive Eviction – An action taken by the landlord that makes the licensed premises unfit to be occupied.

Total Eviction – The tenant is totally deprived of his or her right to the leased property.

Partial Eviction – The tenant is deprived of only some of his or her right to the leased property.

CONCLUSION

General property law deals with the rights and responsibilities related to possession of real property. This includes the possession, sale, and leasing of real property. A person who owns property has an estate in the property, the ownership interest. The ownership can be in fee simple absolute, which is total ownership of property, or the owner could lose the property if a certain event happens (fee simple determinable) or only have ownership if a certain event does happen (fee simple conditional). Ownership can be shared by several people either by joint tenancy with right of survivorship, tenancy in common, or tenancy by the entirety.

Possession of property can be given to another without transferring ownership through a bailment, whereby property is left with someone for safekeeping, or a lease, whereby a person enters into a contract for the use of land. The lease can be for possession of the property for a set period of time or at the discretion of the landlord, or it can be to remove something from the land, a mineral lease.

The use of property can be limited by easements, the right another person or the public has to use someone else's land; covenants, promises that run with the land; or zoning laws, restrictions that are placed on what can be done with or what can be built on property.

These are general principles that apply in many other areas of law. Some areas of property law are even more specialized.

KEY WORDS AND PHRASES

abstract of title
access easement
adverse possession
bailee
bailment
bailment for hire
bailor
cloud on title
cluster zoning
color of title
concurrent lease
conditional estate
conditional zoning
constructive eviction
covenant
deed
easement
estate
eviction
fee simple absolute
fee simple conditional
fee simple defeasible

fee simple determinable
fee tail
grant
gross lease
ingress
joint tenancy with right of
  survivorship
landlord
landlord warranty
lease
life estate
life estate pur autre vie
mineral deed
mineral lands
mineral lease
mineral right
mineral royalty
notice to quit
periodic tenancy
personal property
property
public easement

quiet title action
quitclaim deed
real property
remainder
remainderman
rent
special use permit
spot zoning
sublease
tenancy at sufferance
tenancy at will
tenancy by the entirety
tenancy in common
title
title search
variance
warranty deed
warranty of habitability
zoning

REVIEW QUESTIONS

SHORT ANSWER

1. What is an estate?
2. What is a warranty deed?
3. What is a quitclaim deed?
4. What is a cloud on title?
5. What is color of title?
6. What is fee simple defeasible?
7. What is a fee tail?
8. What is a tenancy in common?
9. What is joint tenancy with right of survivorship?
10. How do married couples jointly possess property?
11. What is the difference between a mineral lease and a mineral deed?
12. What is considered to be constructive eviction?

FILL IN THE BLANK

1. Someone has the right to use property for as long as he or she is alive. The interest he or she has is a _____.

2. A limitation that is placed on the use of the land that runs with the land is a _____.

3. When someone has the right to cross over another person's property, this person has an _____.

4. Government limitations on what can be done with property are _____.

5. The authorized use of one piece of property is changed without taking into account the uses of the surrounding property. This is known as _____.

6. Land in a housing development is set aside for public use. This is known as _____.

7. A deviation from authorized zoning is a _____.

8. A permitted exception to a zoning ordinance is _____.

9. The amount of rent a landlord can charge is limited by law. This is known as _____.

10. A tenancy for a set period of time is a _____, and a tenancy where the tenant is allowed to stay by the landlord is a _____.

FACT SITUATIONS

1. Gold is discovered on Harry's property. In order to get to the property, the mining company has to cross over Sara's property. While on Harry's property, they erect a fence that includes Stan's property without Stan's permission. Identify the different property interests involved.

2. Wilma gives her daughter Holly an interest in a piece of land for as long as Holly's husband is alive. What estate does Holly have in the land? What estate would Holly have if it was as for long as she was alive?

3. Ralph is left property by his uncle provided he is married by the time he is thirty-five. If he is single when he is 35, the property goes to his sister Deborah. What interest do Ralph and Deborah have in the property?

4. Dale, Joe, and Dennis are given property by their father. Each has an equal interest in all the land. Joe sells his interest to Peter. What interest did Joe, Dale, and Dennis have? Under what circumstances will Peter receive title to the property?

5. Sarah and David divorce. David signs a deed giving Sarah whatever interest he has in the property. What type of deed is this?

6. Gus leases out the mineral rights to his property to the Lion Oil Company. He then leases out the property to Louie for Louie to farm the land. What lease does the Lion Oil Company have? What lease does Louie have? Can both these leases exist at the same time?

7. Jerry gives Harold the right to use property for twenty years. Then it goes to Samantha for Samantha's life. Finally, it goes to Sally, who will own it outright. What interest do Harold and Samantha have? What interest does Sally have? How will she own the property?

8. Carmen leases a house from Rafael and signs a year-long lease. After six months, the roof starts to leak, the basement floods, the kitchen is overrun with insects, and the hot water heater quits working. Can Carmen leave the premises and not be liable for rent? How? What has Rafael committed?

9. The property Wells and Audrey purchase has limitations on the type of fence they can erect, forbids storage sheds from being built, and requires cars to be kept in the garage. These are part of the deed. What are these restrictions called?

10. When Wells and Audrey purchase the property, they receive assurances from Vito that no one else has a claim to the property. What is this promise from Vito called?

CHAPTER 12

Real Estate Transactions

INTRODUCTION

Real estate transactions are governed by property law, and there is some overlap in legal terminology. However, several words and phrases apply specifically to the sale and purchase of real property. Some of these terms apply to the people who arrange for the sale of homes and what their responsibilities are. Other terms apply to the negotiation and finalization of the sale. Because most people cannot pay cash for a home or real estate, they arrange for financing, and this chapter discusses terms related to that process. The chapter concludes with an explanation of terms that apply to the closing of the sale of real estate.

SELLING OF REAL ESTATE

Real estate is another term used to describe real property, which was defined in Chapter 10 as land, items that are fixed to the land, and whatever is erected or growing on the land. The selling of real property is different from any other type of sale because of the nature of what is being sold.

SELLERS OF REAL ESTATE

If a person wants to sell his or her property, he or she may use the services of a **real estate broker**—someone who is licensed to negotiate the sale, purchase, lease, or exchange of property. The broker is paid on commission, with payment of the commission based on the success of the transaction. In other words, the real estate broker is paid only if he or she is successful in arranging the sale of the property. A **real estate agent** is a person whose business it is to sell, and offer for sale, real estate for others, to rent buildings or real estate, or to collect rents for others. The real estate agent is also paid on a commission basis, which means the transaction must be completed for the agent to be paid. See Exhibit 12-1.

EXHIBIT 12-1 | SELLERS OF REAL ESTATE

Real Estate Broker – Person who is employed to negotiate *the sale, purchase, lease, or exchange of property*. The broker is paid on a commission basis, with payment of the commission based on the success of the transaction.

Real Estate Agent – A person whose business it is to *sell, and offer for sale*, real estate for others, rent buildings or real estate, or collect rents for others. The real estate agent is also paid on a commission basis.

LISTING THE PROPERTY

Turnor, who wishes to sell his house, selects Roddy to be his real estate agent for the sale of the property and they enter into a listing agreement. A **listing** is the agreement between the owner of the real property and the real estate agent regarding the sale of the real estate. Under the terms of the listing, the agent agrees to attempt to locate a buyer for the property at a certain price and at certain terms for a fee or commission.

Listings are classified in a number of ways. An **open listing** is one that may be given to more than one agent at a time. The seller of the real estate is obliged to pay the commission of the real estate agent who locates a buyer if that agent is one of the authorized agents. The real estate agent who actually locates the buyer of the property is the person who collects the fee, even if he or she was not the real estate agent with whom the property was originally listed. If the owner of the property finds the buyer, however, he or she is under no obligation to pay a commission to the real estate agent. For example, Roddy, the real estate agent, shows the home to a person who offers $100,000 for the property. However, before Turnor is told about the $100,000 offer, a person who is not using an agent offers him $120,000 for the property. Turnor may accept the $120,000 offer and owe Roddy nothing because Turnor found the buyer.

An **exclusive agency listing** gives one agent the exclusive right, other than the right of the owner, to sell a property for a specified period of time. Under the terms of this type of listing, no other real estate agent can show a prospective buyer the property for a specified period of time. If an exclusive agency listing is the agreement that is entered into between the agent and the owner, then the agent will have the owner sign an exclusive authorization to sell the listing. Under the terms of an **exclusive agency listing agreement,** the real estate agent will receive a commission even if the owner is the one who finds a buyer. Under the terms of a **nonexclusive listing,** the agent has an exclusive listing, but if the owner sells the property without using the agent, he or she does not owe the agent any commission.

A listing may also be a **multiple listing,** one that is shared with other members of a real estate association. Under this type of listing, the agent who originally had the listing, and the agent who actually found the buyer, will each receive part of the commission from the sale.

A **net listing** allows the owner of the property to set the minimum price he or she will accept for the property. The real estate agent's **commission** is the amount that the property sells for over the minimum amount that has been established. If the property sells for either the minimum amount established by the owner or less than the minimum amount, then the agent receives no commission. For example, Turnor lists the property with Roddy as a net listing, setting the minimum amount he will accept as $100,000. If the property sells for $106,000, Roddy has earned a $6,000 commission. If the property sells for $100,000 or less, Roddy receives no commission for the sale. See Exhibit 12-2 for the types of listing.

EXHIBIT 12-2 | **TYPES OF LISTING AGREEMENTS**

Open Listing – The property is listed with more than one real estate agent.

Exclusive Agent Listing – Only the real estate agent or the owner of the property can sell the property for a certain period of time. The agent earns a commission if the owner sells the property.

Nonexclusive Listing – Only the real estate agent or the owner can sell the property for a certain period of time. The agent only earns commission if he or sells the property.

Multiple Listing – An exclusive listing shared between agents of a real estate association.

Net Listing – The owner sets the minimum price he or she will accept for the property. The real estate agent must sell for more than the minimum set in order to earn a commission.

Another provision of the listing agreement may be a **guaranteed sale** provision. Under a guaranteed sale provision, if a specified length of time has passed and the property still has not been sold, the real estate firm or agent will buy the property. This agreement to purchase may be under particular terms and conditions and the purchase may be at a substantial discount from the listed price.

EARNEST MONEY

When an offer is made on a property and it is accepted, the buyer of the property will pay **earnest money** at the time the contract for the sale of the home is signed. Earnest money indicates the willingness, the intention, and the ability of the person to purchase the property. The earnest money is applied to the price of the property, and if the buyer defaults on the sale, the money is forfeited to the seller. For example, Paul and Susan make an offer to buy Turnor's home for $100,000. Turnor accepts the offer, so a contract for the sale of the home is entered into. Paul and Susan pay $2,000 in earnest money, showing their intention to complete the transaction. When the sale of the home is completed, they will have to pay $98,000 because the $2,000 paid as earnest money will apply to the purchase price of the home. See Exhibit 12-3.

EXHIBIT 12-3	EARNEST MONEY

$100,000 – Agreed upon sale price of the real estate.

$2,000 – Earnest money, money paid to insure the completion of the sale. Binds the seller to the buyer and the buyer to the seller.

$98,000 – The amount the buyer will still have to pay the seller at closing because the earnest money is applied to the sale of the real estate.

MORTGAGES

IN GENERAL

Susan and Paul are planning on paying $10,000 in cash for the home and financing the remaining $88,000, borrowing this amount to complete the sale. They will apply for a **mortgage,** a written agreement that gives the person or institution that is lending them the money an interest in the property. The mortgage provides the lender some security for the repayment of the amount borrowed, something the lender can use to recoup its money if the mortgage is not repaid. (See Chapter 19 for more information about debtor/creditor relationships.) The real property secures the loan, and the loan will be used to purchase the property that secures the loan. The mortgage gives the lender an interest in the property, a claim to the property in case the person who borrowed the money does not repay the loan. *Mortgage* is a generic term that applies to many different types and classifications of mortgages. See Exhibit 12-4.

EXHIBIT 12-4	MORTGAGES IN GENERAL

Step One – Paul and Susan apply at a bank or other lender for money to buy a home. They are applying for a mortgage.

Step Two – The bank approves the loan, lending Susan and Paul the money needed to complete the transaction.

Step Three – At closing, Paul and Susan sign the paperwork that gives the bank a security interest in the real property in return for the loan. This gives the bank the right to take possession of the home and sell it if Paul and Susan fail to pay back the loan.

CLASSIFICATIONS OF MORTGAGES

Mortgages are classified based on who issues them, payment type, and interest rate. A **conventional mortgage** is a contract that uses all or part of the property to secure the loan that is used to purchase the property; the borrower retains possession of the property. A person will usually apply for a conventional mortgage from a bank, a mortgage company, or a finance company. The conventional mortgage is used to purchase the property, the property secures the mortgage, and the borrower has possession of the property subject to the mortgage.

A **FHA mortgage** is insured by the Federal Housing Administration in whole or in part. If the buyer defaults on the mortgage, the FHA will pay the balance of the mortgage, and then initiate proceedings against the person who defaulted on the mortgage.

A **VA mortgage** is given to veterans of the U.S. armed forces and their spouses and is guaranteed by the Veterans Administration. Only veterans or their spouses are eligible for this type of mortgage. If there is a default on the loan, the VA will pay the balance of the mortgage and then proceed against the person who defaulted on the loan.

A **blanket mortgage** is one that creates a security interest on a substantial portion or all of the borrower's assets (property). The real property is not enough to secure the loan, so more than the real property is used to insure payment; personal property is used. If the borrower defaults on the loan, the lender can go after all of the other property of the borrower that secured the mortgage in order to satisfy the debt.

A **chattel mortgage** is secured by the personal property of the borrower rather than the real property that is the subject of the transaction. Chattel mortgages are not used very much anymore because other credit devices contained in the Uniform Commercial Code have replaced them.

A **fixed rate mortgage** specifies an interest rate that remains fixed for the life of the mortgage regardless of what happens with regard to interest rates. The interest rate that is charged initially stays the same throughout the life of the loan; the rate does not go up or down. An **adjustable rate mortgage,** on the other hand, is one whose interest rate is tied to an index and is periodically adjusted as the rate index moves up or down. The rate may or may not have a maximum limit. An adjustable rate mortgage may also state that the rate cannot go up more than a certain percentage each year. For example, Paul and Susan have an ARM mortgage; the terms of the mortgage state that the maximum interest rate that can be charged is 12% and that the interest rate can increase by a maximum of 1% a year. Thus, the most the interest rate can go up in a year is 1%; the highest the rate can go is 12%, regardless of what the rate index is.

A **balloon payment mortgage** is one that requires interest payments for a specified period and full payment of the principal at the end of that period. For example, Hubert has a balloon payment mortgage for $50,000. The mortgage states that for twenty years, Hubert will pay 10% interest per year on the amount borrowed, or $5,000 in interest per year. At the end of twenty years, Hubert will have to pay the $50,000 that was originally borrowed because the payments made were for interest only—none of the amount paid was used to reduce the amount borrowed.

The opposite of a balloon payment mortgage is the **amortized mortgage,** a mortgage whereby the borrower pays the current interest charges each month as well as a portion of the principal amount borrowed. For example, Jackson's mortgage payment is $1200 a month; $400 goes to pay the interest and $800 is credited toward the amount borrowed. A **closed end mortgage** is one that stipulates that neither the property originally used to secure the mortgage nor the amount borrowed can be changed during the term of the mortgage. Refer to Exhibit 12-5 for a summary of the different types of mortgages.

EXHIBIT 12-5	WHICH MORTGAGE IS RIGHT FOR YOU?

Conventional – The property secures the loan. The property can be used to assure payment.

Veterans Administration – The VA, as well as the property itself, secures the loan. The VA can be used to assure payment.

Federal Housing Authority – The FHA, as well as the property itself, secures the loan. The federal government can be used to assure payment.

Blanket Mortgage – Real and personal property is used to secure the loan.

Chattel Mortgage – Only personal property is used to secure the loan.

Fixed Rate Mortgage – The interest rate remains the same during the term of the loan.

Adjustable Rate Mortgage – The interest rate can go up or down during the term of the loan.

Amortized Mortgage – Loan payment includes interest and part of the principal amount that was borrowed.

Balloon Payment Mortgage – Loan payment is all interest. Entire amount of money borrowed is due at the end of the loan term.

An **open end mortgage** allows the borrower to borrow additional money under the same mortgage and mortgage terms provided additional property is available to be used to provide security for the loan.

MORTGAGE BONDS AND ASSUMPTION

A **mortgage bond** is a bond where payment of the bond is pledged, secured by real estate. In other words, a borrower borrows money to buy property and the person or business that loaned the money receives a bond (see the definition of *bond* in Chapter 20, Commercial Paper). The payments on the loan go to paying off the bond, and if the borrower fails to make payments, payment of the bond is secured by the real estate. For example, a company issues a mortgage bond for $100,000 to Paul and Susan who use the $100,000 to purchase a home. The couple will repay the $100,000 plus interest to the company that has the bond until the loan is repaid. If they fail to repay the loan, the person or company who has the bond can sell the property to recover the amount that was loaned. See Exhibit 12-6 to see how bond money is used to finance a mortgage.

EXHIBIT 12-6	USE OF BOND MONEY FOR A MORTGAGE

Borrower	**Lender**
Gets – Money to purchase the real estate.	**Gives** – Money to purchase the real estate.
Gives – A bond whereby payment is secured by the real estate.	**Gets** – A bond whereby payment is secured by the real estate.

Another option that may be available to a purchaser of real estate is **assumption of the mortgage.** A buyer may qualify to take over the current owner's existing mortgage. However, the mortgage must be one that is designated as assumable.

OBTAINING THE MORTGAGE

In order to apply for the mortgage, Paul and Susan can go to a **mortgage banker,** a person or business that deals in mortgages, including the servicing, refinancing, and reselling of a mortgage to other investors. The couple may also go to a **mortgage company,** a business that originates and closes mortgages, which are then assigned or sold to other investors. The banker will service the mortgage, while the mortgage company may not. **Mortgage servicing** includes procedures such as collecting the payments due, releasing the lien on the property when the mortgage is paid in full, and starting foreclosure proceedings if necessary.

Quite often, the mortgage bank or company that originally loaned the money will sell the mortgage to another person or company. The new mortgage bank or company has the mortgage assigned to it as part of the purchase. **Assignment of a mortgage** accords the right to collect any payments due to another person or business, one different from the person or company that originally loaned the money. The company or bank that purchases the mortgage purchases the right to collect the debt from the person who borrowed the money. That company or bank may keep the mortgage and collect the payments or may sell the mortgage yet again. A mortgage may be sold many times during the term of the loan before the loan is finally paid back.

If Susan and Paul are approved for a loan, they become the **mortgagors,** the people who borrowed the money that creates the mortgage. The person or business where they obtained the mortgage is the **mortgagee.**

CONDITIONS OF A MORTGAGE

As a condition of allowing the mortgage, the bank may require Paul and Susan to pay mortgage points or obtain mortgage guarantee insurance. A **mortgage point** is a percentage of the loan charged by the mortgagee as part of the cost of the loan. A mortgage point is usually 1% of the loan, so if the mortgagor has to pay four points, then he or she must pay 4% of the loan as part of the cost of obtaining the loan. The purchase of mortgage points usually lowers the interest rate charged on the loan. For example, Paul and Susan borrow $80,000 at 6% interest, but they are required to purchase one and a quarter ($1\frac{1}{4}$) mortgage points as part of receiving the mortgage. They would pay an additional $1,000 ($80,000 × $1\frac{1}{4}$%) at closing, and the interest rate on the loan would be $4\frac{3}{4}$% because of the mortgage points purchased. See Exhibit 12-7.

EXHIBIT 12-7	MORTGAGE POINTS

Mortgage Point – A percentage of the loan charged by the mortgagee as part of the cost of the loan. Points lower the interest rate on the loan.

Loan reads 8% plus 1.5 points. $100,000 is the amount of money borrowed.

$100,000
× 1.5% (.015)
$1,500 Amount that will be paid to the mortgagor at closing.

The actual interest rate is 6.5% (8% − 1.5%).

Mortgage guarantee insurance will pay the mortgagee a portion of the loss suffered by the mortgagee if the mortgagor defaults on the loan. For example, Clarice defaults on a loan and still owes $30,000 on her mortgage. The bank seizes her property, but can sell the property for only $20,000. The bank is still owed an additional $10,000. Mortgage guarantee insurance would pay the $10,000 the bank would lose because it could not collect that amount. See Exhibit 12-8 for an explanation of mortgage insurance.

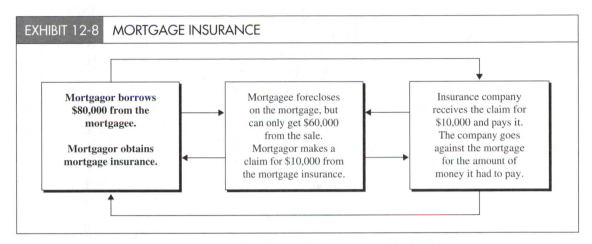

EXHIBIT 12-8 MORTGAGE INSURANCE

When a buyer makes an offer on real estate, there may be a clause in the offer similar to the following statement: "This offer is subject to the buyer's being able to obtain suitable financing." This statement is known as a **mortgage contingency clause;** the purchase of the real property is contingent on the buyer's being able to acquire a mortgage or "suitable financing." The mortgage contingency clause is designed to protect the buyer of the property in the event he or she is unable to obtain a loan to purchase the property. If the buyer cannot obtain a loan to buy the real estate, the mortgage contingency clause provides that he or she is under no obligation to purchase the property because a condition of the sale has not been met. In this situation, the buyer will receive his or her earnest money back. Inability to obtain financing is not considered a default on the agreement because one of the conditions of the sale was not met. (See Chapter 10, Contracts, for more information about breach of contract and conditions.)

CLOSING

When Paul and Susan have obtained a mortgage and the survey and title search have been completed, the next step in the process is closing. **Closing** is the term used to refer to the final steps of the real estate transaction. It is a separate procedure.

WHAT HAPPENS AT CLOSING

During closing, the following things happen:

1. The purchase price for the real estate is paid.
2. The mortgage is secured. The mortgagor is given the interest in the property that secures the loan of the money (see Chapter 18, Debtors Rights and Creditors Remedies).

3. The deed is delivered or is placed in escrow. By way of **escrow,** a legal document is delivered to a third party who holds it until a contingency has been fulfilled or a condition has been met. The deed is held in escrow until the revenue stamps required are paid and affixed to it.

RESPA

If Susan and Paul obtained their loan from a bank or other institution that is insured by the federal government, RESPA applies to the closing. RESPA, or the **Real Estate Settlement Procedures Act,** is a federal statute that requires disclosure of settlement costs in the sale of a residential improved property that is being financed by a bank or other lender that is insured by the federal government through the FDIC. RESPA applies any time the purchaser of a home obtains the mortgage through a bank or other institution that is insured by the federal government. The term **residential** is defined as "a property for one to four families." The term **improved property** refers to real estate that has had its value increased by the addition of such things as buildings, streets, sidewalks, utilities, or even landscaping. See Exhibit 12-9 for a summary of what happens during closing.

EXHIBIT 12-9	WHAT HAPPENS AT CLOSING

1. The purchase price for the real estate is paid.
2. The mortgage is secured. The mortgagor is given the interest in the property that secures the loan of the money (see Chapter 18, Debtors Rights and Creditors Remedies).
3. The deed is delivered or is placed in escrow. If the Real Estate Settlement Procedures Act applies, then
4. There is full disclosure of all the costs associated with closing the sale.

CLOSING COSTS

Certain costs are associated with the purchase of real property, and these costs are paid at closing. **Closing costs** are expenses or costs that are in addition to the purchase price of the property. Some typical closing costs include:

1. Costs associated with the obtaining of the loan (mortgage points, for example)
2. Cost of the title search and survey
3. Cost of the premiums for title insurance
4. Costs of real estate taxes and insurance, which are placed in an escrow account. (This is an account that holds funds for the payment of real estate taxes and insurance. These funds are payable to a third party [the government or the insurance company] when the taxes or premiums are due.)
5. Cost of **revenue stamps,** which are a state tax on the sale of property. When the tax on the transaction has been paid, stamps are attached to the deed indicating the amount of tax that was paid. The deed cannot be recorded without these revenue stamps being attached to it.
6. Appraisal fees

7. Cost of obtaining the credit report
8. Cost of document preparation and notarization. See Exhibit 12-10 for a summary of closing costs.

| EXHIBIT 12-10 | BRING PLENTY OF CHECKS: THIS IS WHAT IS PAID AT CLOSING |

1. Purchase price of the real property
2. Cost of obtaining the loan (loan origination fee and any mortgage points)
3. Title search and survey
4. Title insurance premiums
5. Real estate taxes
6. Real estate insurance
7. Revenue stamps
8. Cost of document preparation
9. Appraisal fees
10. Cost of credit report

SETTLEMENT AND CLOSING STATEMENTS

These costs are set out on the **settlement statement,** a document prepared by an escrow agent or the lender that gives a complete listing of all the costs involved in the sale. See Exhibit 12-11 for the elements of a settlement statement.

| EXHIBIT 12-11 | SETTLEMENT STATEMENT |

Purchase price of the real property–$100,000
Loan origination fee–$300
Mortgage points–$1500
Title search and survey–$400
Title insurance premiums–$250
Real estate taxes–$400
Real estate insurance–$150
Revenue stamps–$445
Cost of document preparation–$35
Appraisal fees–$150
Cost of credit report–$35
TOTAL PAID AT CLOSING–$100,000 less escrow money plus $3665 in closing costs

---

There may also be a **closing statement,** a document that analyzes the closing and sets out the costs with regard to how much money the seller will actually receive. The closing statement will set out the purchase price less the amount of money needed to pay off the existing mortgage as well as any taxes due. The statement will also indicate if there are any credits that will be added. The purchase price, minus paying off the mortgage and any other amounts due, plus any credits is the amount of money the seller will receive. For example, Turnor has sold the property for $100,000. He has an existing mortgage in the amount of $50,000. The taxes due for the year that have been prorated (adjusted for the partial year) are $1,000, and there are no credits. The closing statement would show the $100,000 purchase price minus the amount used to pay off the existing mortgage ($50,000) and the $1,000 tax bill. Turnor will actually receive $49,000 for the sale of the property. See Exhibit 12-12.

EXHIBIT 12-12	CLOSING STATEMENT

$100,000 – Purchase price for the real estate

– $50,000 – Pay off existing mortgage

– $1,000 – Prorated property taxes

+ 0 – Amount of any credit due the seller

$49,000 – Amount the seller will actually receive for the sale of the property

Upon completion of this process—the finding of the property, offer and acceptance, the tendering of earnest money, the qualifying for a loan, the title search, the survey, and the closing—Paul and Susan will have successfully purchased the property from Turnor.

CONCLUSION

Real estate transactions constitute a more specialized area of property law than general property law. Real estate brokers and real estate agents are people who sell real estate for others. The listing is the agreement between the owner and the agent regarding the sale of the property. Listings can be open, exclusive, nonexclusive, or multiple.

The purchase of real estate is usually financed by a mortgage or security interest. The mortgage can be conventional, FHA, or VA. The mortgage can be a blanket mortgage or a chattel mortgage. The mortgage can have a fixed or variable rate of interest.

The real estate transaction concludes with the closing, the culminating steps taken to finalize the sale. The purchase price is paid, as well as any outstanding mortgage, fees, taxes, and insurance. Only then does title pass to the new owners.

KEY WORDS AND PHRASES

adjustable rate mortgage	FHA mortgage	mortgagor
amortized mortgage	guarantee sale	multiple listing
assignment of mortgage	improved property	nonexclusive listing
balloon payment mortgage	listing	open listing
closing	mortgage	real estate
closing costs	mortgage banker	real estate agent
closing statement	mortgage bond	Real Estate Settlement
conventional mortgage	mortgage contingency	Procedures Act
earnest money	clause	revenue stamps
escrow	mortgage points	settlement statement
exclusive agency listing	mortgage servicing	VA mortgage

REVIEW QUESTIONS

SHORT ANSWER

1. What is a blanket mortgage?
2. What happens during assumption of a mortgage?
3. What is the difference between a mortgage bank and mortgage company?
4. What is an escrow account?
5. What is earnest money? Why is it paid?
6. What is an adjustable rate mortgage?
7. What is a balloon payment?
8. What is the difference between a conventional mortgage and a FHA mortgage?
9. What are mortgage points?
10. What is the effect of paying mortgage points?
11. What is a wraparound mortgage?
12. What is an improvement?
13. What is closing?
14. What is shown on a closing statement?
15. What is a revenue statement?
16. What is the difference between a real estate broker and a real estate agent?
17. What is mortgage servicing and who does it?
18. What is an open listing?
19. What is a guarantee sale clause?
20. What do revenue stamps represent?

FILL IN THE BLANK

1. Identify the following types of mortgages.
   a. The interest rate can go up or down during the term of the mortgage. _____

   b. The borrower can borrow additional money under the mortgage with the same terms, provided there is additional property to secure the mortgage. _____
   c. The borrower pays a portion of the principal as well as the monthly service charges. _____

   d. Interest payments for a specified period of time and full payment of the principal at the end of the mortgage period. _____
   e. All or part of the property is used to secure the loan, and the borrower retains possession of the property. _____
   f. Mortgages are secured by different departments of the federal government. _____ and _____
   g. The value of the real property is not enough to secure the loan, so different assets are used. _____
   h. Personal property rather than real property is used to secure the mortgage. _____

   i. The interest on the loan stays the same regardless of what interest rates do. _____

2. _____ is a percentage of the loan charged as part of the cost of the loan.

FACT SITUATIONS

1. Herman buys a home. His mortgage has a payment at the end of the mortgage that is most of the principal that was borrowed. What type of mortgage is this?
2. When Doug and Candy put their home on the market, different agents are allowed to show the home. What type of listing is this?
3. What kind of listing would be in effect if only one agent were allowed to show Doug and Candy's home?
4. Fred and Ginger find the home they want to purchase. Along with their offer, they pay $1000. What is the $1000 called? What does it do?
5. Fred and Ginger's offer also contains the statement, "Contingent upon finding suitable financing and selling our current home." What is this known as?
6. Tameka fills out the paperwork to apply for permission to take over someone else's payments on the home she wishes to buy from them. What is this known as?
7. Sasha takes out a mortgage from Metro Bank. Two weeks after she closes on her home, she receives a notice saying her payments must now be made to Wells Fargo Bank. A month later, she gets another notice saying payments now go to Chase Manhattan. What is happening to her mortgage?
8. Jasmine has sold her home for $120,000. She owes $20,000 on the mortgage, $1,200 in taxes, and $350 for insurance. She has a credit of $200 that will be applied. How much money will Jasmine receive from the sale of her home?
9. Jacob lists his home with a real estate agent and signs an agreement saying only this agent can show the home to prospective buyers. What type of listing is this?
10. If Jacob finds a seller, and they enter into an agreement without using the real estate agent, will the agent or be entitled to a commission? Why or why not?

CHAPTER 13

Agency

INTRODUCTION

Most people have heard the term *agent.* We use a real estate agent to buy a house, and we use an insurance agent to buy insurance. Celebrities and famous athletes have agents to represent them in business negotiations. In this chapter, terms that describe the agency relationship are discussed as well as the many types of agency. How this relationship is formed, the powers and duties of the different types of agents, and who is liable for the actions of the agent are also covered.

AGENCY IN GENERAL

In general, an **agent** is a person authorized by another to act for or in place of him or her, one who represents or acts for another under contract or because the agency relationship exists. For example, someone might hire someone else to negotiate a contract on his or her behalf.

FIDUCIARY DUTY

Agency is a **fiduciary duty,** a duty to act for someone else's benefit, making one's own interests secondary to that of the other person. This fiduciary duty is created when one person consents to act on the other person's behalf and be under that person's "control." For example, when the NBA drafts Sidney, he will consent for David to represent him in negotiations with the team that drafted him. Sidney is the **principal,** the person who has authorized another to act for his benefit and be subject to his direction and control. The actions of the agent can be binding upon the principal. David is the agent because he will be representing Sidney during the contract negotiations with the team. David and Sidney have an **agency relationship,** an employment arrangement for the purpose of representation in establishing a legal relationship between the principal and a third party. Using the previous example, David has been hired by Sidney to negotiate a contract for Sidney with the NBA team that drafted him. Once David and the team agree on the terms of a contract, Sidney will be bound by the terms of that contract because he authorized David to negotiate on his behalf. See Exhibit 13-1.

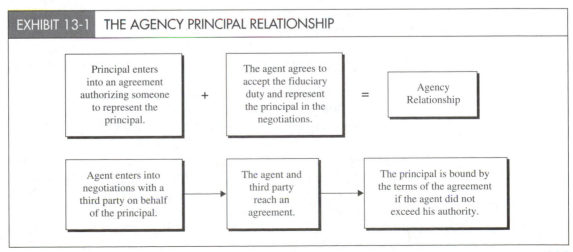

EXHIBIT 13-1   THE AGENCY PRINCIPAL RELATIONSHIP

Principal enters into an agreement authorizing someone to represent the principal.   **+**   The agent agrees to accept the fiduciary duty and represent the principal in the negotiations.   **=**   Agency Relationship

Agent enters into negotiations with a third party on behalf of the principal.   →   The agent and third party reach an agreement.   →   The principal is bound by the terms of the agreement if the agent did not exceed his authority.

TYPES OF AGENCY

There are several ways to classify the type of agency that has been created: by whether or not the identity of the principal is known, by how much authority the agent is given, or by what duties the agent will be performing.

DISCLOSED AND UNDISCLOSED PRINCIPALS

Because the NBA team would know whom David is representing, they are on notice that the agent is acting for the principal. The team knows the identity of the principal, so David would be considered a **disclosed principal.** If the other party has notice that the agent is working for someone else but does not know who the principal is, then the principal is a **partially disclosed principal.** If the third party has no notice that the agent is acting for a principal, and thinks the agent is acting for himself, then the principal is an **undisclosed principal.** See Exhibit 13-2.

EXHIBIT 13-2	IDENTITY OF THE PRINCIPAL

Disclosed Principal – The third party knows he or she is dealing with an agent and he or she knows who the agent is representing.

Partially Disclosed Principal – The third party knows he or she is dealing with an agent, but does not know who the agent is representing.

Undisclosed Principal – The third party does not know that he or she is dealing with an agent. He or she thinks the agent is negotiating on his or her own behalf, not on behalf of someone else.

GENERAL TYPES OF AGENCY

There are three general types of agency with three general types of agent, each with different levels of authority. In a **general agency,** the power to perform all the acts connected with a particular trade, business, or employment is delegated to a **general agent,** the person who is authorized to act for the principal in all matters concerning a particular business. While this agent has the authority to perform any activity that is connected with a particular business, he or she can do nothing that is not connected with the business.

A **special agency** is one in which a **special agent** is authorized to conduct a single transaction or series of transactions that does not involve a continuation of services. Once the transaction or series of transactions is conducted, the agency relationship ends. The services performed by the agent cannot be continuous services—ones that are performed over and over again.

A **universal agency** is a relationship whereby an agent is empowered to conduct every transaction that can lawfully be delegated by a principal to an agent. This agent is referred to as a **universal agent.**

AGENCY BASED ON AGREEMENT AND IMPOSED AGENCY

There are several further classifications of agents and agencies. An **agency in fact** is an agency relationship established by agreement between the principal and the agent. The agency relationship actually exists, and there is agreement between the parties involved that it exists. This is also known as an **actual agency.**

Agency by estoppel is an agency relationship that is imposed by the law because of the actions of one of the parties involved. Specifically, the actions of the principal could reasonably lead a third person to believe that an agency relationship exists. The "principal" is estopped—prevented—from saying that the agency relationship does not exist because his or her actions helped create the impression that an agency relationship existed. See Exhibit 13-3.

EXHIBIT 13-3 | GENERAL TYPES OF AGENTS AND AGENCY

General Agency – The power to perform all the acts connected with a particular trade, business, or employment is delegated to the general agent.

General Agent – The person who is authorized to act for the principal in all matters concerning a particular business. This agent has the authority to perform any activity that is connected with a particular business, but can do nothing that is not connected with the business.

Special Agency – The agent is authorized to conduct a single transaction or series of transactions that does not involve a continuation of services.

Special Agent – The person authorized to conduct the single event or series of events on the behalf of the business or person.

Universal Agency – An agency relationship where the agent has the power to conduct every transaction that can lawfully be delegated by the principal to the agent.

Universal Agent – The person who has the power to conduct every transaction that legally can be delegated to him. The universal agent is the agent who has the most authority to act on behalf of the principal.

Agency by estoppel can also be created if the principal is negligent in supervising the actions of the agent and allows the agent to exercise powers not granted to him or her. Because the agent is exercising powers that were not given to him or her, this can create the impression to third parties that the agent does possess the authority to act. The principal cannot say the agent does not have the authority to act because the principal was allowing the agent to perform acts the agent did not have the authority to perform. The principal is the one most capable of stopping the unauthorized activities, but takes no action. The "agent" in this situation is an **apparent agent,** one whom the principal either intentionally or because of negligence, causes a third person to believe the person is actually his or her agent. This situation is also known as **ostensible agency** with an **ostensible agent;** the principal helped create the impression that an agency relationship existed.

Implied agency is created when the conduct of the principal and the agent imply or indicate that there is an agency relationship, although no formal agency agreement was established. See Exhibit 13-4 for a summary of how these agencies are created.

EXHIBIT 13-4 | CREATION OF AGENCY RELATIONSHIPS

AGENCY IN FACT

An agency relationship established by an agreement between the principal and the agent. There is an actual agreement between the agent and the principal about their relationship. An agency in fact is also known as *actual agency.*

AGENCY BY ESTOPPEL

An agency relationship that is created by law when the actions of the principal reasonably lead a third person to believe that an agency relationship exists. The principal is estopped—prevented—from saying that the agency relationship does not exist. The principal took positive action to create the impression that a person was his or her agent acting on his or her behalf.

This agency can also be created if the principal is negligent in supervising the actions of the agent and allows the agent to exercise powers not granted to him or her. The agency relationship already exists, but the agent exercises more authority than he or she was given. The principal is negligent in supervising the agent's actions, even though he or she is in the best position to stop the agent's actions.

IMPLIED AGENCY

An agency is created when the actions of both the principal and the agent imply or indicate that there is an agency relationship even though there is no formal agency agreement. The parties intended to create the agency relationship, and their conduct indicates that such a relationship does in fact exist, but there is no formal agreement creating the agency. There must be conduct from both the agent and the principal indicating or implying there is an agency relationship.

PUBLIC AND PRIVATE AGENTS

A **private agent** is a person who is representing a principal in his or her private affairs, which are usually not open to the general public. An example of a private agent is a **high managerial agent,** whose power is comparable to the authority of an officer of a corporation to formulate corporate policy or supervise subordinate employees in a managerial capacity. A **corporate agent,** another private agent, is authorized to act for and on behalf of a corporation. An example of a corporate agent acting on behalf of a company is the corporate agent receiving the service of process on behalf of the corporation when the corporation is being sued.

A **public agent** is an agent of the public—a state or federal government. This individual is appointed to act for the public in some matter pertaining to the administration of government. One example of a public agent is a **diplomatic agent,** who represents a domestic government in its dealings with a foreign government.

CO-AGENTS, AGENCY COUPLED WITH AN INTEREST, AND GENERAL AGENT

A **co-agent** shares authority to act as an agent with another person who has also been appointed and authorized to act by the principal. The term **agency coupled with an interest** refers to a relationship in which an agent has an interest in the property or subject matter with which he or she is dealing. A **general agent business** is a person who is not engaged as an agent for a single firm or person, but holds himself or herself out to the public as being engaged in the business of being an agent. A sports agent who represents many different clients is a general business agent. See Exhibit 13-5.

EXHIBIT 13-5 | PUBLIC AND PRIVATE AGENTS

Private Agent – A person who is representing a principal in his or her private affairs—something that is not open to the general public.

Example: High Managerial Agent – An agent with power comparable to the authority of an officer of a corporation to formulate corporate policy or supervise subordinate employees in a managerial capacity.

Corporate Agent – An agent who is authorized to act for and on behalf of a corporation.

Public Agent – An agent of the public, the state, or the federal government; a person appointed to act for the public in some matter pertaining to the administration of government.

Example: Diplomatic Agent – An agent representing a domestic government in its dealings with a foreign government.

MERCANTILE AGENTS

A **mercantile agent** is employed for the sale of goods or merchandise. There are two types: brokers and factors. A **broker** is an agent who is employed to make bargains and contracts for a fee. The broker is an intermediary who has no control over the property, and the sale is in the name of the principal. For example, Donny has stock in a company that he wants to sell because he wants to play the market. He decides to use a stockbroker, Marie, to sell the stock on his behalf. Marie can enter into a contract for the sale of the stock, but she has no control over the property. She does not own the stock; all she does is arrange the sale. The sale will be in Donny's name.

A **factor** is an agent who is hired by a principal to sell **consigned** merchandise— property delivered to the agent for sale on behalf of the principal, but in the agent's name. The agent is entrusted with the possession and control of the goods and is compensated by a commission that is usually termed a **factorage.** For example, Dina takes her clothes to a consignment shop to be sold. The shop owner maintains a record of what Dina brought in, and the clothes are now considered to be consigned merchandise. When the clothes sell, the shop keeps part of the proceeds—the factorage—and sends Dina the rest of the proceeds from the sale. See Exhibit 13-6 for a summary of mercantile agents.

EXHIBIT 13-6	MERCANTILE AGENTS

Broker – An agent who is employed to make bargains and contracts for a fee (compensation). The broker is an intermediary who has no control or possession of the property; the sale is in the name of the principal.

Factor – An agent who is hired by the principal to sell consigned merchandise, property delivered to the agent for sale on behalf of the principal. The sale may be in the agent's name. The agent is entrusted with the possession and control of the goods and is compensated by commission.

REAL ESTATE AGENTS

A **real estate agent** is a person whose business it is to sell, and offer for sale, real estate for others, to rent buildings or real estate, or to collect rents for others. The real estate agent and the seller may enter into an **exclusive agency** arrangement, which is a grant of the exclusive right to sell within a particular market or area. The real estate agent would then be an **exclusive agent,** one who has the exclusive right to sell within a particular market or area. There may also be an **exclusive agency listing**—an agreement between a property owner and a real estate agent that the owner will pay the agent's commission if the real property is sold during the listing period regardless of whether the agent is responsible for the sale. (See Chapter 12, Real Estate Transactions.)

FOREIGN, LOCAL, MANAGING, INDEPENDENT, AND SUB-AGENTS

A **foreign agent** is a person who registers with the federal government as a lobbyist representing the interest of a foreign nation or corporation. The agent may lobby about such things as import quotas, tourism, and foreign aid. A **local agent** is a person appointed to act as the representative of a corporation and to transact its business at a given place or within a defined area. A **managing agent** is a person who has exclusive supervision and control of some department of a business. The management of the division requires the agent to exercise independent judgment and discretion.

An **independent agent** is one who exercises his or her own judgment and is subject to the one who hired him or her only for the results of the work performed. The person you hire to build your home—an independent contractor—is an independent agent. You do not tell him how to build the house: You tell him what you want built and then hold him responsible for the end product. How the actual construction is done is up to the contractor, and he will be held legally responsible for the end results.

A **sub-agent** is a person hired by an agent to perform functions for the principal. Usually there must be express or implied authority from a principal for an agent to be able to hire a sub-agent. The authority may be express authority (the agent is told that he or she has the authority to hire sub-agents), or it may be implied authority (the authority is implied because of the relationship). For example, the agent you hire to build your home uses implied authority to hire a sub-agent to build a certain part of your home. The contractor is very good with structure, but does not know electrical wiring or plumbing. The agreement with the contractor only states that the contractor is responsible for building the home. Because the contractor is not licensed to put in electricity or plumbing, his ability to hire sub-agents—a sub-contractor—is implied. This allows the contractor to sub-contract with an electrician and a plumber to do the wiring and the plumbing for the house. See Exhibit 13-7.

EXHIBIT 13-7   OTHER TYPES OF AGENTS

Foreign Agent – A person who registers with the federal government as a lobbyist representing the interest of a foreign nation or corporation.

Local Agent – An agent appointed to act as the representative of a corporation and to transact its business at a given place or within a defined area.

Managing Agent – An agent who has exclusive supervision and control of some department of a business.

Independent Agent – An agent who exercises his or her own judgment and is subject to the one who hired him or her only for the results of the work performed.

Sub-Agent – A person hired by an agent to perform a function for the principal.

Certain terms and principles further define the relationship between an agent and a principal. An agent may have actual authority, implied authority, or apparent authority to act on behalf of the principal. The principal may also ratify or reject actions of the agent that were beyond his or her authority.

AUTHORITY OF THE AGENT

ACTUAL, IMPLIED, AND APPARENT AUTHORITY

Actual authority is the power a principal gives an agent by way of express or implied agreement. A principal may not be bound to an agreement entered into by an agent if the agent exceeded his or her actual authority. Generally an agent cannot bind the principal to an agreement if the agent is not authorized to enter into that type of agreement.

Implied authority is the power of an agent to act on behalf of a principal that is inferred or implied from the responsibility given to the agent. Implied authority is the authority the agent has that is necessary for the agent to carry out the principal's wishes. This authority is not expressly given to the agent, but because it is necessary for an agent to use this authority to complete the principal's wishes, it is implied that the agent has the authority. For example, when you hire a contractor to build your home, you may not expressly give him the authority to purchase supplies. But because the contractor must have supplies to build the home, the contractor's authority to purchase supplies is implied.

Apparent authority is the authority the principal knowingly or negligently allows the agent to assume or the power the principal indicates the agent actually has. The agent does not have actual or implied authority, but the principal, by his or her action or non-action, gives the impression that the agent has the authority to act. The principal can be bound by the agent's actions in the case of implied or apparent authority because the principal has the ability to stop the actions of the agent but does not. The principal can be held responsible because he or she is the one who can stop the unauthorized activity, but chooses not to. See Exhibit 13-8 for a summary of the authority of agents.

EXHIBIT 13-8	AUTHORITY OF AN AGENT

Actual Authority – The power of an agent to bind the principal when the power comes from an express or implied agreement between the principal and agent. This is the authority the principal gives to the agent because of an express agreement or an implied agreement.

Implied Authority – The power of an agent to act on behalf of the principal that is inferred or implied from the responsibility given to the agent. Implied authority is the authority the agent has that is necessary for the agent to carry out the principal's wishes. This authority is not expressly given to the agent.

Apparent Authority – The authority the principal knowingly or negligently allows the agent to assume or the power the principal indicates the agent actually has. The agent does not have actual or implied authority, but the principal, by his or her action or non-action, gives the impression that the agent has the authority to act.

RATIFICATION

If the agent is acting outside the scope of his or her authority, whether express or implied, the principal can still be responsible for the agent's actions if the principal ratifies the agent's conduct. **Ratification** occurs when someone who, at the time of the act or agreement did not have the authority to act on the "principal's" behalf, did enter into an agreement or did act on the "principal's" behalf. The principal, who has knowledge of all the material facts, then accepts the act performed or contract entered into. The ratification, the actual acceptance of what was done, may either be express or implied.

Express ratification is a ratification that is made in express and direct terms. The principal expressly accepts—clearly states—that he or she accepts the benefits of the act or contract. **Implied ratification** is ratification that is established by the law and based on the actions of the principal. The principal does not expressly accept the benefits of the "agent's" actions; he makes no statement, but he accepts and takes advantage of what the "agent" has done. See Exhibit 13-9 for a flow chart showing the ratification of an agent's actions.

EXHIBIT 13-9	RATIFICATION OF AN AGENT'S ACTIONS

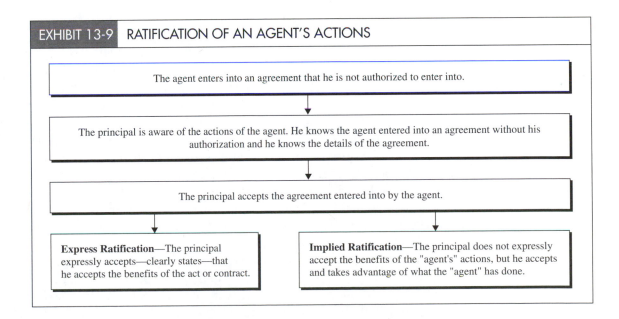

LIABILITY FOR THE AGENT'S ACTIONS

Because an agent acts on behalf of a principal, the principal may be liable for the actions of the agent. Whether the principal will be liable depends on the circumstances surrounding the actions of the agent.

RESPONDEAT SUPERIOR

What if an agent commits a tort while acting as an agent for the principal? Under the doctrine of **respondeat superior,** which literally means "let the master answer," the principal (the "master") can be held responsible for damages caused by the agent's tortious conduct if the agent was acting within the course and scope of the agency. This doctrine was applied in the case of *McMillian v. Monroe County, Alabama.* See Sidebar 13-1.

SIDEBAR 13-1 *MCMILLIAN V. MONROE COUNTY, ALABAMA*

Facts: The appellant had sued Monroe County, Alabama under 42 U.S.C. § 1983 for allegedly unconstitutional actions taken by Monroe County Sheriff Tom Tate. After spending six years on Alabama's death row, petitioner's capital murder conviction was reversed on the ground that the State had suppressed exculpatory evidence. Petitioner then sued respondent Monroe County and others under 42 U.S.C. § 1983 for the allegedly unconstitutional actions of, inter alios, County Sheriff Tom Take in suppressing the evidence. A county is liable under § 1983 for those actions of its sheriff that constitute county "policy."

If the sheriff's actions constitute county "policy," then the *county* is liable for them under the doctrine of respondeat superior.

Issue: Could the county be held liable for the actions of the sheriff when he was acting in his law enforcement capacity?

Holding: The State's constitutional provisions concerning sheriffs, the historical development of those provisions, and the interpretation given them by the State Supreme Court strongly support Monroe County's contention that sheriffs represent the *State* when acting in their law enforcement capacity. The State of Alabama would be liable under respondeat superior for the actions of the sheriff, not Monroe County.

Source: Alabama Reports

IMPUTED KNOWLEDGE

The principal answers for the harm caused by his or her agent if the agent was acting as and within the scope of his or her authority as an agent; the agent's conduct is **imputed** to the principal. This means the principal has a duty or responsibility applied to him or her not because he or she is aware of the act that gave him or her the duty or responsibility, but because another person who he or she has control over is aware of the act. In other words, the principal is not held responsible because he or she knows about the act, but he or she *is* held responsible because his or her agent was aware of the act. In the area of agency law, the term **imputed knowledge** refers to the idea that notice of facts brought to the attention of the agent acting within the scope of his or her employment is the same as bringing the facts to the attention of the principal. In other words, if the agent is aware of the facts—is aware of a duty or responsibility that is imposed upon the principal—then the principal is deemed or considered to also be aware of the facts.

The term **imputed negligence** refers to the negligence of an agent that may be charged to a principal if the agent was acting within the scope of his or her authority. The principal may be held responsible for the harm caused by his or her agent's negligent acts if the agent was acting with the scope of his authority as an agent. See Exhibit 13-10.

EXHIBIT 13-10	PRINCIPAL RESPONSIBLE FOR THE ACTIONS OF THE AGENT

Respondeat Superior – The principal is responsible for the actions of the agent when the agent is acting in his or her capacity as an agent because of the relationship between the agent and the principal.

Imputed Negligence – The negligence of the agent may be charged to the principal if the agent was acting within the scope of his or her authority.

PAYMENT OF AGENTS

Generally agents are to be compensated, or paid, for their services. In order to ensure compensation, the agent may want an agent's lien from the principal. The **agent's lien** is the legal right agreed to in advance for payment from the principal to the agent for services rendered. This gives the agent the right to make a claim for compensation against the principal.

CONCLUSION

An agency relationship is one that is either entered into between two people or that is created by law as a result of the conduct of the two people. What an agent can do, how much authority he or she has, and when he or she can bind the principal are either determined by agreement of the parties or is created by their conduct. The agent may have authority to represent the principal that is either expressly given or implied from the conduct of the principal.

There are several classifications of agent, depending on the number and types of transactions that occur in the agent/principal relationship. In sales transactions, an agent can be a broker or a factor, depending on possession of the property and on whose behalf the sale takes place.

An agent can have actual, implied, or apparent authority; the principal can be bound under all three types, depending on the circumstances. A principal can be held liable for the actions of the agent under the doctrines of respondeat superior and imputed negligence.

In all circumstances, regardless of the amount of authority given or how the relationship came about or what was intended, a principal has an obligation to be fully aware of the actions his or her agent is taking because he or she may be held liable for those actions.

KEY WORDS AND PHRASES

actual authority	express ratification	principal
agency	fiduciary duty	private agent
agency by estoppel	general agency	public agent
agency coupled with an	general agent	ratification
interest	implied agency	respondeat superior
agent	implied authority	special agency
agent's lien	implied ratification	special agent
apparent authority	imputed knowledge	sub-agent
broker	imputed negligence	undisclosed principal
disclosed principal	independent agent	universal agency
exclusive agency	managing agent	universal agent
exclusive agent	partially disclosed principal	

REVIEW QUESTIONS

SHORT ANSWER

1. What is the difference between implied authority and actual authority?
2. What is an agent's lien?
3. What is an apparent agent?
4. When is an agency an agency coupled with an interest?
5. What is a broker?
6. When is a person a corporate agent?
7. What is a local agent?
8. What is a general agency business?
9. What is a factor?
10. What is diplomatic agency?
11. What is a factorage?
12. What is the difference between a broker and a factor?
13. What is the difference between a public agent and a private agent?
14. How does one become an agent coupled with an interest?
15. Under what theory is the knowledge of an agent's actions attributable to a principal?
16. How may a principal be held responsible for the negligent acts of an agent?
17. How can a principal ratify the actions of an agent?
18. What is implied authority?
19. What is the difference between actual authority and implied authority?

FILL IN THE BLANK

1. When someone sells property on another person's behalf for a commission, the person is a _____.

2. An agent who is employed to sell goods or merchandise is a _____.

3. An agent who has all the authority that can be given to an agent is a _____ agent.

4. An agent who has the authority to conduct a certain business transaction is known as a _____ agent.

5. The authority to act given by a principal to an agent that is stated in an agreement is _____.

6. The authority an agent has because of the negligence of a principal is _____.

7. A principal's being held responsible for the negligence of an agent is known as _____.

8. An agent who can perform a series of actions for the principal is known as a/an _____ agent.

9. "Let the master answer" is the literal translation of _____.

10. _____ is ratification that is established by the law based on the actions of the principal.

FACT SITUATIONS

1. Ralph enters into an agreement with Norton that Norton will represent him in all business transactions. What type of agency has been created?

2. Richard enters into an agreement with Herman and James for both of them to represent him in business transactions. What type of agency has been created?

3. Mario enters into agreements on behalf of Robin even though Robin has not agreed to Mario's representing him. When Mario finds out about the deals, he accepts them as negotiated. Has an agency relationship been formed? If it has, what type of relationship is it?

4. Tom, who is a minor, performs an act that damages Richard's property. Richard sues David for the harm because David is Tom's parent. Which theory of liability will Richard use to sue David?

5. Alexander is Charles's agent. Charles authorizes his agent to perform tortious activity. Who can be held liable for Alexander's actions and why?

6. While acting within the course and scope of agency, Alexander performs a negligent act that causes harm. The conduct was not authorized by Charles. Charles also did not supervise Alexander when Alexander was acting on Charles's behalf. Can Charles be held responsible for Alexander's actions? Why or why not?

7. Inez goes to an exclusive art auction to bid on art work on behalf of Montel. Prior to the auction, Inez notifies the art gallery that she will represent someone but is not at liberty to state who. What sort of relationship exists between Montel and Inez?

8. Inez does not inform the art gallery that she is there bidding for someone else. The gallery thinks Inez is bidding for herself. Identify the relationship between Montel and Inez.

9. Victor goes to an auction of antique furniture and informs the sellers that he is there representing Mohammed. Mohammed is aware that Victor is saying he is Mohammed's agent, but no such relationship exists. Mohammed takes no action to correct what people think or to stop Victor from making these statements. Would Mohammed be bound by any sales contract Victor entered into on his behalf? Why or why not?

10. If Mohammed had no idea that Victor was making these statements and did nothing to create the impression that such a relationship exists, would he be bound by any sales contract entered into by Victor's "acting on Mohammed's behalf." Why or why not?

CHAPTER 14
Business Organizations

INTRODUCTION

There are several different ways of organizing the entity that is responsible for the operation of a business. Each business organization has its own method of inception, its own way of operating, its own way of going out of business, and its own types of owner liability. The business organization can be very simple or very complicated, with different levels of responsibility.

SOLE PROPRIETORSHIP

One type of business organization is the **sole proprietorship** (sole pro-*pry*-ə-ter-ship). In this type of business, one person owns the business and all of its assets. The **sole proprietor** (sole pro-*pry*-ə-ter), the person who owns the business, is personally responsible for all the debts of the business. If the sole proprietor retires, dies, or otherwise goes out of business, the sole proprietorship ends. For example, a young man named Vincent Gates creates software for the most realistic wrestling video game ever developed. Gates starts his own business, selling the software locally from a store he has opened. He has put his own money into the business, is the only one operating the business, and is the only person responsible for all the debts of the business. All of the profits are his, but so are all debts of the business and the risks. See Exhibit 14-1.

EXHIBIT 14-1	SOLE PROPRIETORSHIP

Owner of the Business – Sole proprietor
Assets – Come from the sole proprietor
Responsibility for Day-to-Day Operations – Sole proprietor
Responsibility for Debt of Business – Sole proprietor; unlimited liability for the debts of the business

PARTNERSHIPS

A second type of business organization is the **partnership** (*part*-ner-ship), an association of two or more persons to carry on, as co-owners, a business for profit. A **partner** (*part*-ner) is the actual person who has united with others to form the partnership in business; he or she is a member of the partnership or firm.

PARTNERSHIP DEBTS AND ASSETS

Generally, each partner is totally responsible for all the **partnership debts,** a specified sum of money owed by the partnership to another person or entity. Each partner contributes **partnership assets** (*part*-ner-ship *ass*-ets), both real and personal property, tangible and intangible property belonging to the partnership, and each partner shares in the profits. When

237

one of the partners leaves the business, the partnership ends. However, this does not mean the business of the partnership ends. It only means that the partnership that was conducting the business has ended; the business can continue in another form—a sole proprietorship, for example—or a new partnership can be formed.

Return, briefly, to the previous example. Gates's software is selling well. He decides to expand, but he needs a partner to help him. He decides to approach his college friend, Steve Ventura. Ventura agrees to go into business with Gates, and they begin to consider what type of partnership they want to enter into.

GENERAL PARTNERSHIP

A **general partnership** is one in which the parties carry on their business, sharing the profits and losses as well as the management of the partnership regardless of their capital contributions. Ventura and Gates would be **general partners:** Each would contribute to the assets of the business and share equally and fully in the profits, losses, and management of the partnership. Each partner in a general partnership is totally responsible for the debts of the partnership. See Exhibit 14-2.

EXHIBIT 14-2	GENERAL PARTNERSHIP

Owner of the Business – The general partners

Assets – Come from the partners

Responsibility for Day-to-Day Operations – The general partners

Responsibility for Debt of Business – Each general partner has unlimited liability for all of the debts of the partnership

Gates and Ventura have several options for their partnership. They could agree that Ventura will be a **junior partner,** one whose participation in the business is limited to profits and management. They might decide Ventura will be a **nominal** (*nŏh*-mə-nal) **partner.** His name will appear in connection with the business as a member of the partnership, but he will have no real interest in it. They may determine that Ventura will be a **dormant** (*door*-mant) **partner** who does not take an active role in the operation of the partnership. If Ventura becomes a dormant partner, he might also be a **silent partner;** his name will not appear as a partner and his identity as a partner will not be known, but he will be entitled to part of the profits.

Ventura might be an **ostensible** (os-*ten*-si-ble) **partner**—one who may or may not be a partner, but who is held out as if he were a partner. For example, his name may appear on the firm name as if he were a partner when in reality he may or may not be a partner. He might also be a **quasi-** (*qwa*-si) **partner,** who is a person who has joined in a business with other people as if they had formed a partnership, but who may or may not be a partner in actuality.

If the Gates/Ventura partnership has to go out of business, it will **liquidate**—convert its assets to cash and then adjust or settle its debts. When a partnership liquidates, a **liquidating partner** is appointed to settle the accounts, collect assets, adjust claims, and pay the debts of the partnership.

LIMITED PARTNERSHIP

A second type of partnership is a **limited partnership,** in which there are one or more general partners and one or more limited partners. A **limited partner's** involvement in a business is limited by agreement, and he or she is not liable for the debts of the partnership beyond the amount of capital he or she contributed. For example, if Ventura gave $10,000 to the partnership as a limited partner, the amount of his potential liability is limited to $10,000. See Exhibit 14-3.

EXHIBIT 14-3	LIMITED PARTNERSHIP

Owners of the Business – The general and limited partners

Assets – Come from the general and limited partners

Responsibility for Day-to-Day Operations – The general partners only

Responsibility for Debt of Business – Each general partner has unlimited liability for all of the debts of the partnership; limited partner's liability is limited to the amount of capital he or she contributed to the partnership

---

The limited partner cannot participate in the management of the business and keep the status of limited partner. If a limited partner does participate in the day-to-day operations of the business, he or she can be considered to be a general partner and has the potential to be held totally responsible for the debts of the business.

FAMILY PARTNERSHIP

A **family partnership** is controlled by family members, who are considered partners in the business. Even children can be partners for tax purposes; the children are taxed on the partnership income rather than the parents, which can reduce the overall taxes that have to be paid. But the children should be given complete control over their part of the business or all the profits of the business will be considered the income of the adult partners and taxed to them.

PARTNERSHIP AT WILL, BY ESTOPPEL, AND IMPLIED

A **partnership at will** will continue in business for no fixed period of time; it remains in business at the discretion of the partners. A partnership at will can be dissolved at any time by one of the partners without any notice to the other partner(s). A **partnership by estoppel** (es-*top*-əl) is a situation where at least two people hold themselves out as partners to a third person when in fact they are not partners. If this happens, the people who held themselves out as partners are prevented from claiming they are not partners. An **implied partnership** is not a real partnership; rather, the court declares a partnership exists because of the conduct of the parties. The effect of an implied partnership is that during litigation involving the people, they are prevented from arguing that a partnership did not exist.

SUBPARTNERSHIPS AND TIERED PARTNERSHIPS

A **subpartnership** is formed when one partner in a firm shares his or her profits with someone not affiliated with the firm. A subpartnership is not a true partnership, but rather an arrangement where a partner agrees to share his or her profits (or losses) in the partnership with another person. The other partners do not share their profits or losses with the subpartner. A **tiered** (teerd) **partnership** is an ownership agreement where one partnership is a partner in one or more other partnerships. The partnership that is the partner in the business organization is called the *parent* or *first tier partnership*; the other partnerships are called *subsidiaries* or *second tier partnerships*. See Exhibit 14-4.

EXHIBIT 14-4 | TYPES OF PARTNERSHIPS

General Partnership – Partners carry on a business and share in the profits, the losses, and management. Each partner is 100% responsible for all of the partnership debt.

Limited Partnership – General and limited partners. Limited partners contribute capital, share in profits and losses, but do not participate in management. Limited partners responsibility for partnership debt is based on the amount of capital contributed.

Family Partnership – Members of a family make up the partnership. Each member should be allowed to control his or her part of the business. Profits and losses are shared.

Partnership at Will – Any partner can dissolve the partnership without notice to the other partners.

Partnership by Estoppel – The people act like a partnership exists so they are prevented from saying that one does not exist.

Subpartnership – A person makes another person his or her partner to share in the profits. The partner who brought in the sub-partner shares his or her profits.

Tiered Partnership – A person is a partner in more than one partnership.

JOINT VENTURES AND SYNDICATES

Gates and Ventura could enter into a **joint venture,** a one-time undertaking of a particular transaction involving two or more people for mutual profit. A joint venture is in the nature of a partnership and is taxed like a partnership, but ends when the venture ends.

They could also agree to form a **syndicate** (*sin*-də-kit), which is an association of individuals formed for the purpose of conducting and carrying out a particular business transaction in which the members are mutually interested. Syndicates are usually formed to provide the financing for a business transaction. The syndicate can be a partnership or a corporation.

PARTNERSHIP AGREEMENT AND DISSOLUTION

Gates and Ventura decide to enter into a general partnership and sign a **partnership agreement.** This is the written document that contains the terms and conditions of the partnership; it is sometimes referred to as the *articles of partnership*. The two may also issue a **partnership certificate,** which is a document giving evidence of the existence of the partnership and that is commonly provided to a financial institution when a partnership wants to borrow money.

If, after they enter into the partnership, Ventura decides he wants out, the partnership can go through **dissolution** (dis-ə-*loo*-shen). The dissolution of the partnership is the change in the relationship of the partners caused by any partner's ceasing to be associated with the carrying on of the partnership. The business can continue, but one of the partners is no longer associated with the partnership or the business. The partnership has been dissolved.

The Gates/Ventura partnership thrives, and the two continue to market the software, *Maximum Body Slam.* The software is so popular they are able to expand and start writing software for other sports video games. Soon they have a chance to expand their business, but they realize they do not have the capital necessary to accomplish this. They decide to form a corporation.

CORPORATIONS

In general, a **corporation** (kore-per-*ay*-shən) is a legal entity created by or under the laws of a state that is treated by the law as being a separate legal entity. Thus, a corporation is considered an artificial person with a life of its own, separate and apart from the people who formed it. There are many types of corporations.

TYPES OF CORPORATIONS

A **public corporation** is created by the state for political purposes and to act as an agency in the administration of government, generally within a particular area or subdivision of the state. (See Chapter 6 for examples of public corporations.) The corporation can be a **domestic corporation,** one that is created by or organized under the laws of a particular state, or it can be a **foreign corporation,** one doing business in one state, but created by or under the laws of another state, government, or country.

The corporation may be for profit, or it may be a **non-profit corporation**—one that is formed for a charitable or benevolent purpose. No part of the income of a non-profit corporation can be distributed to its members, directors, or officers. The non-profit corporation may be exempt from paying taxes on its income if it is operated exclusively for one of the specified purposes. See Exhibit 14-5 for some of the purposes of a non-profit corporation.

EXHIBIT 14-5	PURPOSES OF NON-PROFIT CORPORATIONS
1. Religious	5. Literacy
2. Charitable	6. Education
3. Scientific	7. Prevention of cruelty to animals
4. Testing for public safety	8. Prevention of cruelty to children

A **de facto corporation** is one existing under color of law and in pursuance of the law if an attempt was made in good faith to organize it under the appropriate statute. In other words, there was an attempt or a good faith effort to comply with the law that creates the corporation, but an essential requirement was unintentionally omitted. A **shell corporation** is a corporate frame—a shell—containing few, if any, assets. It is kept in existence by the required filing of documents, and is generally for the future use of the incorporators.

The owners of a **non-stock corporation** do not own stock in the company because none is issued; ownership of the company is usually through a membership charter or agreement. A non-stock corporation is usually a religious, charitable, or **mutual company,** whose shares are held exclusively by the members. The profits of the company are distributed to the members based on how much business each member did with the company. The more business the member did with the company, the larger his or her share of the profits.

A corporation can be formed for the benefit of its owners or for a limited purpose. One such type of corporation is the **cooperative** (koh-*op*-er-a-tive), which is organized for the purpose of rendering economic services to the shareholders who own and control it. A **cooperative corporation** is primarily organized to provide services and profits to its members, not to earn corporate profit. An example of a cooperative is a farmers cooperative, an organization that pools the purchasing power of many farmers to purchase farm supplies. Individual farmers do not have the ability or need to purchase large amounts of supplies in order to receive a discount on the supplies purchased. By pooling their needs and resources, the cooperative is able to purchase the supplies at a reduced cost, saving its members money.

A **limited liability company** is a company that is organized for a limited purpose for a limited period of time. The liability of each owner is limited to the amount of that person's contribution to the company. For example, Craig and Cathy form a limited liability company to operate a retail store that sells model railroad supplies. Their limited liability company will be in existence for a maximum of seventy-five years, and the amount of liability Craig or Cathy is responsible for is limited to the amount of capital each contributed to the company.

Corporations can also be categorized according to how their income is taxed. An **S corporation** is a small business corporation whose stockholders are limited in number by statute. The corporation has decided, under certain conditions, to have the corporation's taxable income taxed to the stockholders at regular individual income tax rates. In other words, the income of the corporation is taxed as income to the individual stockholders. A **C corporation** is a regular corporation whose income is taxed at the corporate level rather than to the stockholders at the individual level.

Vincent Gates and Steve Ventura, from the earlier example, want to form a **business corporation**—a corporation formed for the purpose of transacting business in the broadest sense of the term. Gates and Ventura also decide that this will not be a **close** (*kloz*) **corporation** where the voting shares are held by a single person or by a closely knit group. In a close corporation, there are no public investors and shareholders are active in the business. See Exhibit 14-6 for a summary of the types of corporations that can be formed.

EXHIBIT 14-6 | TYPES OF CORPORATIONS

Public Corporation – A corporation created by the state for political purposes and to act as an agency in the administration of government, generally within a particular area or subdivision of the state.

Private Corporation – A corporation founded and composed of private individuals for private purposes.

Domestic Corporation – A corporation that is created by or organized under the laws of a particular state.

Foreign Corporation – A corporation that is doing business in one state, but was created by or under the laws of another state, government, or country.

Non-profit Corporation – A corporation that is formed for a charitable or benevolent purpose; no part of the income can be distributed to the members, directors, or officers.

De facto Corporation – A corporation existing under color of law and in pursuance of the law if an attempt was made in good faith to organize a corporation under the appropriate statute.

Shell Corporation – A corporate frame—a shell—containing few, if any, assets; maintained by the required filing of documents; generally for the future use of the incorporators.

Non-stock Corporation – A corporation where the owners do not own stock in the company because none is issued; ownership of the company is usually through a membership charter or agreement.

FORMATION OF THE CORPORATION

Gates and Ventura are the **incorporators** (in-*kore*-per-ay-tors), the people who will prepare and execute the articles of incorporation. **Incorporation** (in-kore-per-*ay*-shən) is the act or process of forming or creating a corporation; the process used is determined by each state's statutes governing the incorporation process. The **articles of incorporation** comprise the instrument or document that is a legal statement identifying the name of the corporation, how long it will be in existence, and its purpose and powers.

The articles contain the **corporate by-laws,** which are the regulations, rules, or laws adopted by the corporation. The by-laws define the rights and obligations of the different officers, persons, and groups within the corporation. The by-laws also declare the rules for routine corporate matters, such as the calling of meetings.

The articles of incorporation will also contain the company name. Sometimes the incorporators will have a different name for the business that is different from the corporation name. The name for the actual business is known as **DBA** or **(doing business as).** In the example, Gates and Ventura state in the articles of incorporation that the company name is *Miniware,* doing business as (DBA) *Slamco,* which is another name for the company. The articles of incorporation will list the corporate offices provided for, such as president, vice president, secretary, and treasurer. The people who will be selected to fill those offices and run the corporation on a day-to-day basis are referred to as **corporate officers.** They will be selected by a **board of directors,** a governing body selected by the shareholders of the company. A board of directors is usually made up of officers of the corporation and outside directors—people who are not employed by the corporation. The board of directors not only elects officers, it also may appoint agents to act on behalf of the corporation, declare dividends, and act on other major matters that affect the corporation. See Exhibit 14-7.

EXHIBIT 14-7 | PEOPLE INVOLVED IN A CORPORATION

Incorporators – People who actually form the corporation; they arrange for the preparation and filing of the articles of incorporation.

Stockholders – People who own stock in the corporation; the corporation's owners.

Board of Directors – Persons selected by the stockholders to form corporate policy; the board makes major decisions regarding the corporation.

Corporate Officers – Persons selected by the board of directors who are responsible for running the corporation on a day-to-day basis.

When the articles of incorporation are filed with the secretary of state's office or other appropriate state agency, the agency will issue a **corporate charter,** which is the document that grants the corporation legal existence and the right to conduct business as a corporation. See Exhibit 14-8 for a summary of the ownership and liability for a corporation.

EXHIBIT 14-8 | CORPORATIONS

Owner of the business – The stockholders/shareholders of company stock

Assets – Come from the sale of stock and the incorporators

Responsibility for day-to-day operations – The officers of the corporation that are selected by the board of directors and the managers selected by the corporate officers

Responsibility for debt of business – A corporation is an artificial person; it has its own lifetime, so the corporation is responsible for corporate debt. Stockholders can be liable if creditors are able to pierce the corporate veil.

STOCK

Ownership interests in the corporation are represented by **stock.** When a person owns shares of stock, he or she owns part of the company. The more stock a person owns, the more of the corporation he or she owns. Corporations raise money to go into business, to expand a current business, and for a variety of other reasons through the sale of stock.

AUTHORIZED STOCK, CAPITAL STOCK, AND STOCKHOLDERS

The articles of incorporation will also state the amount of **authorized stock** as well as the classes of stock that can be issued. Stock, or **capital stock,** in a corporation is a security: It represents an ownership interest in the company and it gives the owner the right to participate in the management of the corporation and to share proportionally in the net profits or earnings of the corporation. Stock ownership also gives the owner of the stock the right to share in the distribution of corporate assets upon dissolution of the corporation.

A person who owns stock in a company owns **shares of corporate stock,** the units into which the property interests in a corporation are divided. The shares of stock a person owns indicate the proportional part of certain rights in a corporation that the person has during that corporation's existence. Shares of stock indicate what interest in the assets upon the termination of the corporation a person has and are evidence of the stockholder's share in the distribution of the assets of the corporation. To put it simply, when you own a share of corporate stock, you own a part of that company; how much of the company you own depends on the number of shares you own. The more shares of stock of a company you own, the bigger the part of the company you own.

COMMON AND PREFERRED STOCK

The corporate charter can authorize two classes of capital stock: common and preferred. **Common stock** represents an ownership interest in the company and the amount of liability a corporation has to a stockholder after the creditors' claims against the corporation have been paid. If there is no preferred stock in a company, the terms *common stock* and *capital stock* can be used interchangeably.

Preferred stock is stock that is given priority over common stock in respect to the payment of dividends. The holders of preferred stock are entitled to receive dividends out of the earnings or profit of the corporation at a fixed annual rate and before any distribution is made to owners of common stock. A **dividend** (*div*-e-dend) is the distribution of current or accumulated earnings to the shareholders pro rata (proportionately), based on the number of shares of stock owned. A dividend may be paid in cash or may be issued in the form of more stock or property.

If there is not sufficient income to pay both classes of stock, preferred stock is paid first; preferred stock must be paid in full before common stock is paid. If earnings are sufficient to pay preferred stock in full with money left over, the remaining amount may be paid to holders of common stock.

Preferred stock can be broken down into two categories. If the holder of the preferred stock is not paid in full, and the amount due carries over to the next year and continues to carry over until the total amount due is paid, then that type of preferred stock is known as **cumulative preferred stock.** With **noncumulative preferred stock,** the amount due does not carry over from year to year. If the holder of noncumulative preferred stock is not paid the amount due in full for that year, the right to payment ends when the year is over. See Exhibit 14-9.

EXHIBIT 14-9 PRIORITY OF PAYMENT OF DIVIDENDS

Preferred Stock, Cumulative – Paid dividends first, and if the dividend is not paid in full, the amount due carries over to the next year.

Preferred Stock, Noncumulative – Paid dividends before common stock. If the dividend is not paid in full, the amount does not carry over to the next year.

Common Stock – Paid dividends last if there is enough left to pay a dividend. The amount not paid does not carry over to the next year.

BLUE CHIP, CONTROL, ISSUED, AND LISTED STOCK

Blue chip stock is distinguished by its high-grade financial record; this rating indicates the best type of stock to purchase. **Control stock** is the amount of capital stock that allows the owner to control the corporation. However much stock is needed to control the company is how much stock is designated as control stock. The term **issued stock** refers to stock that is authorized for sale, available for sale, and is actually sold to a person. **Unissued stock** is authorized, but it has not been distributed to stockholders or made available for sale. All types of stock are either **listed** for sale on a stock exchange or **unlisted,** which means they are traded over the counter or privately.

In their articles of incorporation, Gates and Ventura state that the corporation will make available two classes of stock: preferred and common. The two men will retain enough of the preferred shares to maintain control of the company; the remaining shares of preferred stock and the common stock will be offered for sale. See Exhibit 14-10.

EXHIBIT 14-10	CLASSIFICATIONS OF STOCK

Common Stock – Stock that represents an ownership interest in a company

Preferred Stock – Stock that is given preference in the payment of dividends; this classification is paid before common stock

Blue Chip Stock – Stock in a company that has an excellent financial record

Control Stock – The amount of stock that allows someone to control the corporation

Issued Stock – Stock that has been issued for sale, is available for sale, and is actually sold

Unissued Stock – Stock that has been issued but not actually offered for sale

PROSPECTUS

Prior to the shares being offered for sale and in accordance with regulations of the **Securities and Exchange Commission (SEC),** the governmental agency that regulates the buying and selling of stock and the stock exchanges, Slamco will issue a prospectus. A **prospectus** (pro-*spek*-tus) is a document that sets out all the material facts concerning a company and its operations so that a potential investor may make an informed decision about the merit of his or her investment.

A prospectus must be issued prior to any stock's being offered for sale. All potential investors should receive a copy of the prospectus. The prospectus will also be used to establish the **par value**—the face or stated value—of the stock.

STOCK MARKETS

When stock in Slamco is first issued, it is referred to as **floating stock**—a term relating to the act or process by which stock is issued and sold. If the stock is issued by means of a stockbroker, it is referred to as **outstanding stock.** The stock may be listed for sale on the **stock exchange,** which is the place where shares of stock are bought and sold; one such stock exchange is the New York Stock Exchange.

Stock may also be listed on the **over-the-counter market.** This is a broad securities market where the brokers purchase or sell securities by computer hookup or telephone rather than through a regular stock exchange. The NASDAQ Exchange is an example of an over-the-counter market. NASDAQ and the New York Stock Exchange are part of the **stock market,** which is the organized trading of securities through the various stock exchanges and over-the-counter markets. The stock market is not a specific exchange or market itself; rather it is all of the exchanges and markets combined.

STOCKBROKERS

When a person buys stock, he or she may use the services of a **stockbroker,** a person who buys or sells stock as an agent of another. After purchasing the stock, the person will receive a **stock certificate** issued by the corporation and stating that the named person is the owner of a designated number of shares of stock. A stock certificate is written evidence of the ownership of stock. A **stockholder** is a person who owns shares of stock in a corporation or a joint stock company; the terms *stockholder* and *shareholder* are often used interchangeably. In order to encourage the sale of their stock, Gates and Ventura offer stock options with the sale of the shares of stock. A **stock option** is the right to buy a designated stock, if the holder of the option chooses to, at any time within a specified period of time at a determined price.

ANNUAL MEETINGS

Miniware, DBA (doing business as) Slamco officially goes into business and has immediate success. The stock is doing well, software and video game sales are breaking records, and the future looks promising. After a year of operation, Slamco has its first **annual meeting of stockholders.** The purpose of the annual meeting is to elect officers and directors, to ratify actions of officers and directors, and to vote on corporate matters. Before the annual meeting is held, each stockholder will receive a copy of the **annual report.** The annual report contains a balance sheet, an income statement, a statement of changes in the financial position, the auditor's report, and comments from management about the year's business and prospects for the next year.

Every stockholder has the right to attend the annual meeting, but if a stockholder cannot attend or does not want to attend, he or she can give his or her proxy to someone else. A **proxy** (*prox*-ee) is the written authorization given by the stockholder to another person so the newly designated proxy can act on the stockholder's behalf. The proxy will represent the stockholder and will vote his or her shares at the annual meeting. Before the proxy can be issued, the stockholder is to receive a **proxy statement,** which is information that must be provided to allow the stockholder to make an intelligent decision as to how his or her shares should be voted. The stockholder gets this statement so he or she can tell his proxy how he or she wants the proxy to vote on corporate issues.

DIVIDENDS

One issue that may be decided at the board of directors meeting is whether or not to declare a dividend on the stock. A dividend is the distribution of current earnings or accumulated earnings to the stockholders of the corporation on a pro rata basis that is based on the number of shares the person owns. The more shares a person owns, the larger his or her share of the profits will be.

CLASSIFICATIONS OF DIVIDENDS

Whereas the dividend paid on preferred stock is usually a set amount per share, the dividend paid on common stock varies depending on corporate earnings and the amount of cash available to pay dividends. There are several classifications of dividends depending upon how they are paid, when they are paid, or the effect of their payment.

A **cash dividend** is a portion of the profits and surpluses paid to the stockholders in cash; it is taxed when the dividend is paid to the stockholder. A **stock dividend** is a dividend that is paid in the form of stock rather than cash; this is done usually to preserve the cash of the corporation. A tax benefit exists for this type of dividend because the "income" from the dividend is not taxed until the stock is actually sold.

A **bond dividend,** which is very rare, is a dividend received in the form of a bond rather than cash or property. A **property dividend** is paid using the property of the corporation rather than cash or stock; an **asset dividend** is paid using an asset of the company. The asset used to pay the dividend is usually one of the products of the company.

EXTRA, YEAR END, AND EXTRAORDINARY DIVIDENDS

An **extra dividend** is one that is paid in addition to a regularly declared dividend; it is paid because of exceptional profits of the corporation during the declared dividend period. A **year end dividend** is an extra dividend paid at the end of the fiscal year of the corporation.

An **extraordinary dividend** is paid at irregular times because of some unusual event. This dividend is not declared from the regular profits of the business; rather, it is declared because of some unusually large amount of income or an unexpected increase in the value of the capital assets of the corporation that were not under the control of the corporation. This type of dividend is non-repetitive; it may never be repeated because these circumstances may not exist again. See Exhibit 14-11.

EXHIBIT 14-11	CLASSIFICATIONS OF DIVIDENDS BASED ON HOW AND WHEN THEY ARE PAID

Extra Dividend – A dividend that is paid in addition to the regularly declared dividend

Year End Dividend – An extra dividend that is paid at the end of the fiscal year of the corporation

Extraordinary Dividend – An extra dividend that is paid at irregular times because of some unusual event

CUMULATIVE AND NONCUMULATIVE DIVIDENDS

A **cumulative dividend** is a dividend of preferred stock, and because the dividend for preferred stock must be paid before any dividends are paid to common stock, any past due dividend must be paid before any common stock dividends can be paid. An **accumulated dividend** is the sum of cumulative dividends that have not yet been paid; these must be paid before any dividend of common stock can be paid. However, dividends of preferred stock can also be **noncumulative.** This means that if the dividend is not paid during a particular year or period, it is gone and there is no obligation to pay the past dividend when the present dividend is paid.

An **unpaid dividend** is one that has been declared but has not yet been paid; these appear as a liability on the company's records until paid. Unpaid dividends can be broken down into two categories: deferred and passed. A **deferred dividend** is one that has been declared, but is not payable until some future date. For example, a board of directors may declare a dividend of $2 per share, but this amount will not be paid until six months later. A **passed dividend** is a dividend that has been declared by a company that has a history of paying regular dividends but was not paid when it was due. See Exhibit 14-12.

EXHIBIT 14-12	CLASSIFICATION OF DIVIDENDS BASED ON THE EFFECT OF PAYMENT

Cumulative Dividend – Dividend on preferred stock that is paid before any other dividend.

Accumulated Dividend – Cumulative dividends that have not yet been paid; must be paid before any dividend on common stock can be paid.

Noncumulative Dividend – If the dividend is not paid during a particular year or period, there is no obligation to pay it in the future.

Unpaid Dividend – Dividend that has been declared but not yet paid; these are a liability on the company records until they are paid.

Deferred Dividend – Dividend that has been declared but is not payable until some future date.

Passed Dividend – Dividend that has been declared but not paid by a company that has a history of paying regular dividends.

STOCK SPLITS

If stock sells well, a board of directors may propose a **stock split,** which is the issuance of a number of new shares of stock in exchange for each old share of stock held by a stockholder.

SPLIT UPS AND REVERSE SPLITS

A stock split results in a proportional change in the number of shares owned by each stockholder; the number of shares owned can increase or decrease. Stock splits can be **split ups**—one share of stock is split into a larger number of shares—or **reverse splits,** where a number of shares are combined to create a smaller number of shares. To return briefly to the Gates/Ventura scenario, because business is going so well, the shareholders and proxies vote for a split up: two shares for every one share of Miniware stock owned.

CORPORATE MERGERS

Several things can happen to a corporation during its "lifetime." One such event is a **merger** (*mer*-jer): two companies join together as one according to statutory provisions. One company survives while the other is absorbed into it, losing its legal identity. The surviving corporation keeps its own name and identity and receives the assets, liabilities, franchises, and powers of the absorbed company. The corporation that is absorbed—the one that disappears—is the **acquired corporation.** Mergers are categorized according to the type of companies involved or how they are accomplished.

CASH, CONGLOMERATE, AND DE FACTO MERGERS

A **cash merger** is a merger transaction in which some shareholders in a corporation accept cash for their shares and others accept new shares in the new corporation. A **conglomerate** (kon-*gloh*-mer-ate) **merger** is the merger of corporations that are not competitors, that are not potential or actual customers, or that are not suppliers of each other. Microsoft's merger with Tyson Foods would be a conglomerate merger: The two corporations do not compete or do business with each other. A **de facto merger** happens when one corporation absorbs another, but without complying with the statutory requirements for a merger. See Exhibit 14-13.

EXHIBIT 14-13	CLASSIFICATION OF MERGERS BASED ON HOW THE MERGER TAKES PLACE

Cash Merger – The stockholders receive either cash or stock in the new company for their shares of stock.

Conglomerate Merger – Companies that do not compete with each other or that are not potential or actual customers of each other merge.

De Facto Merger – One company has merged with another, but there has been no compliance with statutory requirements.

DOWNSTREAM, UPSTREAM, HORIZONTAL, AND VERTICAL MERGERS

A **downstream merger** happens when a parent company is merged into one of its subsidiaries; an **upstream merger** happens when a subsidiary corporation is merged into its parent corporation. A **horizontal merger** is a merger of businesses who compete in the same market area. A **vertical merger** is a merger of a corporate customer with its supplier. See Exhibit 14-14.

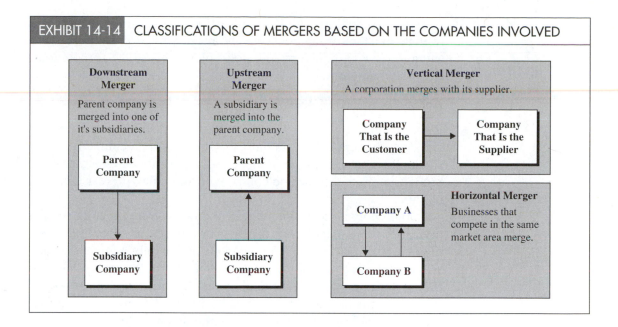

EXHIBIT 14-14 CLASSIFICATIONS OF MERGERS BASED ON THE COMPANIES INVOLVED

Downstream Merger

Parent company is merged into one of it's subsidiaries.

Parent Company → Subsidiary Company

Upstream Merger

A subsidiary is merged into the parent company.

Parent Company ← Subsidiary Company

Vertical Merger

A corporation merges with its supplier.

Company That Is the Customer → Company That Is the Supplier

Horizontal Merger

Businesses that compete in the same market area merge.

Company A ⇄ Company B

SUBSIDIARIES

A company might become the subsidiary of another company. A **subsidiary corporation** is a company whose parent corporation owns at least a majority of the shares of stock and thus has control over it.

Recall the example. Slamco wants to merge with Nony Corporation, a smaller company that makes the equipment used to play video games. Slamco foresees a cash merger, with money and stock being offered for Nony stock. If Nony Corporation is not interested in being merged with Slamco or any other company, or if it is not interested in becoming a subsidiary of Slamco, it could conduct a **stock redemption,** buying back its own stock. Stock redemption usually occurs when a company goes private or when a company defends itself against a hostile takeover attempt. However, Nony Corporation shareholders agree to the merger. They want the cash or the stock in Slamco, so Slamco is able to merge with Nony.

If Slamco wanted to get out of the retail business altogether, it could become a holding company of Nony or other companies. A **holding company** is a company that limits its activities to owning enough stock to have a controlling interest in one or more companies and supervising the management of those companies. The holding company is not directly involved in the manufacture or sale of a product; it simply manages the company that manufactures and sells the product. A holding company may benefit from certain tax advantages, but only if the company owns at least 80% of the voting stock of the corporation.

LEGAL ACTIONS

Because the corporation is a legal entity—an artificial person—it can sue and be sued. Because they are the owners of the company, stockholders can also sue on behalf of the corporation.

STOCKHOLDER'S DERIVATIVE ACTION

If a corporation has been wronged—for example, if someone commits a tort or breaches a contract—the corporation can sue on its own behalf. However, if the corporation has been wronged and has taken no action, a stockholder can file a **stockholder's derivative** (de-*riv*-ə-tiv) **action.** The stockholder files the cause of action in his or her own name, even though the corporation would be an appropriate party. Because the corporation is not suing to remedy the wrong, the stockholder can use the corporation's right to sue to file his or her own lawsuit.

ANTITRUST ACTIONS

If the corporation performs a wrongful act, it can be sued as a corporation. When the U.S. government brings an antitrust suit against a company, it may sue the majority stockholder as well as the company as a separate defendant. An **antitrust suit** can be brought to protect trade and commerce from unlawful restraints, price fixing, and monopolies.

A **monopoly** is the exclusive right or power a company has to carry on a particular business or trade, to manufacture a particular product, or to control the sale of the whole supply of a particular good. In a monopoly, one or only a few companies dominate the total sales of a product or service; because they control the market, they can fix prices. An **antitrust act** is a statute that prohibits the formation of a monopoly. The **Antitrust Civil Process Act** is the federal statute that permits the filing of an antitrust case in federal district court. (See Chapter 16 for more information on Antitrust.)

PIERCING THE CORPORATE VEIL

Another suit that can be brought against a corporation is one to **pierce the corporate veil,** a judicial process used to disregard the immunity of corporate officers, directors, and stockholders from liability for the wrongs of the corporation. The court can hold the corporate directors, officers, and stockholders personally liable for the harm caused by the corporation only if it is proven that the corporation was established solely for the purpose of fraud. The corporation can also be sued in tort law, contract law, or any type of law—including criminal law—where someone can be held liable for his or her actions.

TERMINATION OF THE CORPORATION

The last thing that can happen during the lifetime of a corporation is its dissolution. Dissolution is the termination of a corporation's legal existence. It may be voluntary, initiated and approved by the board and the stockholders, or involuntary, initiated by the legislature, by the state, by the attorney general, by unpaid creditors, or by the stockholders themselves. If the corporation is going through dissolution, the last event in its life will be a **winding up**—the process of settling its accounts and liquidating its assets for the purpose of distributing the net assets to the shareholders. See Exhibit 14-15 for the life cycle of a corporation.

BUSINESS ORGANIZATIONS SIMILAR TO CORPORATIONS

There are two types of business organizations that have some of the characteristics and benefits of a corporation but are not true corporations. A **joint stock company** is an unincorporated business enterprise with ownership represented by shares of stock. A joint stock company is generally treated as a corporation for certain purposes, but it is more a mix of partnership and corporation. A **professional corporation (PC)** is authorized by statute and allows people who practice a profession that requires a license (doctors, lawyers, accountants, counselors, veterinarians, etc.) to form a "corporation." The professional corporation is treated like a partnership for day-to-day management purposes and like a corporation for income tax purposes.

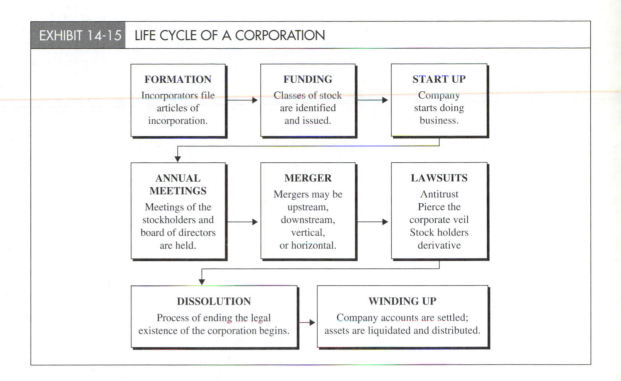

EXHIBIT 14-15 LIFE CYCLE OF A CORPORATION

FRANCHISES

Another type of business organization is the **franchise,** a license from the owner of a trademark or trade name that allows another to sell a product or service under that name or mark. Wendy's, McDonalds, Burger King, Pizza Hut, and TCBY are franchises.

The **franchisee,** the person or company that receives the franchise, agrees to conduct the business or sell the product or service in accordance with the methods and procedures prescribed by the **franchiser,** the person or company that granted the license. A person who receives a Wendy's franchise must agree to run his or her Wendy's the way the company tells him or her to. The franchiser will assist the franchisee with advertising, promotion, and advisory services; the local dealer will benefit from national advertising, provided by the franchiser.

A **franchised dealer** is a retailer who sells the product or service of a manufacturer or supplier under a franchise agreement that protects the territory for the retailer and provides advertising and promotion support to the retailer. A franchise can be granted to a sole proprietorship, a partnership, or a corporation.

CONCLUSION

There are many ways an entrepreneur can form a business. The type of business formed depends on the number of people entering the business, the purpose of the business, the tax consequences, and what happens to the business during its lifetime. It is possible for a business to start out as a sole proprietorship and eventually wind up as a major corporation.

Sole proprietorships are owned by one person. That person is totally liable for all of the debts of the business. The sole proprietorship ends when the owner dies or goes out of business.

There are many forms of partnership. Generally, two or more people agree to go into business together; they share in the business's profits and losses. Each partner can be totally liable for all of the debts of the partnership. In a limited partnership, liability of the limited partner(s) is limited to the amount of capital contributed.

A corporation is a separate legal entity, an artificial person, that has a life all its own. Distinct groups function in the corporation, but a person can be a member of more than one of these groups. Incorporators actually form the corporation, stockholders own the corporation through shares of stock, the board of directors sets corporate policy, and the corporate officers run the company on a day-to-day basis.

Corporations can become subsidiaries, can merge with other corporations, and can be sued as corporations. Just like any other business, corporations can dissolve and cease to exist.

KEY WORDS AND PHRASES

accumulated dividend
annual meeting of
  stockholders
antitrust act
articles of incorporation
authorized stock
blue chip stock
board of directors
capital stock
close corporation
common stock
cooperative
corporate officers
corporation
dividend
domestic corporation
foreign corporation
franchise
general partner
general partnership

holding company
horizontal merger
joint venture
limited liability company
limited partner
limited partnership
merger
monopoly
mutual company
over-the-counter market
par value
partner
partnership
passed dividend
pierce the corporate veil
preferred stock
professional corporation
 (PC)
prospectus
proxy

proxy statement
public corporation
share of corporate stock
shareholder
sole proprietor
sole proprietorship
stock
stock certificate
stock dividend
stock exchange
stock market
stock options
stock split
stockholder
stockholder's derivative
 action
subsidiary corporation
syndicate
winding up

REVIEW QUESTIONS

SHORT ANSWER

1. Identify the liability for the owners of each of the following types of business organizations.
   a. Sole proprietorship
   b. Partnership
   c. Limited partnership
   d. Corporation
   e. Limited liability company

2. When does a sole proprietorship end?

3. When does a partnership end?

4. Can the business continue when the partnership ends? Explain.

5. What is a limited partnership?

6. How is it formed?

7. Who owns the corporation?

8. What is a limited liability corporation?

9. What is the difference between common stock and preferred stock?

10. What is a dividend?

11. What is the difference between a cumulative and noncumulative dividend?

12. What is redemption?

13. What is a franchise?

14. What does the phrase *piercing the corporate veil* mean?

15. What is the difference between a stock dividend and a cash dividend?

16. How is a professional corporation different from a regular corporation?

17. How can a person lose his or her status as a limited partner?

18. What is the effect of a person's losing her status as a limited partner?

19. What is a proxy statement?

20. When is a company a parent company?

FILL IN THE BLANK

1. Stock that has been authorized but is not for sale is _____.

2. A company's merger with a subsidiary is known as a _____.

3. When two competitors in the same market merge, this is a _____ merger.

4. The partner who is responsible for ending the partnership is _____.

5. The people who form the corporation are known as _____.

6. A company that controls another company's stock but does not take part in the every-day management of the company is a _____.

7. _____ stock receives a dividend before common stock.

8. The New York Stock Exchange is a _____ market.

9. A merger where cash and stock are given for the company's stock is a _____ merger.

10. The _____ are the people who run the corporation on a day-to-day basis.

11. A dividend that is paid using company assets is a _____ dividend.

FACT SITUATIONS

1. Tom, Roger, and Sid form a general partnership. Sid dies. What happens to the partnership? What happens to the business?

2. Nolan decides to sell stock in his company. What type of company has it become?

3. Steven, David, and Lee enter into a partnership. Lee does not take part in the day-to-day operations of the business—only Steven and David do that. Lee only contributed capital to the business.
   a. What type of partnership is this?
   b. Who runs the business on a day-to-day basis?
   c. What type of liability does Lee have in the business?
   d. What happens if Lee starts to participate in the day-to-day running of the business?
   e. If the partnership dissolves, when does Lee get his money?

4. When John joins a corporation, part of his compensation is the right to purchase company stock at reduced prices at certain times. What does John have?

5. When Roger takes his company public, he establishes how much the shares of stock he is selling are worth. What is this termed?

6. Colleen starts out in business by herself. What type of business is this?

7. Francine goes into business with someone else for a limited purpose. The business will expire when its limited purpose has been achieved. What type of business agreement is this?

8 Sheldon and Margaret buy stock in a company. What are they now known as?

9. What will Sheldon and Margaret receive to indicate they own stock in the company?

10. Sheldon and Margaret turn their stock in to the company in which they invested. They receive three shares for every one share they turn in. What is this called?

CHAPTER 15
Securities

INTRODUCTION

Securities law relates to the types of securities that are traded or sold and the people who trade or sell them. This chapter introduces and explains the terms used to describe the people who sell and buy securities, how they are bought and sold, the types of securities available, and the regulations concerning their sale. The chapter also explores how securities can be bought and sold illegally.

SECURITIES IN GENERAL

SECURITIES

Securities are generally defined as stocks, bonds, notes, convertible debentures (see below), warrants (see below), or other documents that represent an ownership share in a company or by a company or a debt owed by government. Securities are evidence either of a debt owed or a right to receive distribution of a company's profits or assets. A security is a document stating that a company owes money to a person; in essence, the document indicates ownership interest in a company. Also orders to pay someone money are all considered either securities or evidence of securities. These securities are bought and sold at stock exchanges and other markets as described in Chapter 14. Securities can also include other investment opportunities that must be in compliance with securities law.

Whether an instrument was actually a security was the issue before the Supreme Court in the case of *Securities and Exchange Commission v. W. J. Howey Co.* The court established the **Howey test** to determine if an instrument is a security. See Sidebar 15-1. According to the Howey test, if the following is found to exist, then the instrument is a security. See Exhibit 15-1.

SIDEBAR 15-1 *SECURITIES AND EXCHANGE COMMISSION V. W. J. HOWEY CO.*

Facts: The Howey Company was offering for sale title to citrus grove acreage and a service contract where the Howey Company would cultivate, harvest, and sell the citrus grown on each parcel. The people who purchased the parcels could purchase a service contract from whomever they wanted, but were encouraged to buy the contracts from the Howey Company. The contracts gave the Howey Company the exclusive right for ten years to harvest and market the crops. The owners would receive payments based on the sale of the fruit. The SEC said this was a security that had to be registered with the Commission before it could be offered for sale to the general public.

Issue: Were these contracts, when taken together, an investment contract that had to be registered with the SEC before it could be sold to the general public?

Decision: In order for something to be considered an investment contract—a security—there must be an investment of money, that is in a common enterprise, with the expectation that profits will be generated from the efforts of others. Applying these factors to the contracts, the court determined that the contracts were a security and were subject to SEC regulations.

Source: United States Reports

---

1. There is an investment of money;
2. in a common enterprise;
3. with the expectation that profits will be generated from the efforts of others.

EXHIBIT 15-1	THE HOWEY TEST: WHEN IS SOMETHING A SECURITY?

1. **Investment of Money** – Someone gave money to someone as an investment.
2. **Common Enterprise** – Investment is in the property of another person.
3. **Expectation of Profits** – Someone other than the investor makes the effort to make money.

The term an **investment of money** is construed as meaning that an investor has turned over some money to someone else for the purpose of investment, that is, to make even more money. The phrase **common enterprise** refers to the fact that the investment is not the property of the investor; the money the investor paid is pooled with other investors' money so each person owns an undivided interest in the investment. The final element of the definition of a security, the **expectation of profits,** means that the investor does not have any direct control over the work that leads to a profit or loss; people other than the investor make most of the effort to generate a profit.

REASONS TO ISSUE SECURITIES

Securities are issued to provide funding or capital to a business that the business will then invest into itself. Two types of financing are based on securities: debt financing and equity financing. **Debt financing** is the selling of bonds—the security—or the borrowing of money. The **debt instrument** that is issued by the corporation usually contains the following information:

1. The amount of the debt
2. The length of the debt period
3. The method of paying the debt back
4. The rate of interest that will be paid for borrowing the money

Debt financing creates an obligation on the part of a company to repay an amount borrowed.

Equity financing is the raising of capital through the sale of stock in a company. Because stock gives the holder of the share an ownership interest in the company, the holder has an equitable interest in the company; the shareholders have a claim on any future profits of the company. (See Chapter 14, Business Organizations.) However, there is no requirement on the part of the company to pay shareholders for the amount of money they spent to purchase the stock. Any return the shareholder receives on his or her investment is in the form of the payment of dividends. See Exhibit 15-2.

EXHIBIT 15-2	TWO TYPES OF CORPORATE FINANCING

Debt Financing – Bonds are sold or money is borrowed. The debt instrument will state how the money will be paid back, how long it will take, and at what interest.

Equity Financing – Money is raised by selling ownership interest in the company. There is no requirement that the money be repaid. All the owners may receive is a share of the profits of the company.

CATEGORIES OF SECURITIES

Categories of securities are based on where they are sold, who issues them, what can be done with them, and even on when payment is made on them.

MARKETABLE AND NONMARKETABLE SECURITIES

In order for a security to be sold on the open market, it must be marketable—that is, able to be sold in the "market" to a buyer. The term **marketable security** has two different definitions, depending on the context in which it is used. The term can refer to a security that is of reasonable investment caliber and is therefore easily sold; in other words, it is a good investment and because it is a good investment will be easy to sell. *Marketable security* can also refer to stocks and bonds of other companies that are held by one company that can readily be sold on stock exchanges or over-the-counter markets. (See Chapter 14, Business Organizations.) The company that is holding the stocks and bonds of another company plans to sell the stocks and bonds when capital is needed. The key factor in both definitions is that the security can be readily sold; it is something people will be willing to buy on the stock exchange or other market.

A **government security** is either issued by or has principal or interest payment guaranteed by the United States. If the United States issues the security or guarantees that either the principal or interest will be paid, then it is a government security. Such a security may be a **nonmarketable security,** one that cannot be sold on the open market; it can only be redeemed by the holder. A nonmarketable security has no investment quality because it cannot be sold on the open market. Certain types of government bonds and notes are classified as nonmarketable securities. See Exhibit 15-3.

EXHIBIT 15-3	MARKETABLE OR NONMARKETABLE SECURITY?

Marketable Security

1. A security that is a good investment, so it can be sold easily.
2. The stocks and bonds of one company that are owned by another company and that can be sold easily.

KEY—the security can easily be sold on the stock exchange or other market.

Nonmarketable Security

A security that cannot be sold on the open market. It can only be redeemed by the owner of the security.

Certain types of government bonds and notes.

HYBRID, OUTSTANDING, CONVERTIBLE, OR CONSOLIDATED SECURITIES

A **hybrid security** has the features of both a debt security and an equity security. It is hybrid because it has some of the characteristics of a bond—a debt—and some of the characteristics of stock—ownership interest or equity in a company. A **voting security** is any security that gives the owner the right to vote for the members of the board of directors of a company.

An **outstanding security** is held by an investor and has not been redeemed by the investor or bought back by the corporation or other entity that issued the security. A **convertible security** is a bond, a debenture, or a preferred stock that can be exchanged by the owner for common stock or for some other security. There may be a ratio of how much of the new security the owner gets in exchange for the old convertible security. For example, a bond may state that the owner can convert three of the convertible bonds for one new bond from the same company. A **consolidated security** is an issue of securities that is large enough to provide the funds to pay off or retire two or more outstanding issues of securities. For example, a company may issue a new series of bonds. The income generated from the sale will be used to pay the amount due on two series of bonds that had been issued earlier. See Exhibit 15-4.

EXHIBIT 15-4	OUTSTANDING, CONVERTIBLE, OR CONSOLIDATED SECURITIES

Outstanding Security – A security that is owned by an investor. The investor has not redeemed it; the corporation or issuer of the security has not bought back the security.

Convertible Security – The owner of this type of security can convert it—exchange it for common stock or some other security. The new security usually comes from the same company.

Consolidated Security – A large issue of securities that will generate enough income so the company can use the funds to pay off two or more sets of outstanding securities.

SHORT-TERM, SENIOR, AND JUNIOR SECURITIES

A **short-term security** is a bond or other security that matures and is payable within a very short period of time. This type of security is usually purchased for almost immediate income rather than for long-term investment. A **senior security** is a security that takes precedence or priority over other securities when the time comes for the security to be paid. In other words, a senior security will be paid before any other security. A **junior security** is subordinate to a senior security; it will be paid only after the senior security is paid. See Exhibit 15-5.

EXHIBIT 15-5	SENIOR SECURITY OR JUNIOR SECURITY?

Senior Security – A security that takes priority over every other security when it comes to payment. Senior securities are paid first.

Junior Security – A security that is subordinate to a senior security. These securities are paid only after all senior securities are paid.

SELLERS OF SECURITIES

Some of the people who deal in stocks and securities were discussed in Chapter 14, Business Organizations. Additional terms, some general and some more specific, are introduced and discussed here.

ADVISORS, BROKERS, AND DEALERS

An **investment advisor** engages in the business of advising others in their investment in, purchase, or selling of securities. This service is provided to others for compensation. Securities brokers and dealers are investment advisors. Generally, a **broker** is an agent employed to make contracts for compensation. (See Chapter 13, Agency.) More specifically, a broker is a dealer in securities for others; it is his or her business to bring a buyer of securities together with a seller of securities and then to arrange the sale.

More specialized classifications of brokers include institutional brokers, note brokers, and securities brokers. An **institutional broker** is a broker who trades (buys and sells) securities for institutional clients: mutual funds, banks, pension funds, and insurance companies. A **note broker** negotiates the sale of commercial paper. (See Chapter 20.) A **securities**

broker buys and sell stocks, bonds, government securities, or other securities for the principal, the person who hires him or her, only. A **securities dealer** buys and sells securities for a principal, and also for himself or herself.

BROKERAGE AGREEMENT

In order for a broker to represent someone, a **brokerage contract** is usually signed. A brokerage contract is the agreement that actually employs the broker to make the type of contracts agreed to on behalf of the principal. Such a contract also sets out how much the broker will be paid for this service. For example, if Leah visits an office of Merrill Lynch and hires someone to be her broker, she is authorizing the broker to buy and sell securities on her behalf in return for a commission. The term **brokerage** refers to the wages or commission a broker receives when the trade of the security is arranged. A **brokerage listing,** which is a unilateral contract (see Chapter 10, Contracts), provides that the broker find or procure a purchaser ready, willing, and able to buy the security, and who will accept the terms stated in the offer.

DISCOUNT BROKERS AND UNDERWRITERS

A **discount broker** is one who discounts bills of exchange and promissory notes and also advances money on securities. Discount brokers perform buy-and-sell orders at a rate *lower* than full-service brokers. An **underwriter** is a firm that handles the marketing of securities to the public, which can be accomplished in two ways. Either the underwriter buys all the securities that are being offered for sale and then sells them to the general public; or the firm does not buy the securities but charges a commission on each security it actually sells. See Exhibit 15-6 for a descriptive summary of the sellers of securities.

EXHIBIT 15-6 SELLERS OF SECURITIES

1. **Investment advisor** – Person who advises others on whether they should buy or sell securities.
2. **Broker** – Agent who makes contracts for the buying and selling of securities for other people or businesses.
   a. **Institutional Broker** – Broker who buys and sells securities for institutional clients: mutual funds, banks, pension funds, and insurance companies.
   b. **Note Broker** – Broker who buys and sells commercial paper.
   c. **Securities Broker** – Broker who buys and sells stocks, bonds, government securities, or other securities for the person who hired him or her, the principal.
   d. **Discount Broker** – Broker who performs buy-and-sell orders at a lower rate than a full-service broker.
3. **Securities Dealer** – Person who buys and sells securities not only for the principal, but for himself or herself as well.
4. **Underwriters** – Generally a firm that deals with the selling of securities to the general public.
   a. The underwriter buys all of the securities and then sells them to the public.
   b. The firm charges a commission for each security it sells.

OTHER TYPES OF COMPANIES

Some companies appear to be engaged in the securities exchange business but either do not conduct business for the general public or do not buy and sell securities. A **bucket shop** is an office or other place where persons accept an order to buy and sell securities or commodities, but never execute the purchase or sale. This is referred to as **bucketing.** An **investment company** is any corporation that is in business to own and hold the stock of other corporations.

SECURITIES MARKETS

Brokers will arrange for the sale of securities at different markets for such securities; the New York Stock Exchange is an example of such a market. Two terms are used to describe the current state of the market for securities: *bull market* and *bear market.* In a **bull market,** the price of securities is either rising or expected to rise. In a **bear market,** the price of securities is either falling or expected to fall. See Exhibit 15-7.

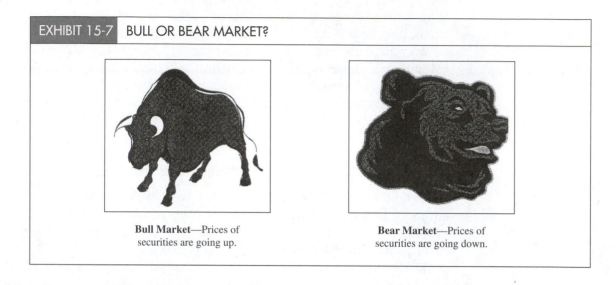

EXHIBIT 15-7 BULL OR BEAR MARKET?

Bull Market—Prices of securities are going up.

Bear Market—Prices of securities are going down.

TYPES OF SECURITIES

What is generally considered a security has already been defined. However, there are many classifications and subclassifications of investments that can be termed *securities.* General terms apply to securities in general; more specific terms apply to specific securities. Certain terms define different classes of securities.

STOCKS AND BONDS

Stock or **capital stock** in a corporation is a security that represents an ownership interest in the company. **Registered stock** has been registered with the Securities and Exchange Commission as a new issue of stock or a secondary offering of stock. (See below for definition of secondary offering.)

A **bond** is a security that is evidence of a debt for which a company or the government promises to pay a specified amount of interest for a specified period of time and to repay the loan on the expiration date of the bond. A **discount bond** is sold for less than face value (below its value at maturity). Interest on a discount bond is not paid annually, but at maturity. A **note** is a security that contains an express and absolute promise of the company to pay a definite sum of money at a specified time. (See the chapters on corporations and commercial paper for more specific types of stock, bonds, and notes.)

WARRANTS AND DEBENTURES

A **warrant** is an order whereby one person authorizes another person to pay a particular sum of money. An **indenture** is a written contract for the issuance of a bond. The contract or indenture will state the type of bond being issued, its maturity date, the amount of the issue, a description of the assets that secure the bond, the interest rate, and any other terms of the bond. Assets of the company are used to secure the bond. A **debenture** is an unsecured debt that is backed only by the general credit and earnings history of the corporation; it is not secured by a mortgage or a lien on specific property. A **debenture bond** is a bond that is not secured by any specific property. Rather, it is issued against the general credit of a corporation or a government; it has nothing backing it other than a promise to repay money. The reliability of the promise to pay the money back is based on the company's or government's history of paying similar bonds. A **convertible debenture** may be changed into some other security, usually at the option of the holder of the debenture. For example, Patty owns debentures of Slamco Corporation; she may be allowed to convert those debentures into stock of the corporation. See Exhibit 15-8 for a summary of indentures and debentures.

EXHIBIT 15-8 | INDENTURE OR DEBENTURE?

Indenture – Written contract for a bond issue that sets out the type of bond, the date the bond matures, the total amount of the bonds issued, the interest rate, and the property that secures the bond.

Debenture – Long-term unsecured debt that is backed only by the company's history of paying its debt and its promise to repay the debt.

   a. **Debenture Bond** – A bond that is not secured by any specific property. These bonds are backed only by the company's credit history.
   b. **Convertible Debenture** – A security that may be changed into some other security, usually at the option of the holder of the debenture.

CLASSIFICATIONS OF STOCK

Certain classifications of stock serve as securities. A **growth stock** has the prospect of an increase in market value, but not necessarily a good dividend return. The value of the stock is in the prospect that its value in the market may go up rather than in the dividends the stock pays. **Letter stock** is stock that is not registered with the Securities and Exchange Commission. It is not registered because the buyer gives the seller a bonus as payment for labor, services, or property. **Penny stock,** which is low-priced because it is highly speculative, sells for less than $1 a share. Registered stock has been registered with the Securities and Exchange Commission either as new issue or as a secondary offering. See Exhibit 15-9.

EXHIBIT 15-9 | CLASSIFICATIONS OF STOCK

1. **Growth Stock** – A stock that has the possibility of an increase in market value but may not have a good dividend return. The value of this stock comes from the possibility that the price for it may increase.
2. **Letter Stock** – Stock that is not listed with the Securities and Exchange Commission because the buyer states that he or she has plans to resell the stock to someone else.
3. **Treasury Stock** – Stock that is issued to stockholders as if it has been fully paid for.
4. **Watered Stock** – Stock that is issued for less than its listed value; the value is "watered down."
5. **Penny Stock** – Stock that sells at a low price because it carries high risk.
6. **Registered Stock** – Stock that has been registered with the SEC.

COMMODITIES

A **commodity** is a staple like wool, cotton, wheat, or pork bellies that is traded on a commodity exchange. A **commodity future** is a speculative transaction involving the sale, for future delivery, of a staple such as wool or wheat at a predetermined price. A person buys a commodity future hoping that the price of the commodity will go up in the near future. The buyer can then sell the future for more than what he or she paid, but at less than the current market value. A **futures contract** is a commitment to buy or sell commodities at a later time and place that is specified in the contract. Only a small percentage of these contracts actually lead to delivery of the commodity because the contracts are bought, sold, or liquidated prior to the delivery date. See Exhibit 15-10.

EXHIBIT 15-10 WHAT AN INVESTOR WANTS TO HAVE HAPPEN WITH A FUTURES CONTRACT

1. The investor buys a futures contract for a commodity or for currency, to be delivered at some point in the future, for $100 per contract.

2. If the commodity value goes up, the investor can sell the contract for the commodity for more than he or she paid for it, but less than what the commodity is currently selling for. The investor might sell the contract for $150 because the amount of the commodity is selling for $175.

3. If the contract is for a foreign currency, the investor wants the foreign currency to be stronger against the dollar. The contract is for 100 deutchmarks (DM). The current rate of exchange is $2 for every 1 DM. When the currency is received, the exchange rate is $4 for every 1 DM. The investor will receive 100 DM that are now worth $400 instead of $200.

An investor may also trade in foreign currency by purchasing a contract for sale of currency at some later date. This is known as a **currency futures option.** The investor wants the foreign currency to be stronger against the dollar when it comes time to receive the contract because he or she can then convert the foreign currency into U.S. dollars and receive more money than what he or she paid for the contract.

PURCHASERS OF COMMODITIES

Futures contracts are usually bought by two types of investors: commercial hedgers and speculators. The **commercial hedger** uses a futures contract to minimize price risks that are inherent in a marketing scheme. A commercial hedger purchases a contract at one price, hoping that when it comes time for actual delivery of goods, the price will be higher than when the contract was purchased. A **speculator** is a person who, using venture capital, attempts to make a profit resulting from price changes. When an investor is involved in futures contracts, he or she is engaged in **futures trading,** the buying and selling of futures contracts that usually take place in a futures market. A **futures market** is a commodity exchange where future contracts are traded; an example is the Chicago Board of Trade.

MUTUAL FUNDS

Some investors choose to invest in **mutual funds,** which are managed by investment companies that invest in publicly traded securities. The amount of return on the investment depends upon how the underlying securities are performing. There are two general types of mutual funds: **open end mutual funds** and **closed end mutual funds.** With an open end mutual fund, the amount of **capitalization**—the actual amount of money invested in the stock—is not set and more shares can be purchased at any time. There is also more money to be invested in underlying securities. With a closed end mutual fund, the amount of capitalization is set, and only the number of shares in the fund that was originally authorized can be sold.

A **growth fund** is a mutual fund made up of the stock of companies that are still growing; the purpose of this fund is to increase the investment value of the fund. An **income fund** is made up of securities that pay periodic dividends; usually consists of coupon bonds or other security that provides a steady income. The portfolio of an **index fund** is designed to match the performance of a broad base index; its performance is to mirror the market as indicated by the index. A **statistical index** is a reference used to measure and track the performance of the stock market; Standards and Poors (S & P) is an example of a statistical index. A **load fund mutual fund** is one for which a charge is assessed at the time of purchase of the shares to cover administrative and commission expenses. A **no load mutual fund,** on the other hand, has no service charge assessed. A **money market fund** invests in money market securities; the **money market** deals with short-term debt instruments like U.S. Treasury bills and commercial paper. The **load** is the portion of the price of the shares of the mutual fund open end investment companies that covers sales commissions and all other costs of distribution. An **open end investment company** is a mutual fund that will buy back its shares and that is continuously offering to sell new shares to the public. See Exhibit 15-11 for a summary of the different types of mutual funds.

EXHIBIT 15-11 | MUTUAL FUNDS

Open End Mutual Funds – The amount of money that is invested in the stock is not set; additional shares of stock can be purchased.

Closed End Mutual Funds – The amount of money that is invested in the stock is set. Only the number of shares of stock that was authorized can be sold.

Open end and closed end mutual funds can also be one of the following:

Growth Fund – Fund that is made up of the stock of companies that are still growing.

Income Fund – Fund that is made up of stock that periodically pays stock dividends.

Index Fund – The stock that makes up the fund is designed to mirror what the stock market is doing based on the index used to track the performance of the stock market.

Load Fund – A charge is made at the time the stock is purchased to cover the cost of administering the fund and to pay commissions.

No Load Fund – No charges are assessed for administering the funds or paying commissions.

Money Market Funds – Instead of stocks, the fund invests money in money markets.

OPTIONS

Options constitute another investment opportunity. An **option** is a contract made for consideration to keep an offer open for a set period of time. Options are classified according to the circumstances of the transaction involved. A **commodity option** is a right purchased by the option holder that entitles him or her to either buy or sell, at a stated price and within the stated time, the actual commodity or a commodities futures contract. A **commodity futures option** is the right to buy or sell a futures contract at a specified price within a stated period of time. The option buyer pays a premium to the dealer for the right in addition to the usual commission. Nothing else is paid at the time of the initial transaction, the purchase of the option. The option will contain the **striking price,** which is the price that the option holder is entitled to either buy or sell the commodity for. This is the price that is charged if the option to buy or sell the commodity is ever exercised, or used.

A **call option** is the right of an option holder to buy a commodity or stock at a fixed price for a stated quantity within a stated period of time. For example, Rodney purchases an option to buy 500 shares of stock in Delmar Publishing at $50 per share for a period of six months. Under the terms of this call option, Rodney can purchase up to 500 shares of Delmar Publishing, paying no more than $50 per share for a period of six months. If Rodney does not exercise this option within the six months, he will have to pay the market price for the stock. A **put option** gives the option holder the right to sell a commodity or stock at a fixed price for a stated quantity within the stated period of time. For example, Brenda has a call option on Delmar stock that allows her to sell 400 shares for no less than $60 per share.

A **stock option**—also referred to as a **call**—is the right to buy stock in the future at a specified price that is established in advance. An **incentive stock option** is an option given to an employee of a company to purchase company stock at a specified price for a specified period of time. The purchase price of the stock is usually lower than the market price, giving the employee an incentive to purchase. A **naked option** is sold by investors giving other people the right to buy stock from them—the investors—even though the investors own no stock to back up the commitments created by the sale of the options. For example, the Smith Investment Group sells a naked option to purchase 400 shares of Delmar stock to Benny and Betty. The Smith Group does not own any shares of Delmar, but because Benny and Betty have the option, they can purchase the stock from the Smith Group. If Benny and Betty exercise their option, the Smith Group will have to buy Delmar stock to sell to Benny and Betty. The investment group will make money if they can purchase the Delmar stock for less than or for the same purchase price contained in the option. See Exhibit 15-12 for a summary of different stock options.

EXHIBIT 15-12   TYPES OF OPTIONS

1. **Commodity Option** – The right to purchase or sell either a commodity or a commodity futures contract at a set price for a set period of time.
2. **Call Option** – The option holder has the right to buy a commodity or stock at a set period of time at a set price.
3. **Put Option** – The option holder has a right to sell a commodity or stock at a set period of time at a set price.
4. **Stock Option** – The right to purchase stock in the future at a specified price for a specified period of time.
5. **Incentive Stock Option** – Employees of a company can purchase company stock at a price less than the market price.

In order to have an option and because an option is a contract, the investor must pay consideration to the person who is selling. The **option premium** is the price that is actually paid for the option, the consideration to keep the option open for the stated period of time. When the investor has an option, he or she has the right to exercise that option at any time during the stated period. **Exercise** is the decision of the option holder to require the performance under the option; the option holder can request that the commodity or the commodity future be paid for or sold. The **exercise date** is the final day on which the option holder can exercise the option that he or she has purchased.

PORTFOLIOS AND ASSETS

All of these instruments are designed to be added to the investor's portfolio. **Portfolio** is the collective term for all the securities held by one person or by an institution. **Portfolio income** accrues from the interest, the dividends, the rentals, the royalties, the capital gains, and any other investment sources that make up the portfolio. A **royalty** is compensation for the use of property—usually copyrighted material or natural resources—that is stated as a percentage of the receipts from the use of the property or as an account per unit produced. All of these investments become part of the person's assets in the hope that the person will realize capital gains. **Assets** are comprised of property of any kind a person possesses; **capital gains** are the profit realized from the sale or exchange of a capital asset.

SALE OF SECURITIES

When the SEC has accepted the proposed registration of a security, the security may be sold. Several general terms relate to the sale of securities.

OFFERINGS

An **offering** is the issue of securities put up for sale to the public or to a private group. There are two general classifications of offerings: primary and secondary. The proceeds from the sale of a **primary offering** go to the company to be used for some lawful purpose. This is also referred to as a **new issue** of the security because it is the first time this security has been offered for sale. In a **secondary offering,** the funds from the sale go to a person or entity other than the company.

If the offering is a public offering made to residents of more than one state, it is referred to as an **interstate offering** and is regulated by federal securities law. An **intrastate offering** is a restricted public offering. It is made by a company that:

1. Is organized under the laws of a particular state;

2. Does its principal business in that state;

3. Offers only to bona fide residents of the state; and

4. Ensures that all the proceeds from the sale remain within the state. See Exhibit 15-13.

EXHIBIT 15-13 | **TYPES OF OFFERINGS, PART I**

Primary Offering
Proceeds from the sale of the security go to the company to be used for some lawful purpose.

Interstate Offering
Offering made to residents of more than one state.

Secondary Offering
Proceeds from the sale of the security go to an individual for his or her use rather than being used by the company.

Intrastate Offering
Restricted public offering that is made by a company that meets these requirements:

1. The company is organized under the laws of a particular state.

2. The company does its principal business in that state.

3. The offering is made to residents of that state only.

4. A substantial amount of the proceeds stays in the state.

A **public offering** is the offering of securities at random to anyone who will purchase them; these offerings are governed by state and federal law. An **initial public offering (IPO)** is the first offering of a stock for investment by the general public. A **private offering** is one made to a limited number of investors who are so well-informed about the affairs of the company that they do not require the protection of disclosure requirements. However, in order for a private offering to be valid, investors must have knowledge about the company that would ordinarily be contained in the registration statement. Because of this knowledge, private offerings may be exempt from federal regulation. An **undigested offering** is a new issue of a security that remains undistributed because there is insufficient public demand for the security at the offered price. See Exhibit 15-14.

EXHIBIT 15-14 TYPES OF OFFERINGS, PART II

Public Offering
Offering to sell securities to anyone who will purchase the securities.

Private Offering
Offering to sell securities that is made to a limited number of people who are so well-informed that they do not need a prospectus.

Undigested Offering
A new issue of a security that remains undistributed (unsold) because there is insufficient public demand for the security at the offered price.

TOMBSTONE ADS AND MARKET ORDERS

In order to put people on notice that there is a new issue of a security, the entity offering the security may use a **tombstone ad**—a notice, a circular, or an advertisement that is placed in a newspaper about the new offering. A tombstone ad will provide basic information and must contain language to the effect that this announcement is for information only: It is not an offer to buy or sell any of the securities listed. The actual securities offer can only be made by using the prospectus.

Generally, when someone wishes to purchase or sell a security, he or she will issue a **market order,** an order to buy or sell a stock or other security on a stock or commodity exchange at the current or best price when the order reaches the floor of the exchange. This market order can be issued by the person himself or herself or it can be done through a broker or securities dealer. The decision to buy or sell a security may be based on the latest **market quotation,** the most current price that securities and commodities have been bought or sold at on an exchange or other market.

BUYING ON MARGIN

Sometimes a purchaser of stocks or securities will do so by **buying on margin,** or by paying part of the price in cash and the rest of the price by a loan. A **margin** is a sum of money or its equivalent—another security for example—that is placed in the hands of a broker by the person who is requesting either a sale of securities or a purchase of securities using his or her account. Usually the loan of the purchase price is made by the broker; when the broker extends the credit, he or she will do so using a margin account. A **margin account** enables the securities industry to extend credit to its customers. The customer purchases a specified amount of a security from the securities firm by paying part of the purchase price in cash. The brokerage firm then loans the money to the purchaser for the remaining amount of the purchase price. The firm maintains possession of the stock to use as collateral for the loan and charges interest on the balance. The use of margin accounts by brokers is regulated by federal law. When a person buys stock on margin, the **margin requirement** must be met. This is a requirement that a fraction of the price of a stock must be paid in cash, while putting the stock up as a security against the loan for the balance. In other words, if a person takes out a loan to purchase stock and gives a security interest in the stock to secure the loan, a certain percentage of the price of the stock must be paid in cash. Sometimes when stocks or other securities are purchased on margin, the price of the stock may fall. When this happens, the broker may issue a **margin call,** a demand by a broker to put up money or securities upon the purchase of a stock or to increase the amount of the money or stock that is on deposit with the broker. See Exhibit 15-15 for a flow chart depicting the purchase of stocks on margin.

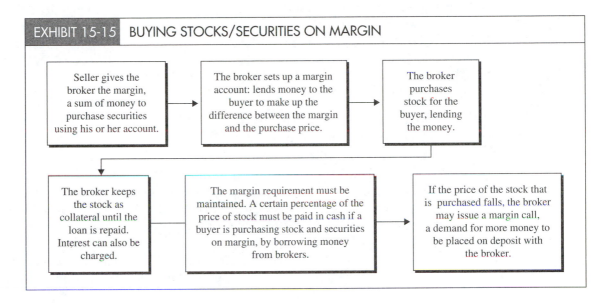

EXHIBIT 15-15 | BUYING STOCKS/SECURITIES ON MARGIN

Seller gives the broker the margin, a sum of money to purchase securities using his or her account.

The broker sets up a margin account: lends money to the buyer to make up the difference between the margin and the purchase price.

The broker purchases stock for the buyer, lending the money.

The broker keeps the stock as collateral until the loan is repaid. Interest can also be charged.

The margin requirement must be maintained. A certain percentage of the price of stock must be paid in cash if a buyer is purchasing stock and securities on margin, by borrowing money from brokers.

If the price of the stock that is purchased falls, the broker may issue a margin call, a demand for more money to be placed on deposit with the broker.

PROGRAM TRADING, CHURNING, AND SCALPING

Another way that securities are purchased is by program trading. **Program trading** is the trading of stock on stock exchanges through the use of computers that are programmed to buy and sell securities at specified prices and when other conditions are met.

Churning, which is a violation of federal securities law, occurs when a broker who can exercise control over the number and the frequency of trades for his or her customers abuses those customers' confidence for personal gain by initiating transactions that are excessive considering the nature of the accounts and the clients' stated wishes. In other words, the broker who churns ignores the orders of his or her customers and uses their accounts for his or her own personal benefit. The broker churns because he or she can make more commission for the trades. Churning is considered fraud.

Another illegal activity is **scalping,** which occurs when a stock professional buys stock for his or her own personal benefit and then urges investors to buy the stock so that its price will rise. The professional can then sell the stock at a higher price than what he or she paid for it. See Exhibit 15-16.

EXHIBIT 15-16 | ILLEGAL BUYING AND SELLING OF SECURITIES

Churning – A broker buys and sells securities for his or her customers without their authorization. These transactions are to increase the amount of commission the broker earns; they are not for the benefit of the investor.

Scalping – A broker buys stock for his or her own portfolio and then urges investors to also buy the stock so the price will rise. If the price rises, the broker will sell his or her stock at the higher price.

ARBITRAGE

Sometimes investors will engage in what is termed *arbitrage* in an effort to make quick profits on their investments. **Arbitrage** is the simultaneous buying of a security or commodity in one market and selling of the same security or commodity in another market by the same person in the hope of making a profit on the small price difference. If a person can buy a security on one exchange and, at the same time, sell the same security on another exchange for more money, then he or she has earned a small profit on the transaction. For example, Phillip discovers that one stock exchange lists the price of a certain stock for 10 cents less than another stock exchange. Phillip purchases the stock on the exchange where the price is cheaper and immediately sells the same stock on the exchange where the price is slightly higher. Phillip would be considered an **arbitrager.**

SELLING SHORT

Another way a person may attempt to make a quick profit on an investment is to sell a stock **short.** This means that the person will sell securities or commodity futures that he or she does not own at the time of the sale. The investor expects to buy back the stock at a lower price than what it was sold for. He or she believes the price of the stock will go down quickly, so he or she sells the stock short. When the stock drops in price, the investor will purchase enough shares to cover the stock he or she sold. **Short interest** is the number of shares a person still needs to purchase in order to return all the stock borrowed to the lender.

Sometimes the investor will not purchase the stock because it has not dropped enough in price. In that situation, the investor finds himself or herself in a **short position** and borrows a stock in order to sell it, figuring the price will go down. The investor is short until he or she purchases stock to replace the stock of the person from whom he or she borrowed the original stock.

The investor is party to a **short sale,** a contract for the sale of shares of stock that a person does not own at the time of the sale. In order to deliver the stock, he or she must borrow the stock so delivery can be made when due. A **short sale against the box** occurs when the investor has enough stock to cover the stock borrowed if necessary. The investor sells the stock short and borrows the stock from someone else. But when it comes time to return the stock, he or she owns enough to replace it without having to purchase stock if he or she needs to. The "box" is a hypothetical safety deposit box where the stocks are kept. **Short covering** is the actual buying of stock to return the stock that was borrowed in order to make the delivery of the short sale.

Regardless of how securities are purchased, they must eventually be paid for. The phrase **settling the account** refers to the process wherein the parties go over the account and agree on the final amount that is due. It is also used to refer to the investor's actually paying any amount still due. The **settlement date** in stock transactions is the date by which an executed or completed order for a transaction must be settled. The buyer is paying for the securities purchased and the seller is delivering the securities that were purchased. For example, through her broker Rita purchases 1,000 shares of stock. The broker arranges to purchase the stock Vic has for sale. When the settlement date arrives, Rita will pay the remaining amount for the stock and Vic will deliver the stock certificates, indicating that ownership of the stock has now changed. See Exhibit 15-17 for a flow chart showing how securities are sold short.

CONCLUSION

This chapter discussed one segment of securities law, an area that is very broad and that covers many principles. First it must be determined if an instrument is indeed a security;

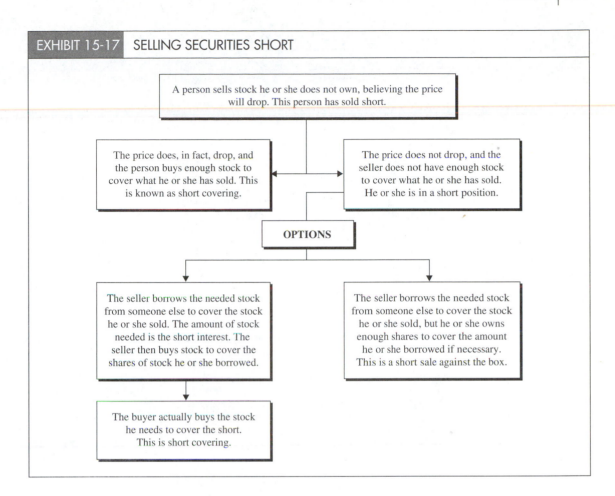

EXHIBIT 15-17   SELLING SECURITIES SHORT

A person sells stock he or she does not own, believing the price will drop. This person has sold short.

The price does, in fact, drop, and the person buys enough stock to cover what he or she has sold. This is known as short covering.

The price does not drop, and the seller does not have enough stock to cover what he or she has sold. He or she is in a short position.

OPTIONS

The seller borrows the needed stock from someone else to cover the stock he or she sold. The amount of stock needed is the short interest. The seller then buys stock to cover the shares of stock he or she borrowed.

The seller borrows the needed stock from someone else to cover the stock he or she sold, but he or she owns enough shares to cover the amount he or she borrowed if necessary. This is a short sale against the box.

The buyer actually buys the stock he needs to cover the short. This is short covering.

the Howey test, announced by the Supreme Court, determines this. In order to be marketable, the security must be able to be sold on the open market, otherwise it is considered a nonmarketable security.

The people who buy and sell securities can be brokers (people who buy and sell securities only for other people) or they can be dealers (people who buy and sell securities for themselves as well). Securities can be stocks, bonds, commodities, and mutual funds. Investors hope for bull markets, periods when prices are high, when they want to sell securities; they hope for bear markets, bear market prices are when stock prices are low, when they want to purchase securities.

An option—the right to purchase a security in the future—may also be a security that is bought and sold. Options can apply to futures contracts or stock. The option can apply to either the sale of a security at a certain price or the purchase of a security at a certain price. Options do not last forever; there is a time period within which the transaction must take place.

Offerings are how securities are usually put up for sale. Offerings can be public or private. An offering might be an undigested offering—one that has not been offered for sale yet.

Securities can be purchased on margin, where only part of the purchase price is paid initially with the rest due at a later time. Churning (ignoring the wishes of the customers) and scalping (urging people to invest in a security to increase the value of the dealer's assets) are two illegal ways of buying and selling securities. Both are violations of federal law. Securities may also be sold short, which means that a person is selling securities he or she does not own, thinking the price will drop and he or she can buy them at a lower price than what he or she sold them for.

CHAPTER 15 REVIEW

KEY WORDS AND PHRASES

arbitrage	debt financing	mutual fund
arbitrager	discount bond	naked option
assets	discount broker	no load mutual fund
bear market	exercise	nonmarketable security
bond	futures contract	note
broker	government security	open end mutual funds
brokerage contract	growth fund	option
bucket shop	growth stock	penny stock
bucketing	Howey test	put option
bull market	hybrid security	registered stock
buying on margin	incentive stock option	scalping
call	indenture	securities broker
capital gains	index fund	settlement date
churning	investment advisor	short
closed end mutual funds	investment company	short covering
commodity	letter stock	short position
commodity future	load fund mutual fund	short sale
commodity futures option	margin	short sale against the box
commodity option	margin account	speculator
convertible debenture	margin call	statistical index
convertible security	margin requirement	stock
currency futures option	marketable security	stock option
debenture	money market fund	tombstone ad

REVIEW QUESTIONS

SHORT ANSWER

1. What is the difference between a bull market and a bear market?

2. What is a brokerage contract?

3. What is a bucket shop?

4. What is a call option?

5. What are considered capital gains?

6. What is a commodity future?

7. What are closed end mutual funds?

8. What is a consolidated security?

9. What is the difference between debt financing and equity financing?

10. What is meant when a mutual fund is described as no load?

11. What is meant when a person's short position is discussed?

12. What is the margin requirement?

13. What is a tombstone ad?

14. What is the difference between a securities broker and a securities dealer?

15. What is a short sale?

16. What must the person do once he or she has completed a short sale?

17. What is a growth stock?

18. What is a futures contract?

19. State the parts of the Howey test.

20. What is a money market fund?

FILL IN THE BLANK

1. A stock that is sold for less than a dollar is referred to as a _____.

2. The amount of money a purchaser of stock must have on deposit with an investment firm in order to buy stock on credit is known as _____.

3. A security that can be exchanged for another type of security is a _____.

4. A person who buys and sells stock for himself or herself as well as for someone else is known as an _____.

5. An office where buy-and-sell orders of securities are received but are never carried out is a _____.

6. A stock that has a potential increase in market value but does not have a history of paying dividends is known as _____ stock.

7. Stock that is issued for less than its listed value is _____ stock.

8. A fund that is made up of securities that pays periodic dividends is known as a _____.

9. An offering of a security that is not distributed because of a lack of interest by the public is known as an _____.

10. A securities firm extends credit to its customers for the purchasing of stocks or other securities by way of a _____.

FACT SITUATIONS

1. Ernie is encouraging his customers to invest in securities that he has also invested in. In what practice is Ernie engaged? Is it legal or illegal?

2. Bert pays part of the purchase price of his stock in cash. He then borrows the rest of the money from the brokerage firm. In what is Bert engaged?

3. A broker requests that a customer pay more money on stock that he or she has purchased using borrowed funds. What is the term for the broker's request?

4. A company decides to issue new shares of stock. What will the company issue to advise potential investors about the stock issue?

5. Martha sells stock she does not have. In what practice is Martha engaging?

6. Roger buys a contract for wheat that is to be harvested three months later. What type of security has Roger purchased?

7. Judy buys securities by paying part of the purchase price in cash and the rest with a loan. How is Judy purchasing the securities?

8. A person pays part of the purchase price of the stock in cash. The stock is then put up as security against the loan that was made for the balance of the purchase price. Why is this being done?

9. Isidore is buying and selling securities for clients that the clients did not authorize. His sole purpose is to generate more commissions. What is this known as? Is it legal?

10. Imelda is selling stock that she does not own at the time of the sale. In what is Imelda engaging? Is it legal?

CHAPTER 16
Securities Regulation

INTRODUCTION

Securities are regulated by state and federal laws and regulations and the cases interpreting those laws and regulations, among them blue sky laws, merit regulations, the Securities Act, and the Securities Exchange Act. This chapter discusses the federal laws that regulate securities: The role of the Securities and Exchange Commission, its divisions, and their powers will also be discussed. The terms and process of registering securities for sale are discussed as well as the different types of registration.

The chapter also explores the issues surrounding insider trading and those federal statutes that attempt to control it. Because ownership of stock means ownership of the company, hostile takeovers can occur. The parties involved, the process that must be followed, the notices that have to be given, and potential defenses against a hostile takeover are covered.

STATE AND FEDERAL LAWS REGULATING SECURITIES

Because of the national scope of companies and the stock market, most laws regulating securities and their sale and purchase are at the federal level. There is some state regulation of securities as well.

STATE REGULATION

In order to regulate securities at the state level, blue sky laws may be passed. A **blue sky law** is a state statute that regulates the sale of securities. One example of a blue sky law is a **merit regulation,** a state securities law provision that allows the state securities commissioner to decide whether a proposed security offering is too risky to be sold to the public in that state. The state commissioner of securities has the authority to prevent an offering of a security for sale if he or she determines that it is too risky an investment for people in his or her state. See Sidebar 16-1.

SIDEBAR 16-1 A STATE MERIT REGULATION

23-42-405. STOP ORDER DENYING, SUSPENDING, OR REVOKING REGISTRATION STATEMENT

(a) The Securities Commissioner may issue a stop order denying effectiveness to, or suspending or revoking the effectiveness of, any registration statement if he finds that:

(1) The order is in the public interest; and

(2) (A) The registration statement, as of its effective date, is incomplete in any material respect or contains any statement which was, in the light of the circumstances under which it was made, false or misleading with respect to any material fact;

Continued

(B) Any provision of this chapter or any rule, order, or condition lawfully imposed under this chapter has been willfully violated;

(C) The security registered or sought to be registered is the subject of an administrative stop order or similar order or a permanent or temporary injunction of any court of competent jurisdiction entered under any other federal or state act applicable to the offering, but:

(D) The issuer's enterprise or method of business includes or would include activities which are illegal where performed;

(E) (i) The offering has worked or tended to work a fraud upon purchasers or would so operate; or

(ii) Any aspect of the offering is substantially unfair, unjust, inequitable, or oppressive;

(F) The offering has been or would be made with unreasonable amounts of underwriters' and sellers' discounts, commissions, or other compensation, unreasonable amounts of promoters' profits or participation, or unreasonable amounts or kinds of options.

Source: Arkansas Code Annotated § 23-42-405

FEDERAL LAW REGULATING SECURITIES—SECURITIES ACTS

Securities acts are federal and state statutes that govern the registration, the offering for sale, and the actual sale of securities. There are two major federal securities acts: the Securities Act of 1933 and the Securities Exchange Act of 1934. The **Securities Act of 1933,** found at 15 U.S.C. § 77a, regulates the registration of securities that are offered for sale to the public. The Act mandates the disclosure of complete information regarding the issue of stock and the stock offering. It also mandates the full disclosure of all material information about a security, the people who are issuing the security, and the intended use of the money that is being raised from the sale. The term **material information** is understood as *all relevant* information that an investor would want to know about a company, its background, its executives, and its plan of operation.

The **Securities Exchange Act of 1934,** found at 15 U.S.C. § 78, governs the operation of the stock exchanges and over-the-counter markets. The Securities Exchange Act also extended federal regulations to securities that had already been issued to the public. The purpose of these acts was not necessarily to protect investors from making bad investment choices but to require disclosure of information so investors could make more *informed* decisions. See Exhibit 16-1.

EXHIBIT 16-1 FEDERAL SECURITIES ACT

Securities Act of 1933 – For securities offered for sale to the general public, there must be complete disclosure of information about the security.

Securities Exchange Act of 1934 – Regulates the operation of stock exchanges and over-the-counter markets.

FEDERAL REGULATION OF UTILITY COMPANIES, BONDS, AND INVESTMENT COMPANIES

The **Public Utility Holding Company Act of 1935** gives the SEC the authority to regulate public utility and holding companies through the use of registration and disclosure proceedings. The **Trust Indenture Act of 1939** gives the SEC the authority to regulate the issuing of bonds for sale to the public and other debt securities. The **Investment Company**

Act of 1940 gives the SEC the authority to regulate the structure and operation of public investment companies. This Act requires companies to register with the SEC, making them subject to the regulations of and liable to the SEC and to private parties if the provisions of the Act are violated. For example, Johnson and Johnson is an investment company that registers with the SEC. If Johnson and Johnson violate any of the provisions of the Investment Company Act, the SEC and private investors can take legal action against the company. See Exhibit 16-2 for a summary of these acts.

EXHIBIT 16-2	FEDERAL REGULATORY ACTS

Public Utility Holding Company Act of 1935 – Gives the SEC the authority to regulate public utility and holding companies because of registration and disclosure requirements.

Trust Indenture Act of 1939 – Gives the SEC the authority to regulate the issuance of bonds and other debt securities to the general public.

Investment Company Act of 1940 – Gives the SEC the authority to regulate public investment companies.

FEDERAL ENFORCEMENT STATUTES

The **International Securities Enforcement Cooperation Act of 1990** gives the SEC the authority to provide securities regulators from other countries information about alleged violators of securities laws in the United States and abroad. In other words, this law allows the SEC to share with officials from other countries information about people who are violating securities laws either in the United States or in other countries.

The **Securities Enforcement Remedies and Penny Reform Act of 1991** grants the SEC more power to regulate the securities industry by giving it the authority to issue cease and desist orders. The Act also gives the SEC the authority to issue potentially substantial monetary fines for violations.

Companies are required to give full disclosure of their prospects of the company when issuing securities. (See Chapter 14, Business Organizations.) At one time, investors could sue these companies when the performance of the securities did not meet their expectations. In order to protect companies that gave complete information detailing factors that could cause actual results to differ from projections, Congress passed the **Securities Litigation Reform Act of 1995.** This law created a **safe harbor**—protection from liability for corporate forecasts that turned out not to be accurate after the fact. The Act provides that a company is protected from liability when its performance does not match the projections *provided* the standards of the Act have been met. If the provisions of the Act have not been met, there is no safe harbor for the company and it can face liability for not meeting the projected performance.

In reaction to this legislation, class action lawsuits against companies began to be brought in state court, where federal law would not apply. In order to prevent this, Congress passed the **Securities Litigation Uniform Standards Act of 1998,** which states that securities lawsuits that involve *nationally traded* securities can only be brought in federal court. In other words, this Act gives exclusive jurisdiction of this type of case to the federal courts. If the attempted class action alleges an untrue statement or an omission of material facts, or that the defendant used any deceptive practice in connection with the sale of a security that is traded nationally, the suit must be filed in federal court. See Exhibit 16-3 for a summary of these statutes.

| EXHIBIT 16-3 | FEDERAL ENFORCEMENT AND LITIGATION STATUTES |

International Securities Enforcement Cooperation Act of 1990 – Gives the SEC authority to share information about securities law violations with security regulators from other countries.

Securities Enforcement Remedies and Penny Reform Act of 1991 – Gives the SEC authority to issue cease and desist orders and to issue substantial monetary fines.

Securities Litigation Reform Act of 1995 – Provides companies with protection from liability for corporate forecasts that were not accurate after the fact.

Securities Litigation Uniform Standards Act of 1998 – Gives exclusive jurisdiction of lawsuits involving nationally traded securities to federal courts.

SECURITIES AND EXCHANGE COMMISSION

The Securities and Exchange Act of 1934 also created the **Securities and Exchange Commission (SEC),** an independent federal agency that is responsible for ensuring investors full and fair disclosure of all material facts with regard to any public offering of securities. The Securities and Exchange Commission is responsible for establishing and enforcing regulations regarding the registration of securities and the prevention of fraud in the registration and trading of securities. The SEC has five commissioners and a chairperson who are appointed by the president and confirmed by the Senate. See Sidebar 16-2.

SIDEBAR 16-2 SECURITIES AND EXCHANGE ACT OF 1934

CREATION OF THE SEC

There is hereby established a Securities and Exchange Commission (hereinafter referred to as the "Commission") to be composed of five commissioners to be appointed by the President by and with the advice and consent of the Senate. Not more than three of such commissioners shall be members of the same political party, and in making appointments members of different political parties shall be appointed alternately as nearly as may be practicable. No commissioner shall engage in any other business, vocation, or employment than that of serving as commissioner, nor shall any commissioner participate, directly or indirectly, in any stock-market operations or transactions of a character subject to regulation by the Commission pursuant to this chapter. Each commissioner shall hold office for a term of five years and until his successor is appointed and has qualified, except that he shall not so continue to serve beyond the expiration of the next session of Congress subsequent to the expiration of said fixed term of office, and except (1) any commissioner appointed to fill a vacancy occurring prior to the expiration of the term for which his predecessor was appointed shall be appointed for the remainder of such term, and (2) the terms of office of the commissioners first taking office after June 6, 1934, shall expire as designated by the President at the time of nomination, one at the end of one year, one at the end of two years, one at the end of three years, one at the end of four years, and one at the end of five years, after June 6, 1934.

(b) Appointment and compensation of staff and leasing authority

(1) Appointment and compensation

The Commissioner shall appoint and compensate officers, attorneys, economists, examiners, and other employees in accordance with section 4802 of title 5.

Source: United States Code

DIVISIONS OF THE SECURITIES AND EXCHANGE COMMISSION

There are five divisions within the SEC. The **Division of Corporate Finance** establishes and enforces standards of financial reporting and disclosure requirements. It reviews all investment statements, prospectuses, and quarterly and annual reports of corporations. The **Division of Market Regulation** regulates national security exchanges—the New York Stock

Exchange and the NASDAQ Exchange, for example—as well as registered brokers (dealers). In order to prevent manipulation and fraud in the issuance, sale, or purchase of securities, the Division of Market Regulations can recommend to the full Commission the suspension of an exchange for up to one year and the suspension or permanent revocation of a license of a broker or dealer.

The **Division of Enforcement** is responsible for the review and supervision of all enforcement activities recommended by the other divisions. The Division of Enforcement also supervises investigations and the initiation of actions by the Commission for injunctions. The **Division of Corporate Regulation** administers the Public Utility Holdings Company Act and advises Bankruptcy Court in Chapter 11 proceedings. The **Division of Investment Management** is responsible for the administration of the Investment Company Act and the Investment Advisors Act. The Division of Investment Management carries out any investigation into wrongdoing by an issuer of or dealer in securities. See Exhibit 16-4.

EXHIBIT 16-4	DIVISIONS OF THE SECURITIES AND EXCHANGE COMMISSION

Division of Corporate Finance – Establishes and enforces regulations regarding financial reporting and disclosure requirements.

Division of Market Regulation – Regulates the national security exchanges and registered brokers. It can recommend the suspension of an exchange or a broker.

Division of Enforcement – Reviews and supervises all enforcement activities recommended by the other divisions.

Division of Corporate Regulation – Administers the Public Utility Holdings Company Act; also advises the Federal Bankruptcy Court.

Division of Investment Management – Administers the Investment Company Act and the Investment Advisors Act.

REGISTRATION OF SECURITIES

Under federal law, in order for securities to be offered to the public for sale, a process of **registration of securities** must be adhered to. Certain documents must be filed with the Securities and Exchange Commission; these documents must indicate the number of securities offered and their dollar value. There is no limitation on the number of securities that can be issued or on the dollar value that can be assigned to them. The term *registration of securities* also refers to the process whereby a company registers or records the name and address of each holder of a bond or certificate of stock in the company records. If the security listed is stock, the records will also contain information about the date of transfer of the stock from one owner to the other, the names of the people involved in the transaction, and other details regarding the transaction.

REGISTRATION STATEMENT

The **registration statement,** which is the document that is required by the Securities Act of 1933 and the Securities Exchange Act of 1934, discloses financial data, the purpose of the offering, and other items that provide information to prospective investors. There are two parts to the registration statement. The first part of the statement is the **prospectus,** a pamphlet produced for distribution to potential buyers of the security. The pamphlet must contain the following information about the security being offered:

1. Descriptive data about the person or company that is issuing the security
2. The purpose of the securities offering
3. The plans for the funds collected
4. The risks involved in the business venture

5. The managerial experience and financial compensation of the person who is promoting the security

6. Financial statements that are certified by an independent CPA

A **red herring** is a prospectus that has been prepared but not yet approved by the SEC. It has a red border on the front to indicate to interested people that the prospectus has not yet been approved for final distribution.

The second part of the registration statement is regulated by **Regulation S-K,** which provides for a more detailed disclosure than the prospectus. Regulation S-K requires more information about the business history of the issuer, particularly the issuer's financial background and past experiences with securities.

APPROVAL BY THE SEC

The SEC may also request additional information about the business and the issuers. The registration becomes effective twenty days after it is filed with the SEC, but the Commission may issue a **deficiency letter** stating that the issuer of the security needs more time to amend the filings to give more detail to the SEC. If the SEC issues a **letter of comment,** it has determined that the proposed registration statement has not met the disclosure and other requirements of the regulations.

If the registration statement is not amended to the satisfaction of the SEC, a **stop order**—an order prohibiting the sale of the securities until the registration statement is amended to the satisfaction of the SEC—may be issued. Once the requirements of the SEC have been met, the stock is considered registered. **Registered stock** is a stock issue that has been registered with the SEC; it is a new security or a secondary offering. See Exhibit 16-5 for a flow chart showing the registration of securities process.

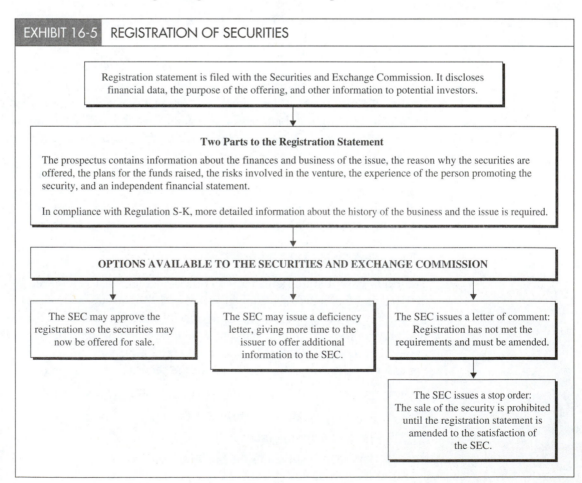

EXHIBIT 16-5 | REGISTRATION OF SECURITIES

Registration statement is filed with the Securities and Exchange Commission. It discloses financial data, the purpose of the offering, and other information to potential investors.

Two Parts to the Registration Statement

The prospectus contains information about the finances and business of the issue, the reason why the securities are offered, the plans for the funds raised, the risks involved in the venture, the experience of the person promoting the security, and an independent financial statement.

In compliance with Regulation S-K, more detailed information about the history of the business and the issue is required.

OPTIONS AVAILABLE TO THE SECURITIES AND EXCHANGE COMMISSION

The SEC may approve the registration so the securities may now be offered for sale.

The SEC may issue a deficiency letter, giving more time to the issuer to offer additional information to the SEC.

The SEC issues a letter of comment: Registration has not met the requirements and must be amended.

The SEC issues a stop order: The sale of the security is prohibited until the registration statement is amended to the satisfaction of the SEC.

DISCLOSURE REQUIREMENT

A **disclosure requirement** exists under federal law calling for the provision of financial and other information that would be relevant to investors who are considering buying the securities. This information is provided so that the investor can make a more informed evaluation of the security before he or she invests. A **misstatement** in securities law is information about an investment that misleads a reasonable investor in making decisions about investments. If the decision is to the investor's detriment, the person who was responsible for giving out misinformation may be liable for the loss suffered by the investor.

CLASSIFICATIONS OF SECURITIES

Once a security has been approved for sale, it has the status of **listed security.** This means it is listed for trading with one of the stock exchanges or that it has been listed with the Securities and Exchange Commission. An **unlisted security** is sold over the counter only and is not listed on a stock exchange. An **exempt security** does not have to be registered under federal law; an example is a **private placement security**—a security that is not offered for sale to the general public but rather is sold to institutional investors, pension funds, or insurance companies. See Exhibit 16-6.

EXHIBIT 16-6	TYPES OF SECURITIES

Listed Security – A security that has been listed for trading with one of the stock exchanges or that has been listed with the Securities and Exchange Commission.

Unlisted Security – A security that is sold over the counter only and that is not listed on a stock exchange.

Exempt Security – A security that does not have to be registered under federal law.

Regulation D sets out the requirements for a security to be considered a private placement security. In order to be a private placement security, the security must be offered only to **accredited investors**—those who are presumed to be sophisticated enough to evaluate investments without need of an SEC-approved prospectus and wealthy enough to endure the loss if the investment loses value. Institutions and individuals are deemed to be accredited investors if they have an annual income of at least $200,000 or a net value of at least $1,000,000. Sales of up to $5,000,000 in private placement securities can be made to up to 35 unaccredited investors if they receive information similar to the information that would be contained in a registration statement. Securities can be sold to an unlimited number of accredited investors. If the private placement securities offering is over $5,000,000, then the securities can be offered for sale only to accredited investors. See Exhibit 16-7.

EXHIBIT 16-7	REQUIREMENTS FOR A PRIVATE PLACEMENT SECURITY UNDER REGULATION D

1. The security must be offered only to accredited investors—those sophisticated enough to evaluate investments and wealthy enough to endure the loss.
2. The security can be sold to up to 35 unaccredited investors if they receive information similar to information available to accredited investors.
3. If the security offering is over $5,000,000 in value, then the securities can only be offered to accredited investors.

Rule 144 A provides another exemption for private placement securities. U.S. and foreign security issuers are exempt from registration requirements if they sell bonds and stocks to institutions with a portfolio of at least $100 million in securities.

If a company wants to be able to issue securities for sale without facing registration delays, it may seek **shelf registration.** The company requests that the SEC register all securities it plans to issue over several years. The company can then issue the securities when it wants to without having to wait during the registration process. If the security issue is small enough, simplified registration filing requirements in **Regulation A** of SEC regulations may apply. Even after registration of a security, the SEC may require **periodic disclosure,** which takes the form of monthly, quarterly, and annual reports regarding the financial status of the company.

INSIDER TRADING

Sometimes an investor may gain access to information about a company that will have an effect on the price of the stock of a company. For example, a drug company may be going to patent a breakthrough medication, or a company that has lost a great deal of money in the last quarter may be looking at layoffs of employees and a decline in business. Depending on who the person is and how he or she acquired this "inside" information, he or she may be accused of insider trading, if he or she used the knowledge for personal financial gain.

INSIDER, INSIDER INFORMATION, AND INSIDER TRADING

Insider trading occurs when a person's access to confidential and unpublished information that gives an unfair advantage over others is used in making a decision about engaging in the trading of a company's securities. An **insider** is a person who has knowledge that is not available to the general public. **Insider information** is information about a company's financial condition that is obtained by an insider before the general public obtains it or has access to it. True insider information is known only to corporate officers or other insiders; no one in the general public has access to the information.

TIPS, TIPPERS, AND TIPPEES

The insider may be a person within the company or a person who is outside the company. If a person is on the "outside," he or she will receive a **tip** about the company. A tip is the basis for the decision to buy or sell a security; it is information that is not shared with the general public. The **tipper** is a person who has the material inside information and who makes a selective disclosure of the information. The **tippee** is an outsider who has acquired inside information from someone who is an insider or who is in such a position that he or she has access to inside information. See Exhibit 16-8 for a chart showing how insider trading can happen.

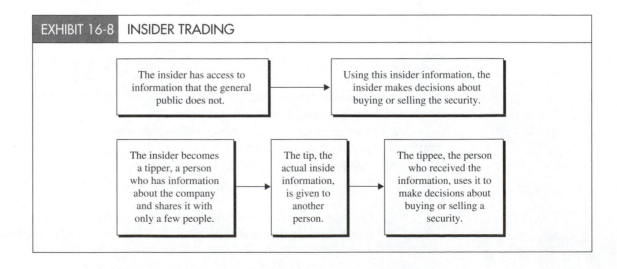

EXHIBIT 16-8	INSIDER TRADING

The insider has access to information that the general public does not. → Using this insider information, the insider makes decisions about buying or selling the security.

The insider becomes a tipper, a person who has information about the company and shares it with only a few people. → The tip, the actual inside information, is given to another person. → The tippee, the person who received the information, uses it to make decisions about buying or selling a security.

FEDERAL LAW REGULATING INSIDER TRADING

Two federal statutes have been passed to deal with the issue of insider trading. The **Insider Trading and Securities Fraud Enforcement Act** is a federal law that governs the enforcement of insider trading laws. This Act provides for bounties or rewards to informants, it provides for the supervision of brokers' employees, and it gives investors the right to sue for damages. The **Insider Trading Sanctions Act** is a federal law that imposes a civil penalty of up to three times an investor's trading profit if he or she violates the law regarding insider trading.

Rule 10(b)(5) is the rule of the SEC that makes it unlawful, when it is in connection with the purchase or sale of any security, to make an untrue statement of a material fact or to forget or fail to make a statement of material fact. Put another way, if a seller has knowledge about a company that could affect whether or not a prospective buyer will actually purchase a security, the seller must disclose the information and refrain from making an untrue statement about the information. See Exhibit 16-9 for a summary of these federal statutes and regulations.

EXHIBIT 16-9	FEDERAL STATUTES AND RULES REGARDING INSIDER TRADING

Insider Trading and Securities Fraud Enforcement Act – Provides for bounties or rewards to informants and for supervision of a brokers' employees. Gives investors the right to sue for damages.

Insider Trading Sanctions Act – Provides for a civil penalty of up to three times the investor's profit if insider trading laws are violated.

Rule 10(b)(5) – Declares that it is illegal, when in connection with the purchase or sale of any security, to make an untrue statement of a material fact or to forget or fail to make a statement of material fact.

Not every use of insider information is a violation of federal law; whether a violation exists depends on the circumstances surrounding the use of the insider information. The Supreme Court has established a test to be used to determine if conduct that is insider trading has violated federal law. In order for a violation to occur, it must be shown that there is an existence of a relationship that allows the trader to access inside information that was intended for corporate use only, and that it would be unfair to allow the insider to take advantage of the information to engage trading in the stock without disclosing to others what he or she knows. The case of *Chiarella v. United States* is an example of the application of insider trading laws to a person who had inside information. See Sidebar 16-3.

SIDEBAR 16-3 *CHIARELLA V. UNITED STATES*

Facts: Chiarella was a printer at a company that printed corporate takeover bids, and he deduced the names of the target companies from information contained in documents delivered to the printer by the acquiring companies. Without disclosing his knowledge, he purchased stock in the target companies and sold the shares immediately after the takeover attempts were made public. Chiarella made $30,000 in profits by using this information. Chiarella was convicted of insider trading.

Issue: Did Mr. Chiarella violate federal law and regulations regarding insider trading?

Decision: Silence in connection with the purchase or sale of securities may be fraud under 10 (b). However, such liability is based upon a duty to disclose arising from a relationship of trust and confidence between the parties to a transaction. Here, petitioner had no affirmative duty to disclose the information as to the plans of the acquiring companies. He was not a corporate insider, and he received no confidential information from the target companies. Nor could any duty arise from petitioner's relationship with the sellers of the target companies' securities, for he had no prior dealings with them, was not their agent, was not a fiduciary, and was not a person in whom the sellers had placed their trust and confidence. A duty to disclose under 10 (b) does not arise from the mere possession of nonpublic market information.

Conviction reversed.

Source: United States Reports

REQUIREMENTS PLACED ON INVESTORS

In an effort to control insider trading, several requirements are placed on certain types of investors. The **disclose or abstain rule** requires that corporate officers, directors, or any other insiders disclose insider information they have prior to trading any stock . If there is failure to disclose information, the investor is to abstain from trading in the stock. Another control on insider trading is the requirement that investors fill out either a **Form 10Q** or the more comprehensive **Form 10K.** These are financial reporting forms that are required to be filed annually with the SEC indicating what stocks and securities the investor owns or has traded in the past year.

Another report that may need to be filed with the SEC is an **insider report.** The SEC requires directors and officers of a company, and its shareholders, to disclose their stock transactions when they own more than 10% of the shares of a company. The SEC is looking for evidence of **short swing profits**—those made by an insider on the purchase and sale of the stock of a corporation within a six-month period. See Exhibit 16-10 for a summary of these SEC regulations.

EXHIBIT 16-10	REGULATIONS TO CONTROL INSIDER TRADING

Rule 10(b)(5) – It is illegal to make an untrue statement of material fact or to not make a statement of material fact when it is in connection with the purchase or sale of a security.

Form 10K and 10Q – Financial reporting forms that investors must fill out.

Insider Reports – When directors, officers, and shareholders own more than 10% of a company's stock, they are required to file this annual report with the SEC.

HOSTILE TAKEOVERS

Because stocks of so many companies are publicly sold, and because stock ownership represents ownership of a company, one company may attempt to take over another company by purchasing the other company's stock. There are several different terms and phrases that apply to situations when this happens.

RAIDERS AND TAKEOVER BIDS

A **raider** is a person or company that attempts to take control of a target company by buying a controlling interest in its stock and installing new management. If a raider accumulates more than 5% of the company stock, he or she must publicly report the purchase according to the Williams Act, 15 U.S.C. § 78.

A **takeover bid** is an attempt by an outside corporation or group—usually termed the *aggressor* or *insurgent*—to take control of a company away from current management. A takeover bid may involve the purchase of shares of stock, a tender offer, a sale of assets, or a proposal that the company merge voluntarily with the aggressor. A **target company** is the object of an attempt at takeover by way of a tender offer or leveraged buyout.

LEVERAGED BUYOUT AND TENDER OFFERS

A **leveraged buyout** is a method used to purchase outstanding shares of publicly traded stock by management or by outsiders. The financing to purchase the stock comes primarily from funds borrowed from investment bankers or brokers. The money used for the buyout is usually secured by the target company's assets, with the money to repay the funds borrowed coming from the company's earnings or sales of some of its assets. Essentially what happens is a company borrows money to purchase enough stock of another company in order to take over and then dismantles all or part of the acquired company to pay back the loans. See Exhibit 16-11 for the leveraged buyout process.

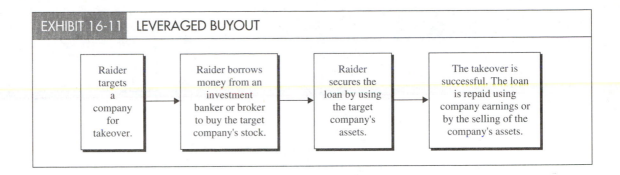

EXHIBIT 16-11 LEVERAGED BUYOUT

| Raider targets a company for takeover. | → | Raider borrows money from an investment banker or broker to buy the target company's stock. | → | Raider secures the loan by using the target company's assets. | → | The takeover is successful. The loan is repaid using company earnings or by the selling of the company's assets. |

Another method the raider may use to take over a company is to make a **tender offer,** a public announcement by a company, a group of investors, or an individual that it will pay a price above the current market price for the shares offered for sale of a particular company. The purpose is to acquire enough stock to be able to take over the company. A **Saturday night special** is a surprise tender offer that usually expires in one week. However, the use of Saturday night specials has been virtually prohibited by federal law.

FEDERAL REQUIREMENTS

When a company is attempting a hostile takeover of another company, there are certain legal requirements that must be met under federal law in order for the takeover to proceed. The raider will have to file a **Schedule 13D**—notice of a potential takeover offer. A **Schedule 14D-1** is a statement made by the offeror when a tender offer begins. A **Schedule 14D-9** is notice to shareholders of a takeover target that gives management's opinion about the offer.

DEFENSES TO TAKEOVER ATTEMPTS

The target company may attempt several strategies to prevent the hostile takeover. Some can be done prior to a takeover bid; others take place after the attempt has begun. Two measures that can be taken prior to a takeover attempt are lock ups and porcupine provisions. **Lock up** is a slang term referring to the company's setting aside securities to be purchased by a friendly interest in order to defeat or make more difficult any takeover attempt. A **porcupine provision** in either the company's by-laws or its articles of incorporation is designed to make takeover attempts either impossible or impractical if the potential acquirer does not have the consent of the management of the company.

A target company may also attempt greenmail or a poison pill. **Greenmail** is the payment made by a target company to buy back shares of stock held by a potential acquirer of a company at a premium over the market value. In return, the person or institution agrees not to continue with the hostile takeover. A **poison pill** is a defensive tactic used by a company to prevent a hostile takeover. The company makes its shares of stock or its financial condition less attractive to the potential acquirer. One method of doing so is to issue a new series of preferred stock that compels redemption at premium prices if there is a hostile takeover of the company. Another method is to burden the company with high debt that will have to be paid by the person or institution attempting to acquire the company if the takeover bid is successful. The target company may also seek for a **white knight:** a potential acquirer who will rescue it from the unwanted takeover attempt.

One thing a raider may attempt to do in an effort to take over a company is to provide golden parachutes to key figures in the corporation. The term **golden parachute** refers to a termination agreement that shelters executives from the effects of a corporate change such as a hostile takeover. It provides for substantial bonuses and other benefits for top management and directors who may be forced to leave the target company, or who otherwise voluntarily leave upon a change in control. See Exhibit 16-12 for a flow chart showing the hostile takeover process.

EXHIBIT 16-12 HOSTILE TAKEOVER OF A PUBLICLY HELD COMPANY

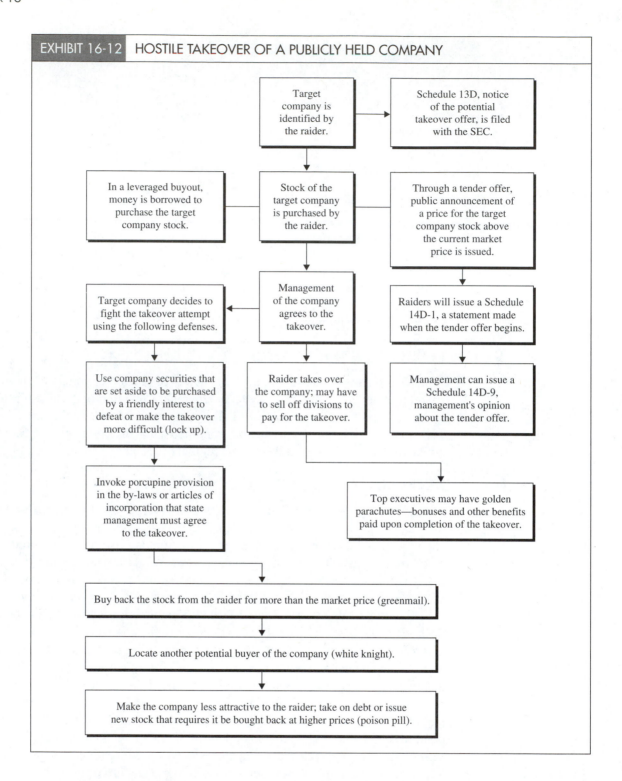

CONCLUSION

Securities regulation is a very complicated area of law. A myriad of terms and phrases apply to different types of securities, how those securities are bought and sold, where they are bought and sold, and the legality of the transaction. There are also terms that describe what can happen because of the purchase of securities and even terms that describe the status of the market where securities are being sold.

KEY WORDS AND PHRASES

accredited investors	periodic disclosure	Schedule 14D-9
blue sky law	poison pill	Securities Act of 1933
deficiency letter	porcupine provision	securities acts
disclosure requirement	prospectus	Securities and Exchange
exempt security	raider	Commission (SEC)
Form 10K	red herring	shelf registration
Form 10Q	registration of securities	short swing profit
golden parachute	registration statement	stop order
greenmail	Regulation A	takeover bid
insider	Regulation D	target company
insider trading	Regulation S-K	tender offer
leveraged buyout	Rule 10(b)(5)	tip
listed security	Rule 144 A	tippee
lock up	safe harbor	tipper
material information	Saturday night special	unlisted security
merit regulation	Schedule 13D	white knight
misstatement	Schedule 14D-1	

REVIEW QUESTIONS

SHORT ANSWER

1. What is the difference between accredited investors and regular investors?

2. What is a blue sky law?

3. What is the disclose or abstain rule?

4. What are the divisions of the Securities and Exchange Commission?

5. What is the purpose of the Division of Corporate Finance?

6. What is a golden parachute?

7. For what is a Form 10Q used?

8. What is a letter stock?

9. What is a porcupine provision?

10. What is Regulation A?

11. What is a Saturday night special?

12. What is shelf registration?

13. When does a company become a target company?

14. When is a security an unlisted security?

15. When is a tender offer made?

16. What is the purpose of Rule 144 A?

17. When is a person considered to be a raider?

18. When is a security exempt from registration?

19. When does the SEC issue a deficiency letter?

20. What is Regulation S-K?

FILL IN THE BLANK

1. A person who has knowledge about a corporation that is not available to the general public is a(n) _____.

2. The report that directors, officers, and shareholders must file with the SEC when they own more than 10% of a company's stock is known as a _____.

3. The federal law that governs insider training is the _____

_____.

4. The federal law that provides for civil penalties for violations of insider trading laws is known as _____.

5. A person or institution that is attempting to take over another company by buying shares of its stock is known as a _____.

6. A public announcement that a person will pay more than the market value of a stock is known as a _____.

7. A tender offer that usually expires in one week is known as a _____.

8. A potential purchaser of a company that is identified by the management of the company is known as a _____.

9. When a company burdens itself with debt to avoid a takeover attempt, this is known as the _____.

10. The _____ is a rule of the SEC that requires corporate officers, directors, or any other insiders to disclose insider information they have prior to trading any stock.

FACT SITUATIONS

1. A person gains knowledge that is not available to the general public and uses this information to engage in the purchase or sale of securities. What is this person called? What is he involved in?

2. In order to prevent a merger, a company borrows a great deal of money, creating a tremendous amount of corporate debt. What is the term for this defense?

3. A company decides to issue new shares of stock. What will the company issue to advise potential investors about the stock issue?

4. When a company is the subject of a takeover attempt, what is the company referred to as?

5. A company set aside securities to be purchased by a friendly company if the first company becomes a target of a takeover attempt. What are these securities known as?

6. A company that is the target of a takeover attempt approaches someone else about purchasing the company. What is this person or entity known as?

7. A corporate raider borrows a sum of money in order to purchase the stock of another company. To obtain the loan, the raider secures the loan by pledging as security divisions of the company that the raider is trying to take over. If the takeover is successful, the raider plans to sell off divisions to repay the loans used to acquire the company. What is this known as?

8. A company whose stock is being bought by a raider decides to pay the raider to buy back the company stock for more than the market value of the stock. What is this known as?

9. A company issues three types of securities. The first type is listed for trading with a stock exchange. The second type is only to be sold over the counter; it is not sold on a stock exchange. The third type of security is not listed for sale at all. What are these types of securities?

10. A company is planning on issuing a new class of securities and files the necessary information with the SEC. The SEC reviews the information, but decides there is not enough information and does not authorize the sale of the security. The company ignores this and issues the securities for sale. What can the SEC do?

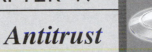

CHAPTER 17

Antitrust

INTRODUCTION

Antitrust is an area of federal statutory law designed to protect consumers from monopolies, which occur when one company so dominates a market that consumers have only one choice for a product or a service. Antitrust laws are enforced primarily by the federal government and were first used to break up the Standard Oil Trust. Most recently, they have been used to break up AT&T and to involve Microsoft in litigation.

ANTITRUST ANALYSIS

In order to determine if a business arrangement or a business practice is, in fact, illegal, an analysis of the organization or the practice must be performed. No one method or test is used to make that determination. Rather, there are several different methods used to ascertain whether a business practice violates antitrust law.

THEORIES

Antitrust laws are designed to guard against unlawful restraints on commerce, price fixing, and the creation of monopolies. The primary purpose of antitrust law—the reason it exists—is to encourage competition, assure fairness, and provide economic opportunity. In order to determine if a trust situation exists, two general theories of antitrust analysis—the Chicago school and the Harvard school—are involved. The **Chicago school** is based solely on the goal of economic efficiency or the maximization of consumer welfare. The **Harvard school** is an approach to antitrust policy based on the desirability of preserving competition to prevent the accumulation of economic and political power, the dislocation of labor, and market inefficiency.

COURT ANALYSIS

Whether or not an action is considered to be a violation of antitrust legislation is made on a case-by-case basis. The courts have looked at business activity in two ways to determine if antitrust laws have been violated. The first method used by the courts is the **per se rule.** This method states that certain business agreements, arrangements, or activity will automatically be held to be illegal by the courts because the courts assume that the arrangement will almost always result in a substantial restraint of trade.

The second method used is the **rule of reason,** which declares that only an unreasonable restraint of trade violates the Sherman Antitrust Act. Using the rule of reason, the court is required to weigh all the circumstances of the case, the history of the restraint, the evil that is believed to exist, the reason for adopting the particular remedy, and the result that is sought. The plaintiff must show that the violating business has produced an anticompetitive effect, or actual harm to the competition. A practice that is unfair or tortuous is not enough to be in violation of antitrust law. If the court determines that an activity is anticompetitive, its effects must outweigh its procompetitive effects for the restraint to be unreasonable. See Exhibit 17-1 for a summary of the per se rule and the rule of reason.

EXHIBIT 17-1	PER SE RULE V. RULE OF REASON

Per Se Rule

Certain business arrangements, agreements, or activities are automatically illegal because it is assumed that the arrangement will result in an unreasonable unrestraint of trade.

Rule of Reason

It is not automatically assumed the business arrangement is invalid. The court has to look at the history of the restraint, the evil that exists, the reason for adopting the remedy, and what result is sought.

FEDERAL ANTITRUST LEGISLATION

Antitrust acts are federal and state statutes that are designed to protect trade and commerce from unlawful restraints, price discrimination, price fixing, and monopolies. Usually laws passed by Congress will specifically state what actions are prohibited. However, when Congress passed antitrust litigation, the laws did not state what activities would actually be illegal. The statutes contain very general language as to the types of activity that are considered illegal. Whether or not a particular activity is considered illegal is determined by the courts applying the general terms to the specific fact situations.

SHERMAN ANTITRUST ACT

The primary federal antitrust statutes are the Sherman Antitrust Act, the Clayton Act, the Federal Trade Commission Act, the Robinson Partman Act, the Celler-Kefauver Amendment, and the Hart-Scott-Rodino Antitrust Improvement Act. The **Sherman Antitrust Act** was passed in 1890 and prohibits any contract or combination that is in the form of a trust or any restraint of trade to be illegal. The act also prohibits monopolies. A **trust** is an association or organization of persons or companies that have the intent and the power to create a monopoly, to control production of a product, to interfere with free trade, or to fix and regulate the supply and price of goods or services. See Sidebar 17-1.

SIDEBAR 17-1 SHERMAN ANTITRUST ACT PROVISIONS THAT MADE TRUSTS ILLEGAL

Section 1. Trusts, etc., in restraint of trade illegal; penalty

Every contract, combination in the form of trust or otherwise, or conspiracy, in restraint of trade or commerce among the several States, or with foreign nations, is declared to be illegal. Every person who shall make any contract or engage in any combination or conspiracy hereby declared to be illegal shall be deemed guilty of a felony, and, on conviction thereof, shall be punished by fine not exceeding $10,000,000 if a corporation, or, if any other person, $350,000, or by imprisonment not exceeding three years, or by both said punishments, in the discretion of the court.

Section 2. Monopolizing trade a felony; penalty

Every person who shall monopolize, or attempt to monopolize, or combine or conspire with any other person or persons, to monopolize any part of the trade or commerce among the several States, or with foreign nations, shall be deemed guilty of a felony, and, on conviction thereof, shall be punished by fine not exceeding $10,000,000 if a corporation, or, if any other person, $350,000, or by imprisonment not exceeding three years, or by both said punishments, in the discretion of the court.

Section 3. Trusts in Territories or District of Columbia illegal; combination a felony

Every contract, combination in form of trust or otherwise, or conspiracy, in restraint of trade or commerce in any Territory of the United States or of the District of Columbia, or in restraint of trade or commerce between any such Territory and another, or between any such Territory or Territories and any State or States or the District of Columbia, or with foreign nations, or between the District of Columbia and any State or States or foreign nations, is declared illegal. Every person who shall make any such contract or engage in any such combination or conspiracy, shall be deemed guilty of a felony, and, on conviction thereof, shall be punished by fine not exceeding $10,000,000 if a corporation, or, if any other person, $350,000, or by imprisonment not exceeding three years, or both said punishments, in the discretion of the court.

Source: United States Code

CLAYTON ACT

The **Clayton Act,** which was passed in 1914, was intended to supplement the provisions of the Sherman Antitrust Act. The Clayton Act gives the federal government the ability to attack business activities when the effect of the activity is to substantially lessen competition or to create a monopoly. Specifically, the Clayton Act prohibits tying arrangements and exclusive dealings arrangements, bans mergers with or acquisition of competitors, and restricts interlocking directors. A **tying arrangement** is a condition imposed by a seller on a buyer that, in order for the buyer to obtain the desired product—the **tying product**—the buyer must also purchase an additional product that he or she may or may not need or want—the **tied product.** In an **exclusive dealing arrangement,** a buyer agrees by contract to purchase all of its needs for a particular product from one supplier. An **interlocking director** is a person who serves at the same time on the boards of directors of at least two corporations that have business dealings with each other. Businesses that supposedly are in competition with each other could have people that serve on both of their boards of directors that set the way the companies will compete against each other in the same markets. See Exhibit 17-2 for a summary of these illegal activities.

EXHIBIT 17-2 ACTIVITY MADE ILLEGAL BY THE CLAYTON ACT

Tying Arrangement – A condition imposed by a seller on a buyer that in order for the buyer to obtain the desired product, the buyer must also purchase an additional product that he or she may or may not need or want.

Exclusive Dealing Arrangement – By contract, a buyer agrees to purchase all of its needs for a particular product from one supplier.

Interlocking Director – A person who serves at the same time on the board of directors of at least two corporations that have business dealings with each other. Businesses that supposedly are in competition with each other could have people that serve on both of their boards of directors that set the way the companies will compete against each other in the same markets.

ROBINSON PARTMAN ACT

The **Robinson Partman Act,** which actually amended Section 2(a) of the Clayton Act, makes it unlawful for any seller to directly or indirectly engage in price discrimination on the sale of commodities of a like grade and quality where the effect may cause injury to or destroy or prevent competition. In other words, the act prohibits price discrimination. The **Celler-Kefauver Amendment** extended the prohibition of mergers to include corporate acquisitions when what is acquired are the assets of another firm. The **Hart-Scott-Rodino**

Antitrust Improvement Act expanded the Department of Justice's power to conduct antitrust investigations; it also requires companies that are planning on merging to give public notice prior to completion of the merger. The law also allows state attorneys general to prosecute antitrust cases. The **Tunney Act** requires the federal district courts to review antitrust settlements negotiated between the Department of Justice and antitrust defendants because of the potential for political influence on the settlement agreement. See Exhibit 17-3 for a summary of federal antitrust legislation.

EXHIBIT 17-3 | FEDERAL ANTITRUST LEGISLATION

Sherman Antitrust Act – Prohibits any contract or combination that is the form of a trust, any restraint of trade, and monopolies.

Clayton Act – Allows the federal government to attack business activities if the activities lessen competition or create a monopoly. Tying arrangements, exclusive dealing agreements, mergers, and acquisitions of competitors are all illegal.

Robinson Partman Act – Amends section 2(a) of the Clayton Act. Any price discrimination is illegal.

Celler-Kefauver Amendment – Prohibits acquisitions of a corporation when what was acquired were the assets of the other firm.

Hart-Scott-Rodino Antitrust Improvement Act –

1. Expands the power of the Justice Department to conduct antitrust investigations.

2. Requires companies that are planning on merging to give public notice prior to the completion of the merger.

3. Allows state attorneys general to prosecute antitrust cases.

Tunney Act – Federal district courts must review antitrust settlements negotiated between the Department of Justice and any antitrust defendants.

Federal Trade Commission Act – Created the Federal Trade Commission, which enforces the provisions of the Sherman Antitrust Act and the Clayton Act. The FTC may promulgate rules and regulations to fill in the gaps in antitrust acts. It is authorized to investigate unfair trade practices.

FEDERAL TRADE COMMISSION

The **Federal Trade Commission Act,** which was passed in 1914, created the Federal Trade Commission (FTC). The Commission has the power to enforce the provisions of the Sherman Antitrust Act and the Clayton Act. It also is authorized to promulgate rules and regulations designed to fill in the gaps in antitrust laws by making certain trade practices that are not covered by the acts illegal. The Commission is authorized to investigate and enforce unfair trade practices. (See Chapter 24, Product Liability and Consumer Protection.)

ANTITRUST ACTIVITIES

ANTITRUST CIVIL PROCESS ACT

Antitrust litigation is initiated according to the provisions of the **Antitrust Civil Process Act,** federal statutes indicating how the litigation commences. The plaintiff initiates the cause of action by filing a petition in U.S. District Court for an order for enforcement of the antitrust laws. In order for a person to have standing to bring an antitrust cause of action under the Clayton Act, there must be an **antitrust injury.** This is an injury that the statutes were designed to prevent and that flows from the activity on the part of the defendant that is illegal. The injury should indicate the anticompetitive effect of the violation or the anticompetitive act that was made possible by violation of the statute. See Exhibit 17-4.

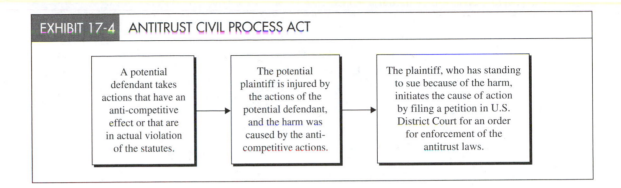

EXHIBIT 17-4 ANTITRUST CIVIL PROCESS ACT

| A potential defendant takes actions that have an anti-competitive effect or that are in actual violation of the statutes. | The potential plaintiff is injured by the actions of the potential defendant, and the harm was caused by the anti-competitive actions. | The plaintiff, who has standing to sue because of the harm, initiates the cause of action by filing a petition in U.S. District Court for an order for enforcement of the antitrust laws. |

MONOPOLIES

A **monopoly** is a form of market structure in which one or only a few companies have the exclusive right or power to conduct a business or trade, to manufacture a product, or to control the sale and supply of a particular product or service. A monopoly under the Sherman Antitrust Act has two elements: possession of monopoly power in the relevant market and the willful acquisition or maintenance of that monopoly power. **Monopolization,** which also violates the Sherman Antitrust Act, occurs when a person or entity combines or conspires to acquire or maintain power in order to exclude competitors from any part of the market, provided the person or entity has the power to exclude actual or potential competition as well as the intent to exercise that power.

MARKET ANALYSIS

In order to determine if a monopoly in fact exists, a market analysis must be conducted. A **market** is a place of commercial activity where goods, services, commodities, or securities are bought and sold. The term **relevant market** refers to the geographic area in which competitors agree to respect the rights of others to sell a product. It also may refer to an area where competitors agree to limit the manufacture and sale of products to either limit or eliminate competition among themselves.

The first step in identifying a relevant market is to determine the geographic market. The **geographic market** in antitrust law is the geographic area where a product is sold without competition. It is used to assess the monopoly power a company has in a certain area. If only one company is competing in a given area, this is used to indicate that there is an agreement giving different areas to each competitor with the understanding that other competitors will not sell in that area.

The next step is to determine the product market. A **product market** is comprised of all the other products that consumers can purchase other than the products of the company that is being investigated for possible violation of antitrust law. The question before the court is whether the different products are perceived by consumers as being reasonably interchangeable. In other words, do consumers perceive the products to be the equal of each other with regard to price, quality, and their use? See Exhibit 17-5 for a summary of the different types of markets.

EXHIBIT 17-5	TYPES OF MARKETS

Relevant Market – The geographic area in which competitors agree to respect the rights of others to sell a product. May refer to an area where competitors agree to limit the manufacture and sale of products to either limit or eliminate competition among themselves.

Geographic Market – For antitrust purposes, the geographic area where a product is sold and there is no competition.

Product Market – All the other products that consumers can purchase other than the products of the company that is being investigated for possible violation of antitrust law.

MARKET SHARE AND MARKET POWER

Once the market has been determined by the court, the court must then determine the alleged monopoly's market share and market power. **Market power,** under the Sherman Antitrust act, is the ability to raise prices significantly above the competitive level without losing all of the company's business. **Market share** is the percentage of the relevant market that a firm controls.

Another method used by the courts in investigating an alleged monopoly is to look at its market concentration in a given market. **Concentration** is the percentage of the market share that one or more companies control in a given product or geographical market. This is used as a way to measure the degree of competition in a market. **Market concentration** is the potential for the exercise of monopoly power, based on the number of firms in the market. The **concentration ratio** is the fraction of the total market sales made by a specific number of the industry's largest firms, usually the largest four to eight. These data are analyzed to determine the amount of the market the business controls and are used to determine if an illegal monopoly exists. See Exhibit 17-6 for a summary of these methods.

WHEN A MONOPOLY IS ILLEGAL

Not all monopolies violate antitrust statutes. To determine if a monopoly is illegal, courts may use the **abuse theory of monopoly,** which is an analysis of both the structure of a market and the conduct of the targeted firm to determine if it is, in fact, a monopoly. The court will look at the use of the market power and monopoly power of the monopoly. **Monopoly power** is the power to fix prices, exclude competitors, or control the market in a relevant geographical area. This must be found in order to establish a violation under the Sherman Antitrust Act. The firm is also illegal if it abuses its market power by performing purposeful acts that harm competitors and consumers. See Exhibit 17-7.

Natural monopolies do not violate antitrust laws. A **natural monopoly** is a business for which a monopoly is more efficient than competition: One firm can adequately supply or produce all of a product that a limited market can absorb. A **legal monopoly** is an exclusive right granted by the government to a business to provide a service. The rates and services that are provided are regulated by the government. For example, the government might give the exclusive right to provide electricity or gas to a particular company. The company has the exclusive right to provide electricity to consumers, but the price that is paid for the service is regulated by the government. See Exhibit 17-8 for a summary of legal monopolies.

| EXHIBIT 17-6 | METHODS USED TO DETERMINE IF A MONOPOLY EXISTS |

Market Share Method

Step One—Relevant market is identified.

1. Geographic market—area where a product is sold without any competition—is determined.

2. Product market—all the other products that consumers can purchase other than the products of the company—is determined.

Step Two—Court determines market share and market power.

1. Market power is the ability to raise prices above competitive levels without losing all the company's business.

2. Market share is the percentage of the relevant market the firm controls.

The Court looks at the market concentration of the alleged monopoly in a given market. The following data are analyzed by the court to determine if a monopoly exists:

1. **Concentration**—The percentage of the market share that a company controls in a market.

2. **Market Concentration**—The potential for the exercise of monopoly power.

3. **Concentration Ratio**—The fraction of the total market sales by a specific number of industries.

| EXHIBIT 17-7 | DETERMINING IF A MONOPOLY IS ILLEGAL |

Abuse Theory of Monopoly – An analysis of both the structure of the market and the conduct of the firm to determine if it is, in fact, a monopoly. The court will look at the use of the market power and monopoly power of the monopoly.

Monopoly Power – The power to fix prices, exclude competitors, or to control the market in a relevant geographical area. This must be found in order to establish a violation under the Sherman Antitrust Act.

| EXHIBIT 17-8 | MONOPOLIES THAT ARE LEGAL |

Natural Monopoly – A business for which a monopoly is more efficient than competition.

Legal Monopoly – An exclusive right granted by the government to a business to provide a service. The rates and services that are provided are regulated by the government.

OTHER ORGANIZATIONS

A monopoly is not the only type of organization that can violate federal antitrust law provisions. Two other entities—a pool and a cartel—are also illegal.

POOLS

A **pool** is a combination of persons or companies that are in the same business, or that is formed for the purpose of engaging in the same business, where all the members contribute to a common fund or give control of all their holdings of a stock or other security to a managing member or committee. The purpose of this arrangement is to eliminate competition between members of the pool. These members may establish a monopoly or control prices or rates by using the power of their combined assets.

CARTELS

Another type of illegal organization is a **cartel,** a group of producers of any product that join together to control the production, sale, and price of the product with the purpose of obtaining a monopoly and restricting competition in a particular industry. Cartels are illegal in the United States because of antitrust laws, but they do exist in Europe. An example of a cartel is the Organization of Petroleum Exporting Countries (OPEC). See Exhibit 17-9 for a summary of pools and cartels.

EXHIBIT 17-9	POOLS AND CARTELS

Pool – A combination of persons or companies that are in the same business, or formed for the purpose of engaging in the same business, where all the members contribute to a common fund or give control of all their holdings of a stock or other security to a managing member or committee.

Cartel – A combination of producers of any product that are joined together to control the production, sale, and price of the product with the purpose of obtaining a monopoly and restricting competition in a particular industry.

MERGERS

As discussed in Chapter 14, a merger is the result of two firms coming together to form a new firm. Because of antitrust implications, mergers are investigated and can be challenged by either the Federal Trade Commission or the Justice Department.

PREMERGER NOTIFICATION

When firms are considering a merger, they must provide premerger notification. The **premerger notification requirement** is legislatively mandated. Certain types of firms must notify the Federal Trade Commission and the Justice Department at least 30 days before finalizing a merger so that these agencies can investigate and challenge any merger they believe may be noncompetitive.

To determine if a merger will be allowed, the Department of Justice and FTC will look at the company's market power, market share, the geographic markets, the product markets, and the relevant market.

ANALYSIS OF COMPETITION

Another factor that will be considered is how the proposed merger will affect competition or potential competition. **Competition** is the effort of at least two parties who are acting independently of each other to secure the business of a third party by offering the most favorable terms. There are two broad types of competition. **Interbrand competition** is competition among the various brands of a particular product. For example, there are several brands of cornflakes available to consumers. **Intrabrand competition,** on the other hand, is competition among retailers in the sale of a particular brand of product. For example, several stores can sell the same brand of cornflakes, and consumers look for the best price among the different retailers.

Potential competition is the consideration given to the amount of competitiveness that exists in the market because of the possibility that companies that are not now in that market may enter it and compete with the existing companies. When weighing potential competition, analysts ask: What is the likelihood that a company will enter a new market? and What will that do to the level of competition? This factor may be enough to prevent a merger: If a company was thinking of entering a market, it could not do so if it was involved in a merger with a company that was already in that market. See Exhibit 17-10.

EXHIBIT 17-10 | TYPES OF COMPETITION

Interbrand Competition – Competition among the various brands of a particular product.

Intrabrand Competition – Competition among retailers in the sale of a particular brand of product.

Potential Competition – The consideration given to the amount of competitiveness that exists in the market because of the possibility that companies that are not now in that market may enter the market and compete with existing companies.

TYPES OF MERGERS

The type of merger may determine if antitrust laws will apply or not. A **horizontal merger** can occur between two companies that compete in the same product market. Whether or not this merger will be allowed depends on the impact it will have on competition in the product market. A **vertical merger** involves two companies, one of whom is a supplier of the other. This type of merger may also be looked at closely because of the union of a company with its supplier.

Diversification mergers involve totally different firms. For example, a manufacturer of sporting goods may merge with a company that provides cellular phone services. A **conglomerate merger** is a merger between two companies that do not buy from each other and that are not in competition with each other. These types of mergers may be allowed more frequently because the potential impact on competition and markets is less. See Exhibit 17-11.

EXHIBIT 17-11 | TYPES OF MERGERS

Horizontal Merger – A merger between two companies that compete in the same product market.

Vertical Merger – A merger of two companies, one of which is a supplier of the other.

Diversification Merger – Combination or merger of totally different firms.

Conglomerate Merger – A merger between two companies that do not buy from each other and that are not in competition with each other.

PRICE DISCRIMINATION

Price discrimination is a method used to force competitors out of a market and can be a form of trust activity. Price discrimination was declared illegal by the Robinson Partman Act. **Price discrimination**—which is a broad, generic term—is charging different prices to different buyers for goods of a like grade and quality. Several activities can be considered forms of price discrimination.

TYPES OF PRICE DISCRIMINATION

One type of price discrimination is **price fixing,** an agreement to set minimum prices or maximum resale prices. **Horizontal price fixing,** which occurs among competitors who operate at the same level of business in the same market, is an agreement among competitors to charge noncompetitive prices. Another type of price discrimination is **predatory pricing,** or pricing a product below what it cost to produce it in order to eliminate competitors in the short run and to limit competition in the long run. In order to show predatory pricing, **predatory intent** must be shown: The alleged price discriminator must have sacrificed present revenue and profits for the purpose of driving a competitor out of the market. Any losses would then be recouped by charging higher prices once the competitor is out of the market. This type of behavior can be used to show a violation of antitrust laws. In order to prove predatory pricing, the plaintiff must prove the following:

1. The defendant priced below cost.
2. The below-cost prices created a genuine prospect that the defendant would monopolize the market.
3. The defendant would enjoy the monopoly at least long enough to recoup the losses suffered during the price cutting.

WHO IS INJURED BY PRICE DISCRIMINATION

Another way price discrimination is classified is based on who is intended to be the object of injury. **Primary line injury** is price discrimination whereby the seller attempts to put a local competitive firm out of business by lowering its prices only in the region where the local firm sells its products. The profits from other sales regions will make up the loss suffered in the targeted region. This is price discrimination aimed at another business.

Secondary line injury is a type of price discrimination by which a seller offers a discount price to one buyer but not to any other buyers. This conduct can be aimed at other businesses or it can be aimed at consumers. **Vertical price fixing** is an agreement between a supplier and a distributor that relates to the price at which the distributor will resell the supplier's product. This type of price discrimination is directed only at consumers: They will have to pay the higher prices agreed to between the supplier and the distributor. An example of vertical price fixing is **resale price maintenance.** This is an agreement among a manufacturer, a supplier, and retailers of a product wherein the retailers agree that they will not sell the product below an established minimum price. See Exhibit 17-12 for a summary of the types of price discrimination.

EXHIBIT 17-12	TYPES OF PRICE DISCRIMINATION

Price Fixing – Agreement to set a minimum or maximum resale price.

Predatory Pricing – Pricing a good below what it costs to make the good in order to eliminate competition in the short run and limit competition in the long run.

Primary Line Injury – The seller attempts to put a local competitor out of business by lowering prices only in the region where the local firm sells its products.

Secondary Line Injury – A seller offers a discount price to one buyer but not to other buyers.

Vertical Price Fixing – Agreement between a supplier and a distributor that sets the price at which the distributor will resell the supplier's product.

RESTRAINT OF TRADE

One type of trust activity is restraint of trade. However, not all restraints of trade violate antitrust law. **Restraint of trade** is a contract or a combination that tends to or is designed to eliminate or stifle competition, create a monopoly, artificially maintain prices, or hamper or obstruct the course of free trade and commerce. In essence, it is the interference with free trade in business and commercial transactions that is designed to control the market to the detriment of consumers. But a restraint of trade may not necessarily create a violation of antitrust law. An **unreasonable restraint of trade** produces a significant anticompetitive effect. This conclusion is based either on the nature or character of the contracts that created the arrangement or the surrounding circumstances that created the impression that the actions were designed to restrain trade and enhance prices. A restraint of trade must be unreasonable in order for it to violate the Sherman Antitrust Act.

MARKET RESTRAINT TRADE

A restraint of trade between companies or organizations can exist in a number of ways. One method is to have restraints of trade apply to the markets of the competitors. A **horizontal division of market** is collusion between two or more competitors to divide the market, customers, or product line among themselves. **Collusion** is an agreement between two or more companies to use fraudulent means to obtain a lawful goal or to use lawful means to accomplish an unlawful purpose.

A **horizontal restraint of trade** occurs when rival firms that operate in the same market and at the same level attempt to restrain trade by restricting output and raising prices. This conduct is usually attempted by a cartel. The arrangement may also be referred to as a **horizontal business arrangement,** which is an agreement among companies that operate at the same level of business in the same market. See Exhibit 17-13.

EXHIBIT 17-13	RESTRAINT OF TRADE BASED ON MARKETS
Horizontal Division of Market – An agreement between two or more competitors to divide the market, the customers, or the product line among themselves.	
Horizontal Restraint of Trade – An agreement between rival firms in the same market at the same level to restrict the output of a product and raise the price of the product.	

GOODS AND SERVICES RESTRAINT OF TRADE

Restraints of trade can also apply to goods and services provided. A **vertical restraint of trade** is a contract or a business combination that reduces or eliminates competition among firms that produce, distribute, and sell the same goods. The restraint of trade is not in a particular market; rather, it is among different firms that produce the same items. **Nonprice vertical restraint** is used by a manufacturer to limit the area where a retailer may sell the manufacturer's products, the number of stores the retailer can operate, and the customers a retailer can serve in an area. A limitation on the area a retailer may sell the manufacturer's product is a **territorial restriction;** a limitation on the customers a retailer can serve is a **customer restriction.** See Exhibit 17-14.

EXHIBIT 17-14	RESTRAINT OF TRADE BASED ON GOODS AND SERVICES

Vertical Restraint of Trade – Contract or business organization that reduces or eliminates competition among firms that deal in the same product.

Nonprice Vertical Restraint – Used by a manufacturer to limit where a retailer may sell the manufacturer's product and the number of stores the retailer can operate.

Territorial Restriction – A limitation on the area a retailer may sell a manufacturer's product.

Customer Restrictions – A limitation on the customers a retailer can serve.

OTHER TYPES OF RESTRAINT OF TRADE

Other restraints of trade may apply to the market where the good is sold, to the price that the good is sold for, or both. A **combination in restraint of trade** is an agreement between at least two people or companies—usually in the form of a contract, a trust, a pool, a holding company, or other form of association—for the purpose of restricting competition or monopolizing trade in a certain commodity. This can apply to different markets or to different products. An **exclusive dealing contract** is an agreement between two companies that they will only deal with each other for certain products or services.

DEFENSES TO ANTITRUST CHARGES

Certain terms refer to defenses that companies can raise when facing allegations of price discrimination or when trying to merge with another company in a move that might be construed as forming a trust.

DEFENSES TO PRICE DISCRIMINATION

In the area of price discrimination, the defenses of cost justification or meeting competition can be raised. **Cost justification,** as a defense, contends that a particular buyer can be offered a good at a lower price than another buyer because of the difference in the costs of serving the two customers. In other words, the difference in the price charged to each buyer exists because, from the seller's perspective, it is cheaper to provide the good or service to one consumer than it is to provide the same good or service to another consumer. **Meeting competition** is another defense to price discrimination charges: A firm shows that it cut its prices to meet the prices of its competitors.

DEFENSES TO MERGERS

When two companies attempting to merge and either the FTC or Justice Department objects to the merger, the firms can raise the **failing firm defense.** This defense allows firms to merge that ordinarily would not be allowed to merge because one of the companies is in danger of going out of business. The rationale is that it is permissible to allow them to merge because one company is going out of business anyway. In order to be successful, the merging companies must prove:

1. The firm being acquired is not likely to survive without the merger.
2. Either the firm has no other prospective buyers, or if there are other prospective buyers, the firm purchasing the firm will affect competition the least.
3. All other alternatives for saving the firm have been tried and have failed.

Yet another defense that can be raised is the **power buyer defense.** The merger is defended by proving that the customers of the companies are sophisticated and powerful buyers—so powerful that they have sufficient bargaining power to ensure that the newly merged firm will be unable to charge monopoly prices. See Exhibit 17-15 for a summary of the defenses to antitrust charges.

EXHIBIT 17-15	DEFENSES TO ANTITRUST CHARGES

Price Discrimination

Cost Justification – A buyer is offered a good at a lower price than another buyer because of the difference in the costs of serving the two customers.

Meeting Competition – A firm shows that it cut its prices to meet the prices of its competitors.

Mergers

Failing Firm Defense – Firms are allowed to merge that ordinarily would not be allowed to merge because one of the companies is in danger of going out of business.

Power Buyer Defense – The customers of the companies are sophisticated and powerful buyers. They are so powerful that they have sufficient bargaining power to ensure that the newly merged firm will be unable to charge monopoly prices.

EXEMPTIONS FROM ANTITRUST LAW

Certain industries and activities are exempt from antitrust laws. For example, the Clayton Act states that nonprofit agricultural cooperatives that are organized to provide assistance to farmers are exempt. The **Capper Volstead Act** extended the same exemption to people who are engaged in agricultural production: farmers, ranchers, dairies, and nut and fruit growers.

A restraint of trade or monopolization that is the result of valid governmental actions is considered to be the **state action exemption** that was created by the Sherman Antitrust Act. In order for the exemption to apply, there has to be a clearly stated policy that permits or requires the particular restraint of trade or activity.

CONCLUSION

Many business initiatives can be considered trust activity. But whether the activity actually is illegal can only be determined on a case-by-case basis. What may be considered illegal activity in one situation may not be considered illegal activity in another situation. Activity such as restraint of trade, price discrimination, price fixing, and monopolization *does* violate antitrust law. Certain standards and tests are used to determine if the activity that is engaged in is, in fact, one of the prohibited activities.

The Sherman Antitrust Act was the first federal legislation designed to limit trust activities. The Clayton Act strengthened the Sherman Antitrust Act, and the Robinson Partman Act amended parts of the Clayton Act. Additional federal legislation has added to or amended existing antitrust law.

A monopoly can be an illegal business activity. To determine if a monopoly exists, market share and market power are analyzed to see if the activity is in violation of antitrust laws. Not all monopolies are illegal: Natural monopolies and legal monopolies are not violations of federal law. Two other business organizations that may violate federal law are cartels and pools. Mergers can also violate federal antitrust law depending on who is merging and for what purposes.

Another form of illegal activity is price discrimination—price fixing and predatory pricing. Restraint of trade, which can consist of a division of the market or restricting the output of a contract can also be illegal trust activity.

Cost justification and meeting the competition are two defenses against allegations of price fixing. If a merger is being questioned, the failing firm defense or power buyer defense may be raised.

The purpose of antitrust legislation is to provide for a free and open marketplace where honest competition determines the price of goods and services that are offered for sale to the general population.

KEY WORDS AND PHRASES

Antitrust Civil Process Act
antitrust laws
Capper Volstead Act
cartel
Celler-Kefauver
 Amendment
Clayton Act
collusion
combination in restraint of
 trade
competition
concentration
conglomerate merger
cost justification
diversification mergers
exclusive dealing
 arrangement
exclusive dealing contract
failing firm defense
Federal Trade Commission
 Act

geographic market
Hart-Scott-Rodino Antitrust
 Improvement Act
horizontal business
 arrangement
horizontal division of
 market
horizontal merger
horizontal price fixing
horizontal restraint of trade
interlocking director
legal monopoly
market concentration
market power
market share
meeting competition
monopoly
monopoly power
natural monopoly
per se rule
pool

power buyer defense
predatory intent
predatory pricing
price discrimination
price fixing
primary line injury
product market
relevant market
restraint of trade
Robinson Partman Act
rule of reason
Sherman Antitrust Act
territorial restriction
tied product
Tunney Act
tying arrangement
vertical merger
vertical price fixing
vertical restraint of trade

REVIEW QUESTIONS

SHORT ANSWER

1. What does the term *antitrust* mean?

2. What is the abuse theory of monopoly?

3. What is an antitrust injury?

4. What is a cartel?

5. What is the difference between the Chicago school and the Harvard school of antitrust analysis?

6. What is a diversification merger?

7. What is a conglomerate merger?

8. What is the failing firm defense?

9. What is a horizontal division of market?

10. What is a horizontal restraint of trade?

11. What is the difference between market power and market concentration?

12. What is market share?

13. What is meant by *meeting competition?*

14. What is a natural monopoly?

15. What does the Robinson Partman Act prevent?

16. What is the state action exemption?

17. What is predatory pricing?

18. What is price discrimination?

19. What are territorial restrictions?

20. What are customer restrictions?

FILL IN THE BLANK

1. A seller offers the same product to two different buyers, charging one buyer a higher price than the other. The seller alleges the price difference is the result of the difference in the cost of serving the two customers. This is the _____ defense.

2. Two companies plan to merge to keep one from going out of business. This is known as the _____ defense.

3. What are the elements of the above defense?

   _____

   _____

   _____

4. A limitation on the area where a retailer can sell a company's product is known as

   _____

5. _____ is an agreement between two or more companies to use fraudulent means to obtain a lawful goal or to use lawful means to achieve an unlawful purpose.

6. _____ is when the alleged price discriminator must have sacrificed present revenue and profits for the purpose of driving a competitor out of the market.

7. An _____ is an agreement between two companies that they will only deal with each other for certain products or services.

8. A _____ occurs when rival firms that operate in the same market and at the same level attempt to restrain trade by restricting output and raising prices.

9. A _____ is a contract or a business combination that reduces or eliminates competition among firms that produce, distribute, and sell the same goods.

10. A _____ is a combination of producers of any product that are joined together to control the production, sale, and price of a product with the purpose of obtaining a monopoly and restricting competition in a particular industry or product.

FACT SITUATIONS

1. A company states that, in order to purchase one product, a retailer also has to purchase another product. What is the agreement known as?

2. A company merges with its supplier of goods. What type of merger is this?

3. A wholesaler gives one price of a good to one retailer and a different, higher price to another retailer. What is this known as?

4. A group of companies joins together and sets limits on how much of a product will be produced and what prices will be charged for the product. What type of organization did the companies form?

5. A company merges with other companies that sell the same product. What type of merger is this?

6. The State of Oregon gives a power company the exclusive right to sell electricity to all customers in the state. What sort of arrangement is this? Is it legal?

7. A manufacturer of goods offers one price to one of its suppliers and offers a second higher price to another of its suppliers for the exact same product. What is the manufacturer doing? Is it legal?

8. Competitors meet and agree to respect each other's territory when it comes to selling products in an area. What is this known as? Is it legal?

9. Farmers in Mississippi form an agricultural cooperative to sell farming supplies. The cooperative is the only place to obtain farm supplies in the area. Is this legal? Why is this arrangement legal?

10. A company that makes electronics is merging with a company that manufactures clothing for children. What type of merger is this? Will this merger be allowed? Why or why not?

CHAPTER 18
Labor and Employment Law

PART I. LABOR LAW

INTRODUCTION

The area of labor law relates generally to unions and their dealings with employers and employees. Labor law did not exist at common law; it was created by federal and state statute. A series of federal statutes allowed the formation of unions, prohibited certain practices of management, and regulated internal union affairs. Other federal law established the National Labor Relations Board, how unions may unionize a work site, how new work agreements are to be negotiated, and what can happen if any of these laws is violated. Other federal laws deal with such issues as workplace safety, time off from work, working hours and overtime, the rights of employees who are injured on the job, and the hiring and firing of employees.

DEVELOPMENT OF LABOR LAW

Labor law developed over time with the passage of different federal laws. Some of the laws dealt with how unions are organized; others outlawed certain employer practices. Still others were passed to deal with the unions themselves to make sure they were not taking advantage of workers.

NORRIS-LAGUARDIA ACT

The first federal statute that was passed regarding organized labor was the **Norris-LaGuardia Act,** which became law in 1932. The Norris-LaGuardia Act gives workers freedom of association, organization, and designation of representation in employment disputes. This Act allows workers to meet and form an organization to represent them, and appoints the organization as the representative of all employees in disputes between employers and employees. The Norris-LaGuardia Act also prohibits the issuing of injunctions in nonviolent labor disputes. In other words, the courts are prohibited from issuing court orders to end a strike and ordering employees back to work if the labor dispute is peaceful. Norris-LaGuardia also prohibits **yellow dog contracts.** These are agreements employees would be forced to sign that stated that, as a condition of employment, they would not join a union and would be fired if they did. See Exhibit 18-1 for a summary of the Norris-LaGuardia Act.

EXHIBIT 18-1	NORRIS-LAGUARDIA ACT

Gives workers freedom of association, organization, and designation of representation in employment disputes. Workers can now meet to form an organization to represent them and to appoint the organization as their representative in all disputes between employers and employees.

Prohibits the courts from issuing court orders to end a strike and ordering employees back to work if the labor dispute is peaceful.

Prohibits yellow dog contracts—employment agreements in which employees promise, as a condition of employment, that they will not join a union and will be fired if they do.

THE WAGNER ACT (NATIONAL LABOR RELATIONS ACT)

The next federal statute, the **Wagner Act of 1935,** also known as the **National Labor Relations Act,** provided employees with the right to organize, form, and join unions; bargain collectively through the unions; and engage in concerted activities to support their bargaining positions. The term **collective bargaining** refers to the negotiations between an employer and organized employees for the purpose of determining by joint agreement the conditions of employment. Employers and representatives of the employees meet and negotiate such terms as salaries, working hours, working conditions, and employee benefits. A **concerted activity** is a joint action by employees, such as a strike or picketing, with the intended purpose of furthering bargaining demands. In order to bring pressure on an employer to enter into an agreement, the employees may go out on strike and then picket the workplace. Such actions stop production, causing the employer to lose money. Negative publicity generated by media attention to a strike or shutdown may result in an employer's being more willing to enter into a labor agreement with employees. See Exhibit 18-2 for a summary of the Wagner Act.

EXHIBIT 18-2   THE WAGNER ACT (NATIONAL LABOR RELATIONS ACT)

Gave employees the right to organize, form, and join unions; bargain collectively through these unions; and engage in concerted activities to support their bargaining positions.

Created the National Labor Relations Board, which prevents and remedies unfair labor practices by employers and labor organizations. The NLRB conducts secret ballot elections to determine if employees wish to be covered by a union shop agreement or whether they want union representation to continue.

The Wagner Act also created the **National Labor Relations Board,** an independent federal agency (see Chapter 6, Administrative Law) that regulates labor relations. The National Labor Relations Board (NLRB) has two principal functions: to prevent and remedy unfair labor practices by employer and labor organizations, and to conduct secret ballot elections to determine if employees wish to be covered by a union shop agreement or whether they want union representation to continue. The NLRB investigates allegations of unfair labor practices, imposes sanctions if unfair labor practices are being conducted by either labor or management, and conducts elections to determine if a job site will be unionized or if the union will cease to represent the employees at a work site.

Unfair labor practices include:

1. Interfering with, restraining, or coercing employees in the exercise of their right to organize a union
2. Interfering with the formation or administration of a labor organization
3. Showing preference in employment, promotion, or other employment benefit to nonunion members
4. Discharging an employee who has testified against his or her employer
5. Refusing to bargain collectively with the representative of the employees
6. Failing to rehire striking employees
7. Refusing to bargain collectively in good faith
8. Threatening to close a plant if the employees unionize
9. Discharging an employee because of union membership or activity. (See Exhibit 18-3.)

EXHIBIT 18-3	EXAMPLES OF UNFAIR LABOR PRACTICES BY MANAGEMENT

1. Management interferes with the organization of a union.
2. Management interferes with how the union is formed or with its administration.
3. Management shows employment and benefit preference to nonunion members.
4. Management fires an employee who testified against management.
5. Management refuses to engage in collective bargaining.
6. Management fails to rehire striking employees.
7. Management threatens to shut down a plant or factory if the workers unionize.
8. Management fires an employee because of his or her union activity.

Management was not the only side that could utilize unfair labor practices. Unions could as well, and in order to better regulate union activity, additional federal laws were passed. The **Taft-Hartley Act of 1947,** which is also known as the **Labor Management Relations Act,** provides for the improved regulation of labor unions. According to Taft-Hartley, certain union activity may be unfair labor practice and therefore illegal. See Exhibit 18-4. Coercion of employees to join a union, refusal to bargain in good faith, secondary boycotts, charging excessive union dues, and featherbedding are all examples of unlawful conduct on the part of a union.

EXHIBIT 18-4	TAFT-HARTLEY ACT (LABOR MANAGEMENT RELATIONS ACT)

Certain activities on the part of labor unions are unfair labor practices. These activities include:
1. Coercing employees to join a union
2. Refusing to bargain in good faith
3. Implementing secondary boycotts
4. Charging excessive union dues
5. Featherbedding

A **secondary boycott** is a refusal by union membership to work for, purchase from, or handle products of an employer that the union has no dispute with in order to force the employer to stop doing business with the employer the union is having a dispute with. The union has no complaint against a second company, but in order to bring more pressure onto the company the union is in dispute with, the union "boycotts" the second company. **Featherbedding** is the creation or spreading of employment by unnecessarily maintaining or increasing the number of employees used on a particular job. For example, a certain job usually takes three people. The union demands that five workers be assigned to that job. Two extra jobs are unnecessarily created.

The **Landrum-Griffen Act,** also known as the **Labor Management Reporting and Disclosure Act,** is designed to curb corruption in labor management and undemocratic practices in internal union dealings. The Landrum-Griffen Act provides for more detailed regulations regarding a union's internal affairs; these regulations are designed to help protect members from improper activities by union leaders. One of the requirements of the Landrum-Griffen Act is that union leadership must give detailed reports regarding the income and expenditures of the union: Where is union money being spent? The Act deals with how candidates for union membership are nominated, how officers are elected, and how one can participate in the day-to-day operation of the union.

All of the preceding legislation is designed to regulate labor-management relations—the broad spectrum of activities involved in the relationship of employees to employers, both union and nonunion. See Exhibit 18-5 for the Union Member's Bill of Rights.

EXHIBIT 18-5	LANDRUM-GRIFFIN ACT (LABOR MANAGEMENT REPORTING AND DISCLOSURE ACT)

UNION MEMBER BILL OF RIGHTS

Members of the union have

1. Equal rights to participate in union activities.
2. Freedom of speech and assembly.
3. A voice in setting the rates for dues, assessments, and fees.
4. Protection of the right to sue.
5. Safeguards against improper discipline within the union.
6. The right to receive and inspect copies of collective bargaining agreements.
7. The right to nominate officers.
8. The right to run for union office.
9. The right to cast a secret ballot.
10. The right to protect the conduct of an election.
11. Right to an adequate procedure to remove union officers.

LABOR UNIONS

A **labor union** is an association of workers organized for the purpose of securing favorable wages, improved labor conditions, and better working hours. Rather than each worker attempting to negotiate with management, one entity—the union—bargains on behalf of all workers. There are several types of labor unions, differing in who can join, who is represented, and the industries in which the union operates.

OPEN AND CLOSED UNIONS

The admission requirements of an **open union** are relatively easy to meet. For example, the dues are low, so all that is required for membership is that a person work for a particular company or in a certain field. A **closed union,** on the other hand, has highly restrictive membership requirements such as costly dues and a long apprenticeship. For example, before a worker can join the electricians' union, he or she must have been trained as an electrician and have served as an apprentice for five years. Only when these conditions have been met can a person join the union.

INDEPENDENT, LOCAL, NATIONAL, AND INTERNATIONAL UNIONS

An **independent union** is one not affiliated with any national organization; it represents workers of a single company or employer only. A **local union** is a union of workers in one plant or location that is affiliated with a parent or larger union. A local union is the bargaining unit of the national union for that particular employer, and because it is also part of the national union, it can call upon the national union for assistance. For example, Local 200 of the AFL-CIO is the union that represents the workers at a particular site, but it is also part of the national AFL-CIO union. A **national union** is the parent union with locals in various parts of the United States, but not outside the country. An **international union** is a parent union with affiliates in other countries, such as Mexico and Canada.

COMPANY, CRAFT, AND INDUSTRIAL UNIONS

A **company union** is one formed or sponsored by a business. Instead of being represented by the local chapter of a national union, the workers would be represented by a "union" formed by the management of the company. Company unions are now illegal because management is prohibited from interfering with union representation. A **craft union** is composed of members who share the same trade or craft—such as carpenters, plumbers, and electricians—regardless of the company for whom they work. The union represents all electricians instead of only the electricians who work for a particular company; the union represents all plumbers instead of just those who work for a particular company. An **industrial union** is composed of workers in a particular industry regardless of their particular trade or craft. For example, the United Auto Workers represents everyone who works for GM, Ford, or Chrysler, regardless of his or her job with the company.

HORIZONTAL AND VERTICAL UNIONS

A **horizontal union** is a craft union that cuts across employer or industry lines. The union represents all the particular classifications of workers who are employed by different companies or in different industries. A **vertical union** is an industrial union that is organized along the lines of industry rather than craft: It represents all employees who work for a particular industry regardless of the job they hold. The UAW is both an industrial union and a vertical union. So if a union is open, local, industrial, and horizontal, it has easy membership requirements, is part of a national organization that represents all the workers in a particular industry regardless of who they work for, and operates only in the United States. See Exhibit 18-6 for a comparison of the different types of unions.

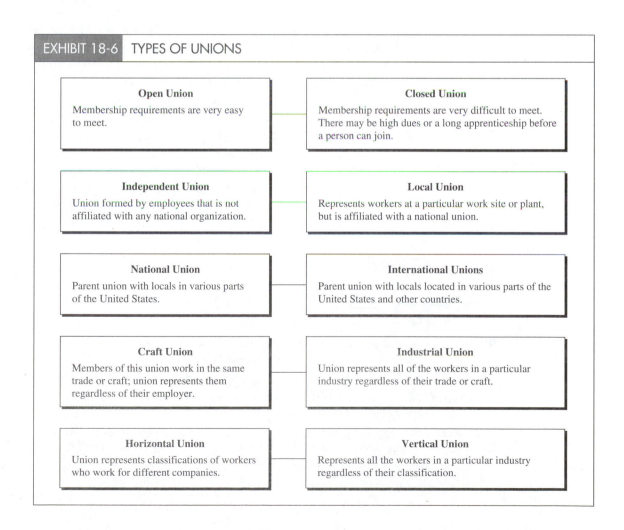

EXHIBIT 18-6 TYPES OF UNIONS

Open Union
Membership requirements are very easy to meet.

Closed Union
Membership requirements are very difficult to meet. There may be high dues or a long apprenticeship before a person can join.

Independent Union
Union formed by employees that is not affiliated with any national organization.

Local Union
Represents workers at a particular work site or plant, but is affiliated with a national union.

National Union
Parent union with locals in various parts of the United States.

International Unions
Parent union with locals located in various parts of the United States and other countries.

Craft Union
Members of this union work in the same trade or craft; union represents them regardless of their employer.

Industrial Union
Union represents all of the workers in a particular industry regardless of their trade or craft.

Horizontal Union
Union represents classifications of workers who work for different companies.

Vertical Union
Represents all the workers in a particular industry regardless of their classification.

UNION SHOPS

There are also several types of "shops" where union membership requirements are determined. What type of shop is at a particular work site or in a particular industry determines if a person must be a member of the union, or when they may join the union. A **union shop** is a site where all workers, once they begin employment, must become a member of the union within a specified period of time as a condition of their continued employment. If the worker does not join the union within the established time frame, his or her employment ends.

OPEN AND CLOSED SHOPS

An **open shop** is a business where union membership is not a condition of securing or maintaining employment. A worker does not have to be a member of the union in order to be considered for employment, and he or she does not have to become a member of the union once employment begins. **Closed shops,** businesses where union membership was required in order to be considered for employment, have been made illegal by the Taft-Hartley Act.

Along with open shops, about twenty states have **right to work laws** that state that employees are not to be required to join a union as a condition of receiving or keeping a job.

PREFERENTIAL AND AGENCY SHOPS

A **preferential shop** is a business that will give preference to union members in hiring and layoff decisions, but nonunion workers may be hired when members of the union are not available. When the business is looking for new employees, it will look to hire union members first. If there are no union members available or qualified to be hired, then the business will look at hiring nonunion employees. If business falls off and the employer has to lay off employees, the first employees laid off will be those who are not members of the union. Union members will be laid off only when all nonunion employees who can be laid off are laid off. An **agency shop** is a business where any nonunion worker, in order to continue employment, pays to the union an amount that is the equivalent of the amount paid by union members. The employee is not a member of the union, and is not required to be a member of the union. However, because the nonunion member is receiving the benefits of the union's efforts on behalf of all employees, the nonunion member pays a fee to the union. This fee can be based on union dues and initiation fees or upon union dues only. It is usually less than regular union dues, but the amount union workers pay is the basis for determining the fee. See Exhibit 18-7 for a summary of union shops.

EXHIBIT 18-7   UNION SHOPS

Union Shop – All workers must join the union as a condition of continuing to work. If the worker does not join the union, then his or her employment ends.

Open Shop – Union membership is not required in order to maintain employment.

Closed Shop – Union membership is required before the worker can even be hired. These shops have been made illegal by the Taft-Hartley Act.

Preferential Shop – Preference is given to union members when hiring and lay off decisions are made. Nonunion workers are hired only when there are no union workers available.

Agency Shop – Nonunion workers pay a fee to the union because the employee is receiving the benefits of the union's efforts without being a member of the union.

FORMATION OF A UNION

If a business is nonunionized, workers can unionize by following a procedure authorized by federal law. If this process is successful, then the union will represent the workers in dealing with management in regard to certain issues.

INITIAL STEPS AND AUTHORIZATION CARDS

If workers decide they want to be represented by a union, they may contact a union about unionizing their place of work. The union will then decide whether it wants to attempt to unionize the work site. Alternatively, a union may determine it wants to try to unionize a worksite that previously has not been unionized. In either case, if the union is interested, it will begin an advertising campaign trying to build support for the unionization. If a worker is interested in having union representation, he or she will sign an **authorization card** indicating that interest. These cards are gathered and turned over to the National Labor Relations Board. The NLRB reviews the cards to determine if a sufficient number of employees (30% of the workers), have expressed an interest in forming a union.

REPRESENTATION ELECTIONS AND UNION CERTIFICATION

If the NLRB determines at least 30% of the workers have turned in authorization cards, it will hold a **representation election** to determine if the work site will be unionized or not. In order to protect the workers from pressure from either the union or the company, the NLRB invokes the **twenty-four-hour rule.** This rule prohibits unions and management from making speeches to a captive audience 24 hours prior to the representative election. The union will also be given an **excelsior list,** which identifies the names and addresses of all employees who are eligible to vote in the representation election. The excelsior list must be prepared seven days after the election order is issued by the NLRB. Under the rules of the NLRB, the list is to be given to the union or the union organizers.

If more than 50% of the workers vote for unionization, then the union is recognized as the collective bargaining agent for all the employees. The term **bargaining agent** applies to unions that have been certified by the NLRB as the *exclusive* representative of all employees in a bargaining unit. A **bargaining unit** is a group of employees who have a similar interest that is appropriate to be used in bargaining. For example, a group of employees may have a similar interest in the amount of wages and benefits that will be available from the employer.

The process outlined in the preceding paragraphs is called **union certification.** If fewer than 50% of eligible workers are in favor of unionization, the union has failed in its efforts to unionize that particular plant or industry. Refer to Exhibit 18-8 for a union certification flow chart.

Not all employers may be happy with their employees forming a union. In response to a successful unionizing effort, an employer may close his or her business temporarily. This is known as a **runaway shop**—a business whose owner moves it to another location or temporarily closes it for antiunion purposes.

If the union is not a certified union, it may still try to represent employees. The company may refuse to recognize the union at all, saying there is no organization that represents the workers. In this situation, workers may use **organizational picketing,** which is picketing designed to force the employer to recognize and bargain with a noncertified union.

SHOP STEWARDS

Once the union is certified, shop stewards may be appointed. **Shop stewards** are union officials elected to represent union members in a plant or a particular department. The duties

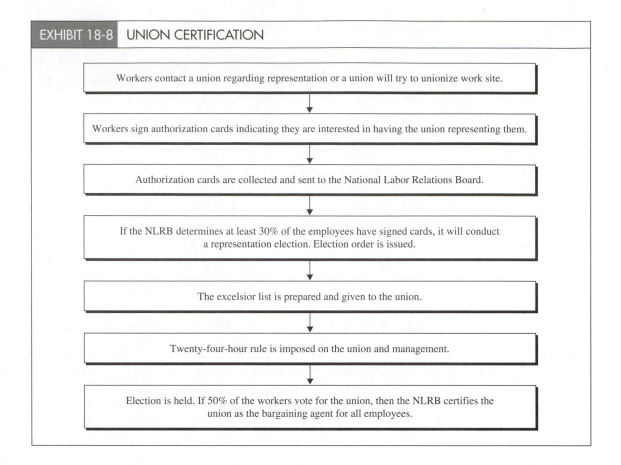

EXHIBIT 18-8 UNION CERTIFICATION

Workers contact a union regarding representation or a union will try to unionize work site.

Workers sign authorization cards indicating they are interested in having the union representing them.

Authorization cards are collected and sent to the National Labor Relations Board.

If the NLRB determines at least 30% of the employees have signed cards, it will conduct a representation election. Election order is issued.

The excelsior list is prepared and given to the union.

Twenty-four-hour rule is imposed on the union and management.

Election is held. If 50% of the workers vote for the union, then the NLRB certifies the union as the bargaining agent for all employees.

of a shop steward include collection of dues, recruitment of new members, and initial negotiations for settlement of grievances. The union will also want to negotiate a **union contract,** a written agreement between the union and the employer covering wages, seniority rights, and working conditions. The union may want to establish a **union rate,** the wage scale set by the union as the minimum wage to be paid and generally stated as an hourly rate or piecework rate. The union may also try to have an **escalator clause** as part of the employment contract, which is a provision that states that the wages of employees will rise or fall in relation to some set standard. The standard may be the cost of living index or a set percentage above the minimum wage: If the minimum wage goes up, so do employees' wages, even though they are still above the minimum wage. The union contract may also contain an **escape period,** a clause that allows workers to withdraw from the union during a set period of time near the end of the current contract and before the start of the next. During this escape period, workers are allowed to cancel their union membership.

COLLECTIVE BARGAINING AND STRIKES

One reason why employees form a union is to be able to engage in collective bargaining with the employer using union representatives. The union representatives will engage in the give-and-take needed to reach an employment agreement that is acceptable to both management and union membership. If the negotiating process is successful, strikes and other labor difficulties can be avoided.

COLLECTIVE BARGAINING

A company that has been newly unionized will meet to hammer out the first employment contract with the newly elected union. If the company and the union are able to reach agreement regarding working conditions and benefits, they will enter into a **collective bargaining agreement** that will regulate the terms and conditions of employment.

A union that is negotiating a collective bargaining agreement is not limited to representing one group of employees with one employer. If the union is representing a group of employees in negotiations with a group of employers or corporations and they enter into an agreement with all the employers, this is known as a **collective labor agreement.** The collective labor agreement applies to all employees of all the employers covered by the agreement. The union negotiates an agreement with several employers within a particular geographical area known as **area bargaining.**

A company and the workers' union might co-exist without conflict during the initial collective bargaining agreement and immediately afterward. However, when it is close to the time to begin negotiating a new agreement and the company's profits begin to increase, the union may determine that its workers should receive a portion of the increased profits. Management, however, may want to maintain the status quo in terms of labor costs. In compliance with the **sixty-day notice rule,** the union may give notice that it wants to renegotiate the contract, not just accept what is in place for another period of time. Notice must be given at least sixty days prior to the date the current contract expires; during those sixty days, there can be no strikes or lockouts. Because the union will seek higher wages, it and the employer will enter into negotiations, each seeking from the other **concessions,** a yielding to a claim or demand of the other side in order to reach a new agreement.

LABOR DISPUTES AND STRIKES

If the employer and the union are unable to reach agreement, they enter into a **labor dispute,** a controversy between employer and employees regarding the terms, tenure, hours, wages, fringe benefits, or conditions of employment. Management and the union may take certain actions to improve their bargaining position, some of which are allowable. Other actions may not be allowable because they are classified as unfair labor practices.

Workers may engage in a work **slowdown**—an organized effort to slow production to pressure the employer. An alternative to a work slowdown is a **strike,** the act of quitting work by a group of employees for the purpose of coercing their employer to agree to some demand that he or she has earlier refused. A **general strike** is the cessation of work by employees effective throughout an entire industry or country. For example, all mine workers or all automobile workers may go out on strike regardless of where they are or which company they work for.

A **jurisdictional strike** results from a dispute by members of one union against members of another union regarding assignment of work; the unions are in dispute as to which workers from what unions are allowed to do certain jobs. An **economic strike** is a cessation of work to enforce economic demands on an employer: Workers might strike for higher wages or increased employer contributions to an employee pension plan. In a **sit-down strike,** employees halt work but do not leave the work premises; they literally sit down at their workstations and do not leave. Their presence prohibits others from working, thereby putting pressure on management. A **wildcat strike** is a strike by a group of employees without the authorization of the union.

Sometimes the workers at one work site who do not have a dispute with their employer will strike in support of another union that has gone on strike. A **secondary strike** is the halting of work by union members of one employer who has business dealings with another employer whose employees are out on strike. The union members who do not have a dispute with their own employer are on strike to try to force their employer to put pressure on the other employer to try to settle the strike. If the original employer is able to reach an agreement with the striking workers, then the second employer's workers will also go back to work.

A union involved in a **sympathy strike** is not seeking gain for itself, but is acting in support of another union that is seeking concessions from an employer. A sympathy strike occurs when more than one union represents workers at the same worksite. For example, in a particular business, one union represents the people who work on the manufacturing line, another union represents the office workers, and a third represents the custodial workers. The union that represents the line workers strike for more money. Because office workers and custodians are satisfied with their wage agreement, they are not seeking any additional concessions from the employer for themselves. However, in order to show support for the union that represents the line workers, the office workers and custodians also go out on strike. Refer to Exhibit 18-9 for a summary of the types of strikes that may be used by employees.

EXHIBIT 18-9	TYPES OF STRIKES BY EMPLOYEES

General Strike – All employees in a particular industry or even an entire country stop working.

Jurisdictional Strike – There is a dispute between members for one union and members of another union regarding work assignments. The workers strike to force the employer to resolve the dispute.

Sit-Down Strike – The workers stop work but do not leave the worksite. They literally sit down on the job.

Wildcat Strike – A group of employees strike without authorization by the union.

Secondary Strike – Workers for one employer go on strike so their employer will put pressure on another employer to settle its dispute with its workers.

Sympathy Strike – Union workers go out on strike in support of another union's workers' strike.

Some employees, even though they are members of a union, may be prohibited from striking. For example, public employees who are unionized may have a **no strike clause** in their contract, stating that employees will not strike for any reason. Any employment disputes will be submitted to arbitration.

MANAGEMENT RESPONSES TO STRIKES

Employers can respond in several ways to a strike by their workers. They may engage in a **lockout,** which is the withholding of work from employees in order to gain concessions from them. The employer can literally lock the doors to the worksite, preventing employees from coming in and performing their job, or employees might be allowed into the worksite, but be given nothing to do.

Another response to a strike is the employment of **strikebreakers,** workers who take the place of those who have left their work. Because the work is still being done, the employer is not facing economic problems; however, the striking workers suffer economic harm. Using strikebreakers is also designed to put pressure on workers to make concessions. Another derogatory term for *strikebreaker* is **scab;** this term also applies to a nonunion worker who passes through a union picket line to go to work.

USE OF MEDIATION

If labor and management are unable to resolve a dispute themselves, they may utilize mediation. **Mediation** is a private, informal dispute resolution process in which a neutral third person—the mediator—helps the disputing parties reach an agreement. The mediator has no power to impose a decision on the parties; the parties themselves must reach an agreement. A special department in the federal government, the **Mediation and Conciliation Service,** is specifically charged with trying to settle labor disputes by conciliation and mediation.

If employees become dissatisfied with representation of the union, they may attempt to decertify the union.

DECERTIFICATION OF THE UNION

Decertification is the process through which a group of employees decides it no longer wants a union to be its bargaining unit. Another vote of the workers is called for to determine whether or not the union will continue to be the agent for the employees in collective bargaining. The vote to decertify the union is also conducted by the National Labor Relations Board. At least 50% of the workers must vote to decertify a union before decertification can occur. Exhibit 18-10 contains a flow chart showing the steps that must be taken to decertify a union.

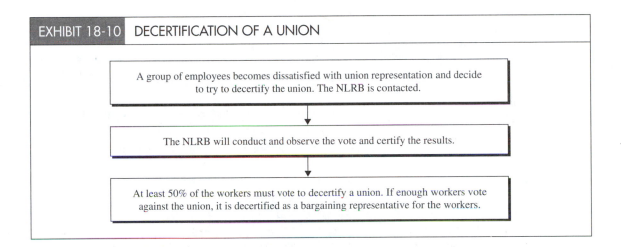

EXHIBIT 18-10 DECERTIFICATION OF A UNION

A group of employees becomes dissatisfied with union representation and decide to try to decertify the union. The NLRB is contacted.

The NLRB will conduct and observe the vote and certify the results.

At least 50% of the workers must vote to decertify a union. If enough workers vote against the union, it is decertified as a bargaining representative for the workers.

PART II. EMPLOYMENT LAW

Unions are not the only way workers have benefits and working conditions established. Workers also have rights and benefits established by state and federal statutory law. Little if any common law concerned the employer/employee relationship, salary, hours worked, leave, and job injuries, so certain federal and state laws set out what rights and responsibilities workers and employers have to each other. These laws govern such issues as wages, leave time, job-related injuries, and unemployment.

FAIR LABOR STANDARDS ACT

Wages are governed by the **Fair Labor Standards Act or FLSA,** which was first passed in 1938 and initially did not apply to government employees. FLSA was amended in 1974 to include government employees, but the Supreme Court decided in 1976 that, even with amendments, the law still did not apply to government employees. However, the Court reversed itself in 1985 and declared that FLSA did cover the wages of government employees. FLSA establishes the minimum wage and the amount of time that must be worked before a person starts to earn overtime.

WORKING TIME AND OVERTIME

Overtime is the amount of time an employee works beyond regular, fixed hours on a week-by-week basis. When an employee works forty hours in a week, all work time over 40 hours is paid at time and a half. **Working time** is time spent at work *actually working*. If an employer has a policy of giving an employee time off with pay, that time does not count when figuring overtime because the employee was not actually at work *working*. Overtime is calculated on a week-by-week basis, regardless of how the employee is paid. For example, if an employee is paid every two weeks, an employer is not allowed to refuse to pay overtime because the employee averaged 40 hours for two weeks. Each week is considered separately.

The portion of wages paid to an employee for services rendered beyond regular, fixed working hours is known as **overtime wages.** If the employer is a government agency, the worker may receive **compensatory time,** an hour and a half of leave time for every hour of overtime worked, rather than overtime wages. See Exhibit 18-11 for an example of how to calculate overtime.

EXHIBIT 18-11	CALCULATION OF OVERTIME

Donna is paid every two weeks. She usually works 40 hours a week. The following are examples of the amount of overtime she would receive.

1. During Week 1, Donna works 43 hours. During Week 2, she works 40 hours. She has worked a total of 83 hours. She is entitled to be paid for three hours of overtime.

2. During Week 1, Donna works five hours extra, but takes eight hours off with pay. During Week 2, she works 40 hours. Donna receives pay for 45 hours for Week 1, but no overtime because she did not spend 40 hours at work working. Eight hours were time off. The fact that she got paid does not matter.

3. During Week 1, Donna works 45 hours. During Week 2, she only works 35 hours; she has to take five hours off without pay during Week 2. She averaged 40 hours a week, but she is still entitled to five hours of overtime pay for Week 1 because the time for each week is calculated separately. The number of hours worked during the pay period is not averaged.

EMPLOYER-EMPLOYEE RELATIONSHIP

The Fair Labor Standards Act applies to the employer-employee relationship only—it does not apply to any other type of relationship. An **employer** is the entity that has the authority to hire and fire, to direct and control the work, and to set working hours. The employer also has an obligation to pay wages. The term **joint employer** refers to an employing entity involving two employers. To determine if there is a **joint employer relationship,** the following factors are considered:

1. Whether a prior arrangement exists between the employers
2. Whether one employer is acting in the interests of the other
3. Whether the employers share control of the employee
4. Whether the operations of the two employers are interrelated
5. Whether the two employers have common management
6. Whether there is common control of labor relations
7. Whether there is common control of finances

An **employee** is a person employed by a business. However, there are situations in which a person is doing work for another, but is not considered an employee. Such persons can be independent contractors, volunteers, or trainees, none of whom is considered an employee. An **independent contractor** is a person who performs a service in the course of self-employment, who contracts to do a piece of work according to his or her own methods, and who is subject to an employer's control only as to the end product or final results. A person is considered to be a **volunteer** if he or she is a nonemployee who volunteers his or her services freely, without coercion, and with no expectation of payment. An employee may volunteer his or her services to an employer if the services are entirely voluntary, if they are provided with no expectation of pay, if the work does not take place during the employee's regular scheduled working hours or scheduled overtime hours, and if the work is not the same type of service the employee performs in his or her regular job.

Whether or not someone is a **trainee** is determined on a case-by-case basis by applying set criteria to each situation. The following criteria are used.

- The training is substantially similar to that provided by a vocational school.
- The training is provided for the benefit of the employee, not the employer.
- The trainee must not displace any regular employees and must work under close observation and supervision.
- The employer does not obtain any immediate advantage from the activities of the trainee.
- The trainee *may* be employed at the end of the training period, but he or she is not *entitled to* employment.
- It is clear in advance that the trainee will not receive wages for the time spent in training.

If all of these conditions are met, then the person is considered to be a trainee and not an employee. Exhibit 18-12 is a summary of when an employee is not considered to be an employee.

EXHIBIT 18-12   WHEN AN EMPLOYEE IS NOT AN EMPLOYEE

INDEPENDENT CONTRACTOR

Performs a service

Is self-employed

Contracts to do work according to his or her own methods

Is subject to an employer's control only as to the end product or final results

VOLUNTEER

Services are entirely voluntary

Services provided with no intention of receiving compensation

If the volunteer is an employee, he or she cannot volunteer during regular working hours or scheduled overtime

Employee must not perform the same type of service performed during regular job

TRAINEE

Training is similar to training provided by a vocational school

Training benefits the employee, not the employer

Trainee does not displace a regular worker; the trainee is closely supervised

Employer gains no immediate advantage

Trainees may be employed at the end of the training period

Trainees are not paid for the period of time in training

EXEMPT AND NONEXEMPT EMPLOYEES

If an employee is **exempt** from FLSA coverage, overtime laws do not apply; that employee does not earn overtime. A **nonexempt** employee is one to whom overtime rules do apply; these are employees who do earn overtime.

Another classification of exempt employee is the **white-collar employee,** one who is paid on a salary or fee basis as opposed to an hourly basis. **Salary** is the amount the employee is paid regardless of the quantity or quality of his or her work. A **fee** is a charge or compensation for a particular act or service. Deductions from a salary or fee cannot be made for absences due to a lack of work or layoff, or absences of less than a full day for sickness or accident. If these deductions are made, then the employee is not on salary; he or she is an hourly employee and is therefore eligible for overtime.

White-collar employees fall into three categories: executive, administrative, and professional. On April 23, 2004, the Wage and Hour division of the Department of Labor issued new regulations that amended the definitions for an executive, administrative, or professional employee. Each one of the categories has a test that can be used to determine the employee's exempt status.

In order for a person to be an **executive employee,** the employee must meet the following factors:

1. The employee is compensated on a salary basis making at least $455 per week.

2. The employee's primary duty is the management of an enterprise, department, or subdivision.

3. The employee customarily and regularly directs the work of two or more employees.

4. The employee has the authority to hire or fire other employees, or his or her recommendation as to hiring, firing, and promotions are given particular weight.

In order to be considered a department or subdivision, the entity must have a permanent status within the organization and have a continuing function. Two or more employees mean two full-time employees or their equivalent. For example one full-time employee and two half-time employees are the equivalent of two full-time employees.

In order for a person to be an **administrative employee,** the employee must meet the following factors:

1. The employee is compensated on a salary *or* fee basis making at least $455 per week.

2. The employee's primary duty is the performance of office or nonmanual work directly related to the management or general business operations of the employer or the employer's customers.

3. The employee's principal duty includes the exercise of discretion and independent judgment with respect to matters of significance.

The phrase *exercise of discretion and independent judgment* means the employee must compare and evaluate possible courses of action and then make a decision after the various possibilities have been considered. The fact that the employee's decision may be reviewed at a higher level does not mean that he or she has not exercised discretion and independent judgment. The term *matters of significance* refers to the level of importance or consequence of the work performed.

In order for a person to be a **professional employee,** the employee must meet the following factors:

1. The employee is compensated on a salary *or* fee basis making at least $455 per week.

2. The employee's primary duty is the performance of work that requires knowledge of an advanced type in a field of science or learning, customarily acquired through a prolonged course of study.

3. The employee must use intervention, imagination, originality, or talent in a recognized field of artistic or creative endeavor.

See Exhibit 18-13 for a summary of these tests.

EXHIBIT 18-13	TESTS FOR WHITE COLLAR WORKERS

The employee must make at least $455 per week in salary (executive) or in salary or fees (administrative and professional) and must meet the following criteria:

EXECUTIVE

Primary duty is the management of an enterprise, department, or subdivision.

Customarily and regularly directs the work of two or more employees.

Authority to hire and fire or make recommendations about hiring and firing decisions.

ADMINISTRATIVE

Primary duty is the performance of office or nonmanual work directly related to the management or general management or general business operation of the employer or employer's customers.

Exercises discretion and independent judgments with respect to matters of significance.

PROFESSIONAL

Primary duty is the performance of work that requires knowledge of an advanced type in a field of science or learning, customarily acquired through a prolonged course of study.

Uses invention, imagination, originality, or talent in a recognized field of artistic or creative endeavor.

HOURS WORKED

Calculation of overtime pay for nonexempt employees is based on the number of hours worked. **Hours worked for overtime purposes** are those spent actually working, on duty, or at a prescribed work place. Certain performance duties may or may not be considered hours worked for overtime purposes.

Preliminary duties are performed before the employee actually starts work. These include duties like clocking in, putting items in a locker, or changing clothes. **Postliminary duties** are performed after the employee has stopped working: changing clothes, washing, or clocking out. Whether or not these duties are **compensable**—entitled to be paid—depends on whether or not they are an integral part of the principal activity. If the duty is a necessary part of the job, the worker is entitled to be compensated for it. Travel time on company premises, time spent waiting to clock in, clock out, or to be paid, and time spent washing up or changing clothes are generally not compensable.

Waiting time is another area where an employee may be compensated. **Waiting time** falls into one of two categories: waiting to be engaged, which is noncompensable, or engaged to be waiting, which is compensable. An employee is **engaged to be waiting** if

- the employer controls the time
- time is an integral part of the job
- the employee is unable to use time effectively for personal purposes
- the periods of time spent waiting are unpredictable
- the periods of waiting time are of short duration

If the employee is engaged to be waiting, he or she is eligible for overtime pay because he or she has been hired to wait to go to work.

The employee is **waiting to be engaged** if

- the employee is completely released from duty
- the employee has enough time to use effectively for personal purposes
- the employee is told in advance that he or she might leave the job
- the employee is told in advance he or she does not have to return to work before a specified time

Exhibit 18-14 is a summary of these two classifications.

EXHIBIT 18-14	ENGAGED TO BE WAITING OR WAITING TO BE ENGAGED?

ENGAGED TO BE WAITING

The employer controls the time.

Time is an integral, important part of the job.

The employee is unable to use the time effectively for personal purposes.

The periods of time spent waiting are unpredictable.

The periods of time spent waiting are of short duration.

WAITING TO BE ENGAGED

The employee is completely released from duty.

The employee has enough time to use effectively for his or her personal purposes.

The employee is told in advance he or she might leave the job.

The employee is told in advance that he or she does not have to return to work before a specified time.

PART III. EMPLOYEES' RIGHTS AND EMPLOYERS' RESPONSIBILITIES

Over the years, federal laws have been passed to provide additional rights and protections to employees. The Family and Medical Leave Act, OSHA, and COBRA are all designed to help workers in a variety of situations.

FAMILY AND MEDICAL LEAVE

The **Family and Medical Leave Act** or **FMLA** was signed into law in 1993. The intent of the Act is to grant eligible employees up to 12 weeks of unpaid leave per year for qualifying conditions.

ELIGIBLE EMPLOYEES

In order to be an **eligible employee,** an employee must have been employed for at least twelve months and have actually worked 1,250 hours in that year. The hours worked must have been spent at the worksite. The definition of *at the worksite working* is the same definition used in the Fair Labor Standards Act. Any time the employee spends away from the worksite does not count, even if he or she is compensated for that time. If an employee receives paid annual leave, sick leave, or paid holidays, none of those hours count toward the 1,250 hours required to be eligible.

In order to be granted leave, an employee must qualify by virtue of one of the following conditions:

- the birth of a son or daughter
- the placement of a child in his or her home for foster care or adoption
- the care of a son, daughter, spouse, or parent who has a serious health condition
- the serious health condition of the employee himself or herself

A **serious health condition** is an injury, illness, impairment, or physical or mental condition that involves inpatient care in a hospital, hospice, or residential care facility, or continuing treatment by a healthcare professional. A **healthcare professional** is a doctor of medicine or osteopathy who is authorized to practice medicine by the state he or she practices.

TO WHOM THE ACT APPLIES

The **parent** is the biological parent of the employee or an individual who stands in **loco parentis**—in the place of a parent—to the employee. This person could be a legal guardian, a relative who raised the employee, or someone with whom the employee has developed a parent/child relationship. The burden is on the employee to prove that this relationship exists. A son or daughter is either a biological child (the child that was born to the parents), an adopted child, a foster child, a stepchild, a legal ward, or a child under the age of 18 of a person standing in *loco parentis*. The Act also applies to a child over the age of 18 who, because of mental or physical disability, is unable to take care of himself or herself. Exhibit 18-15 shows who is considered a child and who is considered a parent under FMLA. Exhibit 18-16 summarizes who is covered by the FMLA.

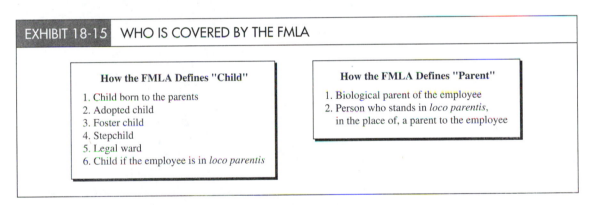

EXHIBIT 18-15 WHO IS COVERED BY THE FMLA

How the FMLA Defines "Child"

1. Child born to the parents
2. Adopted child
3. Foster child
4. Stepchild
5. Legal ward
6. Child if the employee is in *loco parentis*

How the FMLA Defines "Parent"

1. Biological parent of the employee
2. Person who stands in *loco parentis*, in the place of, a parent to the employee

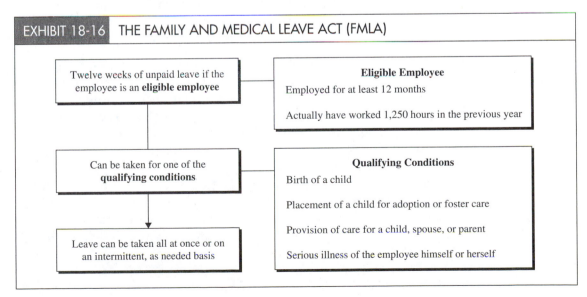

EXHIBIT 18-16 THE FAMILY AND MEDICAL LEAVE ACT (FMLA)

Twelve weeks of unpaid leave if the employee is an **eligible employee**

Eligible Employee

Employed for at least 12 months

Actually have worked 1,250 hours in the previous year

Can be taken for one of the **qualifying conditions**

Qualifying Conditions

Birth of a child

Placement of a child for adoption or foster care

Provision of care for a child, spouse, or parent

Serious illness of the employee himself or herself

Leave can be taken all at once or on an intermittent, as needed basis

HOW THE LEAVE MAY BE TAKEN

Leave may be taken for the 12-week period all at once or on an **intermittent basis**—in shorter, separate periods of time. Leave on an intermittent basis may be for periods of up to one hour or more for several weeks.

KEY EMPLOYEE

FMLA allows leave to be denied to a **key employee,** one who is among the highest paid 10 percent of employees and absence will cause the employer to suffer substantial and grievous economic injury. **Grievous economic injury** is construed as bankruptcy or dissolution of the business. Under this definition, a key employee does not really exist because, as a practical matter, no employee is this important.

WORKERS' COMPENSATION

When an employee is injured on the job, workers' compensation is usually the remedy available for that employee. **Workers' compensation** is set by state statute and provides for fixed awards to workers who are victims of employment-related accidents or injuries and their dependents.

STRICT LIABILITY AND WORKERS' COMPENSATION INSURANCE

The effect of workers' compensation is to make the employer strictly liable for injury sustained by an employee during the scope of and arising out of the course of employment. If an employee is injured on the job and the injury occurred as a result of work being performed, the employer is liable for that injury. This liability is not unlimited; there are statutory limits on how much the injured worker can receive. Workers' compensation is usually an exclusive remedy: If the employee collects workers' compensation, he or she cannot also sue the employer in tort law. **Workers' compensation insurance** is purchased by employees to cover the risks of workers' compensation.

Workers' compensation did not exist at common law; it was created by state statute. Every state has its own workers' compensation law governing employers in that particular state with each law having its own set of definitions. There is no overarching federal law governing workers' compensation that applies to all the states; every state's laws are different. Employees of the federal government are covered by workers' compensation law as provided in the **Federal Employees' Compensation Act.**

DISABILITIES UNDER WORKERS' COMPENSATION

Because there are so many different statutes, a comprehensive discussion of terms that apply to workers' compensation is beyond the scope of this text. However, some terms are commonly found in the statutes. When a person is injured on the job, he or she may suffer what is classified as a **temporary disability.** The term refers to the healing period during which the employee is totally or partially unable to work. Temporary disability continues as long as recovery or improvement of the injured condition can reasonably be expected. An injury might be classified as a **temporary total disability,** one that, during the healing or recovery period, prevents the employee from being able to return to work. *Work* includes whatever skills, activities, duties, or responsibilities the employee performs during the course of his or her regular employment. *Temporary total disability* is also defined as total disability that is not permanent: The employee's total disability is only temporary.

An employee might also suffer a **permanent disability**—an injury that remains substantially the same during the remainder of the employee's life. Such an injury causes a competitive handicap for the employee in the workplace because it impairs the normal use of part of the employee's body. Whether an injury created a permanent disability is determined when the injury has healed as much as it is going to heal. See Exhibit 18-17.

EXHIBIT 18-17   DISABILITIES UNDER WORKERS' COMPENSATION

Temporary disability – Refers to the healing period, the time it takes the injury to heal, where the employee is totally or partially unable to work due to the injury.

Temporary total disability – An injury that, during the healing or recovery period from the accident, prevents the employee from being able to return to work.

Permanent disability – An injury that remains substantially the same during the remainder of the employee's life.

WORKERS' COMPENSATION HEARINGS

Disputes regarding workers' compensation are heard by either a board or a court. Workers' compensation boards/courts have jurisdiction to review cases under workers' compensation law. Because workers' compensation is governed by strict liability principles, there are not many defenses to a workers' compensation claim.

WILLFUL MISCONDUCT

An employer might try to avoid liability by challenging whether an injury actually took place, the severity of the injury, or whether the injury was work-related or caused by employee misconduct. **Willful misconduct** of an employee is more than mere negligence: It is the intentional performance of an act that is likely to result in serious injury and the reckless disregard on the part of the employee of the probable consequences of his or her actions. Willful misconduct is proven by showing one of the following:

- Wanton and willful disregard of the employer's interests by the employee
- Deliberate violation of the rules of the workplace, resulting in injury
- Disregard of the standards of behavior an employer has a right to expect from an employee
- Negligence in conduct so severe as to show culpability, wrongful intent, evil intention, or intentional and substantial disregard for the employer's interests or the employee's duties and obligations. See Exhibit 18-18.

EXHIBIT 18-18   HOW WILLFUL MISCONDUCT IS SHOWN

1. The employee **willfully ignores** the best interests of the employer.
2. The employee **deliberately violates** the rules of the workplace.
3. The employee **ignores the standards of conduct** an employer has a right to expect from an employee.
4. The employee's conduct is **so negligent** that it shows a wrongful intent, evil intentions, or an intentional and substantial disregard for the interests of the employer.

If there is willful misconduct on the part of an employee and that conduct is the cause of injury, then an employer is not liable under workers' compensation law for the injury. For example, Beckman Towing has rules that prohibit employees from drinking on the job, using drugs on the job, or appearing for work under the influence of drugs or alcohol. Laverne shows up at work and is involved in an accident that causes her to be injured. Investigation reveals that Laverne's blood alcohol level is .15, which is over the legal limit. Laverne engaged in willful misconduct because she showed up at work under the influence of alcohol and was injured because she was under the influence. Because of Laverne's willful misconduct, Beckman Towing can avoid liability. Exhibit 18-19 is a flow chart showing the steps involved in a workers' compensation claim.

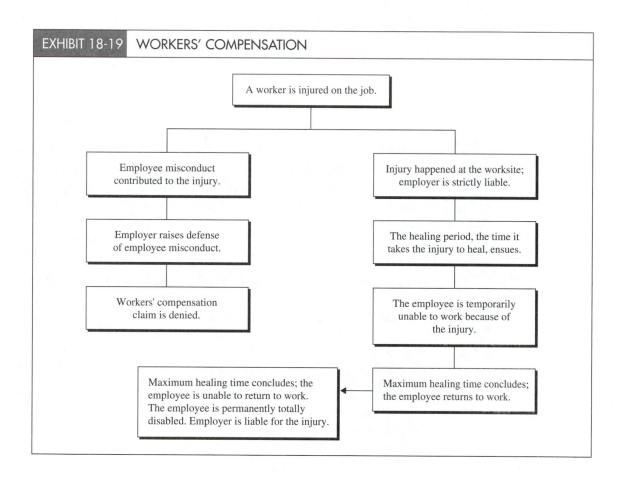

EXHIBIT 18-19 WORKERS' COMPENSATION

A worker is injured on the job.

Employee misconduct contributed to the injury.

Injury happened at the worksite; employer is strictly liable.

Employer raises defense of employee misconduct.

The healing period, the time it takes the injury to heal, ensues.

Workers' compensation claim is denied.

The employee is temporarily unable to work because of the injury.

Maximum healing time concludes; the employee is unable to return to work. The employee is permanently totally disabled. Employer is liable for the injury.

Maximum healing time concludes; the employee returns to work.

POLYGRAPH EXAMINATION

A growing trend has been to subject employees to polygraph examinations as a method of investigating employee misconduct or other issues. The **Employee Polygraph Protection Act,** 22 U.S.C. § 2001, provides for protection for employees from polygraph examinations. For purposes of the Act, an employer is any person who is acting directly or indirectly in the interest of an employer in relation to either an employee or prospective employee. In other words, for purposes of the Act, the term *employer* refers not only to the actual employer, but anyone who is acting *on behalf of* the employer. A **lie detector** is any device— a polygraph, a deceptograph, a voice stress analyzer, a psychological stress evaluator— mechanical or electrical, that is used or the results of which are used to give a diagnostic opinion regarding whether a person is being truthful or not. In other words, it is any device that is used to help render an opinion about the truthfulness of a person. A **polygraph** is an instrument that records continuously, visually, permanently, and simultaneously changes in cardiovascular, respiratory, and electrodermal patterns as minimum instrumentation standards. The results from the measurements must be used for the purpose of giving a diagnostic opinion about the honesty of an individual.

COBRA

In the past, when an employee lost his or her job, he or she also lost any insurance made available by the employer. In 1985, in order to protect workers and allow them to continue to carry insurance, Congress passed the **Consolidated Omnibus Budget Reconciliation Act (COBRA).** COBRA provides that an employee who has lost his or her job can continue to be covered by insurance if he or she can pay the full premium for the policy plus up to a 2% administration fee. This coverage can continue for up to 18 months, or 29 months if the employee is disabled. This option exists for up to 60 days after coverage would normally expire to allow the employee time to decide if he or she wants coverage to continue.

OSHA

In order to provide a safer working environment for workers, Congress passed the Occupational Safety and Health Act. This Act established the **Occupational Safety and Health Administration (OSHA),** the federal agency responsible for setting standards for workplace safety and for enforcing those standards. The **National Institute for Occupational Safety and Health** is an independent agency that identifies occupational health and safety problems. The National Institute develops methods to prevent identified occupational accidents and diseases and publishes its findings. OSHA works with the National Institute in developing safety standards for the workplace.

PROCESS TO DEVELOP SAFETY STANDARDS

OSHA utilizes a four-step process to develop new safety standards. The first step is to determine if a hazard presents a significant risk to workers. The second is to determine if regulatory action can reduce the risk. The third is to determine if OSHA standards can reduce the risk, taking into account technological and economic feasibility. The final step is to analyze the cost effectiveness of various implementation options to determine which option will achieve the goals the most efficiently. See Exhibit 18-20.

EXHIBIT 18-20	OSHA FOUR-STEP PROGRAM

Step One – Does the hazard present a significant risk to the health and safety of workers?

Step Two – Can regulatory action reduce the risk to health and safety?

Step Three – Can OSHA standards reduce the risk to the greatest extent possible taking into account technology and current economics?

Step Four – How cost effective are the options?

OSHA INVESTIGATIONS

OSHA conducts inspections of worksites to determine if they are in compliance with government standards. There are several different levels of OSHA inspections. An **imminent danger inspection** occurs when OSHA learns of a workplace hazard that can reasonably be expected to cause physical harm or death. OSHA conducts a **catastrophic and fatality inspection** when an accident at a worksite either hospitalizes five or more employees or causes a death. It will undertake an **employee complaint inspection** when an employee alleges a violation of a standard and requests an investigation or inspection. The Agency's **special inspection program** is aimed at certain hazards or industries; using the findings of these inspections, OSHA may impose financial or other sanctions against an employer. See Exhibit 18-21.

EXHIBIT 18-21	DIFFERENT TYPES OF OSHA INSPECTIONS

Imminent Danger Inspection – A hazard exists that may cause physical harm or death.

Catastrophic and Fatality Inspection – An accident at the worksite either hospitalizes five or more employees or causes a single death.

Employee Complaint Inspection – An employee alleges a standard violation or requests an investigation or inspection.

Special Inspection Program – Inspection is aimed at certain hazards or industries.

Appeals from the findings of these inspections are filed with the **Occupational Safety and Health Review Commission,** an independent federal review body that evaluates findings by OSHA and the penalties and abatements issued by OSHA if they are contested by an employer. An administrative law judge hears the case and issues his or her findings. The judge's decision becomes final after thirty days unless either the employer or OSHA appeals.

EMPLOYERS' DUTIES UNDER OSHA

The Occupational Safety and Health Act also imposes certain duties on an employer. Under the Act, an employer has a **general duty** to provide employees with a safe work environment that is free from recognized hazards that are likely to cause death or serious physical injury. The **specific duty** under the Act is the employer's obligation to comply with OSHA's regulations affecting particular workplace safety and health conditions.

In order to provide additional incentive to employers to be in compliance with its standards, OSHA offers a **star worksite** designation. This recognition is awarded to worksites distinguished by outstanding safety records and achievements. OSHA also operates a **voluntary protection program.** Under this program, an employer agrees to undergo training from the Agency dealing with workplace safety. Upon conclusion of this training, if the firm passes an inspection, then ordinary inspections will take place only once a year or once every three years depending on the criteria met by the worksite. Additional inspections will occur only if a worker formally complains, a major accident occurs, or there is a chemical spill.

EMPLOYMENT AT WILL

When someone goes to work for a company or a business, he or she may sign an employment contract or be a part of an employment-at-will situation. The term **employment at will** means that, absent an express agreement to the contrary, either the employer or employee may end the employment relationship at any time for any reason, or for no reason at all. An exception to the employment-at-will doctrine is the **public policy exception,** which prohibits terminations that are against established public policy. **Public policy** varies from state to state, but includes such things as dismissals because an employee participated in environmental or consumer protection activities, whistleblowing, serving jury duty or military service, and filing for or testifying at workers' compensation hearings. Another exception to the employment-at-will doctrine is the **employment contract,** an agreement between the employer and employee that sets out the terms and conditions of employment.

CONCLUSION

Over the years, Congress and the individual states have passed laws regarding the rights of employees and the responsibilities of employers. This is an area of law that continues to expand as new laws are passed and more decisions that interpret the laws are handed down.

A major area of federal legislation deals with labor unions. The Norris-LaGuardia Act gives workers the freedom of association, organization, and designation of representation in employment disputes. The Wagner Act provides employees with the right to organize, form, and join unions; to bargain collectively through these unions; and to engage in concerted activities to support their bargaining positions. The Taft-Hartley Act states that certain union activity may be unfair and illegal labor practice. The Landrum-Griffen Act regulates internal union activities and places requirements on union leadership: The unions must submit detailed reports regarding their finances and state how candidates for union membership are nominated, how officers are elected, and how members can participate in the day-to-day operations of the union.

Unions may be classified as open, closed, independent, local, national, or international. These classifications are based on how membership is determined or on how expansive the membership of the union is. Unions can also be company, craft, or trade unions, depending on whom the union represents.

Unions are formed when either the union or the employees at a worksite start to campaign for the union. If enough employees sign authorization cards and the cards are authenticated, then a union election will be held. The election will be overseen by the National Labor Relations Board, which will also certify the results. If the union is certified, it becomes the bargaining agent for all of the workers at the worksite. The union and management will enter into collective bargaining. If that is not successful, both the union and management can take action to improve their bargaining strength. The union might engage in one of several types of strikes; management might use strikebreakers or conduct a lockout, literally locking out the employees from the worksite.

More recent federal legislation sets minimum wages for employees and also establishes what is considered to be overtime and how overtime is to be compensated. Mandatory leave time for illness or the birth of a child has also been established by federal law. Federal law also governs employees' rights regarding polygraph examinations, insurance coverage after employment terminates, and workplace safety.

Workers' compensation is not federally mandated; rather, each state has its own version of law providing for payment to workers who are injured on the job. Workers' compensation terminology may vary by state, but the principle remains the same: to provide compensation to employees who are injured on the job.

KEY WORDS AND PHRASES

administrator exemption
agency shop
area bargaining
authorization card
bargaining unit
closed shop
closed union
collective bargaining
collective labor agreement
company union
compensable
compensatory time
concerted activity
craft union
decertification
economic strike
eligible employee
engaged to be waiting
escalator clause
escape period
Fair Labor Standards Act
  (FLSA)
Family and Medical Leave
  Act (FMLA)
featherbedding
general strike
horizontal union
independent contractor
independent union

industrial union
joint employer
joint employer relationship
jurisdictional strike
key employee
labor dispute
Labor Management
  Relations Act
labor union
Landrum-Griffen Act
local union
lockout
loco parentis
mediation
National Labor Relations
  Board
national union
no strike clause
nonexempt
open shop
overtime
parent
permanent disability
postliminary duties
preferential shop
preliminary duties
representation election
right to work laws
runaway shop

salary
scab
secondary strike
serious health condition
shop steward
sixty-day notice rule
strike
strikebreaker
sympathy strike
Taft-Hartley Act of 1947
temporary disability
temporary total disability
trainee
unfair labor practices
union
union certification
union contract
union rate
union shop
vertical union
volunteer
Wagner Act of 1935
waiting to be engaged
wildcat strike
willful misconduct
workers' compensation
working time
yellow dog contract

REVIEW QUESTIONS

SHORT ANSWER

1. What is a sit down strike?

2. What is a wildcat strike?

3. What is a lockout?

4. What does the FLSA control?

5. What is compensatory time?

6. What makes a person a volunteer?

7. What makes a person a trainee?

8. What makes a person an executive?

9. What is an exempt employee?

10. To whom does the FMLA apply?

11. Who is a key employee?

12. What is the difference between a horizontal union and a vertical union?

13. What is area bargaining?

14. What do employees sign when they want to have a union election?

15. What is concerted activity?

16. What is the difference between a closed shop and an open shop?

17. How is the term *parent* defined under the Family and Medical Leave Act?

18. How is the term *child* defined under the Family and Medical Leave Act?

19. What is a craft union?

20. What is an escape clause?

FILL IN THE BLANK

1. Hiring more workers than needed is known as _____.

2. An employer's preventing employees from working is known as a _____.

3. A business that will give preference to union members in hiring and layoff decisions is a _____ shop.

4. A person who crosses a picket line to work at a company that is in a labor dispute is a _____.

5. The wages a member of a union is supposed to receive are referred to as _____.

6. A union shop where nonmembers of the union still have to pay a fee to the union is a _____.

7. An agreement not to join a union while working for an employer is a _____.

8. The _____ states that if the union gives notice that it wishes to negotiate a new contract and not accept an extension of the old one, negotiations must take place during the first _____ with no strikes or other concerted activity.

9. Union officials elected to represent union members in a plant or a particular department are _____.

10. Three classifications that exempt an employee from the Fair Labor Standards Act are:

   _____

   _____

   _____

FACT SITUATIONS

1. Bob and Carol work for the same company. Carol delivers a healthy little boy. Under the Family and Medical Leave Act, how much leave time can each parent take for the birth of the child?

2. How much leave time can Bob and Carol take if they get sick?

3. Jackson wants to go to work for a company, but he is told he must be a member of the union before he can work for that company. What type of shop is this?

4. Boyd works for a company that is unionized, but Boyd is not a member of the union. However, he pays a fee to the union because it is the collective bargaining unit for the employees. What type of union shop is Boyd's workplace?

5. Marty is sometimes required to wear a beeper when she is off duty. She is limited in the area she can move around in and in her activity while she wears the beeper. Is she engaged to be waiting or waiting to be engaged? Why?

6. Michael is on call, but he has a cell phone with a broad range. When the phone rings, he is expected to respond; however, he has no limitations placed on where he can go and what he can do. His response also can be by telephone. Is he engaged to be waiting or waiting to be engaged? Why?

7. Marvin files a workers' compensation claim alleging he was hurt at work when something broke on the forklift he was driving, causing it to swerve out of control and crash. There are indications that Marvin not only was drinking on the job, but that he was also intoxicated. If he was intoxicated, would he recover workers' compensation? Why or why not?

8. A group of nurses at a hospital want to unionize, so they contact one of the national unions.
   a. What will the nurses have to fill out to have an election?
   b. What sort of election will be held if one is called for?
   c. What will be the end result of the election if enough people vote for a union?
   d. What process will the nurses follow if they no longer want to be unionized?

9. Instead of paying extra wages for overtime, an employer is allowed to give additional vacation time to an employee. What type of time is this?

10. Roger, who works at a nursing home, wants to volunteer his time to come in and help with the residents on his off days. He wants to take them on special outings, participate with them in special events, and take some of them to church with him. His regular job duties include providing direct care to the residents and participating in recreational activities. Could Roger be classified as a volunteer at the nursing home?

CHAPTER 19

Debtor Creditor Relations

INTRODUCTION

When someone lends or borrows money, a debtor/creditor relationship is formed. The debtor/creditor relationship can be informal or formal. The more formal the debtor/creditor relationship, the more it is regulated by different laws.

GENERAL CREDIT TERMS

When a person wants to borrow money from someone or buy something "on time," he or she wants to establish credit. **Credit** is the ability of a person or business to borrow money or obtain goods on time. Instead of paying for the good when it is purchased, the consumer uses credit and agrees to pay for the item over time.

DETERMINING WHETHER TO EXTEND CREDIT

To determine whether or not a person will receive credit, a lender will consult a credit report. A **credit report** is a document from a credit bureau setting out the credit rating and pertinent financial data concerning a person or business entity. A **credit rating** is an evaluation of a person's or business's present ability to pay a debt and past performance in paying debts. This evaluation reveals the potential borrower's current income and the number of times he or she has been delinquent in paying bills. The better the credit report and credit rating, the more likely the person will be to receive the requested credit; the worse the credit report and credit rating, the less likely the person will be to receive the credit requested. The **credit bureau** is the business that collects information relating to the credit, character, responsibility, and reputation of individuals and businesses for the purpose of furnishing a credit report to its subscribers, the people and businesses who pay for the service.

If credit is granted, the person or business will have a **line of credit**—a fixed limit of credit granted by a bank, retailer, or credit card issuer. This is the amount of credit the customer is allowed to use; he or she must not exceed this amount. For example, Maxine applies for and receives a credit card from a department store with a $2,500 limit. Maxine can charge up to $2,500 worth of merchandise from the store, but she is not authorized to charge more than $2,500.

CREDITORS

The **creditor** is the person or business to whom the debt is owed. When a charge is made, the creditor is the person or business that is repaid. There are several types of classifications of creditors depending on their relationship with the debtor or what type of loan is arranged.

GENERAL, DOMESTIC, AND FOREIGN CREDITORS

A **general creditor** has no lien or security for the payment of the debt. The only assurance a general creditor has that the loan will be repaid is the promise of the debtor to repay the money. A **domestic creditor** is situated in the same state or country as the debtor. A **foreign creditor** does not reside in the same state or country as the debtor or in a state or country where the debtor has any property.

CLASSIFICATION OF CREDITORS BASED ON PRIORITY OF PAYMENT

Sometimes the debtor does not have enough money to pay back all of his or her creditors. When there is a limited amount of money available to pay back creditors, creditors are classified based on which will be paid and in what order. A **principal creditor** is a creditor whose claim or demand exceeds the claims of all other creditors; this is the creditor that is first to be paid. A **junior creditor** is one whose claim arose at a later time than the claim of another creditor. A junior creditor's claim ranks below the claims of other creditors to the same property. For example, Mario has a mortgage on his home through Metropolitan Bank. He takes a second mortgage out on the home through Worthen Bank. (See Chapter 12, Real Estate Transactions.) The creditor that has the first mortgage, Metropolitan Bank, is the principal creditor; the creditor who has the second mortgage, Worthen Bank, is the junior creditor.

The right to payment of a **preferred creditor** supersedes the right to payment of a junior creditor. For example, a creditor who holds a mortgage on a home is a preferred creditor because he or she will be paid before any junior creditor who may have only the promise of the debtor that the amount of money borrowed will be repaid. The junior creditor could also be a **secondary creditor,** one whose claim is secondary or inferior to the preferred creditor's claim.

CLASSIFICATIONS BASED ON CLAIMS OF CREDITORS

A **single creditor** has a claim or lien only on a single fund; there is only one resource for the repayment of the debt. A **double creditor** has a lien or claim on at least two funds—there are two resources that can be used for the repayment of the debt. For example, Mario borrows money from First National Bank, and the only source of money to repay the loan is the savings account he has at First National. First National Bank is a single creditor. Maxine borrows money from First Commercial Bank, but she has a savings account and a money market account there, so two sources of money are available to repay the loan. First Commercial Bank is a double creditor. **Joint creditors** are two or more people who are entitled to payment of the same debt. For example, First Commercial Bank and First National Bank join together to loan $1,000,000 to Angel. There is one loan with the amount of the loan coming from two banks, so each bank is entitled to payments on the debt.

A **lien creditor** is a creditor who has acquired a lien, or claim, on the property of the debtor to help secure the debt. If the debtor fails to pay the creditor, the creditor can use **attachment,** which is the legal process by which another person's property is seized pursuant to a court order. The purpose of the attachment is to secure the property in anticipation of receiving a judgment against the debtor. The creditor does not have judgment yet, but this secures the property so the creditor already has the property once judgment is received. The term **attaching creditor** refers to the creditor who has caused the attachment to be issued and levied on the property of the debtor. It is possible for a creditor to fit into more than one category: A creditor can be a preferred, single, lien creditor or a secondary, double, joint creditor. See Exhibit 19-1 for a summary of the types of creditors.

EXHIBIT 19-1	TYPES OF CREDITORS

General Creditor – A creditor who has no security for the repayment of a loan. All that exists is the debtor's promise to pay.

Principal Creditor – A creditor whose claim is superior to the claim of all other creditors.

Junior Creditor – A creditor whose claim is inferior to the claim of another creditor; also known as a *secondary creditor.*

Domestic Creditor – A creditor who lives in the same state or country as the person who is borrowing the money.

Foreign Creditor – A creditor who lives in a different state or country than the person who is borrowing the money.

Single Creditor – A creditor who has claim to a single fund of the debtor.

Double Creditor – A creditor who has a claim to more than one fund of the debtor's.

Joint Creditor – Two or more creditors who are entitled to repayment of the same loan.

Lien Creditor – A creditor who has placed a lien on the property of the debtor in order to help secure the debt.

TYPES OF CREDIT

Different terms are used to describe the types of credit a debtor may receive. Classifications of credit are based on who issues the credit or how the loan is to be repaid.

INSTALLMENT CREDIT

Bank credit is credit granted by a bank based either on a credit rating or security given for the credit to a person who can draw upon the credit up to the set limit. The credit that is granted may be **installment credit,** whereby the buyer pays for an item in more than one payment. Usually payments are of an equal amount, and a finance charge is included. A **finance charge** is an amount of money that is paid for being allowed to purchase an item by paying installments. For example, Emma is financing the purchase of a new car; she will have a set number of payments that are of the same amount. The monthly payment is the amount that is paid each month until the debt is paid in full.

REVOLVING, OPEN, AND REVOCABLE CREDIT

An account may be a **revolving credit** account, one that allows the borrower to purchase goods on a continuing basis as long as the outstanding balance does not exceed a certain limit. This is the type of credit that is most frequently represented by a credit card. The more a person charges, the more his or her monthly payment will be. There may be a minimum monthly payment, but the amount that is due each month is not a set amount but is based on the amount of money borrowed by using the credit.

Open credit is a line of credit extended up to a certain amount without requiring additional security or without having to reestablish the limit. For example, Abdul has an open credit account with a limit of $10,000. She can use up to that amount without having to give any more security for the repayment of the loan. **Revocable credit** can be withdrawn or canceled before the expiration date and without consent of the person to whom it was issued. Revocable credit is primarily used in foreign trade. Exhibit 19-2 is a summary of the types of credit available.

EXHIBIT 19-2	TYPES OF CREDIT

Installment Credit – Set number of equal payments that include a finance charge.
Revolving Credit – Credit limit is set; the monthly payment is based on how much is owed.
Open Credit – Set amount that can be used without having to provide additional security.
Revocable Credit – Line of credit that can be cancelled at any time without consent of the debtor.

TRUTH IN LENDING ACT

The above types of credit are governed by the **Truth in Lending Act,** a federal law that mandates that every customer who is seeking credit is to be given meaningful information about the cost of the credit. The credit cost must be given in the dollar amount of finance charges as well as in an annual percentage rate. The purpose of these requirements is to allow the customer to compare different credit terms available and make an informed choice.

CONSUMER CREDIT

A separate classification of credit just for consumers is known as **consumer credit,** which is a short-term loan to individuals for the purchase of consumer goods and services. **Consumer goods** are goods that are used or bought primarily for personal, family, or household purposes.

CONSUMER CREDIT SALES

A **consumer credit sale** is any sale in which consumer credit is extended or arranged by the seller. In a **consumer credit transaction,** credit is extended to a real person; the money, property, or service that is the subject of the transaction is primarily for personal, family, household, or agricultural use. For example, Luci goes to her local car dealer and arranges financing for a new car through the dealership. The loan that is arranged through the dealership is for five years, and the car will be the primary family car. This is a consumer credit sale because the car—the consumer good—was purchased using credit that was arranged by the dealer, the seller of the consumer good.

CONSUMER CREDIT PROTECTION ACTS

Consumer credit is governed by a number of consumer credit protection acts, federal and state laws that safeguard the consumer by requiring full disclosure of the terms and conditions of finance charges in credit transactions and offers to extend credit. Consumer credit protection acts also restrict the garnishment of wages and regulate the use of credit cards. These acts include the Equal Credit Opportunity Act, the Fair Debt Collection Practices Act (see below), the Fair Credit Billing Act, the Fair Credit Reporting Act, and the Truth in Lending Act (see above).

The **Equal Credit Opportunity Act,** 15 U.S.C. § 1691, is a federal law that prohibits a creditor from discriminating in the granting of credit because of race, color, religion, national origin, age, sex, or marital status. The **Fair Credit Reporting Act,** 15 U.S.C. § 1681, regulates credit reporting agencies to insure that their activities are conducted in a fair and equitable manner. The consumer is granted several rights by this Act, including:

1. A right to privacy of the information collected
2. A right to notice of reporting activities, that is, to know when information about the consumer has been given to someone
3. A right of access to the information in the reports
4. A right to correct erroneous information contained in the credit report and other reports. See Exhibit 19-3.

EXHIBIT 19-3	CONSUMER RIGHTS ACCORDING TO THE FAIR CREDIT REPORTING ACT

1. Right to privacy of the information collected
2. Right to know when information that has been collected has been given to someone
3. Right of access to all of the information contained in credit reports
4. Right to rectify incorrect information in the credit report or any other reports generated

The **Fair Credit Billing Act,** 15 U.S.C. § 1666, provides for the settlement of billing error disputes and places an obligation on credit card companies for the quality of the merchandise purchased by their cardholders. See Exhibit 19-4 for a summary of the consumer credit protection acts.

EXHIBIT 19-4	SUMMARY OF CONSUMER CREDIT PROTECTION ACTS

Equal Credit Opportunity Act – Establishes that a creditor cannot discriminate in the granting of credit because of race, color, religion, national origin, age, sex, or marital status.

Fair Credit Reporting Act – Provides that consumer credit reporting activities must be conducted in a fair and equitable manner.

Fair Credit Billing Act – Sets out how billing errors and disputes are settled and places an obligation on credit card companies to assure the quality of merchandise purchased by the cardholder.

CREDIT DEVICES

There are several ways that credit is extended to businesses and people. There are terms used to define the source of the credit and the type of credit the person is receiving. Loans are also classified according to how the loan is to be repaid, the purpose of the loan, and the interest rate of the loan.

GENERAL LOAN PRINCIPLES

A **loan** is the giving by one party to another party of a sum of money based on an express or implied agreement for repayment either with or without interest. Classifications of loans are based on how they are secured, who borrows the money, what the money is to be used for, or how the money is to be repaid.

An **amortized loan** has periodic payments that are applied to the interest first and then applied to the principal according to the terms of the loan. When Samantha makes a payment on her home loan—an amortized loan—a set amount of the payment is used to pay the interest and the rest is applied to the actual amount borrowed. See Exhibit 19-5 for an example of an amortized loan payment.

EXHIBIT 19-5	AMORTIZED LOAN PAYMENT

$1200 – Amount of the loan payment
$800 – Applied to interest
$400 – Applied to the amount borrowed, the principal
The amount that is applied to principal and interest can change over the term of the loan.

CALL, DEMAND, AND INSTALLMENT LOANS

A **call loan** (also called a **demand loan**) is payable on demand, or when it is "called" by the lender. There may or may not be a definite date that payment is due, but the entire amount can become due if the lender demands payment. An **installment loan** is a loan that is repaid over a period of time in installments that are established in the loan agreement. For example, Debbie and Benny buy new furniture and sign an agreement in which they agree to pay $45 per month for three years for a total of $1620. The furniture listed at $1400: Payments they will make include part of the principal and part of the interest that is being charged. The number of installments and the amount of each payment is set out in the agreement.

A **time loan** is set for a fixed period of time and cannot be repaid before the expiration of time set out in the agreement. If the loan is repaid early, there may be a penalty imposed. A **term loan** has a definite maturity date when the loan is due to be repaid. Exhibit 19-6 shows classifications of loans.

EXHIBIT 19-6	CLASSIFICATION OF LOANS BASED ON REPAYMENT TERMS

Call Loan – A loan that is payable on demand or when it is "called" by the lender.

Demand Loan – A loan where the lender may demand repayment at any time; another term for *call loan*.

Installment Loan – A loan that is repaid over a period of time by installments that are established in the loan agreement.

Time Loan – A loan for a fixed period of time that cannot be repaid before the expiration of the time set out in the agreement.

Term Loan – A loan with a definite maturity date, a specific date when the loan is due to be repaid.

CLASSIFICATIONS OF LOANS BASED ON THE LENGTH OF THE LOAN

Loans are also classified on the basis of the length of repayment term. A **commercial loan** is a short-term loan—usually thirty to ninety days—given to businesses. A **short-term loan** is issued for less than a year and is usually shown to exist by note or other negotiable document. (See Chapter 20, Commercial Paper.) A very short-term loan called a **morning loan** is usually issued to allow a stock broker to carry out his or her business for a particular day.

A **bridge loan** is a short-term loan used to cover the down payment and other costs associated with the purchase or construction of another home pending the sale of the existing home. A bridge loan provides a bridge for the ownership of one home to another. Cathy and Butch own one home but want to start building another home while they wait for the sale of their current home to close. In order to do this, they get a bridge loan to cover the initial costs of the construction of their new home. The rest of the cost will be paid using the proceeds from the sale of their first home. A **construction loan** is a short-term loan used to finance the cost of constructing a building; payments are made periodically as the work is completed. See Exhibit 19-7 for a summary of how loans are classified based on the length of the loan.

EXHIBIT 19-7	CLASSIFICATIONS OF LOANS BASED ON THE LENGTH OF THE LOAN

Commercial Loan – A short-term loan, usually for thirty to ninety days, generally issued to businesses.

Short-Term Loan – A loan for less than a year, usually shown to exist by a note or other negotiable document.

Morning Loan – A very short-term loan, usually to allow a stock broker to carry out business for that day.

Bridge Loan – A short-term loan used to cover the down payment and other costs associated with the purchase or construction of another home pending the sale of the existing home.

Construction Loan – A short-term loan used to finance the cost of constructing a building; payments are made periodically as the work is completed.

FURTHER CLASSIFICATIONS OF LOANS

Loans are also classified based on who is borrowing the money, what the money is to be used for, or on the interest rate. A **consumer loan** is made to a person for family, household, personal, or agricultural purposes. This type of loan is usually governed by the Truth in Lending Act. A **personal loan** is one made for a short period of time for a personal use; it may be secured or unsecured. A **consolidation loan** is used to pay off several debts to create one, more manageable payment.

A **fixed rate loan** carries a set interest rate; this rate does not go up or down regardless of the prime interest rate. In a **variable rate loan,** on the other hand, the interest rate can go up or down depending on the fluctuations in the prime interest rate. See Exhibit 19-8.

EXHIBIT 19-8	CLASSIFICATIONS OF LOANS BASED ON THE PURPOSE OF THE LOAN AND THE INTEREST RATE

Personal Loan – A loan used for personal purposes.

PURPOSE OF THE LOAN

Consolidation Loan – The money is used to pay off several other debts, creating one payment rather than several payments.

Consumer Loan – A loan made for family, household, personal, or agricultural purposes.

INTEREST RATE

Fixed Rate Loan – The interest rate on the loan is set and will not go up or down during the period of the loan.

Variable Rate Loan – The interest rate on the loan can go up or down depending on fluctuations in the prime interest rate.

SECURED AND UNSECURED LOANS

Loans are also classified on the basis of whether or not they are secured and what is used to secure them. A **collateral loan** is secured by property or securities; the property securing the loan can be real property or personal property. A **commodity loan** is a type of collateral loan secured by a commodity such as cotton, wool, wheat, or other products. A **nonrecourse loan** is made only to farmers by the national government in exchange for a particular commodity, such as wheat, rice, or corn. This loan is labeled *nonrecourse* because the government is not allowed (has no recourse) to demand payment of the loan.

An **equity loan** is one available to homeowners based on and secured by the equity an owner has in his or her home. *Equity* is the difference between what the house is worth less the amount the homeowner still owes on the mortgage. The amount that can be borrowed using an equity loan is limited by the amount of equity in the home.

A **participation loan** is a loan that involves several banks. Instead of one bank lending a large sum of money, several banks lend a part of the amount, thereby spreading the risk of the loan over several banks instead of just one. A **loan commitment** is the commitment a lender makes to a borrower that the lender will lend a specific amount at a definite rate on a particular piece of real estate. This commitment is usually for a limited period of time; the amount of time is based on the estimated length of time it will take the borrower to construct or buy a home.

CHARGE ACCOUNTS AND CREDIT CARDS

A person can show he or she has the necessary credit to buy an item using credit in several ways. The ability to use credit may be indicated by the issuance of a **credit card**—a card, plate, or other similar credit device used for obtaining money, property, labor, or services on credit. A credit card can be used for personal or commercial transactions; possession of the card indicates there is a charge account. A **charge account** is a system of purchasing goods and services on credit. Under the terms of the charge account, the consumer agrees to make payments on the balance within a specified period of time. An **equity card** is a type of credit card where the amount of credit is determined by the amount of equity a person has in his or her home. When an item is charged using the equity card, the equity in the home secures the amount charged on the card.

Credit cards are an example of an **open-end credit plan,** which is credit granted pursuant to a plan where it is anticipated that there will not be a one time transaction but rather a series of credit transactions. See Exhibit 19-9. The credit terms are initially established, but there is no fixed amount of debt. For example, Maura has a credit card with a $3,000 credit limit. She does not owe $3,000; that is how much credit she has available. When Maura starts charging items, she will have to start making payments because that is when she has actually "borrowed" some of the $3,000 available to her. When purchases are made, the amount charged is added to the outstanding balance. Each new purchase is another extension of credit.

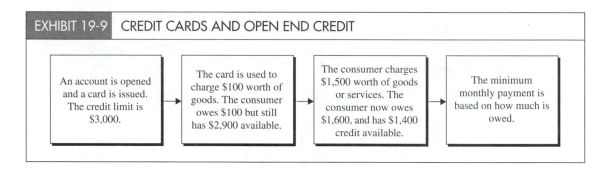

EXHIBIT 19-9   CREDIT CARDS AND OPEN END CREDIT

An account is opened and a card is issued. The credit limit is $3,000. → The card is used to charge $100 worth of goods. The consumer owes $100 but still has $2,900 available. → The consumer charges $1,500 worth of goods or services. The consumer now owes $1,600, and has $1,400 credit available. → The minimum monthly payment is based on how much is owed.

Because of the nature of credit cards, **credit card crime** can occur. In this type of criminal activity, a person uses a credit card to obtain property or services knowing that the card is stolen, forged, revoked, or cancelled.

LETTERS OF CREDIT

The ability to use credit in commercial transactions may be indicated by a letter of credit. A **letter of credit** is an **engagement**—a contract or agreement that is an exchange of mutual promises—made by a bank or person at the request of the customer that the issuer of the letter of credit will honor drafts or other demands for payment based on the conditions stated in the letter. For example, a bank issues a letter of credit for $10,000. The borrower can order payment for things up to $10,000 in value. The credit may either be revocable or irrevocable.

There are several types of letters of credit. In an **irrevocable letter of credit,** the issuing bank agrees that it will not withdraw the line of credit or cancel it before the expiration date. A **revocable letter of credit,** on the other hand, is a letter in which the bank that issued the credit reserves the right to cancel the line of credit after giving proper notice. A **general letter of credit** is addressed to no one in particular. A **special letter of credit** names an individual, a firm, or a corporation. An **open letter of credit** is unrestricted and will be paid when a simple draft is presented. A **revolving letter of credit** is a self-renewing letter; the unused portion of the letter is cumulative. The maximum amount cannot be exceeded, but with payment of the amount borrowed, the debtor has that much credit available again. For example, Gretel has a $20,000 letter of credit, and she uses $2,000 of it. If the letter of credit is a revolving letter, Gretel still has $18,000 in credit available. Once Gretel repays the $2,000 and any other amounts she charged using the letter, she once again has $20,000 in credit available.

A **commercial letter of credit** is used by a person who is purchasing some type of merchandise. This individual sends the letter to a bank in the area that he is doing business in and the seller presents the bill of sale or other proof of the sale to the bank to be paid. The bank that paid the money will then make a demand for payment to the bank that issued the letter of credit. In a **confirmed letter of credit,** a local bank gives a guarantee that a demand for payment from the seller will be honored even if the bank that issued the letter of credit refuses or fails to honor it. If the bank that issued the letter does not pay, the bank that has the letter will pay the amount demanded.

An **export letter of credit** is sent to an exporter of goods explaining that a line of credit has been established in the exporter's favor by a foreign bank and that the bank agrees to honor the exporter's draft for the goods purchased. An **import letter of credit** is issued by a foreign bank to a local seller allowing the seller to write a draft on the foreign bank for the shipment of merchandise. A **traveler's letter of credit** can be used by a borrower when traveling overseas. The issuing bank authorizes the payment of funds in the local currency by a local bank. The borrower writes a check drawn on the issuing bank, and the local bank forwards it to the issuing bank for the credit. A **transferable letter of credit** allows a person to assign the right to use the credit to another person.

DEBT

When a person borrows money (that is, uses a credit card, a line of credit, or a letter of credit), he or she goes into **debt,** a specific sum of money that one person owes to another, including the obligation to pay and the right to receive and enforce payment. The person who borrows money is a **debtor.**

TYPES OF DEBT

A **matured debt** is unconditionally due and owing. If a debt is mature, nothing has to happen in order for it to be collected; it is due now. A debt can be a **liquidated debt,** where it is certain how much is due, or it can be an **unliquidated debt,** which is an obligation that has not been reduced to a specific monetary amount. A debt can be a **fixed debt,** a more or less permanent form of debt that must be paid back. A debt can be a **contingent debt,** one that is not presently fixed, but may become so in the future with the occurrence of some uncertain event.

Debts owed can be categorized in several ways. **Active debt** is a current debt to which interest is added and that is currently due and payable. An example is a monthly credit card bill: The debt is a current debt, and interest is added to the debt monthly until the total amount due is paid in full. If less than the total amount of the debt is paid, interest is added to the remaining amount until the debt is paid in full. A **passive debt** is one on which no interest is payable; this type of debt is based on an agreement between the debtor and creditor. **Consumer debt** is incurred by an individual primarily for a personal, family, or household purpose. **Existing debt** is an existing legal liability—a debt that a person owes that has not been paid in full. **Fraudulent debt** is created by fraudulent practices used by the debtor. A **bad debt** is an uncollectible account receivable, an uncollectible debt. An **unsecured debt** is a debt that is not backed by pledged **collateral,** property that is pledged as security for the satisfaction of the debt, or a security agreement. The only thing the creditor has to help enforce payment of the debt is the promise of the debtor that the debt will be repaid. A **secured debt** is one secured by collateral; the creditor has an interest in the property of the debtor that can be used to satisfy the debt. A secured debt is also a **preferential debt:** it is paid before others in case the debtor becomes insolvent. Exhibit 19-10 is a summary of the different types of debt.

EXHIBIT 19-10 TYPES OF DEBT

Matured Debt – Debt that is currently due. Nothing has to happen in order for the debt to be collected.

Liquidated Debt – The total amount that is due is known with certainty.

Unliquidated Debt – It is not known exactly how much is owed; a specific monetary amount has not yet been determined.

Active Debt – Current debt that has interest added each month and that is due and payable. Interest is added as long as there is debt.

Passive Debt – No interest is being added to the amount that is due. This type of debt is created by an agreement between the debtor and the creditor.

Unsecured Debt – The only thing that helps insure payment of the debt is the promise from the debtor that the money will be repaid.

Secured Debt – Property is pledged as a security for the repayment of the debt. The creditor can make a claim against the property if the debtor does not pay.

DEBT COLLECTION

If a debtor starts falling behind in payments, the collection efforts of the creditor are regulated by the **Fair Debt Collection Practices Act,** a federal act that prohibits abusive debt collection practices by debt collectors. It limits the times collection agencies can call the debtor at home or at work, gives the debtor the right to see proof of the debt in writing, and gives the debtor the right to dispute the amount owed.

SECURITY INTERESTS

If the debtor becomes **insolvent** (is no longer able to pay bills) and **defaults** (fails to pay the amount due), a creditor wants to be a secured creditor. A **secured creditor** is one who holds some special assurance of payment, such as a **security interest.** This is a form of interest in property that provides that the property may be sold if the debtor defaults, so that the obligation for which the security interest was originally granted can be satisfied.

A security interest can be in real property or personal property: Both types of property can be used to secure a debt. In either case, if the debtor fails to pay the amount of money that was borrowed, the secured creditor has the right to seize the property, sell it, and apply the proceeds against the amount the debtor still owes.

An **unsecured creditor** does not have any assurance of payment other than the debtor's agreement that the amount will be paid. The unsecured creditor has no interest in property or any other asset that can be seized and sold to satisfy all or part of the debt. If the debtor becomes insolvent, the unsecured creditor is the last creditor to be paid.

A security interest can be created by a **security agreement**—an agreement granting the creditor a security interest in personal property. A security interest can also be a **purchase money security interest,** which is taken by the seller of an item to secure the item or by a creditor who loans funds to purchase the property so the creditor can have security interest in the item purchased. For example, Kelly uses a credit card to buy a new lawnmower. The company that issued the card, as part of the credit agreement, may have a security interest in the lawnmower because the credit card company advanced Kelly the funds to pay for the item.

If a creditor has a security interest in personal property, the creditor will want to perfect the security interest to make its claim to the property effective. **Perfection of security interest** is the process used to protect a security interest against competing claims to the same collateral. In order to perfect the interest, the secured party is usually required to give public notice that this security interest is in existence. Notification is usually accomplished by filing the notice with the appropriate state official, usually the office of the secretary of state. When notification is filed with the appropriate state office, the process is completed and the security interest is **perfected.** In the event of default, the secured creditor will receive money first, ahead of any unsecured creditor, if the collateral the creditor has a security interest in is sold. See Exhibit 19-11 for a flow chart showing how a security interest is created.

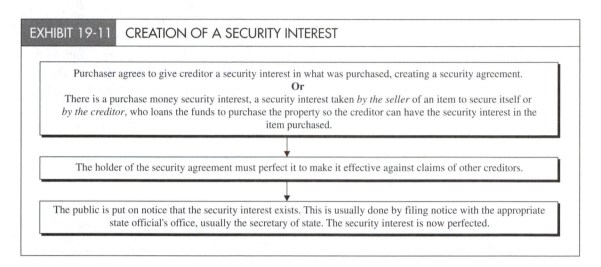

EXHIBIT 19-11 CREATION OF A SECURITY INTEREST

Purchaser agrees to give creditor a security interest in what was purchased, creating a security agreement.

Or

There is a purchase money security interest, a security interest taken *by the seller* of an item to secure itself or *by the creditor*, who loans the funds to purchase the property so the creditor can have the security interest in the item purchased.

The holder of the security agreement must perfect it to make it effective against claims of other creditors.

The public is put on notice that the security interest exists. This is usually done by filing notice with the appropriate state official's office, usually the secretary of state. The security interest is now perfected.

MORTGAGES

As stated in Chapter 12, a **mortgage** is a security interest in real property—land. The security interest is created by a written agreement between the debtor and the creditor. The real property secures the loan, and the loan is used to purchase the property. In the event of default, the real property can be sold and the proceeds applied against the amount of unpaid debt.

SECOND MORTGAGES

A **second mortgage** is the second one in a series of mortgages that ranks immediately after the first mortgage on the property and is entitled to payment out of the proceeds of a sale after the first mortgage has been paid. See Exhibit 19-12.

EXHIBIT 19-12 FIRST AND SECOND MORTGAGES

Amount of the first mortgage: $100,000
Amount of second mortgage: $50,000
Debtor defaults on both mortgages.
Property is seized and sold for $125,000.
First mortgage holder receives $100,000.
Creditor who holds the second mortgage is still owed $25,000.

DEFAULTING ON A MORTGAGE

If a debtor defaults on a mortgage, the creditor has the right to seize and sell the property that secured the mortgage in an attempt to recover the amount of money still owed. If the mortgage was a **blanket mortgage,** the creditor can go after additional property, not just the property that was purchased using the loan. If the property is seized, the debtor has a right of **redemption:** the repurchase (buying back) of property that has been sold. **Right of redemption** is usually limited to the buying back of real property, not personal property. The **redemption period** is the length of time a debtor has to redeem a defaulted mortgage. Under the right of redemption, a debtor who defaults on a mortgage has a limited period of time to pay the amount that is past due and buy back the property.

If a debtor defaults on a mortgage, the holder of the mortgage can start a foreclosure action against the debtor. **Foreclosure** is a termination of all the rights the mortgagor has in the property covered by the mortgage. If the mortgage goes to foreclosure, the debtor loses the right of redemption. In a **foreclosure decree,** the court orders the sale of the premises and the satisfaction of the mortgage out of the proceeds. A **foreclosure sale** is the actual sale of the property to obtain satisfaction of the mortgage out of the proceeds. Exhibit 19-13 is a flow chart showing what happens when a mortgage default occurs.

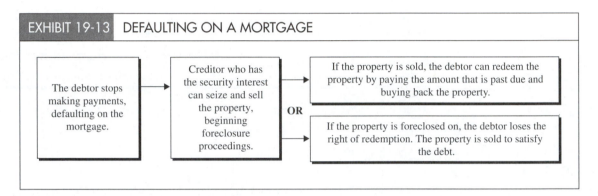

EXHIBIT 19-13 | DEFAULTING ON A MORTGAGE

The debtor stops making payments, defaulting on the mortgage. → Creditor who has the security interest can seize and sell the property, beginning foreclosure proceedings. → If the property is sold, the debtor can redeem the property by paying the amount that is past due and buying back the property.

OR

If the property is foreclosed on, the debtor loses the right of redemption. The property is sold to satisfy the debt.

LIENS

A **lien** is a claim, encumbrance, or charge on property for payment of some debt, obligation, or duty; a lien is also a security interest in the property of the debtor. A **lien creditor** is a creditor whose claim is secured by a lien on a particular piece or type of property. There are several types of liens depending upon how they were created or who holds the lien.

LIENS BY OPERATION OF LAW: ARTISAN'S AND MECHANIC'S LIENS

A **lien by operation of law** is created by the law itself and thus does not require the consent of the parties. If the lien is created by statute, it is a **statutory lien.** An **artisan's lien** is given to a person who has made improvements and added value to another's personal property as security for payment for the services performed. For example, Tyler, an independent computer technician, upgrades Moshe's computer. Tyler has a lien on the computer until his bill is paid because he performed a service that improved Moshe's personal property. A **mechanic's lien** is a statutory lien for the purpose of securing priority payment of an amount owed for work performed and materials furnished in constructing, improving, or repairing a building. A mechanic's lien attaches to the land as well as to the building that was improved or repaired. An artisan's lien applies to personal property; a mechanic's lien applies to real property.

FLOATING LIENS

A **floating lien** is a lien on collateral that applies even when the collateral changes in character or location. For example, a company takes out a loan to buy goods and the creditor is given a lien on the goods. As the goods are sold, the goods that have the lien on them are gone, but the floating lien applies to the new goods that are brought in to replace the goods sold. Under the floating lien doctrine, the lien "floats" over the goods and does not attach to specific goods until the debtor defaults. If the debtor defaults, then the lien "drops down" and attaches to the goods currently in the debtor's possession. See Exhibit 19-14.

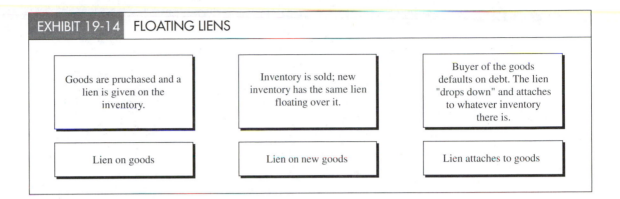

EXHIBIT 19-14   FLOATING LIENS

Goods are pruchased and a lien is given on the inventory.	Inventory is sold; new inventory has the same lien floating over it.	Buyer of the goods defaults on debt. The lien "drops down" and attaches to whatever inventory there is.
Lien on goods	Lien on new goods	Lien attaches to goods

BANKRUPTCY

GENERAL PRINCIPLES

Imagine this: Business is bad and getting worse, but creditors still want to be paid. There are phone calls and threatening letters. A lawsuit has actually commenced. In dire circumstances such as these, there is an option available to businesses and individuals: declare bankruptcy. Being **bankrupt** (*bank*-rupt) is the state or condition of a person, a partnership, a corporation, or a municipality that is unable to pay its debts as they become due. **Contemplation of bankruptcy** is the process by which a debtor considers measures that might need to be taken as a result of financial inability to pay debts.

Bankruptcy is governed by the **Bankruptcy** (*bank*-rupt-see) **Code,** the federal law that provides for the benefit of creditors and the relief of debtors in cases where the debtor is unable or unwilling to pay his or her debts. Because bankruptcy is governed by federal law, the Federal Bankruptcy Court has exclusive jurisdiction to hear all bankruptcy proceedings. The bankruptcy judge is the person responsible for overseeing the proceedings.

FILING THE PETITION

If a person or business decides to declare bankruptcy, the first step is the filing of the **petition in bankruptcy** (pǝ-*tish*-ǝn in *bank*-rupt-see), a document filed with the bankruptcy court by a debtor seeking the relief provided for under the Bankruptcy Code. The petition will have a listing of all of the creditors of the debtor and the amounts each creditor is owed. Bankruptcy can be a **voluntary proceeding** begun by a debtor, or it can be an **involuntary proceeding** initiated by creditors of an insolvent debtor, basically forcing the debtor into bankruptcy. When the voluntary petition is filed, an **automatic stay**—which bars all debt collection efforts against the debtor and his or her property—is issued immediately. All phone calls, all threatening letters, all court proceedings stop. A **stay** is an act that stops a judicial proceeding by an order of the court. However, there is no requirement in the Bankruptcy Code that the bankruptcy court issue an order for automatic stay; the filing of the petition is enough to put the stay in place. The debtor is also required to file a **bankruptcy schedule,** a listing of the debtor's **assets** (*ass*-ets), property of all kinds, real and personal, tangible and intangible, all liabilities, and all secured and unsecured creditors.

BANKRUPTCY ESTATE

When the bankruptcy petition is filed, all the property of the debtor—all legal and equitable interests in property that the debtor owns—becomes part of the **bankruptcy estate.** All assets of the debtor initially become part of the bankruptcy estate; however, some of the debtor's property is **exempt,** (eg-*zempt*), or relieved from the bankruptcy estate. The debtor will claim his or her **exemption** (eg-*zemp*-shən), the privilege allowed by law to the debtor that allows him or her to retain property up to a certain amount or to have certain classes of property free from liability or bankruptcy.

The **Homestead Exemption** (*home*-sted eg-*zemp*-shən) was created by statute, and allows a householder or head of a family to designate his or her dwelling and adjoining land as his or her **homestead.** The homestead is exempt from remaining in the bankruptcy estate: It was included initially, but is removed from the estate by a debtor's claiming the homestead exemption. However, a debtor is not allowed to claim an unlimited amount of property as the homestead; how much a debtor is allowed to claim depends on the homestead exemption claimed. The **state homestead exemption** is the amount a debtor can claim under state law; this amount varies from state to state. The **federal homestead exemption** is the amount of property a debtor can claim as exempt from the bankruptcy estate under federal law. See Exhibit 19-15 for a listing of the state and federal homestead exemptions.

EXHIBIT 19-15	FEDERAL AND STATE HOMESTEAD EXEMPTIONS

FEDERAL EXEMPTION—11 U.S.C. § 522: $17,425 IS EXEMPT FROM BANKRUPTCY ESTATE

Alabama – $5000

Alaska – $64,800

Arizona – $100,000 can be claimed as exempt from bankruptcy estate

Arkansas – Rural, one acre of land with a value of up to $2,500; urban, 160 acres of land with a value of up to $2,500

California – Either $50,000, $75,000, or $100,000, depending on the circumstances

Colorado – $45,000

Connecticut – Market value cannot exceed $75,000

Delaware – Only property held by tenancy by the entirety

Florida – Unlimited in value; cannot exceed one-half acre in municipality or 160 contiguous acres elsewhere

Georgia – $10,000

Hawaii – One acre, maximum value of $30,000, if married or over 63; $20,000 for all others

Idaho – Net value of $50,000 or less

Illinois – $7,500

Indiana – $7,500

Iowa – Unlimited as to value; cannot exceed one-half acre urban; 40 acres rural

Kansas – Rural, 160 acres; urban, one acre

Kentucky – $5,000

Louisiana – $25,000 and a 200-acre limit

Maine – $50,000 or $25,000

Maryland – $2,500

Massachusetts – $300,000

Michigan – $3,500 up to 40 acres

Minnesota – $200,000 to $500,000

Mississippi – $75,000 in value up to 160 acres

Missouri – $8,000

Montana – $100,000 if single; $200,000 if married

Nebraska – $12,500

Nevada – $125,000

New Hampshire – $50,000

New Jersey – No stated homestead exemption

New Mexico – $30,000

New York – $10,000

North Carolina – $10,000

North Dakota – $80,000

Ohio – $5,000

Oklahoma – $50,000

Oregon – $25,000 for one; $33,000 for joint; limited to one block urban; 160 acres rural

Rhode Island – $100,000

South Carolina – $5,000

South Dakota – $30,000

Tennessee – $5,000

Texas – One acre of urban property; 200 acres or rural property

Utah – $20,000 if single; $40,000 if married

Vermont – $75,000

Virginia – $5,000 plus $500 per dependent

Washington State – $40,000

West Virginia – $25,000

Wisconsin – $40,000

Wyoming – $10,000

FIRST MEETING OF THE CREDITORS

Once the bankruptcy petition is filed, a date for the **first meeting of the creditors** will be set. This is the initial meeting called by the court of the listed creditors and the creditors who have filed a proof of claim so their claims can be reviewed and the debtor can be questioned. A **proof of claim** is a statement made under oath, filed as part of the bankruptcy proceeding by a creditor. A **claim** is a right to payment regardless of whether the right is established by a judgment, and regardless of whether it is a secured or unsecured debt. A claim is simply the right to receive payment from a debtor for a debt. A creditor sets out the amount owed him or her through a proof of claim and provides sufficient detail to identify the basis for the claim. The court will also appoint a **bankruptcy trustee** (trus-*tee*), an employee of the court who is to take charge of the estate, collect assets, bring suit if required, defend any actions filed against the estate, and otherwise administer the estate.

TYPES OF BANKRUPTCY

An individual or business debtor has options about which type of bankruptcy to file. A **straight bankruptcy** is a Chapter 7 bankruptcy, the type of bankruptcy most people think about when they hear the term *bankruptcy*. A **rehabilitative bankruptcy** is a Chapter 11, Chapter 12, or Chapter 13 bankruptcy.

For example, Marcus earns $1,200 a month, but has to pay $2,000 per month to keep his bills current. He has little if any assets, no homestead, and not much of anything else. Marcus could choose to file for straight, or **Chapter 7 bankruptcy,** which **liquidates** or converts assets to cash by selling any of the debtor's property that is nonexempt and then paying the creditors using the proceeds from the sale, thereby discharging the debtor from any remaining debt. A Chapter 7 bankruptcy can be voluntary or involuntary. The bankruptcy court supervises the liquidation process through the bankruptcy trustee.

To understand rehabilitative bankruptcy, consider the case of Daryl and Meryl. Hoping to cash in on the popularity of Tex-Mex restaurants, they decide to open a restaurant combining Mexican and Chinese cuisines. They take out several loans and open their restaurant, D and M's Mexanese, hoping to get rich by selling franchises. Unfortunately, monthly income from the restaurant is far below the monthly payments on the loans they took out. Rather than totally wiping out the business, Daryl and Meryl chose to file a **Chapter 11 bankruptcy,** a bankruptcy that allows for **business reorganization.** The debtor business is allowed to continue to operate under court supervision until the plan of reorganization is prepared. The **reorganization plan** specifies how the business will continue to operate and pay its creditors, and must be approved by at least two-thirds of the business's creditors. The plan will operate for a period of five to seven years. If Daryl and Meryl are allowed by their creditors to continue to remain in control of the business, they are the **debtors in possession.**

If the business is insolvent, it may go into **receivership.** A **receiver** is appointed by the court to protect the assets of the business and ultimately sell the assets and distribute the proceeds from the sale to any creditors. The receiver that is appointed is usually the bankruptcy trustee, but it may be someone other than the bankruptcy trustee.

To understand a Chapter 12 bankruptcy, consider Harold's case. Harold his own successful consulting business about how to farm. He also owns a small farm, which has been in his family for generations. Currently, the farm is not doing well because prices for supplies are too high and prices for produce are too low. Harold may decide to file a **Chapter 12 bankruptcy,** which is also known as a **family farmer bankruptcy.** A **family farmer** is defined as a person or a person and spouse who are engaged in a farming operation whose aggregate debts do not exceed $1,500,000; at least 80% of the debt, excluding the debt on a home, comes from the farming operation; and more than 50% of gross income derives from the farm operation. See Exhibit 19-16 for a summary of these requirements.

EXHIBIT 19-16	FAMILY FARMER BANKRUPTCY

1. The person who files for bankruptcy is engaged in a farming operation.
2. Aggregate debts do not exceed $1,500,000.
3. At least 80% of the debt, excluding any mortgage on a home, comes from the farming operation.
4. More than 50% of the gross income comes from the farming operation.

A corporation or partnership can also claim status as a family farm if more than 50% of the stock or equity in the partnership is owned by one family, or one family and its relatives; the family and its relatives run the farming operation; the farming operation's aggregate debts do not exceed $1,500,000; at least 80% of the debt, excluding the debt on a home, comes from the farming operation; and more than 50% of gross income derives from the farm operation. The Bankruptcy Code provides for special debt repayment relief for a family farmer who has regular income that is sufficiently stable and regular enough to enable the farmer to make payments under the plan.

Persons who accumulate too much consumer debt (debt incurred by an individual primarily for personal, family, or household purposes) may choose to file a **Chapter 13 bankruptcy** or **wage earner's plan.** Any insolvent debtor who is a **wage earner** (a person who earns wages, a salary, or commission) can create and file a plan with the court that provides him or her with more time to pay off creditors. In order to file this type of bankruptcy, the wage earner must be an individual with regular income, income that is sufficiently stable and regular to enable the person to make payments under a Chapter 13 plan. The plan must provide that future earnings will be subject to the supervision and control of the bankruptcy trustee until all debts are satisfied. If the wage earner is unable to pay his or her debts using the plan, then he or she can still file a Chapter 7 bankruptcy. Creditors have the right to approve or file objections to the plan. However, the court can confirm (approve) a Chapter 11, 12, or 13 plan over the objections of creditors. This is known as **cram down:** the creditors have the plan forced upon them—"crammed down their throats."

PAYMENT AND DISCHARGE

Once a Chapter 7 bankruptcy is filed and any nonexempt property is sold, proceeds will need to be distributed. Under a Chapter 11, Chapter 12, or Chapter 13 plan, creditors will be paid based on the distribution schedule established in the bankruptcy plan. **Distribution is the sharing or parceling out of money to creditors.** How the money is distributed depends on the **priority** established, the ranking of competing claims to the same property or money. In bankruptcy proceedings, this priority is established by federal statute, the Federal Bankruptcy Code. In a Chapter 7 bankruptcy, priority claims are paid before any other claims; in a Chapter 11 plan, priority creditors must be paid in full before anyone else is paid. Secured creditors have priority claims. The usual order of priority follows:

- secured creditors
- the costs of preserving and administering the debtor's estate
- unpaid wage claims
- certain claims of farmers or fishermen
- refunds of security deposits
- alimony and child support
- taxes
- general (unsecured) creditors who filed a proof of claim

Unsecured creditors are the last to be paid, so there may be nothing left for these creditors to collect. See Exhibit 19-17 for the order of priority of paying debts.

EXHIBIT 19-17	ORDER OF PRIORITY OF PAYING DEBTS IN A BANKRUPTCY

1. Secured creditors
2. Costs of the bankruptcy
3. Unpaid wage claims
4. Certain claims of farmers and fishermen
5. Refunds of security deposits
6. Alimony and child support
7. Taxes
8. Unsecured creditors

Sometimes after a bankruptcy petition is filed, a debtor and creditors enter into a **workout,** an out-of-court settlement by which the debtor enters into an agreement that provides for payment or discharge of debt. In a workout, a debtor may not show preference for one creditor over another. An insolvent debtor shows **preference** by paying or securing all or part of the debt owed to one or more creditors to the detriment of other creditors. One creditor cannot be put into a better position than another creditor with regard to their priority claims to the assets of the debtor. If this happens, the bankruptcy trustee may disallow the preferential payment or transfer of property. The creditor would have to repay the payments received or release the security interest on the property.

Upon the successful completion of a bankruptcy plan or the conclusion of a Chapter 7 bankruptcy, the debtor is **discharged,** or released from all of the debts that were proven as part of the bankruptcy. Any remaining debt is wiped out by the discharge. See Exhibit 19-18 for a flow chart for the different types of bankruptcies.

EXHIBIT 19-18 | BANKRUPTCY

Bankruptcy petition is filed, listing creditors and how much each is owed. Automatic stay goes into effect. Bankruptcy schedule listing all of the debtor's assets is filed.

↓

All assets of the debtor become part of the bankruptcy estate. Exempt property is removed from the estate.

↓

First meeting of the creditors. Listed creditors and creditors who have filed a proof of claim can appear and question the debtor and have their claims reviewed. Bankruptcy trustee is appointed.

Chapter 7 Bankruptcy Straight Bankruptcy	**Chapter 11 Bankruptcy Rehabilitative Bankruptcy**	**Chapter 13 Bankruptcy Rehabilitative Bankruptcy**
Nonexempt property is sold by the bankruptcy trustee.	Business reorganization plan is prepared and presented to the creditors.	Individual reorganization plan is prepared and presented to the creditors.
Debts are paid using the proceeds of the sale. Any unpaid debts are discharged.	Creditors must approve the plan, but the court can accept the plan over the objections of the creditors (cram down).	Creditors must approve the plan, but the court can accept the plan over the objections of the creditors (cram down).
	Debts are paid according to the plan. Plan usually runs from three to five years.	Debts are paid according to the plan. Plan usually runs from three to five years.
	Any remaining debt is discharged.	Any remaining debt is discharged.

However, some debts are exempt from being discharged by bankruptcy. These debts are alimony and child support payments, back taxes, student loans, debts incurred immediately before the bankruptcy petition was filed, debts incurred by fraud against the creditors, and fines owed to the government. These debts are classified as **nondischargeable debts.** See Exhibit 19-19.

EXHIBIT 19-19 | DEBTS THAT ARE NOT DISCHARGED IN BANKRUPTCY

1. Alimony and child support
2. Debts incurred immediately before the bankruptcy was filed
3. Back taxes
4. Debts incurred by fraud against the creditors
5. Student loans
6. Fines owed to the government

ALTERNATIVES TO BANKRUPTCY

Bankruptcy is a drastic remedy to which there are alternatives. One such alternative is **composition with creditors,** an agreement between an insolvent or embarrassed debtor with his or her creditors in which the creditors agree to accept payment that is less than the whole amount of the creditors' claims. Upon payment of this agreed amount, the entire debt is deemed **satisfied,** extinguished by the payment of the agreed upon amount. An **accord and satisfaction** is an agreement between a debtor and only one of his or her creditors. The creditor agrees to take less money in order to satisfy the debt. The accord is the agreement; the satisfaction is the actual performance of the agreement, when the creditor receives full payment.

CONCLUSION

The use of credit has become more and more prevalent in business and personal transactions. Whether a person receives credit depends on his or her credit rating as established by a credit bureau, which issues a credit report. The creditor—the person or business extending the credit—can be a principal creditor, a junior creditor, or other type of creditor, depending on when the credit is granted or what type. The creditor may be secured by way of security interest in property, or unsecured if all that secures the loan is the promise of the debtor to repay.

The credit extended can be installment credit, revolving credit, open credit, or revocable credit. The loan may be an amortized loan, with payments consisting of interest and principal, a call loan, or a demand loan. The loan may be classified as a business loan, a consolidation loan, or a personal loan. The loan may have a fixed interest rate (one that does not change) or a variable interest rate (one that can change over the life of the loan). Proof of the credit may exist by the use of credit cards or by letters of credit.

If a debtor is unable to repay a creditor, he or she may declare bankruptcy. The bankruptcy may be voluntarily filed or may be forced upon the debtor by creditors in an involuntary bankruptcy. Once the petition for the bankruptcy is filed, an automatic stay goes into place that stops all debt collection efforts. The bankruptcy estate—all property of the debtor except for any exempt property—is gathered in by the bankruptcy trustee. The first meeting of the creditors will be held so creditors may present their claims and possibly question the debtor.

A bankruptcy may be a straight bankruptcy (Chapter 7) or a rehabilitative bankruptcy (Chapter 11 for businesses; Chapter 13 for individuals). A bankruptcy may also be a Chapter 12 bankruptcy, a special kind of bankruptcy known as the Family Farmer Bankruptcy. The purpose of all bankruptcies is to relieve the debtor of debt, pay the creditors all, some, or sometimes none of the money they are due, discharge certain debts, and give the debtor a fresh start.

CHAPTER 19 REVIEW

KEY WORDS AND PHRASES

accord and satisfaction
active debt
amortized loan
artisan's lien
attaching creditor
attachment
automatic stay
bad debt
bank credit
bankrupt
bankruptcy
Bankruptcy Code
bankruptcy estate
bankruptcy schedule
bankruptcy trustee
blanket mortgage
bridge loan
business reorganization
call loan
Chapter 7 bankruptcy
Chapter 11 bankruptcy
Chapter 12 bankruptcy
Chapter 13 bankruptcy
charge account
claim
collateral
commercial letter of credit
commercial loan
composition with creditors
confirmed letter of credit
consolidation loan
construction loan
consumer credit
consumer debt
consumer good
consumer loan
contemplation of
  bankruptcy
contingent debt
cram down
credit
credit bureau
credit card

credit rating
credit report
creditor
debt
debtor
debtor in possession
default
demand loan
discharge
distribution
domestic creditor
double creditor
engagement
Equal Credit Opportunity
  Act
equity card
equity loan
exempt
exemption
existing debt
export letter of credit
Fair Credit Billing Act
Fair Credit Reporting Act
Fair Debt Collection
  Practices Act
family farmer
family farmer bankruptcy
finance charge
first meeting of the
  creditors
fixed debt
fixed rate loan
floating lien
foreclosure
foreign creditor
fraudulent debt
general creditor
general letter of credit
Homestead Exemption
import letter of credit
insolvent
installment credit
installment loan

involuntary proceeding
irrevocable letter of credit
joint creditor
junior creditor
letter of credit
lien
lien by operation of law
lien creditor
line of credit
liquidate
liquidated debt
loan
matured debt
mechanic's lien
morning loan
mortgage
nondischargeable debt
open credit
open letter of credit
open-end credit plan
passive debt
perfected
perfection of security
  interest
personal loan
petition in bankruptcy
preference
preferential debt
preferred creditor
principal creditor
priority
proof of claim
purchase money security
  interest
receiver
receivership
redemption
redemption period
rehabilitative bankruptcy
reorganization plan
revocable credit
revocable letter of credit
revolving credit

revolving letter of credit	single creditor	unliquidated debt
right of redemption	special letter of credit	unsecured creditor
satisfied	statutory lien	unsecured debt
second mortgage	stay	variable rate loan
secondary creditor	straight bankruptcy	voluntary proceeding
secured creditor	term loan	wage earner
secured debt	time loan	wage earner's plan
security agreement	transferable letter of credit	workout
security interest	traveler's letter of credit	
short-term loan	Truth in Lending Act	

REVIEW QUESTIONS

SHORT ANSWER

1. What is an active debt?
2. What is an adjustable rate?
3. What is a balloon payment?
4. What is a blanket mortgage?
5. What is a consumer credit sale?
6. What is the difference between a conventional mortgage and an FHA mortgage?
7. What is a confirmed letter of credit?
8. What is considered collateral?
9. What is a commercial letter of credit?
10. What is a contingent debt?
11. What makes up a person's credit rating?
12. Who is a double creditor?
13. What is engagement in debtor creditor relations?
14. What is an export letter of credit?
15. What does the Equal Credit Opportunity Act protect?
16. What is an equity loan?
17. What does the Fair Debt Collection Practices Act prohibit?
18. What is a fixed rate mortgage?
19. What makes a debt fraudulent?
20. What is an installment loan?

FILL IN THE BLANK

1. A security interest is recorded and the public is put on notice that the security interest exists. This is known as _____.
2. A creditor who has a security interest is known as a _____.
3. A lien on personal property is known as a _____.
4. A loan whose interest rate can go up and down depending on the prime interest rate is known as a _____.

5. The house where the head of a household resides is known as the _____ under the Bankruptcy Code.

6. The rehabilitative bankruptcy for an individual is a _____ bankruptcy.

7. Chapter 7 bankruptcy is also known as _____.

8. If the creditors of a debtor disagree with the provisions of the debtor's plan, the court can still force the creditors to accept the plan by _____.

9. A debtor's and creditor's entering into an agreement where the creditor agrees to accept less than the amount that is actually owed is known as _____.

10. _____ occurs when an insolvent debtor pays or secures all or part of the debt owed to one or more of his or her creditors to the detriment of any other creditors.

FACT SITUATIONS

1. Lorna applies for credit at a department store. What will the store issue to indicate Lorna has credit? What type of account will it be?

2. Eldon pledges personal property to help secure a loan. What is the property pledged to secure the loan called?

3. When a person applies for credit, what will the business request a copy of? What does it contain?

4. Craig takes out a loan. He pays on the loan for six months. After six months, he quits making payments. What term applies to Craig as borrower of the money? What term applies to the person or entity who loaned the money? What did Craig do when he quit making payments as called for under the agreement?

5. A couple borrows money and uses the value of their house to help secure the loan. What type of loan is this?

6. A couple takes out a loan to buy a home. The interest on the loan will not go up or down during the life of the loan. What type of loan is this? What type of loan is it if the interest rate can go up or down depending on market conditions?

7. McCarthy quits making payments on his home loan. What action can the bank take to get its money? What sort of court order will the bank try to get? What will the bank or the sheriff do if the bank gets the court order it is seeking?

8. Erv takes out a loan to purchase an automobile. He is to make a set number of payments, each at a set amount. There is no penalty for paying off the loan early. What type of loan is this?

9. What type of credit exists when there is a preset spending limit and the amount of payment that is due depends on the amount of money that is owed?

10. Minnie is in default on several loans. She is getting phone calls at home and at work, and is being threatened with garnishments and lawsuits. If she files for bankruptcy, what stops all of this?

11. A business is unable to pay its debts, but believes it can continue to operate if it has a little time and some relief from its creditors. What type of bankruptcy will the business file? What will it file after the initial bankruptcy petition, and what is the purpose of this filing?

12. Once the bankruptcy petition is filed, about what type of hearing are the people who are owed money notified?

13. What type of bankruptcy will the business file if it still cannot pay its bills at the end of the first bankruptcy filed?

14. Some of the creditors of the business do not like the proposal regarding how they will be paid back. What is an option the bankruptcy court has with regard to their objections?

15. What will the creditors of a debtor who filed for bankruptcy file to prove their claim to repayment?

16. Ralph is the owner of a business that has filed for bankruptcy. His creditors have decided to allow him to continue to run the business. What does this make Ralph? What would happen if the creditors did not want to let Ralph continue to run the business?

CHAPTER 20

Commercial Paper

INTRODUCTION

People use commercial paper every day without knowing it. Commercial paper is considered to be a security under the law; the law that generally governs commercial paper is found in Section 3 of the Uniform Commercial Code. This chapter deals with terms that describe types of commercial paper: notes, drafts, instruments, and bonds. It also explains terms referring to the owners and issuing agents of different types of paper. The chapter concludes with a discussion of how commercial paper ownership can be transferred and when and how it is payable.

GENERAL PRINCIPLES

Commercial paper is a broad term referring to documents such as bills of exchange, promissory notes, bank checks, and other negotiable instruments used for the payment of money. Commercial paper represents money that someone is to be paid or that someone is owed.

INSTRUMENTS

An **instrument** is a written, formal, or legal document that is evidence of a right to the payment of a certain amount of money. In other words, an instrument is proof that a specific person has the right to be paid a certain sum of money. A **negotiable instrument** is a written and signed unconditional promise or order to pay a certain sum of money upon demand or at a definite time. Negotiable instruments do not have to be made out to a specific person; they can be made payable to the bearer, or "to the order of." The **bearer** is the person who is in possession of the document when payment is requested; "**to the order of**" specifically names who is to receive payment. For example, a check reads "Pay to the order of _____." By filling in the space after "Pay to the order of," the person who is writing the check is indicating who is to be paid the amount of money indicated on the check. Exhibit 20-1 is an example of a negotiable instrument.

EXHIBIT 20-1	EXAMPLE OF A NEGOTIABLE INSTRUMENT

```
Your Name                                                          101
Street Address
Anywhere, USA 00000


Pay to the
Order of  _____  $ _____

Exactly  _____  dollars.


Warbucks National Bank
00000–00000–00              0000–0000–000    _____
```

PAYOR, MAKER, DRAWER, PAYEE, AND DRAWEE

Under the law of commercial paper, different terms are used to refer to different persons, depending on the type of commercial paper that is issued. The **payee** is the person or entity to whom an instrument is payable to on issuance, the person who will receive the amount of money that is stated on the check. The **payor/payer** is the one who pays: When a check, bill, or note is presented for payment, the payor is the person who will actually pay the money. A **fictitious payee** is a payee named in a negotiable instrument who has no right to it; the maker (see below) does not intend that a fictitious payee is to receive payment.

A **drawer** is a person who **draws,** or writes, the bill of exchange (the check or the draft) and then signs it. A **drawee** is a person who the bill of exchange, draft, or check is directing to do something. This person—the drawee—is directed to pay the amount of money indicated on the bill of exchange, draft, or check when this item is presented for payment. If the commercial paper is a promissory note or a certificate of deposit, there is a **maker,** the person who creates or **executes** (issues) the note. The maker signs the instrument that promises to pay a certain sum of money to the holder of the note or certificate. See Exhibit 20-2 for a summary of the parties involved with different types of commercial paper.

EXHIBIT 20-2	PARTIES INVOLVED IN COMMERCIAL PAPER		
TYPE OF COMMERCIAL PAPER	*PERSON WHO ISSUES IT*	*PERSON WHO PAYS*	*PERSON WHO RECEIVES PAYMENT*
Check	Drawer	Drawee	Payee
Bill of exchange	Drawer	Drawee	Payee
Draft	Drawer	Drawee	Payee
Promissory note	Maker	Payor	Payee
Certificate of deposit	Maker	Payor	Payee

HOLDER IN DUE COURSE AND HOLDER IN GOOD FAITH

Certain terms are used to designate the owner or possessor of commercial paper and how that person gained possession. A **holder** is a person or entity that has legal possession of the commercial paper because ownership has been signed over to him or her or because the paper was actually issued to him or her. A **holder in due course** is the holder of the instrument who took it for value, in good faith, and without notice of any claim or defense against it. This holder in due course can enforce the instrument—claim payment—free from all other claims and personal defenses against payment. In other words, the holder in due course can demand payment of the instrument regardless of any claims or defenses that would prevent payment. A **holder in good faith** is a holder who takes an instrument without knowledge of any defect in its title, but who did not necessarily give anything of value for it. Because nothing of value was given for the commercial paper, a holder in good faith may not be able to enforce the instrument against all claims or personal defenses. The holder in good faith may not be able to demand and receive payment because the demand for payment may be defeated by a defense or a competing claim to the instrument. See Exhibit 20-3 for a summary of the difference between a holder in due course and a holder in good faith.

EXHIBIT 20-3	DIFFERENCE BETWEEN A HOLDER IN DUE COURSE AND A HOLDER IN GOOD FAITH

Holder in Due Course – Took the document for value (paid money for it), in good faith and without notice of any claim or defense against it.

Holder in Good Faith – Took the instrument without knowledge of any defect in its title but did not give anything of value for it.

ENDORSEMENT

Transfer of ownership of a negotiable instrument may take place by **endorsement,** which occurs when the payee, drawee, or holder writes his or her name on the back of the instrument. The endorsement assigns and transfers ownership of the commercial paper from one person to another. An endorsement is effective for negotiation only when it conveys the entire instrument or any unpaid amount of money. The endorsement, in order to make the commercial paper negotiable (capable of being transferred), must apply to the entire document or be for any amount of money that is still to be paid. A person cannot transfer ownership of just part of the instrument; ownership of the entire instrument must pass when it is endorsed.

The **endorser** is the holder or payee who writes his or her name on the back of the instrument; the **endorsee** is the person to whom or for whose benefit the commercial paper is endorsed. The endorser transfers ownership of the instrument, and the endorsee receives ownership. An **endorsee in due course** is a person who, in good faith, in the ordinary course of business, and for value, without knowledge of its dishonor or any problem with the instrument, acquires an endorsed instrument. For example, Leah writes a check to Home Depot for new tile for her kitchen. Leah's check is telling—ordering—her bank to pay Home Depot a certain sum of money. A representative of Home Depot endorses the check and takes it to Home Depot's bank, where it is deposited into the business's account. Home Depot has essentially sold the check to its bank for its face value. If the check was written for $150, the bank has paid $150 for the check and has deposited that $150 into Home Depot's account. The bank now owns the check and can present it to Leah's bank, asking for the face value of the check.

There are several types of endorsements. A **blank endorsement** is one in which the endorser writes his or her name on the back of the instrument and does not mention the name of any person in whose favor the endorsement is made. For example, Lisa signs her name to the back of an instrument transferring ownership, but does not indicate on the check whom she is transferring ownership to. A **full endorsement** is one whereby the endorser orders the money paid to a particular person by name. A **conditional endorsement** is a **restrictive endorsement:** It limits when the instrument can be paid or transferred because of the condition that a future event must happen first. For example, Rita endorses a check to Vic, but adds the condition that the governor of the state must be elected President of the United States. If the governor is never elected president, then the condition has not been met and the endorsement is not effective. A **special endorsement** specifies the person to whom or to whose order the instrument is payable. The person named in the special endorsement is the only one who can endorse the instrument for the endorsement to be effective. An **unauthorized endorsement** is one that is made without actual, implied, or apparent authority; it is a forged endorsement. See Exhibit 20-4 for a summary of endorsements.

EXHIBIT 20-4 TYPES OF ENDORSEMENTS

Blank Endorsement – A person writes/signs his or her name on the back of the instrument/check. No indication is given as to who is to receive the document.

Full Endorsement – A person writes/signs his or her name on the back of the instrument/check and indicates who is to receive the document.

Conditional Endorsement – A condition must be met before ownership of the document is transferred.

Special Endorsement – Only the person specifically named in the document can transfer ownership by endorsement.

Unauthorized Endorsement – The document is a forgery.

BEARER DOCUMENTS

Some negotiable instruments do not name a specific person they are payable to; these negotiable instruments are payable to the bearer. The bearer is the person who is in possession of the instrument. This means that when the instrument is presented for payment, payment will be made to the person who has *possession* of it. Whoever appears and requests payment of the document is the person who will receive payment because ownership of the instrument is not required. All that is required for payment is for the person to have possession when it is presented for payment. The **bearer instrument** is the negotiable instrument that is payable to bearer, order of bearer, a specified person *or* bearer, "cash," or "to the order of cash." A **bearer document** is negotiated by presentation alone—no proof of ownership has to be given. Anyone in possession of this document is a holder of it and is entitled to payment. For example, Hans, who stole millions of dollars in bearer bonds, appears with one of the bearer bonds and requests payment. Hans is entitled to payment because ownership is not the issue; possession of the bond is enough to be able to receive payment. **Bearer paper** is commercial paper that is payable to the bearer, the person who has possession. Endorsement of a bearer instrument does not transfer ownership; rather, possession of the document transfers ownership.

BILLS

One type of commercial paper is a **bill,** or promissory obligation for the payment of money. A bill in commercial paper is broken into several different categories: a bill of credit, a treasury bill, or a bill of exchange.

TREASURY BILLS AND BILLS OF CREDIT

A **bill of credit** is issued by the government based on its full faith and credit, and is designed to circulate in the community as money. A **treasury bill** is issued by the federal government and represents a short-term obligation, usually for three, six, or twelve months. Treasury bills are sold at a discounted price—a price that is less than the face value of the bill—but pay no interest. These bills are worth their face value only. For example, a bill's face value may be $50, but it sells for $40 because of the discount price. However, the bill is worth $50 because that is what the bill states it is worth. It will never be worth more than $50 because it does not earn interest.

BILL OF EXCHANGE

A **bill of exchange** is an unconditional written order addressed by one person to another, signed by the person giving it, requiring the person that it is addressed to, to pay a definite sum of money either on demand, which is when it is presented, or at a definite time in the future. For example, Lotus and Frannie save aluminum cans for recycling. When they have several trash bags full, they take the cans to a recycling plant that weighs the cans and then writes out a bill of exchange. The bill of exchange tells someone else in the company to pay Lotus and Frannie a specific amount of money for the cans they have turned in. This bill will be paid when the girls present it for payment. Exhibit 20-5 features an example of a bill of exchange.

EXHIBIT 20-5   BILL OF EXCHANGE

TO: Marty Bookkeeper

Pay to Lotus Customer and Frannie Customer _____ $24.00 _____ for _____ 200 _____ pounds of aluminum cans.

Payable on _____ March 13, 2003 _____

_____

Signed – Michael Owner

A **foreign bill of exchange** is drawn in one country and directed to another country that is not governed by the same type of laws. It can also be a bill of exchange drawn in one state upon a person residing in another state in the United States. A **blank bill** is a bill of exchange with the payee's name left blank. An **advance bill** authorizes payment before the actual shipment of goods. A **clean bill** is a bill of exchange with no additional documents attached to it. Exhibit 20-6 is a summary of the types of bills of exchange.

EXHIBIT 20-6   TYPES OF BILLS OF EXCHANGE

Bill of Exchange – A written, signed, unconditional order addressed by one person to another, directing the person addressed to pay a definite sum of money either on demand, which is when it is presented, or at a definite time in the future.

Foreign Bill of Exchange – A bill written in one state or country addressed to a person in another state or country.

Blank Bill – A bill of exchange with the payee's name left blank.

Advance Bill – A bill of exchange authorizing payment before goods are shipped.

Clean Bill – A bill of exchange with no additional documents attached to it.

DRAFTS

A second type of commercial paper is a **draft,** a written order to pay a certain sum of money, signed by a drawer, payable on demand or at a definite time, and payable to order or to bearer. The term **payable to order** means that the instrument is payable to a person that is specified with reasonable certainty. For example, Jay, who is an independent contractor, writes a draft telling Katie, his accountant, to pay Home Depot for supplies that Jay received and is using on his current project. This is a draft because it is a written order to pay a sum of money, it is signed by Jay, it is payable on demand because of the date on it, and it is made payable to Home Depot.

TYPES OF DRAFTS

A **bank draft** involves two banks: one bank is the drawer and another bank is the drawee. One bank writes a draft telling another bank to pay someone or the bearer of the draft a certain sum of money. A **clean draft** has no shipping documents attached; it stands alone. A **sight draft** or **demand draft** is payable when it is presented or upon demand because there is no specific date for payment indicated. A **time draft** is one that is payable a certain number of days after it has been presented for acceptance. For example, the draft may state "payable ten days from this date"; the draft is not to be paid until ten days have passed from the date of the draft. In order for the time draft to be effective, the number of days in it must be specific. Exhibit 20-7 is a summary of the different types of drafts.

EXHIBIT 20-7	TYPES OF DRAFTS

Draft – A written order to pay a certain sum of money, signed by a drawer, payable on demand or at a definite time, and payable to order or to bearer.

Bank Draft – A draft in which the drawer is one bank and the drawee is another bank.

Clean Draft – A draft that has no shipping documents attached.

Sight Draft – A draft that is payable when it is presented or upon demand because no specific date for payment is indicated.

Time Draft – A draft that is payable a certain number of days after it has been presented for acceptance.

Acceptance is the drawee's signed agreement to honor the draft as presented. In other words, it is the agreement to pay the draft.

CHECKS AND CERTIFICATES OF DEPOSIT

Checks and certificates of deposit are types of commercial paper that involve banks. A **check** is a draft written by a drawer, directing a drawee to pay a certain sum of money to a payee. The drawee of a check, the "person" responsible for paying the check, must be a bank with which the drawer has deposited funds. If a bank is not the drawee, then the instrument is not a check. For example, if Bill wrote a draft (check) to Home Depot and listed Home Depot as the entity the draft (check) is payable to, and the draft (check) is directed to the Metropolitan Bank, then the draft is a check.

OVERDRAFTS

A drawer must have deposited sufficient money with a bank so funds are available to pay the check when it is presented. If funds are not sufficient, and a drawer writes a check for more money than is available in the account, he or she has written an **overdraft.** When there is an overdraft, the bank will send out a notice of **insufficient funds,** bank terminology that means the drawer's amount of money on deposit is less than the amount of the check that is drawn on the account. The bank is stating that there is not enough money available in the account to comply with the order to pay the payee the amount written on the check.

TYPES OF CHECKS

A **bogus check** is a check written by a person upon a bank in which the person has no funds; the person has no reason to believe that the check will be honored. For example, Mikhail transfers money from his First Commercial Bank checking account into a checking account at First National Bank. Mikhail closes the checking account at First Commercial, but retains his printed checks from First Commercial Bank. Mikhail writes a check drawn on the closed account at First Commercial; the check is bogus. When the check is presented to First Commercial for payment, the bank does not honor it because the account is closed. Mikhail has no reason to believe that First Commercial will honor the check because the account is closed.

A **cancelled check** carries a notation or stamp indicating it has been paid and that the amount specified has been charged to the drawer. Canceling the check prevents the check from being presented to the bank for payment again. A **certified check** is a check of a depositor that is drawn on the bank that the bank has stamped accepted or certified and dated. It is signed by a bank official. If a check is certified, a bank has the obligation to pay the check when it is presented. When a bank certifies a check, it is indicating that there are sufficient funds to pay the check and that the bank has set aside those funds to pay that specific check. A **registered check** is drawn on funds of a bank that have been specifically set aside to pay the check. However, a registered check is not certified by the issuing bank; the bank is not promising that the money has been set aside. A **cashier's check** is a check drawn by the bank upon itself and is issued by an authorized officer of the bank. The payee of the check is authorized to present and demand from the bank the amount indicated on the check. The funds are present because a person has already paid the bank the amount of money to honor the check. A **postdated check** is one that is made payable after the date the check was written. For example, Boris writes the check on May 8th, but dates it for May 18th. The check is still a negotiable instrument, but it is not payable until the date stated on the check. Exhibit 20-8 sets out the different types of checks and when these checks will be paid.

EXHIBIT 20-8 PAYMENT OF CHECKS

TYPE OF CHECK	ISSUER OF CHECK	PAYMENT OF CHECK
Regular check	Account holder	Funds are available in the account.
Certified check	Account holder	Bank certifies there are sufficient funds available and agrees that the bank will pay the check when it is presented.
Registered check	Purchased by someone	Funds of the bank have been set aside to pay the check. However, it is not certified, so the bank is not promising that money has been set aside.
Cashier's check	Bank official	Funds are present because the person who purchased the check has already paid the bank the amount of money necessary to honor the check.

CHECK KITING

Check kiting is writing a check against a bank account in which the funds are insufficient to pay the check in the hope that there will be sufficient funds in the account before the check is presented. For example, Tasha has two checking accounts at two different banks. One is at First National Bank; the second is at Farmers' National Bank. Tasha cashes a check from First National Bank at Farmers' National Bank, knowing there are insufficient funds at First National to pay the check. Tasha hopes to put enough money into the account at First National before Farmers' presents the check for payment. See Exhibit 20-9.

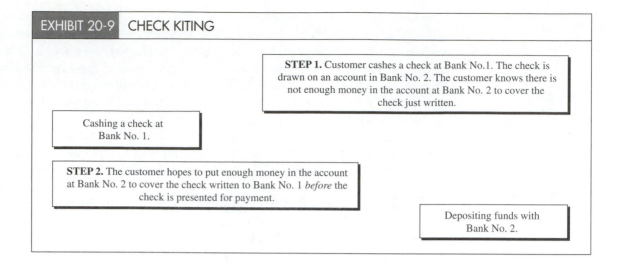

EXHIBIT 20-9 CHECK KITING

STEP 1. Customer cashes a check at Bank No. 1. The check is drawn on an account in Bank No. 2. The customer knows there is not enough money in the account at Bank No. 2 to cover the check just written.

Cashing a check at Bank No. 1.

STEP 2. The customer hopes to put enough money in the account at Bank No. 2 to cover the check written to Bank No. 1 *before* the check is presented for payment.

Depositing funds with Bank No. 2.

CERTIFICATES OF DEPOSIT

Drafts and checks are *orders* to pay. Certificates of deposit, bonds, and notes are *promises* to pay. When a draft or check is written, it is an order telling someone to pay a certain sum of money. Certificates of deposit, bonds, and notes are promises that a certain sum of money will be paid in the future.

A **certificate of deposit,** or **CD,** is a written acknowledgement by a bank that it has received a deposit of a certain sum of money. The bank promises to pay this sum of money plus interest to the depositor at some future point. Payment of the CD is usually upon demand, but there may be a substantial penalty if the demand is made before a certain period of time has elapsed. For this reason—because a certain amount of time must pass before the CD can be paid without incurring a penalty—certificates of deposit are termed **time deposits.** For example, Benny purchases a six-month CD. After six months, the bank will pay Benny his original deposit plus the interest that was earned when Benny requests payment. However, if Benny demands payment before the six months is over, he may have to pay a penalty and actually receive less money than he originally deposited. A **demand deposit** is a bank deposit that may be withdrawn at any time by the depositor without prior notice to the bank. The depositor can go to the bank and demand whatever sum of money he or she wishes up to the total amount on deposit. For example, Keisha opens a savings account that allows her to demand money anytime she wants up to the amount she has on deposit. The savings account she has opened is an example of demand deposit account because she can request payment at any time and without being charged a penalty.

BONDS

GENERAL PRINCIPLES

A **bond** is a certificate that is evidence of a debt. A company or the government promises to pay the holder of the bond a specified amount of interest for a specified period of time and to repay the debt on its expiration date. A bond is one way that companies or government can borrow money. The bond is evidence of the loan; interest is paid on the loan until it is time to repay the debt, and then the amount of the original loan is repaid. The **maturity date** of the bond is when the principal amount of the bond—the amount of money that was borrowed—becomes due and payable. For example, Martindale Company issues bonds for ten years; the amount of money that is used to purchase the bonds is $5,000. The bonds are issued on May 8, 2005, and their maturity date is May 8, 2015. Interest on the bonds will be earned for ten years and may be paid during the ten years. On May 8, 2015, the principal amount of the bond—the $5,000—will be due if it has not been paid over the length of the bond. The term *maturity date* also applies to notes, drafts, and any other debt instrument: This is the date the note or draft is to be paid. The **maturity value** is how much the bond is worth, what is due and payable, on the maturity date of the bond. The maturity value is the amount that was paid for the bond plus any earned, unpaid interest. For example, Company Martindale issues $5,000 bonds that earn 5% interest per year. No interest is paid on the bonds during the ten years, so the interest accumulates. The maturity value of the bond would be the original $5,000 plus the $250 in interest per year that was earned for ten years, for a total of $7,500.

CALLABLE BONDS

A **callable bond** is one that payment may be demanded for prior to its maturity date; the owner of the bond does not have to wait for the maturity date to request repayment of the loan. For example, Cal purchases U.S. savings bonds with a face value of $50, but only pays $25 for them. The maturity date on the bonds is 30 years after the date of purchase, but Cal can demand payment at any time. The amount Cal will receive is the original $25 that was paid plus any interest that was earned on the $25. The **call price** is the price that is paid to retire the bond whose payment is called for prior to its maturity date. The call price on Cal's savings bonds would be the original $25 plus any interest that was earned. A **noncallable bond** is one that cannot be redeemed—bought back—at the option of the entity that issued the bond. In other words, the company or government that issued the bond cannot offer to buy back the bond from the owner; only the owner of the bond can request payment. A **perpetual bond** has no maturity date: It will continue to earn interest until payment is demanded or the government or company that issued the bond redeems it.

ISSUING AND SALE OF BONDS

When a company, government, or any other entity wants to offer bonds for sale, the bonds are **issued,** or offered for sale at a certain time to the general public. The **bond issue** is the entire number of bonds offered for sale to investors at a given time. A **serial bond** is a bond issue where the bonds are all issued at the same time, but have different maturity dates. **Series bonds** are groups of bonds issued at different times with different maturity dates, but under the same agreement. In other words, the bonds are all part of the same overall issue, but are offered for sale at different times and each group offered has a different maturity date.

When bonds are sold, their price may be discounted. A **bond discount** is the difference between the face value or obligation of the bond and the current market price of the bond if the selling price is lower than the face value of the bond. For example, if a bond has a face value of $10,000 but sells for $8,500, there is a bond discount of $1,500. A **bond premium** is the difference between the face value of the bond and the selling price of the bond if the selling price is greater than the face value of the bond. If the face value of the bond is $10,000 but it actually sells for $10,500, then the bond premium is $500.

Because there are so many types of bonds issued by many different entities, investors want some way to determine if a particular bond is a good investment. A **bond rating** is an appraisal of the investment value of a bond made by one of several different companies. This investment value is based on the probability that the issuer of the bond will default on the bond. AAA bonds have the highest rating, which means these bonds have the lowest probability that the issuer will default on payment. An **investment grade bond** is any bond that has a rating of BBB or better by the bond-rating services.

A **registered bond** carries the name of the owner along with the company or entity that issued the bond; ownership is registered with the company that issued the bond. Ownership of this bond can only be transferred when the registered owner endorses the bond; then the new owner is listed as the registered owner of the bond. A **bearer bond** is payable to the person having possession of it. Formal ownership of the bond is not required to receive payment on it: The person who presents the bond for payment is the person who will receive payment. Exhibit 20-10 is a summary of the categories of bonds that can be issued.

EXHIBIT 20-10 | CATEGORIES OF BONDS I

The following are categories of bonds based on *type*.

Callable Bond – Payment on this bond can be demanded before its maturity date.

Noncallable Bond – The issuer of this type of bond cannot redeem it. Only the owner of the bond can redeem it.

Perpetual Bond – This bond has no maturity date. It will continue to earn interest.

Serial Bond – Bond issue in which the bonds are issued at the same time, but groups of bonds have different maturity dates.

Series Bonds – Bonds are issued at different times with different maturity dates, but are issued under the same terms.

Investment Grade Bond – Any bond that is rated BBB or better as an investment by a bond-rating service

Registered Bond – Bond that has the name of the owner registered with the entity that issued the bond.

Bearer Bond – Bond payable to the person who has possession of the bond.

TYPES OF BONDS

There are several types of bonds. How a bond is paid, who issues it, and the purpose it is issued for determines what type of bond has been issued. The collateral of the entity that issued them secures some bonds. Bonds that are secured by the general credit of the issuing government or corporation are called **debenture bonds.** The only thing securing the payment of these bonds is the credit history of the corporation or government that issued the bonds. A **coupon bond** is a bond that has interest coupons attached, each coupon representing an amount of interest that is due. The **bond coupon** is the part of the bond that is cut or "clipped" and surrendered for payment of one of the interest payments. When someone is said to be "clipping coupons," it means he or she is presenting the interest coupons of a bond for payment.

A **joint and several bond** has two or more people or entities who have guaranteed payment of the principal and interest and who can be sued either individually or as a group for nonpayment. The plaintiff cannot collect more than he or she is entitled to under the bond, but one person can be held liable for the entire amount. A **joint bond** is issued by two or more people or entities who are responsible for the payment of the bond and who must be sued together in case of a default on payment. A plaintiff cannot sue just one of the issuers of the bond.

A **consolidated bond** is large enough (worth enough) to pay two or more outstanding issues of bonds. The value of the new bond is sufficiently high to be used to purchase or pay the value of two or more sets of bonds that have already been issued. For example, the city of Warfield issues two series of bonds to help pay for road improvement. Each bond that is issued has a face value of $500. A third series of bonds is issued, with each bond having a face value of $1,500. The proceeds from this third series raises enough money that Warfield can pay the first two series of bonds and still make road improvements. A **convertible bond** can be converted into or exchanged for stock. This conversion or exchange is done at the option of the holder of the bond. For example, Zachary has convertible bonds that have been issued by Pell Corporation. Zachary may exchange those bonds for Pell stock. **Junk bonds** are of two types, both of which pay a high rate of interest, and are considered high-risk investments. The first type of junk bond was originally investment grade (see page 368), but since the bond was issued, it has been downgraded. The second type of junk bond is the bond that was originally issued as a low-grade bond: Its rating was low to begin with.

A **foreign bond** is an international bond whose value is stated in the currency of the country in which it was issued. For example, if a company located in Germany issued international bonds, the value of the bonds would be stated in German Deutschmarks. A **government bond** is issued by a government to fund its operations and is backed solely by the credit of the government. A **municipal bond** is issued by a state, county, city, town, village, or state agency. Generally the interest that is paid on these bonds is exempt from federal, state, and local income taxes within the state that issued the bond. This type of bond is also known as a **tax-exempt bond:** The income that a person receives from this bond is not taxable.

There are two types of **treasury bonds.** The first is one that is reacquired—bought back—or that was never sold by the corporation that issued it. The term *Treasury bond* also applies to bonds issued by the U.S. Treasury. An example of a U.S. Treasury bond is a **U.S. savings bond.** These bonds are issued by the United States and are designed to encourage savings. People buy the bonds at a reduced price and are required to hold them for a period of time before they can be redeemed for their face value. For example, Tina buys a U.S. savings bond with a face value of $100 but pays only $50 for it. In order to be paid the full $100, she must hold onto the bond until its maturity date. A **zero coupon bond** is a treasury bond that has had all the interest coupons removed by the purchaser of the bond. The remaining bond is sold for far less than its face value because the bond will earn no interest. All that the purchaser of a zero coupon bond will receive is the face value of the bond at maturity. The amount that the price of the bond is discounted by is determined by the number of years before the bond can be redeemed for its face value. Exhibit 20-11 is a summary of bonds based on how the bonds are paid, who issued the bond, or what the bond is to be used for.

EXHIBIT 20-11	TYPES OF BONDS II

Bonds are also classified on the basis of how they are paid, who issues the bonds, or what they are used for.

Debenture Bond – Bond issued by a government or corporation that is not secured by specific property. Bond is secured only by the general credit of the issuer.

Coupon Bond – Bond that has coupons attached that can be removed and presented for payment of interest.

Joint and Several Bond – Two or more people or entities have guaranteed payment of the bond. They can be sued separately for payment.

Joint Bond – Two or more people or entities have guaranteed payment of the bond, but they must be sued at the same time for payment.

Consolidated Bond – The value of the bond is high enough that proceeds from the sale can be used to retire two or more outstanding bond issues.

Convertible Bond – Bond that can be exchanged for stock.

Junk Bond – Bond that had a high rating but now has a low rating, or bond that always had a low rating.

Foreign Bond – Bond issued by a foreign country whose value is stated in that country's currency.

Tax-Exempt Bond – Bond that generates income that is not taxable.

Zero Coupon Bond – Treasury bond that has had all of the interest coupons removed by the original purchaser.

Treasury Bond – Bond that has been reacquired by the corporation that issued it or that was never issued by the corporation.

An **improvement bond** is a bond issued by a city or a town to finance improvements within that city or town. For example, the city of Farleigh wants to build a new high school. The city has set aside funds for the school in its budget for the next five years—the length of time it will take to build the school. But it will be five years before the city will have enough money to start building the school. Rather than waiting five years to begin construction, the city issues improvement bonds. The money from the sale of the bonds will finance the new high school, and the bonds will be paid off using the money budgeted over the five-year period to build the high school. An **industrial development bond** is issued by a municipality as a method of attracting businesses to the area. The proceeds from the sale are used to build facilities for new businesses. The rent a business pays the municipality for its facilities will be used to pay the bonds.

A **revenue bond** is one issued by a public agency, municipal corporation, or state for the purpose of raising revenue. The revenue is usually used for a specific project, such as a new sports complex. The proceeds from the project are used to pay the bond obligation. Exhibit 20-12 is a summary of the different types of government bonds.

EXHIBIT 20-12	GOVERNMENT BONDS

Government Bond – Bond issued a government to fund its operations that is backed solely by the credit of the government.

Municipal Bond – Bond that is issued by a state, county, city, town, village, or state agency.

U.S. Savings Bond – Treasury bond issued by the U.S. Treasury; designed to encourage savings.

Improvement Bond – Bond issued by a city or town that is used to finance improvements. The money to repay the bond comes from the improvement fund.

Industrial Development Bond – Bond that is issued to help finance a facility for a private company; used to attract business to a particular area.

Revenue Bond – Issued by a public agency, municipal corporation, or state for the purpose of raising revenue for a specific project.

NOTES

A **note** is an instrument that contains an express and absolute promise of the maker to pay to a specified person, to the order, or to the bearer a definite sum of money at a specified time. A note is a promise to pay that is not a CD; this instrument is also known as a **promissory note.** There are several types of notes: balloon notes, collateral notes, unsecured notes, and demand notes.

BALLOON NOTE

A **balloon note** requires a minimum payment of principal, if any payment of principal is made, and the payment of interest at regular intervals. A balloon note requires a substantial payment of principal at the end of the term of the note. The final payment, which is called the **balloon payment,** frequently is most or all of the principal of the loan. During the term of the note, all that is paid is interest (and maybe a little of the principal amount borrowed). At the end of the term of the note, the principal is due.

COLLATERAL, UNSECURED, DEMAND, AND INSTALLMENT NOTES

A **collateral note** or **secured note** is a two-party instrument containing a promise to pay that is secured by a pledge of property. To guarantee payment, one of the two parties pledges property against the note. If the party that pledges payment does not pay the note, then the other party has a claim to property that may satisfy the remaining amount due. An **unsecured note** contains a promise to pay that is not secured by anything; no property is pledged to secure the note.

A **demand note** is payable on demand: There is no definite due date—it is to be paid when a request or demand for payment is made. An **installment note** requires payments on the note at fixed periods of time. The payments are usually of the same amount, due at the same time each month, and include principal and interest. For example, Calvin goes to a car dealership, buys a new automobile, and signs documents saying he will make monthly payments of $300 for five years. Calvin has signed an installment note—a promise to pay back a sum of money borrowed by making regular payments over a period of time. A **time note** is payable in its entirety at a definite future time. Instead of signing a note that says she will pay $300 every month for five years, Jenn signs a note that says she will pay $18,000 five years from the date she purchased her car. This note is a time note because it is payable at a definite future time and the entire amount is due at that time.

JOINT AND NEGOTIABLE NOTES

A **joint note** is a note in which two or more people agree to be liable for payment. All of the people who agreed must be joined—made a part of the action to recover the amount due. If two people sign a note and say they will be jointly liable, both of them must be sued in order to try to collect the amount due. A **joint and several note** is signed by two or more people who agree to be bound jointly and severally. These people may be sued individually for the full amount of the note, or they may be sued as a group for payment of the entire amount of the note.

Notes, like all other types of commercial paper, can be negotiable—that is, bought and sold. A **negotiable note** must be signed by the maker of the note, contain an unconditional promise to pay a certain sum of money, and must be payable upon demand or at a definite time to the order of or to the bearer. The person who purchases the note has the right to enforce the terms of the note against the maker of the note. If the maker of the note defaults—does not pay—the purchaser can sue the maker for the amount that is due.

CONCLUSION

Commercial paper is essentially a substitute for cash. Bills are promises to pay with a drawer, a drawee, and a payee. They are payable either on demand or at a specific time. A draft is a written order to pay with a drawer, a drawee, and a payee, and they are payable either on demand or at a specific time. A check is a draft whose drawee must be a bank; it is payable on demand. If a bank is not involved, then the document is not a check. A note is a promise to pay with a maker, a payor, and a payee. Notes are payable at a definite time and earn interest. A bond is a promise to pay with a maker and a payee. Bonds are payable at a definite time and they may earn interest. See Exhibit 20-13 for a summary of the different types of commercial paper.

EXHIBIT 20-13	SUMMARY OF THE TYPES OF COMMERCIAL PAPER			
TYPE	**DESCRIPTION**	**PARTIES INVOLVED**	**PAYMENT**	**EARNS INTEREST**
Bill	Promise or order to pay	Drawer, drawee, payee	Upon demand or at a definite time	No
Draft	Written order to pay	Drawer, drawee, payee	Upon demand or at a definite time	No
Check	Written order to pay	Drawer, bank, payee	Upon demand	No
Note	Promise to pay	Maker, payor, payee	Definite time	Yes
Bond	Promise to pay	Maker, payee	Definite time	Yes
CD	Promise to pay	Bank, payee	Definite time	Yes

Ownership of commercial paper can be transferred by negotiation or decided by whoever has actual possession of the document. Ownership of a bearer document is determined by whoever has possession when payment is demanded.

Commercial paper such as bonds can be issued for many different purposes, including municipal improvements, raising capital for a business or government, or to pay off an existing bond issue. Bonds are also classified according to interest payment, tax advantage, or financial rating. Notes can be classified according to how they will be repaid, whether they are secured or not, or whether they are negotiable.

Commercial paper serves as a cash substitute in the business world and offers investment opportunities for individuals and entities.

KEY WORDS AND PHRASES

acceptance	commercial paper	maturity date
advance bill	conditional endorsement	maturity value
balloon note	consolidated bond	municipal bond
balloon payment	convertible bond	negotiable instrument
bank draft	coupon bond	negotiable note
bearer	debenture bond	noncallable bond
bearer bond	demand deposit	note
bearer document	demand draft	overdraft
bearer instrument	demand note	payable to order
bearer paper	draft	payee
bill	draw	payor/payer
bill of credit	drawee	perpetual bond
bill of exchange	drawer	promissory note
blank bill	endorsee	registered bond
blank endorsement	endorsee in due course	registered check
bogus check	endorsement	restrictive endorsement
bond	endorser	secured note
bond coupon	execute	serial bond
bond discount	fictitious payee	series bonds
bond issue	foreign bill of exchange	sight draft
bond premium	full endorsement	special endorsement
callable bond	holder	tax-exempt bond
cancelled check	holder in due course	time deposit
cashier's check	holder in good faith	time draft
certificate of deposit (CD)	installment note	to the order of
certified check	instrument	treasury bill
check	insufficient funds	U.S. savings bond
check kiting	investment grade bond	unauthorized endorsement
clean bill	joint note	unsecured note
clean draft	junk bond	zero coupon bond
collateral note	maker	

REVIEW QUESTIONS

SHORT ANSWER

1. What is the difference between a draft and a check?

2. What is a balloon note?

3. What is bearer paper?

4. What is a bond?

5. What are bond coupons?

6. What is a bearer instrument?

7. What is a bond discount?

8. What is a callable bond?

9. What is the difference between a cashier's check and a certified check?

10. What is a debenture bond?

11. What is a demand deposit?

12. What is a certificate of deposit?

13. What is a bond rating?

14. What is a blank endorsement?

15. Who is a drawer and who is a drawee?

16. What is a fictitious payee?

17. What is the difference between a holder in due course and a holder in good faith?

18. What is meant by *endorse in due course?*

19. What is a premium bond?

20. What is meant by *payable to order?*

FILL IN THE BLANK

1. A _____ bond has no maturity date; it will continue to earn interest.

2. A _____ note has low payments until the end of the note, when a majority of the interest is due.

3. The proceeds for a sale of _____ is used to retire two or more issues of outstanding bonds.

4. Any bond with a rating above BBB is a _____ bond.

5. A _____ is one for which the bank states that money has been set aside to pay the check and promises that the check will be paid.

6. A _____ is one for which the bank states that money has been set aside to pay the check, but does not promise the check will be paid.

7. A bank is the drawer and the drawee of a _____.

8. A bond that is payable to the person who has possession of it is a _____.

9. A bond that has always had a low financial rating or that had a higher financial rating but now has a lower rating is a _____.

10. A bond that can be exchanged for stock is a _____.

FACT SITUATIONS

1. When is a bond payable to the person who has possession of the bond? No proof of ownership is required to be shown.

2. Andy has taken out a note with most of the principal due at the end of the note's period. What type of note is this? What type of payment is due at the end of the note?

3. Frank owns bonds. Periodically he clips part of them off and presents them for payment. What type of bond is this? What does the clipped-off part represent?

4. Madge writes a check on one account, deposits that money into another account, and then writes a check on that account. What is Madge doing?

5. Geoff has an instrument that is payable when it is presented. What sort of instrument does Geoff have?

6. Tiki takes an instrument with assurances that the person who sold it to him was the proper owner and had full title when it was transferred to him. What is Tiki called?

7. Escobar has a bond that has earned all the interest it can earn. What type of bond does he own?

8. Jaomir writes a check, but does not have enough funds in his account to meet the amount of money that is to be paid. What is this termed?

9. If a city wants to generate money for improvements, what sort of bonds might it issue?

10. Ira has a draft that is to be paid at a certain time. What type of draft does Ira have?

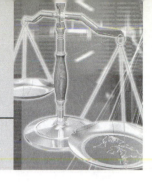

CHAPTER 21

Intellectual Property

INTRODUCTION

The law of property deals with three types of property: real property, personal property, and intellectual property. The law of real and personal property is based primarily on common law, although some areas of the law are based on statutes. The law of intellectual property is based primarily upon statutory law, with some principles finding their basis in common law. Some of the principles of common law have been incorporated into the statutes.

Intellectual property is the physical or tangible result of original thought, the physical manifestation of a person's thoughts or ideas. Four types of intellectual property will be discussed in this chapter: copyrights, trademarks, patents, and trade secrets.

COPYRIGHT

GENERAL PRINCIPLES

Copyright applies primarily to written works. Anything that can be put in writing—books, magazine articles, music, movie scripts, a movie itself, even photographs—may be protected by copyright. **Copyright,** which is governed by the federal 1976 Copyright Act, is an intangible right granted by statute to the author or originator of original works that are created. Refer to Exhibit 21-1 for excerpts from the Copyright Act.

EXHIBIT 21-1	SELECTED SECTIONS OF U.S.C. TITLE 17, COPYRIGHT

Section 102. Subject matter of copyright: In general

(a) Copyright protection subsists, in accordance with this title, in original works of authorship fixed in any tangible medium of expression, now known or later developed, from which they can be perceived, reproduced, or otherwise communicated, either directly or with the aid of a machine or device. Works of authorship include the following categories:

(1) literary works;

(2) musical works, including any accompanying words;

(3) dramatic works, including any accompanying music;

(4) pantomimes and choreographic works;

(5) pictorial, graphic, and sculptural works;

(6) motion pictures and other audiovisual works;

(7) sound recordings; and

(8) architectural works.

(b) In no case does copyright protection for an original work of authorship extend to any idea, procedure, process, system, method of operation, concept, principle, or discovery, regardless of the form in which it is described, explained, illustrated, or embodied in such work.

Continued

Continued

Section 201. Ownership of copyright

(a) Initial Ownership. – Copyright in a work protected under this title vests initially in the author or authors of the work. The authors of a joint work are coowners of copyright in the work.

(b) Works Made for Hire. – In the case of a work made for hire, the employer or other person for whom the work was prepared is considered the author for purposes of this title, and, unless the parties have expressly agreed otherwise in a written instrument signed by them, owns all of the rights comprised in the copyright.

(d) Transfer of Ownership. – (1) The ownership of a copyright may be transferred in whole or in part by any means of conveyance or by operation of law, and may be bequeathed by will or pass as personal property by the applicable laws of intestate succession.

(2) Any of the exclusive rights comprised in a copyright, including any subdivision of any of the rights specified by section 106, may be transferred as provided by clause (1) and owned separately. The owner of any particular exclusive right is entitled, to the extent of that right, to all of the protection and remedies accorded to the copyright owner by this title.

Section 302. Duration of copyright: Works created on or after January 1, 1978

(a) In General. – Copyright in a work created on or after January 1, 1978, subsists from its creation and, except as provided by the following subsections, endures for a term consisting of the life of the author and 70 years after the author's death.

(b) Joint Works. – In the case of a joint work prepared by two or more authors who did not work for hire, the copyright endures for a term consisting of the life of the last surviving author and 70 years after such last surviving author's death.

Source: United States Code

The word **created** in copyright law means that the work is fixed in a copy or record for the first time. The author has, for a specified period of time, the sole and exclusive right to make multiple copies of the work and to publish and sell them. Copyright exists for the life of the author plus the seventy years after his or her death. The copyright of a work can be renewed.

Publication, in copyright law, refers to the distribution of copies of the work to the public by sale or other transfer of ownership or by rental, lease, or lending. In other words, the person who actually created the work is the only person who can copy the work, sell the copies, rent the copies, lease copies, or lend copies to other people. If anyone other than the author (or the person who owns the copyright) publishes the work, this publication can violate the author's copyright in the work.

OWNERSHIP OF COPYRIGHT

Copyright protection applies to a **work of authorship,** which is a work that is fixed in any tangible medium of expression, from which the work can be perceived, reproduced, or otherwise communicated either directly or by a machine or device. Put another way, a work of authorship is anything that is in written form or any other form from which the work can be read, heard, or seen. Exhibit 21-2 lists what can be a work of authorship.

EXHIBIT 21-2	WORKS OF AUTHORSHIP

Works of authorship include the following.

1. Literary works
2. Musical works, including any accompanying words
3. Dramatic works, including any accompanying music

4. Pantomimes and choreographic works
5. Pictorial, graphic, and sculptural works
6. Motion pictures and other audiovisual works
7. Sound recordings
8. Architectural works

The **copyright owner** is the person who owns the exclusive rights of a copyright. This person may or may not be the author of the work because the copyright of a piece of work may be sold, inherited, traded, or given away just like any other piece of property. For example, Paul McCartney, Ringo Starr, and the estates of George Harrison and John Lennon do not own the copyright to many Beatles' songs. These rights were sold to other people who receive the benefits of the copyright.

However, in order to protect and uphold the reputation of the author of the copyrighted material, he or she retains moral rights to the work. **Moral rights** guarantee the author the right to claim or disclaim authorship of the work, and in certain cases, prevent the distortion, mutilation, or other modification of the work. For example, if Charles Schulz's estate decided to sell the right to draw the cartoon strip *Peanuts,* Schulz's heirs could require that the original content of the strip not change. *Peanuts* would always have to be about Charlie Brown and the rest of the gang—children whose characteristics could not change.

There is one type of work for which an author does not own the right of copyright. If the work is a **work for hire,** the person who employed the author of the work is the one who retains the copyright. Even though another person actually wrote the work, the employer of the author is the person who owns copyright of the work. See Exhibit 21-3 for what is considered to be a work for hire.

EXHIBIT 21-3 WORKS FOR HIRE

The following works are work for hire; the author does not own the copyright.
1. A work prepared by an employee within the scope of his or her work
2. A work specially ordered or commissioned for use as a contribution to a collective work
3. A work that is part of a motion picture or other audiovisual work
4. A translation of another's work
5. A supplementary work
6. A compilation
7. A test and the answer material for a test
8. An atlas
9. Any work that the parties agree in writing is a work for hire

---

RIGHTS OF THE OWNER OF THE COPYRIGHT

The owner of a copyright has certain rights. These include the rights of adaptation and compilation. The owner of the copyright holds the **adaptation right,** the exclusive right to prepare **derivative works**—works based on the preexisting copyrighted work. Derivative works include translations of the original work, musical arrangements, fictionalizations, motion picture versions, sequels, or any other form to which the work is transformed or adapted.

The owner of a copyright has the right to agree or disagree to the inclusion of the work in a compilation or collective work. A **collective work** is one in which a number of individual works have been assembled into a collective whole, such as an anthology or encyclopedia. A **compilation** is a collection of preexisting materials that are selected, coordinated, or arranged in such a way that the resulting work as a whole constitutes an original work. See Exhibit 21-4.

EXHIBIT 21-4 | **RIGHTS OF THE OWNER OF THE COPYRIGHT**

The owner of the copyright has the exclusive rights to:

Prepare a Derivative Work – A work such as a sequel, a motion picture based on the work, a translation of the work into different languages, or in the case of nonfiction work, a fictionalization of the work.

Approve Its Use in a Compilation – A gathering together in one volume of the work of several different people.

Literary Property – If a work is literary property, the author has the right to use the property and to profit from its use.

FIRST SALE RULE

It is possible for the owner of a copyright to give up some of the rights of copyright while the other rights remain intact. An example is the application of the **first sale rule.** If the copyright owner conveys title to a particular copy of the work to a **vendor**—a person who transfers goods or property by sale—the owner gives up the exclusive right to sell that copy. This is known as the *first sale rule.* The copyright owner retains all other rights, but the vendor has the right to distribute the transferred copy in whatever manner he or she chooses. For example, when Stephen King enters into a book contract, he is selling the right to distribute his work to a book company. The company pays Stephen King for the right to distribute his book. Mr. King has lost the exclusive right to sell his book, but he retains all other rights in the work. Mr. King's work is a **literary work,** a work expressed in words or numbers or other verbal or numerical symbols. Because it is a literary work, it is also **literary property,** which carries the right that entitles the author to the use and profit of his or her work. No independent right to use the work is created through any act or omission on the part of an author.

VIOLATION OF COPYRIGHT

There are several ways that the rights a person has in copyright can be violated. **Copyright infringement** occurs if someone other than the owner of the copyright prepares a derivative work, or includes the author's work in a collective work or compilation, without the consent of the copyright owner.

A second way a copyright can be violated is by plagiarism. **Plagiarism** is the act of taking the literary work of another—parts or passages of the writings of another person or the ideas or the language used by another person—and then passing the work off as the product of one's own mind. If there was a copyright on the original work, plagiarism becomes a form of copyright infringement as well.

A third type of copyright infringement is **piracy,** the illegal reprinting or reproduction of copyrighted material. For example, Schroeder tapes a popular movie shown on cable TV and then sells copies of the tapes to his associates at work. Schroeder has committed piracy because the work he taped is copyrighted and he does not have permission from the owner to make copies of the work and sell them.

Is using a videotape recorder to record programs for one's own use a violation of copyright laws? The case of *Sony Corporation v. Universal City Studios, Inc.*, which was heard by the U.S. Supreme Court, settled this issue. See Sidebar 21-1 for a summary of this case. A recent example of widespread piracy involved music available on the Internet.

SIDEBAR 21-1 *SONY CORPORATION V. UNIVERSAL CITY STUDIOS, INC.*

Facts: The Sony Corporation builds VCRs and markets them to private individuals. The Sony Corporation also owns the copyright to some of the TV programs that are broadcast. Universal Studios sued Sony, alleging that the customers of Sony, the purchasers of the VCRs, had been recording some of Universal Studios copyrighted television programs and this practice infringed Universal's copyrights. Universal also alleged that Sony was liable for the copyright infringement because of their marketing and selling of the VCRs. Universal sought money damages, an accounting of profits, and an injunction against the manufacture and marketing of the VCRs. The District Court denied Universal all relief, ruling that noncommercial home use recording of material broadcast over the public airwaves was a fair use of copyrighted works and did not constitute copyright infringement. The Court of Appeals reversed the District Court, and Sony appealed to the U.S. Supreme Court.

Issue: Did the sale of VCRs to the general public constitute a violation of copyright laws?

Rulings: The sale of the VCRs to the general public did not constitute "contributory infringement" of Universal's copyrights. Any individual may reproduce a copyrighted work for "fair use"; the copyright owner does not possess the exclusive rights to fair use.

Supplying the "means" to accomplish copyright infringement and encouraging that activity through advertisement are not sufficient to establish liability for copyright infringement.

The only contact between petitioners and the users of the VCRs occurred at the moment of sale. And there is no precedent for imposing vicarious liability on the theory that petitioners sold the VCRs with constructive knowledge that their customers might use the equipment to make unauthorized copies of copyright material. The sale of copyright equipment, like the sale of other articles of commerce, does not constitute contributory infringement if the product is widely used for legitimate, unobjectionable purposes, or, indeed, is merely capable of substantial noninfringing uses.

The record and the District Court's finding show (1) that there is a significant likelihood that substantial numbers of copyright holders who license their works for broadcast on free television would not object to having their broadcast time-shifted by private viewers (i.e., recorded at a time when the VCR owner cannot view the broadcast so that it can be watched at a later time); and (2) that there is no likelihood that time-shifting would cause nonminimal harm to the potential market for, or the value of, respondents' copyrighted works. The VCRs are therefore capable of substantial noninfringing uses.

Source: United States Reports

COPYRIGHT NOTICE AND LICENSES

The owners of copyrights take measures to insure that people are put on notice that a particular work is protected by copyright. People are made aware of the existence of a copyright by **copyright notice,** a necessary notice in the form required by law that is placed in each piece of work that is copyrighted. Usually this is the word *Copyright,* a *C* with a circle around it, and the date of the copyright.

Someone other than the owner of a copyright can legally use a work that is copyrighted through licensing and the fair use doctrine. A person who wants to make use of the copyrighted work to make a compilation or a derivative work or to copy the work can obtain a license from the copyright owner. **License,** in copyright law, means permission to do a particular thing, to exercise the right the copyright owner has. License can allow duplication, preparation of a derivative work, the use of the work in a compilation, or the preparation of a sequel to the original work.

The license to use the copyrighted work may be a **compulsory license,** one that allows certain parties to make certain uses of copyrighted material not only without the explicit permission of the copyright owner but also only upon the payment of a specified royalty. For example, film director George Lucas retained all the licensing rights to *Star Wars* and the characters created in those movies. If a manufacturer wants to market anything related to *Star Wars* or any of its sequels or prequels, that manufacturer must purchase a license to do so from George Lucas.

There are some instances in which someone can use part of a copyrighted work without a license or permission and not violate the copyright. These circumstances are governed by the **fair use doctrine.** Under this doctrine, a person may use copyrighted material in a reasonable manner without the owner's consent. To determine if the use is reasonable, four interests must be taken into account:

1. The purpose and character of the use, including its commercial nature
2. The nature of the copyrighted work
3. The proportion that was taken
4. The economic impact of the "taking" of the copyrighted work

TRADEMARKS

INTRODUCTION

A second type of intellectual property is the trademark. A **trademark** is any word, name, symbol, device, or any combination thereof that is used by a person or business in commerce to identify or distinguish his or her goods from those manufactured or sold by others. A tademark, like a copyright, is protected by federal legislation. The federal **Lanham Act** governs the use of trademarks and is also designed to protect the public so it may buy a product bearing a trademark with confidence that it will get the product it wants. The Lanham Act also protects the holder of the trademark from misappropriation of the mark by others.

TRADEMARK DISTINGUISHED FROM TRADE DRESS AND TRADE NAME

A product or service may be identified in ways other than by trademark. These methods of identification are by the use of trade dress or trade name. The term **trade dress** refers to the total appearance and image of a product. It includes the size, texture, shape, color or color combinations, graphics, advertising, and marketing techniques used to sell the product. Trade dress is also protected by the Lanham Act. Unlike a trademark, trade dress does not have to be registered in order to be protected. Trade dress must be inherently distinctive and must have secondary meaning. A **trade name** is the name used by companies to identify their businesses; a trade name actually symbolizes the reputation of the business.

REGISTRATION OF TRADEMARKS

In order for a trademark to be protected, it must be registered with the **U.S. Patent and Trademark Office,** a federal agency in the Department of Commerce. The Patent and Trademark Office is headed by the Commissioner of Patents and Trademarks. This office receives and examines patent and trademark applications and determines if certain standards are met. If these standards are met, the Office will issue the patent or register the trademark.

A **registered trademark** is one that has been filed and registered with the U.S. Patent and Trademark Office, and that gives the person who registered it the right to use it exclusively. The initial right to use a trademark extends for ten years; this term can be prolonged for another ten years if an application is made prior to the expiration of the ten-year term. See Exhibit 21-5 for an example of a public notice of the registration of a trademark, and Exhibit 21-6 for the actual registration of the trademark.

EXHIBIT 21-5 PUBLIC NOTICE OF A NEW TRADEMARK

SN 76-504, 612 EARNHARDT, TERESA H., MOORESVILLE, NC. FILED 4-8-2003

THE LIKENESS OF "DALE EARNHARDT" DOES NOT PORTRAY A LIVING INDIVIDUAL.

THE MARK CONSISTS OF THE SILHOUETTE LIKENESS OF "DALE EARNHARDT" WITH HIS ARMS HELD UP IN A SIGN OF VICTORY, SUPERIMPOSED OVER A LARGE LETTER "E".

CLASS 6—METAL GOODS

FOR METAL GOODS, NAMELY, KEY RINGS, KEY CHAINS, KEY CLIPS, COLLECTOR TINS SOLD EMPTY, DECORATIVE TINS SOLD EMPTY, LICENSE PLATES, METAL HOLIDAY ORNAMENTS AND METAL HOLDERS FOR DISPLAYING BASEBALLS (U.S. CLS 2, 12, 13, 14, 23, 25 AND 50).

CLASS 14—JEWELRY

FOR BELT BUCKLES, MONEY CLIPS AND HAT PINS OF PRECIOUS METAL; WATCHES AND CLOCKS; JEWELRY, NAMELY, LAPEL PINS, CHARMS, PENDANTS, EARRINGS, RINGS, TIE FASTENERS, TIE CLASPS, NECKLACES, AND WATCH BANDS (U.S. CLS 2, 27, 28 AND 50).

CLASS 16—PAPER GOODS AND PRINTED MATTER

FOR PAPER GOODS AND PRINTED MATERIAL, NAMELY, BROCHURES, MAGAZINES, NEWSLETTERS, PAMPHLETS, PROGRAMS, STATISTICAL SHEETS AND BOOKS, FEATURING SPORTS, MUSIC, AND WILDLIFE; TRADING CARDS; COMMEMORATIVE STAMPS FEATURING SPORTS, MUSIC, AND WILDLIFE; POSTCARDS, NOTE CARDS; POSTERS; STICKERS; DECALS; CALENDARS; PAPER PLACEMATS; PAPER PENNANTS; UNMOUNTED AND MOUNTED PHOTOGRAPHS; MEMO PADS; PENS; PENCILS; BINDERS; FOLDERS; BOOK COVERS, STATIONERY AND STATIONERY TYPE PORTFOLIOS (U.S. CLS. 2, 5, 22, 23, 29, 37, 38 AND 50).

CLASS 18—LEATHER GOODS

FOR LUGGAGE, ATHLETIC BAGS, SHOE BAGS FOR TRAVEL, OVERNIGHT BAGS, BACKPACKS, FANNY PACKS, WAIST PACKS, DUFFEL BAGS, TOTE BAGS, BOOK BAGS, ALL PURPOSE SPORTS BAGS, GYM BAGS, GARMENT BAGS FOR TRAVEL, HANDBAGS, PURSES TOILETRY CASES SOLD EMPTY, COSMETIC CASES SOLD EMPTY, TRUNKS, BRIEFCASES, ATTACHE CASES, SUITCASES, KNAPSACKS, BUSINESS CARD CASES, KEY CASES, BILLFOLDS, WALLETS, LUGGAGE TAGS, AND UMBRELLAS (U.S. CLS 1, 2, 3, 22 AND 40).

Source: United States Patent and Trademark Office

EXHIBIT 21-6 REGISTRATION OF A TRADEMARK

Word Mark	**ARKANSAS RAZORBACKS**
Goods and Services	IC 025. US 039 G & S: CLOTHING, NAMELY, NECKWEAR, JERSEYS, T-SHIRTS, SWEATSHIRTS, JACKETS, SOCKS, SWEATERS, SPORT SHIRTS, SHORT, SWEATSUITS AND RAIN PONCHOS. FIRST USE: 19350000. FIRST USE IN COMMERCE: 19350000
	IC 041. US 107. G & S: EDUCATIONAL SERVICES - NAMELY, PROVIDING COURSES OF INSTRUCTION AT THE COLLEGE LEVEL AND ENTERTAINMENT SERVICES - NAMELY, ORGANIZING AND PROMOTING SPORTS EVENTS. FIRST USE: 19091118. FIRST USE IN COMMERCE: 19091118
Mark Drawing Code	(1) TYPED DRAWING
Serial Number	73747620
Filing Date	August 22, 1988
Current Filing Basis	1A
Original Filing Basis	1A
Published for Opposition	October 31, 1989
Registration Number	1579111

Continued

Continued

Registration Date	January 23, 1990
Owner	(REGISTRANT) BOARD OF TRUSTEES OF THE UNIVERSITY OF ARKANSAS, THE PUBLIC BODY CORPORATE ARKANSAS 2404 N. UNIVERSITY LANE LITTLE ROCK ARKANSAS 72207
Type of Mark	TRADEMARK. SERVICE MARK
Register	PRINCIPAL-2(F)-IN PART
Affidavit Text	SECT 15. SECT 8 (6-YR).
Renewal	1ST RENEWAL 20000306
Live/Dead Indicator	LIVE
Distinctiveness Limitation Statement	AS TO THE WORD "ARKANSAS"

Source: United States Patent and Trademark Office

REQUIREMENTS FOR REGISTRATION OF TRADEMARK

A proposed trademark must meet several requirements before it will be registered as a valid trademark by the Patent and Trademark Office. One of the elements required for registration is a determination by the Trademark Office that the mark has **distinctiveness,** a quality that identifies the goods of a particular merchant and distinguishes them from the goods of others. Another determination that will be made by the Trademark Office is whether the company is trying to trademark the functionality of the product. **Functionality** under trademark is a doctrine that allows trademark protection for a shape, configuration, or color scheme only if it is nonfunctional: The shape, configuration, or color scheme must have nothing to do with how the product works or is used. A company generally cannot trademark functionality.

TYPES OF TRADEMARKS

There are several different types of trademarks, and whether or not one can be registered depends on the type of mark it is. A **descriptive trademark** directly conveys to the buyer the ingredients, qualities, or characteristics of the product; in short, it describes the product to the consumer. A **suggestive trademark,** on the other hand, is one that requires the buyer to use thought, imagination, or perception to connect the goods with the mark. This type of trademark *suggests* what the product is to the consumer, but the consumer must use his or her imagination to *determine* what the product is. A suggestive mark is subject to registration and protection under the Lanham Act. A descriptive mark may also be subject to registration and protection under the Lanham Act.

A **fanciful trademark** is a made-up or coined term or word. Such marks are considered inherently distinctive and are eligible for registration and protection from the time they are first used. A **geographically descriptive mark** is a geographic word used to describe or indicate where the goods are grown or manufactured. A geographically descriptive mark will not be registered unless it can be shown that the term has **secondary meaning,** that the word or device used as a trademark is not distinctive when it is first used, but becomes distinctive over a period of time so that people eventually come to associate the word or device with that particular product.

A **service mark** is used in the sale or advertising of services to distinguish those services from the services of others. A service mark may also be registered with the Patent and

Trademark Office and is entitled to protection under federal law. Titles, character names, and other distinctive features of a radio or television program may be registered as a service mark. A **generic mark** or **term** is a mark or term that lacks the distinctiveness necessary to merit federal trademark protection. A generic mark may have been a trademark at one time, but the use of the trademark has become so connected with the product regardless of the manufacturer that the mark has lost its distinctiveness. See Exhibit 21-7 for examples of the different types of trademarks.

EXHIBIT 21-7	DIFFERENT TYPES OF TRADEMARKS			
ARBITRARY AND FANCIFUL	**SUGGESTIVE**	**DESCRIPTIVE**	**GENERIC** *(no longer trademarks)*	
Exxon	Orange Crush	Raisin Bran	Escalator	
Microsoft	Roach Motel	Motel 6	Zipper	
Chicken of the Sea	Burger King	Yellow Pages	Trampoline	
Virginia Slims	Dairy Queen		Thermos	
Clorox	Hawaiian Tropic		Aspirin	

TRADEMARK INFRINGEMENT AND ABANDONMENT

The Lanham Act also prohibits violation of the rights a person has in a trademark. **Trademark infringement** occurs if someone other than the owner of the trademark prepares a product that is very similar to the owner's product and uses a mark that is the same or similar to the mark used by the owner. In order to show infringement, the holder of the trademark must prove the **likelihood of confusion** between that trademark and another trademark: whether a substantial number of ordinarily prudent purchasers are likely to be misled or confused as to the source of the different products. If the holder of the trademark cannot prove the likelihood of confusion, then trademark infringement has not been established and there is no violation of the Lanham Act.

What protection from infringement a trademark is entitled to also depends on whether the trademark is a strong or weak trademark. A **strong trademark** is one that is generally fictitious, arbitrary, fanciful, and inherently distinctive. A strong trademark is entitled to a greater degree of protection because of its unique usage. A **weak trademark** is a mark that is a meaningful word in common usage or that is merely a suggestive or descriptive trademark; it is entitled to protection only if it has a secondary meaning.

A company can decide to abandon a trademark. **Abandonment of trademark** happens when the trademark is no longer being used and there is intent to give up the use of it permanently.

PATENTS

GENERAL PRINCIPLES

A third type of intellectual property—a patent—provides protection for original, novel inventions for a set period of time. A **patent** is a grant from the federal government that gives an inventor the exclusive right to make, use, and sell an invention for a period of twenty years. After twenty years, the inventor loses this exclusive right. Patents are issued by the U.S. Patent and Trademark Office. Before a patent will be issued by the Patent Office, it must be **patentable,** that is, entitled by law to be protected by the issuance of a patent. The person applying for the patent must show that the invention is new, useful, and nonobvious. See Exhibit 21-8.

EXHIBIT 21-8 | SELECTED SECTIONS OF U.S.C. TITLE 25, PATENTS

Section 111. Application

(a) In General. –

(1) Written application. – An application for patent shall be made, or authorized to be made, by the inventor, except as otherwise provided in this title, in writing to the Director.

(2) Contents. – Such application shall include –

(A) a specification as prescribed by section 112 of this title;
(B) a drawing as prescribed by section 113 of this title; and
(C) an oath by the applicant as prescribed by section 115 of this title.

Section 112. Specification

The specification shall contain a written description of the invention, and of the manner and process of making and using it, in such full, clear, concise, and exact terms as to enable any person skilled in the art to which it pertains, or with which it is most nearly connected, to make and use the same, and shall set forth the best mode contemplated by the inventor of carrying out his invention. The specification shall conclude with one or more claims particularly pointing out and distinctly claiming the subject matter which the applicant regards as his invention. A claim may be written in independent or, if the nature of the case admits, in dependent or multiple dependent form. The following paragraph, a claim in dependent form shall contain a reference to a claim previously set forth and then specify a further limitation of the subject matter claimed. A claim in dependent form shall be construed to incorporate by reference all the limitations of the claim to which it refers. A claim in multiple dependent form shall contain a reference, in the alternative only, to more than one claim previously set forth and then specify a further limitation of the subject matter claimed. A multiple dependent claim shall not serve as a basis for any other multiple dependent claim. A multiple dependent claim shall be construed to incorporate by reference all the limitations of the particular claim in relation to which it is being considered. An element in a claim for a combination may be expressed as a means or step for performing a specified function without the recital of structure, material, or acts in support thereof, and such claim shall be construed to cover the corresponding structure, material, or acts described in the specification and equivalents thereof.

Section 113. Drawings

The applicant shall furnish a drawing where necessary for the understanding of the subject matter sought to be patented. When the nature of such subject matter admits of illustration by a drawing and the applicant has not furnished such a drawing, the Director may require its submission within a time period of not less than two months from the sending of a notice thereof.

Drawings submitted after the filing date of the application may not be used (i) to overcome any insufficiency of the specification due to lack of an enabling disclosure or otherwise inadequate disclosure therein, or (ii) to supplement the original disclosure thereof for the purpose of interpretation of the scope of any claim.

Source: United States Code

PATENT PROCESS

In order to receive a patent, the inventor files an application with the Patent and Trademark Office, providing written information describing the invention and how it works. A drawing of the invention may also be included with the application. The invention may receive the designation of **patent pending,** which means the patent application has been filed and the **patent examination**—the process to determine if the invention is in fact new, useful, and nonobvious—is ongoing. *Patent pending* is usually abbreviated "Pat. Pend." See Exhibit 21-9 for a chart showing the number of patents applied for and actually granted from 1963 to 2001.

| EXHIBIT 21-9 | PATENTS APPLIED FOR AND GRANTED 1963–2001 |

YEAR	APPLIED FOR	GRANTED
1963	90,982	48,971
1964	92,971	50,389
1965	100,150	66,647
1966	93,482	71,886
1967	90,554	69,098
1968	98,737	71,230
1969	104,357	67,964
1970	109,359	81,790
1971	111,095	78,185
1972	105,300	78,185
1973	109,622	81,278
1974	108,011	76,810
1975	107,456	75,388
1976	109,580	69,788
1977	108,377	52,412
1978	108,648	52,412
1979	108,209	66,170
1980	112,379	71,063
1981	113,966	63,276
1982	117,987	61,982
1983	112,040	72,650
1984	120,276	77,245
1985	126,788	76,862
1986	132,665	89,835
1987	139,455	84,272
1988	151,491	102,533
1989	165,748	99,077
1990	176,264	106,698
1991	177,830	107,394
1992	186,507	109,746
1993	188,739	115,587
1994	206,090	113,384
1995	228,238	121,696
1996	211,013	124,068
1997	232,424	163,147
1998	260,889	169,086
1999	288,811	175,980
2000	315,015	173,475
2001	345,723	183,975
Total	**5,950,768**	**3,202,443**

Source: United States Patent and Trademark Office

PUBLIC USE

If, during the patent examination, it is found that the invention was in **public use** (any non-secret use of the completed and operative invention in its intended way) and the invention has been in public use for more than a year prior to the filing of the application for the patent, then the patent will not be granted. If, after the patent has been issued, it is discovered the invention was in public use, then the issued patent will be invalid.

LETTERS PATENT AND THE RIGHTS GRANTED

Dan Hedges, a chemist with a crime laboratory, discovers a new chemical that can be used to detect fingerprints on any type of surface. Dan decides to try to patent this discovery and files an application for a patent. If it is decided by the federal Patent Office that the chemical is indeed new, useful, and nonobvious, then it will issue a patent. The **letters patent** is the instrument issued by the government to Dan Hedges granting or confirming the patent of the new invention.

Mr. Hedges is the **patentee,** the person to whom the patent has been granted. Mr. Hedges has **patent rights,** the right to the exclusive manufacture, use, and sale of the invention. If he wishes to sell these rights, he may use a **patent right dealer,** a person whose job it is to sell, or offer for sale, patent rights. Mr. Hedges, the patentee, may also decide to issue a **patent license,** the right given in writing by the patentee to another person or company allowing that person or company to make use of the patented item for a limited period or in a limited territory.

As patentee, Mr. Hedges could also engage in **patent pooling,** an arrangement by which a number of manufacturers agree to an interchange of their patent licenses among themselves. He might also enter into a cross-licensing agreement. **Cross-licensing** occurs when two patent holders license each other to use their patented objects, but only on the condition that neither one will license anyone else to use the item without the other person's consent. However, such an arrangement is an illegal arrangement. See Exhibit 21-10 for a summary of the rights of a patent holder.

EXHIBIT 21-10 | RIGHTS OF THE PERSON WHO HOLDS THE PATENT

Patent Rights – The right to be the exclusive manufacturer, seller, and user of the invention.

Right of Sale – The right to employ a patent-right dealer to sell or offer for sale patent rights.

Patent License – The right given by the patentee in writing to another person or company allowing that person or company to make use of the patented item for a limited period or in a limited territory.

Patent Pooling – An arrangement whereby a number of manufacturers agree to an interchange of their patent licenses among themselves.

Cross-licensing – Two patent holders license each other to use their patented objects, but only on the condition that neither one will license anyone else to use the item without the other person's consent. **This is an illegal arrangement.**

TYPES OF PATENTS

There are several classifications of patents based on what the applicant is attempting to patent. A **combination patent** is for a specific *combination* or *arrangement* of different items or elements, rather than the elements or items themselves. For example, combination patents are issued for new drugs: Patent is not for the chemicals used to create the drug, but for the *combination* of the chemicals used to make the drug.

A **design patent** protects the unique *design* of an item against duplication, not the item itself. The process used to manufacture a good or to reach a certain result can also be patented. This type of patent is a **process patent,** a patent of the method that was used to produce the result in a new or a useful way that is an improvement. A **pioneer patent** is for an invention covering a function never before performed, or a wholly novel device, or a device that is so novel and so important that it is a distinct step in progress and not just an improvement on what has gone before.

A **plant patent** is for any distinct or new variety of plants, including cultivated sports (a plant that has an intentional genetic change that causes a variation in its growth habits or blossom color from the other plants of its kind), mutants, hybrids, and newly found seedlings. A plant patent does not apply to tuber-propagated plants or to plants found in an uncultivated state. A **utility patent** is the customary patent issued to any novel, nonobvious, and useful machine, article of manufacture, composition of matter, or process. The patent of an invention or discovery that has never been put to commercial use or recognized in the business trade is a **paper patent.** See Exhibit 21-11 for a summary of different types of patents.

EXHIBIT 12-11 | **TYPES OF PATENTS**

Combination Patent – A patent for an invention that is the combination of different existing items or elements, rather than new elements or items.

Design Patent – A patent that applies to the unique *design* of an already existing item. The design is what is patented, not necessarily the item itself.

Process Patent – A patent that applies to a new or improved method used to produce a result. The process used to manufacture a good or to reach a certain result is what is patented.

Pioneer Patent – A patent for an invention covering a function never before pioneered, or a wholly novel device, or a device that is so novel and so important that it is a distinct step in progress and not just an improvement on what has gone before.

Plant Patent – A patent for any distinct and new variety of plants, including cultivated sports, mutants, hybrids, and newly found seedlings.

Utility Patent – A customary patent issued to any novel, nonobvious, and useful machine, article of manufacture, composition of matter, or process.

Paper Patent – A patent of an invention or discovery that has never been put to commercial use or recognized in a business trade.

PATENT INFRINGEMENT

As with every other type of intellectual property, unauthorized use or duplication of a patented item can occur. If that happens, the owner of the patent may have a cause of action for patent infringement. For example, if Mr. Hedges discovered that another manufacturer was attempting to duplicate his chemical without his permission, he could sue that company for **patent infringement,** the unauthorized making, using, or selling of an invention covered by a valid patent during the term or extended term of the patent.

Liability for patent infringement can exist for a person or entity even if that person or entity did not actually violate the patent. Liability exists for actively inducing infringement and for contributory infringement. In other words, if someone encourages or induces someone else to violate a patent, or contributes to the infringement of the patent, then that person is just as liable as the person who actually infringed the patent. However, Mr. Hedges would not have a case for patent infringement if his patent had expired before the competing company began its manufacture of his chemical. Once a patent expires, anyone can manufacture an item. Item duplication can occur because all of the information related to its manufacture is on file with the Patent Office. The information is public record, but can only be used by the patent holder for twenty years.

AMERICAN INVENTOR'S PROTECTION ACT

Some newly patented items must go through a lengthy approval process before they can be marketed. This limits the time a patent is valid, and curtails the amount of time the manufacturer can sell the item under patent. For example, when a pharmaceutical company develops a new drug, it will attempt to patent the drug to prevent other companies from duplicating it. When the new drug is intended for human consumption, the company must obtain FDA approval before it can be marketed and sold. Before the drug is given to the FDA for testing and trials, it will be patented so other manufacturers cannot duplicate it. This means that the time limit of the patent has begun to run; part of the twenty-year time period will be used up even before the drug is available to consumers. The FDA approval process lessens the amount of time a drug company can recoup the costs of developing the drug before the patent expires. In order to benefit drug companies, Congress passed the **American Inventor's Protection Act,** a federal law that authorizes the Patent and Trademark Office to extend the terms of a drug patent if delays in Food and Drug Administration trials continue for more than three years. See Exhibit 21-12 for parts of this statute.

EXHIBIT 21-12	PART OF THE AMERICAN INVENTOR'S PROTECTION ACT

35 U.S.C. § 155   The term of a patent which encompasses within its scope a composition of matter or a process for using such composition shall be extended if such composition or process has been subjected to a regulatory review by the Federal Food and Drug Administration pursuant to the Federal Food, Drug, and Cosmetic Act leading to the publication of regulation permitting the interstate distribution and sale of such composition or process and for which there has thereafter been a stay of regulation of approval imposed pursuant to section 409 of the Federal Food, Drug, and Cosmetic Act which stay was in effect on January 1, 1981, by a length of time to be measured from the date such stay of regulation of approval was imposed until such proceedings are finally resolved and commercial marketing permitted. The patentee, his heirs, successors or assigns shall notify the Director within ninety days of the date of enactment of this section or the date the stay of regulation of approval has been removed, whichever is later, of the number of the patent to be extended and the date the stay was imposed and the date commercial marketing was permitted. On receipt of such notice, the Director shall promptly issue to the owner of record of the patent a certificate of extension, under seal, stating the fact and length of the extension and identifying the composition of matter or process for using such composition to which such extension is applicable. Such certificate shall be recorded in the official file for each patent extended and such certificate shall be considered as part of the original patent, and an appropriate notice shall be published in the Official Gazette of the Patent and Trademark Office.

Source: United States Code

ABANDONMENT OF PATENT

A patent holder may choose not to exercise his or her rights and abandon the patent. **Abandonment of patent** occurs when the patent holder decides to dedicate his or her invention to public use. The intent to abandon the patent is shown by the patent holder's failure to sue infringers, sell licenses, or otherwise make an effort to realize a personal advantage from the patent. The patent holder does not attempt to make money or gain some other advantage from the patent.

TRADE SECRETS

IN GENERAL

A fourth type of intellectual property is a trade secret, a type of property that contains elements of copyright and patent, but that is different from any other type of intellectual property. A **trade secret** is any formula, pattern, plan, process, tool, mechanism, or compound that is used in one's business and is known only by the owner and those employees to whom it is necessary to confide it. A trade secret is information that could be patented or copyrighted; however, because the information becomes public knowledge and patents and copyrights expire, the information is not revealed as part of the patent process or copyrighted. The information about the process, formula, or plan is kept secret within the company. A trade secret may give a company an opportunity to obtain an advantage over competitors who do not know or use it.

MISAPPROPRIATION

Under common law, the only cause of action available to a company if another company discovers and starts to use a trade secret is misappropriation of the trade secret. **Misappropriation of a trade secret** is the unauthorized, improper, or unlawful use of another company's trade secret in the hope of capitalizing on the secret. Trade secret law has been codified into federal law (see below). However, if the trade secret does not meet federal law requirements, the only protection is under common law.

THE SECRET FORMULA

The best example of a trade secret is the secret formula for Coca-Cola. Only a few of the top executives in the company know the exact ingredients and formula for the syrup used to make Coca-Cola. Other employees only know what they need to know about the formula, if anything. The higher a person rises in the company, the more of the formula the person knows. When a person knows all of the formula, he or she is one of the top executives in the company and is locked into the company financially. It is not in these individuals' financial best interests to reveal the secret formula to competitors.

FEDERAL LAW

The definition of trade secret and its protection has been codified in federal law, which is based on the **Uniform Trade Secrets Act.** This Act has been adopted in some form by forty-two states and the District of Columbia. According to the **Protection of Trade Secrets Act,** 18 U.S.C. § 1831 et. seq., a trade secret is any form or type of financial, business, scientific, technical, economic, or engineering information, if the owner has taken reasonable steps to keep the information secret and the information has actual or potential economic value because it is not generally known to or readily ascertainable by the public. See Exhibit 21-13 for the factors used to determine if information is, in fact, a trade secret.

EXHIBIT 21-13	FACTORS USED TO DETERMINE IF INFORMATION IS A TRADE SECRET

1. How extensively is the information known outside the company? The more extensively the information is known outside the company, the less likely it is a trade secret.
2. How many employees in the company know the information? The greater the number of employees who know the information, the less likely it is a trade secret.

Continued

Continued

3. How extensive are the measures taken by the company to guard the secrecy of the information? The greater the security measures taken by the company to keep the information secret, the more likely the information is a trade secret.

4. How valuable is the information to the company and its competitors? The greater the value of the information to the company and to its competitors, the more likely the information is a trade secret.

5. How much time, effort, and money did the company expend in developing the information? The more time, effort, and money expended in developing the information, the more likely the information is a trade secret.

6. How easy or difficult is it for the information to be properly acquired or duplicated by others? The easier it is to acquire or duplicate the information, the less likely the information is a trade secret.

The **owner** of a trade secret is the person or entity that has rightful legal or equitable title to or license in the trade secret. **Theft of a trade secret** is defined as knowingly stealing or without authorization appropriating, taking, carrying away, and concealing the information. Theft of trade secret also includes obtaining the information by fraud, **artifice** (a trick), or deception. Theft of trade secret is also construed as copying, drawing, photographing, downloading, uploading, altering, or destroying the information or transmitting the information by mail or other communication. Theft of trade secret also happens if a person receives, buys, or possesses the information knowing that it was obtained without proper authorization.

ECONOMIC ESPIONAGE

Another form of theft of intellectual property defined by the Uniform Trade Secrets Act is known as **economic espionage.** This form of theft involves foreign governments and agents, and occurs when a person steals or without authorization appropriates, takes, carries away, conceals, or obtains information by fraud, trick, or deception with the intent or knowledge that the offense will benefit any foreign government or agent. It also includes the receiving, buying, or possessing of a trade secret knowing it has been stolen and with the intent of delivering it to a foreign government. A **foreign government** is any agency, bureau, ministry, component, institution, association of government, or any business organization that is substantially owned or controlled by a foreign government. A **foreign agent** is any officer, employee, delegate, or representative of a foreign government. Economic espionage carries a penalty of up to 15 years in prison, up to a $10,000,000 fine, or both. The penalty for theft of a trade secret is up to 10 years in prison, up to a $5,000,000 fine, or both.

CONCLUSION

The law of intellectual property deals with patents, trademarks, copyright, and trade secrets. This area of the law is designed to allow originators and inventors to benefit from their work for a period of time without others taking advantage of their work. Intellectual property law protects ideas from being used improperly by others. The length of protection varies, depending on the type of intellectual property. See Exhibit 21-14.

EXHIBIT 21-14	LENGTH OF PROTECTION FOR INTELLECTUAL PROPERTY

Copyright – Life of the author plus seventy years. This time frame can be extended.

Patent – Twenty years. The time frame can be extended if conditions under the American Inventor's Protection Act are met.

Trademark – Ten years. Registration can be renewed.

Trade Secret – For as long as the secret can be maintained.

Intellectual property law also sets out what rights the person who developed the idea has with regard to the use of the property. A work can be duplicated, sold, licensed, and derivative works prepared. These rights to the work can also be sold.

Intellectual property is protected by either common law or by federal law, depending on the type of property that is protected. Copyright is protected by the Federal Copyright Act, patents and trademarks are protected by the Lanham Act, and trade secrets are protected by common law or by the Protection of Trade Secrets Act.

KEY WORDS AND PHRASES

abandonment of patent
abandonment of trademark
adaptation right
collective work
combination patent
compulsory license
copyright
copyright infringement
copyright notice
copyright owner
derivative work
descriptive trademark
design patent
economic espionage
fair use doctrine
fanciful trademark
first sale rule
geographically descriptive
  mark

intellectual property
Lanham Act
letters patent
license
literary property
literary work
misappropriation of a trade
  secret
moral rights
paper patent
patent
patent examination
patent infringement
patent pending
patent pooling
patent right
patent right dealer
pioneer patent
piracy

plagiarism
process patent
public use
publication
registered trademark
service mark
strong trademark
suggestive trademark
theft of a trade secret
trade dress
trade name
trade secret
trademark
trademark infringement
U.S. Patent and Trademark
  Office
utility patents
work for hire

REVIEW QUESTIONS

SHORT ANSWER

1. What is intellectual property?
2. Which federal act protects trademarks?
3. What are the differences among trademarks, trade names, and trade dress?
4. What is the fair use rule?
5. What are moral rights? To what type of intellectual property do they apply?
6. What is piracy of intellectual property?
7. What makes an invention patentable?
8. What is the difference between a strong and a weak trademark?
9. What is a design patent?
10. What is the first sale rule?
11. What is a work for hire?
12. What is a patent examination?
13. What is the cause of action for a violation of a trade secret?
14. What are the moral rights to a work?
15. How does someone register a trademark?
16. For how long is trademark registration valid?

17. How long does a person own a copyright?
18. How long does a patent last?
19. What is a pioneer patent?
20. What is patent infringement?

FILL IN THE BLANK

1. One company copies the trademark of another and starts using it to mark their product. This is known as _____.

2. A student copies an essay about an author's work straight out of a book, word for word, and turns it in as his own work. The student has committed _____.

3. A trademark that hints at what the product is, is known as a _____ mark.

4. An inventor patents her invention, but before the patent expires, she allows several people to copy her ideas and does not sue them for infringement. This is known as

_____.

5. An inventor files for a patent on a new invention. While the application is being considered, the invention can bear the designation of _____.

6. A person comes up with a new method of manufacturing an item. The person can be granted a _____ on the new method.

7. To promote a new product, a manufacturer comes up with a new term. This is known as a _____.

8. A person who arranges the buying and selling of patents is a _____.

9. The appearance of an item—its color and shape—is known as _____.

10. A work that an author creates for another person who actually owns the copyright is a

_____.

FACT SITUATIONS

1. Roger submits paperwork to the Patent Office about a new way of building filing cabinets. The Patent Office receives it and determines that the invention might be patentable. What type of patent might Roger receive? What will the Patent Office do to determine if a patent should be issued? What designation will the process receive while the determination regarding the patent is being made?

2. What is it called if someone got the information from the patent office regarding the new manufacturing process and started to use the same process before the patent had expired?

3. Susan wants to put people on notice that she has a copyright on her doctoral dissertation. What must she do to insure that people are put on notice that her work is copyrighted?

4. After forty years, the Lion Oil Company decides to change its trademark. They do not renew their existing trademark and register Lionco as their new trademark. What did they do with their old trademark? How might their new trademark be classified?

5. Ava, a chemist, discovers a new chemical formula for a drug that is guaranteed to regrow hair. It has a 100% success rate with no side effects. What type of patent might Ava apply for and why?

6. The Raymond House of Candy has created a wonderful new candy. It does not want competitors to copy their formula—at least not right away. What ways can the company try to keep others from using its formula for a specific period of time or for as long as possible? Which option might the company choose? Why?

7. Two inventors agree to allow each other to use their patents. What is this known as?

8. An artist drew a comic strip for fifty years and then sold the rights to someone else. The person the strip was sold to started to make changes to the characters. What can the artist do to prevent this? How can this be done?

9. A drug company develops a new drug to treat cancer. The drug is patented while FDA approval is pending. The FDA takes three years to approve the new drug. Can the drug company have the patent extended, and if so, how?

10. For what kind of patent would the drug company apply?

CHAPTER 22

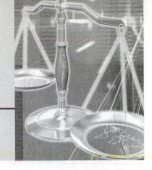

Domestic Relations

INTRODUCTION

Domestic relations (do-*mes*-tick re-*lay*-shenz) is the area of law that deals with matters of family, including divorce, separation, custody, support, and adoption. Domestic relations, in other words, is family law, and family law follows a natural progression—with several variations.

This chapter discusses legal terminology related to living situations before marriage and agreements entered into prior to marriage. The types of marriage that can be entered into are also discussed, as well as the legal requirements for a valid marriage. The chapter identifies and explains issues associated with adoption and surrogate motherhood. Finally, the ending of a marriage by divorce or annulment is explored along with the continuing relationship between the parties after divorce. Terms related to child support, child custody, and remarriage are discussed, along with torts that can arise as a result of marriage.

DOMESTIC RELATIONS PRIOR TO MARRIAGE

"Domestic relations" do not occur only in marriage. The term also refers to relationships that exist prior to or instead of marriage, the circumstances surrounding these relationships, and any formal agreements entered into because of these relationships.

COHABITATION

In order to explain some of these terms, we will make reference to a couple, Bob and Carol. Bob and Carol meet; they like each other. After dating for awhile, they decide to engage in **cohabitation** (ko-ha-bi-*tay*-shən), which is the living together as husband and wife, even though they are not married. Bob and Carol may enter into a **cohabitation agreement,** a contract between a man and a woman who are living together in contemplation of sexual relations and out of wedlock, relating to the property and financial relations of the parties. A cohabitation agreement sets out who gets what property if a couple's live-in arrangement ends. The agreement can also set out a financial agreement if the couple's cohabitation ends. For example, at Bob's insistence, Carol quit work; however, Carol insists that the cohabitation agreement stipulate that Bob will pay her a certain amount of money per month for a set period of time if they end their relationship. See Exhibit 22-1 for a summary of the elements of a cohabitation agreement.

EXHIBIT 22-1	COHABITATION AGREEMENT

1. Agreement between a man and woman who are living as husband and wife but who are not married.
2. Sets out the property settlement if the couple breaks up without getting married.
3. Can include any financial agreement if the couple breaks up without getting married.

COMMON LAW MARRIAGE

If Bob and Carol live together long enough, and if they are living in a state that recognizes it, they may have a **common law marriage.** A common law marriage is one that is entered into without a formal ceremony. The parties agree that they will be husband and wife because they have cohabited and they have held themselves out to be husband and wife. States that do not have common law marriage will recognize other states' common law marriages because of the full faith and credit clause of the U.S. Constitution. (See Chapter 8, Constitutional Law, for more on the full faith and credit clause.) For example, if a couple is recognized as being married in California, then Arkansas—which does not have common law marriage—would also recognize the couple as being married because of the full faith and credit clause. Exhibit 22-2 lists the states that have common law marriage.

EXHIBIT 22-2	STATES THAT HAVE COMMON LAW MARRIAGE
Alabama	New Hampshire (for inheritance purposes only)
Colorado	Ohio (if created before October 1991)
District of Columbia	Oklahoma
Georgia (if created before January 1997)	Pennsylvania (if created before September 2003)
Idaho (if created before January 1996)	Rhode Island
Iowa	South Carolina
Kansas	Texas
Montana	Utah

PALIMONY

If Bob and Carol split up, and a common law marriage were the only type of marriage they had, or they lived in a state that does not have common law marriage, one could be ordered to pay **palimony** (*pal*-i-moh-nee) to the other. Palimony, which is similar to alimony, is the payment of money to one of the parties of a live-in relationship that has ended. *Palimony* is a relatively new term that was created by combining *pal* with *alimony,* giving it the literal meaning of "alimony for a pal." See Exhibit 22-3. Palimony applies only to a nonmarital relationship between parties; it does not apply if a couple were legally married. It came into existence because of the case of *Marvin v. Marvin.* See Sidebar 22-1.

EXHIBIT 22-3	PALIMONY

1. Defined as the payment of money to one of the parties in a live-in relationship that has ended. It applies only to couples who lived together who never married.
2. Can be based on an agreement between the couple. If the only reason the couple entered into the agreement was because of a sexual relationship, then the agreement is invalid.
3. There has to be an agreement of some sort between the parties for palimony to be awarded.

SIDEBAR 22-1 *MARVIN V. MARVIN*

Facts: Lee Marvin, the actor, was being sued by his longstanding live-in girlfriend, Michelle Triolla. Ms. Triolla changed her name to Michelle Marvin, and a short time later filed suit against Lee Marvin using a contract theory. She alleged that she had given up her "lucrative" career as a singer and entertainer to live with Mr. Marvin and to provide domestic service to him. She further alleged that Mr. Marvin had verbally agreed to share all assets accumulated during the course of their relationship and to support her for the rest of her life. She was seeking half the assets acquired during the course of the relationship. The trial court ruled on the pleadings in favor of Lee Marvin. Michelle Triolla Marvin appealed to the California Supreme Court.

Issue: Was the trial court correct when it dismissed Ms. Triolla's claim to half the assets acquired during the relationship?

Ruling of the Court: The California Supreme Court ruled that cohabiting adults could enter into a valid contract and the contract would be enforced to the extent that it does not explicitly rely on sexual services. In other words, if sex was the only consideration for entering into the contract, then there is not a valid contract. The case was remanded, or sent back down to the trial court for further proceedings.

What Happened Next: The ironic twist to the case is that Michelle Triolla Marvin won palimony at the trial level only to have that decision reversed and the entire case dismissed by the California Supreme Court. Ms. Triolla, who helped establish the principle of palimony, never received any palimony as a result of this case.

Source: California Reports

Palimony is not recognized nationwide, and it is not automatically awarded every time two people who lived together break up. The court looks at individual relationships and determines if the couple's conduct demonstrates an implied contract, an agreement of partnership, a joint venture, or some other understanding between the parties. If there is no agreement between the parties regarding their relationship, then palimony cannot be awarded.

MARRIAGE

Bob and Carol continue to co-habitate happily. One day, Bob pops the question; he wants Carol to marry him and Carol says yes.

MARRIAGE IN GENERAL

Marriage (*mehr*-ej) is a legal term defined as the legal union of one man and one woman as husband and wife. Marriage is also a contract binding the parties to each other until one dies or until a divorce or annulment occurs. In order for Bob and Carol to get married, they must first get a **marriage license,** which is permission granted by a public authority to a couple who intend to marry usually addressed to a minister or a magistrate who is to perform the ceremony. In some states, a marriage license is an essential requirement to the lawful solemnization of the marriage. The license grants permission from the state to marry, and lets the person who is to perform the marriage know that the union has been approved by the state. The couple has met the legal requirements for marriage and can be legally married. Because the couple has a marriage license, it is now permissible to conduct the ceremony.

PRENUPTIAL AGREEMENTS

Prior to marriage, some couples sign a prenuptial agreement. **Nuptial** (*nup*-shəl) means "pertaining to marriage," **prenuptial** (pre-*nup*-shləl) means "before marriage"; thus, a **prenuptial agreement** is an agreement that is entered into prior to marriage, but in contemplation and in consideration of marriage. A prenuptial agreement sets out the financial and property arrangements of one or both of the parties to the marriage in the event of divorce or death during the marriage. Another term for a prenuptial agreement is **antenuptial** (an-tə-*nup*-shəl) **agreement.** Contrast these with a **marital** (mehr-i-təl) **agreement,** which can be a prenuptial agreement (before the marriage) or an agreement between two married people who are on the verge of separation. A marital agreement sets out the division and ownership of the **marital property,** which is the property of spouses subject to equitable distribution upon termination of the marriage. See Exhibit 22-4 for a comparison between a prenuptial and marital agreement.

EXHIBIT 22-4	PRENUPTIAL OR MARITAL AGREEMENT?
PRENUPTIAL AGREEMENT	*MARITAL AGREEMENT*
1. Entered into prior to marriage—when marriage is being considered.	1. Entered into prior to or after marriage takes place.
2. Sets out financial and property arrangements for one or both people in the event of divorce or death.	2. Sets out the division of the marital property only.

Because marriage is considered a contract, in order to be married the parties must be able to consent to the marriage. **Consent to the marriage** is a term meaning that each party to the marriage has the mental capacity to enter into a contract, and in this case, has actual intent to marry.

TYPES OF MARRIAGE

Bob and Carol both consent to the marriage. The big day arrives and they have a **ceremonial marriage,** one performed by an appropriate religious or civil official once the parties have met all legal requirements. The actual performance of the marriage ceremony is the **solemnization of the marriage:** both parties, as part of the ceremony, give their consent to be married. See Exhibit 22-5 for the effects of the solemnization of the marriage.

EXHIBIT 22-5	EFFECT OF THE SOLEMNIZATION OF MARRIAGE

1. Both parties give their consent to be married.
2. When the parties give their consent and the couple is pronounced husband and wife, they are now each other's spouse—and marriage partner.
3. The couple is in wedlock—the legal state of being married.

Once the ceremony has been completed and Bob and Carol have been pronounced husband and wife, they are now each other's **spouse.** Bob and Carol are now in blissful **wedlock** (*wed*-lok), or the legal state of being married. Because they are married, they will receive a **marriage certificate,** a document that certifies the marriage. The marriage certificate is executed or completed (signed) by the person officiating at the marriage. The certificate does not necessarily have to be signed by the couple, but it is evidence of the marriage.

There are types of marriage other than the ceremonial marriage entered into by Bob and Carol. A **consular** (*kon*-su-lar) **marriage** is solemnized in a foreign country by a consul or diplomatic agent of the U.S. government. A consular marriage is not recognized as valid in every state. **Proxy** (*prox*-ee) **marriage** is arranged and contracted by one or more agents rather than by the parties themselves. A **putative** (*pew*-ta-tive) **marriage** is one contracted in good faith and in ignorance on one or both sides of some existing impediment to the marriage on the part of at least one of the parties. In other words, the parties intended to be married, but for some reason at least one of them cannot enter into marriage. One or both of the people in this marriage would be a **putative spouse:** a person who believes in good faith that he or she is a part of a valid marriage, even though the marriage is invalid. Very few states recognize a putative marriage as valid; most states rule that a putative marriage is not a marriage at all. In a **covenant** (*cov*-ə-nant) **marriage,** a couple enters into an agreement that they will undergo counseling prior to marriage, and further agree to attend marital counseling prior to either one of them seeking a divorce. A divorce will not be granted unless it is shown that the couple has attended the required counseling. See Exhibit 22-6 for a summary of the types of marriage.

EXHIBIT 22-6	TYPES OF MARRIAGE

Consular Marriage – Marriage performed by a diplomatic agent of the United States; not recognized as valid in all the states.

Proxy Marriage – Marriage is arranged by agents representing the couple, not the couple themselves.

Putative Marriage – The couple intends to wed, but something is preventing them from legally being able to be married. The couple thinks the marriage is valid.

Covenant Marriage – The couple agrees to undergo counseling before they marry and to undergo counseling again prior to either party seeking a divorce.

VOID AND VOIDABLE MARRIAGE AND ANNULMENT

A marriage may be void or voidable. A **void marriage** is a marriage that never legally took place. A marriage might be void because, for example, one of the parties could not consent to the union because of mental illness, disease, or intoxication. A marriage might also be void because it involves an **incestuous relationship**—the man and woman are related to each other to the degree that sexual relationship and marriage are prohibited by law. A marriage also may be void because of bigamy or polygamy. **Bigamy** (*big*-a-me) is willfully or knowingly entering into a second marriage while still being married to the first spouse. Bigamy is a criminal offense, and is classified as a misdemeanor. **Polygamy** (po-*lig*-ə-me) is marrying multiple times while still being married to at least two other people. It also is a crime: Polygamy is not recognized in any state. Polygamous marriages of citizens of other countries who are traveling through or visiting in the United States are regarded as legally valid, as long as polygamy is legal in their home country.

A **voidable marriage** is a valid marriage when entered into and remains valid until either party obtains a court order dissolving the marital relationship. A voidable marriage is binding on the parties until a court declares the marriage to be null and void. A marriage might be declared void if fraud has occurred. For example, the parties may not have had blood tests completed, or one or both of the parties might have been required to obtain parental consent prior to marriage but did not.

So what might happen if Carol found out that her "husband" Bob is a **bigamist** (a person who has committed bigamy)? Carol might have the marriage **annulled** (a-*nulld*), or formally declared to have never existed. Carol would file a petition for **annulment** (ə-*nul*-ment) with the court, and the court would declare that the marriage legally never took place. See Exhibit 22-7 for a definition of void marriage, voidable marriage, and annulment.

EXHIBIT 22-7   VOID AND VOIDABLE MARRIAGE AND ANNULMENT

VOID MARRIAGE

Marriage never legally took place.

GROUNDS
1. Lack of legal consent because of mental disease or incapacity
2. Intoxication
3. Entering into an incestuous relationship
4. Bigamy
5. Polygamy

VOIDABLE MARRIAGE

Marriage is valid until a court declares the marriage null and void.

GROUNDS
1. Blood test or other formal requirement was not complied with.
2. Parental consent for marriage was not obtained when required.

ANNULMENT

Court declares a marriage never took place.

GROUNDS
1. One person is underage.
2. One or both parties were not able to understand what they were agreeing to.
3. Fraud was committed.
4. Inability to consummate the marriage exists on the part of one or both spouses.

Other grounds for annulment include being underage, not being able to understand marriage, giving consent to the marriage as a result of force or fraud, or being physically unable to consummate the marriage. **Consummation** (kon-su-*may*-shən) in the area of domestic relations means the completion of a marriage by sexual intercourse between the spouses.

TENANCY BY THE ENTIRETY

To return to Bob and Carol: Nothing calls the validity of their marriage into question. Living the American dream, they decide to buy a house. When they find the home they want, they will own it as husband and wife. According to the law of real property, when a husband and wife buy a house or land, the two hold it—own it—as a **tenancy by the entirety.** (See Chapter 11, Property.) Only married couples can own real property by a tenancy by the entirety. Tenancy by the entirety exists because the people are married. Each spouse has the right of survivorship, which means that when one spouse dies, the other is entitled to all of the property.

ADOPTION AND SURROGATE PARENTHOOD

Sometimes couples have a difficult time conceiving a child or, for a variety of reasons, are unable to conceive a child. Adoption has long been an option for people who are unable to have children; surrogate parenthood is a newer and sometimes more controversial alternative to adoption.

ADOPTION

After a few years, Bob and Carol decide to start a family. For some reason, they are not successful in getting pregnant. After undergoing fertility treatments with no result, they decide to pursue adoption. **Adoption** (a-*dop*-shən) is the process of creating the relationship of parent and child between persons who do not naturally share that relationship by blood. The court creates the relationship of parent and child when it enters an adoption decree.

Bob and Carol think they have found a young woman who will give up her child for adoption. She is a college student who is looking to place the child with a good family. Bob and Carol talk with her and she decides to let them adopt the child. But when the mother is eight months pregnant, the boyfriend—the **putative** (*pew*-tə-tive) **father,** (the alleged father of a child born out of wedlock)—comes forward and says he is interested in the child. He has even gone so far as to register with the **Putative Father Registry,** a registry where men who think they are fathers of illegitimate children can register. If a putative father is listed in the registry, he is entitled to notice of any adoption action. Because the father has stepped forward, Bob and Carol are no longer interested in adopting the child.

SURROGATE MOTHERHOOD

Because the adoption process is lengthy and quite expensive, Bob and Carol decide to try a more drastic measure: They pursue surrogate motherhood. **Surrogate motherhood** is an arrangement whereby couples who cannot have a child enter into a contract or agreement with a woman to bear a child for them. The surrogate mother carries the fertilized egg to term. The child may be conceived using the couple's own egg and sperm, the egg of a third person and the sperm of the husband, the egg of the wife and the sperm of a third person, a third person's egg and sperm, or the host "mother" may be impregnated with the husband's sperm. If the surrogate mom is impregnated using her egg, she agrees to surrender parental rights when the child is born. All the parties sign a **surrogate parenting agreement,** the agreement between the surrogate mother and the prospective adoptive parents. According to a surrogate parenting agreement, the surrogate mother agrees

1. To be artificially inseminated
2. Conceive a child and carry it to term
3. Assign her parental rights to the birth father and his wife after the birth

The wife of the birth father will adopt the child and she and the father will be regarded as the child's natural parents. The birth mother will have no further contact or legal claim to the child. If the surrogate mother agrees to act as a surrogate for money and part of the agreement is a binding agreement that she will surrender her parental rights, this type of contract is illegal and unenforceable, like the contract in the *Case of Baby M*. See Sidebar 22-2.

SIDEBAR 22-2 *THE CASE OF BABY M*

Facts: William and Elizabeth Stern were a childless couple living in New Jersey. They entered into a contract with Mary Beth Whitehead. Ms. Whitehead agreed to be impregnated with Mr. Stern's sperm and to give up the child to him for a fee of $10,000. The child was born. Three days later, Ms. Whitehead turned the baby girl over to the Sterns. A few days later, Ms. Whitehead, who had changed her mind about giving the child up for adoption, appeared at the Stern home. Very distraught and upset, she pleaded to be given the baby girl temporarily. The Sterns, fearing that Ms. Whitehead would commit suicide, agreed. The next week, Ms. Whitehead informed them that she was keeping the child and that if they began any legal proceedings, she would leave the country. Ms. Whitehead and her husband then fled to New Jersey, where they were able to hide with the child for three months. When Ms. Whitehead was hospitalized with a kidney infection, the Florida police were able to get custody of the child and the child was returned to the Sterns. The Whiteheads returned to New Jersey and sought custody of the child. A year after the child was born, the New Jersey trial court declared the contract was valid; specific performance was justified in part by the best interests of the child. The court awarded custody to the Sterns. Ms. Stern then adopted the child. The Whiteheads appealed to the New Jersey Supreme Court.

Issue: Was the surrogacy contract between the Sterns and Ms. Whitehead an enforceable, valid contract?

Ruling: The New Jersey Supreme Court set aside the adoption and declared the contract void. The contract where the woman was to be paid $10,000, and where there was no showing that the birth mother was an unfit mother, or that the natural father and his wife were fit parents is void as counter to laws governing adoption and termination of parental rights. It also violated the public policy of keeping children with both of their natural parents and treating the rights of the natural parents equally concerning custody of children.

Source: New Jersey Reporter

The main problem with the surrogacy agreement in the Baby M. case was that it violated New Jersey law regarding surrogate mother agreements. See Exhibit 22-8 for the specific reasons the agreement was illegal.

EXHIBIT 22-8 | WHY THE SURROGACY AGREEMENT *IN THE MATTER OF BABY M* WAS ILLEGAL

1. Irrevocable agreement to surrender the child for adoption prior to birth or even conception. New Jersey law only allowed an agreement to surrender the child for adoption to be effective after birth. Birth mother must be given opportunity to revoke agreement.
2. New Jersey law requires the mother to be offered counseling about surrendering the child for adoption prior to signing the agreement. This did not happen.
3. Payment of $10,000 was made for the surrogate mother to carry the child, which violated New Jersey law that prohibited the payment of money in adoption placements.
4. Grounds for adoption in New Jersey are parental unfitness or abandonment. Also, the adoption must be in the child's best interest. The contract required the surrogate mother to agree to all of this prior to the child's being conceived.

Bob and Carol are aware of the case of Baby M., so they use his sperm and her egg. The surrogate mother, Alice, is impregnated. This procedure is successful, and a healthy baby boy is born to Bob and Carol.

However, there is trouble on the horizon. Bob, who has gotten to know Alice quite well before and during her pregnancy, decides to forget the artificial part of the process and engages in an affair with her. Bob is now committing **adultery** (a-*dul*-ter-ee), which is voluntary sexual intercourse by a married person with a person who is not his or her spouse or by a person with a person who is married to someone else. Adultery is a crime in most states, but laws against it are rarely, if ever, enforced.

During his affair with Alice, Bob continues to have sex with his wife. Bob thinks he has it made, but then the inevitable happens: Carol finds out he is having an affair with Alice. Carol is also pregnant, but she does not know this yet. Upset about the affair, Carol decides to commit an act of **cruelty,** the intentional and malicious infliction of suffering upon a human being. To be specific, one night she takes her iron skillet and hits Bob on the side of the head with it. Bob and Carol have both committed acts that establish grounds for divorce.

SEPARATION AND DIVORCE

Divorce (di-*vorss*) is the setting aside of the marriage relationship between a husband and wife. **Dissolution** (dis-ə-*loo*-shən) **of marriage** is another term for divorce.

TYPES OF DIVORCE

Divorce is a generic term. There are different types of divorce. **Absolute divorce** is the total dissolving of the marriage ties: The parties are completely released from their matrimonial obligations. A **divorce from bed and board** is a partial or qualified divorce: The parties are separated and forbidden to live or cohabit together. A **foreign divorce** is obtained out of the state or country where the marriage was solemnized. For example, Bob and Carol could go to Las Vegas and obtain a divorce there. However, they would not want to obtain a **Mexican divorce,** which takes place in Mexico, either through the mail or with one spouse appearing in Mexico and obtaining a divorce without ever having established a Mexican domicile. Carol and Bob would not want this kind of divorce because it is not recognized as valid in the United States. A very specialized type of divorce is **rabbinical divorce**—divorce granted by the authority given to rabbis. In an **ex parte divorce** proceeding, only one party appears and participates; the other spouse does not appear. Whether or not this divorce proceeding is valid depends on the notice given to the spouse who does not appear. In a **no fault divorce,** the parties are not required to prove fault other than the existence of **irreconcilable differences** (ir-rek-ən-*sy*-lebl *dif*-ren-sez). *Irreconcilable differences* are interpreted as dissension and personality conflicts within the marriage relationship: The marriage has been destroyed and there is no reasonable expectation of reconciliation. **Incompatibility**—deep and irreconcilable conflict in personalities or temperament—makes it impossible for the parties to continue a normal marital relationship. See Exhibit 22-9 for a summary of the types of divorce.

EXHIBIT 22-9	TYPES OF DIVORCE

Absolute Divorce – All marriage ties are done away with. The couple is completely released from any marital obligations to each other.

Divorce from Bed and Board – Partial divorce in which parties are separated and ordered to live apart. There is no obligation to support each other or live together.

Foreign Divorce – Is obtained in a different state or country from the one the couple was married in.

Mexican Divorce – Takes place in Mexico but is not recognized as being valid in the United States because the parties do not have to live in Mexico.

Rabbinical Divorce – Divorce granted by a rabbi based on authority granted to rabbis.

No Fault Divorce – Parties are not required to prove fault; all they have to show is irreconcilable differences.

Ex Parte Divorce – Only one of the parties to the divorce appears and participates in the hearing.

SEPARATION

Bob and Carol are not ready for divorce—yet. They decide to try a period of **separation,** agreeing to live apart from each other. A **separation agreement** is a written agreement between a husband and wife who have separated that articulates arrangements concerning child custody, child support, alimony, and property division. If the separation is court ordered, then it is a **legal separation.** As part of a legal separation, the court can order that one spouse provide **maintenance**—the furnishing of support or the means of living—to the other spouse.

Bob and Carol do not have a legal separation; they just separate, and after a few weeks they attempt a **reconciliation** (rek-ən-sil-ee-*ay*-shən), the act of resolving differences. Reconciliation is also the resumption of cohabitation by a couple that has been separated. But the reconciliation fails. Bob misses Alice and decides to move in with her. He and Alice engage in **open and notorious adultery,** residing together publicly as if **conjugal** (*kon*-jugal) **rights**—the right that husband and wife have to each other's company, comfort, and affection—exist and the fact that they are not married must be known in the community.

GROUNDS FOR DIVORCE

This is the last straw for Carol. She hires an attorney and sues for divorce. In her petition, she alleges adultery and **desertion** (de-*zer*-shən)—voluntary separation of one of the parties to a marriage from the other without the consent of or without having been wronged by the second party with the intention to live apart and without any intention to return to the cohabitation. Carol also alleges that Bob treated her with mental cruelty during their marriage. **Mental cruelty** is a course of conduct on the part of one spouse to another spouse that can endanger the mental and physical health of the other spouse. This conduct has the effect of causing the marital relationship to become intolerable. When it is used as grounds for divorce, the person making the claim must show the conduct caused such embarrassment, humiliation, and anguish that his or her life became unbearable.

ALIMONY, CUSTODY, AND PROPERTY

Carol also asks for **alimony** (*al*-i-moh-nee), ongoing support payments by a divorced spouse, usually payment made for the maintenance of the former spouse. She wants to be kept in the standard of living to which she has become accustomed. She also asks for **alimony pendente lite** (*al*-i-moh-nee pen-*den*-te li-*tee*), temporary alimony that is paid while a suit for divorce is pending. Alimony pendente lite can include a reasonable allowance for the cost of preparing the suit for divorce. In other words, one spouse not only pays for the support of the other spouse but also can be paying the costs of the divorce action the other spouse wants to file. Carol also is requesting sole **custody** of her child (the right to care for and control the child), plus a **partition** of property, which is the division of the property belonging to the husband and wife as co-owners. Carol is also seeking **child support**— money paid from one parent to the other for the support of the child or children. Child support follows the child, not the parent; if the child goes to live with someone else, the support follows the child. After her petition for divorce is filed, Carol decides two can play at Bob's game and begins an affair with Ted, an old boyfriend.

DEFENSES TO DIVORCE

Bob is served and hires his own attorney, who files a response to the divorce petition. Two defenses to the divorce are raised. One is **condonation** (kon-do-*nay*-shən), the forgiveness of one spouse of the other's conduct that constituted the grounds for divorce. Bob alleges Carol forgave him his adultery when they attempted to reconcile. The second defense is **recrimination** (re-krim-i-*nay*-shən): Carol is not totally innocent. Bob also has grounds for divorce because Carol struck him in the head with an iron skillet. That deed would be grounds for divorce if Bob were bringing the action against Carol.

PATERNITY

During the initial phase of the divorce proceeding, it is discovered that Carol is pregnant. Bob also finds out that Carol has been having an affair with Ted. The divorce proceeding must wait until after the child is born because the court will not allow a married woman to **bastardize** her child, that is, have the child out of wedlock because of the divorce action. A **bastard,** in legal terms, is a child that is born out of wedlock. Bob and Carol must wait until the birth of a baby boy, Bob Junior (Ted Junior?), to continue their divorce.

Carol amends her petition, requesting that Bob pay child support for two children rather than one. In his answer, Bob states that he is not the father of the second child, that Carol was having an affair at the time the child was conceived, and that someone else is the father of the child. If the couple were not involved in a divorce, a **paternity suit**—a proceeding to establish the paternity of a child born out of wedlock—would be filed. However, the present court can establish **paternity,** the status of being a father, between Bob and Ted. The court enters an order directing that paternity testing be performed to determine who is, in fact, the father of Carol's child. One of two tests may be used to determine paternity. The first is human leukocyte antigen (HLA) testing, which is a blood test that compares the blood chemistry of a fetus and its alleged father. Several states use deoxyribonucleic acid (DNA) testing rather than HLA testing. The DNA of the parent and the child are examined to determine who the father is.

Test results reveal that Bob is indeed the father of Carol's baby. The court must now decide the custody of two children and the division of the property of the couple.

PROPERTY DIVISION

In determining how property is distributed after divorce, the court in some states attempts to distinguish between that which is separate and that which is marital. **Separate property** is property owned by a married person in his or her own right during the marriage or acquired afterwards by gift, devise, or exchange for other separate property. Marital property consists of any assets acquired by either spouse during marriage except those that can be shown to be separate. Other states are community property states. The term **community property** refers to the earnings of either spouse or property acquired by either spouse during the course of the marriage that is considered the property of both spouses. In the event of a divorce, the other spouse is entitled, as a matter of law, to one half of all the marital assets. In a community property state, separate property is property that is brought to the marriage by either spouse or acquired during marriage by gift, bequest, devise, or descents. If a person receives property as a gift or an inheritance, or it passes to the person because of some earlier arrangement, then the property is not subject to community property rules. See Exhibit 22-10 for a listing of the states that have community property laws.

EXHIBIT 22-10	COMMUNITY PROPERTY STATES	
Arizona	Louisiana	Texas
California	Nevada	Washington
Idaho	New Mexico	Wisconsin

Because Bob and Carol do not live in a community property state, the court will set aside Bob's separate property and Carol's separate property, and then make a division of the rest of the property. If one person is found to be at fault for the divorce, he or she may receive more property than the other. If both parties are found to be at fault, then the court may engage in **equitable distribution** (*ek*-wi-tə-bəl dis-tri-*byoo*-shen) of the marital assets: The property is distributed equally and equitably between the parties. Exhibit 22-11 contains a list of everything a court may decide during a divorce proceeding.

EXHIBIT 22-11	ISSUES DECIDED BY THE COURT DURING A DIVORCE CASE

1. **Alimony** – Continuing support payments for the maintenance of one of the former spouses.
2. **Custody** – The right to care for and control the child.
   a. **Sole Custody** – Only one parent has custody of the child.
   b. **Divided Custody** – One parent has legal custody, but the child lives part of the time with one parent and part of the time with the other parent.
   c. **Joint Custody** – Both parents have legal custody of the child and both participate in making major decisions regarding the child.
3. **Partition of Property** – What each spouse receives depends on whether the state is a community property state or a separate and marital property state.
   a. **Separate Property** – Property one of the spouses owned prior to marriage and property acquired during marriage, by gift, inheritance, or exchange.
   b. **Marital Property** – Property that is acquired during marriage unless it meets the criteria to be separate property.
   c. **Community Property** – All property and earnings accumulated during the marriage are community property and are divided in half if the marriage ends.

The court decides that both parties have grounds for divorce and equitably distributes the marital property between Bob and Carol.

TENDER YEARS DOCTRINE

The court must next determine custody of the children. The state Bob and Carol live in no longer practices the tender years doctrine. In states that still recognize it, the **tender years doctrine** provides that courts typically award custody of children of "tender years" to the mother unless she is found to be unfit. In order to insure the best interests of the children are being met, the court appoints a **guardian ad litem** or **next friend** to represent the children. The next friend or guardian ad litem is an officer of the court who is appointed to look after the interests of the minor that he or she represents. Minor children cannot represent themselves, so someone is appointed to represent them.

CHILD CUSTODY AND SUPPORT

One issue that court must deal with during the actual divorce and even after the divorce is granted is determining which parent will receive custody of the children. The court is also charged with determining how much child support the noncustodial parent will have to pay.

TYPES OF CHILD CUSTODY

The court can consider several options for custody of the children. One option is **sole custody**—one of the parties has custody. Another option is **divided custody,** an arrangement wherein the child lives part of the time with one parent and part of the time with the other parent. In divided custody, legal custody remains with only one parent; custody is not shared. A third option is **joint custody:** Both parents retain legal custody of the child and jointly participate in reaching major decisions regarding the child. If there is a noncustodial parent, then that parent has the right of **visitation**—the right to visit the child at such times and places as the court orders.

After hearing the case, the court issues a **divorce decree,** the final order that sets out the rights and responsibilities of the parties who are no longer married. The marital property is split equally, and Carol is awarded sole custody of the children. One reason for this is that Bob is still living with Alice, the surrogate mother. Carol's request for alimony is denied because of her affair with Ted. Bob is ordered to pay child support for the two children until they reach the age of 18.

NONPAYMENT OF SUPPORT

If a parent fails to pay child support, he or she is said to be in **arrears** (ah-*rears*): money (support) is overdue and unpaid. The custodial parent can seek to enforce the child support order even if the noncustodial parent is out of state. The order would be enforced using the **Uniform Reciprocal Enforcement of Support Act (URESA).** This is an act that allows a court decree from one state court ordering child support to be sent to another state where the noncustodial parent resides to have that state's courts enforce the order.

But Bob is a good father and pays his support in full and on time.

EMANCIPATION

The obligation to pay child support will continue until children of divorced parents reach the age of majority or are emancipated. The term **emancipation** (ee-man-sə-*pay*-shən), when used in domestic relations, means that the parents have voluntarily surrendered the right to the care, custody, and earnings of a child and have renounced their duties as parents. The child is now treated as an adult for purposes of parental control over the actions of the child and for the obligation a parent has to support a child. **Complete emancipation** is the full surrendering of the care, custody, and earnings of a child, as well a renunciation of parental duties. **Partial emancipation** frees a child for only a part of the time he or she is a minor. This term is also used when parents have surrendered only some of their rights, or the child is emancipated for some purposes but not for others. An **emancipated minor** is a child under the age of eighteen who is totally self-supporting. In some states, the parents and child must go to court to have the child emancipated.

TORT ACTIONS RELATED TO MARRIAGE

A tort is a civil wrong committed by one person against another. Certain torts are unique to the marital relationship.

ALIENATION OF AFFECTION AND LOSS OF CONSORTIUM

Back to our little drama. Carol is still not satisfied; she wants to get at Alice, the surrogate mother. Carol has an option available to her: She can sue Alice for loss of consortium or alienation of affection. **Consortium** (kon-*sore*-shum) is defined as the rights and duties of a husband and wife to each other resulting from their marriage. Consortium includes companionship, love, affection, assistance, comport, cooperation, and sexual relations. **Loss of consortium** is the loss of the spouse's assistance and companionship or his or her willingness to have sexual relations. **Alienation of affection** is a cause of action in tort law based on willful and malicious interference with a marriage relationship by a third party. See Exhibit 22-12. To prove alienation of affection, the plaintiff must show the following elements:

1. Wrongful conduct on the part of the defendant
2. Loss of the spouse's affection or consortium
3. A causal connection between the conduct of the defendant and the loss of affection

---

EXHIBIT 22-12 | **TORTS THAT ARISE BECAUSE OF MARRIAGE**

1. **Loss of Consortium** – Cause of action in tort law because of the loss of a spouse's assistance, companionship, and willingness to have sexual relations.
2. **Alienation of Affection** – Willful and malicious interference with a marriage relationship by a third party. The plaintiff must show:
   a. Wrongful conduct on the part of the defendant
   b. Loss of the affection or consortium of the spouse
   c. A causal connection between the conduct of the defendant and the loss of consortium

---

Prior to filing suit, Ted proposes to Alice. Rather than engaging in another court battle, Carol accepts Ted's proposal.

SECOND MARRIAGE

Marriage creates certain relationships between a man and a woman in turn that create certain rights and responsibilities. If a couple divorces and then one or both of the parties remarries, different relationships can be created, depending on the circumstances.

STEPPARENTS

When Carol and Ted marry, Ted becomes a **stepparent**—the father (or mother) of a child born during a previous marriage of the other parent. Bob and Alice's children become the **stepchildren,** the children of one of the spouses by a former marriage. Put another way, a stepchild is a child who has a parent by his or her natural parent's second marriage and who has not been adopted by that parent.

After learning that Carol and Ted are marrying, Bob finally proposes to Alice. One reason he does so is to get back at Carol. So Carol marries Ted to get even with Bob, and Bob marries Alice to get even with Carol.

And Bob, Carol, Ted, and Alice live happily ever after.

CONCLUSION

Domestic relations can begin when a couple lives together or cohabitates. They can sign an agreement that sets out what property they will receive if the relationship ends. If the couple stay together and decide to marry, they may sign a prenuptial agreement. The couple may have a common law marriage simply because they have lived together or they may have a more formal marriage.

Children are also part of domestic relations. Adoption is one option for a couple that cannot conceive a child, forming a parent-child relationship where one did not previously exist. Surrogate parenthood is another option; however, the couple must be careful regarding the agreement to make sure it is valid.

When couples no longer desire to be married, they may separate or divorce. A separation may involve the parties simply deciding to live apart, or it can be a more formal, court-ordered separation with support payments being made. Divorce can be total or limited, such as a divorce from bed and board. The court may have to make decisions regarding property division depending on the rules that apply in a particular state. Custody of minor children may also have to be decided; this custody can be joint, divided, or sole.

Simply put, domestic relations is the area of law that deals with families and the issues inherent in family relationships.

KEY WORDS AND PHRASES

absolute divorce
adoption
adultery
alienation of affection
alimony
annulment
antenuptial agreement
arrears
bigamy
child support
common law marriage
community property
condonation
conjugal rights
consummation
custody
desertion
divided custody
divorce
divorce from bed and board

emancipation
ex parte divorce
guardian ad litem
irreconcilable differences
joint custody
legal separation
loss of consortium
marital agreement
marital property
marriage
mental cruelty
no fault divorce
open and notorious adultery
palimony
paternity
paternity suit
polygamy
prenuptial agreement
putative father
Putative Father Registry

putative marriage
reconciliation
recrimination
separate property
separation
solemnization of marriage
spouse
stepchildren
stepparent
surrogate motherhood
surrogate parenting
 agreement
tender years doctrine
Uniform Reciprocal
 Enforcement of Support
 Act (URESA)
visitation
void marriage
voidable marriage

REVIEW QUESTIONS

SHORT ANSWER

1. What is the difference between a void marriage and voidable marriage?
2. What are some of the bases for a void marriage?
3. What are some of the bases for a voidable marriage?
4. What is annulment?
5. What is an absolute divorce?
6. What is an informal marriage?
7. What must a couple possess before they can marry?
8. What is a no fault divorce?
9. What are the types of custody?
10. What is the Putative Father Registry?
11. What is alienation of affection?
12. What is considered to be consummation of marriage?
13. What is the difference between bigamy and polygamy?
14. What is the tender years doctrine?
15. What are the elements of the tort of loss of consortium?

16. What makes property separate property or marital property?

17. What are the elements of open and notorious adultery?

18. What makes a marriage a void marriage?

19. What makes a marriage a voidable marriage?

20. What is a guardian ad litem?

FILL IN THE BLANK

1. One spouse forgives the other for what created the grounds for divorce. This is termed _____.

2. A defendant spouse also has grounds for divorce. This is known as _____.

3. A couple is holding themselves out as husband and wife, even though they are not married. One is married to someone else, and this is known in their community. What term applies to their relationship? _____.

4. Payments made from one spouse to another that are ordered by a court while a divorce is pending are known as _____

5. The grounds used for a no fault divorce are called _____.

6. Both parents having legal custody of a child is known as _____.

7. The right a person has to a spouse's care, comfort, and affection is known as _____.

8. When a noncustodial parent falls behind in child support, the parent is in _____.

9. A man who is claiming to be the father of an illegitimate child but whose paternity has not been established is known as a _____.

10. _____ are the payments one person has to pay another when a live-in arrangement ends.

FACT SITUATIONS

1. A state has a law providing that if a couple live together as husband and wife for a certain period of time they will be considered legally husband and wife. What type of marriage is this?

2. The couple move to another state that does not have this type of marriage. Is their marriage still valid? Why or why not?

3. Jeremy and Rebecca are divorced. The divorce decree states that their son will live with Rebecca and will visit Jeremy every other weekend, on every other holiday, and for ten weeks in the summer. What custody arrangement is this?

4. What type of custody would Jeremy and Rebecca have if they both retained custody of the child and he spent the same amount of time with both parents?

5. Denzel and Cammie are married when Cammie is only 16 years old. The age of majority in the state where they live is 18. What type of marriage is this?

6. Brent and Lisa are seeking a divorce. Lisa is alleging that Brent committed adultery while they were married. Brent admits to the adultery, but says that it happened five years ago and that Lisa allowed him to move back home where they resumed their normal lives as a married couple. What defense is Brent raising to the divorce action?

7. Roberto and Inez have filed for divorce. Inez is alleging that Roberto had an affair while they were married. Roberto, in his answer, alleges that Inez also had an affair while they were married. What defense to the divorce has Roberto raised?

8. Henri alleges he is the father of Monique's baby. What must he do to receive notice if Monique tries to give up the child for adoption?

9. Wesley and Olga undergo counseling before they marry and agree to seek additional counseling prior to filing for divorce. What sort of marriage is this?

10. Nadia has lived on her own since she was 14 years old. She is currently 17 years old, has a job, is finishing high school, and is planning on going on to college. She does not want her parents to have any more control over her. What can she ask the court to grant her?

CHAPTER 23

Decedent Estates

GENERAL PRINCIPLES

The study of **decedent estates** (de-*see*-dent es-*tates*) is the study of property law, wills, and trusts. A **decedent's estate** is property—both real and personal—that the **decedent** (de-*see*-dent), the person who died, possessed at the time of death. The term **estate** (es-*tate*) refers to all the property the deceased owned at the time of death. This estate is used to pay all claims against the estate and the debts of the estate. Once all the debts and valid claims have been paid, the remaining property, if any, is distributed to the decedent's heirs. How the remaining property is distributed is determined by the decedent's will or by state statutes if there is no will. This chapter will deal with laws regarding decedent estates.

WRITING OF WILLS

In order to express her desires as to who should receive what property from her estate, a person will prepare her last will and testament. A **will** is an instrument, in document or some other form, by which a person declares her wishes as to the disposition of her property after death.

ALTERING AND REVOKING WILLS

A will is ambulatory and revocable by the person during her lifetime. The word **ambulatory** (*am*-bu-la-tor-ee) refers to the power the person has to alter her will during her lifetime. If a person changes her mind about property one of her heirs will receive, she is able to alter the will to reflect this change. The term **revocable** means that the will can be canceled or withdrawn at any time. If the person wants to revoke her will and draft an entirely new one she has the power to do so. **Revocation of the will** is the actual cancellation or withdrawal of a will. One way a will can be revoked is by the writing of a new will that cancels any previously existing will; the new will may state that it revokes any and all previous wills written by the decedent.

TESTATOR AND TESTAMENTARY INTENT

A person who makes or writes, or who causes her will to be made or written, is a **testator** (tes-*tay*-tor); a testator is also a person who has died leaving a will. The title of the document is often "The Last Will and Testament of _____." Under English common law, the term *will* referred to a person's real property, and **testament** (*tes*-tə-ment) referred to an individual's personal property. Interpreted literally, *last will and testament* means "the last disposition of a person's real property and personal property." The term *testament* is no longer required for a will to be valid, as the word *will* now relates to real and personal property.

In order for any will to be valid, the testator must have testamentary capacity. The term **testamentary** (tes-tə-*men*-ter-ee) means "pertaining to a will or testament, or derived from or appointed by the will and testament." **Testamentary capacity** (tes-tə-*men*-ter-ee kə-*pass*-i-tee) is the mental ability sufficient for the making of a will; the person must have the intent to create a will and understand that that is what she is doing. Also, in order to have testamentary capacity, a person must understand the effect that her actions will have. There must also be **testamentary intent** (tes-tə-*men*-ter-ee in-*tent*): the testator must intend that the document she is writing will function as her last will and testament. In other words, at the time the will is made, the person must intend for it to be the final disposition of her property. The testator will also make a formal declaration when she signs the will that it is her last will and testament. This is known as **publication.**

ATTESTING TO THE WILL

In order to be considered valid, a will must be attested to. To **attest** (a-*test*) means to bear witness to a fact, to affirm to be true and genuine, or to act as a witness to the formal signing of a document. When a will is attested to, a person watches and affirms that the testator signed the document in his or her presence. **Attestation** (a-test-*ta*-shen) **of the will** is the act of witnessing the performance of the statutorily required actions to make a will valid. For example, state law may require the testator to read each page of the will and initial it to show she has read that page and then sign it indicating this is what she intends. This action will have to be witnessed in order to have attestation of the will. The state statute will indicate the number of people required to witness the testator sign the will and comply with any other statutory requirements. The people who observe this process are known as **attesting witnesses,** and may be required to sign their names to the will for the purpose of proving or identifying it. The **attestation clause** (a-test-*ta*-shən klaws) in a will usually appears at the end of the document where the witness certifies that the will has been **executed** (completed, performed, signed, or carried into full effect) before him or her. See Exhibit 23-1 for a summary of how a will is properly executed.

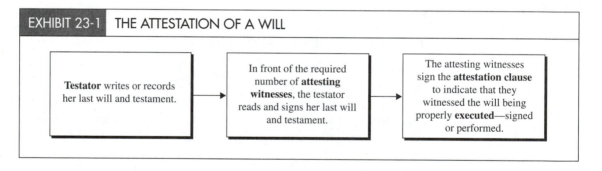

EXHIBIT 23-1	THE ATTESTATION OF A WILL

Testator writes or records her last will and testament. → In front of the required number of **attesting witnesses**, the testator reads and signs her last will and testament. → The attesting witnesses sign the **attestation clause** to indicate that they witnessed the will being properly **executed**—signed or performed.

TYPES OF WILLS

Wills vary depending on the clauses contained in them, how they are written, and even when they are written. Each can be valid, provided the requirements for proper execution have been followed.

AMBULATORY WILLS AND CODICILS

An ambulatory will can be amended, as explained previously. Changes to the will can be made by **codicil** (*kod*-i-sil)—a supplement or addition. The codicil may explain, modify, add to or subtract from, qualify, or amend provisions of a will; however, it does not revoke the entire will. All the codicil does is make an amendment to an existing will.

CONDITIONAL AND JOINT WILLS

A **conditional will** is one that depends on the occurrence of some uncertain event for the will either to take effect or not to take effect, to be defeated. For example, Brenda writes two wills: One is effective if her husband dies first, the other if she dies first. Both wills will be conditional because there is a condition that has to be met for each to be effective. Whoever dies first determines which will is effective and which will is defeated.

A **contingent will** is a will that will take effect only upon the happening of a specified event. If the event does not take place, then the contingent will is never effective. For example, Brenda may write a will that states it is only effective if she lives to be at least eighty years old. If Brenda does not live to be eighty years old, then the will is never effective.

A **joint will** is one shared by two or more persons and is jointly signed by those persons. Joint wills are usually executed to dispose of jointly owned property. For example, Brenda and her husband Rodney jointly own several different plots of land. They have a joint will that states which person is to receive what plot of land when Brenda and Rodney have both passed away.

ORAL, HANDWRITTEN, AND LIVING WILLS

A **nuncupative** (*nun*-kyoo-pay-tiv) **will** is an oral will declared or dictated by the testator during terminal sickness before a sufficient number of witnesses that is written down at a later time. For example, a person who is dying of cancer tells the required number of people what he wants to have happen to his property when he dies. One of the witnesses writes down what was said, and the dying person signs the document creating a nuncupative will.

A **holographic** (hol-o-*graf*-ik) **will** is one that is written, signed, and dated in the handwriting of the testator. If all the conditions for a valid will are met, then the holographic will is a valid will. For example, Dean writes down what property each member of his family is to receive upon his death and then signs the document in front of the correct number of testating witnesses. These witnesses then sign the document. Dean has created a holographic will because he has complied with the statutory requirements for a valid will. Exhibit 23-2 is a summary of the different types of wills.

EXHIBIT 23-2	TYPES OF WILLS

Ambulatory Will – A will that is changeable. The testator can amend—change the will—by using a codicil.

Conditional Will – Some uncertain act must happen or not happen in the future in order for the will to be effective.

Contingent Will – Some future act *must* take place in order for the will to be effective.

Joint Will – A will that is made and signed by two or more people.

Nuncupative Will – A verbal will that is later written down and then signed by the testator.

Holographic Will – A handwritten will that the testator writes, signs and dates.

A **living will** is not a will in the traditional sense. It is a declaration signed by a person that authorizes the withholding or withdrawal of life-sustaining treatment in the event of an incurable or irreversible condition that will cause death within a relatively short time and when the person is no longer able to make decisions regarding his medical care. For example, Harry has cancer that is very advanced; his doctors estimate he has less than a month to live. In case Harry gets to the point where he can no longer decide what medical treatment he wants, he signs a living will stating that he wants no extraordinary measures to be taken to keep him alive.

HEIRS AND THE INHERITANCE OF PROPERTY

One purpose of a will is for the testator to indicate specifically who is to receive what property—personal or real—from the testator's estate. The will lists the testator's **heirs,** the people who inherit the real and personal property of the testator. Heirs can be listed in the will, or they can be the people that the state law states are the heirs and who will inherit if the testator died without a will. There are additional classifications of heirs, depending on their status.

LEGAL, APPARENT, AND NO HEIRS

A **legal heir** is the decedent's next of kin; legal heirs can be sons, daughters, and grandchildren. An **heir apparent** is a person whose right of inheritance is **indefeasible:** It cannot be revoked or be made invalid provided she outlives her ancestor. A **pretermitted** (pre-ter-*mitt*-ed) **heir** is a child or other descendent who is omitted by the testator from the will. If it is established that the heir was excluded unintentionally, the heir will share in the estate as though the testator had died without a will. See Exhibit 23-3. For example, Esther is frustrated and angry with her son Chris. He never calls, writes, or comes to see her, so she omits him from her will, making him a pretermitted heir. However, her attorney made a mistake and also left out her other son, Joseph, and Esther signs the will, not catching this error. Upon her death, if Joseph could establish he was omitted by mistake, he could inherit that part of the estate that he would have inherited if Esther had died without a will.

EXHIBIT 23-3	TYPES OF HEIRS

Generally – An heir is a person who can inherit the real and personal property of someone else.
Legal Heir – The decedent's next of kin: sons, daughters, grandchildren, great-grandchildren.
Heir Apparent – An heir whose right of inheritance cannot be revoked or made invalid.
Pretermitted Heir – An heir who has been left out of the will either intentionally or unintentionally.

Some persons die without having had any children. This is known as a **failure of issue.** If a person dies without issue, state law dictates who inherits the person's property. If a man dies leaving behind a wife who is pregnant, there is no failure of issue; he will have a child, even after he died, in terms of the law.

CONSANGUINITY AND AFFINITY

Certain terms and phrases describe how title to property is transferred from one person to another by inheritance; other terms describe the relationships between people involved in probate matters. The following terms describe the relationship between people when they are involved in probate.

Consanguinity (kon-san-*gwin*-i-tee) is the connection or relation of people descended from a common ancestor. In other words, this is how this group of people—all who have a common ancestor—are related to each other; this term refers to people who are blood relatives. **Affinity** is the connection or relationship of people who are linked because of marriage. Affinity is the relationship between a husband and his wife's relatives, and a wife and her husband's relatives.

LINEAL AND COLLATERAL CONSANGUINITY

Lineal (*lin*-ee-əl) **consanguinity** is the relationship between people who are descended in a direct line from each other. **Collateral** (ko-*lat*-er-əl) **consanguinity** is the relationship between people who have a common ancestor, but who are not in a direct line of descent. For example, a father and son are in lineal consanguinity: They are related to each other in a direct line from a common ancestor. An uncle and nephew are in collateral consanguinity: They have a common ancestor, but they are not in a direct line of descent. See Exhibit 23-4 for a comparison of these two types of consanguinity.

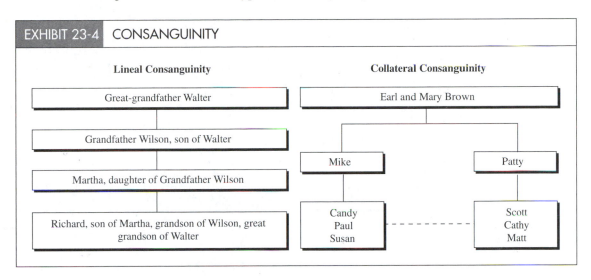

EXHIBIT 23-4 | CONSANGUINITY

In the examples in Exhibit 23-4, Walter, Wilson, Martha, and Richard are in lineal consanguinity: They have a common ancestor, and they are related to each other by a direct line of descent. Mike and Patty are in lineal consanguinity because they have common ancestors—their parents. Mike and Patty are related to each other's children, and their children are related to each other because of collateral consanguinity. They share a common ancestor, Earl and Mary, but they are not in a direct line of descent from each other. Mike is related to Scott, Cathy, and Matt because he is the brother of Sally, their mother.

LINES OF DESCENT

The following terms refer to how title to property is transferred from one person to another by inheritance. Title to the real estate of the deceased will pass by **descent,** or inheritance. Descent is how ownership rights in real property can be passed in probate. **Title by descent** is the title that one person receives to the real estate when the owner dies and the person receiving the property is his or her heir.

Descent can be lineal or collateral. **Lineal descent** is the passing of title in a direct line: from father to son, from mother to daughter, from grandparent to grandchild. **Collateral descent** is descent in a collateral line, that is, from a common ancestor: a grandparent, for example, then to brother from brother, sister to sister, or between cousins.

The term **lines of descent** refers to the order of people who have descended one from the other, or all from a common ancestor, placed in the line according to their birth and showing the connection of all the blood relatives. A **direct line** of descent is traced through those persons who are related to each other directly as descendants only. For example, Hiram and Mary are the parents of Hiram, Jr., whose children are Alfred and William, whose children are Mary, Scott, Martha, and Cindy, whose children are, etc. A **collateral line** of descent connects persons who are not directly related to each other as ascendants or descendants, but who do share a common ancestor. See Exhibit 23-5. For example, Martha and Paul are cousins whose mothers were Madge and Martha, whose parents were Robert and Emmaline. **A maternal line** of descent or relationship exists between two persons who are traced through the mother of the younger. A **paternal line** of descent or relationship exists between two persons who are traced through the father of the younger.

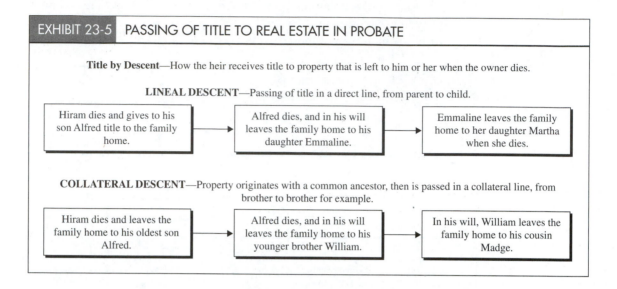

EXHIBIT 23-5   PASSING OF TITLE TO REAL ESTATE IN PROBATE

Title by Descent—How the heir receives title to property that is left to him or her when the owner dies.

LINEAL DESCENT—Passing of title in a direct line, from parent to child.

| Hiram dies and gives to his son Alfred title to the family home. | → | Alfred dies, and in his will leaves the family home to his daughter Emmaline. | → | Emmaline leaves the family home to her daughter Martha when she dies. |

COLLATERAL DESCENT—Property originates with a common ancestor, then is passed in a collateral line, from brother to brother for example.

| Hiram dies and leaves the family home to his oldest son Alfred. | → | Alfred dies, and in his will leaves the family home to his younger brother William. | → | In his will, William leaves the family home to his cousin Madge. |

INHERITING PERSONAL PROPERTY

Transfer of personal property may take place by **bequest** (be-*kwest*), which is a gift transferred by will. To **bequeath** (be-*kweeth*) is to give personal property by will to another person. A **general bequest** is a gift that is payable out of the general assets of the estate, not a bequest of a particular thing or money. For example, "I leave $1,000 to my cousin John" is a general bequest: No specific fund is mentioned that this amount is to be paid out of and it is not a specific statement of a particular piece of personal property.

A **demonstrative bequest** is a gift that must be paid from a specific fund: "I bequeath $3,000 to my nephew, which is to be paid from the sale of my stock in Microsoft." This is a demonstrative bequest because the specific account this bequest is to come from is identified in the will. The purpose of a **charitable bequest** is to benefit religious, educational, political, or general social interest to mankind. An example of a charitable bequest is a provision in a will that states, "I leave $10,000 to the American Cancer Society." A **conditional bequest** is one that takes effect upon the occurrence or nonoccurrence of a particular event: "I leave $100,000 to my grandson William provided he has received his bachelor of arts degree" is a conditional bequest because William will not receive the money until he completes and receives a bachelor of arts degree.

In a **specific bequest,** a testator gives an heir all property of a certain class or kind. "I give all of my stock to my daughter Candy" is a specific bequest because it gives the heir all of a certain kind of property. A **residuary bequest** is a gift of the remainder of a testator's personal estate after the payment of debts and distribution of bequests. "The rest, remainder, and excess of my estate I leave to my cousin Lee" is a residuary bequest because it gives all remaining property to a specific person.

INHERITING REAL ESTATE

A number of terms refer to how real property transfers by inheritance. A **devise** (de-*vize*) is a gift of real property by the last will and testament of the testator. The **devisor** (de-*vize*-or) is the person who is making the gift of the property by will. *Devisor* is a more specific term than *testator*. The **devisee** (de-*vize*-ee) is the person to whom real property is given by the terms of the will.

A **contingent devise** is one that depends on some future event that must happen for the estate to vest under the devise. In a **vested devise,** the future event is referred to merely to determine when the person will come into the use of the estate. A vested devise does not hinder or interfere with the vesting of the estate. For example, "My daughter Estee shall receive the family estate in Oyster Bay when she marries" is a contingent devise: If Estee never marries, she will never inherit the property. But if the will reads, "My daughter Estee shall receive the estate in Oyster Bay when she is 21 years old," the devise is vested because it states when the heir is to receive the estate. See Exhibit 23-6.

EXHIBIT 23-6	DEVISE: THE GIFT OF REAL PROPERTY IN A WILL

Contingent Devise – Some future event *must* happen for the estate to be inherited. To Ralph when he graduates from college. . . . To Martha if she marries before she reaches thirty. . . . To Sam when his first book is published. . . . To Tom if he joins the Air Force. . . .	**Vested Devise** – The future event determines *when,* not *if* the estate is inherited. To Candy when she reaches her 30th birthday. . . . To Bob when he reaches the age of majority. . . . To Mike upon the conclusion of the 2004 World Series. . . . To Frank when he turns 65. . . .

A **general devise** is a devise of land without a specific description of the property. A **specific devise** specifically identifies and describes the land that is passing by the devise. "I leave to my son Henry the home located at 1545 Westchester Lane in Little Rock, Arkansas" is an example of a specific devise.

A **lapsed devise** is a devise that fails because the devisee—the person named in the will who is to receive the property—dies before the testator. A **residuary devise** is a devise of all the property that is not given by devise to someone. See Exhibit 23-7. For example, a will gives to three of the children of a testator specific grants of property. The fourth child is to receive the "rest, residue, and remainder" of the real property of the testator. This is a residuary devise because the property the heir will receive is not specifically listed; the heir will receive all the property that is left.

EXHIBIT 23-7	SPECIFIC AND RESIDUARY DEVISES

Devise is how ownership of real property passes by a will. When he dies, Jay owns two condominiums, three houses, an office building, and an apartment building. He has three children to whom he leaves the property.

Specific Devise "To Keith I leave the condo in Aspen and the home in Atlanta." What Keith receives is specifically described.	**Specific Devise** "To Amy I leave the home in Chicago and the home in Dallas." What Amy receives is specifically described.	**Residual Devise** "To Lee I leave the rest, residue, and remainder of my real property." Lee inherits the condo, the office building, and the apartment building because that property was not specifically given to someone.

Legacy (*leg-ə-see*) is the process of the disposition of personal property by will. An **absolute legacy** is one given without condition and is intended to vest immediately. "I leave to my daughter Ann all my property to have and to hold forever" is an example of an absolute legacy. In an **alternate legacy,** a testator gives one of two or more things without designating which one. For example, a will reads: "I leave to my sister, Sandy, one of my three Rolls Royce automobiles." The testator did not specify which automobile Sandy is to receive.

LEGACIES

A **conditional legacy** is a legacy that may take effect or may be defeated according to the occurrence or nonoccurrence of some uncertain event. For example, the will states that Lorene is to receive her grandmother's engagement and wedding rings if she is married when her grandmother passes away. If she is not married when her grandmother passes away, then the condition has not been met and she will not inherit the rings. A **contingent legacy** is given to a person at a future time that may or may not arrive: "When he reaches the age of thirty, he shall receive $1,000,000." If the heir never reaches the age of thirty, he will never inherit the money.

A **demonstrative legacy** is a gift of a certain sum of money with directions that it be paid out of a particular fund. If the gift fails for any reason, it is entitled to come out of the estate as a general legacy. For example, a will states: "I leave to my grandchild Stuart $1,000 that is to paid from the account maintained at the Good Business Savings and Loan. If this savings and loan should fail for any reason, then this amount is to be paid out of the estate in general."

A **general legacy** is a gift of money payable out of the general assets of the estate. A **specific legacy** is a gift by will of a particular specified item. A specific legacy is limited to a particular item that is specifically identified; thus, the gift cannot apply to any of the other property of the estate. For example, a will states: "I leave to my nephew Wilson my Rhodes College Boston-style rocking chair." The devisor owns other rocking chairs, but there is only one Boston rocker with the seal of Rhodes College on it. The gift of the Rhodes College rocker is a specific legacy because the item is specifically identified; the legacy does not apply to any other property of the estate, and no other rocking chair can substitute for the Rhodes College rocking chair. See Exhibit 23-8 for a summary of types of legacies.

EXHIBIT 23-8	TYPES OF LEGACIES: PERSONAL PROPERTY PASSING BY WILL

1. **Absolute Legacy** – Legacy without condition, intended to transfer ownership immediately.
2. **Alternate Legacy** – Testator gives an heir one item of personal property when there are two or more without specifically designating which item.
3. **Conditional Legacy** – In order for the legacy to be effective, some event must either happen or not happen.
4. **Demonstrative Legacy** – Certain sum of money with instructions that it is to be paid out of a specific fund. If it cannot be paid out of that specific fund, then it is paid out of the general assets of the estate.
5. **General Legacy** – Sum of money that is paid out of the general assets of the estate.
6. **Specific Legacy** – Gift of a specific item of personal property. The property is clearly identified and is limited to that specific item.
7. **Residuary Estate** – Gift of the testator's personal property that is not otherwise disposed of by the will.

RESIDUARY ESTATES AND LAPSED LEGACIES

A **residuary estate** is a gift of all the testator's personal estate not otherwise disposed of by the will. Whatever is not left to someone in the will is the residuary; it is the property that is not left to any specific person. A **lapsed legacy** occurs when the beneficiary dies before the testator or before the legacy is payable. If this happens, the legacy falls into the residue of the estate unless the state has an antilapse statute, in which case the legacy passes as it would if there was no will. Instead of the property falling into the residue of the estate, the property will go to the person according to the state's intestate succession laws. If a person dies and does not leave any heirs at all, then the property **escheats** (ess-cheats)—becomes the property of the state because there is no valid heir to inherit.

INTER VIVOS GIFTS

Sometimes a person may want to give a gift while he is still living. This gift is known as an **inter vivos** (in-ter *vie*-vô) **gift,** one made while the donor is living and that must take effect while the donor is living. In order to be a true inter vivos gift, the gift must be made while the testator is still alive and ownership and possession of the gift must transfer while the testator is still alive. An **inter vivos transfer** is a transfer of property during the life of the owner; possession and ownership transfer while the original owner is still alive.

Sometimes property is given to a minor, and if the state has adopted it, the **Transfer to Minors Act** may apply. This act allows the transfer of any type of property—real, personal, tangible, or intangible—to a **custodian,** a person who takes charge of the property. The custodian has a legal duty to act on behalf of the minor. While the minor is a minor, the custodian is responsible for maintaining and preserving the property for the minor. When the minor reaches the age of majority, the custodianship ends and the inheritor assumes complete control of the property.

PROBATE OF THE WILL

People talk about avoiding probate by writing their own wills, but probate has nothing to do with the writing of the will. When a will is admitted to **probate** (*proh*-bate), the court begins a procedure by which a will is proven to be valid or invalid. While probate has nothing to do with the writing of a will, it has everything to do with whether or not the will that has been written is valid.

PROBATE COURT AND ESTATES

Probate court is the court that has jurisdiction over the probate of wills and the administration of estates. In some states, this court also holds the power to appoint guardians. The **probate estate** is the property of the decedent that is subject to administration by the executor or administrator. An **executor** (eg-*zek*-yoo-tor) is a person appointed by a testator to carry out the directions and requests in his will and to dispose of property according to the will. The executor is named in the will by the testator; if the executor cannot serve for any reason, an administrator may be appointed. An **administrator** (ad-*min*-is-tray-ter) is a person appointed by the court to carry out the directions and requests in the testator's will. In the event that the named executor cannot serve in that capacity, the court—not the testator—selects the administrator.

The executor or the administrator may be required to file a **probate bond,** indicating that the will has been introduced into probate. The purpose of the probate bond is to pay heirs if the executor causes an heir to lose property he or she would have inherited.

The executor or administrator is responsible for the **administration of the estate**—the management of the estate and the settlement of the debts of the estate. Administration of the estate is supervised by the court and usually consists of the executor or administrator collecting the decedent's assets; the paying of debts and claims against the estate; the paying of estate taxes, if any; and the distributing of the remainder of the estate among the people entitled to inherit.

SETTLEMENT OF THE PROBATE ESTATE

Settlement of the estate is the administration of the estate by the executor or administrator. This settlement involves the actual paying of the debts of the estate, the granting to the heirs of their shares of the property of the estate, and doing whatever is necessary prior to final distribution. There may be a **family settlement:** an agreement among the members of a family settling the distribution of the property among themselves. If there is a family settlement, the court does not administer the provisions of the agreement: Whatever the family has agreed to regarding the distribution of property is what controls.

Final settlement is a determination by the court that the estate has been fully administered, and that the administrator has completed his or her job and has accounted for all the money received. All valid debts of the estate have been paid, there has been distribution of the property among the heirs, and any taxes due have been paid. The business of the estate has concluded, and the executor or administrator is discharged from his or her duties. Exhibit 23-9 shows the steps involved in the probate of a will.

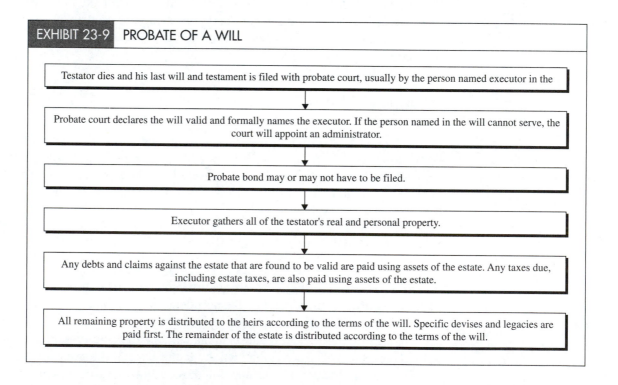

EXHIBIT 23-9 PROBATE OF A WILL

Testator dies and his last will and testament is filed with probate court, usually by the person named executor in the

Probate court declares the will valid and formally names the executor. If the person named in the will cannot serve, the court will appoint an administrator.

Probate bond may or may not have to be filed.

Executor gathers all of the testator's real and personal property.

Any debts and claims against the estate that are found to be valid are paid using assets of the estate. Any taxes due, including estate taxes, are also paid using assets of the estate.

All remaining property is distributed to the heirs according to the terms of the will. Specific devises and legacies are paid first. The remainder of the estate is distributed according to the terms of the will.

WILL CONTEST

If a beneficiary of a will is not satisfied with the will or thinks the will is invalid, he or she may engage in a **will contest,** a direct attack on a decree admitting a will to probate. However, if there is a **no contest clause** in the will, the legacy or devise that is intended for the person who is filing the will contest will be forfeited. A no contest clause places a condition on the receiving of the bequest that no will contest will be undertaken. Put another way, in order for an heir to inherit, he or she must not contest the will. For example, "If any of my children attempt to contest my will, then that child's bequest is specifically revoked and he or she is to receive nothing from my estate" is a no contest clause.

However, the surviving spouse of a testator may challenge a will even if the will has a no contest clause because of a statutory provision called **election by spouse.** State statutes give spouses the right to contest the provisions of a will and take the portion of the estate that is provided to the surviving spouse by statute, or claiming the dower interest. If a spouse chooses not to contest a will, then he or she has elected to receive what is stated in the will.

DYING INTESTATE

If a person dies without a will, then he or she has died **intestate** (in-*tess*-tate). The state's intestate laws—laws that provide for the distribution of the estate of a person who dies without a will—will apply. **Intestate succession** is the actual distribution of the property of the deceased according to the state's intestate laws. For example, if a husband dies without a will, the state statute sets out how much his wife receives, how much his children receive, and how much other relatives will receive if certain conditions are met. If the entire list of potential heirs has been checked and there are no legal heirs at all, then the property usually goes to the state. Exhibit 23-10 is an example of an intestate succession law.

EXHIBIT 23-10	EXAMPLE OF A STATE'S INTESTATE SUCCESSION LAW

ARKANSAS TABLE OF DESCENTS
ARK. CODE ANN. § 28-9-214 – 28-9-215

For purposes of this statute, *intestate* refers to a person who dies without a will.

First – To the children of the intestate and the descendants of any child who predeceased the intestate. If there are no children

Second – To the surviving spouse, unless the intestate and the spouse had been married less than three years, then the spouse only gets half of the estate. If no spouse –

Third – To the intestate's surviving parents or to the sole surviving parent. If no parents –

Fourth – If the spouse and intestate had been married less than three years the portion of the estate not inherited by the spouse passes to the surviving parents.

Fifth – No parents, no children, then the estate passes to any surviving brothers and sisters and their children if any of them have predeceased the intestate. If no surviving brothers or sisters—

Sixth – Surviving grandparents, aunts, and uncles who all share equally in the estate. Or any descendants of an aunt or uncle who predecease the intestate. If no surviving grandparents, aunts, or uncles—

Seventh – Any surviving great grandparents or great aunts or uncles or any descendants of the great aunt and uncle who all share equally in the estate.

Eighth – If no heirs capable of inheriting the estate can be found, then Ark. Code Ann. § 28-9-215 applies.

Ninth – The surviving spouse of the intestate even if they have been married less than three years.

Tenth – If there is no such surviving spouse, then the heirs of the spouse as set out in Ark. Code Ann. § 28-9-214 (go through the entire list again for the deceased spouse), unless the marriage ended because of divorce. In that instance, none of the heirs of the divorced spouse can inherit.

Eleventh – If no heirs can be found, then the property escheats, passes to the county where the intestate resided at the time of death.

Source: Arkansas Code

TRUSTS

A **will substitute** is a document that attempts to accomplish what a will is designed to accomplish: transfer ownership of real or personal property. Some examples of will substitutes are trusts, life insurance policies, or joint ownership of property. A testator may set up a **trust** or **fiduciary responsibility** to manage the trust's property assets and income for the economic benefit of the beneficiaries. In other words, one person manages property and other assets for the benefit of another person.

COMPONENTS OF A VALID TRUST

In order for a trust to be valid, there must be a designated beneficiary and trustee, funds or other property sufficiently identified so title to the property or the funds can pass to the trustee, and the actual delivery of the property to the trustee. Exhibit 23-11 shows the steps needed to establish a valid trust.

EXHIBIT 23-11	THE CREATION OF A TRUST

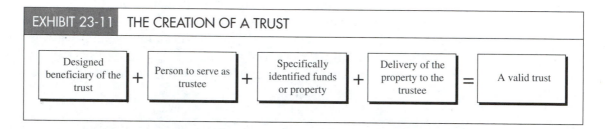

A **trustee** is a person holding a property in trust, and a **trust deed** is a document that represents the trust. A **trust instrument** is a formal document that creates a trust; it contains the powers of the trustee and the rights of the beneficiaries. A **trust fund** is a fund held by a trustee to help meet the specific purposes and goals of the trust. For example, Harold and Holly state in their wills that $50,000 is to be held in trust by First Commercial Bank for the education of their daughter, Samantha. The $50,000 is the trust fund, First Commercial Bank is the trustee, Harold and Holly are the settlors (see below) of the trust, and Samantha is the trust beneficiary. The bank is to use the trust fund—the money that has been deposited with the bank—to see that Samantha completes her education. A trust fund cannot be used for any other purpose other than that specified in the trust document. See Exhibit 23-12.

EXHIBIT 23-12	EXAMPLE OF THE CREATION OF A TRUST

Step 1 – Harold and Holly state in their wills that $50,000 is to be held in trust. Harold and Holly are the settlors of the trust—the people who established the trust.

Step 2 – The trust is for the benefit of their daughter, Samantha. Samantha is the beneficiary of the trust because the trust is to be used for her benefit.

Step 3 – First Commercial Bank is the trustee. It is the entity that will control the trust and is responsible for seeing that the trust is used the way it is supposed to be.

The purpose of the trust is to insure that Samantha receives a college education.

The money in the trust can only be used for this purpose.

INTER VIVOS, LIVING, AND TESTAMENTARY TRUSTS

Trusts vary depending on when they were formed, for whose benefit they were formed, and what conditions they contain. An **inter vivos trust** is created during the lifetime of the set-

tlor, the person who establishes the trust; it is to become effective in the settlor's lifetime. For example, Ricardo establishes a trust fund for each of his children that become effective immediately. Ricardo has created inter vivos trusts because the trusts are created and become effective while Ricardo is alive.

A **living trust** is an inter vivos trust that is created and becomes operative during the lifetime of the settlor and that is commonly for the benefit or support of another person. Ricardo sets up a trust for each of his children and specifies that these trusts are to pay for the living expenses of the children and for their education until they either graduate from college or graduate school or reach the age of thirty. These trusts are living trusts because they are established and become effective during Ricardo's lifetime and are for the benefit and support of his children.

A **testamentary trust** is created by will and is executed with all the formalities required of a will. In the previous example, because Harold and Holly establish the trust that is to be used to pay for Samantha's education in their wills, and the trust was created with all the same formalities as the will, the trust is a testamentary trust.

ACTIVE, PASSIVE, AND BLIND TRUSTS

An **active trust** imposes on the trustee the duty of taking active measures in the execution of the trust. Put another way, there are specific duties and tasks that the trustee must do to insure that the purpose of the trust is met. Title to the property remains with the trustee, and the trustee must be active in meeting the terms and provisions of the trust.

A **passive trust** is in effect when the title to the property that is the subject of the trust is granted to the beneficiaries of the trust, but the trustee still ensures that the property is used for the benefit of the beneficiaries. The beneficiaries of the trust receive legal ownership of the property, but the property is still to be used for their benefit.

A **blind trust** gives management of the investments to an outside person over whom the beneficiary has no control. For example, when a person is elected President of the United States, the president-elect may place all of his or her assets in a blind trust during his or her presidency in order to avoid even the appearance of a conflict of interest. The trustee has the responsibility to perform his or her duties, but the person who is the beneficiary of the trust has no authority over the trustee. In the above example, because the President has no control over the trustee and is unaware of the specific actions of the trustee, he or she could not use the presidential position to influence the trustee or to take advantage of information he or she has access to as President.

CHARITABLE AND CLIFFORD TRUSTS

A **charitable trust** is designed for the benefit of a specific class or group of people or the general public. Because the trust is for the benefit of a specific group of people or the general public, the identity of the beneficiaries of the trust are not established with any certainty. Charitable trusts must be created for charitable, educational, religious, or scientific purposes. For example, Madge establishes a trust for the benefit of the University of Arkansas, her alma mater; the trust is to be used for student scholarships. The trust is a charitable trust: It has been created for educational purposes and the identities of the beneficiaries of the trust are not known because the names of the students who might apply for a scholarship are not known.

A **Clifford trust** is a tax-planning device. According to the terms of the Clifford trust, income-generating property is transferred to a trust that states the income is either to be paid or accumulated for the benefit of a beneficiary who is not the creator of the trust. This trust can exist for up to ten years, at which time the trust terminates and the property reverts back to the grantor. The beneficiary receives the benefit of the property for a period of time, but after this period of time has elapsed, the property reverts back to the owner. During this period of time, the settlor is not considered the owner of the property, so the income generated from the property is not taxed to him or her. The beneficiary is the one responsible for paying any taxes due on the income when the beneficiary receives the income.

EXPRESS, IMPLIED, AND ILLUSORY TRUSTS

An **express trust** is a trust created or declared in express terms. The terms of the trust are usually in writing but can be verbal. In either instance, the terms of the trust are clearly stated. In the example above, Harold and Holly specifically state in their will that the trust for Samantha's education is to be created and specifically state the property that will be placed in the trust. The trust they create is an express trust because the existence of the trust and its purpose are expressly stated. An **implied trust** is a trust that is raised or created by implication or presumption of law based on the circumstances surrounding an arrangement. This type of trust is not expressly created, but because of the parties' statements, actions, and conduct, it is implied that a trust is being created.

An **illusory trust** is a trust arrangement that takes the form of a trust, but because of the powers retained by the settlor, there is not a completed trust. Because the settlor did not give all the necessary powers to a trustee, all the requirements to create a trust have not been met. The arrangement appears to be a trust on the surface, but because the settlor did not comply with all the requirements to have a trust, there is no trust.

CONTINGENT AND DISCRETIONARY TRUSTS

A **contingent trust** is an express trust that will become effective only if a future event happens. For example, Frank sets up a trust for his daughter Candice that will become effective when she reaches her 21st birthday. The trust is not effective when it is created because the condition has not yet been met. The trust only becomes effective when Candice reaches her 21st birthday.

A **discretionary trust** is a trust in which the trustee has discretion as to the types of investments that can be made and also has discretion as to if and when distributions may be made to beneficiaries. The trustee determines when and what type of investments will be made; he or she also decides if and when the beneficiaries will receive any of the money from the trust.

FIXED AND GRANTOR TRUSTS

A **fixed trust** is nondiscretionary: The trustee may not exercise his or her own judgment regarding any aspect of the trust. The trust sets out what investments can be made, if any, as well as the amounts and timing of distribution of the proceeds of the trust to the beneficiaries. In a **grantor trust,** a grantor transfers or conveys property in trust for his or her own benefit or for the benefit of himself and another person. For example, Frank creates a trust, transfers property to the trust, and names himself and Madge as the beneficiaries of the trust. This is a grantor trust because the grantor made himself one of the beneficiaries of the trust.

IRREVOCABLE, REVOCABLE, LIMITED, AND PERPETUAL TRUSTS

An **irrevocable trust** is a trust that cannot be revoked after it has been created; once the trust is created and becomes effective, then it can never be revoked or done away with by the person who created it. A **revocable trust** is one where the settlor retains the right to revoke. For example, Bernardo sets up a trust for his children, but reserves the right to take the trust back at some future time and at his discretion. This is a revocable trust because Bernardo reserved the right to revoke the trust at a later time if he so desires.

A **limited trust** is created or established by a settlor for a specific period of time. If Magda sets up a trust for her daughter Claire that will pay Claire a certain amount of money per year until she reaches the age of 30, then Magda has set up a limited trust. When Claire reaches 30, she will receive the entire remaining amount of the trust and the limited trust will dissolve. A **perpetual trust** will continue as long as the need for the trust exists; it can continue for the lifetime of the beneficiary or for as long as a particular charity exists.

MIXED, POUR OVER, AND TOTTEN TRUSTS

A **mixed trust** is designed to benefit not only a private individual, but also a charity. For example, Joan sets up a trust for her son Ben for his lifetime. Upon Ben's death, the beneficiary of the trust is Rhodes College. This trust is a mixed trust because it is set up for the benefit of a person and then for the benefit of an educational institution that is considered a charity.

A **pour over trust** is actually a provision in a will by which a testator leaves the residue of his or her estate to a trustee of a living trust for the purposes of the pour over trust. Instead of going to a residuary heir, the residue of the estate "pours over" into the trust that has been established. For example Tashi's will provides that the rest, residue, and remainder of his estate is to go into a trust for the benefit of his friend, Sandy. This provision in the will creates a pour over trust because the residue of Tashi's estate, instead of going to a specific person, is going into a trust for Sandy's benefit. A **Totten trust** is a method used to pass property in a bank account after the depositor's death to a designated person through a trust rather than through probate. For example, Craig has a trust document written that states that, upon his death, the money that is in his Metropolitan Bank account will be held in trust for the benefit of his son, Travis.

Sometimes a trust is set up in an effort to preserve assets. A testator may take measures to keep his or her assets from being wasted by heirs who are spendthrifts. A **spendthrift** is a person who spends money profusely and wastefully, one who lavishes or wastes an estate. For example, Mario sees his children fly to Europe every month, watches them buying a new Mercedes every six months, and constantly spending money on clothes and jewelry. Mario does not want the money he is leaving to his children to be wasted, but he wants to make sure they have sufficient income to meet their needs. Mario sets up **spendthrift trusts:** trusts created to provide funds for the maintenance of a beneficiary and at the same time to secure the fund against the beneficiary's incompetence regarding financial management. A spendthrift trust is an effort made by a grantor to preserve what he or she has spent a lifetime earning or maintaining. It can also be an effort by someone to ensure that his or her children do not go broke because of their spending habits.

Exhibits 23-13, 23-14, 23-15, and 23-16 show several classifications of trusts.

EXHIBIT 23-13	CLASSIFICATIONS OF TRUSTS BASED ON HOW THEY ARE CREATED

Testamentary Trust – Trust that is created by a properly executed will. The trust is created using the same formalities.

Express Trust – Trust created or declared by clear verbal or written statements. The intent to create a trust is clear from the verbal or written statements.

Implied Trust – Trust created by the law based on the circumstances surrounding an agreement between the parties.

EXHIBIT 23-14	CLASSIFICATIONS OF TRUSTS BASED ON WHEN THE TRUST BECOMES EFFECTIVE

Living Trust – Trust that becomes effective during the lifetime of the settlor.

Contingent Trust – An express trust that becomes effective only if a stated future event happens.

EXHIBIT 23-15	CLASSIFICATIONS OF TRUSTS BASED ON BENEFICIARY

Charitable Trust – Trust created for the benefit of a specific class or group of people or for the general public. It is created for charitable, educational, religious, or scientific purposes.

Grantor Trust – The grantor transfers property into a trust that is for his or her own benefit or for his or her benefit and the benefit of one other person.

Mixed Trust – Trust created to benefit an individual as well as a charitable purpose.

Spendthrift Trust – Trust created to provide a fund for the maintenance of a person who spends money wastefully and to secure the fund against wasteful spending.

Clifford Trust – Property is put in trust and the income from the property is paid to the beneficiary. This trust can exist for up to ten years. Upon expiration, the property reverts back to the settlor.

EXHIBIT 23-16	CLASSIFICATIONS OF TRUSTS BASED ON THE POWERS THAT CAN BE EXERCISED

Active Trust – The trust imposes duties upon the trustee to insure that the purpose of the trust is met.

Blind Trust – The management of the trust is given to a person over whom the beneficiary has no control or influence. The beneficiary is unaware of the actions of the trustee.

Discretionary Trust – The trustee has discretion as to the types of investments that can be made and regarding any distribution of income or assets to the beneficiary.

Passive Trust – The title of the trust property is granted to the beneficiary of the trust, but the trustee still uses the property for the benefit of the beneficiary.

Fixed Trust – The trustee does not exercise any discretion regarding any aspect of the trust. The trust sets out what investments will be made and the timing and amount of any distribution of assets or income from the trust.

CONCLUSION

Wills and trusts ensure the orderly transfer of a decedent's property to his or her heirs. Certain steps must be taken to ensure that a will is executed properly. There must be testamentary capacity, testamentary intent, publication, attestation of the will, and an attestation clause. Wills can be conditional, contingent, joint, nuncupative, or holographic.

Heirs are those people who inherit property under a will. Heirs can be specifically listed or they can be pretermitted—deliberately omitted from the will. Heirs inherit by bequest for personal property and by devise for real property. Bequests and devises may be general or conditional, demonstrative in the case of personal property, or specific in the case of real property.

Probate of the estate includes filing the will with the proper court and having it declared valid. It also includes the establishing of the amount of the bond, if any, and the appointment of the executor or administrator if no one is named executor. Upon the full administration of the estate, it is declared settled.

Another way a person can control the use and disposition of his or her property after death is by use of a trust. A trust is a fiduciary duty involving a trustee, the settlor, and a beneficiary. A trust can be established and become effective when the settlor is still alive, or it can be created by will. A trust can be active or passive. The trustee must take an active role in the execution of the trust. A beneficiary has legal ownership of a trust, but the property is still controlled by the trustee, who acts in the best interest of the beneficiary.

Trusts can be used for charitable or tax purposes. Spendthrift trusts can be established to prevent assets from being wasted. A trust can be discretionary (the trustee uses his or her own judgment) or fixed (the trustee is very limited in what he or she can do). Trusts can be revocable, irrevocable, limited, or perpetual. The purpose of any trust is to ensure the orderly transfer of ownership of property and to ensure, as much as possible, that the property will be properly used and not wasted.

CHAPTER 23 REVIEW

KEY WORDS AND PHRASES

active trust
administration of the estate
administrator
attestation clause
bequest
blind trust
charitable trust
Clifford trust
conditional bequest
conditional legacy
consanguinity
contingent devise
contingent legacy
contingent trust
decedent's estate
demonstrative bequest
demonstrative legacy
descent
devise
direct line
discretionary trust
election by spouse
escheat
estate
executor
express trust

failure of issue
final settlement
fixed trust
general bequest
general devise
general legacy
grantor trust
heir
holographic will
illusory trust
implied trust
inter vivos gift
inter vivos trust
intestate
intestate succession
irrevocable trust
lapsed devise
lapsed legacy
legacy
limited trust
living trust
living will
no contest clause
nuncupative will
pour over trust
pretermitted heir

probate
publication
residuary devise
residuary estate
revocable trust
revocation of the will
settlor
specific bequest
specific devise
specific legacy
spendthrift trust
testament
testamentary capacity
testamentary intent
testamentary trust
testator
Totten trust
Transfer to Minors Act
trust
trust fund
trust instrument
vested devise
will
will substitute

REVIEW QUESTIONS

SHORT ANSWER

1. What is revocation of a will?

2. What is testamentary intent?

3. What is testamentary capacity?

4. What is publication?

5. What is an attestation clause?

6. What is a codicil?

7. What is a nuncupative will?

8. What is a holographic will?

9. What is an heir?

10. What is a pretermitted heir?
11. What is a maternal line?
12. What is a general bequest?
13. What is a specific bequest?
14. What is a contingent devise?
15. What is a specific devise?
16. What is a legacy?
17. What is a conditional legacy?
18. What is a residuary estate?
19. What is a lapsed legacy?
20. What is an inter vivos gift?

FILL IN THE BLANK

1. The process to determine if a will is valid is referred to as _____.
2. When a person dies without a will, he or she has died _____.
3. A fiduciary relationship to manage property and assets for the benefit of another person is a _____.
4. The formal document that creates the fiduciary relationship is a _____.
5. The person who creates the fiduciary relationship is the _____.
6. A trust that is established by a will is a _____.
7. A trust that is specifically used for tax planning purposes is a _____.
8. A trust that is created by law because of the surrounding circumstances is a _____.
9. The trustee can make decisions regarding types of investments and when to make distributions. This is a _____ trust.
10. A testator leaves the residue of her estate to a trustee of a living trust. This is known as a _____.

FACT SITUATIONS

1. Emmaline inadvertently leaves her daughter Cordelia out of her will. What sort of heir is Cordelia? What are her options?
2. What sort of trust can Brendan set up to prevent his two children from spending their inheritance at a rapid rate?
3. Hank handwrites his will, canceling all other wills he has written. What sort of will is his handwritten will?
4. After his will is written, Ron discovers that his daughter is going to have another child. Ron writes an addition to his will. What is this addition called?
5. Olivia writes a will but does not have it properly witnessed or signed. If the will is declared invalid, how is it determined who will inherit Olivia's property?
6. Vladimir establishes trusts for each of his children. However, two of them do things that anger him so he amends the trusts such that all three are merged into one, which is for the benefit of only one child. What sort of trust allows him to do this?

7. James establishes a trust whose beneficiaries are James himself and his wife Lahoma. What sort of trust has James created?

8. A will names Johann as the executor of his father Ludwig's will. However, Johann refuses the appointment as executor. What can the court do? What will that person be called?

9. Shameka states in her will that all the assets from the sale of her stock portfolio are to go to her daughter Kimbra. What sort of transfer is this?

10. Albert states in his will that he leaves to his daughter LaTasha one of his BMW automobiles. Albert owns four different BMWs, but he does not specify which BMW LaTasha is to receive. What sort of legacy is this?

CHAPTER 24

Product Liability and Consumer Protection

PART I. PRODUCT LIABILITY

INTRODUCTION

Product liability law was originally based on contract law principles, but this worked to the detriment of consumers. Because of the requirement of privity of contract, consumers were not successful in suing manufacturers of defective products. As the law developed, tort law theories began to be applied: There was no requirement for privity of contract, just proximate causation for the injury suffered. The law has further changed to allow for strict liability for product liability. Contract law also still applies because of the use of warranties. Warranties can be express or implied; what is warranted varies with the type of warranty that exists.

The second part of consumer protection relates to the federal laws that have been passed to protect consumers from unsafe food, drugs, and cosmetics. There are regulations regarding what certain words mean when applied to food, as well as regulations governing what consumers have to be told about the nutritional value of foods. Federal laws have also been passed to regulate trade practices, sales, and consumer transactions. The purpose of these laws is to establish and protect consumer rights with regard to credit, leases, and sales.

GENERAL PRINCIPLES

People buy products with the expectation that they will perform as advertised and promised without causing harm to the user. People want the products they buy to do what they are intended to do safely. When products fail to perform as intended, require repair, or cause injury, the law of product liability applies.

CONSUMERS AND DEFECTIVE CONDITIONS

Product liability is the legal liability of manufacturers and sellers to compensate buyers, users, and even bystanders for damages or injuries suffered because of a defect in the goods purchased. Product liability is a tort that makes a manufacturer liable if the product has a defective condition that makes it unreasonably dangerous to the consumer or to a person who uses the product.

A **defective condition** is the tendency of a product to cause physical harm beyond any harm that would be contemplated by an ordinary user or consumer. A **consumer** is the person who buys, uses, maintains, and disposes of the product or service. If a manufacturer produces a product that is defective and this defect makes the product dangerous, and if a consumer would not think the product could cause this type of harm, then the manufacturer can be held liable for any harm caused. For example, Brooke buys hair spray not thinking that, because of a change in the chemical formula, it is now highly flammable. She uses the hair spray and is injured when the spray catches on fire. The manufacturer of the hair spray can be held liable for the harm caused to Brooke. The product was defective, this defect made the product dangerous, and the consumer did not think that the hair spray would catch fire.

LATENT DEFECTS AND INHERENTLY DANGEROUS PRODUCTS

Sometimes a person will inspect a product before he or she purchases it, and then is injured while using the product. For example, Aiden is shopping for a new set of tires for his Volvo. He inspects the set of tires he wants to purchase, seeing nothing wrong with them. However, the tires he selects have a design defect that causes them to fall apart after they have been used for a short period of time. The tires have a **latent defect**—a hidden or concealed flaw that cannot be discovered by reasonable and customary observation. Because the tires fall apart when Aiden has them out on the road, products liability applies.

However, a product is not defective simply because it is possible to be injured while using it. For example, Aiden also buys a chainsaw to cut some limbs off trees in his yard. If he is injured while using the chainsaw, the saw does not necessarily have a defect. It is possible to be injured while using a chainsaw in perfect working condition. A chainsaw is **inherently dangerous:** The danger of an injury arises from the product itself. In both situations, Aiden was injured, but he may only sue under products liability for the injuries caused by the defective tires. See Exhibit 24-1.

EXHIBIT 24-1 DEFECTIVE CONDITION? OR INHERENTLY DANGEROUS?

Defective Condition – A product has the tendency to cause physical harm beyond any harm that would be contemplated by an ordinary user or consumer. There is something wrong with the product that causes it to be more dangerous than a consumer would think the product would be. The manufacturer can be held liable for harm caused because of the defective condition.

Inherently Dangerous – The danger of an injury arises from the product itself. The product is made as safe as it can be, but the very nature of the product makes the product dangerous to use. The manufacturer *cannot* be held liable if the injury was caused as a result of the product's inherent danger.

A person may not sue for injury under products liability if the product causes injury because it is inherently dangerous. Simply using an inherently dangerous product puts a person at risk of injury; the product cannot be made safer. However, if harm is caused by a design defect or something other than a product's inherent danger, then products liability can apply. If Aiden can show that harm was caused to him by a defect in the saw that is separate from the inherent danger in the saw, then he can sue under products liability.

Chemotherapy is another example of an inherently dangerous product. Chemotherapy has the effect of making a cancer patient very sick; it also causes weight loss and hair loss. There is inherent danger in taking chemotherapy; however, the drugs cannot be made safer, so there is no liability for the harm caused by taking them.

DEVELOPMENT OF THE LAW OF PRODUCT LIABILITY

Product liability law was not always based on tort law. Initially, if a consumer was injured by a product, he or she had to sue under contract law. The consumer had to show that he or she had a contract with the manufacturer in order to sue under contract law.

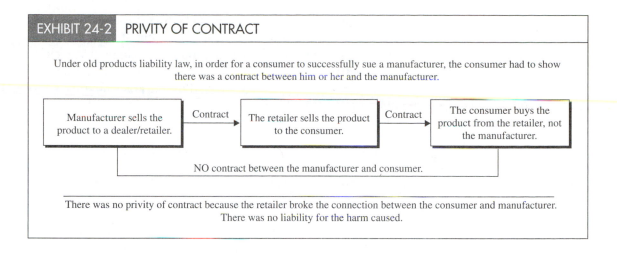

EXHIBIT 24-2 · PRIVITY OF CONTRACT

Under old products liability law, in order for a consumer to successfully sue a manufacturer, the consumer had to show there was a contract between him or her and the manufacturer.

Manufacturer sells the product to a dealer/retailer. → *Contract* → The retailer sells the product to the consumer. → *Contract* → The consumer buys the product from the retailer, not the manufacturer.

NO contract between the manufacturer and consumer.

There was no privity of contract because the retailer broke the connection between the consumer and manufacturer. There was no liability for the harm caused.

PRIVITY OF CONTRACT

The consumer had to show **privity of contract**—a direct contractual relationship between himself or herself and the manufacturer of the product in order to successfully sue for the harm caused. In many cases, there was no privity of contract because the consumer bought the product from a retailer, not from the manufacturer. The manufacturer was able to successfully argue that the contract was not with him, but with the person the consumer bought the goods from, the retailer. Because the retailer was not responsible for the manufacture of the goods, the injured party often collected nothing for any injuries suffered. The doctrine of **caveat emptor**—let the buyer beware—was the rule of law in products liability. See Exhibit 24-2.

The law of products liability began to change with the case of *MacPherson v. Buick Motor Company*. See Sidebar 24-1.

SIDEBAR 24-1 *MACPHERSON V. BUICK CORPORATION*

Facts: Buick manufactured an automobile and then sold it to a retail dealer. The retailer then sold it to the plaintiff. While the plaintiff was in the car, it suddenly collapsed. He was thrown out and injured. One of the wheels was made of defective wood, and its spokes crumbled into fragments.

Issue: Was Buick liable for the harm caused to MacPherson? Buick raised the defense of no privity of contract.

Decision: If the nature of a thing is such that it is reasonably certain to place life and limb in peril when negligently made, it is then a thing of danger. If to the element of danger there is added knowledge that the thing will be used by persons other than the purchaser, and used without new tests, then, *irrespective of contract,* the manufacturer of this thing of danger is under a duty to make it carefully.

The nature of an automobile gives warning of probable danger if its construction is defective. Unless its wheels were sound and strong, injury was almost certain. The defendant knew the danger. It knew also that the car would be used by persons other than the buyer.

Source: New York Reporter

REASONABLE CARE REPLACES PRIVITY OF CONTRACT

Because of the case of *MacPherson v. Buick,* the doctrine of privity of contract was replaced with the tort doctrine of reasonable care. If the producer of a product is shown to have been negligent in constructing and placing the product on the market, the producer is liable in tort for the foreseeable injuries that result from not using reasonable care in the manufacturing of the product. **Reasonable care** is the degree of care a careful person would use in the same or similar circumstances to prevent injury.

Foreseeable injuries are those it would be reasonable to anticipate considering certain acts or omissions. It would be reasonable to assume that, if the wheels of an automobile broke while it was being driven, that automobile would be involved in an accident and injuries and property damage could be the result. This theory of product liability was quickly adopted by other states and is still applied today. For a summary of the development of product liability law, see Exhibit 24-3.

EXHIBIT 24-3	DEVELOPMENT OF THE LAW OF PRODUCT LIABILITY

Early Law – The law of contracts applied, but the consumer had to have a direct contract with the manufacturer. The consumer had to buy the product directly from the manufacturer. Caveat emptor—let the buyer beware—was the theory.

Initial Change – After *MacPherson v. Buick Motor Company*, tort law replaced contract law as the theory of law to be used. A manufacturer must use reasonable care in producing a product. If not, then the manufacturer is liable for any foreseeable harm caused by the defective product.

Current Law – Tort law: negligence and strict liability; contract law: warranties.

STRICT LIABILITY IN PRODUCT LIABILITY

The next development in this area of product liability law was the application of **strict liability**—liability without fault—to product liability.

PROVING STRICT LIABILITY

The doctrine of strict liability imposes liability on any manufacturer for any and all defective or hazardous products that threaten a consumer's personal safety. In order to prove strict liability, the plaintiff must show that the product was defective, that the defect created an unreasonable risk of harm to the user, and that the defect was the proximate cause of or a substantial factor in causing the injury. Even if the manufacturer used reasonable care, if the criteria are met for strict liability, the manufacturer is liable for the harm caused.

The first case that applied the doctrine of strict liability was *Greenman v. Yuba Power Products*. See Sidebar 24-2.

SIDEBAR 24-2 *GREENMAN V. YUBA POWER PRODUCTS*

Facts: Greenman purchased a combination power tool—the Shopsmith—that could be used as a saw, drill, and wood lathe. He saw it demonstrated and read the brochure prepared by the manufacturer. He also purchased the attachments necessary to use the Shopsmith as a lathe. After he had worked on the piece of wood several times, it flew out of the machine and struck him in the forehead, inflicting serious injury. Experts testified that inadequately set screws were used to hold parts of the machine together, and that there were other ways of fastening the parts that would have prevented the accident.

Issue: Is the manufacturer strictly liable for the injury complained of as a result of a defect in the Shopsmith?

Decision: The purpose of strict liability is to insure that the costs of injuries resulting from defective products are borne by the manufacturer that put such products on the market rather than by the injured persons who are powerless to protect themselves. Implicit in the machine's presence on the market was a representation that it would safely do the jobs for which it was built.

To establish the manufacturer's liability, it was sufficient that the plaintiff proved that he was injured while using the Shopsmith in a way in which it was intended to be used. A defect in design and manufacture, of which the plaintiff was not aware, made the Shopsmith unsafe for its intended use.

Source: California Reporter

FAILURE TO WARN, DESIGN DEFECT, AND UNKNOWN HAZARD

There are three major areas of product liability law where strict liability has been applied: failure to warn of dangers involved in the use of a product, design defect, and unknown hazard. **Failure to warn** concerns dangers involved in the use of the product that the producer knew or should have known about and should have notified the consumer about. This places a burden on producers to anticipate anything adverse that can happen with their product even when the product is not used as intended. For example, the failure to warn doctrine is the reason why warnings are printed on plastic bags indicating that these bags are not toys and pose a suffocation hazard. Manufacturers of plastic bags realize that children sometimes play with such bags, putting them over their heads and thereby risking suffocation. Well-intentioned caregivers might use the plastic bags to line an infant's or toddler's mattress, again posing risk of suffocation. Manufacturers must warn consumers about such potential dangers; failure to do so could result in the manufacturer being held strictly liable for the harm caused by the product.

A **design defect** occurs when a product is manufactured in conformity with the intended design, but the design itself can cause an unreasonable danger to consumers. The test of design defect is whether there is a reasonable alternative design that the producer knew about or should have known about. If there is a reasonable alternative, then the manufacturer can be held strictly liable for the harm caused. Some states have adopted the **consumer expectation test,** which asks: What level of safe performance would an ordinary consumer expect of the product under the circumstances?

The third area of strict liability in products liability is the unknown hazard. An **unknown hazard** is a risk or peril that was not known at the time the product was first marketed. Only later did the harm caused become known. Some of the more familiar examples of unknown hazards are those associated with asbestos, silicone breast implants, and the Dalkon shield. At the time these products were released, it was not known that they could cause harm to consumers or to people who were exposed to them. Over time, harm was caused, and thus manufacturers were held liable. The rationale behind this doctrine is that the manufacturer of any product is in the best position to test the safety of that product and should continue to test that product to monitor its performance over time. See Exhibit 24-4 for a summary of the principles of strict liability.

EXHIBIT 24-4 | **STRICT LIABILITY AS APPLIED TO PRODUCT LIABILITY**

General Rule: Plaintiff must show the product was defective, that the defect created an unreasonable risk of harm, and that the defect was the proximate cause of the injury to the consumer.

STRICT LIABILITY HAS BEEN APPLIED IN THREE AREAS

1. **Failure to Warn** – The manufacturer has a duty to warn consumers of the dangers related to product use that are known and that should be known by the manufacturer.
2. **Design Defect** – The design is defective, the defect caused the harm, and there were reasonable design alternatives that the manufacturer knew about or should have known about.
3. **Unknown Hazard** – The danger in using the product was not known when it was first used; only later did the danger become known. Manufacturers are held liable because they are in the best position to continue to test the product for potential hazardous performance.

MARKET SHARE LIABILITY AND JOINT AND SEVERAL LIABILITY

When a product has an unknown hazard, sometimes it is impossible to determine which manufacturer made the product that caused the specific injury to the consumer. Two doctrines of liability have been used to determine who is liable when it is impossible to identify the origin of the hazardous product.

The first of these doctrines is **market share liability,** which provides that each manufacturer of the product shares liability based on the percentage of the market it had at the time of the injury. If a company had 10% of the market, the company is considered to be responsible for 10% of the injuries and therefore is liable for 10% of the damages. This was the doctrine used in the case of *Sindell v. Abbot Laboratories.* See Sidebar 24-3.

SIDEBAR 24-3 *SINDELL V. ABBOT LABORATORIES*

Facts: The plaintiff's mother took a prescription drug called DES while she was pregnant with the plaintiff. DES is a synthetic compound of the female hormone estrogen. The drug was administered to plaintiff's mother for the purpose of preventing miscarriage. Twenty years later, it was discovered that this drug caused cancer in the female children of the women who took it; male children were not affected. The plaintiff could not identify which manufacturer made the drug her mother took, so she sued major drug companies. The trial court dismissed her case.

Issue: Can the drug manufacturing companies be held liable even though the plaintiff cannot show they manufactured the drug that actually caused the injury?

Decision: The circumstances of the injury appear to render identification of the manufacturer of the drug ingested by plaintiff's mother impossible by either plaintiff or defendants, and it cannot reasonably be said that one is in a better position than the other to make the identification.

As between an innocent plaintiff and negligent defendants, the latter should bear the cost of the injury. The plaintiff is not at fault in failing to provide evidence of causation, and although the absence of such evidence is not attributable to the defendants either, their conduct in marketing a drug, the effects of which are delayed for many years, played a significant role in creating the unavailability of proof.

The manufacturer is in the best position to discover and guard against defects in its products and to warn of harmful effects; thus, holding it liable for defects and failure to warn of harmful effects will provide an incentive to product safety.

We hold it to be reasonable in the present context to measure the likelihood that any of the defendants supplied the product which allegedly injured plaintiff by the percentage which the DES sold by each of them for the purpose of preventing miscarriage bears to the entire production of the drug sold by all for that purpose. Each defendant will be held liable for the proportion of the judgment represented by its share of that market unless it demonstrates that it could not have made the product which caused plaintiff's injuries.

Source: California Reports

The second doctrine is **joint and several liability,** which means that each manufacturer of the product can be held totally liable for all the harm caused by the hazardous product. (See Chapter 9, Torts, for more about joint and several liability.)

DEFENSES TO STRICT LIABILITY

There are several defenses in tort law to a claim of strict liability in products liability. The first defense is **product misuse:** The product is being used in a manner neither intended nor reasonably foreseeable by the manufacturer. This defense declares that the product is safe for its **intended use**—what the product is *meant* to be used for—but that the consumer is using it in a way contrary to its intended use and unforeseeable by the product's manufacturer. The manufacturer will have to show that it applied the **intended use doctrine,** which states the manufacturer takes into account the environment in which the product will be used in determining the intended use of the product. If product misuse is the primary cause of injury, this can relieve the manufacturer of any liability or reduce the amount of liability.

A manufacturer can also raise the defense of **assumption of the risk.** This defense declares that the plaintiff knew the product was dangerous, but chose to expose himself or herself to the known and appreciated danger. The danger must be known: If the danger is not known, there can be no assumption of the risk. The defense of voluntary assumption of the risk applies to products that are **unavoidably dangerous,** those that, given the current state of science, cannot be made any safer, and have potentially harmful effects. This defense applies to pharmaceuticals—prescription drugs—but only to known side effects. A person taking a medication has assumed the risks for the known side effects, but has not assumed any risk for unknown side effects because one cannot assume something of which he or she has no knowledge.

Prescription drug manufacturers have attempted to use FDA approval as a defense to products liability, arguing that a drug is safe because the FDA has approved it. However, the courts have taken the position that FDA approval is evidence of safety only; it is not a total shield to liability. However, if a drug is improperly administered—because the physician makes a dosage error, for example—and a person is harmed, the drug's manufacturer is shielded from liability because of the **learned intermediary doctrine.** This doctrine states that the injury was not caused by the product itself, but rather was caused by improper administration of the product by a learned intermediary—the doctor. The improper dosage was the cause of injury, making the doctor liable for the harm. The manufacturer is not responsible for the actions of the doctor, so the manufacturer is not responsible for any harm caused.

Another defense to strict liability in products liability is that of **sophisticated purchaser.** The defense declares that the sophisticated purchaser has more knowledge about the product in question than ordinary consumers and thus is expected to know actual and potential hazards and should not have to be told about them every time the product is purchased. For example, a manufacturer buys toxic chemicals to clean its products and machines every month. Because the manufacturer uses this product in the course of everyday business, it should be familiar with the hazards of the chemicals and should not have to be made aware of such hazards with every purchase. See Exhibit 24-5 for a summary of defenses to strict liability.

| EXHIBIT 24-5 | DEFENSES TO STRICT LIABILITY: WHAT THE DEFENSE MUST PROVE |

ASSUMPTION OF THE RISK

1. The plaintiff knew the product was dangerous.
2. The plaintiff appreciated the danger the product presented.
3. The plaintiff chose to expose himself or herself to the danger.
4. The product is unavoidably dangerous. The product cannot be made any safer, given the current state of technology.

PRODUCT MISUSE

1. The product is safe when it is used the way it is supposed to be used.
2. Consumer is using the product in a way it is not intended to be used.
3. The manufacturer could not know that the product would be used this way.
4. The manufacturer took into account the environment that the product would be used in to determine how the product might be used.

LEARNED INTERMEDIARY DOCTRINE (USED FOR PHARMACEUTICAL PRODUCTS)

1. The drug is safe when it is administered properly.
2. The learned intermediary, a doctor, improperly administered the drug.
3. The improper dosage or other administration of the drug is what caused the injury.

SOPHISTICATED PURCHASER

1. The business uses the product frequently.
2. The business has greater knowledge about the product and its dangers.
3. The business is expected to know more about the product than a regular consumer.
4. The business does not have to be warned about the dangers every time it buys the product.

WARRANTIES

Contract law also governs part of product liability law because warranties are considered to be contracts. A **warranty** is a statement or representation made by the seller of goods, as part of a contract of sale, that refers to the quality or fitness of the product. A warranty is a promise by the seller that the goods have a certain quality and that certain facts are or shall be as he represents them.

EXPRESS WARRANTIES

An **express warranty** is a promise—either written or oral—in which the quality, description, or performance of a good is assured. The manufacturer, distributor, or retailer will preserve or maintain the use or performance of the good or provide compensation if the good fails. Put another way, the manufacturer, distributor, or retailer promises that the quality and performance of the product will be at a certain level. If the product fails to meet that level of performance, it will be either repaired or replaced, or the consumer will get his or her money back.

MAGNUSON-MOSS WARRANTY ACT

The Federal Trade Commission (FTC) is the federal agency responsible for insuring that warranties meet certain standards and that they are complied with. In order to give the FTC this authority, the **Magnuson-Moss Warranty Act** was passed. This Act sets standards regarding what written warranties must contain and delineates the differences between full and limited warranties. See Exhibit 24-6 for a summary of the warranties provided for under this act.

EXHIBIT 24-6 | MAGNUSON-MOSS WARRANTY ACT WARRANTIES

Written Warranty – Written document that is proof of the promises made when the product was sold. The warranty must contain:

1. The parts of the product or types of problems the warranty covers and what it does not cover.
2. The term of coverage.
3. What will be done to correct any problem.
4. How the consumer can get warranty services.
5. How state law affects the warranty, if at all.

Full Warranty – A warranty that covers all parts and labor. This warranty must contain the following provisions:

1. Warranty service is provided to anyone who owns the product while the warranty is effective, even if the owner is not the original purchaser.
2. The warranty service is provided free of any charge.
3. If the product cannot be repaired, then the product will be replaced or its purchase price refunded.
4. The warranty is in effect even if the consumer did not return the warranty card.

Limited Warrant – Any warranty that is limited to parts or labor for a specified period of time. Also, any warranty that does not contain all of the provisions of a full warranty is a limited warranty and must identify itself as such.

A **written warranty** is proof of the promises made in connection with the sale of a particular product. The written warranty will contain all of the provisions of the warranty, including the parts of the product or the types of problems the warranty covers and the parts or problems it does not cover. The warranty must also specify the time period of coverage, what will be done to correct any problems, how the customer can get warranty service, and how state law may affect the warranty.

A **full warranty** is a warranty of full performance, one that covers the cost of materials and labor required to repair the product. To be considered a full warranty, the warranty must state that warranty service is provided to anyone who owns the product during the warranty period, even if that individual is not the original purchaser. The warranty must also state that warranty service is provided free of charge, and that if the product cannot be repaired, the consumer may choose either a replacement or a full refund. A full warranty must also state that the warranty service is provided even if the consumer did not complete and return the warranty card, and that any implied warranty is not limited by the written warranty. Under a full warranty, the **warrantor**—the person who made the warranty—must remedy the defect within a reasonable period of time without charge.

If a warranty does not include all of the above provisions, then it is a limited warranty and must be identified as such. A **limited warranty** is a warranty that is limited to the costs of parts and labor for a specified period of time. An **extended service warranty** is an additional warranty, usually sold with appliances, motor vehicles, and other goods, to cover repair costs not covered by the standard warranty.

IMPLIED WARRANTY OF MERCHANTABILITY

A warranty can also be implied by operation of the law. One such warranty is an **implied warranty of merchantability,** which is imposed by the Uniform Commercial Code. The term **merchantability** means that the article sold is of the general kind described and is reasonably fit for the general purpose for which it was sold. The phrase **fitness for a particular purpose** means that the seller, at the time of the sale, has a reason to know the purpose for which the goods are being purchased and that the buyer is relying on the seller's skill or judgment to select the suitable good. See Exhibit 24-7.

EXHIBIT 24-7	ELEMENTS OF THE IMPLIED WARRANTY OF MERCHANTABILITY

Created by the Uniform Commercial Code and applicable to the sale of goods.
1. **Merchantability** – The article sold is reasonably fit for the general purpose for which it was sold.
2. **Fitness for a Particular Purpose**
   a. Seller knew what the purchaser was planning on using the good(s) for.
   b. Purchaser was relying on the seller's skill and judgment to select the appropriate good(s).
3. **Merchantable** – The good(s) will be fit for the ordinary purpose for which such goods are to be used.

The implied warranty of merchantability means that a good that is sold will be **merchantable**—fit for the ordinary purpose for which such goods are to be used. For example, if a consumer goes to the hardware store looking for supplies to fix the tile in his or her bathroom, he or she may rely on what the salesman says about different products. Because the consumer relied on what the salesman said, an implied warranty of merchantability may be found to exist. If this warranty is violated—if the product is not fit for the ordinary purpose that it is used for—the seller can be held liable for any harm caused by his or her actions.

All of these principles of law are designed to protect the consumer from defective goods that may cause injury. However, products liability is the area of law that critics point to most often when they argue for tort reform and limits on the amount of damages a person can recover.

PART II. CONSUMER PROTECTION

Many different federal laws establish and protect consumer rights. These laws apply to food and drug safety, nutrition, unfair trade practices, advertising, leases, and sales. Consumers are also protected by laws governing consumer loans, credit cards, billing, and access to credit.

FOOD AND DRUG REGULATION

One of the first areas to be regulated by the federal government was food and drug safety. The Food and Drug Administration (FDA), an agency of the Department of Health and Human Services, is responsible for setting safety and quality standards for food, drugs, cosmetics, and other household items that are sold as consumer products. A **consumer product** is any tangible personal property that is distributed in commerce and that is normally used for personal, family, or household use.

FOOD, DRUG, AND COSMETIC ACT

The FDA is responsible for the enforcement of the provisions of the **Food, Drug, and Cosmetic Act,** the federal law that prohibits the transportation in interstate commerce of any adulterated or misbranded food, drug, or cosmetic. A food product, drug, or cosmetic is considered to be **adulterated** if something is added to it that makes it unfit for consumption. The Act also prohibits the false advertising of drugs, gives the FDA added enforcement powers, calls for the maintenance of an inspection system, and sets safe levels of food additives.

In 1958, the **Delaney Clause** was added to the Food, Drug, and Cosmetic Act. This clause gives the FDA the authority to set the safe-use level of food additives. The original standard was **zero risk,** which meant that the additive posed no threat whatsoever to the health and safety of consumers. That standard has been replaced with the **reasonable certainty of no harm standard,** which states that any direct or indirect additive to a product must have no more than a one in a million lifetime chance of causing cancer.

NUTRITION LABELING AND EDUCATION ACT

In 1973, the FDA began issuing regulations for nutrition labeling. In 1994, as required by the **Nutrition Labeling and Education Act of 1990,** the FDA began issuing new regulations regarding nutrition labeling. According to this Act, the following components must be listed on a food label based on the amount in a serving size: total calories, calories from fat, total fat, saturated fat, carbohydrates, cholesterol, calcium, fiber, iron, sodium, proteins, Vitamin A, and Vitamin C. Regulations also exist concerning what certain words mean when applied to food. For example, *fresh* can only refer to raw food that has never been frozen, processed, or preserved. *Low fat* designates three or fewer grams of fat per serving and per 100 grams of the food. *Light* can only be used to label foods that have one-third fewer calories than a comparable product.

PRESCRIPTION DRUGS

The Food, Drug, and Cosmetic Act also applies to **prescription drugs,** which are defined as drugs that may be used only under a physician's orders. These are drugs a consumer can only purchase legally if a doctor has written a prescription for them; they are not over-the-counter medications. According to the 1962 **Kefauver Amendment** to the Food, Drug, and

Cosmetic Act, drugs that are sold must actually do what the manufacturer claims they can do. Prior to the Kefauver Amendment, all that was required of a drug was that it had to be safe for human use; the drug did not actually have to do what the manufacturer claimed the drug could do.

TRADE PRACTICES

The Federal Trade Commission is a federal administrative agency created to provide protection to consumers. The FTC is responsible for preventing unfair and deceptive trade acts or practices. It also regulates advertising and sales practices.

TRADE DECEPTION

The FTC has a **deception policy statement** that contains a three-part test (see Exhibit 24-8) to determine if a particular act or practice is deceptive. If the following are found, then the act is considered to be deceptive:

- There is a misrepresentation or omission of information that is communicated to consumers.
- The deception is likely to mislead consumers.
- The deception is material—important—and therefore detrimental to the consumer.

EXHIBIT 24-8	FEDERAL TRADE COMMISSION DECEPTIVE PRACTICE TEST

If the following are found to exist, then the act or practice is considered to be deceptive.
1. There is an omission of information or misrepresentation of information that is provided to consumers.
2. The misinformation or misrepresentation is likely to mislead a consumer.
3. The deception is about something important. It is likely to be misleading and is detrimental to the consumer.

The FTC has also issued a policy statement to determine if a trade practice is **unfair.** In order for a trade practice to be considered unfair, the following must apply:

- There is substantial harm caused to the consumer.
- The consumer cannot reasonably avoid injury.
- The injury is harmful in its net effects.

ADVERTISING

The FTC is also responsible for regulating advertising and does so using an **advertising substantiation program.** Under this program, advertisers and advertising agencies must have a reasonable basis for making a claim before they can make that claim in advertising. In order to determine if the advertiser has a reasonable basis, the FTC looks at the product and the type of claim being made about the product. The Commission also looks at the consequences of a false claim and the benefit of a truthful claim, the cost of developing substantiation for the claim, and the amount of substantiation that experts believe is reasonable.

TRADE REGULATION RULES

Certain industries are prime candidates for deception when dealing with consumers. These include mail order companies, used car dealers, and some retailers. **Trade regulation rules** are promulgated by the FTC to regulate and prevent the use of certain deceptive trade practices by certain industries. One such practice used by retailers is the **bait and switch,** which occurs when a seller stocks a limited supply of inexpensive merchandise that is advertised for sale in order to lure or attract customers into the store. Efforts are then made to sell these customers higher priced goods.

One example of a regulation that applies to the mail order industry is the **mail order rule.** This rule states that if a company sells merchandise by mail, it must have a reasonable basis for believing it can ship the merchandise within the time frame stated in its advertising. Shipping dates must be stated on the offers, or the merchandise must be shipped within thirty days of the order being received.

The **used car rule** is another regulation aimed at a specific industry—the sale of used cars. The used car rule states that used car dealers must provide clear information about who is responsible for paying for repairs after the car has been sold. Dealers are also required to post a buyer's guide that states the terms of any warranty offered with the car and that includes a prominent statement of whether or not the dealer is selling the car "as is." The buyer's guide must advise that, if the car is being sold as is, then there must be a written statement indicating that the consumer is responsible for all repairs needed after the car is bought. It must also warn that any oral promise is difficult to enforce, that all promises should be put in writing, and it must contain a suggestion that the consumer get an independent evaluation of the car before it is purchased. See Exhibit 24-9 for a summary of these rules.

EXHIBIT 24-9 | FEDERAL TRADE REGULATIONS

Mail Order Rule – If a company sells merchandise by mail, it must have a reasonable basis for believing it can ship the merchandise within the time frame stated in its advertising.

Used Car Rule – Used car dealers must provide clear information about who is responsible for paying for repairs after the car has been sold. Dealers are also required to post a buyer's guide that states the terms of any warranty offered with the car and that includes a prominent statement of whether or not the dealer is selling the car "as is."

CONSUMER CREDIT AND LEASES

Another area of consumer protection that the federal government has become involved in is the area of consumer credit. In 1968, Congress passed several different federal laws. Taken as a whole, these laws are referred to as the **Consumer Credit Protection Act.** They include the Truth in Lending Act, the Fair Credit Reporting Act, the Equal Credit Opportunity Act, the Fair Debt Collection Practices Act, the Electronic Funds Transfer Act, the Consumer Leasing Act, and the Fair Credit Billing Act. See Exhibit 24-10.

EXHIBIT 24-10 | STATUTES THAT MAKE UP THE CONSUMER CREDIT PROTECTION ACT

Truth in Lending Act – Consumer must be given information about finance charges and annual percentage rates.

Fair Credit Reporting Act – Regulates consumer credit reporting agencies. If a consumer is denied credit, the consumer can see the report that led to the denial of credit.

Equal Credit Opportunity Act – Credit cannot be denied to any applicant because of race, color, religion, national origin, age, sex, or marital status.

Fair Debt Collection Practices Act – Debt collection agencies are prohibited from using obscene language, threatening people with jail, and making phone calls in the middle of the night. The debtor is also entitled to the following information:

1. The amount of the debt
2. The name of the creditor
3. A statement that if the consumer does not dispute the debt within 30 days, it is presumed to be valid
4. A statement that the collection agency must show proof of the debt if the consumer disputes the debt within the 30-day period

Electronic Funds Transfer Act – Governs electronic transfer of funds and sets out the limits of a consumer's liability for fraudulent transfers:

1. If the bank is notified within two days, liability is limited to $50
2. If the bank is notified after two days but within 60 days, liability is limited to $500
3. If the bank is notified more than 60 days after the event, the consumer faces unlimited liability

Consumer Leasing Act – Applies to leases of personal property that is used for personal family or household use. The consumer must receive information about the following:

1. The number, the amount, and the length of time lease payments must be made plus the total amount of the payments
2. Any express warranties
3. The identity of the person responsible for maintaining and servicing the property
4. Whether the consumer has the option to purchase the property and the terms of the option to purchase
5. Any penalties if the consumer ends the lease early

Fair Credit Billing Act – Consumer has 60 days to notify the credit card company of any disputed charges. The creditor must acknowledge the complaint within 30 days and is given 90 days to resolve the dispute.

TRUTH IN LENDING ACT

The **Truth in Lending Act,** 15 U.S.C. § 1601, was passed to ensure that every consumer is given sufficient information about the cost of credit. The consumer must be given information about the **finance charge,** the amount that the consumer contracts to pay for the privilege of purchasing goods or services by installments. The finance charge does not include the amount paid for insurance premiums, late charges, over the limit charges, or other charges. The cost must be stated in dollar amounts of the finance charges as well as the **annual percentage rate**—the actual cost of borrowing money stated in terms of a percentage of the amount due. For example, the annual percentage rate for a credit card is 19.8% per annum, which means that the amount of interest that will be charged on an annual basis is 19.8% on any amount that is not paid.

Regulation Z was promulgated by the Federal Reserve Board and it implements the Truth in Lending Act. Under Regulation Z, the following items are to be listed as part of a finance charge: service, activity, and carrying charges, loan fees and points, charges for credit life and credit accident and health insurance, and the fees for credit reports and appraisals.

FAIR CREDIT REPORTING ACT

The **Fair Credit Reporting Act,** 15 U.S.C. § 1681, regulates the consumer reporting industry and consumer reporting agencies. A **consumer reporting agency** is an agency that gathers or evaluates information about consumers in order to provide this information to third parties that are engaged in commerce. Consumer reporting agencies include all **credit**

bureaus, organizations that collect information about the credit, character, responsibility, and reputation of people and businesses for the purpose of sharing this information with people and businesses that subscribe to their service. These subscribers include investigative reporting agencies, detective and collection agencies, lenders' exchanges, and computerized information reporting companies.

According to the Act, if a person is denied credit, that person is entitled to see the information that led to the denial of credit. Credit bureaus must also respond to consumer complaints about inaccurate information within thirty days and tell consumers, if so requested, who has asked for copies of their credit history in the past year. The credit bureau must also provide a toll-free number for consumers, and obtain consumers' permission before giving a report to an employer or before releasing a report that contains medical information.

EQUAL CREDIT OPPORTUNITY ACT

The **Equal Credit Opportunity Act,** 15 U.S.C. § 1691, is federal law that prohibits a creditor from discriminating against any applicant on the basis of race, color, religion, national origin, age, sex, or marital status. This criteria are known as **prohibited basis:** a lender cannot use any of these basis to deny credit. **Credit discrimination** is the denial of credit to a person because of his or her race, color, national origin, age, sex, marital status, or religion.

Regulation B, issued by the Federal Reserve Board, specifies activities that may constitute credit discrimination.

1. Making any written or oral statement about a prohibited basis intended to discourage a person from applying for credit. For example, a representative of a credit card company is prohibited from saying that a person over the age of forty should not apply for credit because the company only gives credit to people who are under the age of forty.

2. Requesting or making use of information about a credit applicant's children or denying credit on the basis of an applicant's income being reduced because he or she has children.

3. If the applicant so requests, any credit history evaluation must include not only the person's **direct credit history** (an account that the applicant is liable for), but also the person's **indirect credit history**—any account in the name of a spouse or former spouse that reflects on the person's credit history.

4. Asking about a spouse or former spouse unless the spouse will also be liable for the debt, the spouse's income is to be considered, or the person receives alimony, maintenance, or child support payments, or the person lives in a community property state or community property is involved.

FAIR DEBT COLLECTION PRACTICES ACT

The **Fair Debt Collection Practices Act,** 15 U.S.C. § 1692(e), is federal law designed not only to eliminate the use of abusive debt collection practices by collection agencies but also to ensure that those collectors who do not use abusive techniques are not at a competitive disadvantage. Forms of debt collection that are prohibited include using obscene language, threatening people with jail, and making phone calls in the middle of the night.

The Act also requires that certain information must be sent to the debtor within five days of initial contact. The information the debtor is to receive includes the amount of the debt, the name of the creditor, and a statement that, if the consumer does not dispute the debt within thirty days, it is presumed to be valid. The debtor is also to receive a statement that the agency that is attempting to collect the debt must show proof of the debt if the consumer disputes the debt within the thirty-day period.

ELECTRONIC FUNDS TRANSFER ACT

The **Electronic Funds Transfer Act,** 15 U.S.C. § 1693, governs the rights and liabilities of consumers, financial institutions, and retailers who use electronic funds transfer systems. An **electronic funds transfer** is a transaction that involves a financial institution and that is performed using a computer, a telephone, or other electronic instrument. The electronic funds transfer is usually initiated by a bank customer, the **originator,** who requests the bank to transfer credit to the account of another person, the **beneficiary,** who usually has an account in a another bank. One of the protections of the Act is the amount of liability a consumer faces if there are unauthorized transactions.

Regulation E, promulgated by the Federal Reserve Board, sets out the consumer's liability. Regulation E states that if the bank is notified within two days of the consumer's learning about the unauthorized transaction, the consumer's liability is limited to $50. If the bank is notified more than two days after the unauthorized transaction but within 60 days, the amount of liability is limited to $500. If more than 60 days have passed since the unauthorized transaction, the consumer faces unlimited liability.

CONSUMER LEASING ACT

The **Consumer Leasing Act,** 15 U.S.C. § 1667, applies to consumers' leasing of personal property for personal, family, or household use. The Consumer Leasing Act does not apply to leases of personal property that are for business purposes. In order for the Act to apply, the lease must be for longer than four months, and the amount of the lease must be less than $25,000. If the Act applies, the consumer must be told the number, the amounts, and the period of lease payments. He or she must also be told the total amount of the payments and be informed about any express warranties offered by either the leasing party or the manufacturer of the property. The consumer is also to be told the identity of the person responsible for maintaining or servicing the property, whether he or she has an option to buy the property and the terms of that option, and what happens if he or she ends the lease before the lease expires.

FAIR CREDIT BILLING ACT

The **Fair Credit Billing Act,** 15 U.S.C. § 1666, is a federal law designed to facilitate the settlement of billing errors and to make credit card companies more responsible for the bill that contains the disputed charge. The creditor must acknowledge the complaint within 30 days and has 90 days to resolve the dispute. The Act also prohibits the mailing of unsolicited credit cards and establishes a process to report lost or stolen cards.

CONCLUSION

Consumer protection and products liability are two growing areas of law designed to protect consumers from the practices of some manufacturers and retailers. They are based on two broad areas of common law: torts and contracts. Product liability was originally based on contract law: The consumer had to show privity of contract in order to be successful when suing for injury caused by a defective product. The contract theory was eventually rejected by the courts and replaced with the tort theory of the duty to use reasonable care in the manufacture of products. If reasonable care was not used, then the manufacturer could be held liable for the harm caused.

The tort principle of strict liability also began to be applied to products liability. The injured consumer no longer has to show a lack of reasonable care to prove liability. All the consumer has to prove is that a product is defective, the defect creates an unreasonable risk of harm, and the defect is the proximate cause of the harm. Strict liability has been applied in cases involving failure to warn, design defect, and unknown hazard. Product misuse, assumption of the risk, unavoidable danger, learned intermediary, and sophisticated purchaser are defenses to a claim of strict liability.

Contract law is still a part of product liability law through the use of warranties, which are statements about the quality or fitness of a product. A warranty can be written or oral, express or implied, or full or limited, depending on the circumstances and the agreement.

Consumer protection occurs primarily by federal law and regulations implemented and regulated by the Federal Trade Commission and the Food and Drug Administration. The FDA regulates food products to make sure food has not been adulterated and made unsafe. The FDA also requires proper labeling so consumers will be informed about what they are eating or taking as medication.

The FTC also regulates unfair trade practices and issues industry-wide regulations such as the mail order rule and the used car rule. Federal legislation also protects consumer's rights with regard to credit and debt collection practices, leases, electronic transactions, and billing.

As commerce continues to grow through the use of the Internet and the rise of the global economy, this is an area of law that will continue to develop and evolve.

KEY WORDS AND PHRASES

annual percentage rate
assumption of the risk
caveat emptor
Consumer Credit
 Protection Act
consumer expectation test
Consumer Leasing Act
consumer reporting agency
credit bureau
credit discrimination
defective condition
design defect
direct credit history
electronic funds transfer
Equal Credit Opportunity
 Act

express warranty
extended service warranty
failure to warn
Fair Credit Billing Act
Fair Credit Reporting Act
Fair Debt Collection
 Practices Act
finance charge
fitness for a particular
 purpose
full warranty
implied warranty of
 merchantability
indirect credit history
inherently dangerous
intended use

intended use doctrine
limited warranty
market share liability
product liability
product misuse
prohibited basis
Regulation B
Regulation E
Regulation Z
sophisticated purchaser
Truth in Lending Act
unavoidably dangerous
unknown hazard
warrantor
warranty

REVIEW QUESTIONS

SHORT ANSWER

1. What doctrine did manufacturers use to avoid liability for harm caused by their products?
2. What theory underpinned this doctrine? How were manufacturers able to avoid liability using this doctrine?
3. What case began to change this doctrine?
4. What areas of law are used to hold manufacturers liable for the harm caused by their products?
5. What is meant by the term *products liability?*
6. What is an inherently dangerous product?
7. What is a latent defect?
8. What is a defective product?
9. What is a design defect?
10. What is the consumer expectation test?
11. What must be shown to hold a manufacturer liable when the theory is strict liability?
12. What is meant by intended use?
13. What are the possible defenses to strict liability? What are the elements of the defenses?
14. Which Act gives consumers the right to challenge incorrect information contained on their credit report?
15. Which Act prohibits the mailing of unsolicited credit cards?

16. What information about lease payments must be disclosed to consumers under the Consumer Leasing Act?

17. What are the time frames and the limits on consumer liability under the Electronic Funds Transfer Act?

18. What is a direct credit history?

19. What must be revealed to consumers under the Truth in Lending Act?

20. What is a consumer reporting agency and what does it do?

FILL IN THE BLANK

1. A person or business who uses a product every day and is familiar with the product is known as a _____.

2. Liability based on the percentage of the market a manufacturer had at the time of the harm is _____.

3. The amount that a consumer agrees to pay for the privilege of purchasing goods or services by installments is _____.

4. _____ implemented the Truth in Lending Act.

5. _____ is the federal law that regulates the collection of debts.

6. A manufacturer's amount of liability is based on the percentage of the market that manufacturer had at the time of the injury. This is known as _____.

7. In order to prove strict liability in products liability, the consumer must show:

   _____

   _____

   _____

8. _____ is the degree of care a careful person would use in the same or similar circumstances to prevent injury.

9. If the danger of injury from using a product comes from the use of the product itself, then the product is _____.

10. If a product will cause harm beyond any harm that an ordinary consumer thinks it would, then the product has a _____.

FACT SITUATIONS

1. Steve goes to the home improvement store to purchase the materials and equipment he needs to put a new floor in his bathroom. He describes the project to the salesperson in charge of that area of the store. The salesperson tells Steve what supplies and tools he will need to perform the job. Steve relies on this advice and buys what the salesperson recommended. What warranty has been formed?

2. Georgia is taking a new medication for her illness. She has been warned of the side effects of the drug, but she agrees to take the medication anyway. She suffers all of the side effects the doctors told her she could suffer. She sues the manufacturer of the drug in products liability. What defenses does the drug company have against Georgia's claim?

3. Georgia is taking the same new drug and she has been warned of the known side effects. She considers the risks and takes the drug. However, she suffers from a side effect that was not mentioned by the doctor that the manufacturer did not know about. Can the manufacturer be held liable for the harm caused by the unknown side effect? If so, why?

4. Gus sues a manufacturer for harm caused by a chemical he uses every day in his business. He claims that the manufacturer did not warn him of the possible dangers when he purchased the product this time. However, he had been warned several times before when he bought the same product. What defenses does the manufacturer have to the claim of products liability?

5. When Belva buys her new car she also buys an agreement that covers the car longer than the original warranty does. What has Belva purchased?

6. The Acme Chainsaw Company has done everything it can to make its saws as safe as possible. They have tested them extensively and have patented several safety devices. Max is injured using the chain saw. What defense or theory of products liability can Acme use to shield itself from liability?

7. Sean leases a TV from a company that leases personal property. What is Sean entitled to know when he signs the lease agreement?

8. Sheila, who is over the age of 40, divorced, and African American, applies for credit from a credit card company. Sheila has an excellent credit history, has never been late on a payment, and has an excellent work history. The company turns Sheila down because of her age and race. What laws have just been violated? How?

9. Duane applies for a home loan. When he receives his credit report, there are numerous mistakes on it. Does Duane have the right to correct those mistakes? If so, what law gives him that right?

10. Carlos is turned down for credit. Is Carlos entitled to find out why he was denied? If so, what law gives him that right?

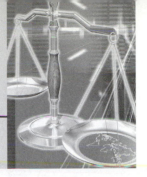

CHAPTER 25

Discrimination in Employment and by State Action

PART I. EMPLOYMENT DISCRIMINATION

INTRODUCTION

Despite numerous federal and state laws prohibiting it, discrimination still occurs in the workplace, in employment decisions, in the provision of employment benefits, in work assignments, in wages, and in all other aspects of employment. Claims of employment discrimination are investigated by the Equal Employment Opportunity Commission (EEOC), a federal agency. The EEOC looks for evidence of either disparate treatment or disparate impact as it analyzes claims of discrimination based on national origin, age, race, religion, disability, or sex.

This chapter introduces and discusses terms related to employment discrimination. It describes the remedies available to those who are victims of workplace discrimination, and explains the defenses commonly invoked in responding to claims of discrimination. The exhibits in this chapter feature important data that both employers and employees should find interesting.

The chapter concludes with a discussion of government action that is discriminatory and an examination of general defenses to charges of workplace discrimination.

GENERAL PRINCIPLES

Discrimination is the unfair treatment of or denial of normal privileges to people because of some inherent characteristic, such as race, age, sex, nationality, or religion. Discrimination is the failure to treat all persons equally where no reasonable distinction can be found. Persons of racial or ethnic **minorities**—African Americans, Hispanics, Asians, Pacific Islanders, American Indians, or Alaskan Natives—are protected from discrimination. People are also protected if they are covered by one of the antidiscrimination statutes, for example, people who are over forty or who have a disability.

THE EEOC

The federal agency responsible for investigating charges of discrimination is the **Equal Employment Opportunity Commission** or **EEOC.** The EEOC is responsible for enforcing laws that prohibit discrimination in employment. The federal government and private individuals can sue in federal court for acts of discrimination not related to employment.

DISPARATE IMPACT AND TREATMENT

Two types of discrimination are recognized by the EEOC: disparate treatment and disparate impact. **Disparate treatment** is the act of treating people differently because of their race, sex, religion, color, national origin, or disability. Disparate treatment is intentional discrimination proven either through direct evidence, comparative evidence, or statistical evidence. **Disparate impact** results when an employment practice appears to be neutral on its face, but in fact falls more harshly upon one group than another and cannot be justified by business necessity. For example, ABC Company offers group health insurance to all of its employees, making sure the rate is the same for all employees. However, the policy does not cover sickle cell anemia, a disease particular to people who are African-American. This insurance would have a disparate impact because it falls more harshly on one group than another: It does not cover a particular disease that affects one group more than others.

INVESTIGATION PROCESS

When the EEOC first receives a claim, it reviews the claim to make sure the complaining party is in a **protected class**—one of the groups the law seeks to protect from discrimination. To determine if a violation took place, the EEOC will look for evidence of disparate impact or disparate treatment. Investigators will look for direct evidence of discrimination: memos, minutes of meetings, or testimony of employees regarding statements made about or against certain employees. For example, a memo from a supervisor telling an employee that he considers the workplace to be a place of God and that the employee better straighten out his life according to God's wishes might be considered evidence of discrimination based on religion. Investigators can also look for circumstantial evidence of discrimination: Only certain employees are granted promotions or pay raises; only certain employees get preferred shifts or days off.

The EEOC may use **comparative evidence**—a statistical analysis of the workforce of an employer—to determine if that force is representative of the overall racial makeup of the area. In other words, if the population in an area is 30% African American and 15% Hispanic, the workforce should be representative of those percentages, otherwise the possibility of employment discrimination in relation to hiring practices might be raised.

If the EEOC finds there is discrimination, it may encourage the parties to enter into a settlement known as *conciliation.* **Conciliation** is the adjustment and settlement of a dispute in a "friendly," nonconfrontational manner: Complaining party, what do you want? Employer, what are you willing to agree to? If the EEOC finds no violation or makes no determination, it issues a **right to sue letter** informing the complaining party that the investigation is complete, that the EEOC found no violation or cannot determine if a violation took place, and that the plaintiff has a right to sue the employer within 90 days of the date of the letter. The person cannot file suit until the right to sue letter has been issued by the EEOC. However, the complaining party does not have to wait for the EEOC to complete its investigation: He or she can ask for the letter if 90 days has elapsed since the complaint was filed with the EEOC. Refer to Exhibit 25-1 for a summary of the EEOC process.

DEFENSES TO A CHARGE OF DISCRIMINATION: MIXED MOTIVE AND AFTER ACQUIRED EVIDENCE

In some situations, an employer's action may be motivated by discrimination only in part: the action in question may have been motivated by other reasons as well. In a **mixed motive case,** discrimination is paired with other factors that precipitate the action the plaintiff finds objectionable. For example, DEF Company fires Pablo because of his ethnic background but also because he stole from the company. One reason Pablo was fired was because of discrimination; the other reason—the theft—would also lead to the action being taken. If a case is one of mixed motive, the only remedy the complaining party is entitled to is an injunction prohibiting future discrimination and attorney's fees. No other remedy is available to the complaining party. See Exhibit 25-2.

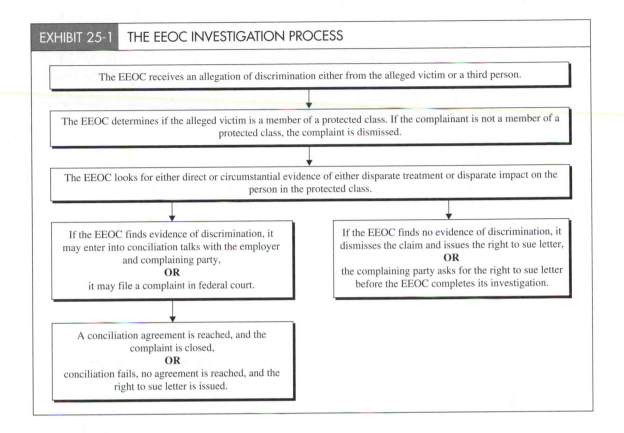

EXHIBIT 25-1 THE EEOC INVESTIGATION PROCESS

The EEOC receives an allegation of discrimination either from the alleged victim or a third person.

The EEOC determines if the alleged victim is a member of a protected class. If the complainant is not a member of a protected class, the complaint is dismissed.

The EEOC looks for either direct or circumstantial evidence of either disparate treatment or disparate impact on the person in the protected class.

If the EEOC finds evidence of discrimination, it may enter into conciliation talks with the employer and complaining party,
OR
it may file a complaint in federal court.

If the EEOC finds no evidence of discrimination, it dismisses the claim and issues the right to sue letter,
OR
the complaining party asks for the right to sue letter before the EEOC completes its investigation.

A conciliation agreement is reached, and the complaint is closed,
OR
conciliation fails, no agreement is reached, and the right to sue letter is issued.

EXHIBIT 25-2 DEFENSES TO A CHARGE OF DISCRIMINATION

1. **Mixed Motive Case** – One reason the action was taken was because of discrimination. The action was also taken for valid, nondiscriminatory reasons. The only remedies available are an injunction prohibiting further discrimination and attorney's fees.
2. **After Acquired Evidence** – After the discriminatory action was taken, a valid reason to take the same action is found. The same action would have been taken once the valid reason had been discovered. This affects the remedies available.

There are also cases where personnel action was taken because of discrimination, but after the action was taken, the employer discovers information that would have caused the same action to be taken. When information is discovered after a discriminatory act has taken place that would lead to the same action, this is known as **after acquired evidence.** For example, Archie, who is openly racist, is a supervisor at a large department store. He fires a black employee "just because." After the employee's termination, it is discovered that she was stealing from the store. The theft of property would have led to the termination. In other words, the store would have fired the employee because of the theft, regardless of race. The employee was discriminated against initially but then a valid reason was discovered that would have caused the employee to be fired. Because of the after acquired evidence, what damages the former employee can receive are different from those granted in a regular discrimination case.

The issue of what damages are available was presented to the U.S. Supreme Court in the case *McKennon v. Nashville Banner Publishing Company*. See Sidebar 25-1. The plaintiff sued the Nashville Banner Publishing Company for discrimination under the Age Discrimination Act. The court stated that liability for discrimination does not end because of after acquired evidence; the employee is entitled to back pay, reinstatement, and front pay.

SIDEBAR 25-1 *MCKENNON V. NASHVILLE BANNER PUBLISHING CO.*

Fact: Christine McKennon worked for respondent Nashville Banner Publishing Company. She was discharged, the Banner claimed, as part of a workforce reduction plan necessitated by cost considerations. McKennon, who was 62 years old when she lost her job, thought she had been discharged because of her age. During her deposition, she testified that, during her final year of employment, she had copied several confidential documents bearing on the company's financial condition. She had access to these records as secretary to the Banner's comptroller. McKennon took the copies home and showed them to her husband. A few days after these deposition disclosures, the Banner sent McKennon a letter declaring that removal and copying of the records was in violation of her job responsibilities and advising her (again) that she was terminated. The Banner's letter also recited that, had it known of McKennon's misconduct, it would have discharged her at once for that reason.

Issue: Would the discovery of the after acquired evidence bar any recovery for damages because of discrimination?

Decision: Such after acquired evidence is not a complete bar to recovery. After acquired evidence of the employee's wrongdoing must be taken into account in determining the specific remedy, lest the employer's legitimate concerns be ignored. The proper boundaries of remedial relief in cases of this type must be addressed on a case-by-case basis. However, as a general rule, neither reinstatement nor front pay is an appropriate remedy. It would be both inequitable and pointless to order the reinstatement of someone the employer would have terminated, and will terminate, in any event and upon lawful grounds.

Once an employer learns about employee wrongdoing that would lead to a legitimate discharge, it cannot be required to ignore the information, even if it is acquired during the course of discovery in a suit against the employer and even if it might have gone undiscovered absent the suit. The beginning point in formulating a remedy should therefore be calculation of back pay from the date of the unlawful discharge to the date the new information was discovered.

Source: United States Reports

REMEDIES AVAILABLE BECAUSE OF DISCRIMINATION

Several different remedies are available to an individual or a group of people who have been discriminated against. One remedy is **back pay**—accrued but uncollected salary. In a case of after acquired evidence, back pay is calculated from the time of the discrimination to the time of the discovery of the new information. The employee must be paid for the time he or she would have been at work had he or she not been discriminated against up to the time the employment action would have taken place when the information that would have led to termination was discovered. For example, if Jordanna was fired on September 1 because of discrimination and evidence of theft on her part was discovered on December 15, she can receive back pay from September 1 to December 15.

Reinstatement is the restoration of the complainant to the position he or she held prior to the discrimination. Reinstatement is not available as a remedy in a case of mixed motive discrimination or a case of after acquired evidence. **Front pay** is the salary paid to a person who was discriminated against when there is no vacancy for that person at the time reinstatement is ordered. The individual receives the salary he or she would have received if he or she had not been discriminated against, even if there is no vacancy at the time. In essence, the employee is paid although he or she is not working during the period he or she waits for a job vacancy.

Affirmative action is an employment program to remedy past discriminatory practices and past facially neutral employment practices that had a disparate impact on minorities. **Artificial seniority** is a remedy that gives minority workers extra years of work credit to make up for past acts of discrimination. Refer to Exhibit 25-3 for a summary of the remedies available.

EXHIBIT 25-3	REMEDIES AVAILABLE FOR DISCRIMINATION

Back Pay – Salary the employee would have earned if he or she had not been discriminated against.

Reinstatement – Restoration of the person to the position he or she held before the discrimination.

Front Pay – Salary paid to a person who was discriminated against while he or she waits for a vacancy to occur so that his or her employment can be resumed.

Affirmative Action – Employment program to remedy past discrimination giving preference to members of the group that was discriminated against.

Artificial Seniority – Giving minority workers extra years of work credit to make up for past discrimination.

RELIGIOUS DISCRIMINATION

Religious discrimination is discrimination based on religion. Religious entities or institutions are exempt from antidiscriminatory policies. See Exhibit 25-4 for a summary of the number of religious discrimination charges filed in the United States between 1992 and 2002 and the costs of settlement.

EXHIBIT 25-4	RELIGIOUS DISCRIMINATION CHARGES FILED WITH THE EEOC AND SETTLEMENT AMOUNTS

1992 – 1,388 charges filed; $1.4 million paid

1993 – 1,449 charges filed; $2.1 million paid

1994 – 1,546 charges filed; $1.5 million paid

1995 – 1,581 charges filed; $1.5 million paid

1996 – 1,564 charges filed; $1.8 million paid

1997 – 1,709 charges filed; $2.2 million paid

1998 – 1,786 charges filed; $2.3 million paid

1999 – 1,811 charges filed; $3.1 million paid

2000 – 1,939 charges filed; $5.5 million paid

2001 – 2,127 charges filed; $14.1 million paid

2002 – 2,572 charges filed; $4.3 million paid

Dollar figure represents the amount cases were settled for. The figure does not include the amount won in litigation.

Source: Equal Employment Opportunity Commission

WHAT IS RELIGION?

In employment law, the term **religion** refers not only to traditional religious views, but also to any moral or ethical beliefs as to what is right and wrong that are sincerely held by an individual with the strength of traditional religious views. The fact that no organized religious group espouses such beliefs does not matter. Freedom of religion also includes the freedom *not* to believe, so the rights of atheists and agnostics are also protected under the law.

COERCION AND HOSTILE WORK ENVIRONMENT

This type of religious discrimination is divided into two broad categories. The first is **coercion,** or being compelled to be in compliance with other employees in the participation or nonparticipation in religious activities. For example, in a real-life case previously referred to, a born-again Christian informed an employee that she considered the workplace a place of God, and that if the employee was unwilling to shape up and play by God's rules, then he would be replaced. This employer clearly attempted to coerce the employee, thus engaging in religious discrimination.

The second category of religious discrimination is the creation of a **hostile work environment.** A hostile work environment is a workplace characterized by enmity or antagonism toward an employee or a group of employees that is created by either supervisors or co-workers. The test used to determine if a hostile work environment exists is whether the harassing conduct is sufficiently severe or pervasive enough to alter the conditions of employment. If the conditions of employment are altered sufficiently, then the hostile work environment exists and discrimination has taken place.

AGE DISCRIMINATION AND RACIAL DISCRIMINATION

Age discrimination is targeted toward those who are forty years old or older; there is no upper age limit. Age discrimination policies apply to employers who have 20 or more employees, employment agencies, and labor unions. See Exhibit 25-5 for a summary of the number of age discrimination charges filed between 1992 and 2002 in the United States and the costs of settlement.

EXHIBIT 25-5	AGE DISCRIMINATION CHARGES FILED WITH THE EEOC AND SETTLEMENT AMOUNTS

1992 – 19,573 charges filed; $57.3 million paid
1993 – 19,809 charges filed; $41.7 million paid
1994 – 19,618 charges filed; $42.3 million paid
1995 – 17,416 charges filed; $29.4 million paid
1996 – 15,719 charges filed; $31.5 million paid
1997 – 15,785 charges filed; $44.3 million paid
1998 – 15,191 charges filed; $34.7 million paid
1999 – 14,141 charges filed; $38.6 million paid
2000 – 16,008 charges filed; $45.2 million paid
2001 – 17,405 charges filed; $53.7 million paid
2002 – 19,921 charges filed; $55.7 million paid

Dollar figure represents the amount cases were settled for. The figure does not include the amount won in litigation.

Source: Equal Employment Opportunity Commission

PRIMA FACIE CASE: AGE DISCRIMINATION

A prima facie case of age discrimination is shown when the person is in an age-protected group (40 or older); the person applied for the job and was qualified; the person was rejected for the job; and the job remained open and the employer continued to see applicants. Also, if a complaining party is terminated because of age, the person replacing him or her does not need to be younger. All that matters is that the person who was terminated is 40 years old or older.

RACIAL DISCRIMINATION

Racial discrimination is targeted toward someone because of his or her race. The standards of disparate treatment and disparate impact apply. A prima facie case of race discrimination is shown when the complainant is a member of a recognized minority group; he or she applied for the job and was qualified; he or she was rejected for the job; and the job remained open and the employer continued to see applicants. See Exhibit 25-6 for a summary of race discrimination charges filed between 1992 and 2002 in the United States and the costs of settlement.

EXHIBIT 25-6	RACE DISCRIMINATION CHARGES FILED WITH THE EEOC AND SETTLEMENT AMOUNTS

1992 – 29,548 charges filed; $31.9 million paid
1993 – 31,695 charges filed; $33.3 million paid
1994 – 31,656 charges filed; $39.7 million paid
1995 – 26,986 charges filed; $30.1 million paid
1996 – 26,287 charges filed; $37.2 million paid
1997 – 29,199 charges filed; $41.8 million paid
1998 – 28,820 charges filed; $32.2 million paid
1999 – 28,819 charges filed; $53.2 million paid
2000 – 28,945 charges filed; $61.7 million paid
2001 – 28,912 charges filed; $86.5 million paid
2002 – 29,910 charges filed; $81.1 million paid

Dollar figure represents the amount cases were settled for. The figure does not include the amount won in litigation.

Source: Equal Employment Opportunity Commission

SEX DISCRIMINATION

Sex discrimination is discrimination in the workplace against someone because of his or her sex. Antidiscriminatory policies relate to sexual harassment, unequal pay, pregnancy, and parental leave. The term **sexual harassment** refers to sexual advances, requests for sexual favors, and other verbal and physical conduct of a sexual nature. Such conduct must be **unwelcome conduct:** This means that the employee did not solicit or incite it, but rather regarded the conduct as undesirable or offensive. See Exhibit 25-7 for a summary of the number of sex discrimination charges filed between 1992 and 2002 in the United States and the costs of settlement.

EXHIBIT 25-7	SEX DISCRIMINATION CHARGES FILED WITH THE EEOC AND SETTLEMENT AMOUNTS

1992 – 21,796 charges filed; $12.7 million paid   **1998** – 24,454 charges filed; $34.3 million paid
1993 – 23,919 charges filed; $25.1 million paid   **1999** – 23,907 charges filed; $50.3 million paid
1994 – 25,860 charges filed; $22.5 million paid   **2000** – 25,194 charges filed; $54.6 million paid
1995 – 26,181 charges filed; $24.3 million paid   **2001** – 25,140 charges filed; $53.0 million paid
1996 – 23,813 charges filed; $27.8 million paid   **2002** – 25,536 charges filed; $50.3 million paid
1997 – 24,728 charges filed; $49.5 million paid

Dollar figure represents the amount cases were settled for. The figure does not include the amount won in litigation.

Source: Equal Employment Opportunity Commission

QUID PRO QUO AND HOSTILE WORK ENVIRONMENT

There are two forms of workplace sexual harassment: quid pro quo and hostile work environment. In **quid pro quo** sexual harassment (something for something), sexual favors are sought in return for job benefits or opportunities: "Have sex with me if you want that raise." "Have sex with me or you are fired." "Your position with this company would be improved if you would loosen up." Only a supervisor or manager can commit quid pro quo sexual harassment because only a person with supervisory authority can carry out the threat: Only a supervisor or manager has the power to condition job benefits or opportunities on submission to sexual conduct.

The demand for sexual favors in return for job benefits can be explicit or implied. The benefit must be a tangible job benefit, such as the job itself, promotion, leave, pay raises, preferential assignments, and job evaluations. One instance of quid pro quo sexual harassment is sufficient to constitute a violation of Title VII.

The second form of workplace sexual harassment is the hostile work environment. This term refers to sexual comment or conduct that has the purpose or effect of unreasonably interfering with a person's work performance or creating an intimidating, hostile, or offensive working environment. A supervisor or co-worker can be responsible for creating a hostile work environment; this type of harassment does not have to affect a tangible job benefit. Rather, it affects the intangible work environment—the work situation itself. The key issues are frequency and severity: The more frequent the objectionable conduct, the less severe it has to be; the less frequent, the more severe the objectionable conduct has to be. The EEOC presumes that one instance of unwelcome, intentional touching of a person's intimate body part is sufficient to create a hostile work environment. See Exhibit 25-8.

EXHIBIT 25-8 | TWO TYPES OF SEXUAL HARASSMENT

Quid Pro Quo – Tangible job benefits are offered in return for sexual favors. Only a manager or supervisor can commit this type of sexual harassment.

Hostile Work Environment – The intangible work environment is affected. The conduct has the purpose or effect of unreasonably interfering with the person's work performance or creates an intimidating, hostile, or offensive work environment.

If the conduct under examination by the EEOC is verbal, the Commission will look at the following factors: Did the alleged harasser single out the charging party? Did the charging party participate? What was the relationship between the charging party and the alleged harasser? Were the remarks hostile and derogatory?

AMERICANS WITH DISABILITIES ACT

The **Americans with Disabilities Act,** or **ADA,** prohibits discrimination against a person because of disability. A **disability,** as defined by the ADA, is any physical or mental impairment that substantially limits one or more of the major life activities of a person. A person who has a record of such impairment, or who is regarded as having such impairment, is also considered to be a person with a disability.

WHO IS DISABLED UNDER THE ADA?

The United States Supreme Court has handed down three decisions that clarified who, in fact, is disabled under the ADA. In *Sutton v. United Air Lines,* two people with severe myopia sued claiming United Air Lines discriminated against them because of their disability. They also alleged the airline *considered* them to be disabled because of their eyesight. The plaintiffs were applying to be pilots with United Air Lines, but they did not meet the vision requirements. See Sidebar 25-2 for the decision of the Supreme Court.

SIDEBAR 25-2 *SUTTON V. UNITED AIR LINES*

Facts: Two job applicants with severe myopia alleged the airline violated the ADA when it did not offer them positions as commercial pilots. The plaintiffs both have severe myopia that was corrected by glasses. Both alleged they were disabled.

Issue: Were the plaintiffs "disabled," using the definition of *disability* under the ADA?

Decision: "Looking at the Act as a whole, it is apparent that if a person is taking measures to correct or mitigate a physical or mental impairment, the effects of those measures—both positive and negative—must be taken into account when judging if the person is substantially limited in a major life activity and thus disabled under the Act."

Looking at the language of the Act, specifically "substantially limits," the court said the language is properly read as requiring that a person be presently, not hypothetically or potentially, substantially limited in order to demonstrate a disability. If corrective measures correct or control the condition, then a person is not substantially limited in a major life activity. The Court stated that if did not take corrective measures into account, then the disability determination is made "based upon general information about how an uncorrected impairment usually affects individuals rather than the individual's actual condition."

According to the Court, the correct procedure is to determine if, with the corrective device, is the person still limited in a major life activity.

Source: United States Reports

In *Murphy v. UPS*, a mechanic with high blood pressure sued UPS alleging the ADA had been violated when he was terminated. The mechanic was fired because his blood pressure levels exceeded Department of Transportation rules. He did not usually drive the trucks, but when he repaired some, he would be required to road test them. Because of the road testing, he fell under the Department of Transportation rules. The Supreme Court, citing its decision in *Sutton* as controlling, upheld the decision to dismiss his case because when the plaintiff was taking his medicine, he was not substantially limited in a major life activity.

In *Albertsons, Inc. v. Kirkinburg*, a truck driver with amblyopia—a condition that severely weakened vision in his left eye—alleged that his employer violated the ADA when it terminated his employment. There was testimony that the plaintiff had developed subconscious compensatory skills to deal with his vision limitation. The Supreme Court said such compensatory measures also needed to be taken into account when determining whether a person is disabled, not just artificial aids like glasses. See Exhibit 25-9 for a summary of these three decisions.

EXHIBIT 25-9	WHO IS DISABLED UNDER THE ADA?

Sutton v. United Air Lines – Is the person limited in a major life activity, taking into account the use of corrective measures? If the person is not limited in a major life activity after taking into account corrective measures, then the person is not covered by the ADA.

Murphy v. UPS – Citing *Sutton v. United Air Lines*, the Court declared that because the plaintiff's high blood pressure was controlled by medication, he was not considered a person with a disability.

Albertsons, Inc. v. Kirkinburg – Corrective measures are not limited to artificial aids like eye glasses or medication. The way a person subconsciously deals with a disability has to be taken into account to determine if a person is disabled under the ADA.

ESSENTIAL FUNCTIONS OF THE JOB AND REASONABLE ACCOMMODATIONS

The ADA requires an employer to identify in writing the **essential functions** of each job. These "essential functions" are the reason why the job exists. A person with a disability must be able to perform those functions either with or without reasonable accommodation. If the person cannot perform the essential functions of the job, then he or she is not covered by Title I.

An employer is required to make reasonable accommodations to allow a person with a disability to perform the essential functions of a job. **Reasonable accommodations** include assigning the nonessential functions to someone else (this does *not* mean hiring someone else to do the disabled person's job), restructuring how the work is done, providing flexible working hours, altering the work site, or providing special equipment. Personal items like eyeglasses and hearing aids do not have to be provided by the employer. Reasonable accommodations can also include transfer to a vacant position, provided the position is, in fact, vacant and the person is qualified for the position.

The accommodation provided does not have to be the one requested, as long as it is effective. The provision of accommodations does not mean that a person is held to a different standard as everyone else: The person with a disability is held to the same standards as everyone else. The accommodation is to help the person meet those standards. See Exhibit 25-10 for a summary of the number of disability discrimination charges filed in the United States since the ADA was passed and the costs of settlement.

EXHIBIT 25-10	DISABILITY DISCRIMINATION CHARGES FILED WITH THE EEOC AND SETTLEMENT AMOUNTS

1992 – 1,048 charges filed; $0.2 million paid	**1998** – 17,806 charges filed; $53.7 million paid
1993 – 15,274 charges filed; $15.9 million paid	**1999** – 17,007 charges filed; $55.8 million paid
1994 – 18,859 charges filed; $32.6 million paid	**2000** – 15,864 charges filed; $54.4 million paid
1995 – 19,798 charges filed; $38.7 million paid	**2001** – 16,470 charges filed; $47.9 million paid
1996 – 18,046 charges filed; $45.5 million paid	**2002** – 15,964 charges filed; $50 million paid
1997 – 18,108 charges filed; $41.3 million paid	

Dollar figure represents the amount cases were settled for. The figure does not include the amount won in litigation. The EEOC started accepting ADA cases on July 26, 1992.

Source: Equal Employment Opportunity Commission

WHISTLEBLOWERS

Recent news reports have made reference to whistleblowers. A **whistleblower** is an employee who reasonably believes his or her employer is violating the law by committing fraud or waste, is abusing its position, or is causing unnecessary expenditures and who notifies the authorities of the employer's actions. A whistleblower cannot be discriminated against because of his or her status as whistleblower. Discrimination can include taking an adverse employment action against either an employee or an applicant or failing to perform a positive employment action for an employee or applicant. For example, an employer might terminate an employee because the employee reported wasteful spending, or a prospective employer might refuse to hire the best qualified applicant because the applicant reported fraud at his or her previous job. Whistleblowers are protected by several federal statutes. In addition, several states have passed whistleblower statutes. See Exhibit 25-11 for a list of statutes that have a whistleblower provision.

EXHIBIT 25-11	FEDERAL LAWS THAT CONTAIN WHISTLEBLOWER PROVISIONS

1. Clean Air Act, 42 U.S.C. § 7622
2. Energy Reorganization Act, 42 U.S.C. § 581
3. Federal Water Pollution Control Act, 42 U.S.C. § 1367, 1369
4. Comprehensive Environmental Response, Compensation, and Liability Act of 1980, 42 U.S.C. § 9610
5. Pipeline Safety Improvement Act of 2002, PL No. 107-335
6. Safe Drinking Water Act, 42 U.S.C. § 300j-9
7. Sarbanes-Oxley Act of 2002, 18 U.S.C. § 1514A
8. Solid Waste Disposal Act, 42 U.S.C. § 6971
9. Surface Transportation Assistance Act, 49 U.S.C. § 31101, 31105
10. Toxic Substance Control Act of 1982, 15 U.S.C. § 2622

WAGE DISCRIMINATION

The **Equal Pay Act** of 1963, which is an amendment to the Fair Labor Standards Act, is federal law that prohibits **wage discrimination**—paying wages to employees at a rate less than the rate paid to workers of the opposite sex. The work done must be equal work on jobs that require equal skill, effort, and responsibility and that are performed under similar working conditions.

EQUAL PAY AND SKILL

Under the Equal Pay Act, the word *equal* means substantially the same in terms of skill, effort, responsibility, and working conditions. *Skill* is defined as the experience, education, training, and ability required to perform the job. *Effort* is defined as the physical or mental exertion needed to perform the job. *Responsibility* is defined as the economic and social consequences that would result from the failure of the employee to perform the job duties in question. The phrase **similar working conditions** means the safety hazards, physical surroundings, and hours of employment are the same.

EXTRA DUTIES

Sometimes an employer will justify pay inequities on the basis that employees of one sex are given extra duties that justify the extra pay. If the listed conditions are met, the duties are **extra duties** and there is no discrimination.

DEFENSES TO WAGE DISCRIMINATION

There are four defenses to a charge of wage discrimination that are listed in the statute. The first is the existence of a **bona fide seniority system,** a system that pays higher wages the longer a worker has worked for a company. The second is a **bona fide merit system** that requires that pay be based on an employee's ability. The third defense is that pay is based on a **quality or quantity of output:** Employees are paid based on the amount or quality of their output. The fourth defense is **factors other than sex.** This is a fairly broad defense that is applied on a case-by-case basis. See Exhibit 25-12.

EXHIBIT 25-12	DEFENSES TO WAGE DISCRIMINATION

Bona Fide Seniority System – Pay is based on a system that pays higher wages the longer a worker has worked for a company.

Bona Fide Merit System – Pay is based on an employee's ability.

Quality or Quantity of Output – Pay is based on the quantity or quality of the employee's output.

Factors Other Than Sex – This defense is applied on a case-by-case basis.

PART II. DISCRIMINATION BY STATE ACTION

Sometimes a person or business complains that a government action is discriminatory. Several terms are associated with this type of discrimination, which is referred to in legal circles as *state action*.

STATE ACTION

State action is an improper government intrusion into the life of a person or the operations of a business. In order to determine if something is state action, the courts determine whether there is enough of a connection between the activity of the state and the challenged action so that it is actually an action by the state. For example, a state passes a law that draws a distinction between different businesses. A person whose business is hurt by the new law files suit, claiming discrimination by state action.

STRICT SCRUTINY

If the law is found to adversely affect a fundamental right, then the state action will be subjected to **strict scrutiny.** In order to pass the strict scrutiny test, the state must show that there is a compelling interest in the law or regulation and that this is the least restrictive alternative available. In other words, this law is necessary and there is no less restrictive way to accomplish the same results. If there is another way to achieve the same results, then the law or regulation has failed the strict scrutiny test.

PART III. DEFENSES TO CHARGES OF DISCRIMINATION

There are general defenses to a charge of discrimination that may be raised by a defendant. Which defense can be raised, if any, is determined on a case-by-case basis. Not every defense will apply to every allegation of discrimination.

BONA FIDE OCCUPATIONAL QUALIFICATION

The first defense is one of **bona fide occupational qualification.** If it can be shown that a characteristic is required of employees as a matter of business necessity, there may be no discrimination based on religion, national origin, or sex. For example, if it is shown that it is a business necessity that all employees must be male, it is not discrimination not to hire female workers.

MERIT DEFENSE

Another defense to an allegation of discrimination is the **merit defense:** Employment and promotion decisions are based on professionally developed tests that are manifestly related to job performance.

There are three types of validation used to determine if, in fact, ability tests are valid and job related. The first is **criterion-related validity:** There is statistical validation between the test scores and the objective criteria of job performance. The second is **content valid-**

ity: a skill used on the job is isolated and the testing directly tests that skill. The third is **construct validity:** A psychological trait needed to perform a particular job-related task is measured.

SENIORITY SYSTEM

A third defense is the use of a **seniority system.** Such a system may perpetuate discrimination, but the use of the system is bona fide and not a violation of federal law if the following criteria are met:

1. The system applies equally to all persons.
2. The seniority units follow industry practices.
3. The seniority system was not started with the intent to discriminate.
4. The system is free from any illegal discriminatory purpose.

BUSINESS NECESSITY

Another defense to workplace discrimination is **business necessity;** the justification for the usually prohibited discrimination in an employment situation is that the prohibited practice is essential for the safety and efficiency of the business. A business that invokes this defense is required to show that there was no reasonable alternate with a lesser impact. If the business cannot do this, it has not met the criteria for the defense.

CONCLUSION

Discrimination is a continuing problem in the workplace. Employers and employees can face liability for acts of discrimination. Discrimination can be based on age, religion, race, national origin, and sex. Discrimination can be seen in disparate treatment or in disparate impact.

The EEOC is the federal administrative agency responsible for investigating allegations of discrimination in the workplace. If the EEOC finds there has been discrimination, it may attempt to enter into conciliation with the employer and employee. If the situation is serious enough, the EEOC may file a complaint in federal court. The remedies to discrimination include reinstatement, back pay, front pay, and injunctions.

Religious discrimination can be by coercion or by the creation of a hostile work environment. The religion does not have to be one recognized as mainstream: As long as a person is sincere in his or her beliefs, he or she is protected from discrimination.

Sex discrimination in the workplace can take two forms: quid pro quo harassment and hostile work environment. The term quid pro quo refers to the demand for sexual favors in return for tangible job benefits. Only a supervisor can carry out quid pro quo harassment. A supervisor or fellow employee can create a hostile work environment.

Disability discrimination applies to people who are disabled according to the terms of the Americans with Disabilities Act and as further defined by the Supreme Court. A person who is legally disabled must be limited in a major life activity after corrective measures have been taken into account.

Defenses to discrimination include after acquired evidence, mixed motive, bona fide occupational qualifications, merit defense, seniority system, and business necessity. However, the best way to avoid liability for discrimination is to insure that it never takes place.

CHAPTER 25 REVIEW

KEY WORDS AND PHRASES

affirmative action
after acquired evidence
age discrimination
Americans with Disabilities
  Act (ADA)
artificial seniority
back pay
bona fide merit system
bona fide occupational
  qualification
bona fide seniority system
business necessity
coercion
disability
discrimination

disparate impact
disparate treatment
Equal Employment
  Opportunity Commission
  (EEOC)
Equal Pay Act
essential functions
front pay
hostile work environment
mixed motive case
protected class
quality or quantity of
  output
quid pro quo
racial discrimination

reasonable accommodation
reinstatement
religion
religious discrimination
right to sue letter
sex discrimination
sexual harassment
similar working conditions
state action
strict scrutiny
unwelcome conduct
wage discrimination
whistleblower

REVIEW QUESTIONS

SHORT ANSWER

1. After it has terminated an employee, an employer finds out that the employee was stealing from the business. What is this called?

2. An employer fires an employee as a result of age discrimination, but also terminates the employee because of poor work performance, inconsistent work attendance, and poor interpersonal skills. What is this termed?

3. What is meant by quid pro quo harassment?

4. What are the protected classes in discrimination cases?

5. What is considered state action?

6. What must the person who is complaining about discrimination receive before he or she can sue for discrimination?

7. If the EEOC finds that there was discrimination, what will it enter into with the complaining party and the employer?

8. What is considered religion in discrimination cases?

9. What is a whistleblower?

10. What is considered strict scrutiny?

11. A person was discriminated against, resulting in their being fired. They are allowed to return to work, but there is no position for them at the time of reinstatement. What is the person entitled to receive until an appropriate position for him or her opens up?

12. What is meant by artificial seniority?

13. What is affirmative action?

14. The Equal Pay Act prohibits what type of discrimination?

15. What is disparate impact?

16. Under the ADA, what is a disability?

17. What is the merit defense to a claim of discrimination?

18. What is the extra duties defense to a claim of wage discrimination?

19. What is the business necessity defense?

FILL IN THE BLANK

1. The Supreme Court case of _____ established the rule that corrective measures must be taken into account to determine if a person is disabled.

2. That pay is based on an employee's ability is the _____ defense.

3. Treating people differently because of their age, race, or sex is known as _____.

4. Being compelled to be compliant with other employees' religious beliefs is _____, and is a type of discrimination.

5. A workplace marked by antagonism toward an employee or group of employees is known as a _____.

6. Giving extra years of work to minorities when they did not actually work those years to make up for past discrimination is known as _____.

7. Salary an employee would have earned had it not been for discrimination is known as _____.

8. The full name of the federal agency responsible for investigating discrimination is the _____.

9. Discrimination is one reason why employment action was taken. However, there were legitimate reasons for taking the action that later came to light. This is referred to as a _____ case.

10. That pay is based on the quality or amount of an employee's work output is the _____ defense to a charge of wage discrimination.

FACT SITUATIONS

1. A business offers insurance to its employees. The insurance costs the same for all employees, regardless of age. However, the coverage for people over the age of forty is less than the coverage provided to people who are under the age of forty. What type of discrimination is this? Why is it discrimination?

2. An employee engages in the telling of sexual jokes that another employee finds upsetting, and continues to tell the jokes even after he is asked to stop. What type of discrimination is this? Why?

3. An employee was fired because of age discrimination. After the employee was terminated, it was discovered the she had been embezzling from the company. What defense would the company have to a claim of discrimination?

4. The EEOC receives an allegation of racial discrimination. An investigation shows that the employer's workforce is 15% minority, and that the racial makeup of the surrounding area is 20% minority. Would discrimination be found to exist? Why?

5. In the above scenario, what method did the EEOC use to determine if discrimination was taking place?

6. Lupe's supervisor takes her aside and says that her position in the company would be greatly improved if she would just loosen up a little bit and learn how to have fun. Lupe has applied for a promotion and the supervisor will be making the selection. Were the supervisor's comments a form of harassment? If so, what type?

7. Antonio is hard of hearing and has poor eyesight. He wears glasses that correct his vision and he has a hearing aid that helps him hear. He is on medication for high blood pressure. His job performance for the past year has been very poor, so his employment is terminated. Antonio claims he is disabled under the ADA and needs reasonable accommodations. Is Antonio disabled under the ADA? Why or why not?

8. Miguel reported his former employer to authorities for padding their bills to the federal government. Miguel is applying for another position with another company that has several federal contracts. He is the best qualified applicant, but does not receive the job. Is this discrimination? Why or why not?

9. GHI Company pays some employees more than others. A group of employees files a charge of wage discrimination. GHI raises the defense of extra duties. What will GHI have to show to prove this defense applies to the situation?

10. XYZ Corporation bases promotions on tests that are given to all interested employees. Some employees allege that the tests are not valid—they are just an excuse not to promote minorities. What must XYZ prove to establish the validity of the test used to promote employees?

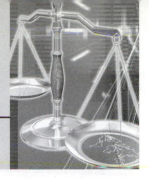

CHAPTER 26
Environmental Protection

INTRODUCTION

In recent years, concerns about the environment have led to the creation of new federal agencies and the passage of new laws that deal with different types of pollutants. Prior to the 1970s, pollution was dealt with by citizens, local government, and the states. The federal government was not involved with environmental concerns at all; and because there were no federal statutes, common law had to be relied on in dealing with pollution issues. Tort law theories were used to protect the environment with limited success.

In 1970, Congress passed the first of many federal statutes designed to protect the environment. The first statutes established the Environmental Protection Agency and the Clean Air Act. The Clean Air Act set national priorities regarding air quality standards and how those standards are to be met and maintained. Legislation dealing with land and water pollution was also created. This chapter discusses terminology related to environmental law and explains major legislation designed to protect our planet from misuse and abuse.

GENERAL PRINCIPLES

Before 1970, there were no federal laws designed to protect the environment and no federal agencies to establish environmental goals or to monitor compliance with environmental laws. Concerns about diminishing natural resources and environmental abuses gradually led to the creation of the Environmental Protection Agency and numerous federal laws and regulations to help protect the environment.

ENVIRONMENTAL PROTECTION AGENCY

In 1970, Congress created the **Environmental Protection Agency (EPA).** Its purpose is to implement and enforce the provisions of federal environmental legislation. The EPA is primarily responsible for four major areas of pollution: air pollution, water pollution, pollution of the land, and pollution connected with certain products.

Also in response to the problem of pollution, Congress established the requirement of environmental impact statements. An **environmental impact statement (EIS)** must be prepared for every major federal activity that would significantly affect the quality of the human environment. The creation of an EIS is mandated by the National Environmental Policy Act of 1979. An EIS must be prepared when these three elements are present:

- The action must be federal—the granting of a license, the making of a loan, or the leasing of property by a federal agency.
- The action must be major—it requires a substantial commitment of resources.
- The action must have a significant impact on the human environment.

The EIS must contain the following.

1. A description of the environmental impact of the proposed action
2. An explanation of any adverse environmental effects that cannot be avoided if the proposal is implemented

3. Identification of any alternatives to the proposed action

4. An explanation of the relationship between local short-term uses of the environment and the maintenance and enhancement of long term productivity

5. A statement regarding any irreversible or irretrievable commitment of resources that would be involved in the activity if it is implemented.

Refer to Exhibit 26-1 for a summary of when an EIS must be obtained and what it must contain.

EXHIBIT 26-1 ENVIRONMENTAL IMPACT STATEMENTS

WHEN AN EIS IS REQUIRED

1. The action must be a federal action, the granting of a license, the making of a loan, or the leasing of property by a federal agency.
2. The action must involve a substantial commitment of resources.
3. The action must have a significant impact on the human environment.

WHAT THE EIS MUST CONTAIN

1. The environmental impact of the proposed action.
2. Any adverse environmental effects that cannot be avoided.
3. Any alternatives to the proposed action.
4. The relationship between the short-term uses of the environment and the maintenance and long-term enhancement of long-term productivity.
5. A description of the irreversible or irretrievable commitment of resources that would be involved in the activity if it is implemented.

The EPA and Environmental Impact Statements are intended to help deal with the problems of pollution, particularly toxic waste. **Pollution** is the contamination of the environment from different sources, including hazardous substances, organic chemicals, toxic substances, and waste. **Toxic waste** is hazardous or poisonous and includes substances like PCBs and DDT.

AIR POLLUTION

The first piece of federal legislation that dealt with the environment was the **Clean Air Act** of 1970. The Clean Air Act established federal air quality standards that the states are required to meet.

AMBIENT AIR STANDARDS

The Act authorizes the EPA to establish **national ambient air quality standards,** federal standards that set the maximum concentration levels for pollutants in the atmosphere. For example, the maximum levels for sulfur dioxide, particulate, ozone, carbon monoxide, nitrogen oxides, or lead that can be in the atmosphere are set by the EPA. The term **ambient air** is defined as the air outside of buildings or other enclosed areas.

The states are required to develop **state implementation plans** (see Exhibit 26-2) that indicate how certain air pollutants are going to be controlled by certain dates in order to meet the national air quality standards. In order to be valid, state implementation plans must include the following:

1. Enforceable emission limits
2. Schedules and timetables for compliance
3. Measures for monitoring air quality and emissions from pollution sources
4. Adequate funding, personnel, and authority for implementing and enforcing the state implementation plan

---

EXHIBIT 26-2	STATE IMPLEMENTATION PLANS

Required by the Clean Air Act of 1970, the plan must contain the following.

1. **Enforceable** emission limits
2. **Schedules and timetables** for compliance
3. Measures for **monitoring air quality and emissions** from pollution sources
4. **Adequate funding, personnel, and authority** for implementing and enforcing the state implementation plan

---

Pollution may be emitted by a **moveable source,** one that migrates from place to place (such as an automobile), or a **stationary source,** such as a factory or an electrical power plant.

PERMIT SYSTEM

The Clean Air Act sets up a permit system to determine where new plants can be built and the amount of pollution they can expel into the air. How much—if any—pollution can be expelled into the air depends on how the area is classified. Some areas are designated as **attainment areas:** in those areas, the federal standards for major pollutants have been met. In other words, in these areas the air contains the maximum amount of pollutants allowed by federal law. Attainment areas will not be allowed to become more polluted.

In a **prevention of significant deterioration area,** the air quality is better than the national standard. Because the air quality is better than what is required by federal standards, only a slight increase in pollution is allowed. This slight increase of pollution in a prevention of significant deterioration area is known as the **maximum allowable increase.** Any plant or business that would cause the maximum allowable increase amount to be exceeded is prohibited from being built in the prevention of significant deterioration area. Prevention of significant deterioration areas and attainment areas are also known as **clean air areas.**

In a **nonattainment area,** the air quality for certain pollutants fails to meet national ambient air quality standards. Because of this, nonattainment areas are also referred to as **dirty air areas.** The requirements for new construction in nonattainment areas are even more stringent than in clean air areas because federal standards are not being met. One of the requirements that must be met for construction to take place in a nonattainment area is **emission offset,** which states that before a new polluting facility can be built or an existing facility expanded, the owner is required to reduce certain air pollutants by as much or more than the amount of air pollution the new factory will produce. One method used to accomplish this reduction is to pay other factories in the area to reduce their amount of pollution. See Exhibit 26-3.

EXHIBIT 26-3 | AIR POLLUTION

Governed by the Clean Air Act

Attainment Areas – Areas where federal standards for air pollution are being met.

Prevention of Significant Deterioration Area (clean air) – Air quality is better than the national standard. Only maximum allowable increase is allowed in these areas. If a plant will exceed this increase, it cannot be built in this area.

Nonattainment Area (dirty air) – Area where national air standards are not being met. In order to build in this area, there must be a reduction of air pollution by at least the amount of pollution that will be produced by the new factory.

EMISSIONS OFFSET POLICY

New construction is also governed by the **emissions offset policy,** which places three requirements on the owners of new plants or plants that have been expanded.

1. A new plant's pollution must be controlled to the maximum degree possible. The plant must use the **lowest achievable emission rate**—the most stringent technology use by any similar plant in the country.

2. New plant owners must certify that the other plants they own in the area meet the state implementation plan requirements.

3. A new plant can only be built in this area if the air pollution from the new plant is offset by a reduction in pollution from other established plants. When the new plant starts operations, the air quality must improve as a result of a reduction in pollution from other established plants in the area.

See Exhibit 26-4 for a summary of the Emission Offset Policy.

EXHIBIT 26-4 | EMISSION OFFSET POLICY

This policy places three requirements regarding air emissions on the owners of new plants or plants that have been expanded.

1. A new plant's pollution must be controlled to the **maximum degree possible.** The plant must use the lowest achievable emissions rate and the **most stringent technology** used by any similar plant in the country.

2. New plant owners must **certify** that the other plants they own in the area meet the state implementation plan requirements.

3. A new plant can only be built in this area if the air pollution from the new plant is **offset by a reduction in pollution from the other plants.** When the new plant starts operations, the air quality has to improve as a result of a reduction in pollution from the other plants in the area.

The EPA also uses the bubble concept, which is similar to the emissions offset policy. The **bubble concept** applies when a factory or factories in the same complex that pollute the air or a geographical area are treated as a single pollution source. A "bubble" is placed over this area, and the entire complex is treated as if it had only one source of pollution. See Exhibit 26-5.

Additional factories may be built in this area provided the overall pollution in the area—in the "bubble"—decreases. One factory can exceed the amount of pollution allowed as long as pollution from the other factories under the "bubble" is below the maximum allowable amount. The most common way this reduction is accomplished is by shutting down

---

EXHIBIT 26-5 | THE BUBBLE CONCEPT

Factories in the same complex that pollute the air are treated as a single pollution source. A "bubble" is placed over this area and the entire complex or area is treated as if it has one smokestack, one source of pollution. Additional factories may be built in this area, provided the overall pollution in the area, in the "bubble," decreases.

---

the factories in the area that are the worst polluters and transferring their production to the newer facility.

The purpose of all these measures is to maintain the quality of air we breathe and to prevent such hazards as acid rain. **Acid rain** is precipitation with high acidic content caused by atmospheric pollution. Acid rain has a pH level of less than five, which means it is highly acidic. Another type of air pollution is referred to as **sick building syndrome**—indoor air pollution caused by the absence of fresh air in overly insulated new buildings and by the emissions of harmful substances found in the building's materials and furniture. See Exhibit 26-6.

EXHIBIT 26-6 | TYPES OF AIR POLLUTION

Acid Rain – Precipitation with a high acidic content that is caused by atmospheric pollution. Acid rain has a pH level of less than five, which means the rain has high acidic quality.

Sick Building Syndrome – Indoor air pollution caused by the absence of fresh air in overly insulated new buildings and by the emissions of harmful substances found in the building's materials and furniture.

WATER POLLUTION

The consumption of water used to be governed by common law riparian rights. **Riparian rights** give the owner of the land that is bounded by a river or body of water or over which water passed the right to reasonably use that water. However, the landowner must not damage the water to the point that a landowner further downstream would find it unusable.

CLEAN WATER ACT

Prior to 1972, the federal government had little if any control over pollution expelled into the nation's waters. The **Clean Water Act,** passed in 1972, gave the federal government control over water pollution. The goal of the Clean Water Act is to protect the integrity of the national water system. There are five major components to the Clean Water Act.

1. It allows the EPA to establish **national effluent** (pollution) **standards,** which set water pollution limits for every industry that discharges liquid wastes into national waterways. The term **effluent limitation** refers to the maximum allowable amounts of pollution that can be discharged from a point source within a given period of time.

2. Water quality standards set by the states must have EPA approval.

3. A discharge permit program establishes water quality standards that can be put into enforceable pollution limits.

4. Special provisions for toxic chemicals and oil spills.

5. Provisions for construction grants and loans from the federal government for publicly owned treatment works.

Refer to Exhibit 26-7 for a summary of the Clean Water Act.

EXHIBIT 26-7 COMPONENTS OF THE CLEAN WATER ACT

1. The EPA is authorized to set national effluent standards for each industry. These standards establish the water pollution limits for every industry that discharges liquid waste into national waterways.
2. Water quality standards set by the states must have EPA approval.
3. A discharged permit program establishes water quality standards that can be put into enforceable pollution limits.
4. Special provisions for toxic chemicals and oil spills.
5. Provision of construction grants and loans from the federal government for publicly owned treatment works.

POINT AND NONPOINT SOURCE POLLUTION

Water pollution is identified as either point source pollution or nonpoint source pollution. **Point source pollution** is emitted from a definitive place of discharge, such as a pipe, ditch, or channel. The location where point source pollution originates is easy to identify and usually easy to treat. **Nonpoint source pollution** is created by several sources, making it impossible to specifically identify where it originated. Nonpoint source pollution includes runoff from streets, agricultural runoff, and pollution from construction, logging operations, and mining sites. There are regulations in place that attempt to control this type of pollution, but because the exact source cannot be identified, nonpoint source pollution is more difficult to regulate and control.

The treatment of sewage from point source pollution usually takes place at a **publicly owned treatment works (POTWs)**, a publicly owned facility that removes pollutants from the water. Because most of the pollutants treated at POTWs are nontoxic, the **sludge**—material that is removed from the water during treatment—is often used for fertilizer.

THE NATIONAL POLLUTANT DISCHARGE ELIMINATION SYSTEM

If an industry is discharging something other than sewage into the water, it is subject to the **National Pollutant Discharge Elimination System.** Under this system, industrial polluters list the amount of discharge and the types of discharge going into the water. See Exhibit 26-8.

EXHIBIT 26-8 NATIONAL POLLUTANT DISCHARGE ELIMINATION SYSTEM

1. Industry lists the amount and types of discharge going into the water.
2. Industry receives a discharge permit that allows it to legally discharge pollution into the water.
3. The permit sets the amount and types of pollution that can be discharged.
4. Industry must prepare a discharge monitoring report that lists the types and amounts of pollutants it has released into the water.

Before an industry can legally discharge pollutants into the nation's waterways, it must receive a **discharge permit** from the federal government. The discharge permit sets the amount and types of pollution that can be discharged into the water. If an industry does not have a permit or exceeds the amount or type of pollution allowed by the permit, the polluter may face an **effluent charge**—a fee or fine imposed on the illegal polluting activity.

An industry is also required to file a **discharge monitoring report** listing the types and amounts of pollutants it has released into the water. A discharge monitoring report is a self-reporting tool; there are serious penalties for lying in the report.

CONTROL TECHNOLOGY FOR WATER POLLUTION

Industries are required to be in compliance with the effluent standards set by the EPA for water pollution. In order to meet those standards, controls are placed on point source pollution released into the water system. Three levels of control or technology are used to limit water pollution. **Best conventional technology** is a term referring to the technology used to control conventional pollutants, such as human waste. For toxic or unconventional pollutants, which are subject to tighter control, the **best available technology** applies. *Best available technology* is defined as the very best control and treatment measures that have been or are capable of being achieved. As better technology is invented to control pollution, the polluter must use that technology to lessen the pollution produced. When a new plant is built or a new source of pollution is discovered, the plant or pollution is subject to **new source performance standards,** the greatest degree of pollution reduction possible through the use of the best available control technology, processes, operating methods, and other alternatives, including, where practical, standards permitting no discharge of pollutants. See Exhibit 26-9.

EXHIBIT 26-9	CONTROL TECHNOLOGY USED TO LIMIT WATER POLLUTION

Best Conventional Technology – Technology used to treat conventional waste.

Best Available Technology – Used for toxic or unconventional pollutants; the very best control and treatment measures that have been or are capable of being achieved.

New Source Performance Standards – Greatest degree of pollution reduction possible through the use of the best available demonstrated control technology, processes, operating methods, and other alternatives.

DRINKING WATER

In addition to passing laws regulating the discharge of pollution into water, the federal government has also created laws designed specifically to protect our country's drinking water supply. The **Safe Drinking Water Act** sets standards for the drinking water supplied by public water supply systems. A **public water supply system** is any system that has at least fifteen service connections or that serves twenty-five or more people.

Under this Act, the EPA is required to establish two levels of drinking water standards: primary standards and secondary standards. **Primary standards** protect human health and **secondary standards** protect the aesthetic quality of drinking water. Primary standards are based on **maximum contaminant level goals**—levels where there are no potential adverse health effects. Maximum containment level goals are not enforceable standards, but rather are goals the industry tries to meet. Primary standards are also based on **maximum contaminant levels**—the maximum amount of pollutants that could have potential adverse human health effects. Maximum contaminant levels are enforceable by the EPA.

WETLANDS

The last area of pollution control regarding water is the regulation of wetlands. **Wetlands** are those areas of land covered by water for at least part of the year. Wetlands are saturated by either surface or groundwater of sufficient frequency and duration to support vegetation typically adapted for life in saturated soil conditions. Wetlands include swamps, marshes, bogs, areas that hold water for just part of the year, and large areas that are always covered by water. The definition of *wetland* continues to evolve as environmental law develops. Anyone wanting to alter a wetland must have a permit from the Army Corps of Engineers.

LAND POLLUTION

Business produces millions of tons of hazardous or toxic waste each year; and this waste has been dumped onto land, stored on land, buried underground, and even injected into the ground. The disposal of the toxic waste is one of the primary causes of land pollution.

SOLID WASTE DISPOSAL ACT

To deal with the problem of land pollution, Congress passed the Resource Conservation and Recovery Act, also known as the **Solid Waste Disposal Act.** This Act controls toxic substances once they are on the market, and sets out how these substances are to be properly disposed of. The Act defines **hazardous waste** as a solid waste which, because of its quantity, concentration, or physical, chemical, or infectious characteristics, may cause a serious, irreversible, or incapacitating reversible illness. Hazardous waste is ignitable, corrosive, reactive, or toxic when ingested or absorbed. Hazardous waste poses a substantial present or potential hazard to human health or to the environment. A **toxic pollutant** is defined by the Act as one that may cause an increase in mortality, death, or serious illness.

MANIFEST SYSTEM

One method used to control hazardous waste pollution is the **manifest system,** which is the requirement that certain chemicals have documentation concerning their production, distribution, and disposal to ensure proper handling and disposal of the substances. A company that produces hazardous waste is required to complete the manifest form setting out the nature of the materials and identifying their source, their routing, and their final destination. The hazardous materials must be properly labeled and packaged.

The company that transports the waste must have a copy of the manifest, which they sign and give to the owner of the treatment site. A **treatment, storage, and disposal site (TSD)** is defined by the Act as a site that has a permit from the EPA to treat, store, or dispose of these waste products. The owner of this site must return the manifest to the company that generated the waste. See Exhibit 26-10 regarding the manifest system process.

TOXIC DUMP SITES

The manifest system deals with current hazardous waste, but does not deal with the major issue of waste dumped in the past. The **Comprehensive Environmental Response, Compensation, and Liability Act (CERCLA)** is the federal law that deals with the issue of closed or abandoned toxic dump sites. CERCLA determines when hazardous waste sites must be cleaned up and who is responsible for the cost. Such sites could be located at **brownfield sites,** where factories, manufacturing plants, and military bases have recently closed.

Another term for CERCLA is the **Superfund.** The term *Superfund* comes from the trust fund that was set up by the Act for meeting the costs of cleaning up the sites pending reimbursement from the parties responsible for the damage. The Superfund authorizes the estab-

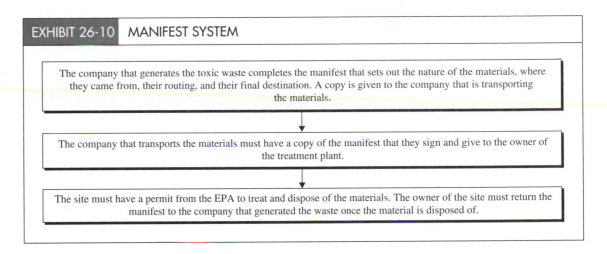

EXHIBIT 26-10 MANIFEST SYSTEM

The company that generates the toxic waste completes the manifest that sets out the nature of the materials, where they came from, their routing, and their final destination. A copy is given to the company that is transporting the materials.

The company that transports the materials must have a copy of the manifest that they sign and give to the owner of the treatment plant.

The site must have a permit from the EPA to treat and dispose of the materials. The owner of the site must return the manifest to the company that generated the waste once the material is disposed of.

lishment of a **National Priority List,** which identifies the worst sites as determined by the EPA that must be cleaned up and returned to nearly original condition. The Superfund also designates who is ultimately responsible for the cost of cleaning up toxic waste dump sites.

SITE EVALUATION PROCESS

A step-by-step evaluation of a potential hazardous waste dump site is followed before that site is placed on the National Priority List. The first step is a **preliminary assessment,** a limited-scope investigation performed on every potential site. Preliminary assessment investigations collect readily available information about a site and its surrounding area. The assessment is designed to distinguish, based on limited data, between sites that pose little or no threat to human health and the environment and sites that may pose a threat and require further investigation.

If the preliminary assessment results in a recommendation for further investigation, a **site inspection** is performed. This inspection identifies sites that will be considered for entry onto the National Priority List. See Exhibit 26-11. This inspection also provides the data needed for hazard ranking system scoring and documentation. Site investigators typically collect environmental and waste samples to determine what hazardous substances are present at a site. They determine if these substances are being released into the environment and assess if they have reached nearby targets.

EXHIBIT 26-11 STATES WITH PROPOSED NPL SITES

Alabama—2	California—2
Colorado—2	Connecticut—1
Florida—1	Georgia—1
Idaho—3	Illinois—5
Indiana—1	Iowa—1
Kansas—2	Louisiana—2
Maryland—1	Massachusetts—1
Michigan—2	Mississippi—2
Montana—1	New Hampshire—1
New Jersey—3	New Mexico—1
New York—1	Ohio—6
Oklahoma—1	Oregon—1
Pennsylvania—2	Tennessee—1
Texas—2	Utah—4
Wisconsin—1	

Source: Environmental Protection Agency

The **hazard ranking system** is the principal method used by the EPA to place controlled waste sites on the National Priorities List. This is a numerically based screening system that uses information from initial, limited investigations, the preliminary assessment, and the site inspection to assess the relative potential of sites to pose a threat to human health or the environment. Sites with an HRS score of 28.50 or greater are eligible for listing on the NPL and require the preparation of an HRS scoring package.

RESPONSIBLE PARTIES

The cost of cleaning up a toxic waste dump site can run into the millions of dollars. This is not a cost that should be borne by the government and taxpayers; the businesses and industries responsible for dumping the waste should pay for cleanup costs. The parties that may be responsible are referred to as **potentially responsible parties (PRPs)**. See Exhibit 26-12. The list of PRPs includes:

1. The current site owners holding title to the property
2. Any prior owner who held title at the time of hazardous waste disposal
3. Any generator of waste who arranged for the disposal of waste at the site
4. Any transporter of waste who selected the site for disposal

All PRPs are jointly and severally liable for clean-up, regardless of how much or how little waste they dumped or allowed to be dumped.

EXHIBIT 26-12	WHO MAY BE RESPONSIBLE FOR CLEANUP

1. The current site owners holding title to the property
2. Any prior owner who held title at the time of hazardous waste disposal.
3. Any generator of waste who arranged for the disposal of waste at the site.
4. Any transporter of waste who selected the site for disposal.

CONCLUSION

The highly specific words and phrases associated with environmental law all deal with the important issue of protecting the environment and trying to prevent further damage by pollution. The Environmental Protection Agency is the federal agency charged with implementing federal legislation regarding the environment. The EPA also establishes regulations and criteria used to regulate, limit, and reduce pollution.

Air pollution is regulated by the Clean Air Act. This Act establishes national air standards and requires the states to create implementation plans that will indicate how they will meet clean air guidelines. The permit system is used to regulate industrial air pollution by placing limitations on how much pollution a new factory is allowed to produce. This amount is determined by the different attainment areas created by the federal statute.

The Clean Water Act established national effluent standards—limitations on the amount of pollution industries can discharge into the nation's waterways. The Act regulates point source and nonpoint source pollution. The Act also established the discharge permit system, a requirement that industry must have a permit before any pollution may be discharged into waterways. Federal legislation also mandates which control technology must be used, provides for the protection of the nation's drinking water system, and establishes protection of wetlands.

Land pollution is concerned with solid and liquid toxic wastes that have been dumped on land and that may still be disposed of by dumping the waste on land. In order to control the disposal of toxic wastes, the manifest system has been created: Waste is tracked from its producer to its final disposal site. To clean up old toxic dump sites, the Superfund was created along with a National Priority List. The National Priority List is a listing of the worst sites as determined by the EPA; these sites have priority in being cleaned up.

CHAPTER 26 REVIEW

KEY WORDS AND PHRASES

acid rain
ambient air
attainment area
best available technology
best conventional
 technology
brownfield sites
bubble concept
Clean Air Act
clean air areas
dirty air areas
discharge monitoring report
discharge permit
effluent charge
effluent limitation
emission offset
emission offset policy

environmental impact
 statements
Environmental Protection
 Agency (EPA)
hazardous waste
lowest achievable emission
 rate
manifest system
maximum allowable
 increase
moveable source
national ambient air quality
 standards
national effluent standards
National Pollutant
 Discharge Elimination
 System

National Priority List
nonattainment area
nonpoint source pollution
point source pollution
pollution
prevention of significant
 deterioration area
riparian rights
sick building syndrome
Solid Waste Disposal Act
state implementation plan
stationary source
toxic pollutant
toxic waste
wetlands

REVIEW QUESTIONS

SHORT ANSWER

1. What is ambient air?

2. What is best conventional technology?

3. To what type of pollution does it apply?

4. What is an attainment area?

5. What is the difference between best available technology and best conventional technology?

6. What is the "bubble concept"?

7. What are clean air areas?

8. What are dirty air areas?

9. What is an emission offset?

10. What is an effluent charge?

11. What is the maximum allowable increase?

12. To what type of pollution does it apply?

13. What is moveable source pollution?

14. What is the National Priority List?

15. To what type of pollution does it apply?

16. What is point source pollution?

17. What is a nonattainment area?

18. To what sort of pollution does it apply?

19. What are new source performance standards?

20. To what sort of pollution do they apply?

FILL IN THE BLANK

1. Indoor air pollution caused by the absence of fresh air and the emissions of harmful substances is known as _____.

2. Pollution that comes from a definite source of discharge is known as _____.

3. _____ is the maximum allowable amount of pollution that can be discharged from a source within a given period of time.

4. A fee or fine that is imposed on an industry that does not have a permit or exceeds the amount of pollution that can be discharged is a/an _____.

5. Technology that is used to control conventional pollutants in water is known as _____.

6. When a new source of pollution is discovered being discharged into water, that pollution is known as _____.

7. The _____ established standards for the water supplied by a public water supply system.

8. For drinking water, _____ is the standard used to protect human health.

9. The requirement that certain chemicals have documentation concerning their production, distribution, and disposal is known as _____.

10. Areas where factories, manufacturing plants, or military bases have recently been closed are known as _____.

FACT SITUATIONS

1. A company wants to build a new factory in an area where the air quality exceeds the national standard. What is this area known as? What is the level of pollution that can be generated?

2. The same company wants to build a factory in an area where the air quality is below the national standard. What is this area known as? What must the company do in order to obtain permission to operate in this area?

3. A company is discharging pollution into water. The company files a report listing the amounts and types of pollution that are being discharged. By filing this report, what is the company requesting?

4. A company is discharging toxic and unconventional pollutants into the water. What level of technology is used to control this type of pollution?

5. A business is producing toxic waste that it wishes to dispose of in a landfill. The company fills out the paperwork indicating the type of waste, where it came from, where it is to go, and the route that is to be taken. What is the business complying with in the disposal of this waste?

6. Under this system, what must the transporter of the waste do with the documentation? What happens to the documentation after the hazardous waste is delivered?

7. The following parties owned or were involved in the dumping of waste at a site that is now on the National Priority List:

   - Armand was the owner of the property prior to the site being used as a dump site.
   - Margot and Sidney owned the property for a two-month period when it was first used as a dump site.
   - Sherman owned the property after Margot and Sidney, and owned it while most of the toxic waste was dumped on the site.
   - Chemco directed the hazardous waste to be dumped on the site.
   - West Chemical relied on York Transporting to arrange for disposal of its toxic waste.

   Which of these parties can be held responsible for the costs of cleaning up the site? Why?

8. Yuri wants to build a housing development on a piece of land that includes a parcel of land that is covered by water most of the year. He wants to dredge this part of the property so the water will drain off and be made suitable for construction. What is this land known as? Who must he get a permit from for construction to take place?

9. The Clavell Company operates several factories at one site, all of them producing air pollution. The Clavell Company wants to build a new factory at this site and is seeking permission to do so. How might the EPA treat this site? Under what circumstances can a new factory be built?

10. Cohen Industries wishes to build a new plant in an area where air pollution measurements greatly exceed established levels because of several old plants producing air pollution. What is this area known as? What will Cohen Industries have to do in order to build a new factory in this area?

CHAPTER 27

Cyberspace Law

INTRODUCTION

Cyberspace law is an emerging area. With the proliferation of personal computers, the growth of the Internet, the expanding use of e-mail in business and in private life, the law has had to adapt to the new technology. New crimes can now be committed, issues regarding intellectual property have emerged, personal privacy issues are the focus of increased attention, and issues regarding civil procedure have burgeoned. In some instances, while a certain conduct may have been deemed illegal, it has been difficult for prosecutors to match the charges to an alleged crime. It is apparent that law must keep up with technology. This chapter introduces and discusses words and phrases that are currently used in conjunction with the legal aspects of cyberspace.

BASIC TERMS

Certain words and phrases that are part of the computer lexicon must be understood before any discussion of cyberspace law can begin. A fundamental computer term is **domain,** which can be understood as a sphere of influence. A domain is part of the Internet. A **domain name** is the title that describes the territory covered by a Web site owner.

HACKERS

A **hacker** is a person skilled in programming computers and in writing computer programs. The term has come to refer to people who find ways to break into secure computer programs. **Hacking** is the gaining of access to computers where no access was intended. Hacking may or may not be a crime, depending on the jurisdiction where the hacking took place and what system is being hacked into.

TOOLS OF THE HACKER

Hackers use several methods, tools, or programs to break into a computer program. These include worms, viruses, Trojan horses, and logic bombs. A **worm** is a computer program that travels from one computer to another, but does not attach itself to the operating system. A worm is used more often for obtaining information, but it can also be used to destroy data. A **virus** is a computer program that does attach itself to the operating system of any computer it enters. A virus destroys, damages, rearranges, or replaces computer data; a virus can infect any other computer that uses files from the infected computer. Some viruses, like the "I Love You" virus, can go to the address book in a user's e-mail system and send itself to every person in the address book.

  Virus writing is the act of writing a program that has the ability to attach itself to other programs in other computers, allowing the program to replicate itself. A program **replicates** itself when it has the ability to go from one group of computer addresses to another group. The program has the ability to copy itself by sending itself to other computers and infecting those computers.

Some of the programs used by hackers have the ability to hide within a system and then become active. A **Trojan horse** is a program that has the ability to hide itself, usually as legitimate software, and then replicate itself. A **logic bomb** is a program that remains undetected in a computer system until it detonates because of an event or a specific date. A **firewall** is a computer between computers on a network that is designed to secure the system from unauthorized access.

One way people break into computer systems is by using a **password sniffer,** a program that monitors and records the names and passwords of network users. Information obtained through the password sniffer can be used to access restricted information. When one computer is disguised electronically to look like another computer in order to gain access to a restricted system, it is referred to as **spoofing.** See Exhibit 27-1 for a summary of the tools of the hacker.

EXHIBIT 27-1	TOOLS OF THE HACKER

Logic Bomb – A program that remains undetected in a computer system until it detonates, set off on a specific date or triggered by a specific event.

Password Sniffer – A program that monitors and records the names and passwords of network users as they log onto a system.

Trojan Horse – A program that has the ability to hide itself, usually as legitimate software, and then replicates itself.

Virus – A computer program that attaches itself to the operating system of any computer it enters. A virus destroys, damages, rearranges, or replaces computer data; a virus can infect any other computer that uses files from the infected computer.

Worm – A computer program that travels from one computer to another but does not attach itself to the operating system. It can be used to obtain information and to destroy data.

ACCESSING THE INTERNET, FRAMING, AND SPAM

In order to gain access to the Internet, computer users utilize a provider. The customer enters into an **access contract,** a contract for electronic access to information. The contract can be with Internet service providers, remote data processing, and e-mail systems.

Sometimes a person may want to view more than one Web site at a time; framing allows this to happen. **Framing** is displaying parts of two Web sites simultaneously. Framing is also used for other purposes such as **spam,** electronic mail sent by marketers as a form of direct solicitation. Spam can be likened to electronic junk mail. Spam often appears as pop up ads; the ads are framed so the viewer still sees part of the Web site he or she accessed.

E-commerce is a general term that refers to any commercial transaction involving the exchange of goods, services, or information over the Internet. Because of the growing use of e-commerce, electronic signatures, or e-sign, are being accepted. **E-sign** is the recognition of electronic signatures. Electronic contracts with electronic signatures have the same validity as traditional printed contracts and handwritten signatures.

JURISDICTION OVER WEB SITE OPERATORS

A legal issue with regard to the Internet was when or if a particular state could exercise jurisdiction over a Web site owner or operator who "conducted business" within that state. When were there sufficient minimum contacts with a state to allow a court within that state to exercise long arm jurisdiction over the Web site owner or operator? Or could there ever be sufficient minimum contacts, considering the very nature of the Internet? (See Chapter 4,

Civil Procedure.) The courts have begun to address this issue of civil procedure, looking at the amount of interaction between a Web site and a person who has accessed the Web site.

PASSIVE OR INTERACTIVE WEB SITES

In order to ascertain the amount of interaction between a site and a visitor, the type of Web site that is being accessed is determined. A **passive Web site** is one that transmits information only; a passive Web site does not solicit any business. An **interactive Web site** is one that does actively seek and solicit business from customers. This site allows for more to happen than just the transmission of information.

INTERACTIVITY AND THE SLIDING SCALE OF JURISDICTION

Interactivity is the extent to which a Web site involves two-way communication between the site and the user. This is used to obtain jurisdiction over the owner/operators of the Web site. The more interaction that is required, the more likely there has been sufficient minimum contacts with the state where the user is located for that state to exercise long arm jurisdiction. **Sliding scale of jurisdiction** is a method used to determine if a state will have jurisdiction over a Web site owner based on the amount of interactivity. It was developed in the case of *Zippo Manufacturing Co. v. Zippo Dot Com, Inc.* See Sidebar 27-1.

SIDEBAR 27-1 *ZIPPO MANUFACTURING CO. V. ZIPPO DOT COM, INC.*

Facts: Zippo Manufacturing Company is a Pennsylvania corporation that makes, among other things, the well-known Zippo tobacco lighters. It is the holder of a trademark on the name *Zippo*. Defendant Zippo Dot Com, Inc., is a California corporation that operates a Web site and Internet news service, and it is the holder of the rights to the domain names Zippo.com, Zippo.net, and Zipponews.com. Zippo Manufacturing alleged that by using the trademark name *Zippo* in numerous locations on its Web site and news group messages, Defendant has violated the Federal Trademark Act and state intellectual property laws. Zippo.com filed a motion to dismiss the case for lack of proper jurisdiction.

Issue: How can a court exercise jurisdiction over a company that conducts business on the Internet?

Decision: In recent years, businesses have begun to use the Internet to provide information and products to consumers and other businesses.

Personal jurisdiction that can be constitutionally exercised is directly proportionate to the nature and quantity of commercial activity that an entity conducts over the Internet. This sliding scale is consistent with well-developed personal jurisdiction principles. At one end of the spectrum are situations where a defendant clearly does business over the Internet. If the defendant enters into contracts with residents of a foreign jurisdiction that involve the knowing and repeated transmission of computer files over the Internet, personal jurisdiction is proper. At the opposite end are situations where a defendant has simply posted information on an Internet Web site that is accessible to users in foreign jurisdictions. A passive Web site that does little more than make information available to those who are interested in it is not grounds for the exercise of personal jurisdiction. The middle ground is occupied by interactive Web sites where a user can exchange information with the host computer. In these cases, the exercise of jurisdiction is determined by examining the level of interactivity and commercial nature of the exchange of information that occurs on the Web site.

Source: U.S. Reports

The standards used for the sliding scale jurisdiction test follow.

1. When the defendant clearly transacts business over the Internet, does the defendant enter into contracts that require knowingly and repeatedly transmitting computer files over the Internet? If so, then the state has jurisdiction.

2. Does the defendant sell goods over the Internet? The more accessible the site is in a particular state or area, the more commerce that is transacted, and the more likely it is that in personam jurisdiction will be found to exist.

3. Does the user exchange information with the Web site? How much does the site interact with the user? The more interaction there is, the more likely it will be that in personam jurisdiction will be exercised.

4. If the Web site is passive, that is, the defendant merely advertises services on the Web, then this is not enough to establish in personam jurisdiction. See Exhibit 27-2.

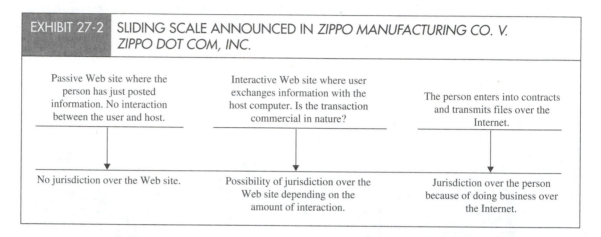

EXHIBIT 27-2   SLIDING SCALE ANNOUNCED IN *ZIPPO MANUFACTURING CO. V. ZIPPO DOT COM, INC.*

Passive Web site where the person has just posted information. No interaction between the user and host.	Interactive Web site where user exchanges information with the host computer. Is the transaction commercial in nature?	The person enters into contracts and transmits files over the Internet.
No jurisdiction over the Web site.	Possibility of jurisdiction over the Web site depending on the amount of interaction.	Jurisdiction over the person because of doing business over the Internet.

COPYRIGHT ISSUES

When computer programs were first being written and the use of personal computers became more popular, issues about the copyright of the program were raised. Which part of the program could be copyrighted? How would people be put on notice about the copyright and would it be binding?

COPYRIGHT OF THE PROGRAM

One of the first areas of concern for copyright violation was the program itself. **Abstraction** is the analysis of a software program's sequence, structure, and organization for the purpose of revealing its functions. Companies would attempt reverse engineering in the hope of discovering the source code or the object code. **Object code** is computer software that is in machine readable form. Programmers use **source code** in writing their programs. Because of these issues and because it was questioned whether existing copyright law adequately protected computer programs, new federal law was passed by Congress. The **Computer Software Copyright Act** is federal law that protects software—both source code and object code—as literary works under copyright law. See Exhibit 27-3.

EXHIBIT 27-3   COMPUTER CODE PROTECTED BY COPYRIGHT

Object code is computer software that is in machine-readable form.
Source code is computer software in the form written by programmers.
Protected by the **Computer Software Copyright Act.**

COPYRIGHT PIRACY

Another issue related to copyright of software is the illegal copying of existing software. **Software piracy** is the term referring to the illegal copying and distribution of software. Piracy is widespread because software is easy to copy, a copy works as well as the original, and a copy costs a great deal less than the original. When a consumer purchases software, the manufacturer can ensure that the purchaser is aware of copyright restrictions and agrees to be bound by the terms of the license agreement. This method is the **shrink wrap agreement,** a standardized license agreement that is enclosed with a piece of software and that is visible through the plastic wrapping. Acceptance of the license is inferred from opening the product. The term **accept or return** applies to the user's options with regard to a shrink wrap agreement: The user will either accept all of the terms of the license of the software or return the product to the seller.

Another method that is used to protect copyright is the **click wrap agreement,** an agreement where access to a Web site or installation of software is prevented unless the person/user clicks to accept the terms of the agreement.

In an effort to limit piracy of software, **antitrafficking provisions** are incorporated into the law. Such provisions prohibit the manufacture or sale of software or devices that circumvent access or use controls over copyrighted material. In other words, software or any other devices designed to help get around controls put in copyrighted material to prevent duplication are illegal.

WEB SITES

Another issue related to cyberspace and copyright involves copyrighted material on Web sites. **Contributory copyright infringement** occurs when a Web site encourages users to violate copyright law by appropriating copyrighted material posted on the site. Notices of copyright are included on Web sites to inform users that material posted is protected by copyright law. There is also federal law that applies specifically to copyrighted material on the Internet: The **Digital Millennium Copyright Act** contains a **notice and takedown** provision that requires an Internet service provider to remove or block access to materials that infringe on copyrights.

CYBERCRIME

With computer use growing and access to information, products, and services made easier because of computer networks, new crimes and new ways to commit existing crimes have been created. **Cybercrime** is crime committed by using a computer and telecommunications networks.

CYBERSTALKING, CYBERTERRORISM, AND CYBERTRESPASS

Some of the more traditional crimes that can be committed by computer are stalking, terrorism, and trespass. **Cyberstalking** is a form of stalking that involves telecommunication devices, the interception of e-mail, or interaction with a person in a chat room. The term **cyberterrorism** refers to criminal activities committed against a computer system rather than a person. Cyberterrorism activities include theft of information, malicious destruction of information, spying, and fraud. **Cybertrespass** is the invasion of another person's property interest in an electronic database by a physical act that is committed on site or by remote access. See Exhibit 27-4.

EXHIBIT 27-4 | TRADITIONAL CRIMES COMMITTED BY A COMPUTER

Cyberstalking – A form of stalking that involves telecommunication devices, e-mails, or interaction with a person in a chat room.

Cyberterrorism – Criminal activities that are committed against a computer system rather than a person. Cyberterrorism activities include theft of information, malicious destruction of information, spying, or fraud.

Cybertrespass – The invasion of another person's property interest in an electronic database by a physical act that is committed on site or by remote access.

NEW COMPUTER CRIMES

Several new crimes are unique to the misuse of a computer system. **Cracking** is the intentional, malicious hacking into a computer system. **Malware** is a term that applies to any harmful software or hardware that harbors viruses, worms, and logic bombs. Malware is made possible because a hacker cracks into a computer system. Once the hacker has access to the system, he or she can insert viruses, worms, logic bombs, Trojan horses, sniffer programs, and denial of service attacks.

Data manipulation occurs when a hacker changes or erases existing information. A **computer network break-in** occurs when a hacker, using software installed on a computer in one location, breaks into different computer systems to steal data or plant viruses or Trojan horses.

A hacker can also commit less serious acts that are generally regarded as nuisances. For example, he or she might change user names or passwords so people cannot log onto their computers. In **mail bombing,** software is written to command a computer to repeatedly send electronic mail to a specific e-mail address. The victim's e-mail account may become overloaded and his or her entire system may shut down. A **denial of service attack** is a crime that occurs when a hacker clogs a Web site's equipment by sending it too many requests for information.

Spoofing, which is a type of con game, involves setting up "phony" Web sites to look like other legitimate Web sites. This creates a copy of the Internet on another person's computer. When the person logs onto the Internet, the information they send is funneled through a hacker's computer and the hacker is allowed to monitor all of the person's activities, passwords, and account numbers. This allows the hacker to engage in the much-publicized crime of identity theft. **Identity theft** occurs when personal identifying information such as social security numbers, credit card numbers, or account numbers are "stolen" and then used to obtain financial services. **Web site defacement** is an activity wherein an attacker gains access to a Web server—usually through identity theft—and then corrupts or alters the content of the site's page. See Exhibit 27-5 for a summary of these new crimes.

EXHIBIT 27-5 | NEW TYPES OF COMPUTER CRIME

Computer Network Break-in – Using software installed on a computer in one location, a hacker breaks into different computer systems to steal data and plant viruses or Trojan horses.

Cracking – The intentional, malicious hacking into a computer system.

Data Manipulation – The alteration or erasure of information by a hacker.

Denial of Service Attack – A hacker clogs a Web site's equipment by sending it too many requests for information.

Identity Theft – Personal identifying information such as social security numbers, credit card numbers, or account numbers are "stolen" and then used to obtain financial services.

Mail Bombing – Software is written to command a computer to repeatedly send electronic mail to a specific e-mail address.

Spoofing – Setting up Web sites to look like other existing Web sites, which creates a copy of the Internet on another person's computer. This allows a hacker to monitor all of the person's activities, passwords, and account numbers.

Web Site Defacement – An attacker gains access to a Web server, usually through identity theft, and then corrupts or alters the content of the site's page.

CYBERPORNOGRAPHY

Cyberporn is defined as obscene material that is transmitted over the Internet or through e-mail. To determine if something is pornographic, the tests created by the U.S. Supreme Court regarding obscenity are used. (See Chapter 5, Constitutional Law.) The transmitting of cyberporn over the Internet was made illegal by the **Communications Decency Act.** In order for a defendant to be found guilty of violating the Communications Decency Act, the material must be obscene and the person transmitting the information must have actual knowledge that the material is obscene.

The intent of the Communications Decency Act was to protect minors from seeing or receiving pornography on the Internet. However, certain portions of the Act were challenged as unconstitutional limitations on freedom of speech. Two cases decided by the Supreme Court, *Reno v. American Civil Liberties Union* and *United States v. Playboy Entertainment Group, Inc.,* declared separate provisions of the Communications Decency Act to be unconstitutional. See Sidebar 27-2 and Sidebar 27-3.

SIDEBAR 27-2 *RENO V. AMERICAN CIVIL LIBERTIES UNION*

Facts: Two provisions of the Communications Decency Act of 1996 (CDA) were written to protect minors from harmful material on the Internet. 47 U.S.C. § 223(a)(1)(B)(ii) makes a criminal offense if there is a "knowing" transmission of "obscene or indecent" messages to any recipient under 18 years of age. Section 223(d) prohibits the "knowing," sending, or displaying to a person under 18 of any message "that, in context, depicts or describes, in terms patently offensive as measured by contemporary community standards, sexual or excretory activities or organs." A number of plaintiffs filed suit challenging the constitutionality of §§ 223(a)(1) and 223(d). An injunction was issued prohibiting the government from enforcing these two provisions of the law.

Issue: Are Section 223(a)(1) and 223(d) unconstitutional?

Decision: The CDA differs from the various laws and orders upheld in those cases in many ways, including that it does not allow parents to consent to their children's use of restricted materials; is not limited to commercial transactions; fails to provide any definition of "indecent" and omits any requirement that "patently offensive" material lack socially redeeming value; neither limits its broad categorical prohibitions to particular times nor bases them on an evaluation by an agency familiar with the medium's unique characteristics; is punitive; applies to a medium that, unlike radio, receives full First Amendment protection; and cannot be properly analyzed as a form of time, place, and manner regulation because it is a content-based blanket restriction on speech.

Regardless of whether the CDA is so vague that it violates the Fifth Amendment, the many ambiguities concerning the scope of its coverage render it problematic for First Amendment purposes. For instance, its use of the undefined terms "indecent" and "patently offensive" will provoke uncertainty among speakers about how the two standards relate to each other and just what they mean.

The CDA lacks the precision that the First Amendment requires when a statute regulates the content of speech. Although the Government has an interest in protecting children from potentially harmful materials, the CDA pursues that interest by suppressing a large amount of speech that adults have a constitutional right to send and receive. Its breadth is wholly unprecedented. The CDA's burden on adult speech is unacceptable if less restrictive alternatives would be at least as effective in achieving the Act's legitimate purposes. The Government has not proved otherwise.

The Judgment of the District Court was affirmed.

Source: United States Reports

SIDEBAR 27-3 UNITED STATES V. PLAYBOY ENTERTAINMENT GROUP, INC.

Facts: Section 505 of the Communications Decency Act required that cable operators, providing channels "primarily dedicated to sexually-oriented programming," either to "fully scramble or otherwise fully block" those channels or to broadcast those channels during the "safe-harbor" hours of 10 p.m. to 6 a.m.—times when young children were unlikely to be watching. The purpose of Section 505 was to protect nonsubscribers, and their children, from "signal bleed," or when audio and visual portions of the scrambled programs might be heard or seen. In February 1996, Playboy Entertainment Group, Inc. filed suit challenging Section 505's constitutionality. The District Court found that Section 505's content-based restriction on speech violated the First Amendment because the Government might further its interests in less restrictive ways. The court also found that the Act provided for a less restrictive alternative than Section 505, in that Section 504 stated that cable operators had an obligation to block channels at a customer's request.

Issue: Did Section 505 of the Communication Decency Act violate First Amendment freedom of speech rights?

Decision: The Court held that because the federal government failed to show that Section 505 was the least restrictive means to further its interests, requiring cable television operators to fully scramble or limit time when sexually-oriented programming was transmitted, violated the First Amendment's free speech guarantee. In finding Section 505 a content-based regulation, "[i]f a statute regulates speech based on its content, it must be narrowly tailored to promote a compelling Government interest. If a less restrictive alternative would serve the Government's purpose, the legislature must use that alternative."

Source: United States Reports

There are several defenses to a criminal charge or civil liability under the Communication Decency Act. The first is the **access provider defense:** The defendant is not the *content* provider, the defendant is just the *access* provider. Another defense is the **blocking access defense,** which argues that the defendant used technology designed to block the transmission of pornography. A third defense is the **Good Samaritan defense,** which protects an online service provider or user of an interactive computer service from *civil liability* as a publisher or speaker of information that is provided by another content provider. In other words, if a provider or a user of an interactive computer service publishes material that is considered obscene, the provider or user is not liable if the material came from another provider.

SECURITIES TRANSACTIONS AND THE CARNIVORE PROGRAM

Another area of computer crime relates to online securities transactions. Existing law did not cover all the aspects of securities transactions that were performed over the Internet. In order to regulate this aspect of securities transactions, the **Office of Internet Enforcement** was created. A division of the SEC, this office oversees securities offerings, trading, and fraudulent scams on the Internet.

In order to help combat cybercrime, the FBI utilizes a special computer program referred to as the **Carnivore program.** This program intercepts and collects communications on the Internet. The program is designed to act like a sniffer, and only intercepts messages the FBI has the authorization to collect. The use of the program is monitored by the Department of Justice, internal FBI controls, and by the court that issued the order.

INTERNET DOMAINS

Still another issue in cyberspace law relates to the use of domain names. Who has the right to use a particular name for a domain, for a Web site? What happens when someone has the right to a well-known trademark or trade name who is not affiliated with the company that has the right to the trademark or trade name?

CYBERSQUATTERS/PIRATES

A **cybersquatter** or a **cyberpirate** is a person or business that intentionally obtains a domain name registration for a company's trademark. Their purpose is to sell the domain name back to the trademark owner. The term **warehousing** refers to the process of registering domain names in the hope that the name can be sold later to a business.

THE ANTICYBERSQUATTING CONSUMER PROTECTION ACT

In order to prevent people from cybersquatting, Congress passed the **Anticybersquatting Consumer Protection Act.** This Act makes it illegal to traffic in domain names that are identical or similar to distinctive marks that are protected under either state trademark laws or the Lanham Act. A person must be acting in **bad faith** to be found guilty of violating the ACPA. Bad faith is the cybersquatter's intent to divert Internet traffic from the trademark owner, or his or her offer to sell or ransom the name of the trademark owner.

FEDERAL LEGISLATION CONCERNING CYBERLAW

Because of the national and international aspects of the Internet, most of the legislation regarding it has come from the U.S. Congress. The laws that have been upheld have dealt with pornography on the Internet, economics, privacy, and copyright.

COPYRIGHT AND TRADEMARK

The Anticybersquatting Consumer Protection Act, referred to earlier, is federal legislation that protects registered trademark holders from online cyberpiracy, the registering as domain names another person's or company's trademark. The **Computer Fraud and Abuse Act** created civil and criminal penalties for unauthorized access or molestation of protected computer systems. The Digital Millennium Copyright Act, also referred to earlier, makes it a crime to traffic in devices that are primarily designed to circumvent technological devices designed to protect against cyberpiracy.

PROTECTION OF CHILDREN

The Communications Decency Act of 1996 discussed earlier, makes it a crime for anyone to knowingly transport obscene material for sale or distribution either in foreign or interstate commerce or through the use of an interactive computer service. To combat child pornography on the Internet, the **Child Pornography Protection Act** of 1996 prohibits and criminalizes electronic trafficking in child pornography. See Exhibit 27-6.

EXHIBIT 27-6	KEY DEFINITIONS IN THE CHILD PORNOGRAPHY PROTECTION ACT OF 1996

For the purposes of this chapter, the term—
(1) "minor" means any person under the age of eighteen years;
(2) "sexually explicit conduct" means actual or simulated –
    (A) sexual intercourse, including genital-genital, oral-genital, anal-genital, or oral-anal, whether between persons of the same or opposite sex;
    (B) bestiality;
    (C) masturbation;
    (D) sadistic or masochistic abuse; or
    (E) lascivious exhibition of the genitals or pubic area of any person;

Continued

Continued

(3) "producing" means producing, directing, manufacturing, issuing, publishing, or advertising;

(4) "organization" means a person other than an individual;

(5) "visual depiction" includes undeveloped film and videotape, and data stored on computer disk or by electronic means which is capable of conversion into a visual image;

(7) "custody or control" includes temporary supervision over or responsibility for a minor whether legally or illegally obtained;

(8) "child pornography" means any visual depiction, including any photograph, film, video, picture, or computer or computer-generated image or picture, whether made or produced by electronic, mechanical, or other means, of sexually explicit conduct, where –

    (A) the production of such visual depiction involves the use of a minor engaging in sexually explicit conduct;

    (B) such visual depiction is, or appears to be, of a minor engaging in sexually explicit conduct;

    (C) such visual depiction has been created, adapted, or modified to appear that an identifiable minor is engaging in sexually explicit conduct; or

    (D) such visual depiction is advertised, promoted, presented, described, or distributed in such a manner that conveys the impression that the material is or contains a visual depiction of a minor engaging in sexually explicit conduct.

Source: United States Code

The **Child Online Protection Act** of 1998 expanded the provisions of the Child Pornography Protection Act to include online transmissions by service providers and e-commerce site providers. The **Protection of Children from Sexual Predators Act** of 1998 expanded liability to those who attempt to use the Internet for the purpose of child pornography. The act specifically targets commercial child pornographers.

CONCLUSION

Cyberlaw is a growing area with established principles being amended and applied to computers and the Internet. An example is the principles of jurisdiction being applied to conducting business over the Internet: Under what circumstances can a court exercise jurisdiction over an Internet company? The exercise of jurisdiction is determined by whether the site is a passive site or an interactive site. This is determined by using the sliding scale of jurisdiction.

Cyberlaw deals with situations that did not exist before the widespread use of computer technology. For example, hackers can break into computer systems by using worms, Trojan horses, and password sniffers and do damage to the systems by planting viruses or mail bombing a site.

Because computers operate using codes, copyright law applies to those codes and to the images those codes create. New measures had to be taken to inform users of the copyright and to protect the author's interest in the work. Shrink wrap agreements, click wrap agreements, and accept or return are methods used to inform consumers of copyright and to protect copyright in computer software.

Computers have made possible the commission of old crimes in new forms: cyberstalking, cybertrespass, and cyberterrorism. Computers have also made possible new crimes: cracking data manipulation, and denial of service. A more serious new crime is identity theft, which occurs when social security numbers, credit card numbers, or account numbers are "stolen" and then used to obtain financial services.

Cyberporn is another issue created by the increase in the use of computers and the Internet. Because of the ease of access to information created by the Internet, a concern is that children will be exposed to pornography. Congress has attempted to protect children from the "dangers" of the Internet by passing federal legislation. However, various provisions of these statutes have been declared unconstitutional by the U.S. Supreme Court.

This remains an area of the law that is undergoing change and expansion as more issues are presented to the courts for decision.

CHAPTER 27 REVIEW

KEY WORDS AND PHRASES

accept or return
Anticybersquatting
  Consumer Protection Act
blocking access defense
Carnivore program
Child Online Protection Act
Child Pornography
  Protection Act
click wrap agreement
Communications Decency
  Act
Computer Fraud and
  Abuse Act
computer network breakin
Computer Software
  Copyright Act
contributory copyright
  infringement
cracking

cybercrime
cyberpirate
cyberporn
cybersquatter
cyberstalking
cyberterrorism
cybertrespass
data manipulation
denial of service attack
Digital Millennium
  Copyright Act
domain
domain name
firewall
framing
Good Samaritan defense
hacker
identity theft
interactive Web site

logic bomb
mail bombing
malware
passive Web site
password sniffer
Protection of Children from
  Sexual Predators Act
replicates
shrink wrap agreement
sliding scale of jurisdiction
software piracy
spam
spoofing
Trojan horse
virus
virus writing
warehousing
Web site defacement
worm

REVIEW QUESTIONS

SHORT ANSWER

1. What is a hacker?

2. What is the difference between a virus and a worm?

3. What is a cybersquatter? What does he or she do?

4. What law is designed to help prevent cybersquatting?

5. What is warehousing?

6. What is bad faith?

7. What do courts look at to determine if they can exercise jurisdiction over Web site owners or operators?

8. What is a shrink wrap agreement?

9. What does a person do if he or she does not want to accept a shrink wrap agreement?

10. What is cyberterrorism?

11. When does a person commit cybertrespass?

12. What is a domain name?

13. What is the purpose of a Trojan horse?

14. What is spoofing?

15. What is the difference between a passive Web site and an interactive Web site?

16. What happens when a program replicates itself?

17. What is a logic bomb?

18. What is a notice and takedown provision?

19. What is considered to be malware?

20. What is data manipulation?

FILL IN THE BLANK

1. A hacker breaks into different computer systems by using software installed on a computer in another location. This is known as _____.

2. A hacker gains access to a Web server and then alters the Web site's page. This is known as _____.

3. A defendant is not the content provider in a case of the transmittal of pornography over the Internet. This is the _____ defense.

4. The FBI program that intercepts and collects communications on the Internet is the _____ program.

5. A person who intentionally obtains a domain name registration for a company's trademark is a _____.

6. The _____ is the title that describes the territory covered by a Web site owner.

7. A _____ is a program that remains undetected in a computer system until it goes off because of an event or a specific date.

8. A _____ is a computer program that attaches itself to the operating system of a computer it enters.

9. An _____ is a contract for electronic access to information.

10. _____ is displaying parts of two Web sites at the same time.

FACT SITUATIONS

1. Malcolm programs his computer to send hundreds of e-mails to a specific Web site. This causes the Web site to be jammed. What crime has Malcolm committed?

2. Roz breaks into a company's computer system and changes people's passwords and steals company information. What offense has Roz committed?

3. Kurt has purchased the rights to dozens of potential Web sites. Some of these Web sites have names that are the same or similar to several companies. What has Kurt done?

4. Diandra uses a sniffer program to gather social security numbers, ID numbers, and account numbers. She then uses the information to apply for credit cards in another person's name. What cybercrime has Diandra committed?

5. A company creates a program that sends unsolicited e-mail to computer users that pop up on their screens when they are using the Internet. What is this e-mail known as?

6. Ingrid is ordering products over the Internet. She is required to answer several questions about her shopping habits and preferences before she can complete her purchases. She must also respond to a series of questions regarding her payment method and shipping address before the order is completed. What type of Web site is this?

7. Torvall is writing a computer program that has the ability to attach itself to other programs in other computers. This allows the program to replicate itself. In what is Torvall engaged?

8. In order to protect its computer system, a company sets up another computer that is between the computers on the company's network and the network that is set up to prevent unauthorized access. What has the company set up?

9. Simon is analyzing a competitor's software, looking at its sequences, its structure, and how it is organized. He is trying to determine the purpose of the software. In what is Simon engaged?

10. A software company sends out new software that requires any user to click an acceptance of an agreement regarding the use of the software before the purchaser can use the software. This is to help protect the company's copyright in the software. What is this agreement known as?

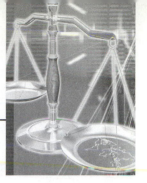

APPENDIX A

The Constitution of the United States

We the People of the United States, in Order to form a more perfect Union, establish Justice, insure domestic Tranquility, provide for the common defense, promote the general Welfare, and secure the Blessings of Liberty to ourselves and our Posterity, do ordain and establish this Constitution for the United States of America.

ARTICLE I.

SECTION 1.

All legislative Powers herein granted shall be vested in a Congress of the United States, which shall consist of a Senate and House of Representatives.

SECTION 2.

Clause 1: The House of Representatives shall be composed of Members chosen every second Year by the People of the several States, and the Electors in each State shall have the Qualifications requisite for Electors of the most numerous Branch of the State Legislature.

Clause 2: No Person shall be a Representative who shall not have attained to the Age of twenty five Years, and been seven Years a Citizen of the United States, and who shall not, when elected, be an Inhabitant of that State in which he shall be chosen.

Clause 3: Representatives and direct Taxes shall be apportioned among the several States which may be included within this Union, according to their respective Numbers, which shall be determined by adding to the whole Number of free Persons, including those bound to Service for a Term of Years, and excluding Indians not taxed, three fifths of all other Persons. *(See Note 2)* The actual Enumeration shall be made within three Years after the first Meeting of the Congress of the United States, and within every subsequent Term of ten Years, in such Manner as they shall by Law direct. The Number of Representatives shall not exceed one for every thirty Thousand, but each State shall have at Least one Representative; and until such enumeration shall be made, the State of New Hampshire shall be entitled to choose three, Massachusetts eight, Rhode-Island and Providence Plantations one, Connecticut five, New-York six, New Jersey four, Pennsylvania eight, Delaware one, Maryland six, Virginia ten, North Carolina five, South Carolina five, and Georgia three.

Clause 4: When vacancies happen in the Representation from any State, the Executive Authority thereof shall issue Writs of Election to fill such Vacancies.

Clause 5: The House of Representatives shall choose their Speaker and other Officers; and shall have the sole Power of Impeachment.

SECTION 3.

Clause 1: The Senate of the United States shall be composed of two Senators from each State, chosen by the Legislature thereof, for six Years; and each Senator shall have one Vote.

Clause 2: Immediately after they shall be assembled in Consequence of the first Election, they shall be divided as equally as may be into three Classes. The Seats of the Senators of the first Class shall be vacated at the Expiration of the second Year, of the second Class at the Expiration of the fourth Year, and of the third Class at the Expiration of the sixth Year, so that one third may be chosen every second Year; and if Vacancies happen by Resignation, or otherwise, during the Recess of the Legislature of any State, the Executive thereof may make temporary Appointments until the next Meeting of the Legislature, which shall then fill such Vacancies.

Clause 3: No Person shall be a Senator who shall not have attained to the Age of thirty Years, and been nine Years a Citizen of the United States, and who shall not, when elected, be an Inhabitant of that State for which he shall be chosen.

Clause 4: The Vice President of the United States shall be President of the Senate, but shall have no Vote, unless they be equally divided.

Clause 5: The Senate shall choose their other Officers, and also a President pro tempore, in the Absence of the Vice President, or when he shall exercise the Office of President of the United States.

Clause 6: The Senate shall have the sole Power to try all Impeachments. When sitting for that Purpose, they shall be on Oath or Affirmation. When the President of the United States is tried, the Chief Justice shall preside: And no Person shall be convicted without the Concurrence of two thirds of the Members present.

Clause 7: Judgment in Cases of Impeachment shall not extend further than to removal from Office, and disqualification to hold and enjoy any Office of honor, Trust or Profit under the United States: but the Party convicted shall nevertheless be liable and subject to Indictment, Trial, Judgment and Punishment, according to Law.

SECTION 4.

Clause 1: The Times, Places and Manner of holding Elections for Senators and Representatives, shall be prescribed in each State by the Legislature thereof; but the Congress may at any time by Law make or alter such Regulations, except as to the Places of choosing Senators.

Clause 2: The Congress shall assemble at least once in every Year, and such Meeting shall be on the first Monday in December, unless they shall by Law appoint a different Day.

SECTION 5.

Clause 1: Each House shall be the Judge of the Elections, Returns and Qualifications of its own Members, and a Majority of each shall constitute a Quorum to do Business; but a smaller Number may adjourn from day to day, and may be authorized to compel the Attendance of absent Members, in such Manner, and under such Penalties as each House may provide.

Clause 2: Each House may determine the Rules of its Proceedings, punish its Members for disorderly Behavior, and, with the Concurrence of two thirds, expel a Member.

Clause 3: Each House shall keep a Journal of its Proceedings, and from time to time publish the same, excepting such Parts as may in their Judgment require Secrecy; and the Yeas and Nays of the Members of either House on any question shall, at the Desire of one fifth of those Present, be entered on the Journal.

Clause 4: Neither House, during the Session of Congress, shall, without the Consent of the other, adjourn for more than three days, nor to any other Place than that in which the two Houses shall be sitting.

SECTION 6.

Clause 1: The Senators and Representatives shall receive a Compensation for their Services, to be ascertained by Law, and paid out of the Treasury of the United States. They shall in all Cases, except Treason, Felony and Breach of the Peace, be privileged from Arrest during their Attendance at the Session of their respective Houses, and in going to and returning from the same; and for any Speech or Debate in either House, they shall not be questioned in any other Place.

Clause 2: No Senator or Representative shall, during the Time for which he was elected, be appointed to any civil Office under the Authority of the United States, which shall have been created, or the Emoluments whereof shall have been increased during such time; and no Person holding any Office under the United States, shall be a Member of either House during his Continuance in Office.

SECTION 7.

Clause 1: All Bills for raising Revenue shall originate in the House of Representatives; but the Senate may propose or concur with Amendments as on other Bills.

Clause 2: Every Bill which shall have passed the House of Representatives and the Senate, shall, before it become a Law, be presented to the President of the United States; If he approve he shall sign it, but if not he shall return it, with his Objections to that House in which it shall have originated, who shall enter the Objections at large on their Journal, and proceed to reconsider it. If after such Reconsideration two thirds of that House shall agree to pass the Bill, it shall be sent, together with the Objections, to the other House, by which it shall likewise be reconsidered, and if approved by two thirds of that House, it shall become a Law. But in all such Cases the Votes of both Houses shall be determined by yeas and Nays, and the Names of the Persons voting for and against the Bill shall be entered on the Journal of each House respectively. If any Bill shall not be returned by the President within ten Days (Sundays excepted) after it shall have been presented to him, the Same shall be a Law, in like Manner as if he had signed it, unless the Congress by their Adjournment prevent its Return, in which Case it shall not be a Law.

Clause 3: Every Order, Resolution, or Vote to which the Concurrence of the Senate and House of Representatives may be necessary (except on a question of Adjournment) shall be presented to the President of the United States; and before the Same shall take Effect, shall be approved by him, or being disapproved by him, shall be repassed by two thirds of the Senate and House of Representatives, according to the Rules and Limitations prescribed in the Case of a Bill.

SECTION 8.

Clause 1: The Congress shall have Power To lay and collect Taxes, Duties, Imposts and Excises, to pay the Debts and provide for the common Defense and general Welfare of the

United States; but all Duties, Imposts and Excises shall be uniform throughout the United States;

Clause 2: To borrow Money on the credit of the United States;

Clause 3: To regulate Commerce with foreign Nations, and among the several States, and with the Indian Tribes;

Clause 4: To establish an uniform Rule of Naturalization, and uniform Laws on the subject of Bankruptcies throughout the United States;

Clause 5: To coin Money, regulate the Value thereof, and of foreign Coin, and fix the Standard of Weights and Measures;

Clause 6: To provide for the Punishment of counterfeiting the Securities and current Coin of the United States;

Clause 7: To establish Post Offices and post Roads;

Clause 8: To promote the Progress of Science and useful Arts, by securing for limited Times to Authors and Inventors the exclusive Right to their respective Writings and Discoveries;

Clause 9: To constitute Tribunals inferior to the supreme Court;

Clause 10: To define and punish Piracies and Felonies committed on the high Seas, and Offences against the Law of Nations;

Clause 11: To declare War, grant Letters of Marquee and Reprisal, and make Rules concerning Captures on Land and Water;

Clause 12: To raise and support Armies, but no Appropriation of Money to that Use shall be for a longer Term than two Years;

Clause 13: To provide and maintain a Navy;

Clause 14: To make Rules for the Government and Regulation of the land and naval Forces;

Clause 15: To provide for calling forth the Militia to execute the Laws of the Union, suppress Insurrections and repel Invasions;

Clause 16: To provide for organizing, arming, and disciplining, the Militia, and for governing such Part of them as may be employed in the Service of the United States, reserving to the States respectively, the Appointment of the Officers, and the Authority of training the Militia according to the discipline prescribed by Congress;

Clause 17: To exercise exclusive Legislation in all Cases whatsoever, over such District (not exceeding ten Miles square) as may, by Cession of particular States, and the Acceptance of Congress, become the Seat of the Government of the United States, and to exercise like Authority over all Places purchased by the Consent of the Legislature of the State in which the Same shall be, for the Erection of Forts, Magazines, Arsenals, dock-Yards, and other needful Buildings;—And

Clause 18: To make all Laws which shall be necessary and proper for carrying into Execution the foregoing Powers, and all other Powers vested by this Constitution in the Government of the United States, or in any Department or Officer thereof.

SECTION 9.

Clause 1: The Migration or Importation of such Persons as any of the States now existing shall think proper to admit, shall not be prohibited by the Congress prior to the Year one thousand eight hundred and eight, but a Tax or duty may be imposed on such Importation, not exceeding ten dollars for each Person.

Clause 2: The Privilege of the Writ of Habeas Corpus shall not be suspended, unless when in Cases of Rebellion or Invasion the public Safety may require it.

Clause 3: No Bill of Attainder or ex post facto Law shall be passed.

Clause 4: No Capitation, or other direct, Tax shall be laid, unless in Proportion to the Census or Enumeration herein before directed to be taken.

Clause 5: No Tax or Duty shall be laid on Articles exported from any State.

Clause 6: No Preference shall be given by any Regulation of Commerce or Revenue to the Ports of one State over those of another: nor shall Vessels bound to, or from, one State, be obliged to enter, clear, or pay Duties in another.

Clause 7: No Money shall be drawn from the Treasury, but in Consequence of Appropriations made by Law; and a regular Statement and Account of the Receipts and Expenditures of all public Money shall be published from time to time.

Clause 8: No Title of Nobility shall be granted by the United States: And no Person holding any Office of Profit or Trust under them, shall, without the Consent of the Congress, accept of any present, Emolument, Office, or Title, of any kind whatever, from any King, Prince, or foreign State.

SECTION 10.

Clause 1: No State shall enter into any Treaty, Alliance, or Confederation; grant Letters of Marquee and Reprisal; coin Money; emit Bills of Credit; make any Thing but gold and silver Coin a Tender in Payment of Debts; pass any Bill of Attainder, ex post facto Law, or Law impairing the Obligation of Contracts, or grant any Title of Nobility.

Clause 2: No State shall, without the Consent of the Congress, lay any Imposts or Duties on Imports or Exports, except what may be absolutely necessary for executing it's inspection Laws: and the net Produce of all Duties and Imposts, laid by any State on Imports or Exports, shall be for the Use of the Treasury of the United States; and all such Laws shall be subject to the Revision and Control of the Congress.

Clause 3: No State shall, without the Consent of Congress, lay any Duty of Tonnage, keep Troops, or Ships of War in time of Peace, enter into any Agreement or Compact with another State, or with a foreign Power, or engage in War, unless actually invaded, or in such imminent Danger as will not admit of delay.

ARTICLE II.

SECTION 1.

Clause 1: The executive Power shall be vested in a President of the United States of America. He shall hold his Office during the Term of four Years, and, together with the Vice President, chosen for the same Term, be elected, as follows

Clause 2: Each State shall appoint, in such Manner as the Legislature thereof may direct, a Number of Electors, equal to the whole Number of Senators and Representatives to which the State may be entitled in the Congress: but no Senator or Representative, or Person holding an Office of Trust or Profit under the United States, shall be appointed an Elector.

Clause 3: The Electors shall meet in their respective States, and vote by Ballot for two Persons, of whom one at least shall not be an Inhabitant of the same State with themselves.

And they shall make a List of all the Persons voted for, and of the Number of Votes for each; which List they shall sign and certify, and transmit sealed to the Seat of the Government of the United States, directed to the President of the Senate. The President of the Senate shall, in the Presence of the Senate and House of Representatives, open all the Certificates, and the Votes shall then be counted. The Person having the greatest Number of Votes shall be the President, if such Number be a Majority of the whole Number of Electors appointed; and if there be more than one who have such Majority, and have an equal Number of Votes, then the House of Representatives shall immediately choose by Ballot one of them for President; and if no Person have a Majority, then from the five highest on the List the said House shall in like Manner choose the President. But in choosing the President, the Votes shall be taken by States, the Representation from each State having one Vote; A quorum for this Purpose shall consist of a Member or Members from two thirds of the States, and a Majority of all the States shall be necessary to a Choice. In every Case, after the Choice of the President, the Person having the greatest Number of Votes of the Electors shall be the Vice President. But if there should remain two or more who have equal Votes, the Senate shall choose from them by Ballot the Vice President.

Clause 4: The Congress may determine the Time of choosing the Electors, and the Day on which they shall give their Votes; which Day shall be the same throughout the United States.

Clause 5: No Person except a natural born Citizen, or a Citizen of the United States, at the time of the Adoption of this Constitution, shall be eligible to the Office of President; neither shall any Person be eligible to that Office who shall not have attained to the Age of thirty five Years, and been fourteen Years a Resident within the United States.

Clause 6: In Case of the Removal of the President from Office, or of his Death, Resignation, or Inability to discharge the Powers and Duties of the said Office, the Same shall devolve on the Vice-President, and the Congress may by Law provide for the Case of Removal, Death, Resignation or Inability, both of the President and Vice President, declaring what Officer shall then act as President, and such Officer shall act accordingly, until the Disability be removed, or a President shall be elected.

Clause 7: The President shall, at stated Times, receive for his Services, a Compensation, which shall neither be increased nor diminished during the Period for which he shall have been elected, and he shall not receive within that Period any other Emolument from the United States, or any of them.

Clause 8: Before he enter on the Execution of his Office, he shall take the following Oath or Affirmation:—"I do solemnly swear (or affirm) that I will faithfully execute the Office of President of the United States, and will to the best of my Ability, preserve, protect and defend the Constitution of the United States."

SECTION 2.

Clause 1: The President shall be Commander in Chief of the Army and Navy of the United States, and of the Militia of the several States, when called into the actual Service of the United States; he may require the Opinion, in writing, of the principal Officer in each of the executive Departments, upon any Subject relating to the Duties of their respective Offices, and he shall have Power to grant Reprieves and Pardons for Offences against the United States, except in Cases of Impeachment.

Clause 2: He shall have Power, by and with the Advice and Consent of the Senate, to make Treaties, provided two thirds of the Senators present concur; and he shall nominate, and by and with the Advice and Consent of the Senate, shall appoint Ambassadors, other public

Ministers and Consuls, Judges of the supreme Court, and all other Officers of the United States, whose Appointments are not herein otherwise provided for, and which shall be established by Law: but the Congress may by Law vest the Appointment of such inferior Officers, as they think proper, in the President alone, in the Courts of Law, or in the Heads of Departments.

Clause 3: The President shall have Power to fill up all Vacancies that may happen during the Recess of the Senate, by granting Commissions which shall expire at the End of their next Session.

SECTION 3.

He shall from time to time give to the Congress Information of the State of the Union, and recommend to their Consideration such Measures as he shall judge necessary and expedient; he may, on extraordinary Occasions, convene both Houses, or either of them, and in Case of Disagreement between them, with Respect to the Time of Adjournment, he may adjourn them to such Time as he shall think proper; he shall receive Ambassadors and other public Ministers; he shall take Care that the Laws be faithfully executed, and shall Commission all the Officers of the United States.

SECTION 4.

The President, Vice President and all civil Officers of the United States, shall be removed from Office on Impeachment for, and Conviction of, Treason, Bribery, or other high Crimes and Misdemeanors.

ARTICLE III.

SECTION 1.

The judicial Power of the United States, shall be vested in one supreme Court, and in such inferior Courts as the Congress may from time to time ordain and establish. The Judges, both of the supreme and inferior Courts, shall hold their Offices during good Behavior, and shall, at stated Times, receive for their Services, a Compensation, which shall not be diminished during their Continuance in Office.

SECTION 2.

Clause 1: The judicial Power shall extend to all Cases, in Law and Equity, arising under this Constitution, the Laws of the United States, and Treaties made, or which shall be made, under their Authority;—to all Cases affecting Ambassadors, other public Ministers and Consuls;—to all Cases of admiralty and maritime Jurisdiction;—to Controversies to which the United States shall be a Party;—to Controversies between two or more States;—between a State and Citizens of another State;—between Citizens of different States,—between Citizens of the same State claiming Lands under Grants of different States, and between a State, or the Citizens thereof, and foreign States, Citizens or Subjects.

Clause 2: In all Cases affecting Ambassadors, other public Ministers and Consuls, and those in which a State shall be Party, the supreme Court shall have original Jurisdiction. In all the other Cases before mentioned, the supreme Court shall have appellate Jurisdiction, both as to Law and Fact, with such Exceptions, and under such Regulations as the Congress shall make.

Clause 3: The Trial of all Crimes, except in Cases of Impeachment, shall be by Jury; and such Trial shall be held in the State where the said Crimes shall have been committed; but when not committed within any State, the Trial shall be at such Place or Places as the Congress may by Law have directed.

SECTION 3.

Clause 1: Treason against the United States, shall consist only in levying War against them, or in adhering to their Enemies, giving them Aid and Comfort. No Person shall be convicted of Treason unless on the Testimony of two Witnesses to the same overt Act, or on Confession in open Court.

Clause 2: The Congress shall have Power to declare the Punishment of Treason, but no Attainder of Treason shall work Corruption of Blood, or Forfeiture except during the Life of the Person attainted.

ARTICLE IV.

SECTION 1.

Full Faith and Credit shall be given in each State to the public Acts, Records, and judicial Proceedings of every other State. And the Congress may by general Laws prescribe the Manner in which such Acts, Records and Proceedings shall be proved, and the Effect thereof.

SECTION 2.

Clause 1: The Citizens of each State shall be entitled to all Privileges and Immunities of Citizens in the several States.

Clause 2: A Person charged in any State with Treason, Felony, or other Crime, who shall flee from Justice, and be found in another State, shall on Demand of the executive Authority of the State from which he fled, be delivered up, to be removed to the State having Jurisdiction of the Crime.

Clause 3: No Person held to Service or Labor in one State, under the Laws thereof, escaping into another, shall, in Consequence of any Law or Regulation therein, be discharged from such Service or Labor, but shall be delivered up on Claim of the Party to whom such Service or Labor may be due.

SECTION 3.

Clause 1: New States may be admitted by the Congress into this Union; but no new State shall be formed or erected within the Jurisdiction of any other State; nor any State be formed by the Junction of two or more States, or Parts of States, without the Consent of the Legislatures of the States concerned as well as of the Congress.

Clause 2: The Congress shall have Power to dispose of and make all needful Rules and Regulations respecting the Territory or other Property belonging to the United States; and nothing in this Constitution shall be so construed as to Prejudice any Claims of the United States, or of any particular State.

SECTION 4.

The United States shall guarantee to every State in this Union a Republican Form of Government, and shall protect each of them against Invasion; and on Application of the Legislature, or of the Executive (when the Legislature cannot be convened) against domestic Violence.

ARTICLE V.

The Congress, whenever two thirds of both Houses shall deem it necessary, shall propose Amendments to this Constitution, or, on the Application of the Legislatures of two thirds of the several States, shall call a Convention for proposing Amendments, which, in either Case, shall be valid to all Intents and Purposes, as Part of this Constitution, when ratified by the Legislatures of three fourths of the several States, or by Conventions in three fourths thereof, as the one or the other Mode of Ratification may be proposed by the Congress; Provided that no Amendment which may be made prior to the Year One thousand eight hundred and eight shall in any Manner affect the first and fourth Clauses in the Ninth Section of the first Article; and that no State, without its Consent, shall be deprived of its equal Suffrage in the Senate.

ARTICLE VI.

Clause 1: All Debts contracted and Engagements entered into, before the Adoption of this Constitution, shall be as valid against the United States under this Constitution, as under the Confederation.

Clause 2: This Constitution, and the Laws of the United States which shall be made in Pursuance thereof; and all Treaties made, or which shall be made, under the Authority of the United States, shall be the supreme Law of the Land; and the Judges in every State shall be bound thereby, any Thing in the Constitution or Laws of any State to the Contrary notwithstanding.

Clause 3: The Senators and Representatives before mentioned, and the Members of the several State Legislatures, and all executive and judicial Officers, both of the United States and of the several States, shall be bound by Oath or Affirmation, to support this Constitution; but no religious Test shall ever be required as a Qualification to any Office or public Trust under the United States.

ARTICLE VII.

The Ratification of the Conventions of nine States, shall be sufficient for the Establishment of this Constitution between the States so ratifying the Same.

AMENDMENT I

Congress shall make no law respecting an establishment of religion, or prohibiting the free exercise thereof; or abridging the freedom of speech, or of the press; or the right of the people peaceably to assemble, and to petition the government for a redress of grievances.

AMENDMENT II

A well regulated militia, being necessary to the security of a free state, the right of the people to keep and bear arms, shall not be infringed.

AMENDMENT III

No soldier shall, in time of peace be quartered in any house, without the consent of the owner, nor in time of war, but in a manner to be prescribed by law.

AMENDMENT IV

The right of the people to be secure in their persons, houses, papers, and effects, against unreasonable searches and seizures, shall not be violated, and no warrants shall issue, but upon probable cause, supported by oath or affirmation, and particularly describing the place to be searched, and the persons or things to be seized.

AMENDMENT V

No person shall be held to answer for a capital, or otherwise infamous crime, unless on a presentment or indictment of a grand jury, except in cases arising in the land or naval forces, or in the militia, when in actual service in time of war or public danger; nor shall any person be subject for the same offense to be twice put in jeopardy of life or limb; nor shall be compelled in any criminal case to be a witness against himself, nor be deprived of life, liberty, or property, without due process of law; nor shall private property be taken for public use, without just compensation.

AMENDMENT VI

In all criminal prosecutions, the accused shall enjoy the right to a speedy and public trial, by an impartial jury of the state and district wherein the crime shall have been committed, which district shall have been previously ascertained by law, and to be informed of the nature and cause of the accusation; to be confronted with the witnesses against him; to have compulsory process for obtaining witnesses in his favor, and to have the assistance of counsel for his defense.

AMENDMENT VII

In suits at common law, where the value in controversy shall exceed twenty dollars, the right of trial by jury shall be preserved, and no fact tried by a jury, shall be otherwise reexamined in any court of the United States, than according to the rules of the common law.

AMENDMENT VIII

Excessive bail shall not be required, nor excessive fines imposed, nor cruel and unusual punishments inflicted.

AMENDMENT IX

The enumeration in the Constitution, of certain rights, shall not be construed to deny or disparage others retained by the people.

AMENDMENT X

The powers not delegated to the United States by the Constitution, nor prohibited by it to the states, are reserved to the states respectively, or to the people.

AMENDMENT XI

The judicial power of the United States shall not be construed to extend to any suit in law or equity, commenced or prosecuted against one of the United States by citizens of another state, or by citizens or subjects of any foreign state.

AMENDMENT XII

The electors shall meet in their respective states and vote by ballot for President and Vice-President, one of whom, at least, shall not be an inhabitant of the same state with themselves; they shall name in their ballots the person voted for as President, and in distinct ballots the person voted for as Vice-President, and they shall make distinct lists of all persons voted for as President, and of all persons voted for as Vice-President, and of the number of votes for each, which lists they shall sign and certify, and transmit sealed to the seat of the government of the United States, directed to the President of the Senate;—The President of the Senate shall, in the presence of the Senate and House of Representatives, open all the certificates and the votes shall then be counted;—the person having the greatest number of votes for President, shall be the President, if such number be a majority of the whole number of electors appointed; and if no person have such majority, then from the persons having the highest numbers not exceeding three on the list of those voted for as President, the House of Representatives shall choose immediately, by ballot, the President. But in choosing the President, the votes shall be taken by states, the representation from each state having one vote; a quorum for this purpose shall consist of a member or members from two-thirds of the states, and a majority of all the states shall be necessary to a choice. And if the House of Representatives shall not choose a President whenever the right of choice shall devolve upon them, before the fourth day of March next following, then the Vice-President shall act as President, as in the case of the death or other constitutional disability of the President. The person having the greatest number of votes as Vice-President, shall be the Vice-President, if such number be a majority of the whole number of electors appointed, and if no person have a majority, then from the two highest numbers on the list, the Senate shall choose the Vice-President; a quorum for the purpose shall consist of two-thirds of the whole number of Senators, and a majority of the whole number shall be necessary to a choice. But no person constitutionally ineligible to the office of President shall be eligible to that of Vice-President of the United States.

AMENDMENT XIII

Section 1. Neither slavery nor involuntary servitude, except as a punishment for crime whereof the party shall have been duly convicted, shall exist within the United States, or any place subject to their jurisdiction.
Section 2. Congress shall have power to enforce this article by appropriate legislation.

AMENDMENT XIV

Section 1. All persons born or naturalized in the United States, and subject to the jurisdiction thereof, are citizens of the United States and of the state wherein they reside. No state shall make or enforce any law which shall abridge the privileges or immunities of citizens of the United States; nor shall any state deprive any person of life, liberty, or property, without due process of law; nor deny to any person within its jurisdiction the equal protection of the laws.

Section 2. Representatives shall be apportioned among the several states according to their respective numbers, counting the whole number of persons in each state, excluding Indians not taxed. But when the right to vote at any election for the choice of electors for President and Vice President of the United States, Representatives in Congress, the executive and judicial officers of a state, or the members of the legislature thereof, is denied to any of the male inhabitants of such state, being twenty-one years of age, and citizens of the United States, or in any way abridged, except for participation in rebellion, or other crime, the basis of representation therein shall be reduced in the proportion which the number of such male citizens shall bear to the whole number of male citizens twenty-one years of age in such state.

Section 3. No person shall be a Senator or Representative in Congress, or elector of President and Vice President, or hold any office, civil or military, under the United States, or under any state, who, having previously taken an oath, as a member of Congress, or as an officer of the United States, or as a member of any state legislature, or as an executive or judicial officer of any state, to support the Constitution of the United States, shall have engaged in insurrection or rebellion against the same, or given aid or comfort to the enemies thereof. But Congress may by a vote of two-thirds of each House, remove such disability.

Section 4. The validity of the public debt of the United States, authorized by law, including debts incurred for payment of pensions and bounties for services in suppressing insurrection or rebellion, shall not be questioned. But neither the United States nor any state shall assume or pay any debt or obligation incurred in aid of insurrection or rebellion against the United States, or any claim for the loss or emancipation of any slave; but all such debts, obligations and claims shall be held illegal and void.

Section 5. The Congress shall have power to enforce, by appropriate legislation, the provisions of this article.

AMENDMENT XV

Section 1. The right of citizens of the United States to vote shall not be denied or abridged by the United States or by any state on account of race, color, or previous condition of servitude.

Section 2. The Congress shall have power to enforce this article by appropriate legislation.

AMENDMENT XVI

The Congress shall have power to lay and collect taxes on incomes, from whatever source derived, without apportionment among the several states, and without regard to any census or enumeration.

AMENDMENT XVII

The Senate of the United States shall be composed of two Senators from each state, elected by the people thereof, for six years; and each Senator shall have one vote. The electors in each state shall have the qualifications requisite for electors of the most numerous branch of the state legislatures.

When vacancies happen in the representation of any state in the Senate, the executive authority of such state shall issue writs of election to fill such vacancies: Provided, that the legislature of any state may empower the executive thereof to make temporary appointments until the people fill the vacancies by election as the legislature may direct.

This amendment shall not be so construed as to affect the election or term of any Senator chosen before it becomes valid as part of the Constitution.

AMENDMENT XVIII

Section 1. After one year from the ratification of this article the manufacture, sale, or transportation of intoxicating liquors within, the importation thereof into, or the exportation thereof from the United States and all territory subject to the jurisdiction thereof for beverage purposes is hereby prohibited.

Section 2. The Congress and the several states shall have concurrent power to enforce this article by appropriate legislation.

Section 3. This article shall be inoperative unless it shall have been ratified as an amendment to the Constitution by the legislatures of the several states, as provided in the Constitution, within seven years from the date of the submission hereof to the states by the Congress.

AMENDMENT XIX

The right of citizens of the United States to vote shall not be denied or abridged by the United States or by any state on account of sex.

Congress shall have power to enforce this article by appropriate legislation.

AMENDMENT XX

Section 1. The terms of the President and Vice President shall end at noon on the 20th day of January, and the terms of Senators and Representatives at noon on the 3d day of January, of the years in which such terms would have ended if this article had not been ratified; and the terms of their successors shall then begin.

Section 2. The Congress shall assemble at least once in every year, and such meeting shall begin at noon on the 3d day of January, unless they shall by law appoint a different day.

Section 3. If, at the time fixed for the beginning of the term of the President, the President elect shall have died, the Vice President elect shall become President. If a President shall not have been chosen before the time fixed for the beginning of his term, or if the President elect shall have failed to qualify, then the Vice President elect shall act as President until a President shall have qualified; and the Congress may by law provide for the case wherein neither a President elect nor a Vice President elect shall have qualified, declaring who shall then act as President, or the manner in which one who is to act shall be selected, and such person shall act accordingly until a President or Vice President shall have qualified.

Section 4. The Congress may by law provide for the case of the death of any of the persons from whom the House of Representatives may choose a President whenever the right of choice shall have devolved upon them, and for the case of the death of any of the persons from whom the Senate may choose a Vice President whenever the right of choice shall have devolved upon them.

Section 5. Sections 1 and 2 shall take effect on the 15th day of October following the ratification of this article.

Section 6. This article shall be inoperative unless it shall have been ratified as an amendment to the Constitution by the legislatures of three-fourths of the several states within seven years from the date of its submission

AMENDMENT XXI

Section 1. The eighteenth article of amendment to the Constitution of the United States is hereby repealed.

Section 2. The transportation or importation into any state, territory, or possession of the United States for delivery or use therein of intoxicating liquors, in violation of the laws thereof, is hereby prohibited.

Section 3. This article shall be inoperative unless it shall have been ratified as an amendment to the Constitution by conventions in the several states, as provided in the Constitution, within seven years from the date of the submission hereof to the states by the Congress.

AMENDMENT XXII

Section 1. No person shall be elected to the office of the President more than twice, and no person who has held the office of President, or acted as President, for more than two years of a term to which some other person was elected President shall be elected to the office of the President more than once. But this article shall not apply to any person holding the office of President when this article was proposed by the Congress, and shall not prevent any person who may be holding the office of President, or acting as President, during the term within which this article becomes operative from holding the office of President or acting as President during the remainder of such term.

Section 2. This article shall be inoperative unless it shall have been ratified as an amendment to the Constitution by the legislatures of three-fourths of the several states within seven years from the date of its submission to the states by the Congress.

AMENDMENT XXIII

Section 1. The District constituting the seat of government of the United States shall appoint in such manner as the Congress may direct:

A number of electors of President and Vice President equal to the whole number of Senators and Representatives in Congress to which the District would be entitled if it were a state, but in no event more than the least populous state; they shall be in addition to those appointed by the states, but they shall be considered, for the purposes of the election of President and Vice President, to be electors appointed by a state; and they shall meet in the District and perform such duties as provided by the twelfth article of amendment.

Section 2. The Congress shall have power to enforce this article by appropriate legislation.

AMENDMENT XXIV

Section 1. The right of citizens of the United States to vote in any primary or other election for President or Vice President, for electors for President or Vice President, or for Senator or Representative in Congress, shall not be denied or abridged by the United States or any state by reason of failure to pay any poll tax or other tax.

Section 2. The Congress shall have power to enforce this article by appropriate legislation.

AMENDMENT XXV

Section 1. In case of the removal of the President from office or of his death or resignation, the Vice President shall become President.

Section 2. Whenever there is a vacancy in the office of the Vice President, the President shall nominate a Vice President who shall take office upon confirmation by a majority vote of both Houses of Congress.

Section 3. Whenever the President transmits to the President pro tempore of the Senate and the Speaker of the House of Representatives his written declaration that he is unable to discharge the powers and duties of his office, and until he transmits to them a written declaration to the contrary, such powers and duties shall be discharged by the Vice President as Acting President.

Section 4. Whenever the Vice President and a majority of either the principal officers of the executive departments or of such other body as Congress may by law provide, transmit to the President pro tempore of the Senate and the Speaker of the House of Representatives their written declaration that the President is unable to discharge the powers and duties of his office, the Vice President shall immediately assume the powers and duties of the office as Acting President.

Thereafter, when the President transmits to the President pro tempore of the Senate and the Speaker of the House of Representatives his written declaration that no inability exists, he shall resume the powers and duties of his office unless the Vice President and a majority of either the principal officers of the executive department or of such other body as Congress may by law provide, transmit within four days to the President pro tempore of the Senate and the Speaker of the House of Representatives their written declaration that the President is unable to discharge the powers and duties of his office. Thereupon Congress shall decide the issue, assembling within forty-eight hours for that purpose if not in session. If the Congress, within twenty-one days after receipt of the latter written declaration, or, if Congress is not in session, within twenty-one days after Congress is required to assemble, determines by two-thirds vote of both Houses that the President is unable to discharge the powers and duties of his office, the Vice President shall continue to discharge the same as Acting President; otherwise, the President shall resume the powers and duties of his office.

AMENDMENT XXVI

Section 1. The right of citizens of the United States, who are 18 years of age or older, to vote, shall not be denied or abridged by the United States or any state on account of age.

Section 2. The Congress shall have the power to enforce this article by appropriate legislation.

AMENDMENT XXVII

No law, varying the compensation for the services of the Senators and Representatives, shall take effect, until an election of Representatives shall have intervened.

Alabama
District Court—one in each county
Circuit Court—covers several counties
Court of Criminal Appeals
Court of Civil Appeals
Alabama Supreme Court

Arizona
Justice and Municipal Courts
Superior Court of Arizona
Court of Appeals
Supreme Court of Arizona

California
Small Claims Court ($5,000 or less)
California Superior Court
Courts of Appeal (6 appellate districts)
Supreme Court of California

Connecticut
Probate Court
Superior Court (Civil, Criminal, Family and Juvenile Divisions)
Appellate Court
Connecticut Supreme Court

Florida
County Courts
Circuit Courts (20)
District Court of Appeal s (5)
Supreme Court of Florida

Hawaii
Small Claims Court (Up to $3,500)
District Court (Up to $25,000)
Circuit Court (Over $25,000)
Intermediate Court of Appeals
Supreme Court of Hawaii

Illinois
Circuit Court of Illinois
Illinois Court of Appeals
Illinois Supreme Court

Alaska
Magistrate Courts
District Court
Superior Court (Trial Court)
Court of Appeals
Alaska Supreme Court

Arkansas
District and City Courts
Circuit Court
Court of Appeals
Arkansas Supreme Court

Colorado
County Courts (64)
District Courts (22 districts)
Courts of Appeal
Colorado Supreme Court

Delaware
Family Court
Justice of the Peace Court
Court of Common Pleas
Superior Court (Trial Court)
Delaware Supreme Court

Georgia
State, Juvenile, Probate, Magistrate Courts
Superior Court
Court of Appeals
Georgia Supreme Court

Idaho
Youth Courts
District Court
Idaho Court of Appeals
Idaho Supreme Court

Indiana
Indiana Trial Courts
Indiana Tax Courts
Indiana Court of Appeals
Supreme Court of Indiana

Iowa
District Court
Iowa Court of Appeals
Iowa Supreme Court

Kentucky
District Court ($4,000 or less)
Circuit Court (Over $4,000)
Kentucky Court of Appeals
Kentucky Supreme Court

Maine
Drug Court—Adult and Juvenile
District Court
Superior Court (Trial Court)
Supreme Judicial Court

Massachusetts
Municipal Court
Juvenile Court
Probate and Family Court
District Court
Superior Court
Appeals Court of Massachusetts
Superior Judicial Court of Massachusetts

Minnesota
District Court (10 districts)
Minnesota Court of Appeals
Minnesota Supreme Court

Missouri
Circuit Court
Missouri Court of Appeals
Missouri Supreme Court

Nebraska
Juvenile Court
Workers Compensation Court
County Court
District Court
Nebraska Court of Appeals
Nebraska Supreme Court

New Hampshire
District Court (Local Courts)
Probate Court
Superior Court (Trial Court)
New Hampshire Supreme Court

Kansas
Municipal Court
District Court
Kansas Court of Appeals
Kansas Supreme Court

Louisiana
City Court
Family Court
District Court
Circuit Court of Appeals (5)
Louisiana Supreme Court

Maryland
Circuit Courts
District Courts
Court of Special Appeals
Court of Appeals

Michigan
Municipal Court
Small Claims Division District Court
Probate Court
District Court (up to $25,000)
Claims Court (Claims against the State)
Circuit Court
Michigan Court of Appeals
Michigan Supreme Court

Mississippi
Circuit Court
Chancery Court
Mississippi Court of Appeals
Mississippi Supreme Court

Montana
Municipal Court
Justices' Court
District Court
Montana Supreme Court

Nevada
Municipal Court
District Court
Nevada Supreme Court

New Jersey
Municipal Court
Superior Court Trial Division
Superior Court Appellate Division
Supreme Court of New Jersey

New Mexico
Municipal Court
Probate Court
Metropolitan Court
Magistrate Court
District Court
New Mexico Court of Appeals
New Mexico Supreme Court

North Carolina
Special Courts (Business and Family Courts)
Superior Courts
District Courts
Court of Appeals of North Carolina
Supreme Court of North Carolina

Oklahoma
District Court
Court of Civil Appeals
Court of Criminal Appeals
Supreme Court of Oklahoma

Pennsylvania
Magistrate
District Court
Common Pleas
Commonwealth Court
Superior Court
Pennsylvania Supreme Court

Rhode Island
Traffic Tribunal
Workers Compensation Court
District Court
Family Court
Superior Court
Rhode Island Supreme Court

South Dakota
Magistrate Courts
Circuit Courts
South Dakota Supreme Court

Texas
Justice of the Peace Courts
Municipal Courts
Statutory County Courts
Constitutional County Courts
District Courts
Foster Care Courts
Probate Courts
Texas Court of Criminal Appeals
Texas Court of Appeals
Supreme Court of Texas

New York
City and County Courts
Family Court
Surrogate Court (Equity Court)
Court of Claims
Supreme Court (Trial Court)
Appellate Division of the Supreme Court
Court of Appeals (Highest appellate court)

North Dakota
District Court
North Dakota Supreme Court

Ohio
Court of Common Pleas Municipal Court
Probate Court
General Court
District Court of AppealsSupreme Court of Ohio
Court of Criminal Appeals

Oregon
Justice Courts
Municipal Court
County Courts
Circuit Courts
Tax Courts
Oregon Court of Appeals
Oregon Supreme Court
Pennsylvania Supreme Court

South Carolina
Magistrate Courts
Probate Courts
Family Court
Circuit Court
Court of Appeals
South Carolina Supreme Court

Tennessee
Court of General Sessions
Circuit Court
Chancery Court
Tennessee Court of Appeals
Tennessee Supreme Court

Utah
Justice Courts
Juvenile Courts
District Courts
Utah Court of Appeals
Utah Supreme Court

Vermont
Small Claims Court
Superior Court
District Court
Vermont Supreme Court
Juvenile and Domestic Relations Court

Washington
Municipal Court
District Court
Superior Court
Washington Court of Appeals
Supreme Court of Washington

Wisconsin
Circuit Court
Court of Appeals
Wisconsin Supreme Court

Virginia
Juvenile and Domestic Relations Court
General District Courts
Circuit Courts
Court of Appeals of Virginia
Supreme Court of Virginia

West Virginia
Court of Claims
County Commissions
County Magistrates Court
Circuit Court
Supreme Court of Appeals

Wyoming
Municipal Courts
Circuit Courts
District Courts
Wyoming Supreme Court